The National Interest and the Human Interest
An Analysis of U.S. Foreign Policy

*Written under the auspices of the Center of International Studies,
Princeton University. A list of other Center publications appears
at the back of this book.*

The National Interest and the Human Interest

An Analysis of U.S. Foreign Policy

ROBERT C. JOHANSEN

PRINCETON UNIVERSITY PRESS

Copyright © 1980 by Princeton University Press
Published by Princeton University Press, Princeton, New Jersey
In the United Kingdom: Princeton University Press, Guildford, Surrey

All Rights Reserved
Library of Congress Cataloging in Publication Data will be
found on the last printed page of this book

This book has been composed in VIP Baskerville

Clothbound editions of Princeton University Press books
are printed on acid-free paper, and binding materials are
chosen for strength and durability

Printed in the United States of America by Princeton
University Press, Princeton, New Jersey

To Martin Luther King, Jr.,

WHO HELPED US UNDERSTAND WHAT IT MEANS TO BE A PLANETARY CITI-
ZEN, AND TO ALL THOSE WHO SEEK TO LIVE ACCORDING TO THIS
UNDERSTANDING.

Contents

Contents

List of Tables

xi

List of Illustrations

Acknowledgments

THIS book has been influenced by values that took root during my childhood and college years. That early learning was pruned and strengthened as I and our society responded to the experiences of activists in the civil rights, peace, feminist, and environmental movements. All of the persons who have touched my life during those years and shaped this book cannot be acknowledged here. But I am confident that these friends will sense, in the following pages, their influences. This book is partly a product of our agonizing together about the inadequacies of the present and envisioning an alternative future.

Some influences have been so profound and my indebtedness so great as to deserve special mention. My parents' inspiration and continuing support for my work are foremost among these. For knowledge of fundamental values, a sense of responsibility to implement them, and a determination to face even unpleasant truths, I happily acknowledge my parents' compassionate and morally sensitive instruction. For an encompassing understanding of the preciousness and precariousness of life, I thank my brother, whose short but humane life strengthened my own commitment to resist the politics and economics of human fragmentation and their accompanying prejudice and violence.

While I was a student at Manchester College, several wise though not widely known professors nurtured the growth of some ideas contained herein. When I returned there to teach, many courageous students of the late 1960s and early 1970s helped temper these ideas further by expressing their acute sense of planetary citizenship both inside and outside the classroom. During and since those years I have benefited enormously from the intellectual stimulation and ethical affirmation of my teacher, colleague, and friend, Kenneth L. Brown.

My own professional life and the intellectual orientation for this book have been heavily influenced by Richard A. Falk. His insight, his unique ability to combine normative inquiry with empirical, scholarly rigor, his constant encouragement, penetrating criticism, and ground-breaking scholarship have been a strong example and inspiration for me. Without his support, this project would not have borne fruit. This book also has been influenced by the pioneering work of the Institute for World Order, by the talented transnational group of scholars in the World Order Models Project, and especially by the intellectual contributions of its director, Saul H. Mendlovitz.

Cyril E. Black and others at the Center of International Studies provided an ideal setting at Princeton University where I wrote the first draft. While there, it was possible to enjoy the luxury of full-time study because of financial support from the University Consortium for World Order Studies as a James P. Warburg Fellow, from Princeton University as a John Parker Compton Fellow of the Center of International Studies, and from Manchester College as a professor on sabbatical leave.

I am deeply grateful to Catherine Smith for her outstanding secretarial and administrative talents. These plus her cheerfulness helped make a pleasant task out of what otherwise would have been a lengthy burden in preparing an unwieldly manuscript. Her commitment to the values undergirding the project gave its completion a unity of purpose for which all co-workers hope.

No one has contributed more to this effort than my wife, Ruthann. She has shared with me her own ideas about and commitment to building a more just world order. These have been invaluable. I thank her also for her empathy, her eagerness to debate substantive questions, her self-sacrifice in giving me uninterrupted hours to write, and her liberated unwillingness to let the writing dominate both of our lives completely. By their questions, laughter, hopes, and frustrations, our children Erik and Sonia have made it possible—and necessary—to understand more fully the unfathomable human stakes that await all children in future foreign policy choices. They have given concrete meaning to abstract discussions about the human consequences of foreign policy decisions. In addition, more than it is fair to expect, Erik and Sonia have been quick to forgive and to accept a father who has seemed forever seated at the typewriter.

While accepting responsibility for the contents of this book, I happily express gratitude to all of these people.

Abbreviations

ABM	*Antiballistic missile*
AEC	*Atomic Energy Commission*
AID	*Agency for International Development*
CIA	*Central Intelligence Agency*
DAC	*Development Assistance Committee of* OECD
IAEA	*International Atomic Energy Agency*
ICA	*International Cooperation Administration*
ICBM	*Intercontinental ballistic missile*
IDB	*Inter-American Development Bank*
IMCO	*International Maritime Consultative Organization*
ISRA	*International Seabed Resource Authority*
ITT	*International Telephone and Telegraph*
IWC	*International Whaling Commission*
JCS	*Joint Chiefs of Staff*
MaRV	*Maneuverable reentry vehicle*
MIRV	*Multiple independently-targetable reentry vehicle*
MNC	*Multinational corporation*
NIE	*National Intelligence Estimate*
NSC	*National Security Council*
OAS	*Organization of American States*
OECD	*Organization for Economic Cooperation and Development*
OPEC	*Organization of Petroleum Exporting Countries*
PDC	*Christian Democratic Party (of Chile)*
PN	*National Party (of Chile)*
psi	*pounds per square inch*
SALT	*Strategic Arms Limitation Talks*
SALT I	*Interim Agreement and* ABM *Treaty of 1972*
SLBM	*Submarine launched ballistic missile*
UNCTAD	*United Nations Conference on Trade and Development*
V_1	*Peace without national military arsenals*
V_2	*Economic well-being*
V_3	*Universal human rights and social justice*
V_4	*Ecological balance*

Foreword

In truth, Americans have always been ambivalent about foreign policy. In the foreground is the special view of American innocence that has existed since the beginning of the Republic. The United States, it was then widely believed, could only be kept pure by remaining aloof from the entanglements of the Old World. Such aloofness always competed with a contrary vision of the United States as a country with a special mission to create a better world. In many respects, the sensibility and outlook of Thomas Jefferson gracefully embodied this ambivalence that has by now deeply insinuated itself into national political consciousness. It was Jefferson who eloquently defended the virtues of detachment while simultaneously working to realize visions of empire, most tangibly, perhaps, by negotiating the Louisiana Purchase and giving, late in his life, a hearty endorsement to the Monroe Doctrine.

This dual heritage is still alive, although its forms are new. The perils and imperatives of involvement are mainly discussed these days in relation to the Third World, and the weight of debate has shifted from goals to tactics. Yet considerable uneasiness persists; witness the tension between the rhetorical respect given by U.S. leaders to nonintervention, self-determination, and sovereign equality as guiding principles of foreign policy and the actualities of an interventionary, even a counterrevolutionary diplomacy. In recent years, really since the late 1960s when the Vietnam failure became apparent, there has been a domestic mood of despair and discontent about the global role of the United States. Indeed, current attitudes of the American public toward foreign policy waver somewhere between apathy and anger, reflecting both feelings of frustration that nothing effective can be done and resentment about the inability of the government to arrest the relative decline of U.S. power and stature in the world system. As matters now stand United States foreign policy is likely to fail both pragmatic and idealistic tests for most citizens, thereby assaulting that aspect of national character preoccupied with success, as well as that concerned with virtue. Besides, the earlier fear of being drawn into foreign wars is being displaced by the insistence that the United States display

a greater willingness to use military capabilities to uphold overseas interests.

Lurking in the shadows are formidable issues that compose
the novel and largely repressed agenda of world order challenges. Underlying these challenges are doubts about the
framework of state sovereignty, especially questions about
whether the old order can provide a satisfactory basis for the security and prosperity of the American people in the nuclear age.
Most fundamental here is whether the deterrence system, including its costly and nerve-wracking arms race, will prove morally acceptable and practically effective as a peace system over
time, and whether, of course, there are attainable alternatives.

Pressing more directly on public awareness is a set of demands
emanating from the countries of Asia, Africa, and Latin
America, summarized by their insistence upon "a new international economic order." Interacting with this North-South confrontation are concerns about "resource diplomacy," about the
status of rich countries using a disproportionate share of the
planet's stock of nonrenewable resources and injecting into the
environment a disproportionate share of pollution in forms and
quantities that do ecological and hygienic damage. This novel
agenda greatly complicates the global setting. Its tone is best
suggested by the emergent eco-equity struggle to devise development paths for countries at various stages of industrialization, development paths that would combine environmental
protection with the fulfillment of essential human needs and
basic societal aspirations for a good life. Such a vision of positive
world order seems remote from the reality of arms races, mass
poverty, widespread warfare, demographic pressures, and repressive governing tactics. Where in this tangle of torments can
one find first the transnational understanding and then the national will in the major countries of the world, to build, in the
phrase of one impressive movement for change active in
America, "a strategy for a living revolution"?

It is hardly surprising that the current language of political
discourse for foreign policy matters in the United States seems
vague, hypocritical, and irrelevant. The inconsistent requirements of servicing an empire while claiming to be the benefactor
of human society at home and abroad are at the root of the difficulty, yet the actualities of declining power and the political need
to disguise the trend and its consequences from the American
people have added to the strain. Of course, other great powers
with liberal traditions have faced a similar challenge. The expe-

riences of England and France provide recent examples; both countries have undergone many difficulties while adjusting psychically and materially to the loss of empire.

Yet a difference of utmost significance pertains. The rationale of imperial policies and the adjustment to increases and reduction of power relative to other states has been carried on for several centuries within a relatively secure geopolitical framework. The game of nations has often been waged for high stakes, and yet the survival of the system never seemed at issue. Even in the seventeenth century when the transition from feudalism to statism culminated in the Thirty Years War the outcomes of international conflict did not imperil the destiny of the human species. In our era the circumstances are different. Threats of nuclear war and ecological catastrophe carry with them apocalyptic dangers of irreversible damage, even of total collapse. People have, of course, long wondered before about whether life on this planet was or should be sustainable; religious imagery, especially in the West, has been filled with prophetic anticipations of death, transfiguration, and last judgment since Biblical times. Yet today, with global communications and interactions so prominent, we have a crisis of confidence among the prosperous peoples of the North, growing doubts about whether the future will seem an improvement on the past, and even deeper fears about whether the secular materialism of a technology-based image of progress can sustain the morale of modern, affluent, and liberal states.

Such a crisis provokes fundamental rethinking. It becomes natural to consider as a matter of urgency whether the values, beliefs, and techniques of the past are adequate for the future. Obvious questions about the viability of the sovereign state are inevitably raised and yet the issues are confused by that other dominant political reality of our time, namely that of surging nationalism. The numerous peoples of the South are struggling with enthusiasm to create genuine full-fledged states. Nationalism is also on the rise in the North as evidenced by the flourishing of separatist movements in the most settled of states. Considering the world as a whole as the ground upon which foreign policy is enacted also reveals an extraordinary unevenness and diversity of aspiration, situation, and heritage.

Occasionally, elements of the new world order agenda break into public consciousness, as briefly during the early 1970s when the Club of Rome's report stimulated "the limits to growth" debate. Such a break in the ice is bound to be temporary at this stage; old patterns of thought quickly reassert themselves, especially if the challenge cannot be handled within orthodox problem-solving frameworks. The leaders of most states are too preoccupied with the short-run management of foreign policy to cast their gaze on longer-term interpretations that are bound to be exceedingly controversial and for some sectors of society, usually those most influential under present arrangements, exceedingly threatening and costly. As a consequence, the more drastic items on an appropriate world order agenda are continually repressed, and the foreign policy process, unless overtaken by war or economic emergency, reverts to short-term managerial maneuvering and blustering self-confidence.

This assessment leads to one further observation. It is a mistake to rely on government for diagnosis or response to the longer-term, underlying, yet very real, world order challenges. It is a mistake easily made as modern governments, and especially ours, claim the allegiance of the citizenry partly because of their supposed omnicompetence. Confusion is increased, also, by the tendency of governments to preempt and harmlessly ritualize much of the rhetoric of global concern, inducing both complacency and cynical disregard of substance. In our culture where the main instruments of this alleged omnicompetence are technology and military prowess, the prognosis is scary. The tension between short-term maneuver and long-term readjustment is illustrated by debates about both the military and civilian aspects of nuclear policy, where the preferences of official elites increasingly collide with the anxieties of the citizenry. Especially in foreign policy, the government feels the growing burdens of omnicompetence at an historical time of apparently diminishing capabilities. Leaders search for ways to provide reassurance and the public grows increasingly restive and narrow-minded as various developments are blamed for erosions of prosperity, security, and serenity. This process of dissolution goes on throughout the trilateral world of North America, Western Europe, and Japan with perhaps its most acute expressions involving recourse to terror as political stratagem and to drugs as private consolation.

Despite the severity of indictment, lines of deeper analysis of our political situation as a nation have so far aroused very little scholarly interest among social scientists. Traditional inquiry into relative economic and political power continues to share the foreign policy scene with an array of modernist methodologies designed to make interpretation less impressionistic. The focus is mainly on a conventional agenda of foreign policy priorities: maintaining reliable access to sufficient overseas oil, keeping the Soviet Union contained without provoking World War III, and holding back Third World demands for major reforms in the international economic order.

The foreign policy literature continues to be dominated by managerial appraisals and proposals, with some revival of the "classical" inquiry into how to achieve equilibrium under conditions of changing global configurations of power and alignment. Little attention is being given to the gaps between words and deeds, between deeds and needs, and between needs and values as these pertain to U.S. foreign policy. It is one thing to discern the gaps and quite another to depict these gaps concretely enough to suggest what might be an alternative foreign policy based on the longer term imperatives of the country.

Against this background, Robert Johansen's book strikes me as a major achievement. Proceeding on a solid foundation of empirical depth, Johansen demonstrates the character of the first gap between declared ends and performance in U.S. foreign policy. Not only do his carefully constructed cases reveal the extent of the gap, but also its quality, especially the consistent interplay between pious rhetoric and expedient activity. As such, the public justification of American foreign policy sets up a distorting filter between the government and the citizenry that inhibits informed discussion and trivializes public discourse on momentous matters.

Johansen's cases lend both concreteness and structural depth to his argument. Each case is inherently significant as an illustration of a specific set of choices by American makers of foreign policy and suggestive of a recurrent theme that can be reexamined in the light of earlier and later "cases." For instance, the CIA role in Allende's Chile can be considered in relation to Arbenz's Guatemala (1954) or the movement that drove the Shah from power in early 1979. Context, as well as structure, matters. We cannot be sure what has been "learned" from the Chilean case and what results from an analysis of American goals and capabilities in the Iranian case. Has American statecraft shifted? If so, does the shift reflect a new willingness to accommodate revolutionary nationalism in Third World countries or merely the provisional acquiescence by a given group of U.S. leaders to a political outcome beyond their capacity to control? American foreign policy toward Iran might revert to an interventionary approach as a consequence of either an electoral mandate in the United States or as a result of a further challenge to American interests in the Gulf region. The response of the United States to internal political developments in a foreign country perceived as adverse to American interests is both a structural feature of American foreign policy and a distinctive "instance." By putting his case studies within an overall framework Johansen illuminates our understanding of both policy and structure.

More impressive, still, Johansen links this revealing critique of American foreign policy to the longer term framework of global reform. In the past decade, "world order" has started to supplant "balance of power" as a focus for the ends of foreign policy, and yet this allegedly new perspective is often deceptive. It often seems to mean no more than finding verbal formulations suitable for the expanded scope of a global system to stabilize relations (including economic relations) among sovereign states. Johansen, in contrast, uses world order to mean the realization of those values which he believes necessary to achieve a humane and secure existence for the peoples of the world. Such a program of global reform implies for Johansen a series of structural changes in the framework of international relations, although it doesn't imply or propose shifting from the state system to world government. At root, Johansen associates the dynamic of change with value shifts in the advanced industrial sectors of world society that will spontaneously erode the legitimacy of the highly coercive structures of the modern state. His image of a different future for American foreign policy places as much emphasis on destructuring the state from within as it does on the growth of external central guidance capabilities to achieve the levels of coordination and regulation required for activity that is of planetary scale and significance. In the end, Johansen insists that a mixed moral and prudential challenge calls for the reorientation of American foreign policy. We must do what we say, seek what we need, and affirm what we want for the future.

It is, of course, too soon for policymakers to heed such wisdom. They are too constrained by their own immediate concerns to confront seriously the argument that their cosmology is outmoded. Instead, as with astronomers throughout the ages, they tinker with old beliefs, long after these have been discredited, devising various ingenious schemes to obscure the realities of their failure, and as with any establishment they will do their best to discredit the new astronomers who propose a different cosmology. Of course, the stakes are higher than achieving a more satisfying apprehension of reality. An inquiry into global reform is, at minimum, a quest for a safer, saner world political system. It involves nothing less than evaluating and influencing the evolutionary destiny of the human race. It also challenges our passivity at a time of danger and turbulence. It is one of the prime opportunities available to scholars in a free society to set forth the unfashionable case for drastic reform, and it is a call to the rest of us to listen and respond as openly as we can. Very few books on American foreign policy have ever set forth so forceful and fundamental a challenge as this one.

Johansen's scholarly inquiry is informed by a citizen's passionate insistence on a foreign policy fit for the American people before it is too late. It is also informed by an understanding that to be a patriotic American late in the twentieth century is indistinguishable from being a loyal citizen of the planet as a whole. In this respect his participation in the World Order Models Project where diverse orientations toward global reform interact gives his outlook a cultural depth that is a happy contrast with the sort of vague globalism that is the sentimental substance of Sunday sermons.

Issuing planetary death warrants is neither novel, nor helpful. At the same time, we require no mysterious or inspired being to warn us that ours is a time of jeopardy for earth and earthlings. The United States, with its awesome capacity to wreck, whether by weapons or its intricate life style, is in an especially responsible position. What we do and don't do in relating to others will seriously, possibly decisively, influence the unfolding of the future.

If Americans are going to stop acting like subjects and start acting like citizens, then they have to become informed and caring about the foreign policy of their nation. Knowledge can be profoundly empowering. Indeed, this conviction underlies Johansen's animating vision of a preferred, alternate world order that is peaceful and just. It can happen, but only if we make it happen, if we move from realms of feeling through realms of thought to realms of actions and activities.

Johansen tells us that by being true to ourselves we will also help forge the still uncreated conscience of the human race, embarking thereby upon what may be the most exciting (and perilous) voyage of discovery ever contemplated. Reality is fundamentally encouraging, but only if we act accordingly, out of a sense of urgency, yet with patience and perseverance (the most revolutionary of virtues).

Richard Falk

The National Interest and the Human Interest
An Analysis of U.S. Foreign Policy

ONE · *The Elusiveness of A Humane World Community*

PURPOSE

WE live on a planet possessing the potential for peace and fulfillment for all, but societies have been distressingly unsuccessful in achieving these conditions for most of the human race. Why? This book begins to answer this fundamental question by examining two others: What has been the United States role in helping to achieve a secure and humane existence for all people? In pursuit of this goal, what should be the content of U.S. foreign policy now and during the remainder of this century?

In addressing these questions, my purpose is to examine recent U.S. foreign policy in order to clarify its impact on insuring the survival and well-being of U.S. citizens and the entire human race. Does the past conduct of U.S. foreign policy justify confidence that it can meet the unprecedented challenges of the 1980s? This analysis assesses the influence of U.S. policies on the prospects for realizing widely shared humanitarian values and for transforming the international system into one with an improved capacity to implement those values.

The present chapter will (1) illustrate the unprecedented foreign policy problems that will confront political leaders in the last quarter of the twentieth century; (2) explain why the complexity and worldwide dimensions of these problems demonstrate a pressing need for different normative standards for policy making than have been used historically; (3) describe the guidelines which seem essential to insure human survival and to facilitate the realization of other important values, such as the promotion of human rights and the abolition of worldwide poverty; and (4) explain the analytic approach employed in this study.

THE CHALLENGE TO HUMANITY'S FUTURE

Global Problems in a National Context

Why should scholars, politicians, and ordinary citizens reassess the goals of U.S. foreign policy at this time? The answer is

3

rooted in considerations of both prudence and morality. First of all, some fundamental policy adjustments will be required to satisfy the basic drive for security and survival in the future. Second, the fulfillment of our most cherished humanitarian values can be greatly facilitated by some modifications in the present national approach to policy decisions.

THE THREAT TO SURVIVAL

In the first instance, unprecedented problems that are global in scope increasingly exceed the capacity of traditional diplomatic practices and institutions to resolve. In general, our perception of foreign policy problems and opportunities has failed to stay abreast of rapidly changing world realities. This has meant that many policies have been growing increasingly unrealistic in the sense that they simply cannot achieve the ends sought. To oversimplify only slightly, the political leadership and attentive public apply essentially nineteenth-century diplomatic ideas[1] to the solution of twenty-first-century problems, the technical and social origins of which are in the present. Nineteenth-century diplomatic ideas encourage (1) the continued emphasis on serving the national interest defined largely in terms of military power and sovereign control over a carefully defined piece of territory and segment of humanity; and (2) the assumption that the present system of competing national sovereignties either cannot or should not be fundamentally changed, and that it both can and will respond adequately to the foreseeable problems of national security, widespread poverty and resource shortages, severe ecological damage, and pervasive denial of human rights. Under the influence of old diplomatic habits and strong vested interests in the political and economic system inherited from the past, officials continue diplomacy as usual to confront newly emerging twenty-first century problems. For example, traditional diplomatic ideas and institutions persist even though their inadequacy is obvious for averting misuse of nuclear technology, the consequences of which cannot be confined to a carefully defined piece of territory, layer of the atmosphere, or segment of humanity. Traditional uses of military power and sovereign control, however sincerely and faithfully practiced, are impotent in the face of irresponsible behavior by a relatively small number of people who could affect millions of others in many countries for decades, centuries, or millennia to come.

A stark reality faces all inhabitants of the earth: through consequences resulting from major war or ecological imbalance, widespread suffering for millions of people and even eventual extinction of the human species are possibilities. Such statements have become commonplace, and thus they have lost their ring of urgency.[2] Yet predicaments mount while time slips away, making remedial action more difficult and perhaps less likely. Even without major war or ecological collapse, existing political institutions prevent a billion of the world's people from having sufficient food, often resulting in permanent mental or physical disability, even though adequate nutrition is technically feasible. In brief, the decentralized structure of world power and authority, distributed among many sovereign states, perpetuates a relatively anarchic international system in which the danger of war, the shortage of food and other resources, and the presence of persistent ecological hazards threaten the survival of many people, if not, in the long run, of all human civilization. The survival question will not be examined in detail here, but a few brief comments about the political impact of nuclear technology and ecological hazards will illustrate the need to consider an alternative approach to the conduct of U.S. foreign policy.[3] Subsequent chapters will substantiate this argument in greater detail.

The existence of nuclear weapons without their use in warfare since 1945 has produced a perhaps unjustified confidence that weapons of mass destruction will never be used. Yet, many dangers remain inherent in a strategy of nuclear deterrence.[4] Although the United States is the most powerful nation on earth, it has no effective defense against a nuclear attack. The government can only hope to *deter* an attack. Yet as nuclear weapons technology spreads to additional countries, the likelihood that such weapons will be used in war increases. A well-known group of strategic experts in a Harvard-M.I.T. Arms Control Seminar have predicted that nuclear weapons will be used in combat before the end of the century—most likely by middle-range powers.[5] Other experts have calculated that the probability of a *general* nuclear war is increasing.[6] The danger of nuclear war will grow further as tactical nuclear weapons become smaller, lighter, "cleaner," and more mobile, because they will be more easily purchased, transported, and viewed as similar to conventional explosives. Although any single national government may believe that its security is increased if it accumulates more and more advanced weapons, for world society as a whole both the likelihood and the potential destructiveness of future wars are increased by the growth of military equipment and the spread of militarism around the world.

With the dispersal of command and control required by submarine-launched missiles and tactical battlefield weapons, an excessively eager team of officers or a miscommunicated signal could initiate the use of nuclear weapons. While the probabilities for accidental war are no doubt low, the impossibility of eliminating the danger of accidents completely is a rather unsatisfactory condition given the awesome consequences of a mistake.[7]

Nuclear war could also begin through miscalculation by some officials about the anticipated actions of another government. Since deterrence is based on the ability of government X to make government Y believe that X will use nuclear weapons in the face of certain provocations, the only way to insure the credibility of one's posture is to use nuclear weapons occasionally. If the threat to use nuclear weapons is only a bluff by X, then Y could rationally proceed to ignore the threat. Thus the leadership in Y could miscalculate the seriousness of X, and precipitate war.

Furthermore, given the absence of dependable screening procedures in selecting government officials, an emotionally unstable person may, in some country, at some time in the future, exercise decisive power in a government equipped with nuclear weapons. Similarly, political leaders who assume office with normal emotional maturity may, when under political pressure, emotional stress, or fatigue, make decisions with some degree of diminished rationality. President John F. Kennedy deliberately raised the risk of nuclear war to odds he estimated as "even,"[8] because he did not like having Soviet missiles ninety miles away in Cuba, even though nuclear missiles could exist legally as close as twelve miles away, in submarines cruising just outside United States territorial waters.

Although there was no apparent security need to risk nuclear war, U.S. officials executed policies that, by their own admission, brought nuclear war frightfully closer: "Not one of us at any

6

time believed that any of the choices before us could bring anything but either prolonged danger or fighting, very possibly leading to the kind of deepening commitment of prestige and power from which neither side could withdraw without resort to nuclear weapons."[9] A key participant in the decisions, Robert Kennedy, reported that, while they hoped to avoid war, "the *expectation* was a military confrontation."[10] During the discussions, FBI Director J. Edgar Hoover informed U.S. officials that the FBI had received information that Soviet personnel in New York were preparing to destroy all sensitive documents in the belief that the United States would "probably be taking military action against Cuba or Soviet ships, and this would mean war."[11] Robert Kennedy summed up his own and President Kennedy's feelings: "There was the realization that the Soviet Union and Cuba apparently were preparing to do battle. And there was the feeling that the noose was tightening on all of us, on Americans, on mankind, and that the bridges to escape were crumbling."[12]

The tension and anxiety accompanying such a crisis often lead to overreactions. Attorney general Kennedy reported that, for a brief time at least, nearly all advisers favored an air attack: "At first there was almost unanimous agreement that we had to attack early the next morning with bombers and fighters and destroy the SAM [surface to air missile] sites."[13] During the brief time that the President was waiting for a Soviet response to the United States demand for withdrawal of Soviet missiles, Theodore Sorensen reported growing support among Presidential advisers for a direct air strike and invasion of Cuba: "The pressures for such a move . . . were rapidly and *irresistibly* growing, strongly supported by a minority in our group and increasingly necessitated by a deterioration in the situation."[14] During one day of long, almost continuous discussions in the White House, the crisis produced rising tempers and irritability among the small group of decision makers. "Pressure and fatigue, he [the President] later noted privately, might have broken the group's steady demeanor in another twenty-four or forty-eight hours."[15]

Great exhilaration followed the "successful" U.S. testing of Soviet will. Sorensen reported the President "had, as Harold Macmillan would later say, earned his place in history by this one act alone. He had been engaged in a personal as well as national contest for world leadership and he had won."[16] Contesting for the personal and national leadership of the world (or a region of the world) through military confrontation is a motivation that other leaders may have in the future and that can hardly avoid questions of human survival.

The possibilities for nuclear war or for terrorist use of nuclear technology are increased by the spread of fissionable materials to additional private organizations and governments. In addition to the six nuclear weapons countries, a score of other states have the resources and technical skills to produce nuclear weapons within one or two years. No existing international organization can prevent even a signatory to the nonproliferation treaty from *deliberately* diverting materials to weapons purposes. Moreover, the purchase of nuclear weapons and delivery systems could become a serious possibility. Even without nuclear weapons a determined group could inflict catastrophe on other states. A few pounds of plutonium distributed as a finely ground powder could devastate a city like New York with lethal radiation lasting for centuries. Such an act might even be committed by persons representing no nation-state against which the United States could retaliate. The destruction of civilian nuclear reactors also could cause the loss of thousands of lives. These conditions make deterrence ineffective because no one can genuinely be defended against a determined opponent.

It may bear repeating that major nuclear war would kill most of the urban populations of the antagonists. It would destroy most industry and commerce. Perhaps more than half of the populations in small towns and rural areas would die from fallout, depending on weather conditions, wind direction, and the height of detonations. Living standards and life expectancies would be substantially reduced for any persons remaining. Millions of cancer and leukemia deaths would occur outside the territories of the two antagonists. Untold numbers of genetic problems and birth deformities would await those still living. There would be dangerous effects on the atmosphere, the soil, and the water, as well as consequences presently unanticipated. As Herbert York, former director of defense research and engineering for the Department of Defense, has written:

> If for any political, psychological or technical reasons deterrence should fail, the physical, biological and social consequences would be completely out of line with any reasonable view of the national objectives of the United States or Soviet Union. . . . [T]here would be a substantial chance that the whole civilized world could go up in nuclear smoke. This is

simply too frightful and too dangerous a way to live indefinitely; we *must* find some better form of international relationship than the current dependency on a strategy of mutual assured destruction.[17]

Given the dangers of nuclear technology, a prudent foreign policy would convey a sense of urgency about establishing the new
values and institutions that could make the prohibition of nuclear weapons a feasible, enforceable, compulsory, universal obligation.

Although less dramatic in its immediacy, pollution of the atmosphere and oceans also illustrates a long-range challenge to
survival and to the quality of our lives—a challenge that again
demonstrates the interconnection of every life on the planet. Although all earthly plant and animal life depends upon the air
and the sea, no one exercises sovereignty over or protects vast
expanses of the atmosphere and oceans. Nations now pollute
them without much regard for long-range consequences to the
planet or even for short-range effects outside their national
jurisdiction. Yet all ecosystems are part of a delicate ecological
balance; all have limits of deterioration beyond which they cannot recover. In many cases we do not know the planetary limits
which, if surpassed, would endanger our species.

The consequences of depleting the amount of ozone in the
stratosphere illustrate the problem. Without ozone protection,
ultraviolet light would break down molecules on earth that are
essential to life. Crops, bacteria, and micro-life in general would
be affected. Ultraviolet light also causes skin cancer and genetic
damage that can severely endanger both animal and plant life.
In addition to protecting life from extraplanetary lethal radiation, ozone, by absorbing ultraviolet light, contributes substantially to heating the upper atmosphere surrounding the planet.
The depletion of ozone could radically alter the climate of the
earth, as well as eventually expose all forms of life to deadly
radiation. Even a small drop in density would increase the incidence of birth defects and skin cancer.

Ozone is threatened by some aerosol sprays, nitrogen fertilizers, exhaust gases of supersonic planes, and atmospheric nuclear explosions. Fred Iklé, Director of the Arms Control and
Disarmament Agency, has reported that nitric oxides injected
into the stratosphere by nuclear war could seriously damage the
ozone layer.[18] The effects of some harmful substances will increase for years after their release because of the time required

9

for them to rise to the stratosphere. All of the threats to the earth's ozone shield produce consequences that obviously transcend national boundaries and exceed the capacity of separate state sovereignties to combat effectively.

A similar conclusion emerges from an examination of marine pollution. The oceans play a vital role in maintaining dependable rainfall, climate, and carbon dioxide levels for the planet. More than a third of the earth's oxygen supply is produced by the process of photosynthesis in plants living in the oceans of the world. Pollutants harmful to these plants could affect the earth's oxygen supply. Even the wastes of landlocked states affect the oceans, because pollutants are transported to the sea through rivers and the atmosphere.

The oceans are a major source of animal protein, the lack of which contributes to malnutrition for one third of the human population. Even though a majority of marine fish remain palatable, nearly all species now contain DDT residues. Pollution diminishes the protein supply by decreasing the reproductive capacity of marine life, killing larvae and untold tons of fish, making some fish unfit for human consumption, and harming marine plant life on which fish feed.[19] Despite more intensive attempts to catch fish, total world harvest has declined since 1970. Overfishing and pollution are the primary causes. Neither is now effectively regulated to produce the maximum sustainable yield.

The preceding discussion of the dangers of unregulated nuclear technology and environmental hazards poses the question whether past foreign policy values, diplomatic habits, and institutions can meet the demands of modern technology and human interaction for global control. We have examined here only two of many possible examples that demonstrate the need for a fundamental reassessment of foreign policy goals and international institutions.

THE THREAT TO PREFERRED VALUES

A reassessment is also useful because present goals and institutions make it increasingly difficult to implement our most cherished values and ethical principles. Indeed, the existing international structure of power in itself violates these principles. For example, the globe is presently divided into nation-states with power unsystematically and inequitably related to population. This means that the simple exercise of sovereignty

10

by a superpower violates the principle of self-determination on a global basis. It is doubtful that any democratic society can long survive with its democratic principles intact if those principles are repeatedly denied in its own conduct. Yet in following the traditional approach to serving the national interest the U.S. government regularly carries out policies that affect millions of people outside its borders who have no control over the making of U.S. policies. When the United States pursues economic policies and consumption patterns that stimulate world inflation, thus decreasing the buying power of non-U.S. citizens, this is a modern, global equivalent of taxation without representation. Similarly, United States citizens are touched directly by the acts of other great powers, although we are unrepresented in their political processes. If other governments put radioactive substances in the atmosphere, American citizens suffer contamination without representation.[20]

Even though he has kept his administration well within the guidelines of traditional diplomacy, President Jimmy Carter seemed to acknowledge part of the representation problem when he delivered a message to the "citizens of the world" immediately after his inaugural address: "I have chosen the occasion of my inauguration . . . to speak not only to my own countrymen—which is traditional—but also to you, citizens of the world who did not participate in our election but who will nevertheless be affected by my decisions."[21]

Rapidly changing technology and patterns of social interaction are making societies inseparable from one another, but the present pattern of international political participation remains relatively unchanged. As long as this system remains constant, it authorizes some people to make decisions that affect other people who are unrepresented in the decision-making process. As this incongruity between political institutions and social needs is allowed to deepen, self-government will be undermined in a national context because it will be unable to respond to citizens' needs. It will fail to take root and flourish in a global context because intra- and inter-societal inequities will not diminish, and severe inequities of wealth and power make it impossible to fulfill the democratic principle in which power must be widely shared. Democracy cannot indefinitely survive within a global political structure that prevents people from participating in decisions that affect their own lives.

Consider the capacity of present political institutions to fulfill a person's most basic need and right—adequate food. The world today faces—for the first time in its history—shortages in each of the four basic agricultural resources: land, water, energy, and fertilizer. No nation can isolate itself from these scarcities or their economic and political consequences. Japan imports more than half of its total cereal supplies. Egypt imports about 40 percent. The farmers of the European Economic Community import 80 percent of their high protein feed for livestock. Nearly all their petroleum is imported. The United States is the supplier of 85 percent of all soybeans on the entire world market, so when in 1973 it ordered an export embargo in order to curb price rises at home, numerous other people, with no opportunity to influence the U.S. decision, were adversely affected. In another example, when Thailand once restricted its rice exports, the action "wreaked havoc with efforts to prevent runaway food prices in other Southeast Asian countries."[22]

Each year approximately one billion people suffer from malnutrition. Fifteen million children die annually before reaching age five because of insufficient food and infections that become lethal due to malnourishment. That is one quarter of all deaths in the world. Almost all children born to poor parents in the less developed countries suffer some degree of malnutrition at one time or another.[23] In the early 1970s, experts estimated that an average of 10,000 people died weekly from lack of food.[24]

Overpopulation is not the only source of this human tragedy. Because of the petroleum-based fertilizer shortages partially resulting from the oil embargo imposed by the Organization of Oil Exporting Countries (OPEC) in 1973-74, the United States suspended its usual fertilizer exports. This action contributed to a 1.5-million-ton fertilizer shortage in the less developed countries, which cost them 15 million tons in lost grain production in 1974. Yet, during the same year, people in the United States used on lawns, cemeteries, and golf courses about 3 million tons of fertilizer—twice the shortage in the poor countries.[25] Obviously, no food grew from this U.S. usage. Moreover, for each pound of fertilizer applied to grain production in the nearly saturated soils of the United States, farmers could increase their yields by an average of only two to three pounds. But in nutrient-starved India, each pound of fertilizer could have yielded an additional production three times as large as the increment derived from U.S. use of the fertilizer.[26] Thus, a slight decrease in U.S. productivity would have yielded a major increase in productivity for fertilizer-poor countries.

Of the total grain produced in the United States, much is fed to cattle, which are inefficient converters of grain into protein. Georg Borgstrom estimates that the world's cattle eat as much food as would be required to feed 8.7 billion people, or twice the world's present population.[27] By including less meat and more grain in their diets, people in the rich countries could enable existing food supplies to extend to far more persons on the globe. In India, where the major source of protein is feed grains, direct and indirect consumption averages about 400 pounds of grain per person per year. In the United States, where much protein is eaten in the form of meat, eggs, or milk, the grain consumed directly or indirectly through production of meat is almost 2000 pounds per person per year.[28] Thus, the average North American consumes five times as many agricultural resources as the average person in India. U.S. average consumption exceeds by two to four times the quantity of protein that the human body can utilize. The remainder is excreted. If Americans were to reduce their meat consumption by only 10 percent, in one year 12 million tons of grain would be freed for human consumption. This amount would feed 60 million people for one year, enough to have prevented famine in parts of India and Bangladesh in 1974.

Sufficient resources exist to feed everyone *if* the resources are shared fairly. Many demographers believe this condition would also cause population growth to decline. However, past policies of food distribution have been governed by traditional diplomatic habits. As the former Secretary of Agriculture, Dr. Earl Butz once explained: "Food is power. Food is a weapon. It is now one of the principal tools in our negotiating kit."[29] A CIA research study, written shortly before the World Food Conference in Rome in 1974, concluded that the world grain shortages in the future "could give the United States a measure of power it had never had before—possibly an economic and political dominance greater than that of the immediate post-World War II years." The report predicted that "in bad years . . . Washington would acquire virtual life-and-death power over the fate of the multitudes of the needy." (Without exaggeration, the hungry might view such a condition as starvation without representation.) The report warned that when societies became desperate the hungry but powerful nations (which possessed nuclear weapons) might engage in nuclear threats or in massive migration backed by force. They might even seek to induce climatic changes, such as "trying to melt the Arctic ice cap."[30] Despite the exaggerated expression of alarm in the image of a rising tide of poor people engulfing the United States, the report accurately described the power of life and death that can be exerted by the world's largest food exporter.

More effectively than existing international organizations, a global food authority could maximize world production, bank grains for periods of drought or famine, ration and allocate fertilizer for optimal increases in production, encourage less consumption of grain by cattle, and decrease the use of food as a diplomatic weapon to gain political influence over other governments. Without increased global coordination of food policies, resentment, repression, and unnecessary human misery are likely to continue throughout the 1980s.

In summary, the decentralized and inequitable distribution of power among states perpetuates an international system in which the most powerful countries maintain privileged positions at the expense of the weak and poor societies. However, even the citizens of the great powers are unable to escape the consequences of other governments' policies that they have no authority to influence. This arrangement of power and authority denies further realization of global justice and basic human rights. Not only is the denial of justice undesirable in itself, it also contributes to the difficulty and detracts from the desirability of maintaining peace. Thus the present distribution of power threatens both the quality of life for a substantial number of coinhabitants of the globe and ultimately the survival of human civilization. Whether one wants to be politically prudent or morally sensitive or both, modern technology has now made it necessary to consider an alternative basis for making foreign policy decisions.

The Westphalian System in a Post-Westphalian Era

The previous discussion of several global problems calls into question the widely held assumption that prevailing political responses are equal to the challenges. If profound problems with historic consequences are not resolved, is this due to unwise foreign policies? If so, then foreign policy could be corrected by getting additional information to officials, improving the policy-making machinery, or selecting new leadership in Washington. Alternatively, one may conclude that global challenges are unmet because the international system is poorly structured to meet present political and economic needs. If that is true, then fundamental structural changes are required to overcome the threats to survival and to preferred values. Finally, the difficulty may be a combination of unwise policies and structural defects, in which case the necessary changes are even more risky to undertake and difficult to bring about.

To increase our understanding of these questions, it is useful to consider the present international system in historical perspective.

THE LIMITS OF DECENTRALIZED, TERRITORIALLY-BASED AUTHORITY

The Peace of Westphalia at the conclusion of the last of the great religious wars of Europe is a convenient benchmark for noting the major shift in European political organization which produced the current international system. Although the selection of any particular date to note systemic changes is somewhat arbitrary, the political changes symbolized by the Peace of Westphalia of 1648 stand in sharp contrast to the political organization of the Middle Ages before the religious wars. In medieval society the Christian commonwealth was hierarchically organized and subject to the authority of the Pope and the Holy Roman Empire. The Roman Catholic Church and its appointed representatives exercised centralized authority across the territorial boundaries of feudalism. Although subunits throughout Europe exercised some power, it was on behalf of and subject to the authority of Pope and Emperor. This continental system gradually changed as authority, power, wealth, and loyalties shifted to a subcontinental or state level. The Peace of Westphalia acknowledged the development of independent, secular, sovereign states, no longer subject to the centralized authority of the Pope or Emperor.[31]

In the Westphalian model, political authority was decentralized on the continent and based on territory, thus making boundaries very important. National governments were all-powerful within their boundaries; no outside authority could legally intrude within each national shell. As the Pope's influence declined and there was no overreaching political authority to regulate conduct between sovereigns, there could be no prohibition of war. Because authority was tied to territory, there was little possibility of establishing sovereignty over the oceans.

The existing international system corresponds to the Westphalian model of a decentralized system of independent states, each exercising dominant authority within its territorial domain.

15

However, mounting evidence of social interpenetration, such as that presented earlier, indicates that we are living during a period pregnant with possibilities for system change. These are similar in significance to the structural transformation registered at Westphalia. This era is marked by rising needs to transform the nation-state or Westphalian system into a new system of order that is in some ways reminiscent of two principal attributes of medieval society. (Of course, one should not assume that the changing world order either should or will develop an authority structure similar to that of the Holy Roman Empire.) First, there is the need to establish a transnational structure of power and authority with increased capacity at the center for coordinating policy and enforcing it on national governments. Second, there is a need for a new structure of authority not limited to a piece of territory for either its sources of legitimacy or the domain of its directives. It must be global in scope and extend its authority even to outer space.

In the emerging system, national boundaries are becoming less important than they were in the nineteenth century. This is illustrated by the growth of multinational corporations and the international regulation of travel, commerce, and communication. The need for additional forms of central guidance is reflected in negotiations about regulating the use of the oceans and the seabed. Incipient supranational institutions are perhaps present in the European economic community. Although governments tenaciously guard their sovereignty, they also advance occasional claims that international organizations may have the right to intervene, such as against apartheid, in areas of traditionally national jurisdiction. In the League of Nations and the United Nations, governments made their first modern effort, although without major success, to control and prohibit aggressive war. The need for international guarantees against war reflects the decline of the invulnerable, impermeable state in the nuclear age.[32]

Yet, the systemic transition now under way reveals a sharp asymmetry. Industrialization and advanced technology have made the earth a post-Westphalian functional unit, but the world remains politically fragmented by Westphalian national divisions of the planet and of human loyalties. Threats posed by the pollution of the atmosphere and oceans, the instability in the supply of food and oil, and the all-encompassing consequences of nuclear war are feebly confronted by a system of sovereign

16

states that recognize no coordinating authority above their national governments.

THE TRAGEDY OF THE COMMONS

The unprecedented scope of the foreign policy problems facing Washington emerges from the incongruity between the *functional unity* and the *political disunity* of the globe. Serving human needs requires cooperative efforts based upon a recognition of the unity of the ecosystem and the universal impact of some political decisions. The Westphalian disunity of political organization encourages self-seeking, competitive efforts. The consequences of this incongruity were illustrated by biologist Garrett Hardin in his well-known discussion of the "tragedy of the commons." He pictured a pasture held in common by a village of cattle herdsmen. As rational beings, the herdsmen seek to maximize their gains from pasturing their animals. Each herdsman asks himself: "What is the utility *to me* of adding one more animal to my herd?" This utility, Garrett explained, has one negative and one positive component. The positive component is nearly +1 because of the increment of one animal; the negative component is a function of the additional overgrazing created by one more animal. Excessive overgrazing can lead to severe soil erosion and eventual destruction of the pasture. However, unlike the positive component which accrues entirely to the owner, the negative effect of overgrazing is shared by all the herdsmen. As a result, the negative utility for any particular herdsman is only a small fraction of −1. After adding the utilities of the positive and negative components, the rational herdsman concludes that the most sensible course for him to pursue is to add another animal to the herd. Following the same calculation, a second is added—and then a third, fourth, and so on. The same conclusion is reached by all rational herdsmen sharing the commons. It makes little sense for any one of them to exercise self-restraint and not add to his herd because the pasture will eventually be destroyed anyway due to the overgrazing by others. As Hardin concluded: "Therein is the tragedy. Each man is locked into a system that compels him to increase his herd without limit—in a world that is limited. Ruin is the destination toward which all men rush, each pursuing his own best interest in a society that believes in the freedom of the commons. Freedom in a commons brings ruin to all."[33]

A similar problem was raised much earlier by Jean-Jacques

Rousseau.[34] He described a primitive hunting party in which a small group of hungry men attempted to catch a deer to satisfy their appetites. If, during the hunt, one man noticed a hare which would satisfy the man's hunger, he would pursue it even if his action would provide no food for the rest of the group and would allow the deer to escape because he had left his post. By this simple example, Rousseau demonstrated his belief in a natural inclination to put self-interest above mutual, general interest. Rousseau did not elaborate upon his story, but we might speculate about the alternatives the hunter faced.[35] He might have thought that rational self-interest dictated that he remain faithful to his hunting partners and refuse to pursue the hare. This would be especially true in the long run, because it would establish a precedent for securing future meals. He could have predicted that, by pursuing the hare, his abandonment of the group would enable the deer to escape. He would have regretted that result, but he also knew that if he did not pursue the hare, it would be possible that the second hunter would see the hare, make calculations similar to his own, and then catch the hare for his own meal. In that case also, the deer would escape, leaving many empty stomachs, including that of the first hunter. With these thoughts in mind, the first hunter then left the hunting party to catch the hare.

The story demonstrates that, in the absence of a central administrative system to help coordinate human behavior and make it more dependable, even a sincere, rational actor fails to engage in otherwise desirable cooperation. This is true even though the rational person at first is willing to cooperate to satisfy common needs as basic as food itself. If a central authority existed and required that the captured hare be divided equally among all hunters, then the hunters would ignore the hare as long as there was a reasonable chance of catching the deer.

Today's slow movement toward central, worldwide administration of some aspects of life, such as carried out by multinational corporations and international regulatory organizations controlling transnational air transportation and electronic communication, suggests that the question no longer is: Will there be a worldwide system of order? Instead, the sobering issue has become: What will be its nature? This is true despite the failure of a majority of the world's people to recognize that a global system is in the making. If one acknowledges that, barring nuclear suicide or ecological collapse, the economic and political structures of the world are becoming enmeshed with one another on a global basis, an issue of high importance is to assess whether the incipient system serves the values that one believes are most worthy of support. Given the value orientations of the dominant actors in today's world, it is possible that new forms of inequity or exploitation may be established.

Because the developing system is global in scope, it is especially important that avoidable errors be averted, since there will be no sanctuaries to which to flee should the evolving system prove tyrannical or inhumane. Therefore, it is imperative to construct a normative basis for international transactions to insure that through inadvertence or moral callousness we do not create a system that eventually destroys our highest values.

In summary, citizens in one state or group of states have no way of assuring that actions of other governments will not be harmful to or catastrophic for the lives of all. Means do not exist to insure that various national interests will harmonize with the human interest. The international structures of power and authority and the prevailing criteria for selecting foreign policies are unable (1) to satisfy the security and survival requirements that a prudent foreign policy must, and (2) to implement the preferred values that a just foreign policy should. The apparent need to establish a system of policy coordination commensurate with the global dimensions of modern human behavior poses two remaining questions: First, what are the most useful standards for assessing whether foreign policies are helping to achieve a more secure and humane global community? These standards will be discussed in the remainder of the present chapter. Second, are U.S. foreign policies in fact implementing the values and transforming the structures without which survival will be in question and human dignity indefinitely denied? The answer to this question is pursued in subsequent chapters which contain detailed analyses of four case studies of U.S. foreign policy.

A GLOBAL HUMANIST RESPONSE

In developing a framework around which to build a foreign policy capable of moving safely into the 1990s, it is useful to begin by clarifying the values that one wants to realize. Of course, one's fundamental values are chosen or assumed, not

19

proven. To be sure, students and practitioners of foreign policy frequently justify one particular policy or another by saying that the national interest "requires" it. A certain policy, they say, is "necessary." This language conveys the false impression that the policy is a direct outgrowth or an empirical expression of what *is*, rather than a statement of what someone thinks the policy *ought* to be. A policy is "required" or "necessary" only in the sense that its proponents believe it is necessary for serving certain other values which are usually not stated explicitly. The highly acclaimed concept of the national interest is not scientifically determined. It is a cluster of goals and strategies derived from more fundamental values. Traditionally, foremost among these is the preservation of the security and prosperity of the government and its supporters. This includes maintaining sovereign control over a defined territory and population. The competitive accumulation of military power and, secondarily, of economic resources, are the principal means for pursuing the values of security and prosperity.

If one chooses to depart from traditional definitions of the national interest, one is not less scientific or less empirically oriented than the defenders of traditional definitions. An untraditional orientation may simply mean that one endorses a slightly rearranged hierarchy of values.

An Alternative Framework for Decision Making

The earlier discussion of mounting foreign policy problems called into question the capacity of national societies to provide security and reasonable opportunities for the fulfillment of humanitarian values as long as governments continue acting in accordance with traditional diplomatic precepts. The challenge for policymakers now and in the future will be to bring policies, which in the past have served the national interest as traditionally defined, into harmony with the human interest in abolishing war and poverty and in halting gross denial of human rights and ecological decay. These four problems can also be stated as world order values: peace without national military arsenals (V_1), economic well-being for all inhabitants on the earth (V_2), universal human rights and social justice (V_3), and ecological balance (V_4).[36] It is imperative to make progress in achieving these values if we seek to insure the long-range survival of the species and to improve the quality of human life for all people.

Although these values may appear uncontroversial, they provide a different set of standards for policymaking than are found in traditional understandings of the national interest. Three clarifying principles will establish points of difference between the two approaches. First, the value framework proposed here rests upon the assumption that the human race is the important constituency to consider in policymaking. The world's people should benefit from policy decisions. The traditional approach gives priority to the people of one nation. It also provides more benefits for the governmental elite and its supporters within the nation than for the national population in general. Thus my proposed emphasis on the human interest differs in two ways from traditional diplomacy. First, the scope of human identity extends across national boundaries rather than remains confined to the people within them. Second, human identity expresses bonds of community between those at the top and at the bottom of the class structure. Compared to the traditional foreign policy approach, human community is expanded horizontally to include all nations and vertically to encompass all classes.

A second idea that undergirds the proposed value framework is that the service of human needs should be the guiding principle for major economic and political decisions, rather than the maximization of national power or corporate profit. This does not mean that nationhood or profit are excluded, but only that they should rank lower in the hierarchy of values than service to basic human needs. A corollary of this value orientation is that human transactions based on cooperation and a sense of human solidarity would increase, while transactions that are competitive and based on a denial of community would decrease. Competitiveness among large social groups is less useful when the human race is the subject of concern than when only a national group is the focal point for protection, production, and consumption. If fulfilling human needs is to become the guiding principle for policymaking, then those most in need should be the first to receive attention. A politics of liberation, which the fourfold value framework is designed to advance, is like the practice of medicine at its best: to help first those people who are most in need. It differs sharply from theories of politics that call for triage, the lifeboat ethic, or the trickle-down theory of development.

Third, the *entire* planet, the atmosphere around it, and the high seas are of prime concern. They are to be protected and

21

conserved for both present and unborn generations. In contrast, the exponents of the national interest place the exercise of sovereignty over one *part* of the planet's territory at the top of their hierarchy of values. They are concerned with securing advantages for "their" segment of the planet and of the human race, and they pay little attention to the needs of future generations.

The four preferred world order values and the three clarifying principles provide the value framework that I call *global humanism* in the course of this analysis. The *human interest* is the collection of goals and strategies that are consistent with and will advance the values of global humanism. The term *humane world community* is used to mean a universal human identity or all-inclusive sense of human solidarity combined with social norms and institutions that aim at achieving a life of dignity for all through an equitable sharing of decision-making powers, opportunities, and resources. *Global populism* refers both to (1) the emphasis on a citizens' movement to mobilize and empower the poor and politically weak and (2) the introduction of structural reforms inspired by the preferred values and designed to help the dispossessed.

In the course of this study, U.S. foreign policy is evaluated by the extent to which it implements or is designed to implement the values of global humanism.[37] In earlier discussion, I have argued that a foreign policy informed by such a value framework is necessary to insure human security and is desirable to achieve other values on which there is a high degree of consensus in our own society. To assess the impact of U.S. foreign policy upon the prospects for preferred world order reform, a representative case study has been selected to illustrate U.S. performance in each of the four value areas. This performance cannot be understood merely by comparing officially professed values with the values of global humanism. As in any political system, a wide gap often exists between rhetoric and reality. To account for this possible discrepancy, the analyses below will distinguish *professed values* from *implicit values*. The former are the goal values expressed in official statements about U.S. foreign policy. Implicit values are the unspoken value preferences that are embedded in actual political behavior and revealed in the value impact of the policy.

With these definitions in mind, the effort to explain the global meaning of U.S. foreign policy will proceed as follows: The first section of each case study consists of an empirical description of U.S. policy, with an emphasis on revealing the professed and implicit values of U.S. policy. The analysis clarifies whether the real value impact was consistent with the goals proclaimed in the rhetoric. Next, the implicit values are juxtaposed against the values of global humanism to determine whether U.S. policy was helping to realize a humane world community. Fourth, the· global humanist value framework is used to develop specific recommendations for future policy in the area of each case study. Finally, some indicators of world order progress are provided in order to enable scholars or political activists to check on future progress in realizing the preferred values.

One purpose of this analysis is to provide a fresh global framework by which to examine the wisdom and utility of U.S. foreign policies. This framework ideally should transcend both the idiosyncracies of this historical era and one's own political culture. I doubtless have been unable to accomplish that fully; thus the framework should be viewed as tentative and subject to refinement and modification.

Before examining U.S. policy itself, it will be useful to look at some implications and applications of the value-centered approach proposed here. We turn now to that discussion.

The Utility of a Value-Centered Approach

This study of foreign policy is a value-centered approach. It delineates the values that guide decision makers in their policy choices and that are expressed in official behavior.[38] A value-centered approach to foreign policy analysis is admittedly a break with the prevailing intellectual tradition. Most foreign policy analysis falls into one of two categories. Some authors treat foreign policy as history. They emphasize a chronological description of events. In contrast, behavioral scientists focus on the processes by which policy is made, negotiated, or executed. They discuss the interactions of officials, the effects of policy-making machinery, the politics of bureaucratic bargaining, or occasionally the psychological origins of policy. In both of these approaches, past scholarship has usually focused on the use of power, without giving much attention to the value impact of policy and to who benefits or should benefit from policies. Traditional approaches have impoverished reality and discouraged use of the imagination by excessive emphasis on the way things are and by inattention to the way they ought to be. In contrast, when a value-centered approach incorporates a rigorous empiricism with explicit attention to values embedded in policy, it yields several advantages.

In the first place, one's understanding of political events is enhanced if international politics is viewed as a value-realizing process. The observer's focus shifts away from examining the processes of political interaction by themselves and from viewing policy consequences merely as discrete events. For example, the values of officials as expressed in several policies may be compared to the global humanist values that this analysis suggests are useful guides for political action. The value impacts of specific foreign policies then provide intellectual handles by which one may grasp the normative direction in which a changing system of world order is moving.

Moreover, if observers examine foreign policy as a value-realizing process, they are able to see more clearly the recurring values that apparently idiosyncratic policies often are advancing. If similar values are repeatedly served by political leaders, one can extrapolate from this the structure of interests or the classes that benefit from the ruling group's policies. This is particularly important in attempting to define the nature of a more just world polity and in developing strategies to attain one. By assessing the desirability and consequences of political action in light of a set of explicit norms, a value-centered approach facilitates a structural analysis of social problems and remedies. This in turn helps to identify both the structures that need reform and the people who can be expected to resist or to support such change.

Whenever a state executes foreign policy, some values are advanced and others are negated. Every major policy issue contains within it a moral issue. Practitioners of foreign policy often disguise the moral code that a state follows in order to obscure the real beneficiaries of acts by the state. A value-centered approach directly attacks this problem by clarifying the implicit values of the ruling group. This provides information essential for the practice of self-government. Because many ordinary citizens implement the leadership's political values by paying taxes or sacrificing their own lives in war, they understandably want not to be deceived about the value impact of their own government's policies.

A value-centered approach also is useful for establishing preferred goals for future behavior. It encourages imaginative thinking about the possibility of change in the international system. Because a value-centered approach explicitly emphasizes human preferences, it helps chart action to reform the existing system. If in making foreign policy officials react to crises as they arise, they are unlikely to think about changing the structure of international relations. If instead they ask themselves how to implement preferred values, they would be more likely to develop alternative visions of future world order systems.

Political leaders seldom follow this approach, but when they do the results stand out boldly against the backdrop of routine diplomacy. For example, when Adlai E. Stevenson was U.S. Representative to the United Nations, he once delivered a speech entitled "Working Toward a World Without War." In it he said, "We do not hold the vision of a world without conflict. We do hold the vision of a world without war—and this inevitably requires an alternative system for coping with conflict. We cannot have one without the other."[39]

To emphasize values does not mean that one must proceed with an idealistic or optimistic view of the future. A value-centered approach may lead to a pessimistic assessment of the prospects for world order reform. One might conclude that the prevailing value perspective of officials departs widely from one's own value preferences. In such a case, the tendency of the actors within the system would be to make the future worse than the present in terms of preferred value realization.

Of course, no process of value clarification can eliminate arbitrariness or subjectivity in selecting preferred values. But this approach underscores the need to make deliberate choices and tradeoffs in the interaction of different values. In the short run at least, some preferred values may conflict with others; all cannot be grasped without the right hand knowing what the left hand is doing. To maximize food production, for example, one may need to use chemical fertilizers or pesticides that pollute. An approach that does not emphasize values obscures the choice among conflicting goals.

Moreover, value clarification can diminish unintended consequences of government behavior. The more explicit and accurate a value impact statement is, the more possible it becomes to make behavior implement value preferences. Without a clear statement of the value impact of a given policy, the possible gap between governmental rhetoric and political reality may go un-

25

noticed. Such a condition could lead citizens to support policies that in practice negate a preferred value that officials have embraced only rhetorically. This could produce citizen behavior that in practice resisted rather than encouraged a desirable change.

A value-centered approach also helps overcome the level-of-analysis problem. That is, by adopting a value framework that can be deliberately constructed so as to reflect planetary rather than strictly national concerns, it is easier to avoid the trap of looking at international relations from a parochial nation-state view. Officials can then give adequate attention to both the total world system and the subsystems within it. Sensitivity to double standards is enhanced by this approach because explicit norms can be universally applied.

It is instructive to examine one example of the level-of-analysis problem that is a central issue in this study and that traditional approaches have seldom clarified. From the nation-state vantage point, diplomacy should protect the interests of the state, usually measured in terms of power. But that is a laissez-faire approach to the interests of the *planet*. The nation-state vantage point is the international variant of the "invisible hand" of classical capitalism. Proponents of this doctrine assumed that separate people or businesses each maximizing their private economic advantages would produce desirable results for the entire society. Likewise, proponents of serving national interests assume that separate nations maximizing their national advantages will produce desirable results for world society. Such an approach is sensitive to the needs of the nation but indifferent to the interests of the planet. It oversimplifies reality by assuming that what is good for the nation is good for the world.

The weakness of the laissez-faire approach is evident in both economics and international relations. There is often a fundamental contradiction between the pursuit of private profit and the service of human needs. Some things that are profitable ought not to be done; some things that ought to be done are not profitable. Similarly, there is often a fundamental contradiction between the pursuit of national advantage of separate states and the service of global human needs. For example, taking fertile land out of production in Kansas or Iowa may be good for U.S. farmers who want to sell wheat or corn at a higher price, but not for malnourished south Asians who want to buy grain at low cost. By using preferred world order values for assessing national policies we are sensitized to this possible contradiction.

Finally, a value-centered approach also holds promise for deepening our understanding and improving the quality of decisions made in the context of a presently inescapable lack of knowledge. For example, no one knows the risks of war that are inherent in the strategy of nuclear deterrence. No one knows whether Indians are more or less secure because their government conducted one nuclear explosion in 1974. No one knows the range of values that would be sacrificed or fulfilled by a deliberate U.S. decision to disarm. When there is little knowledge available for calculating the consequences of decisions, value presuppositions become more important in the choice of behavior. In such cases values determine the outcome of decisions at a more primitive stage. The less certain we are about how to achieve our ends, the more we let our values influence the means we select for immediate action. Thus it is extremely important for policy analysts and citizens to know whether national officials value, say, national power or human life more highly.

To clarify this point, consider the following example of a dearth of knowledge. If U.S. citizens knew that the U.S. nuclear arsenal would eventually involve the United States in a nuclear war that would kill 100 million Americans and leave an additional 50 million with radiation sickness or genetic damage, presumably there would be more intense public pressure to disarm. National power or sovereignty might even be restricted in order to protect human lives. But in the absence of dependable knowledge about the risks inherent in using nuclear deterrence as a means to prevent war, the public prefers to protect national power through augmenting the nuclear arsenal. This preference may take priority over other values, including the value of human life. But the nuclear priority does not *appear* to sacrifice the value of human life because uncertain knowledge about negative consequences enables us to hope for indefinite postponement of nuclear war. The lack of knowledge about risks makes this hope plausible, although the probability of avoiding war permanently may in fact be very remote.

In contrast, abundant knowledge clarifies the relationship between means and ends. In such cases, the means chosen to implement policy must conform to the terminal values one professes to serve, or else the inappropriateness of the means can be

27

quickly shown. For example, if a man living in Chicago values a reunion with friends in Long Island, when making travel plans he would not select a flight to San Francisco. If he did, a travel agent could quickly demonstrate the inappropriateness of the action. On the other hand, lack of knowledge lets a decision maker choose *any* means which his or her value system may prefer, because no one can show that the means selected will not lead to the end professed. (Without dependable information, a flight to San Francisco appears as good as a flight to New York for one's trip to Long Island.)

Thus on foreign policy issues where imponderables abound, alarming results can occur. Decision makers are most likely to choose means that serve their vested interests. If the way to peace is seen as uncertain, then policies might as well benefit the leadership's interests while they pursue peace. Yet an elite's vested interests seldom are congruent with the global human interest, either in its domestic or global manifestations. In this example, the policy decisions might be based on a desire to protect power and wealth for national decision makers and their group of supporters within the nation, not to achieve peace or a humane world community. Who benefits most from the world-wide growth of armaments and the accumulation of U.S. power overseas? A political and economic elite? All U.S. citizens? Humanity? A plausible case could be made that the value impact of additional armaments contributes more certain and immediate benefits to the power and wealth of decision makers than to the achievement of security for the human race in the long run. Until the contrasting values—privileges for national security managers or security for ordinary people—are clear, intelligent policy for world order reform is impossible. A value-centered approach helps reveal the occasionally vested nature of the values being realized.

The Application of a Global Humanist
Framework to Alternative Images of World Order

In addition to the benefits of a value-centered approach listed above, both citizens and officials could use the four values of global humanism to construct a range of future world order options, to compare the value-realizing potential of each, and to select the foreign policies most likely to achieve the preferred values. In contrast to the waning Westphalia system, one might envisage at least four types of future world order systems:[40] a concert of great powers, a concert of multinational corporate elites, world government, and global humanism.[41]

CONCERT OF GREAT POWERS

One possible future system of world order is a slightly remodeled version of the existing system, with new emphasis on cooperation among the great powers. This could be thought of as a global, twentieth-century equivalent of Metternich's effort to achieve a concert of European great powers after the Congress of Vienna in 1815. The United States, the Soviet Union, Western Europe, Japan, and China could lower tensions among themselves and together administer many of the economic and political affairs of the rest of the world. Because such a system would be hierarchical and inequitable, it would doubtless be exploitative. It probably would not attack worldwide poverty, political repression, or ecological decay. It would flourish with client states and sphere-of-influence politics. It would also work to repress terrorism, to stabilize the world economy, and to exploit ocean resources.

If United States policy aimed to implement this option for achieving international stability, it would give priority to protecting or enhancing its power position vis-à-vis the other great powers, to seeking consensus among the great powers while ignoring the grievances of smaller powers, to defending the dollar in the world monetary system, and to developing strategies to insure access to vital raw materials from foreign markets. The government would be unconcerned about Third or Fourth World countries except insofar as liberation movements or political instability might jeopardize the opportunities for U.S. corporations to invest, buy, or sell abroad, and insofar as the former's political orientation might bear upon the power of the United States within the concert of great powers. When threats to U.S. power would arise, counterrevolutionary intervention by the United States would be likely after seeking concurrence from, or at least neutralizing the opposition of, the Soviet Union or any other relevant great powers.

CONCERT OF MULTINATIONAL CORPORATE ELITES

A second variant of future world order is global, private government by multinational corporations. In this model, corporate

29

elites act together to maximize profit and economic growth, to secure worldwide markets, and to protect the wealth and privilege of relatively few owners and managers against the protests of the poverty-stricken masses. Multinational corporate elites managing global resources would probably lead toward dampened international political conflict, increased transnational class conflict, rapid but uneven economic growth in the private sector, use of resources to maximize profit rather than the service of human needs, and relative unconcern about environmental and humanitarian issues. The Trilateral Commission, a group of wealthy, influential business people from North America, Japan, and Western Europe, illustrates this possibility. Its purposes include a transnational effort to adapt corporate capitalism to changing economic and political forces to insure capitalism's future in a nonterritorially-oriented economy facing possible conflicts with territorially-based national governments or dispossessed classes.

Multinational corporations may have some advantages over states in the approaching play of social forces leading to a new system of world order. For the first time in history, managerial skills and technology make the management of the globe as an integrated unit a genuine possibility.[42] Multinational corporations, as private agencies, can respond with more flexibility and speed to the functional unity of the globe than many national governments, which are restrained by nationally-oriented ideological and political inertia. Markets and the field for investment, after all, are nonterritorial and include the planet, whereas national governments still operate from a territorial base. The nonterritorial perspective of corporate managers maximizing profits may put them at odds with the national government ruling the territory in which the corporation is primarily based. For example, when the price of crude oil increases, this may be much less objectionable to U.S.-based multinational oil corporations than to the United States government, representing a constituency territorially more limited in scope than the oil companies themselves. Multinational corporations place less emphasis than national governments on the interests of one state in the system or the well-being of its domestic population.

U.S. foreign policy could serve this image of world order by facilitating the movement of capital abroad, by allowing corporations to escape the domain of any national government's effective regulation, by not restricting high profits on the corporate provision of vital resources, and by declining to insure that the major corporations scrupulously respect the environment or serve the general public rather than private interest. If large corporations are able to influence governmental policies sufficiently, either through the placement of members of the business elite in positions of political decision making or through financial support and control of government officials recruited from outside the business elite, the government itself will serve the interests of multinational corporations more directly, meanwhile giving less attention to national interests more traditionally defined as territorially-based security and prosperity.

WORLD GOVERNMENT

The prescriptions favored by most traditional advocates of world government are contained in *World Peace Through World Law* by Grenville Clark and Louis Sohn. They described a greatly strengthened United Nations with modified voting procedures, world disarmament, and world federation on a sufficient scale to prevent future military buildups. This model aims to create "an effective system of *enforceable* world law in the limited field of war prevention."[43] It gives less attention to the other values of global humanism.

If U.S. policy were to aim at achieving this option, policymakers would seek to amend the UN Charter in order to democratize the voting procedures and qualify the veto principle. In addition, after accepting enhanced decision making and enforcement authority for the UN, the United States would need to undertake substantial arms reductions. Until an effective strategy is developed for implementing this vision, its very low political feasibility makes it unrealistic in the foreseeable future. Its implementation rests on agreement among national governments to restrict their sovereignty voluntarily. This is unlikely given present political attitudes and institutions.

GLOBAL HUMANISM

A system based on global humanism can be illustrated by the image of world order developed by the North American team of participants in the World Order Models Project. Richard A. Falk has elaborated this model in *A Study of Future Worlds*.[44] It calls for drastic changes in the existing configuration of power, wealth, and authority during the next thirty years. The transition strategy calls for widespread education, attitudinal changes, and

31

populist mobilization to realize substantial gains in preferred values without recourse to violence and without the traumas that would attend nuclear war, widespread famine, or ecological collapse.

This model, slightly revised by the present author, is described here in greater detail than the other models because it provides a tentative vision of how the world might look if global humanist values were pursued in U.S. foreign policies.

One particularly appealing feature of the model is that it avoids merely a transferal of state power and authority to a unified world government. Instead, authority and power are dispersed in *two* directions from the national level: "downward" toward provincial or local governments as well as "upward" toward a central guidance agency. The happy result is a form of policy coordination that increases the capacity for global administration without increasing the overall bureaucratic presence in human life at various levels of social organization. Two countervailing organizational tendencies would be present: (1) *centralization* of functional control and planning to enable more equitable allocation of scarce resources, to protect endangered values in the "commons," and to enforce provisions for disarmament; and (2) *decentralization* of political structures combined with localization of identification patterns. The focus of human identity, now pinpointed upon national symbols, would be dispersed to include global human solidarity on the one hand, and increased subnational identification and participation in political and economic decisions on the other.

This model avoids the hierarchical centralization implicit in most classical schemes for world government. It seeks to create global policy coordination with wide dispersion of authority and distribution of power among various actors, such as global and regional intergovernmental organizations, national governments, local or provincial governments, and transnational coalitions of people or private organizations acting in the global arena without going through their respective national governments.

In general, this constitutional structure would tolerate less efficiency to achieve diverse, equitable participation and to inhibit the abuse of concentrated powers. Proposed governing machinery might include the following:

1. A world assembly would set general policy respectful of global humanist values. It would be organized to represent

peoples, nongovernmental organizations, states, and regional groups.

2. A smaller council would apply the policy of the assembly and act in its place during emergencies.

3. Supporting administrative agencies would assure that directives of the former bodies are carried out by other actors in the system. It would also provide feedback useful for tailoring policies to fulfill the values of global humanism. Agencies for implementation would be organized around the following four functions.

a. A world security system would include a transnational peace force, a world disarmament service, and a world grievance system. The latter would insure that all states could respond to policy decisions. It would also facilitate peaceful change to avoid the danger that a global system did not merely enforce a peace of the status quo. Individuals and nongovernmental organizations, as well as governments and intergovernmental organizations, could forward complaints to this body.

b. A world economic system would include agencies for economic planning, equity, world monetary policy, taxing authority, and development. This cluster of agencies would facilitate economic development aimed at insuring economic well-being for all, promoting intergroup and intragroup economic equity and achieving balance between human activity and ecological capacities for disposal and resource use. Economic policies would be tailored to curtail wasteful growth and to encourage growth aimed at fulfilling human needs.

c. A human rights commission and court would enhance the prospects for respecting human dignity and human rights. Any person or group could take grievances to these bodies.

d. A global environmental authority would establish procedures to monitor pollutants, to set and enforce waste disposal standards, and to conserve and allocate scarce resources fairly. The authority would seek to implement a humane transition from a growth orientation to an equilibrium orientation respectful both of nature and of human needs. An effort would be made to establish an index of Gross National Quality to highlight the qualitative rewards that may compensate for the quantitative decline in Gross National Product which some wealthy societies may encounter during the effort to equalize world incomes and to avoid injury to the environment.

The benefits from this system, as well as the strategy for

Table 1-1
A Summary Comparison of Alternative
World Order Systems, 1980-2000[a]

Leadership	Westphalian nation-state system	Concert of great powers
Basic aspirations	Sovereign independence, unregulated governmental behavior	Geopolitical stability, political and economic inequity
Strategy for fulfillment of aspirations	Competitive power-seeking in decentralized international system	Consensus of dominant governments, stratified inter-governmental system, regional spheres of influence
Performance in implementing global humanist values:		
Peace	Low	Medium
Economic well-being	Low	Low
Social justice	Low	Low
Ecological balance	Low	Medium
Performance in achieving human solidarity:		
Vertical (transclass) identity	Medium	Medium
Horizontal (transnational) identity	Low	Low

[a] Several of the categories in this table are adapted from Richard A. Falk, "A New Paradigm for International Legal Studies," p. 1001.

achieving it, are consistent with populism in a global context. This image of world order seeks to avoid both the multinational corporate elite's tendency to put corporate profit and growth above human needs and conservation, and the national governmental elite's tendency to impose nationalist advantages and values upon major political and economic activity, with little regard for global implications.

In contrast to the world government approach, the populist

Table 1-1 (cont.)

Concert of multinational corporations	World government	Humane world community
Unregulated economic growth, profit maximization, capital intensive technology, high consumption	Enforced disarmament, strengthened international institutions	Dependable peace, economic well-being for all, respect for human rights and social justice, ecological balance
Consensus among privileged elites, stratified transnational system	Negotiations among national governments	Global populist movement, major attitudinal and value change
High	High	High
Low	Medium	High
Low	Low	High
Low	Medium	High
Low	Medium	High
High	Medium	High

image places greater emphasis on the likelihood of political conflict with entrenched elites in the process of transforming the existing system, and on the need to mobilize support among dispossessed peoples presently not influential in government processes. The global humanist perspective emphasizes values that transcend the limits of class and national boundaries and that anticipate the emergence of a system of nonterritorial central guidance. This perspective is based on an understanding that the outcome of the present transition period will be determined by the interplay of statist, business, and populist social forces.

35

This approach reflects a belief that the most beneficial future world order system will be responsive to populist demands for peace, economic equity, social and political dignity, and ecological balance.

The global humanist vision offers a humane alternative to the neo-Darwinian trend in the establishment of a concert of great powers or multinational corporate elites. This trend is encouraged by resource scarcity and political or economic competition, in which both national governmental and corporate elites seek to accumulate more power and prosperity for their respective national or corporate constituencies, neither of which represents humanity at large. The global humanist option seeks to reorient institutions so they will serve the needs of all people rather than the wants of a privileged minority.

Images of the Future and the Content of Foreign Policy

The preceding four images of alternative futures help us understand the present. With an awareness of several alternatives it is easier to appraise the meaning of contrasting foreign policies for the future of humanity. Without some reflection about alternative futures, policymaking is little more than tactical calculation to maintain an unsatisfactory status quo or to gain a short-range advantage in an otherwise aimless drift on the expansive, uncharted waters of the future. Or even worse, some narrowly based but powerful elites may seek to implement an image of the future that the majority of people would oppose if the future world prospects were openly exposed.

The preceding models also enable one to take steps toward the particular future that one desires. Of the four options discussed, world government seems politically unfeasible, and the concerts of great powers or corporate elites are deficient in realizing one or more important values. Therefore, the global humanist image of world order will be used to assess the performance of U.S. policy in the remainder of this study.

The political attractiveness of a vision of world order based on an open, self-correcting understanding of the values of global humanism could be critically important in determining which of several alternative models of the future will in fact become reality. What people implicitly believe about how the world functions and will function in the future contributes to making it function that way in the present as well as in the future. It is commonplace to say that past events influence or determine the

36

present, but growing evidence suggests it is no less accurate to say that one's image of the future determines the present.[45] For example, when a foreign policy bureaucracy views the present international system as continuing indefinitely into the future, that bureaucracy constructs policy in ways that prevent another future from being realized.

In making decisions, an official must extend lines of action into the future and select among alternatives according to his or her expectations about future events.[46] An official's image of the immediate future, even if not explicitly stated, influences current governmental behavior. That behavior opens some doors and closes others for the future. As sociologists Wendell Bell and James A. Mau have correctly warned: "Today's images of the future need elaboration, refinement, and revision; the actual future is rolling over people and whole societies before they are prepared; the possibilities of a better life are not being fulfilled as adequately as they could be."[47]

Taking this advice into account, the chapters that follow seek to clarify (1) the image of world order upon which current U.S. foreign policies are based and (2) the image of a preferred future that could inspire future foreign policies that will be likely to produce a more humane world community.

TWO · *The Strategic Arms Limitation Talks*

THE possibility of nuclear war is an obvious and immediate threat to all human civilization. Permanent peace remains one of the most profound yet unrealized human yearnings. Approximately since the incineration of Hiroshima, technological conditions have existed for both (1) an irreversible disaster for the human race in event of war and (2) a truly worldwide, demilitarized system of public order. Political and social institutions have conditioned human beings more for acceptance of world war than for promotion of world community. Since the Second World War, more than ten million persons have been killed in various wars. Every person on the planet lives under the threat of unfathomable destruction or inescapable radiation hazards posed by the prospect of even distant nuclear conflicts. Since 1945, the worldwide quantity of resources devoted to military purposes has more than tripled. The proportion of world output going to military uses has increased to about 6.5 percent, roughly twice the proportion of output during the years preceding World War I.[1]

Although many persons would deny its attainability, few would dispute the desirability of the first value of global humanism: to minimize collective violence and eventually to establish permanent peace without massive military arsenals. V_1 aims at the elimination of war; disarmament; and the establishment of dependable procedures for peaceful change, adjudication of disputes, and enforcement of disarmament. Advocates of global humanism do not view the minimization of collective violence in isolation from the other world order values. Its realization, for example, is both more desirable and more feasible with the concomitant achievement of worldwide human rights and justice.

It is difficult to assess governmental performance in implementing the first value of global humanism because of our inability to predict the causes, scope, duration, and probability of wars. Nonetheless, some commonsense assessments are possible about the merits of national security policies, the destructive capabilities of states, and, perhaps, even the countries most likely to engage in war.[2] Destructive capability, speed of inflict-

38

ing injury, the indiscriminate character of weaponry, and the vulnerability of human civilizations to extinction by military technology have all increased in this century. At the same time, the weapons of mass destruction have not substantially reduced the perceived likelihood of war. On the contrary, government officials of the superpowers perceive a constant need for continued increments to their arsenals, with the tacit assumption that some day the weapons may be used in lethal conflict. In the meantime, the arsenals are instruments of psychological and diplomatic conflict, confirming a second tacit assumption that the major actors in the international system are unprepared to move away from a system of mutual threat that is ultimately based on massive military firepower.

Progress toward minimizing collective violence could be measured in part by various indexes:

—total battlefield casualties per year;

—total military expenditures, or military expenditures as a percentage of total world output;

—the rate of change in military expenditures compared to expenditures in other fields of social endeavor;

—the size and configuration of arms sales or transfers;

—the spread of knowledge and capability to produce weapons of mass destruction;

—the growth and utilization of nonlethal procedures for settlement of disputes;

—the fluctuation of patterns and objects of loyalty for national and global political or economic structures;

—the growth of international restraints, such as arms control agreements, upon deployment of weapons.

Even these relatively simple indicators present unresolvable controversies and uncertainties. For example, it is widely believed among government officials that the best way to prevent war is to be able to win (or, in the nuclear age, at least, not to allow the opponent to win) any war that may occur. For those who believe that violence is minimized by building the most powerful and efficient instruments of death, a decrease in military expenditures represents regress. For those who believe that present wars must be fought to avoid future wars, even a decline in battlefield casualties for one or several years may be cause for discouragement. Proponents of these and other defense postures are inclined to maintain that a high probability for particular wars may come and go, but the war system is here to stay.

Thus, they give their attention to relatively short-run calculations about specific conflicts breaking into war. The analysis that follows is less concerned with the slightly fluctuating odds for war—significant though they are in any particular year—than with assessing the progress toward supplanting the existing militarized international system with a security system that would eventually make possible the elimination of large national military establishments.[3]

Recognizing the controversy that will surround any effort to assess the realization of a demilitarized world system, I have attempted to select an illustrative case study that offers some analytic promise for those who seek peace through the military equality of the superpowers, as well as for those who seek disarmament.[4] This analysis focuses on United States military expenditures, capabilities, and strategic doctrine within the context of efforts for armament limitations. The development of arms control policy represents the most accessible and important effort by the United States to build a more peaceful system of world order. Officials as well as the general public have widely embraced arms control as one of the most promising approaches to halting the arms buildup and setting the stage for disarmament. Perhaps most important, the focus on arms control makes sense because dependable world peace is unlikely without disarmament. The perpetuation of nuclear deterrence encourages a permanent war mentality because a well-armed "enemy" is never more than a few minutes away. Moreover, the technical requirements of deterrence as a mechanism for security will ensure an influential role in policymaking for the military-industrial complex which has a built-in propensity to press for new armaments.

The Vladivostok agreement of November 23, 1974, provides an instructive case study for examining the impact of United States policy on the first value of global humanism. Rooted in the Strategic Arms Limitation Talks (SALT) which began in 1969, it was the result of long planning by senior officials of the United States, and of a major diplomatic initiative spanning two administrations. In addition, the Vladivostok agreement was a product of efforts by both the United States and the Soviet Union to promote an atmosphere of détente. It came at a juncture of technological development (before deployment of multiple independently targetable reentry vehicles [MIRVs] by the Soviet Union) during which a major new step in arms competition was likely, but not yet politically impossible to prevent. If the Vladivostok agreement was not typical of arms control negotiations, then it was an atypically positive experience, insofar as it actually provided the basis for an arms control agreement that may be formally consummated in the Carter administration. The accord and the earlier SALT agreements of 1972 are the most important strategic products of arms control negotiations since 1963. Thus, the Vladivostok agreement presents the prospects for arms control in a favorable context.

U.S. policies on arms control negotiations and strategic military doctrine, the trend of military spending and foreign arms sales, and the extent of international structural change that officials have envisaged were all revealed by SALT. The accord mirrors the accomplishments and failures of previous negotiations, extending back to 1946.[5] By scrutinizing the accord's provisions and omissions in the context of earlier negotiations, the principal recurring interests of the United States—whether defended or ignored—are vividly portrayed.

The process of continually increasing and modernizing U.S. armaments involves far more than merely adding to the number of missiles or submarines in the arsenal. More than half of the undesignated funds in the national budget are spent annually for military purposes; the executive and legislative branches are therefore heavily preoccupied with military power and its possible applications around the world. The governing process itself becomes militarized. With the consideration of force always near the center of foreign policymaking, many civilian officials of the vast defense bureaucracies and chairmen of the influential armed services and appropriations committees in Congress develop a military mind-set not unlike that of career military officials. Military planners, administrators, employees, weapons researchers, arms producers, and labor unions dependent on military production represent a formidable array of talent and sheer numbers. They are well financed, and many are strategically located to influence the policy process in order to encourage lavish military spending and the dominance of military considerations in foreign policy.

The mere availability of military power, as well as the desire to enhance it, often influences the outcome of decision making. For example, the existence of sophisticated counterinsurgency equipment encouraged officials to think first about a military response to events in Indochina in the 1960s, and only secondarily

41

about a political settlement without violence. The application of military power makes officials insensitive to the human consequences of policies where force is never far from the central consideration. Governments with enormous military power at their disposal usually react less compassionately than they would without such power. A continuing arms buildup has led the United States to seek military allies and to arm other governments, thus contributing to the militarization of the political processes in other countries. A refusal to cut back military expenditures generally decreases support for human rights as well as the resources available for the economic development of less developed countries.

This analysis will proceed as follows: first, by describing the fruits of U.S. policy in the SALT I and Vladivostok agreements; second, by explaining the professed values and policy goals of U.S. officials in justifying United States policy; third, by comparing these professed values with the values implicit in governmental behavior itself; and fourth, by comparing the value impacts of United States policy with those sought by advocates of global humanism.

DESCRIPTION OF U.S. ARMS CONTROL POLICIES

Antecedents of the Vladivostok Agreement

The Vladivostok agreement of 1974 grew out of efforts that began in 1969, and that had produced the earlier agreement known as "SALT I," which included two documents signed on May 26, 1972. The first of these limited antiballistic missile systems (ABMs) to no more than two sites. The parties also agreed not to develop, test, or deploy ABM systems that were sea-based, air-based, space-based, or mobile land-based. These obligations were of unlimited duration.[6]

The second document, called the Interim Agreement, limited strategic offensive arms.[7] It prohibited the construction of additional fixed land-based intercontinental ballistic missile launchers for a period of five years. The two governments also agreed not to convert existing land-based launchers for "light" ICBMs into launchers for heavy ICBMs. In practice, this agreement restricted, to a maximum of 313, the deployment of the very large Soviet SS-9 missile, capable of carrying a 25-megaton warhead. In addition, the parties were prohibited from exceeding the numbers of submarine-launched ballistic missiles (SLBMs) then in operation and under construction, except by following special conditions for replacement. These conditions enabled the United States to increase its SLBM launchers from the existing 656 to 710 on a one-for-one replacement basis for ballistic missile launchers deployed on land before 1964, or for older submarine launchers. On the same basis, the Soviet Union could increase its SLBM launchers to 950. In practice, therefore, SALT I limited ABMs to two sites in each country, and ICBMs and SLBMs to levels operational or already under construction.

Because of the technological lead of the United States in developing MIRVs, the Interim Agreement enabled the United States to have more than twice the number of deliverable warheads that the Soviet Union could deploy (5,700 to 2,500 at the time of signing). United States missiles were also generally recognized to be more accurate than Soviet missiles, and those installed on submarines had a longer range than their Soviet counterparts. In addition, because of U.S. submarine-tending bases overseas, it took three Soviet submarines for every two in the U.S. fleet for equivalent numbers "on station." The Soviet Union had larger warheads on many of its launchers than did the United States, but this factor was less important in calculating total destructive capability (in terms of number of targets) than the accuracy and number of independently targetable warheads. In both of these areas, the United States had large advantages.

The United States and Soviet Union also agreed that further negotiations should aim to limit strategic weapons for longer than the five years covered in the Interim Agreement itself. The accord at Vladivostok was the product of those efforts.

The Vladivostok Agreement

At Vladivostok, President Gerald Ford and Party Secretary Leonid Brezhnev agreed to limit strategic offensive weapons to 2,400 launch vehicles, with no more than 1,320 of them containing MIRVs. The ceilings, which were to continue until 1985, included ICBMs, SLBMs, and strategic bombers. The "mix" of the three types of launchers could be determined and changed unilaterally by each party. Construction of new missile silos and enlargement of existing silos beyond 15 percent of existing capacity were prohibited. NATO forces and U.S. vehicles part of the

NATO European force were not counted in the total launch vehicles. Although the terms of the agreement appeared to be simple and apparently equal, the picture became complicated and controversial when assessments were made of the meaning of Vladivostok for future arms competition. Indeed, after more than four years had passed since the Vladivostok ceilings were announced, they had not yet been incorporated into a legally binding treaty. When the Carter administration took office in 1977, it tried to lower the ceilings from the Vladivostok levels, and preliminary reports suggested that they would be reduced by approximately 10 percent. Given the large numbers involved in the original ceilings, plus the range of subjects not covered by either the Ford or Carter proposals, the conclusions drawn from the following analysis of the Vladivostok accord apply also to the SALT II agreement.

From a global perspective, the central question is whether the potential agreement will lay the groundwork for reversing the general arms buildup. To answer that question, we will examine, first of all, official statements explaining U.S. policy and, secondly, that policy's concrete impact on the arms competition.

OFFICIAL RATIONALE COMPARED TO THE VALUES IMPLICIT IN U.S. POLICY

Nearly all officials in both the executive and legislative branches agreed that the most important goals in the conduct of foreign policy were to promote national security and international stability and peace. For most, these three were inseparable. Only a secure United States, the argument went, could help secure the world. And international stability, which perpetuated U.S. preeminence, was seen as the essential condition for peace.

Arms control, among other means, could help achieve stability. The government declared that the Strategic Arms Limitation Talks served the purposes of "enhancement of national security, strategic stability, and détente through dialogue and agreements with the Soviet Union." The negotiations were "aimed at the limitation and reduction of both offensive and defensive strategic arms."[8] Officials maintained that an arms control agreement, such as one based on the Vladivostok accord, would contribute to security because it would (1) slow the arms race; (2) curtail military spending; (3) pave the way for future arms reductions; and (4) reduce international tensions that caused war. Let us examine these instrumental values and then assess whether they were implemented in United States arms control policy.

Professed Value 1: To Slow the Arms Race

Executive officials hailed the Vladivostok agreement as a major step toward stopping the arms competition between the United States and the Soviet Union. President Ford described the agreement as "a real breakthrough [that] puts a cap on the arms race." He announced that "we put a firm ceiling on the strategic arms race which has heretofore eluded us since the nuclear age began. . . . [W]e have . . . set firm and equal limits on the strategic forces of each side, thus preventing an arms race with all its terror, instability, war-breeding tension and economic waste."[9]

Secretary of State Henry Kissinger appeared equally certain of the historic importance of the agreement. He said that the agreement "marks the breakthrough with the strategic arms limitation negotiations that we have sought to achieve in recent years."[10] He promised that when it was formally ratified, it would "be seen as one of the turning points in the history of the post-World War II arms race."[11] The secretary declared that "a cap has been put on the arms race for a period of ten years. . . . The element of insecurity, inherent in an arms race in which both sides are attempting to anticipate not only the actual programs but the capabilities of the other side, will be substantially reduced."[12] Moreover, he stated: "For the first time in the nuclear age . . . the arms race will not be driven by the fear of what the other side might be able to do but only by the agreed ceilings that have been established. That can be justly described as a major breakthrough."[13] The president and the secretary of state even declared that the agreement "actually reduces a part of the buildup at the present time. . . . [W]e actually made some reductions below present programs."[14] Secretary of Defense James Schlesinger echoed these sentiments in describing the agreement as "a very major step forward . . . and a major accomplishment."[15]

NEW CEILINGS COMPARED WITH EXISTING ARMS

The truthfulness of this promising rhetoric can be tested by comparing the missiles deployed before the Vladivostok agreement with those allowed afterwards. Two principal elements of the agreement must be examined: the maximum permissible number of strategic launch vehicles for nuclear weapons and the sublimit established for the maximum number of vehicles that could carry MIRVs. As Table 2-1 indicates, a total of 4,473 strate-

Table 2-1

Comparison of the Vladivostok Ceilings for Strategic Delivery Vehicles
with the Total Number of Vehicles Deployed by 1974

	Launch vehicles deployed by 1974	*Launch vehicles allowed by the Vladivostok Agreement*
U.S.		
ICBMs	1,054	
SLBMs	656	
Bombers		
(B-52s)	420[a]	
Subtotal	2,130	2,400
USSR		
ICBMs	1,567	
SLBMs	636	
Bombers		
(Mya-4s and Tu-20s)	140	
Subtotal	2,343	2,400
Total deployed	4,473	Ceiling set 4,800
Increase of 327 launchers or 7.3 percent		

NOTE: [a] The Department of Defense has often considered FB-111s capable of strategic bombing missions. Their range is 3,300 nautical miles. (See, for example, James R. Schlesinger, *Annual Defense Department Report*, FY 1976, p. II-19.) However, FB-111s are not included in this table because they were excluded from the original Vladivostok ceilings. The United States possessed 76 of them.

gic launchers were deployed by the two countries at the time the Vladivostok agreement set a new ceiling of 4,800. The new ceiling represented an increase of 7.3 percent, or a total of 327 launch vehicles, which, if MIRVed, contained far more than enough power to devastate any national society on earth.

The MIRV ceiling most fully revealed the true significance of the agreement. At the time of the Vladivostok meeting, the United States had deployed 832 MIRVed vehicles, 352 on submarines and 480 Minutemen. The Soviet Union had no MIRVs. President Ford's "very major step forward" allowed a total of 2,640 MIRVed vehicles, an increase of 217 percent. The ceilings allowed 1,808 new MIRVed vehicles resulting in a total that was 3.3 times higher than the existing levels. (See Table 2-2.)

Conservatively estimated, a MIRVed missile may carry an average of 4 warheads more than an un-MIRVed missile; on that basis the Vladivostok agreement allowed a total superpower increase

Table 2-2
Comparison of the Total MIRVs Deployed by 1974
with the Vladivostok Ceilings

	MIRVs *deployed by 1974*	MIRVs *allowed by the Vladivostok Agreement*
U.S.	832	1,320
USSR	0	1,320
Total	832	2,640
	Increase of 1,808 MIRVed vehicles, or 217 percent	

of 7,232 warheads, or nearly three times the total existing Soviet arsenal of 1974. The increase was almost equivalent to the existing number of warheads in the total U.S. strategic arsenal. Poseidon nuclear missiles carried a maximum of 14 warheads, and a convention among strategists was to use a figure of 10 warheads per Poseidon to figure their average capacity. (Decreasing the number of warheads allowed the missile to fly further or also to carry penetration aids, such as decoys.) The Trident C-4 missile will carry 20 warheads. If one assumed a less conservative average of 9 extra warheads per missile over the number possible without MIRVs, the destructive potential added by the Vladivostok agreement was nearly equal to twice the combined United States-Soviet ICBM and SLBM capacity of 1974.[16]

Throughout the years before, during, and after the Interim and Vladivostok agreements, the United States set the pace for warhead deployment. The United States had a three-to-one lead over the Soviet Union in 1974. Nonetheless, between mid-1974 and mid-1975, the United States increased its number of warheads by 850. In the same period, the Soviet Union increased its force by 300. During the five years in which the Interim Agreement was in force (1972-77), the number of warheads in the U.S. strategic missile arsenal increased by 100 percent.[17]

The replacement of a single warhead on a launch vehicle by multiple independently targetable warheads generally de-

47

Figure 2-1
Total U.S. and U.S.S.R. Strategic Delivery Vehicles[a]

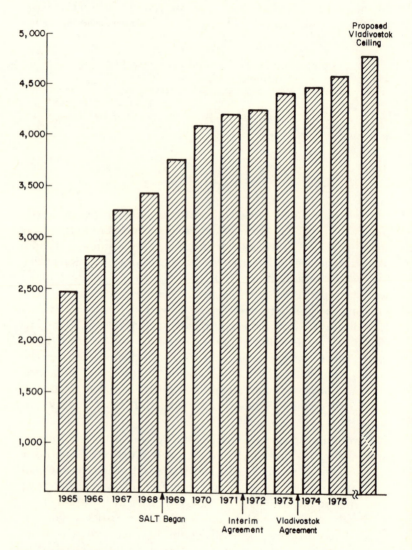

[a]This graph excludes 66 U.S. FB-111's which were not included in the original Vladivostok agreement. See note, Table 2-1.

Figure 2-2
Total U.S. and U.S.S.R. Warheads on Strategic Delivery Vehicles[a]

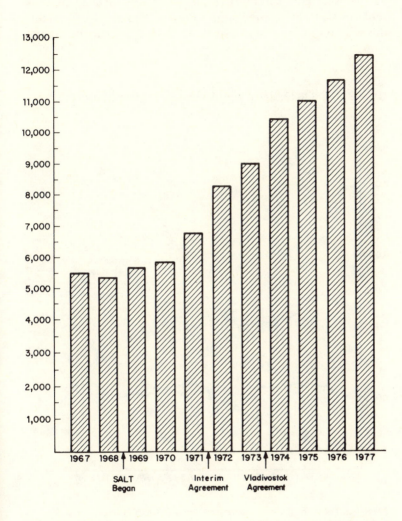

Source: Robert C. Johansen, "A Global Humanist Critique of National Policies for Arms Control," *The Journal of International Affairs*, Vol. 31 (Fall/Winter, 1977), p. 226. Reprinted with permission.

[a] Totals include U.S. FB-111's.

creased the total megatonnage that a given missile could carry, due to added weight of the separate warheads and triggering mechanisms. For example, a single 3-megaton warhead might be replaced with three .7-megaton MIRVs on the same missile. Thus, the MIRVing of launchers usually increased destructive capabil-

Figure 2-3
U.S. and U.S.S.R. Strategic Vehicles and Strategic Warheads[a]

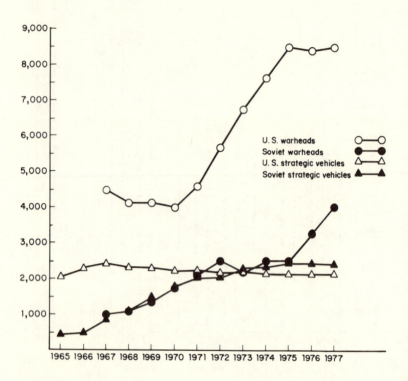

Source: Data taken from Stockholm International Peace Research Institute, *World Armaments and Disarmament: SIPRI Yearbook 1974* (Cambridge: MIT Press, 1974), pp. 106-07, and *SIPRI Yearbook 1977* (Stockholm: Almquist & Wiksell, 1977), pp. 24-25

[a] Totals include U.S. FB-111's.

ity, in terms of the number of targets that could be hit, although it did not increase megatonnage per launcher. Three .7-megaton warheads, if delivered on target, could destroy three cities, whereas one 3-megaton weapon would destroy only one city and some surrounding suburbs.[18]

Compared with the ceilings allowed for launchers in the accord of 1972, with the quantities of vehicles deployed at the time of the Vladivostok meeting, or with the total number of deliverable warheads possessed by both sides in 1974, the new ceilings set by the Vladivostok agreement allowed substantial increases in the size of the forces.

Even the preceding analysis, however, does not fully reveal the extent to which the arms race continued unabated after the Vladivostok agreement. The omissions of the agreement nullified the significance of its prohibitions. A country's destructive capability, one must recall, depended not only on the number of its launchers, but also on the number of its warheads, the yield of the various warheads, and the accuracy of the vehicles in delivering the warheads on target. Of these four factors, the agreement sought only to regulate the first, which was becoming less and less important in the then current stage of weapons development. Given the areas of competition that remained uncontrolled, what was the significance of the agreement?

First of all, even the highly acclaimed limit on the number of strategic launchers was far less significant than officials asserted. The ceiling meant little, since new, more accurate, and more powerful vehicles could replace the old. Existing silos could be loaded with indefinitely "improved" missiles of similar diameters, or the silos themselves could be increased by 15 percent to accommodate even larger missiles. In defending the agreement's "flexibility," Kissinger noted that the United States could, through technical improvements, deploy missiles with larger throw weight, "so there is no effective limit on the increase in our throw weight."[19] Except for retaining the freeze on the deployment of the Soviet SS-9 or other equally "heavy" ICBMs, as established in the Interim Agreement, no limits were set on the throw weight of replacement missiles.

The refusal of the superpowers to limit throw weight to that of existing deployments was significant, because they also chose to set no ceiling on the number of warheads and bombs each side might possess. Neither did the two governments place a maximum upon the total megatonnage each side could deploy.

51

By increasing the throw weight of their missiles, the parties could also increase the number of warheads per missile and the yield per warhead. Since modifications in the capabilities of the launchers were allowed, even the absolute limit on launchers, which was the central "accomplishment" of the accord, meant very little.

The failure to restrict improvements in missiles, increases in the number of warheads, and total deployable megatonnage also undermined the Vladivostok agreement's second major accomplishment—the sublimit on MIRved vehicles. To begin with, the ceiling of 1,320 MIRVs was well above existing levels. More importantly, since each MIRved vehicle could carry an unspecified number of warheads, the overall limit of 1,320 had little restrictive significance.

Any constraining quality of the already weak accord was eroded further by Soviet and American unwillingness to ban the testing and development of new missiles, bombers, and guidance systems. Technological competition would continue without limits. With no restraint on testing and development of missiles, totally new weapons—such as strategic cruise missiles launched from mobile platforms on land, sea, or air—could be deployed. U.S. programs to improve the accuracy of missiles and the yield-to-weight ratios of warheads would increase the U.S. capacity to destroy a large portion of the Soviet land-based ICBM force. Although well behind the United States in such technology, the Soviet Union could eventually develop a similar capability. Testing could also proceed on "cold launch" or "pop-up" missile launchers. This technique would facilitate heavier payloads and, when perfected, allow rapid firing of a second or third missile from a single silo. (The missile would be ejected from the silo before the main engines were ignited, thus sparing the silo from the fire damage that normally prevents the silo from being used again immediately.) Should these techniques be successfully developed, the limit on even the number of silos would be insignificant.[20]

Futhermore, the agreement's failure to prohibit underground testing of nuclear weapons allowed both sides to continue the type of testing that would enable them to increase the explosive power per pound of warhead. The result would be to add more independently targetable warheads to each missile. The Atomic Energy Commission's test program was actually *accelerated* after the Vladivostok accord, so a more destructive warhead could be prepared for deployment on the Minuteman.[21]

In addition, the SALT I sublimits on SLBMs were completely abandoned at Vladivostok. This opened the way for military officials to deploy the new Trident submarine, already under development. The previous arms control agreement could be cast aside when it inhibited deployment of a new weapon that officials wanted to manufacture.

There were no limits placed on *any* intermediate-range weapons, including missiles and bombers, any number of which could be stationed within appropriate range for large-scale attack. Thus, technical breakthroughs which occurred during the unrestricted testing and development could be incorporated in unlimited numbers in a country's nuclear arsenal if it were deployed in a "non-strategic" role. This possibility, of course, was facilitated by not establishing a limit in the total megatonnage either side could poise for attack. The possession by the United States of about 7,000 nuclear weapons in Europe that did not come under the strategic limitations demonstrated that this potential was by no means small. Some tactical weapons contained three times the explosive power of the Hiroshima bomb. Paul Nitze, the former deputy secretary of defense and defense department representative on the U.S. SALT delegation, declared that by not including the Soviet "Backfire" and the U.S. FB-111 (medium-range bombers) and by not restricting tankers (which can give long-range capability to medium-range aircraft), "the entire concept of a 2,400 ceiling on ICBMs, SLBMs, and heavy bombers becomes essentially meaningless."[22] Finally, as Secretary Kissinger confirmed, the Vladivostok agreement did not curtail any weapons program then in progress or planned before the agreement.[23] "In fact," said Air Force Secretary John McLucas, "SALT II proposed ceilings generally consistent with our previously planned programs."[24]

In order to slow the arms race, the most important areas to control were those in which the agreement was unrestrictive. The single exception to this was the MIRV ceilings, but these were so high as to constitute little dampening effect during a ten-year period. Well before the Vladivostok agreement, Malcolm R. Currie, the director of defense research and engineering, testified that the most disquieting aspects of the arms competition were "qualitative improvements," such as sophistication of ICBMs and SLBMs, improved accuracy, increased throw weight, and MIRVed warheads.[25] Of all these, only MIRVs were limited by a ceiling; and that became a target toward which each side would *increase* its arsenals.

In trying to refute the criticism that the agreement's ceilings were too high, the Ford administration argued that, in spite of the continued buildup permitted in the agreement, it kept the levels of weaponry lower than they would have been otherwise. It was, of course, impossible to know what might have occurred without the agreement. Nevertheless, some evidence cast doubt on the Ford-Kissinger contention. Secretary Schlesinger offered detailed information supporting his belief that the agreement encouraged larger strategic forces than previously planned. Given the very high MIRV ceilings, defense officials perceived a major "restructuring" of strategic forces as even more necessary than before the accord. The restructuring would place less emphasis on land-based missiles and more emphasis on the relatively invulnerable submarine-based missiles and highly flexible manned bombers. After the Vladivostok agreement was signed, Schlesinger announced the United States would need (1) to build two more Tridents than the ten already planned, at a cost of about $2 billion each; (2) to keep ten Poseidon submarines in service longer than planned; (3) to decide definitely in favor of manufacturing a new strategic bomber; (4) to develop and deploy a new, larger ICBM in existing silos; and (5) to develop larger and more accurate warheads for the existing Minuteman missiles. To be sure, each of these categories of weapons had been under development before the Vladivostok agreement. But Schlesinger believed the agreement confirmed and, in some cases, expanded the need for deployment of these new weapons.[26]

Space does not permit a listing here of the scores of weapons programs that were initiated or pushed forward after the Vladivostok agreement. But some of the most important should be mentioned. Research, development, and in some cases deployment of the following were carried forward after the Vladivostok agreement:

—the Trident submarine with 24 missile tubes;

—the long-range Trident missile;

—a maneuverable reentry vehicle (MARV) with pinpoint accuracy;

—additional ICBM research, to provide greater yield, accuracy, and throw weight for the Minuteman;

—the Command Data Buffer System, permitting the Minuteman III to be retargeted remotely and rapidly;

—the M-X, an entirely new, larger ICBM;

—alternative basing modes for warheads, such as land-mobile or aircraft-launched missiles;

—the cruise missile, which could maneuver and target itself after being launched from a submarine, ship, aircraft, or mobile land base;

—a new aerial tanker for airborne refueling, to give bombers greater range and carrying capacity;

—various sophisticated guidance and command technologies, such as the Advanced Ballistic Reentry System (ABRES), which would give warheads increased penetrativeness, maneuverability, and terminal guidance;

—a totally new reentry vehicle capable of carrying a higher yield warhead;

—a worldwide communication satellite system, called NAVSTAR Global Positioning System, which was designed to give pinpoint accuracy even to SLBMs.[27]

In summary, the Vladivostok agreement was neither "a firm ceiling on the strategic arms race," nor "a cap . . . on the arms race," as the president and the secretary of state had claimed. It merely registered a recognition that for ten years at least no more than 2,400 strategic launchers should be built, while the arms race shifted to perfecting multiple warheads and guidance systems, and sophisticating underwater launching, cruise missiles, and new bombers. The accord merely emphasized and accelerated a shift toward qualitative improvements of weapons while establishing only a porous quantitative ceiling toward which the governments would build. The agreement allowed the continuation of an unabated arms buildup in areas preferred by military officials, while appearing to regulate arms deployment in directions that were no longer of interest to them. Vast qualitative and substantial quantitative dimensions of the arms race would continue.

Using the Vladivostok agreement to slow the arms race is analogous to attempting to dam a wide stream by dropping one large rock in its middle. No water will pass through the space actually displaced by the rock, but the stream will flow around it without decreasing its volume by increasing its speed on both sides of the rock. If implemented in a treaty, the Vladivostok ceilings would be relatively insignificant limits through which neither side would pass for ten years. But the arms competition would swirl undiminished around those barriers. Official rhetoric lacked even minimal resemblance to reality. Contrary to professed value 1, the behavior of officials as registered in the Vladivostok agreement contained an alternative, operative value: *to allow the arms buildup to continue without significant restriction* (implicit value A).

THE ACCORD AND LEGITIMATION OF COUNTERFORCE STRATEGY

The case for implicit value A—that the Vladivostok agreement allowed the arms race to continue—can be so strongly substantiated that it suggests a further question: did SALT in fact legitimize and accelerate the arms race?

The question cannot be easily answered, but some significant evidence is available on four dimensions of the issue:

a) Were the Vladivostok ceilings serious limits for deployment of launchers or, instead, goals for additional deployment?

b) Did the two ceilings slow down, or stimulate, development in related areas?

c) Did the use of bargaining chips at SALT become, in fact, an easy way for officials to overcome objections to otherwise controversial arms initiatives?

d) Did the Vladivostok agreement undermine political opposition to the procurement of additional weapons?

Ceilings or targets? After the meeting at Vladivostok, the figures of 2,400 launch vehicles and 1,320 MIRVs became accepted almost overnight as targets for planning in the next ten years. Before November 24, 1974, the public had had no inclination to regard those levels as legitimate. After that date, the political forces that earlier would have opposed such major increases did not wage a serious struggle against them. As Fred Iklé, the director of the U.S. Arms Control and Disarmament Agency warned, "one of the dangers of prolonged bargaining in arms control negotiations is that if you do not watch out it could lead to agreements to *augment* arms, arms augmentation agreements instead of arms reduction agreements. . . . You compare all these numbers and before you know it you have to level *up* to what the other side has instead of leveling down."[28]

President Ford clearly expected that the United States would build up to the levels enumerated in the agreement: "We do have an obligation within the limits of 2,400 on delivery systems and 1,320 on MIRVs to keep our forces up to that level." He repeated this view later in the same news conference on the Vladivostok agreement: "We do have an obligation to stay up to that ceiling, and the budget that I will recommend will keep our strategic forces either up to or aimed at that objective."[29]

In the Defense Department's annual report, Secretary Schlesinger rhetorically offered to stay below the ceilings if the Soviet Union did. But rather than exercise self-restraint in an effort to implement such an idea, he declared: "Until we obtain solid evidence of Soviet restraint, we shall plan for deployment of approximately 2,400 strategic delivery vehicles and 1,320 MIRVed missiles." Even though the United States clearly held the technological lead and had deployed far more warheads than the Soviet Union, he advised that "we should plan toward the Vladivostok goals."[30]

After the Vladivostok meeting, most officials assumed that the Soviet Union would build up to the ceilings. Since few people wanted to be accused of advocating that the United States deliberately fall behind Soviet military capability, U.S. deployment which was aimed at the ceilings encountered criticism far less vigorous than would have been likely had there not been a Vladivostok agreement. The latter set a level *below* which advocates of arms control could aim only by opening themselves to the charge that they wanted to make the United States a second-class power. After hearing exhaustive testimony on the Department of Defense requests for post-Vladivostok weapons, Senator Stuart Symington, a member of both the Armed Services Committee and the Arms Control Subcommittee, concluded that the Vladivostok agreement had fixed ceilings that were targets for *increased* deployment of weapons.[31]

The former U.S. chief negotiator at SALT and head of the Arms Control and Disarmament Agency commented, "the MIRVed missile ceiling was apparently chosen to permit the United States to *complete* programs for land- and sea-based MIRVed missiles."[32] Indeed, the U.S. proposal of 1,320 MIRVs reportedly exceeded by 30 percent the number of MIRVs the Soviet Union had been willing to accept in the spring of 1974.[33]

Stimulus in related areas. In addition to setting goals for a continued arms buildup of strategic launchers and MIRVs, the agreement also stimulated new development in related areas, such as guidance systems, throw weight, and yield. It focused energies on the most dangerous, destabilizing, and volatile components of arms competition: technological "advances" to increase the lethal capability of the launchers within the set limit.

57

As Malcolm Currie explained, "Because it limits total numbers of weapons and weapon carriers, the accord on strategic nuclear weapons at Vladivostok re-enforces our need for technological progress." The Vladivostok agreement, therefore, did not merely maintain the past pace of technological "progress" in arms competition; the accord also encouraged officials to pour more energy into the process of technically refining the instruments of destruction: "The Vladivostok agreement . . . inevitably . . . *places a premium* on steady technological progress and on . . . qualitative improvements to maintain deterrence, which new technology can change overnight."[34] The increased attention given to accelerating technological innovation was most often expressed as a need to increase lethal capacity per weapon, since the number of launchers was limited. General David C. Jones, chief of staff of the U.S. Air Force, explained that, "as ceilings are imposed on *quantity* of systems, the *qualitative features of remaining systems assume even more importance.*"[35]

This consequence of the Vladivostok agreement, described as the need for "high unit performance," also meant that officials sought to erode the influence of budgetary limits as a restraint on military spending. As Secretary of Defense Schlesinger explained to the Senate Armed Services Committee in discussing his desire to have a new strategic bomber, "given the strict limitation on bomber numbers [due to the Vladivostok accord] . . . *there is much less relevancy to the cost-quantity trade-off that would automatically apply were a procurement decision to be inherently less limited.* Given the limitation on numbers, there is a powerful incentive to achieve high unit performance—associated with the lesser degree of relevance of the cost-quantity trade-off."[36] In other words, the usual need to justify weapons purchases on economic grounds no longer applied when an arms control agreement went into effect. The Vladivostok agreement could subvert its professed purpose and facilitate arms procurement.[37] It undermined budgetary limits which in the past had been the single most effective restraint on the purchase of new weapons.

Bargaining chips. Although there was no outright conspiracy between the military officials of the Soviet Union and the United States to prolong the arms race, the practical consequences of their respective policies were almost the same as if there had been. During informal discussions with Soviet military advisers at the SALT negotiations, the Soviet advisers indicated that an arms control agreement on launchers would merely mean there would be a race in technology.[38] Each side's actions or anticipated actions were used to justify deployments by the other.

Continuous rounds of arms negotiations enabled advocates of weapons innovations to initiate research, testing, and development of a wide variety of new weapons under the pretense that a U.S. lead in weaponry could be used either as a bargaining chip to be traded off for some Soviet compromise in negotiations or as a demonstration of such superior U.S. technology that the Soviet Union would be persuaded to halt the arms race rather than try to imitate U.S. technological progress.[39]

Since the Soviet Union has sought no less than equality in armaments since World War II, neither the bargaining-chip strategy nor the negotiation-from-strength approach was likely to work. In the former case, the Soviet Union would be unwilling to prohibit development of weapons that the United States had tested but the Soviet Union had not. The latter approach was unworkable because the United States was reluctant to ban what it had developed, and the Soviet Union refused to freeze a position of U.S. superiority. As a result, U.S. bargaining chips and arms advantages were seldom negotiated away; instead, they launched new stages of arms competition. As a study group of the Federation of American Scientists concluded: "First weapons systems are moved toward procurement as bargaining threats, and then the subsequent negotiations ratify the procurement of everything in the pipeline. [The Vladivostok accord] did exactly that, approving or leaving room for all weapons already used as 'chips.' Under such conditions, it would be preferable not to put discussion of new armaments on the arms control agenda where negotiations could serve as a pretext for further development of bargaining chips."[40]

Official arguments for developing MIRVs illustrated how arms control negotiations could provide a convenient rationale for weapons that lacked a good military justification on their own merits. Given the U.S. possession of a deterrent capable of assured destruction, plus overall strategic advantages and technological superiority over the Soviet Union, the MIRV was not an important addition to United States security.[41] For several years during its development, the MIRV was justified and funded not as a weapon necessary for security but as an item useful for arms control negotiations. In the late 1960s, officials argued that the MIRV should be developed as a bargaining chip to secure an agreement on ABM limitation with the Soviet Union or, if no agreement were possible, as a necessary device to penetrate possible future Soviet antiballistic missile forces. However, when SALT I limited ABMs to a militarily insignificant number, officials justified the continued deployment of MIRVs as a bargaining chip for negotiations to prohibit the deployment of MIRVs.[42] But, as development and deployment proceeded, officials dropped efforts to prohibit MIRVs.

At that time, there were no Soviet MIRVs ready for deployment. It was widely acknowledged, however, that U.S. deployment would, within a few years, stimulate a similar Soviet effort, thus casting doubt on the survivability of a majority of both sides' land-based ICBMs in a first strike.[43] Such a development would also generate new pressures for creation of alternative weapons systems, less vulnerable than Minuteman, as well as for the perfection of precise guidance systems to enable the destruction of hardened silos. The latter technology would be highly destabilizing in a case where one side thought its ICBMs were truly vulnerable. But, rather than slow the unilateral U.S. deployment of the MIRV, installation continued at a steady rate both during and after SALT I, justified substantially by the professed desire to make SALT successful. By the end of 1974, the United States had deployed a total of 7,940 deliverable nuclear warheads (including non-MIRVed warheads) on its strategic vehicles, as opposed to the Soviet Union's 2,600.[44]

Negotiations encouraged weapons proponents to move programs along faster than opponents could prepare to control them, thus providing a stimulus for the arms race that had nothing to do with any external military threat. Such *intra*national arms racing occurred between those who wanted disarmament and those who wanted more arms. As Herbert York, former director of defense research for the Department of Defense and a member of the General Advisory Committee on Arms Control and Disarmament, concluded: "[The MIRV program] has some of the earmarks of being something that the military is trying to get done before the arms control people can stop it."[45] The bargaining-chip ploy strengthened the hand of the arms advocates by speeding the forces for development and slowing those for self-restraint.

Reading the testimony of various defense officials during the years of the SALT negotiations, one gets the clear impression that the arms talks made it harder to cut the defense budget and restrain arms procurement. Officials would tell their critics: "We must build these weapons to make the Soviet Union negotiate seriously at SALT." In the case of the MIRV and ABM, the bargaining-chip argument was used to gain support for weapons systems which would not have been supported on their merits, thus stimulating the arms competition rather than the negotiations. "In retrospect . . . it is clear that on balance the bargaining chip tactic as it has been used has raised the military competition to levels more difficult to bring under control."[46]

Neutralization of opposition. If there had been no arms control negotiations, it would have been clearer to Congress and the public that they were paying for an open-ended arms race, whereas during SALT many people were led to believe that they were supporting limited arms increments for the purpose of facilitating arms control. In addition, arms talks seemed to place the burden for continuing buildups on the "enemy," because the latter failed to come to an agreement. Without such negotiations, the responsibility of one's own country for the buildup would have been at least as visible. Deeper awareness of U.S. responsibility for the arms competition could have nurtured the idea that self-restraint might have produced more restrictive results than SALT. With the prospect of an agreement continuously being raised, people presumed that the United States should build new weapons until an agreement halted the buildup. This presumption for going ahead in the absence of an agreement was so strong that the Joint Chiefs of Staff unhesitatingly rejected a Senate inquiry about conducting a yearly review of the impact of Defense Department programs on arms control: "An annual analysis of the arms control implications of the defense budget would seem to be of little or no value."[47] Finally, in the absence of arms negotiations, the assumption that advanced technology should be exploited for new weapons could have been challenged more directly. The justification for weapons programs, at the least, would then have had to rest on military rather than on arms control needs.[48]

Although it cannot be conclusively demonstrated, it is possible that, in the early 1970s, congressional opposition to MIRVs was bothersome enough to military officials that they decided that an arms control "ceiling" for MIRVs would be a good way to facilitate MIRV deployment and harmlessly vent the pressure for MIRV reductions. To be sure, there would have been pressures to develop the MIRV even without SALT, but the belief was widespread that there was no genuine deterrence *need* for MIRV. The convenient SALT justification for MIRV substantially increased the chances for its initial deployment. This was especially true since the liberal critics of the new weapons were the same persons who supported arms control. Precisely because of the liberals' enthusiasm for arms control, military officials could use the SALT negotiations to entice liberals to support an arms buildup. Although never stated explicitly, an implicit theme of many discussions was that more weapons were needed for arms control than for military security. The arms control negotiations transformed political opposition to arms spending into initial support for new programs.

In terms of public expectations, defense planning, and military appropriations, the Vladivostok agreement actually helped *to legitimize a further arms buildup* (implicit value B). The editors of the *New York Times* commented after the Vladivostok meeting that, if both sides deployed weapons to the limits specified, the arms race would go on "just about as now planned, and possibly a little faster in some areas—*legitimized*, in fact, by international compact."[49] After conducting extensive hearings on arms control and the shifting rationales for weapons innovation, Senator Edmund Muskie correctly observed, "my suspicion is that the SALT talks actually stimulated the arms race rather than stabilized it."[50]

Because of SALT, officials created an atmosphere designed to convince the public that all was being done that could be done to achieve a disarmed world. The arms control talks legitimized existing arms programs as well as justified new ones as bargaining chips. To some extent, the negotiations actually deterred meaningful efforts at disarmament.[51]

THE SIGNIFICANCE OF VLADIVOSTOK-LEGITIMIZED
SHIFTS IN STRATEGIC DOCTRINE

What was the significance of the changes in strategic doctrine and arsenal size that occurred during the arms control negotiations? Since the first days of its nuclear monopoly, the United States had pursued a "countercity" or "countervalue" strategy of nuclear deterrence based on the capacity to destroy the cities and industrial centers of the Soviet Union in event of war. After the Soviet Union acquired a formidable nuclear arsenal of its own, the two deterrents produced a balance of terror based on "mutual assured destruction" (MAD). In maintaining this posture, both sides possessed enough nuclear weapons to suffer a first strike from the other side and still be able to inflict assured destruction on the attacker in a retaliatory response. Both governments assumed that such a capability would be sufficient to deter nuclear war.

A second approach, called "counterforce" strategy, had also been a subject of discussion since the mid-1960s. A counterforce strategy selects Soviet military capability, such as ICBM silos or airports, as targets instead of Soviet cities. A "first-strike" or "damage-limiting capability" is one in which the counterforce capacity is so large and effective as to enable one side to disarm the opponent in a massive first strike. An essential condition of a first-strike strategy is to destroy the opponent's ability to retaliate against the attacker.

For many reasons, a genuine first-strike capability, with high promise of disarming the opponent, remains unattainable by either side at the present time.[52] For example, an entire fleet of nuclear submarines cannot be located and destroyed instantaneously. Neither can weapons be launched at precisely the same time in a coordinated attack on SLBMs, ICBMs, and bomber bases. If weapons were launched at different times, the warning period would be sufficient for the potential victim to employ the undestroyed segment of its deterrent in a retaliatory response.[53]

During SALT, U.S. strategy moved markedly from being based primarily—though not entirely—on a countercity and assured destruction approach to one that included an extensive counterforce capability far in excess of the forces needed for assured destruction only. Critics of this shift feared that the enlargement of the counterforce arsenal would be destabilizing because it was likely to stimulate Soviet fears that the United States was moving toward a first-strike strategy. Even if these fears were not fully substantiated, a mere step in that direction could stimulate Soviet planners to take countermeasures in order to avoid leaving part of their deterrent in a vulnerable position. A counterforce capability short of a first-strike potential might conceivably be used to destroy most of the land-based missiles of one side while holding back further missiles to destroy the cities of the victim in order to deter the victim from retaliating with its SLBMs. Although such a scenario, with its assumed precise and restrained responses, seems implausible, it nonetheless influenced defense planners and was used by them to justify deployment of more weapons.[54]

The potential for development of new weapons vastly increased the appeal of counterforce strategy to Pentagon officials because the new weapons they desired (MIRVs, pinpoint accuracy in guidance systems, cruise missiles, Trident, and larger yield reentry vehicles) could be militarily justified by movement toward a counterforce strategy. The new weapons were not needed for deterrence (MAD) in itself. Military officials were possessors of a technology in search of a strategic rationale. Aside from counterforce strategy, the only possible justification for MIRVs was the bargaining-chip argument—to build MIRVs in order to negotiate an agreement for banning them. Counterforce strategy and cynical, bargaining-chip use of the SALT talks professedly to *avert* counterforce deployment were used to provide the needed rationale for which military officials had been searching. And because the Soviet Union would not agree to freeze its own inferiority in an agreement, military planners made sure, by remaining ahead of the Soviet Union in deployment of MIRVs, that the bargaining chips would never serve as the basis for a genuine ban of the new technology.

Deployment of MIRVs was a major technological and strategic innovation of doubtful security value because MIRVs allowed a single missile with multiple warheads to destroy several enemy missiles, thus giving an advantage to the side launching a first strike. For example, one missile with six warheads could destroy three enemy missiles if two warheads were targeted on each missile to insure penetration and nearly certain destruction. In pre-MIRV days, the attacker would have needed to use two missiles (given only one warhead per missile) to destroy each enemy missile, at the same two-to-one ratio. Thus the attacker would always deplete its missile arsenal faster than it would destroy its opponent's missiles. MIRVs reversed the balance of advantages. Since the Vladivostok agreement did not prohibit MIRVs or limit their number to a low level, it facilitated and encouraged movement toward a counterforce strategy. That was doubtless one of its most serious weaknesses.

In the years preceding the Vladivostok meeting, the United States had taken the earliest steps toward deploying a first-strike capability in the arms race with the Soviet Union. The United States had long deployed far more warheads than were required for assured destruction of the Soviet Union and its allies. In addition, the United States began development of the single most crucial technological prerequisite of a counterforce strategy, the MIRV, early in the 1960s.

The United States also outpaced the Soviet Union in the second most important condition for establishing a first-strike capability: vehicle accuracy. Without high accuracy, even the delivery of many warheads would not insure the destruction of an opponent's missiles. The Minuteman III and Poseidon missiles had relatively high accuracy (.25 to .15 of a nautical mile). Soviet ICBMs of the same period were credited with an accuracy of about one mile.[55] In computing the ability of a warhead to destroy a silo, accuracy was far more important than yield, an area in which the Soviet deployment exceeded U.S. weapons.[56] In terms of counterforce capability, the heavier throw weight and larger warheads of the Soviet Union did not compensate for U.S. advantages in accuracy and multiple warheads and did not constitute any *technological* advantage. The United States had in hand the technology to increase both of these factors whenever it sought to imitate Soviet forces. (The United States had unilaterally decided years earlier that it did not need more throw weight or warheads of larger yield.) The Soviet Union, on the other hand, could not match United States forces because it lacked the technology possessed by the United States in accuracy, yield-to-weight ratios, and MIRVs.

Congressman Robert L. Leggett, a California Democrat on the House Armed Services Committee, analyzed the counterforce capability of the United States and Soviet Union, using predictions based on weapons then deployed or in the process of development.[57] As Table 2-3 shows, the Vladivostok agreement legitimized vast increases in counterforce capability, expressed as index K. In 1974, K for both sides totaled 31,243. Leggett predicted it would increase by more than 3½ times by the early 1980s, and could jump by 169 times to 5,277,275 by the late 1980s. Most of those who disputed Leggett's estimates maintained only that the Soviet Union would have a *higher* counterforce capability than his tables showed, thus further confirming the point that the Vladivostok agreement was anything but an arms limitation agreement.

To Soviet observers, United States armament policies also might have seemed designed to attain a partial first-strike capability because all one thousand of the modern ICBM silos, which were hardened with concrete and steel to withstand nuclear blast overpressure of 300 pounds per square inch (psi), were scheduled to be hardened further. The new silos were designed to withstand 900 psi and perhaps as much as 1,200 psi.[58] Ninety of the latest Soviet silos were believed to withstand 600 psi. But

65

Table 2-3

Counterforce Capability of 1974 Compared with Predicted
Counterforce Capability after the Vladivostok Agreement

Missile	Yield, megatons (per warhead)	Accuracy nautical miles	Warheads (per missile)	Number of missiles	K^a (per missile)
		PRESENT PROGRAMS			
		U.S.			
Minuteman III	(.17) 280	.2	(3) 1,650	550	(22.1) 12,127
Minuteman II	(1) 450	.3	(1) 450	450	(11.1) 5,000
Titan	(5) 270	.5	(1) 54	54	(11.7) 631
Poseidon	(.04) 198	.3	(10) 4,960	496	(12.8) 6,393
Polaris A-3	(.6) 96	.7	(1) 160	160	(1.5) 240
U.S. total	1,294		7,274	1,710	24,391
		USSR			
SS-9	(25) 7,200	.7	(1) 288	288	(17.4) 5,011
SS-11	(1) 1,010	1.0	(1) 1,010	1,010	(1.0) 1,010
SS-13	(1) 60	.7	(1) 60	60	(2.0) 120
SS-8	(5) 545	1.5	(1) 109	109	(1.3) 142
SS-7	(5) 500	2.0	(1) 100	100	(0.7) 70
SS-N-6	(1) 528	1.5	(1) 528	528	(0.4) 211
SS-N-8	(1) 180	.8	(1) 180	180	(1.6) 288
USSR total	10,023		2,275	2,203	6,852
Combined U.S. and USSR totals			9,549		31,243

Missile	Yield, megatons (per warhead)	Accuracy nautical miles	Warheads (per missile)	Number of missiles	K^a (per missile)
		EARLY 1980s			
		U.S.			
Minuteman III	578 (.35)	.1	1,650 (3)	550 (148)	81,675
Minuteman II	450 (1)	.3	450 (1)	450 (11.1)	5,000
Titan	270 (5)	.5	54 (1)	54 (11.7)	631
Trident II	230 (.08)	.18	2,880 (20)	144 (114)	16,416
Trident I	499 (.08)	.18	6,240 (10)	624 (57)	35,568
Polaris A-3	96 (.6)	.7	160 (1)	160 (1.5)	240
U.S. total	2,123		11,434	2,095	139,480
		USSR			
SS-18	1,878 (1)	.3	1,878 (6)	313 (66)	20,658
SS-19	1,208 (.2)	.3	6,042 (6)	1,007 (23)	22,825
SS-13	60 (1)	.7	60 (1)	60 (2.0)	120
SS-8	545 (.5)	1.5	109 (1)	109 (0.4)	142
SS-N-8	910 (1)	.5	910 (1)	910 (4)	3,640
USSR total	4,601		8,999	2,399	47,385
Combined U.S. and USSR totals			20,433		186,865

Table 2-3 (cont.)

Missile	Yield, megatons (per warhead)	Accuracy nautical miles	Warheads (per missile)	Number of missiles	K^a (per missile)
		LATE 1980s			
		U.S.			
Minuteman III	412 (.25)	.02	1,650 (3)	550	1,212,750 (2205)
Minuteman II	450 (1)	.3	450 (1)	450	5,000 (11.1)
Titan	270 (5)	.5	54 (1)	54	631 (11.7)
Trident II	345 (.06)	.02	5,760 (20)	288	1,822,000 (6500)
Trident I	288 (.06)	.02	4,800 (10)	480	1,560,000 (3250)
U.S. total	1,765		12,714	1,822	4,650,381
		USSR			
SS-18	3,756 (2)	.1	1,878 (6)	313	296,724 (948)
SS-19	2,417 (.4)	.1	6,042 (6)	1,007	326,268 (324)
SS-13	60 (1)	.7	60 (1)	60	120 (2.0)
SS-8	545 (5)	1.5	109 (1)	109	142 (0.4)
SS-N-8	910 (1)	.5	910 (1)	910	3,640 (4)
USSR total	7,678		8,999	2,399	626,894
Combined U.S. and USSR totals			21,713		5,277,275

SOURCE: Robert L. Leggett, "Two Legs Do Not a Centipede Make," *Armed Forces Journal* (February 1975), pp. 30-32. Reprinted by permission.

NOTE: [a] Index "K" measures the capability of one state's nuclear forces to destroy an opponent's unlaunched nuclear weapons. This capability is determined by the number of warheads, their yield, and their accuracy. In figuring K, accuracy is far more important than yield. See note 56.

only two-thirds of the then current Soviet ICBM force was emplaced in silos of the 300 psi grade, with the remainder substantially less hard.[59] Thus Soviet ICBMs were clearly more vulnerable to counterforce attack than United States missiles, and since the Soviet Union's deterrent was proportionately more dependent on ICBMs than the U.S. triad of ICBMs, SLBMs, and bombers, U.S. policy was far more threatening to the Soviet Union than vice versa.

The United States further demonstrated an intention to enhance its counterforce potential by the development of "remote retargeting" of missiles from central launcher control facilities. This procedure provided speed and flexibility in enabling commanders to target *replacement* missiles for first-round missiles that had been observed to fail. Such a capability was unnecessary in countercity strategies, but was useful for a first-strike or damage-limiting capability to insure the destruction of all Soviet retaliatory vehicles.

The United States also sought to improve its SLBMs to give them more counterforce capability. Development was being conducted before and after the Vladivostok agreement to increase the accuracy of the warheads through use of a Global Positioning System to provide "a continuous, worldwide, all-weather positioning capability with an accuracy of tens of feet in three dimensions."[60]

In sum, during the years preceding the Vladivostok agreement, the Soviet Union did far less to increase the counterforce capabilities of its strategic forces than did the United States. The Soviet Union did not even test a MIRV until mid-1973[61]—three years after the first U.S. *deployment*. To be sure, the Soviet Union had laid the groundwork for the subsequent development of a counterforce capability by constructing missiles with large throw weight. It seemed reasonable to conjecture, however, that the original intention of developing such large missiles was to compensate by the use of heavier warheads for inferior Soviet technology in yield-to-weight ratios and accuracy compared to U.S. advanced technology even in the pre-MIRV stage. The United States, on the other hand, had most of the needed counterforce technology available and had begun deploying weapons that were useful primarily as an enlargement of its counterforce capability. In the wake of the Vladivostok accord, both parties—with the United States far in the lead—pursued deployment of counterforce capability even more seriously.

69

Although the Vladivostok accord certainly was not the cause of initial pressures within the United States for shifting to a counterforce posture, it facilitated the process and proved more useful to advocates of arms buildup than of arms control. By legitimizing MIRVs and channeling arms competition into technological innovation, the accord facilitated a doctrinal shift—from emphasis on deterrence of war through assured destruction, to deployment of more sophisticated weapons useful for counterforce targeting. This shift also meant the central strategic premise changed—from traditional deterrence of major nuclear war, toward deploying precise instruments of nuclear war-fighting ability useful for "limited" nuclear war.[62] Bernard T. Feld, a physicist with long experience in weapons research for the United States, concluded that "the main result of SALT has been to initiate a new phase of the nuclear arms competition, in which both sides are moving steadily, from their earlier posture of reliance on nuclear weapons for the sole purpose of deterring a first-strike by the other side, towards postures that can only be interpreted as preparations for use of these weapons in any conflict against any kind of target, regardless of the actions of the other side."[63]

The Vladivostok agreement legitimized MIRVs at the very moment when there remained the last, easy opportunity to prohibit them altogether or to restrict them to very low levels. Once the number 1,320 was included in an international agreement, it meant legitimation of weapons that had been understood, throughout the years of congressional debate about research and development, not to be needed in themselves.

In facilitating the shift to counterforce strategy and limited war-fighting capability, the Vladivostok accord kept open the military's desires for "flexible options." With MIRVs and precise accuracy, officials could attack a few or many specific and small targets. Counterforce strategy required continued arms development in the areas of accuracy, yield, throw weight, and global guidance systems. The Vladivostok accord neatly avoided significant restraints in all these areas. By legitimating MIRVs and "flexible response," it supported a principle in fundamental contradiction with the purpose of arms control, which by definition must *restrict* flexibility and constrain behavior. A chronic desire for increased flexibility meant unlimited weapons development, and could be perceived by the opponent as movement toward a first-strike capability.[64]

Schlesinger used the Vladivostok agreement in another way to buttress his argument for additional weapons. The agreement, he argued, enshrined the principle of equality in weaponry for the two superpowers. By projecting the Soviet *potential* for MIRV-ing on heavier Soviet throw weight, U.S. officials justified the procurement of many new weapons in order to maintain equality with the Soviet Union.[65] As Secretary Schlesinger stated, "There is just no possibility that a high confidence disarming first strike is attainable for either side, even against the ICBM components of the strategic forces on both sides."[66] In short, despite higher Soviet throw weight, under *no* foreseeable circumstances could the Soviet Union achieve a first-strike capability. Nonetheless, if Soviet leaders put MIRVs on their ICBMs, and developed more accurate warheads, and deployed more MIRVs than the United States, then the Soviet arsenal could give the Soviet Union "a capability that we ourselves would lack, and it could bring into question the sense of equality that the principles of Vladivostok so explicitly endorse."[67] Additional weapons were necessary not primarily for security but for fulfilling the principle of equality—which was included in an agreement ostensibly intended for reduction of armaments. By using graphs and slides based on cleverly manipulated statistics, the secretary of defense showed congressional committees what the Soviet Union might be able to deploy in the 1980s, given its great throw weight potential.[68] Military officials argued that the United States ought to begin deploying in 1975 what they estimated the Soviet Union might have in the 1980s.[69] The United States had to remain the number one military power in the world.[70]

Officials also announced a new condition for an adequate deterrent: "perceived balance." "Political sufficiency" or "perceived balance" meant that "no major asymmetrics should exist in the basic factors which determine force effectiveness, and that the forces and capability are perceived by everyone, ourselves, our enemies, and third countries, to be in relative balance."[71] Even if there were no security need for additional weapons, the United States should procure them if United States intelligence predicted that the Soviet Union would eventually deploy such forces.

As Senator Thomas McIntyre, chairman of the Armed Services Subcommittee on Research and Development, explained, "The real Pentagon justification for counterforce is, in fact, not military, but political or diplomatic. They primarily justified

these programs on the basis of what they call 'political perception.' " Military officials asserted that without such a capability,
the political position of the United States might be adversely affected in the world. The enlargement of U.S. counterforce
capability "was designed not to perform a military function in
the classic sense but to be used as a diplomatic device or tool in
world politics."[72]

In sum, the shift in strategic doctrine that was facilitated by
the SALT negotiations produced an extraordinarily provocative
chain of political and technological events that were likely to
stimulate the arms buildup at a substantially higher level than
had been occurring during the 1960s.

Although space does not permit a comprehensive treatment
of the ways an enlarged counterforce capability can exacerbate
the arms race,[73] one aspect of the rationale for counterforce
strategy bears examination here because it is related to the Vladivostok agreement. The question that confronted officials was:
if the Soviet Union deployed a counterforce capability, should
the United States increase its own counterforce, *offensive* arsenal,
leading toward a first-strike strategy; or should it pursue *defensive* development programs aimed at nullifying any Soviet effort
to acquire a first-strike capability?

In weighing the pros and cons of counterforce strategy, opponents of the shift in strategic doctrine argued that movement
toward an enlarged counterforce capability would exacerbate
the arms race (since the Soviet Union would probably seek to
match U.S. efforts); increase the lethal capacity of both sides
without any increase in security; raise the cost of weapons; cause
"crisis instability" either by providing an incentive for a preemptive, disarming first strike by a country fearing attack (in order
to insure that its missiles would not be destroyed in their silos),
or by putting nuclear weapons on a hair trigger (in the sense that
the side fearing a first strike by its opponent would aim to launch
its missiles on warning of attack, rather than wait for unambiguous evidence of a first strike before retaliating as would occur in
the old deterrence doctrine); increase the likelihood that nuclear
weapons would be used in war, not so much between the United
States and Soviet Union, as against other countries (since the
United States was shifting to a doctrine based on limited war-
fighting capability); and, by perpetuating the further sophistication of weapons in ways that would make them easier to use on

limited battlefields, pose a threat to smaller powers, and encourage them to procure nuclear weapons themselves.

Advocates of the new U.S. strategy asserted that it would make the use of nuclear weapons possible at lower thresholds of violence. This possibility, they said, would increase the credibility of the threat to use them, and thus provide a better deterrent.[74] Nevertheless, proponents of the counterforce doctrine were unable to demonstrate that the vast new expenditures and risks would appreciably increase deterring capacity beyond that of the old doctrine, since limited counterforce strategy was possible by simply targeting existing weapons on Soviet military installations instead of on cities. Obviously, something more was required to justify the vast increase in warhead deployment sought by the Pentagon.

Even the prediction that the Soviet Union would deploy a counterforce capability was not a persuasive argument for a U.S. counterforce strategy, because the most economical and militarily least destabilizing response to such a Soviet deployment would have been to decrease the vulnerability of the U.S. deterrent, not to increase U.S. offensive capability. The latter would stimulate an equivalent Soviet response and encourage the further development of Soviet counterforce weapons. In short, the United States could have nullified the effects of Soviet counterforce deployment by hardening its own silos, by putting some ICBMs on mobile platforms, or by deploying more launchers at sea where they could not be found, so that a Soviet first strike could serve no purpose. Serving no purpose, such costly deployments would have been unlikely, as the ABM case has demonstrated. But such a rational response of self-restraint would not have fulfilled the desire of U.S. military officials for vast new weapons deployments. Thus they rejected it.

Military officials intended first to complete research on the technologically most difficult foreseeable innovations (before the arms controllers could restrict them)—innovations such as MIRVs and MARVs, increased accuracy, and better yield-to-weight ratios. Afterwards, the argument of arms controllers that Soviet counterforce efforts should be met by making U.S. forces less vulnerable would still remain valid and could be used for further weapons innovations. Officials sought to avoid the possibility that the defensive path toward less vulnerability be taken first, because then the country might never deploy offensive, counter-

73

force, hard-target weapons. The same bureaucratic strategy had been used when officials decided not to deploy the technologically easy, high throw-weight missile, and instead sought first to develop the technology for more accurate and higher yield-to-weight, multiple warheads. Development of additional throw weight could come later, if desired, as the technology was near at hand. This in fact happened in the development of the new M-X. Thus the arms control negotiations not only accelerated the pace of certain weapons development, they also encouraged military officials to concentrate their efforts on the most advanced and often most destabilizing technology in order to have it perfected before arms controllers could close off their preferred options.

The negotiations thus encouraged a game of technological leapfrog, in which military planners always jumped ahead to the most advanced technology anticipated. Later on, they could favor the deployment of more stabilizing weapons based on an intermediate stage of technology more suitable for defensive than offensive purposes. This kept up a steady flow of new research and weapons, but it also meant that the least provocative measures to provide for defense, based on intermediate technology, were taken only *after* the more provocative steps of arms innovation, based on advanced technology, were well under way and difficult to stop. The military planners emphasized technological progress much more than genuine defense or protection of people.

Thus officials rejected the militarily most sensible and least costly response to the possibility of Soviet MIRV deployment. The discussions leading to the Vladivostok accord aided this rejection by providing the rationale to build counterforce weapons as a pretext for encouraging the Soviet Union to limit counterforce weapons in arms control negotiations. Before congressional committees, military officials frequently expressed reluctance to develop counterforce weapons; they coupled this professed reluctance with arguments of the necessity to do so in order to help the SALT negotiations. Without this cynical approach, the authorization for such needless and provocative weapons would have been far more difficult. The Vladivostok agreement signaled that the bargaining-chip argument had worked to the advantage of the proponents of more arms and that the crucial doctrinal corner of following a war-fighting strategy with significant counterforce capability had been turned. The pressures for increased armaments had been in part sustained and inflated by the very people who professed to favor arms control.

74

In brief, the consequences of the shifts in strategic doctrine legitimized at Vladivostok further confirm the accuracy of implicit values A and B. Military officials used the arms control negotiations to help justify and marshal support for development of weapons for which there was no clear security necessity.

Professed Value 2: To Curtail Arms Expenditures

The Ford administration maintained that the Vladivostok agreement provided a substantial saving in military expenditures compared to what would have been spent without an agreement—even though officials announced no major cutbacks in previously planned, upcoming programs. The president declared: "I can say this without hesitation or qualification: if we had not had this agreement, it would have required the United States to substantially increase its military expenditures in the strategic areas." The Vladivostok accord limited the strategic forces of both countries, "thus preventing an arms race with all its . . . economic waste."[75] Kissinger supported this view, telling Congress that it would need to appropriate $5 to $10 billion more than currently requested if it did not support the agreement. Intelligence estimates indicated, according to Kissinger, that in the absence of an agreement, Soviet armaments would have been substantially higher than under the agreement.[76]

The actual amount that would have been spent in the absence of an agreement cannot be known with any reasonable degree of certainty. One can, however, note actual spending patterns and compare levels that were foreseen before the agreement with those favored afterwards, in order to gain some rough estimation of the agreement's consequences.

Before making comparisons, it is necessary to acknowledge several difficulties surrounding the use of data on military expenditures. First of all, only limited data are available for estimating the size of Soviet military expenditures. Even after the rouble figure is determined, the exchange rate to be used for comparative purposes is a second difficult estimate, since official exchange rates do not reflect equivalent purchasing values between roubles and dollars.

Moreover, the relationship between expenditures and armaments is not perfect. Inflation aside, it may be true that in some cases destructive capability—which we seek to measure here—does not rise with a commensurate increase in expenditures. Or, possibly, a decrease in expenditures does not result in a decrease in destructive capability; for instance, if a state purchased a nuclear arsenal during a ten-year period and then stopped all further strategic spending for several years, the nuclear arsenal would still represent enormous firepower. Moreover, two countries with similar expenditures in one year may not have equivalent lethal power, especially if one has previously maintained higher expenditures than the other for a period of years.

In spite of these problems, overall expenditures for military purposes remain the most convenient index of destructive capacity.[77] Especially if one examines data for numerous countries over the long run, it is possible to obtain a fairly accurate picture of the trends in weapons procurement. Regardless of the much-debated causal linkage between arms expenditures and the likelihood of war, it is widely acknowledged that high levels of military spending are undesirable, given a world of scarcity, and that they are considered necessary only because of the continued expenditures of one's opponent.

As the experienced authors of the *SIPRI World Armaments and Disarmament Yearbook* have pointed out, expenditure data are useful for several reasons. First, "the growth in the lethal power of the world's armaments results not so much from increases in the number of men under arms or in the stock of weapons, as from the replacement of existing arms by new and more effective ones."[78] Thus it is necessary to examine the deployment of new weapons or improvements in old ones—both of which require new funds—rather than simply count guns or rockets. Second, expenditure data often reveal trends in weapons development, such as the transfer of resources from constructing new ballistic missile silos to developing multiple independently targetable warheads. Such data are crucial to understanding an arms race that may be in process but is obscured by examination of aggregate expenditures alone. Even a constant or slightly declining level of spending, therefore—if it goes for new research or weapons instead of for maintenance, payroll, and overhead costs—is a likely sign of a continuing arms buildup. Finally, for the limited purposes of this analysis, none of the conclusions drawn would be substantially affected by the somewhat varying estimates of expenditures provided by alternative sources.

With these caveats in mind, one must begin by noting that doubt is cast on the claim that the SALT agreements restricted spending (professed value 2) by the evidence already presented (for implicit values A and B), which demonstrates that the agreement curtailed no major U.S. weapons program in the planning or development stage.

Furthermore, the testimony of officials themselves substantiated the idea that future United States expenditures for new, advanced weapons would be equivalent to or somewhat higher than expenditures of the past. For example, the president explained that the Vladivostok agreement meant "we must continue our present strategic research, development, deployment [and] maintenance program. . . . The net result is that costs will probably go up as we phase out some [weapons] and . . . phase in some."[79] The secretary of defense publicly announced that the Vladivostok agreement would require some "upward adjustment" of spending.[80] Tens of billions of dollars were needed, he said, to shift to greater reliance on new bombers and mobile missiles on land, in aircraft, and at sea.[81] The shift was, in his mind, a necessary response to the agreement's legitimation of deploying enough MIRved vehicles to destroy nearly all land-based ICBMs in a first strike.

The SIPRI data in Table 2-4 show that United States and Soviet outlays from 1970 through 1975 declined slightly in constant

Table 2-4
Military Expenditures

	1970	1971	1972	1973	1974	1975	1976
	Billions of Current Dollars						
United States	77.9	74.9	77.6	78.4	85.9	90.9	99.1
Soviet Union	63.0	63.0	63.0	63.0	61.9	61.1	61.1
Total	140.9	137.9	140.6	141.4	147.8	152.0	160.2
	Billions of 1973 Dollars and 1973 Exchange Rates						
United States	89.1	82.1	82.5	78.4	77.4	75.1	77.4
Soviet Union	63.0	63.0	63.0	63.0	61.9	61.1	61.1
U.S. and USSR Total	142.1	145.1	145.5	141.4	139.3	138.2	138.5
World total	254.1	252.9	258.4	258.5	263.0	268.2	276.0
U.S. and USSR as % of total	56	57	56	54	53	51	50

SOURCE: Tables are compiled from data reported in Stockholm International Peace Research Institute, *World Armaments and Disarmament: 1977*, pp. 222-225.

dollars and increased slightly in current dollars.[82] The decline in U.S. real expenditures during 1970-75 was due more to the eroding effects of inflation than to any scaling down of arms because of the Interim Agreement.[83] In current dollars, the FY 1976 budget climbed 28 percent above the FY 1972 budget that was in effect when the Interim Agreement was signed. But purchasing power had not kept pace with inflation. Inflation "has achieved what the Pentagon's Congressional critics never could do. It has reduced the nation's defense program."[84] Most significantly, the slight decline in real expenditures from 1970-75 was *reversed* during the first complete fiscal year following the Vladivostok accord. (See Table 2-5.) After the Vladivostok

Table 2-5
Total Obligational Authority of United States Military Expenditures

Billions of Current Dollars		Billions of Constant 1979 Dollars
Fiscal Year		
1970	75.6	144.9
1971	72.9	131.1
1972	76.6	127.1
1973	79.0	121.8
1974	81.8	115.5
1975	86.2	111.6
1976	95.9	116.4[a]
1977	108.3	122.6
1978	116.8	123.7

SOURCE: Department of Defense, "Total Obligational Authority," mimeo., p. 21.
NOTE: [a] First complete fiscal year after the Vladivostok Accord.

agreement was signed, Pentagon requests for expenditures were far above previously authorized levels. Secretary Schlesinger presented what he called a "turnaround defense budget" that, in addition to maintaining the existing military establishment, would purchase new strategic weapons and provide a large initial down payment for future growth in military spending. Officials designed the budget request for fiscal 1976 to reserve an unusually large portion of the appropriation increment for future years, thus providing the basis for a steadily increasing defense budget. Even taking inflation into account, officials requested an $8.2 billion increase over the previous, pre-Vladivostok year.[85] Despite unusually large congressional cuts in the requested defense budget for FY 1976—cuts made primarily to stay within a self-imposed congressional limit on total governmental spending—the increase in the budget over the previous year exceeded the anticipated rate of inflation by more than 1 percent, thus permitting a slight real growth in the defense program.[86]

In its projected budgets after the Vladivostok agreement, the Defense Department sought an increase in its *real* purchasing power of 2 to 4 percent annually between 1976 and 1981.[87] By contrast, in the Defense Department's *Annual Report* for the fiscal year preceding the Vladivostok agreement, the Pentagon had projected a smaller real increase of about 1.5 percent yearly. By 1980, the Pentagon planned to be spending $148 billion annually.[88] Part of the increase was earmarked for the accelerated development of new strategic weapons that were increasingly stressed in the wake of the Vladivostok accord.[89]

Although the Vladivostok agreement covered strategic weapons, Pentagon officials estimated that a 25 percent increase in strategic spending was necessary over the two or three years following the signing of the accord.[90] Defense Department officials said they needed 40 percent more for equipment in fiscal 1976 than in the previous fiscal year (during which the Vladivostok accord was agreed upon), in order to modernize forces and increase weapon inventories. The Air Force asked for $600 million more than in the previous year and made requests for fourteen new programs.[91] Requests for aircraft and missiles in 1976 were higher by 30 percent than amounts spent in 1975.[92]

The size of increases within the budget category of research and development, which influenced the size and direction of future budgets, also revealed that the arms competition was continuing without restraint. The budget increased by eight times from 1950 to 1978, even after discounting the effect of inflation. (See Table 2-6.) Expenditures for research, development, testing, and evaluation fluctuated but generally rose from 1950 to 1964, after which they declined somewhat in real terms until FY 1976. However, during the second budget year following the Vladivostok accord, the Pentagon was able to reverse the decline. Director of Defense Research and Engineering, Malcolm Currie, said that the fiscal year 1976 request of $10.2 billion, compared with $8.6 billion appropriated in 1975, represented a "conscious decision to reverse the downward trend in . . . RDT & E [Research, Development, Testing, and Evaluation] in the last decade . . . and establish an overall RDT & E program for the long haul." New exploratory research and development "have been increased purposefully to enhance and revitalize our base of technology options for the future."[93] The United States goal was "to maintain world leadership in defense-related technology."[94]

According to Currie, increased spending for research and development of new weapons was vital because "Vladivostok limits

Table 2-6
Department of Defense Budget for Research, Development,
Testing, and Evaluation

Fiscal Year	Millions of Current Dollars	Millions of 1978 Dollars
1950	$ 413	$ 1,394
1951	867	2,796
1952	1,490	4,413
1953	1,953	5,612
1954	2,178	6,080
1955	2,400	6,547
1956	3,080	7,970
1957	3,961	9,733
1958	4,270	10,131
1959	4,652	10,783
1960	5,310	11,960
1961	6,131	13,526
1962	6,319	13,734
1963	6,376	13,629
1964	7,021	14,753
1965	6,236	12,867
1966	6,259	12,578
1967	7,160	13,898
1968	7,746	14,505
1969	7,457	13,351
1970	7,166	12,064
1971	7,303	11,629
1972	7,881	11,928
1973	8,157	11,802
1974	8,582	11,491
1975	8,866	10,750
1976	8,923	10,132
1977	9,993	10,604
1978	11,416	11,416

SOURCE: Department of Defense mimeo.

the total [number of launchers]. It obviously places a premium, a growing premium, on technological progress." Currie reported and agreed with a Soviet Communist Party statement that "the scientific technological revolution has become the most important part of the competition between the two opposed world systems."[95] In a prepared statement, Secretary James Schlesinger said: "The stringent limits on bomber numbers under present circumstances and a prospective arms limitation agreement . . . both reduces the relevance of cost-quantity tradeoff calculations and enhances the incentive for higher performance in deployed units."[96] The Vladivostok accord thus failed to slow the most important and potentially destabilizing part of the arms buildup—the race for technology. At the same time that the latter brought with it the likelihood of increasing military expenditures for weapons technology, the secretary of defense said the arms control agreement weakened traditional budgetary restraints.

In sum, military spending did not decrease after the Vladivostok agreement. The eroding effect of inflation curtailed expenditures, as the secretary of defense pointed out, more than the Vladivostok agreement did. New budget requests and appropriations, even in real terms, were higher than had been appropriated or anticipated before the agreement. Similarly, projected budgets increased after the Vladivostok agreement. It would be a mistake to conclude that the Vladivostok accord caused all of these increases but clearly the accord did not dampen spending.

Some evidence demonstrated that spending increased because the accord speeded the shift toward a partial counterforce strategy and away from existing land-based stationary missiles. Equally important, arms spending continued at high levels for the purpose of purchasing weapons that did not substantially increase either side's ability to deter an attack. By increasing their relative lead in military technology over other countries, and by taking no serious steps to diminish the role that military power played in international affairs, the Vladivostok agreement stimulated military expenditures in other countries and encouraged the continued consumption of scarce resources for construction of weapons of mass destruction. Thus, U.S. policy served another unarticulated value: *to maintain*—rather than curtail— *high levels of United States and world military expenditures* (implicit value C).

Professed Value 3: To Lay the Foundation for Future Arms Reductions

Secretary Kissinger stated that the Vladivostok agreement was extremely valuable because, once ceilings were established for launch vehicles, "reductions will become much easier."[97] President Ford similarly declared, "we have . . . created the solid basis from which future arms reductions can be . . . negotiated."[98]

The official view that the Vladivostok agreement would lead to arms reductions was based upon the assumption that past arms races had produced self-generating forces for an armaments buildup. Each side aimed to counteract the anticipated potential buildup of the opponent. Once the Vladivostok accord stabilized competition, anticipatory weapons develment would be nipped in the bud and reductions could be made. As Kissinger explained, "Once a ceiling exists, both military establishments can plan without the fear that the other will drive the race through the ceiling, which is one of these self-fulfilling prophecies which has fueled the arms race." The Ford administration thus portrayed the agreement as "one of the turning points in the history of the post-World War II arms race."[99]

In spite of official pronouncements supporting the professed value, there were many actions that negated it. In the first place, the preceding discussions of implicit values A, B, and C cast doubt on the likelihood of any future reductions. On the basis of Secretary Kissinger's own logic, Vladivostok would lead to arms reductions only if the agreement had, in fact, stopped an open-ended arms race. The earlier analysis has demonstrated that the accord did not accomplish this. The premise upon which Kissinger's conclusion depended was absent and thus the conclusion was faulty.

By their own concrete acts, officials have shown that they accepted and anticipated a continued arms buildup. The ceilings were targets for enlarging lethal capacity and future defense budgets. Official statements and proposed policies for the post-Vladivostok years demonstrated the unlikelihood of any arms reductions. In the president's words, "we must continue our present strategic research, development, deployment, maintenance programs. And we are going to move into the present program some additional new weapons systems." Ford felt an "obligation to stay up to that ceiling" of 2,400 launchers and 1,320 MIRVs. Despite the need to build *up* to those levels, he predicted that "the new agreement . . . will constrain our military competition over the next decade."[100] Even the latter assertion, one should note, contained the assumption that the arms competition would continue, not that reductions would follow in the wake of the Vladivostok meeting. Kissinger's defense of the agreement's virtues also demonstrated the prevailing assumption that disarmament would not occur: "for a 10-year period the arms race will not be driven by the fear of what the other side might be able to do but only by the agreed ceilings that have been established."[101]

The absence of any serious intention to reduce armaments

was substantiated by the failure of the original wording of the agreement to call for any reductions before the expiration of the accord in 1985. However, between the signing of the agreement on November 24 and the detailed, public explanation of it by the president on December 2, intense public criticism condemned the ceilings as being far too high. As a result, Kissinger successfully sought to change the language of the aide-mémoire to *allow*, at least, for reductions before 1985, if they could be mutually agreed upon. Kissinger acknowledged that the language had been changed to meet criticism of the accord.[102]

It is equally revealing of the administration's attitude toward disarmament that Kissinger admitted that the ceilings for MIRVed vehicles could possibly have been lower, but that he had made no effort to establish a lower limit:

> . . . the MIRV limits resulted substantially from American proposals and not from Soviet proposals. Basically, the judgment of our Defense Department was that once the MIRVs went beyond the point where, over a period of time, the land-based missiles might become vulnerable, a difference of a *few hundred* was not decisive. And therefore we geared the MIRV limits to a minimum program that we had established as being in the interest of our own security and made the proposed number consistent with that program. *No major attempt was made to see whether a hundred less would have worked.*[103]

This is an astonishing statement when one recognizes that 100 extra MIRVed vehicles for each side might easily represent 1,000 additional nuclear weapons for each country. One should recall that the Soviet Union, for example, has only about 240 cities in excess of 100,000 people. Thus this "negligible" increase to the U.S. arsenal would be far more than enough to constitute a satisfactory deterrent in itself. A prime candidate for transporting some of these additional MIRVs would be the new Trident submarine, which can carry 24 missiles, and which costs about $2 billion. At that rate, even 100 fewer MIRVs on Tridents, for which Kissinger made no effort to negotiate, could have saved $8 billion.

Of course, officials did not ordinarily express so clearly their indifference to reducing weapons. For example, Kissinger later asserted that, "The only way we could plausibly have achieved lower numbers is to begin building up our strategic forces dramatically in order to produce an incentive to reduce numbers on the other side."[104] In spite of Kissinger's earlier admission that he had not even tried to get a lower MIRV level in negotiations with the Soviet Union, he illogically argued that to have gotten a lower ceiling, the United States would have had to build up to higher levels. Without attempting to reduce or even restrict arms to the U.S. deployments then existing, Kissinger advocated building to higher levels to achieve arms control. While negotiations proceeded, of course, both sides would deploy more weapons, making an agreement to reduce armaments even less likely. This was typical of the specious thinking and the familiar bargaining-chip arguments that had stimulated the arms race many times since the end of World War II. Despite Kissinger's own illogic, he chided critics: "It doesn't make any sense to instruct us to get better numbers without at the same time being prepared to pay the price of the arms buildup that will be the *only* possible incentive by which an agreement for lower numbers could be achieved."[105]

The *New York Times* reported that, toward the end of the Nixon Administration, the Soviet Union accepted a ceiling of 1,100 MIRVed vehicles for the United States to 1,000 for the Soviet Union, with the expectation that the five-year ceiling would probably continue after 1980. (In 1978, the Carter administration sought to return the MIRV ceiling to roughly this level.) As Kissinger acknowledged, the 1,320 level was a U.S. proposal. "All this suggests that the impetus for the high MIRV ceiling came from the Pentagon, rather than the Kremlin."[106] According to Alton Frye, "the Air Force and Navy were so committed to MIRV deployment that neither within the Defense Department nor at the committee of principals was there a concerted campaign to include a MIRV ban in the SALT package."[107]

The press also reported that the United States had offered a lower MIRV ceiling only four months earlier. But Kissinger argued that the earlier U.S. proposal was not lower than the November agreement. "The July proposal, first of all, called for a five-year agreement. If you double the number that we proposed for the five-year agreement, you would have a higher number than the one we settled on for 10 years."[108] Kissinger inexplicably assumed that the number of arms by 1985 would be twice the number in 1980, and that the five-year levels would not be extended another five years, a possibility the Soviet Union reportedly was willing to consider. In addition, the statement demonstrated Kissinger's presumption that any arms control agreement would simply ratify the armament procurement plans already in existence, and that the buildup would continue indefinitely. It contradicted his earlier public stance, taken in praise of the Vladivostok agreement, that one arms control treaty would increase the chances for comprehensive reductions in the future. Following the Interim Agreement, the behavior of the United States demonstrated its assumption that the arms race would continue in the face of agreements professedly concluded for the purpose of arms control. SALT I, which limited the deployment of ABMs, had indicated that both sides would adopt a no-damage-limiting posture.[109] That is, each side would accept as a fact that it was vulnerable to destruction by the other side in case of war. No efforts would be undertaken to try to erode the other side's nuclear capability to inflict unacceptable damage on an attacker, because to do so would stimulate the other side to new weapons deployment. By not deploying ABMs in more than one site, both sides seemingly recognized the futility of any arms programs that moved toward a counterforce capability.

However, in the Vladivostok agreement officials completely eliminated that assumption of SALT I. MIRVs meant that damage-limiting capability would be developed, even though sufficient capability could not be developed to make one side or the other really invulnerable to attack.

Since the Interim Agreement already had limited all strategic vehicles except bombers, the existing *pre*-Vladivostok limitation removed any pretext for enlarging offensive forces. If arms reductions would in fact follow the establishment of a ceiling, as claimed, then the Vladivostok accord (SALT II) should have set ceilings lower than the number of weapons allowed in SALT I. At the least, the Vladivostok negotiations should logically have extended the Interim Agreement in slightly modified form and unconditionally banned multiplication of offensive warheads.[110] Instead, negotiators paved the way not simply for adding more sophisticated weapons to existing arsenals, but also for legitimizing the deployment of hundreds of new warheads.

Furthermore, the Vladivostok agreement failed to increase the prospects for general disarmament because it did nothing to decrease incentives for weapons procurement by other countries. Among the most relevant of these incentives was the pace-setting role of the United States and Soviet Union in armaments development. If the superpowers deployed more sophisticated weapons and moved quickly from one weapon generation to

85

another, other countries were bound to feel a need to update their forces also. If the major powers gained prestige, power, wealth, and psychological dominance from their possession of arms, it was hypocritical and discriminatory for them to ask the weaker countries of the world to refrain voluntarily from also seeking to obtain instruments of military power.

For example, the nuclear Non-Proliferation Treaty was an effort at enforcing inequity.[111] Only the countries without nuclear weapons accepted obligations for international inspection of nuclear installations. The countries that had nuclear weapons did not. If honored, such controls would in practice make it impossible for the militarily weaker states to produce nuclear explosions while the superpowers would continue development, increasing their hegemony even more. In Article VI, the superpowers undertook to negotiate "in good faith on effective measures relating to cessation of the nuclear arms race at an early date and to nuclear disarmament, and on a treaty on general and complete disarmament." If implemented, that measure would have begun to decrease the power differential between nuclear and nonnuclear states. However, neither superpower has taken the provision seriously.[112] Similarly, the Limited Test Ban Treaty of 1963 had included a promise of "seeking to achieve the discontinuance of all test explosions of nuclear weapons for all time."[113] After more than fifteen years, that goal has yet to be realized.

The SALT negotiations did not take into account the hopes or fears of the nonnuclear-weapons countries. Limiting ABMs and establishing high ceilings on strategic launchers meant little to the nonnuclear states; even a 50 percent cut in existing launchers would still have left the superpowers in an overwhelmingly superior position in strategic weapons. What the Vladivostok agreement allowed and even encouraged—the qualitative side of the arms race—carried the greatest risks for the small powers. Miniaturization, increased accuracy, and improved yield-to-weight ratios of nuclear explosives make such weapons more appropriate for fighting "limited" wars in the weaker countries. The battlefields for such new weapons, as Alva Myrdal has pointed out, are not likely to be the homelands of the superpowers, protected by strategic weapons, but the homelands of other nations.[114] President Ford's public declaration (even if merely a verbal threat) only seven months after the Vladivostok meeting, that nuclear weapons were a serious option for use in war against North Korea, could not help but increase North Korea's desire for nuclear weapons.[115]

Because the superpowers were unwilling to work toward international equity, the societies that were cast, through no fault of their own, into inferior conditions and status, were likely to seek to redress the imbalance of power and wealth against them by imitating the least desirable features of superpower behavior: in the quest for achieving genuine equity as full members of the planetary family, they would be tempted—encouraged by the militaristic values and actions of the superpowers—to waste resources on expenditures for items such as aircraft and nuclear explosives.

The prospects for disarmament were dimmed further by growing Soviet and U.S. arms exports. The estimated value of worldwide arms exports by all suppliers rose from $4.4 billion in 1963 to $8.7 billion by 1973 (in constant 1972 dollars).[116] During the year of the Vladivostok agreement, the United States government alone sold about $8.3 billion worth of military equipment to seventy different foreign countries. Direct sales by manufacturers, plus aid provided by the U.S. government, brought the 1974 total of arms given or sold by Americans to $12.5 billion,[117] or more than twice the level of the previous year and about ten times the average level of the late 1960s. U.S. arms exports from 1972 through 1974, the years of the SALT I and Vladivostok agreements, exceeded total sales in the previous two decades.[118] On the basis of a growing number of multi-year contracts, Pentagon officials predicted that a high volume of foreign sales would continue for the foreseeable future.[119]

The United States exported more arms in 1973 than all other countries combined.[120] Because of the long U.S. tradition of arms sales, about two-thirds of world armaments outside of the Soviet Union and the United States are U.S.-made and -distributed.[121] If one includes the lesser munitions exported by hundreds of small companies, the value of military equipment the United States either sold, lent, or has given away since World War II totals about $100 billion. Selling munitions to foreign armies has been so lucrative that over 1,000 U.S. corporations produce or export arms. Of the fifty largest industrial companies in the United States, thirty-two make or export munitions. The State Department's Office of Munitions Control has reported in vivid detail the extent to which United States wealth and many working people's livelihoods are intertwined with arms sales. The munitions manufactured by General Motors Corporation, for example, required ten pages simply to list the categories of weapons, ranging from rifles, bayonets, and flame throwers to "biological agents adapted for use in war to produce death or disablement in human beings or animals, or to damage crops and plants." Even smaller companies, long associated with consumer goods, produce an imposing array of equipment. The Bulova Watch Company, for instance, turns out "mechanical and electronic ammunition manufacturing machines, devices for activation and devices for detonation of missiles . . . missile . . . arming devices, [and] missile fusing devices."[122]

In order to increase United States power and profits, officials sought to promote rather than to restrict the sale of armaments.[123] As the Department of Defense and Secretary of Defense James Schlesinger have acknowledged, arms exports have enhanced the political hegemony of the United States. Officials specifically designed the supply of weapons to foreign governments to increase U.S. influence over those governments, and "to maintain the political and economic advantages that accrue from the resultant supplier relationship."[124] When Senator Edward Kennedy proposed slowing arms transfers to the Persian Gulf area, Schlesinger rejected the idea, saying "We are engaged in attempting to maintain influence in these areas."[125] In another instance, he explained, "The degree of influence of the supplier is potentially substantial, and typically, those relationships are enduring."[126]

Military advisers and technicians usually followed military sales. In the year after the Vladivostok agreement, the Defense Department sent out 132 technical assistance and training teams to 34 foreign governments because of foreign military sales contracts.[127] Since 1950 the United States has trained 428,000 foreign military personnel.[128] These missions not only increased United States influence abroad, but also made foreign military establishments more sympathetic toward U.S. strategic interests and more dependent on continued good relations with the United States in order to receive maintenance support, spare parts, technical improvements, and training.

A related objective in providing military assistance and sales has been to continue "an uninterrupted access to bases and facilities important to the worldwide U.S. military posture."[129] To protect its hegemony, the United States has promoted the transfer of arms to other governments to increase their stake in U.S.

predominance and to make them more pliable in allowing this hegemony to continue.

The United States also has sold arms abroad in order to lower the per unit cost of weapons to the Department of Defense. As General Fred C. Weyand, Chief of Staff of the U.S. army, explained: "From the pure economics of it, [the military equipment] the foreign military buy pays for a share of the research, development, and engineering, and the tooling up costs."[130] In addition to subsidizing the production of weapons, selling arms to the Third World also has been a convenient way to enlist the poor of the world to aid an unstable United States economy, to redress shortages in its balance of payments, to recover petrodollars, and to expand the profits of arms manufacturers.[131]

The United States further promoted military assistance and sales in order to maintain political stability—sometimes through repression of reform movements—in the recipients' domestic politics in the hope that that would in turn contribute to stability of the international order in which the United States enjoyed preeminence. The vast arms exports increased the political and economic power of military persons and institutions in all of the recipients' societies. Because military organizations are inherently authoritarian and therefore uncongenial to democratic processes, to augment the power of such organizations with money, weapons, and training programs made it more difficult to build a world in which military power would play a decreased role.

In sum, the superpowers have contributed greatly to the arms competition among smaller nations. This competition is so difficult to dampen that some officials of smaller powers have argued that the problems of regional arms races can be solved only in the context of worldwide disarmament.[132]

Future arms reductions were also unlikely to flow from the Vladivostok agreement because it did not prohibit enough weapons to reduce the number of people in military production who in the long run exerted pressures for more armaments. This was an important deficiency because the arms race since World War II had been fueled by a combination of domestic bureaucratic, corporate, and labor pressures for military spending, as well as by the perceived threat of the Soviet Union. Determining the extent of the various influences is beyond the scope of this study. Nevertheless, there is substantial evidence that domestic pressures for weapons development constituted a significant driving force in the arms buildup—a force often more influential than either the capability or the intention of the Soviet Union.[133]

These pressures included corporate desires for easy profits, labor unions' thirst for more jobs and higher wages, a national political obsession and official psychological need to remain the strongest military power in the world, bureaucratic pressures for continuing or expanding ongoing programs, and the scientific community's inclination to exploit and expand the limits of technology for weapons purposes.[134]

The high profitability of defense contracts to major corporations has been well documented.[135] It would be an exaggeration to suggest that arms producers determined U.S. national security policy; still, the Vladivostok agreement was clearly constructed in such a way that corporate interests were not harmed by the ceilings. Insofar as the agreement legitimized the deployment of weapons at new levels, it aided the future profits of defense industries and at the same time kept the unions happy. Many legislators translated votes on military appropriations into jobs in their respective districts.

The desire to maintain the United States as the most powerful military force in the world also inflated budgets and arsenals beyond actual security needs.[136] Secretary Schlesinger declared: "I am convinced . . . the American public wishes to remain [militarily] second to none. There may be difficulties in any fiscal year or any program year, but over the course of a decade or more . . . the United States will not consent to a position of being second to anyone else."[137] Since not all other countries of the world were happy with the superior position of the United States, this attitude encouraged arms competition. If there were benefits for the United States in being number one, there were costs to some of those who were not number one. In their efforts to diminish the United States lead, rivals deployed more weapons, and the United States in turn sought to meet or exceed these new efforts. Precise equality between the United States and the Soviet Union was hardly possible, given the biased perspectives from which each set of leaders viewed the opponent's arsenals. In any case, each side doubtless preferred superiority to equality. As long as those conditions prevailed, the simple notion that the United States should be second to none made arms reductions impossible.

The widespread belief that additional military capability would contribute to the bargaining power of a country in its international relations has also encouraged the growth of arsenals, even if such growth was unrelated to the enhancement of security. Admiral Moorer, for example, said that if the Soviet Union achieved strategic superiority, "we will pay a very high price in the effectiveness of our diplomacy . . . even were that superiority to have no practical effect on the outcome of an all-out nuclear exchange."[138] Secretary Schlesinger believed that the never-ending drive to stay ahead of the Soviet Union "is also important for symbolic purposes, in large part because the strategic offensive forces have come to be seen by many—however regrettably—as important to the status and stature of a major power."[139]

The desire to remain the biggest military power was buttressed by the familiar argument that the Soviet Union would take arms control seriously only if the United States negotiated from a "position of strength." That statement was an older, more general version of the bargaining-chip argument. As Kissinger told those who wanted lower ceilings, an "arms buildup . . . will be the only possible incentive by which an agreement for lower numbers could be achieved. . . . The only way we could plausibly have achieved lower numbers is to begin building up our strategic forces dramatically."[140] According to Kissingerian logic, in order to hit the target of disarmament, one should aim at armament. Of several weaknesses in this approach, the one relevant here is that such a negotiating strategy encouraged powerful domestic economic and bureaucratic constituencies to coalesce behind new programs and made them difficult to stop in subsequent arms control proceedings.[141]

Malcolm Currie advanced a technological variation of the argument for seeking superiority over other countries: "[Military] technology . . . appears to offer us our place in the sun—the means to insure our security and economic vitality."[142] Currie believed that the best way "to protect our technological lead is to continue to advance and exploit our technological base. In so doing, we can show the Soviets that they will never catch up, that the military balance will be maintained because the technological balance will always be in our favor." Currie warned, "The stakes in this [technological] competition are high. They involve national survival."[143] By seeking military and technological superiority, the United States stimulated the arms race and demonstrated its unwillingness to limit its military programs to a minimum necessary for security.[144]

Furthermore, misleading government statements nullified effective domestic political action by critics of the arms race and thereby facilitated continued military expenditures. For example, officials virtually promised that arms reductions would follow the Vladivostok agreement, but, in fact, they were hardly any more likely than before. Kissinger's skillful manipulation of language either confused or convinced reporters sufficiently that they failed to press him for concrete elaboration of his claim that the Vladivostok agreement reduced armaments.[145] Kissinger said the accord's "significance becomes all the more clear if one compares the numbers not with some hypothetical model that one might have in mind but with what would have happened in the absence of this agreement. . . . [I]t is not a fair comparison to compare these [Vladivostok] figures with some abstract model."[146] In that manner he silenced critics who called for lower ceilings by accusing them of forming judgments based on "hypothetical models" of the future, in contrast to his policies based on "what would have happened in the absence of this agreement." The latter, of course, was merely a prediction, which was also unavoidably hypothetical. Kissinger did not estimate what would have happened if the United States had offered to dismantle its MIRVs before the Soviet Union deployed any at all.

Some critics said that the United States had such a strong deterrent, including sizable overkill, that there was no need for more weapons, even if the Soviet Union developed them. Kissinger said this condition "would be true at almost any foreseeable level, or at any level that has been publicly suggested by any of the protagonists in this debate. This is a problem that is inherent in the nature of nuclear weapons and in the size of existing nuclear stockpiles." Astonishingly, reporters apparently accepted this as a reasonable explanation for why the United States should have more weapons. Kissinger had said that overkill would exist at any of the contemplated strategic ceilings, thus the ceilings might as well be higher (to have more overkill). In other words, since both sides had more than enough weapons to destroy the other several times, a ceiling high enough to deploy several thousand more weapons needed no new justification. Kissinger also commented upon the criticism that the Vladivostok accord did not stop the qualitative arms race: "It is of course extremely difficult to stop qualitative changes in the best of circumstances, because it is very difficult to control what one is not able to describe, which is inherent in the nature of technological change."[147]

Although that explanation seemed reasonable on an abstract level, it was simply untrue in practice. MIRVs, an important part of the qualitative arms race, could have been reduced or prohibited relatively easily. Under the Vladivostok guidelines both sides planned to distinguish, through national means of verification, between MIRVed and non-MIRVed vehicles. If that could be done, there was no technical reason why all MIRVs could not have been banned on all land-based ICBMs and, if desired, even on SLBMs. The rule agreed upon was that any vehicle tested in a MIRV mode would be counted against the MIRV total, so the limit could have been set at any level. Similarly, it would have been easy in 1974 to prevent deployment of the even newer maneuverable reentry vehicles (MARVs) by prohibiting their testing (which could be verified). Once they had been tested, control would become more difficult. Moreover, the Interim Agreement's ban on future deployment of MIRVed or otherwise more sophisticated ABMs demonstrated that weapons yet undeveloped *could* be banned.[148] Kissinger misled reporters and the public by suggesting that control became easier after weapons had been developed and tested, when actually the opposite was true. Because national verification of testing programs was simpler than controlling deployment once the technology was in hand, a ban on each of the following major weapons would have been technically easier to achieve before they were tested than afterwards: the atomic bomb, the hydrogen bomb, ICBM, SLBM, ABM, MIRV, and MARV. The problem was not to control the unknown, as Kissinger described it, but to prevent the testing of the experimental.

The preference of military and State Department officials for developing rather than banning new weapons was clearly revealed in the negotiation over mobile missiles. The United States, in late 1974 or early 1975, proposed that mobile missiles be prohibited. U.S. officials thought the Soviet Union would have several advantages in mobile missiles if they were allowed. First, U.S. citizens and Congress might disapprove of mobile missiles moving around the country on truck or rail launchers. Second, such missiles could be stolen more easily by terrorist groups, if not in the United States, then in other countries that might eventually get them. Third, the Soviet Union had more territory in which to hide mobile missiles than did the United States. As a result, the Air Force began to test an air-launched intercontinental missile in order to use it as a bargaining chip to induce the Soviet Union to give up their land-mobile missiles. But after the Soviet Union agreed to the U.S. position, the United States reversed itself and decided that it was more important to keep new missile options open than to prohibit them.[149] The U.S. later developed the M-X, which avoided most of the problems indicated in the first and second reasons above. In brief, a prohibition on a new weapon was deliberately rejected by the U.S. government at the time when verification of the ban would have been most feasible.

Moreover, Kissinger claimed that the Vladivostok agreement "reduces substantially the incentive of an unlimited arms race. The nightmare in qualitative changes had always been the linkage of qualitative change with quantity."[150] Again, it was deceptive to say that the Vladivostok agreement reduced the incentive for qualitative improvements. As indicated above, the limits on the number of launchers *emphasized* additional sophistication and destructive power per unit. Kissinger's distortions undermined consciousness-raising efforts by those genuinely seeking disarmament. By reporting but failing to probe Kissinger's specious explanations, the press aided the administration in its deception of the public.

The continued and largely uncontested existence of bureaucratic pressures for military procurement also undermined the propects for arms reductions resulting from the Vladivostok meeting. The creation of powerful bureaucratic and economic forces in arms production had changed the face of American politics since World War II. These forces showed a Parkinsonian proclivity to resist any decline in their institutional expressions and to promote their own expansion. Many of the requests for new weapons were buttressed by arguments that the Pentagon should be able to spend a certain percentage of total U.S. output. Military officials sought to convince Congress that the military establishment had a "right" to maintain a given percentage of spending regardless of more narrowly defined security needs. They tried to establish expenditures for military equipment on an economic footing similar to that for education, roads, and environmental protection. In their minds, military spending should be viewed as a value in itself. Yet, none explained why military spending should grow as the total economy or national budget grew, despite an era of détente, a widely acclaimed arms control agreement, and an abundance of nuclear weapons on hand from previous purchases.

Pentagon officials also sought to preserve their status within the government as a whole. Moderate as the effects of the Interim Agreement were, Admiral Moorer testified before the Senate Appropriations Committee that the Joint Chiefs of Staff (JCS) agreed to the Interim Agreement only after receiving "assurances" from the White House that in return they would get "a very extensive research and development program, and . . . aggressive improvement and modernization programs to include the B-1 and the Trident." The Joint Chiefs approved the 1972 five-year accord because it was a temporary, stop-gap measure, not a permanent treaty: "No matter what we did during this 5-year period, there was no way we could add to our force levels. . . . We had made the decision to level off our force levels [even in the absence of any agreement]. . . . Now we never would have accepted this [Interim] agreement as a treaty; we accepted it as an interim agreement for that 5-year period because we felt we knew that we could not add to our forces during that time."[151] It is clear, therefore, that the SALT I agreement was not designed to stop the arms buildup. In 1972, Melvin Laird, then secretary of defense, proposed a cruise missile program as part of a package of "strategic initiatives" designed to win the Joint Chiefs of Staff's approval of the accord. Since such missiles would not be covered by the Interim Agreement, Laird suggested them as a legal way to evade the restrictive impact of the agreement upon defense planners.[152] As indicated below, later U.S.-Soviet arguments over the cruise missile jeopardized the effort to transform the Vladivostok accord into a more formal agreement.

Obviously, the SALT ceilings were determined heavily by what the Pentagon wanted to deploy;[153] they were maintained only for as long as the Defense Department thought they would not be restrictive. In return for accepting the admittedly non-restrictive provisions of the Interim Agreement, the Pentagon received promises that it could later deploy its new weapons then undergoing research and development. To the extent that

95

an agreement might have meant a serious halt to arms procurement, the Pentagon's enormous bureaucratic forces would have opposed it.

Finally, the desire of some groups of scientists and government bureaucrats to exploit the limits of technology for weapons advances contributed to the drive for new armaments.[154] The intense exploitation of technology for military purposes has been more pronounced since 1945 than ever before. Between the First and Second World Wars, military support for science and technology absorbed less than 1 percent of the military budgets of the major powers. The share of major military budgets devoted to research and development ranged from 10 to 15 percent during the late 1950s, and has remained at that level. U.S. research and development costs rose from about $30 million in 1939 to 330 times that in 1975.[155]

One of the most important features of the technological process that has stimulated the armaments buildup has been the long lead-time required for new weapons. Ten years may pass between the initial stage of development and eventual deployment. This has meant that each side has felt it is necessary to begin immediately the development of weapons that the other side *might* deploy only ten years later. In any case of uncertainty, officials have wanted to go ahead with development to prepare for the worst possible contingency. Each side has therefore built weapons not for current security needs, but to counteract weapons anticipated for some years in the future. Since the range of possibilities for the opponent's arsenal has been almost limitless, a full range of development programs has continued on both sides.

Once various programs have been begun, of course, the energies and money put into them for research have been used as arguments to justify eventual production and deployment. Moreover, as the opposing side has probably developed similar weapon prototypes independently, this development has been used as a "justification" for deployment of the weapons that years earlier were studied only because of a possibility that the other side might seek to gain a qualitative technological advantage. The MIRV was a case in point.

The rapid pace of applying technological innovations to new weapons often has little to do with any external military threat. First the technology is developed—as in the case of the MIRV—and then officials search for a strategic doctrine that will justify the "need" for the technology.[156] The unilaterally determined pace of innovation has, in the long run, no doubt *decreased* U.S. security. Although the United States has been in the vanguard of military power, other states have followed—buying, borrowing, or copying the technology for destructive weapons that the United States invented, and which, when possessed by others, will later come to haunt us.

Once new weapons were off the drawing boards and in production, officials tailored strategic doctrine to justify military "requirements" that were pegged to production capability rather than to objective security needs. Alain C. Enthoven, former assistant secretary of defense for systems analysis, testified that in preparing budget requests for "necessary" weapons, "year after year the *requirement* came out to use all of the available production capability."[157]

The technological emphasis on weapons development has had another self-generating feature. Because development of modern military equipment requires highly skilled people and specialized resources, the laboratories and industries engaged in development are regarded as national assets. Persons employed there cannot be allowed to drift away to other tasks because of fear that new development might be missed in one year, which would have dangerous consequences ten years later. To keep these resources intact means that they must be fully employed at all times, and this in itself creates many new technical possibilities for sophisticating weapons.[158]

As weapons become more complex and expensive, the number of persons involved at the peak of development on any given weapon becomes larger. An ever-growing technological agenda is therefore required to keep those additional research teams employed. The reason that the employment capacity at the peak of a program's development cannot be held constant is that officials consider it impossible to increase the length of time required for the development process. If it took longer, the weapon might become obsolete before it had been deployed. The development process therefore not only required that research and development teams be fully employed at all times, but also meant that the increase in their size was difficult to control.

Although it is beyond the scope of this chapter to explain the reasons for the arms buildup, the preceding discussion offers evidence that the arms race has not been exclusively a pattern of action and reaction in which each side responds to the minimum level necessary to protect its security in the face of incremental changes in the arsenal of the opponent. On the contrary, there is little evidence to suggest that the action-reaction pattern even is the most important influence in the arms race.[159] The rate of increasing armaments has not been noticeably influenced by any improvement in the relations of the two countries. Bureaucratic pressures for weapons development, coupled with a desire to exploit technological opportunities as they arise, have led to a much more rapid sophistication of weaponry than would have resulted from an arms race stimulated merely by the action-reaction pattern.

In assessing the consequences of the arms control negotiations, Senator Edmund Muskie observed: "SALT doesn't mean anything unless it is going to produce some reductions on both sides of capabilities which we both [the United States and Soviet Union] regard as important to our respective strategic policies. If we are giving away nothing, the thing isn't worth anything."[160] By that standard, the Vladivostok accord was worth very little.

As the foregoing discussion suggests, instead of laying the foundation for future arms reductions (professed value 3), the Vladivostok agreement mirrored and conformed to the desires of the forces seeking more armaments. It expressed implicit value D—*to reach an agreement (1) that was tailored to the officially held assumption that the arms competition would continue indefinitely; (2) that maintained political and military incentives for other countries to increase the size and cost of their arsenals; (3) that enjoyed the support of those persons and institutions with vested interests in continuing the arms buildup; and (4) that avoided deflating economic, bureaucratic, and technocratic pressures at home for more arms spending.*

Professed Value 4: To Reduce International Tensions Exacerbated by the Arms Race

General George J. Brown, the Chairman of the Joint Chiefs of Staff, told the Senate Armed Services Committee that the Vladivostok agreement "is a significant milestone toward improving relations between the U.S. and U.S.S.R., reducing the risk of war, and enhancing the chances of world peace."[161] In explaining the significance of the accord, President Ford said that it would "prevent . . . an arms race with all its terror, instability, [and] war-breeding tension."[162] In his state-of-the-world message to Congress, Ford said that a treaty incorporating the Vladivostok agreement "would mark a turning point in postwar history and would be a crucial step in lifting from mankind the threat of nuclear war."[163]

The conclusion that the Vladivostok agreement would decrease tensions rested on the assumption that it had stabilized armaments significantly. However, the agreement allowed the deployment of new submarines, bombers, missiles, warheads, cruise missiles, and the development of additional "improvements." It encouraged movement away from a posture of finite deterrence based on assured destruction, toward the less stable posture of attaining a damage-limiting capability against land-based missiles. The legitimization of MIRVs increased the possibility that in time of crisis one side might launch a preemptive strike in an effort forcibly to disarm its opponent, at least in part. "Crisis instability—the penultimate danger of the nuclear era, second only to the ultimate horror of an actual nuclear exchange—clearly has been brought closer by the failure at Vladivostok to limit MIRV missiles to low levels."[164] In assessing the political impact of the Vladivostok conference, the editors of the *New York Times* wrote, "The new agreement seems almost calculated to increase instability. By vastly increasing the number of warheads, it enshrines the doctrine that a nuclear war-fighting capability is needed. Planning to fight a nuclear war, rather than merely to deter one, is certain to reduce the inhibitions against using nuclear arms."[165] Tensions arising among various other countries would also be exacerbated by continuing United States-Soviet buildups, rapid technological innovation, and the export of advanced weapons. Precision-guidance systems increase the prospects for nuclear weapons being used against third parties.

To summarize, the Vladivostok agreement may have increased military instability between the superpowers. It also failed to discourage superpower participation in intrastate violence. Neither did the accord do anything to dampen tensions arising from growing militarism and internal class or ideological conflicts in other countries that often, at least since World War II, precipitated violence involving direct or indirect military participation by the superpowers. Once again, the Vladivostok accord produced a value impact that contrasted sharply with professed values. By enabling the arms race to continue without significant restriction, its practical effect was *to perpetuate an international political process heavily influenced by military power and therefore to*

99

continue both the intranational and international tensions arising from further militarization of the planet (implicit value E). To the extent that tensions were lessening during the 1970s, détente was less a product of restraint in military procurement than of general great-power realignments due to changing political conditions.

Table 2-7
A Comparison of Professed and Implicit Values
in U.S. Policies for Arms Reduction

Professed Values	*Implicit Values*
1. To slow the arms race.	A. To allow the arms buildup to continue without significant restriction.
	B. To legitimize a further arms buildup.
2. To curtail arms expenditures.	C. To maintain high levels of U.S. and world military expenditures.
3. To lay the foundation for future arms reductions.	D. To reach an agreement (1) that was tailored to the officially held assumption that the arms competition would continue indefinitely; (2) that maintained political and military incentives for other countries to increase the size and cost of their arsenals; (3) that enjoyed the support of those persons and institutions with vested interests in continuing the arms buildup; (4) that avoided deflating economic, bureaucratic, and technocratic pressures for more arms spending.
4. To reduce international tensions exacerbated by the arms race.	E. To perpetuate an international political process heavily influenced by military power and, therefore, to continue both the intranational and international tensions arising from further militarization of the planet.

An Opposing View of the Arms Buildup

The present case study demonstrates that the Vladivostok accord did not reverse or even significantly limit the arms buildup. Nor, it seems, did officials really try to take any steps toward a disarming world. Both superpowers were intent upon deploying their newest generation of weapons and keeping their options open for future deployments. To some extent, each side was locked in competition to develop new technology as soon as the other side did. There are of course some who may dispute these findings. It is instructive to examine briefly the views of one of the most respected and informed critics of some of the conclusions reached in this case study. Albert Wohlstetter, in an exchange with other students of arms control,[166] has argued at some length that there has been no arms race between the two superpowers for at least fourteen years. According to Wohlstetter, U.S. intelligence predictions of future Soviet strategic deployments in the 1950s and 1960s underestimated actual Soviet deployments. Because predictions had consistently been too low, the U.S. did not overreact to Soviet deployments, and thus there was no action-reaction pattern between the two states that could have stimulated an arms race. "If we underestimated, then exaggerated fears cannot have driven us in a race."[167] Second, Wohlstetter presented data showing that in recent years Soviet expenditures for strategic deployments were increasing while U.S. strategic expenditures were decreasing.

Because Wohlstetter's analysis typifies so much of official and academic thinking, it is useful to respond briefly to these two points. The fact that Wohlstetter showed U.S. intelligence predictions to have been too low in anticipating Soviet deployments does not refute the notion that U.S. officials may have exaggerated the threat posed by Soviet hardware actually in existence. This possible exaggeration could have produced unwarranted U.S. strategic deployments and an excessively confrontational diplomatic posture that stimulated the arms buildup. Wohlstetter seemed to recognize the possibility of exaggerating the Soviet threat when he criticized the Vladivostok agreement in another context: "Vladivostok also illustrates the absurdity of the exaggerated threat/'worst case' dynamic. Here, overblown estimates of future Russian programs may lend a specious urgency to rapid agreement—another 'miracle' for the Secretary [of State]."[168] But Wohlstetter did not acknowledge that an "overblown estimate" or exaggerated threat based on an intelligence underestimate makes the *under*estimate little different from an overestimate in terms of the practical consequences for deployments and for the action-reaction pattern. Such an acknowledgment would, of course, have negated Wohlstetter's argument that underestimates could not have produced an overreaction.

More importantly, there is another reason why an action-reaction pattern could have come into play in spite of intelligence underestimates by the United States. Arms proponents like Wohlstetter seem to assume that U.S. weapons procurement was somehow linked to intelligence predictions, and that, if predictions were low, then U.S. deployments could not have been too high. However, since 1945 the U.S. government has simply wanted to be first among all nations in military technology and power. (Wohlstetter curiously overlooks frequent official statements and actions embracing this goal.) U.S. officials have deployed weaponry far in excess of security needs in order to perpetuate United States superiority. In doing so, they have encouraged the Soviet government—itself not satisfied with being an inferior power—to deploy a vast arsenal. One need not necessarily believe that the United States overestimated Soviet forces and then overreacted to these predictions, to know that as a matter of historical fact the United States has deployed more weapons than needed for deterrence, and the Soviet Union has spent most of its strategic effort during the 1950s and 1960s trying to catch up to the United States.

In addition, it is at least possible that because of the U.S. lead—and regardless of U.S. intelligence underestimates—the Kremlin may have deployed its weapons at an even faster pace than originally planned. If so, American actions could very well have stimulated Soviet reactions that made potentially accurate U.S. intelligence predictions appear too low with the passage of time.

Moreover, regardless of the extent to which one believes that Wohlstetter has successfully argued that the weapons buildup was not due to an action-reaction pattern, his argument in no way refutes the idea presented in this case study that unilateral U.S. decisions, unrelated to security needs, were an important stimulus to the annual appropriation of billions of dollars for more strategic weapons. Domestic pressures for more arms may produce vast deployments, regardless of whether intelligence predictions are too high or too low. Such pressures also discourage intensive efforts to develop models of a disarming world.

To recapitulate: (1) the presence of U.S. intelligence underestimates fails to prove that an action-reaction pattern of arms competition could not have developed anyway, and (2) the alleged absence of an action-reaction pattern fails to prove that the United States did not deploy far more weapons than were necessary for security or than were desirable for achieving a disarmed world.

If, for the sake of arguing Wohlstetter's second point, we assume that U.S. expenditures on strategic weapons have recently decreased in real terms, this decline does not constitute convincing evidence that a race for weapons superiority has ended. The United States had a considerable headstart in the arms competition, and has recently been able to remain in the competition even with declining strategic expenditures. Except over a long period, strategic expenditures in themselves may prove little about whether the United States is vigorously competing at the forefront of important strategic innovations. That is especially true for U.S. breakthroughs which have produced more sophisticated weapons at less cost.

In two of the articles in *Foreign Policy*, Wohlstetter insisted that the term "race" should not be used to describe the strategic rivalry between the United States and Soviet Union. To justify the word "race," he argued, the United States government must be "rapidly increasing its strategic budgets and forces."[169] This statement reveals Wohlstetter's assumption—one also held by many officials—that a constant level of annual expenditures for strategic weapons is a norm. If the U.S. government spent less this year than last, Wohlstetter would think of this as a decrease in the amount spent for strategic weapons, even though there is clearly an increase in the accumulated total expenditures for strategic arms. Buying missiles is not like buying groceries, where the food is soon eaten and must be resupplied. Once missiles and submarines are purchased, they remain in the arsenal for years. Wohlstetter ignored that U.S. expenditures annually exceeded the amount that would have been necessary simply to pay for maintenance of old weapons. The government in fact has been upgrading its forces each year, even when less is spent than previously.

Wohlstetter's idea that the word "race" must be reserved for only a "rapidly increasing" rate of expenditure may be contrasted with the view of long-distance runners who consider themselves in a race even though for much of the race they are not increasing their pace at all. Any movement toward a goal can be a race—even without any increase in pace—if in the process one competes with another.

103

Since the United States has decreased its real expenditures for strategic weapons while the Soviet Union had increased that segment of its annual budget, Wohlstetter commented that "it is surely stretching it to talk of a 'race' between parties moving in quite different directions."[170] In a later article, he again declared that the superpowers "have been moving not only at different speeds, but in *opposite directions*. If that doesn't do lethal damage to the arms race metaphor, nothing will."[171]

For Wohlstetter and other strategic analysts to say that the United States was moving in an "opposite direction" to the Soviet Union is the equivalent of telling the front-runner in a marathon race that if he decreased his rate of progress, he would be running in the opposite direction to the runner in last place who is picking up speed. In fact, the front-runner is moving in the same direction, and he will win the race if he does not decrease his pace too far. Similarly, both the Soviet Union and the United States have been expending additional money every year for more sophisticated weapons—even if the United States has spent less per year than in some previous years.[172] The two states are headed in the same direction, but at different speeds, at least insofar as budgetary statistics reflect the pace of "progress." Because Wohlstetter judges arms procurement from the norm of a constant level of expenditure rather than from the norm of a disarming world, he sees a decline in annual strategic expenditures as a "different direction." Even if United States strategic expenditures declined when compared to previous years, annual expenditures for new hardware may still be to the advocates of disarmament an undesirable continuation of the same direction.

In the preceding discussion, I have assumed the validity of Wohlstetter's data in order to point out the contrast in perspective between one who assumes that ongoing arms policies are largely satisfactory and one who believes that policies should aim toward the minimization of collective violence. Without going into detail about the actual data, however, one should note that some of Wohlstetter's critics have disputed his interpretation of recent spending trends in the strategic area.[173]

Wohlstetter also denies that U.S. destructive capability has increased. He comes to this conclusion by emphasizing a decline in the total yield of all deployed strategic weapons. Any decrease in overall strategic megatonnage available for destroying soft targets means little, since both sides have far more capability than required to destroy all soft targets even in a second strike. Hard-target destructive capability, however, has increased enormously because improvements in accuracy and increases in the number of warheads more than offset any decline in total megatonnage deployed in 1975 as compared to pre-MIRV deployments.

Why has Wohlstetter worked so hard to prove that there has been no arms "race?" Perhaps because he believes that, "We may want, in general, to stop or curb a race, but not a competition in arms."[174] By demonstrating that no arms race has occurred, Wohlstetter facilitates continued weapons development and deployment. Therefore, according to Wohlstetter, it is not a race for the United States and the Soviet Union to spend billions and billions of dollars for strategic arms year after year; it is competition that one should not stop. Regardless of whether one uses the word "race" or "competition" to describe the continuing application of massive energies and resources to producing military equipment, it is clear that present policies in Washington and Moscow have failed to make progress in arms reductions.

A GLOBAL HUMANIST APPROACH

Comparison of Professed Values, Implicit Values, and the Minimization of Collective Violence

This analysis began by examining the widely professed value of promoting international peace, stability, and national security through arms control. Officials articulated four instrumental values in their program for realizing the terminal value: to stop the arms race, to curtail military expenditures, to pave the way for future arms reductions, and to lessen tensions caused by arms competition. These values are in harmony with the first value of global humanism, but in contrast to official practice. U.S. policy actually served interests reflecting an alternative set of implicit values. The following were imbedded in United States behavior: (A) to allow the arms buildup to continue without significant restriction; (B) to legitimize and stimulate arms procurement; (C) to maintain high levels of military expenditures; (D) to reach an agreement that enjoyed the support of persons with vested interests in continuing the arms buildup, and that in the domestic area avoided deflating economic, bu-

105

reaucratic, and technocratic pressures for more arms spending; and (E) to perpetuate the tensions arising from a continued military buildup.

No doubt most officials would deny that they preferred any of the preceding consequences of policy as an end in itself. However, they rated the preservation of the U.S. economic-political position higher than other values, and to accomplish their ends they selected militarily oriented instruments. Thus, in practice, officials served values A through E, and often furthered interests that produced value impacts which no one endorsed publicly. Both the executive and legislative branches preferred these five implicit values to the consequences that would attend a scaling down of U.S. military strength.

If these implicit values express the operational code of official behavior, then the professed value itself must be qualified. A more accurate statement of the central value impact of United States arms control policy would be: to harm the long-range security of U.S. citizens and the prospects for world peace. When the values implicit in U.S. behavior—as opposed to rhetoric— are stated explicitly, it becomes clear that they directly contradicted the aim of minimizing collective violence.

Two principal differences separate the values expressed in United States policies at Vladivostok from the first value of global humanism: U.S. policies represent a willingness to maintain and even increase the destructive capacity of the superpowers' nuclear deterrents, whereas advocates of global humanism seek to nurture an *un*willingness to use or to possess nuclear weapons. Global humanists search for ways to undermine the legitimacy of massive national arsenals and to facilitate disarmament by transforming the existing international system into a demilitarized system of world order. In contrast, U.S. officials did not question the legitimacy and utility of the sovereign-state worldview as a guide for policymaking. (The contrasting perspectives are more fully summarized in Table 2-8.)

Because the preceding conclusion—that U.S. policy damaged the long-range prospects for security and peace—may at first appear too severe a judgment, it deserves further elaboration. It rests, of course, primarily upon the delineation of implicit values. In general, the agreement at Vladivostok facilitated a further arms buildup, continued the East-West and North-South tensions resulting from arms competition, and prolonged the poverty of the Third and Fourth Worlds by wasting human and material resources on military technology and hardware. The accord also discouraged effective political activity by opponents of military spending and proponents of disarmament because it appeared to demonstrate serious governmental efforts to stop weapons buildups.

Even if one believes that the preceding statement of implicit values is too harsh an indictment of U.S. policy, two consequences stand out among the various SALT proceedings: neither party demonstrated any intention to disarm or to change the structure of the international system in order to make disarmament more feasible. Regardless of the differences among governmental opponents and proponents of the Vladivostok agreement, the notion that nuclear weapons were a legitimate instrument of foreign policy was never in question.[175] Even if the agreement is viewed in the glowing terms of its most ardent advocates, it unequivocally embraced as legitimate both nuclear deterrence and growing destructive capability. Arms control in its modern Vladivostok variant would not lead to disarmament even if continued indefinitely.

The SALT negotiations also discouraged a reassessment of foreign policy priorities and the development of a strategy for international systemic change as a long-range technique for minimizing violence. Without a fundamental reassessment no new initiatives can replace incremental arms control which at best only slightly adjusts the balance of terror, the particular mode of the arms competition, and the gradual spread of nuclear weapons around the world. Such limited arms control does not substantially increase human security. As Senator Edmund Muskie, chairman of the Subcommittee on Arms Control, concluded after extensive hearings on armaments: "Without control of the arms race, there can be no long-term security. In an arms-race situation, the continuous effort to maintain an ever-changing strategic balance simply dooms us to buying more and more defense with no net increase in our national safety."[176] Officials preoccupied with remaining number one militarily did not think about building a new global system to implement disarmament. Nor did they publicly consider the extent to which current armaments were an inevitable consequence of the existing international system.

Genuine security in the long run can come only through a dismantling of the weapons of mass destruction and the creation of a global system to facilitate peaceful change and prevent fu-

107

Table 2-8

Selected Values of Global Humanism Compared to U.S. Policies for Arms Reductions

Global Humanism	U.S. Policy
Peace	
1. Major arms reductions are desirable. First steps toward disarmament are presently possible.	1. In the foreseeable future, major arms reductions are neither desirable nor feasible. Despite rhetoric, officials have sought to retain nuclear deterrence as a national security policy.
2. An international norm against the use of nuclear weapons should be strengthened.	2. Officials have sought to increase the preparedness of the United States to use nuclear weapons.
3. The United States should make a unilateral declaration never to be the first to use nuclear weapons.	3. Officials have refused a no-first-use pledge.
4. By showing greater political and military self-restraint, the role of military power in international relations should be diminished.	4. Officials have sought to retain the role of military power in diplomacy because such power helps keep the United States "number one."
5. It is more important to slow nuclear proliferation through self-restraint in weapons deployment than to stay equal in overkill to the Soviet Union.	5. Although officials have been unhappy with nuclear proliferation, they have sacrificed little to prevent it. Officials have shown less interest in discouraging proliferation than in deploying more sophisticated weapons and maintaining massive arsenals with substantial overkill.
6. Profit or other material benefits from foreign arms sales should be discouraged.	6. U.S. officials have favored foreign arms sales in order to increase U.S. influence abroad, recover petrodollars, provide jobs at home, and solve balance-of-payments problems, as well as to increase the profits of U.S. manufacturers.
7. The power and authority of the superpowers should be shared more equitably within a global security system that could make disarmament feasible.	7. Officials have sought to retain and increase the national power of the United States within the world system.
8. Security policy should be guided by a sense of human solidarity that transcends the nation rather	8. The sovereign state system in which states compete for more and more power is the appropriate worldview

than by a desire to maximize national military power.

9. The security of people must be met more by satisfaction of human needs than by accumulation of national power.

10. Pursuit of security for the human race should influence policy at least as much as the drive for security for any national government

Economic Well-being

1. Military spending distracts from the effort to eliminate world poverty and the general achievement of economic and social well-being.

Human Rights and Social Justice

1. Maintaining present levels of military spending by the superpowers undermines global justice by perpetuating inequity of wealth.

2. Because of an overemphasis on military power, corrupt, elitist, and repressive foreign governments are often supported because they will be loyal U.S. allies. Emphasis on these types of military allies should end.

Ecological Balance

1. Present arms buildups exacerbate the problems of wasteful resource depletion, unnecessary pollution, and ecocide.

for guiding national security policy.

9. U.S. officials have emphasized the security of the state by enhancing its military power

10. People's security is less important than the security of the state.

Economic Well-being

1. Military spending is more important than promoting the economic and social well-being of the world's poverty-stricken people.

Human Rights and Social Justice

1. The U.S. should not decrease its military spending in order to eliminate inequity. In fact, the U.S. should keep spending high enough to be able to defend its present position of wealth from threats posed by other nations.

2. Whether a foreign government is pro- or anti-United States is more important than whether the government deals justly with its own people.

Ecological Balance

1. Environmental concern should not be allowed to distract from weapons innovation and production. Conservation of resources has been of no significant influence on military policy.

ture weapons deployments. By discouraging steps for transforming the international system, by exacerbating the arms buildup, and by legitimizing a less stable strategic doctrine, the Vladivostok agreement contributed to a loss of security for Americans.[177]

From a global, humanitarian perspective, the national security policies of the superpowers could with some justification be viewed as a conflict of interests between the national security managers in Moscow and Washington implicitly working together on the one hand, and the security interests and humanitarian needs of the majority of the people of the world on the other. The most important disagreement in the debate about weapons policy was not between the military establishments of the two countries; it was between the officials of both countries on one side, who wanted more arms, and the few people of both countries working for arms reductions and system change on the other. The editors of the *New York Times* correctly observed that the Vladivostok agreement was "an agreement between the military on both sides—achieved through the intermediary of the chiefs of government—to permit the build-ups each desired."[178] One reason for the agreement and its particular timing was the desire of Brezhnev, Ford, and Kissinger to perpetuate the atmosphere of détente and to resist pressures mounted against it by military and civilian hard-liners in both the United States and Soviet Union.[179] To the extent that this appraisal was accurate, there existed two unpromising alternatives: either to accept a Vladivostok-type agreement in order to decrease the influence of militarists, even though they virtually dictated the terms of the agreement anyway; or to achieve no agreement at all and allow the opponents of détente to exercise their influence more openly.

Events since the Vladivostok meeting confirmed the reality of this pessimistic set of alternatives. At the meeting, officials expressed the intention soon to conclude a more formal treaty based on the Vladivostok accord. However, serious disagreement erupted in drafting the formal document. The military officials of both the United States and Soviet Union raised new issues. They pressed their respective governments so intensely that the entire Vladivostok accord was jeopardized and delayed for more than four years. Because of pressures by the Department of Defense, the United States reneged somewhat on its earlier positions and insisted upon restrictions for the new Soviet medium-range "Backfire" bomber.[180] The Soviet Union attempted to restrict development and deployment of the U.S. cruise missile.

The United States strongly resisted limits on the cruise missile.[181] It could evade Soviet radar and, with its terminal guidance, strike within thirty yards of a target after flying thousands of miles.[182] It could carry nuclear warheads and be launched from land, airplanes, or submarines. Secretary Kissinger reported that the United States could potentially deploy 11,000 cruise missiles on existing bombers and transport planes and 10,000 more on nuclear submarines. All would be capable of reaching targets in the Soviet Union.[183] New weapons such as these made the Vladivostok ceilings virtually meaningless in terms of halting the weapons race. When one or the other side insisted that such weapons be included, then even a relatively nonrestrictive agreement like the Vladivostok accord could hardly be consummated—precisely because banning the new weapons would make the agreement too restrictive. The folly of trying to stop the arms race without imposing serious restrictions was clearly exposed.

Without going into detail, it is possible to see that the Carter administration has failed to overcome the gap between professed and implicit values that characterized previous administrations. During his campaign for the presidency and in several important presidential addresses, Carter pledged to reduce armaments and military expenditures.[184] None occurred. In his inaugural address, Carter promised to persevere in efforts "to limit the world's armaments to those necessary for each nation's own domestic safety. We will move this year a step toward our ultimate goal—elimination of all nuclear weapons from this earth."[185] However, Carter increased the United States' destructive capability and deployed more advanced equipment for improved nuclear warheads early in his presidency.[186] These acts increased the U.S. capacity to fight a nuclear war but contributed little to, and possibly detracted from, U.S. "domestic safety." Testing and development proceeded on a wide range of new strategic equipment, such as the M-X missile and the Trident submarine. Only the B-1 bomber was cancelled. But that decision was taken less to halt the arms buildup than to take advantage of the militarily more useful and technologically more sophisticated cruise missile, which had overtaken the B-1 during its long and costly development.

Carter at first predicted an early SALT II agreement based on revisions of the Vladivostok principles, but negotiations faltered, in part because the Carter administration would not accept a ban on cruise missiles or the inclusion of them within ceilings for strategic launch vehicles in an eight-year agreement. The cruise missile programs, one should recall, were started in part because the Interim Agreement of 1972 put a five-year limit on ballistic missiles. Thus the cruise missile program, which helped the Pentagon circumvent the spirit of SALT I limitations on ICBMs and SLBMs, became a stumbling block for SALT II. Once cruise missiles were tested and prototypes produced, verification of future ceilings would become so complicated that new SALT efforts to prohibit the missile appeared unpromising.

A SALT II agreement on other matters, however, remained within the realm of possibility. During 1978 the United States and the Soviet Union appeared to be reaching agreement on a treaty incorporating most of these provisions:

(1) A seven-year treaty (in contrast to ten years discussed previously) that would set these restrictions: (a) a top limit of 2,250 strategic launch vehicles, or slightly less than a 10 percent reduction from the Vladivostok limits; (b) a maximum of 1,320 MIRVs (as agreed at Vladivostok), including within this total ICBMs, SLBMs, and bombers equipped with cruise missiles; (c) no more than 1,200 of the 1,320 could be ICBMs and SLBMs, and no more than 800 could be ICBMs; and (d) the large Soviet land-based missile, the SS-18, would be restricted to 308.

(2) A three-year protocol limiting the deployment of the cruise missile. The protocol would place a range restriction of 1,500 miles on cruise missiles launched by bombers and a range limit of 360 miles on the testing and deployment of cruise missiles launched from ships, submarines, or land. It would also ban for a three-year period, the deployment of the M-X.[187]

Although the potential agreement is somewhat more restrictive than the Vladivostok limits, the conclusions drawn from analyzing the Vladivostok accord still largely apply. The most positive new development in the potential treaty is clearly the possibility of achieving some qualitative limits on deployment of new weapons. However, it appears that such limits may continue only for a period of three years, and the limits apply only to weapons that will not be ready to deploy anyway until the protocol has expired. Reminiscent of the first deployment of MIRVs, one must note that this potential treaty will, in fact, reject the opportunity to ban the cruise missiles before they are deployed. Instead it will legitimize their deployment, albeit with restricted ranges at first. Surely the Pentagon knows that later it will be almost impossible to verify range restrictions with only satellite observation. Hence once the Soviet Union matches the limited U.S. cruise missile capability, the door will be open for deployment of cruise missiles of ever greater ranges, justified by the United States' inability to know with certainty what the Soviet Union has deployed. Whether this will occur depends heavily upon whether the restriction can be extended indefinitely, once a three-year ban is achieved. If it cannot be made permanent, then on this point U.S. officials carefully tailored their position to allow the continued development of the cruise missile on a limited basis for three years with the testing and deployment of it coming at approximately the time that technology will have advanced sufficiently to provide an effective cruise missile of greater range.

The slight reduction in overall strategic vehicles, while welcome, is not very significant. The limits will still legitimize vastly greater destructive capability than was deployed when the Vladivostok accord was reached. With the prospect of adding numerous warheads to allowable launch vehicles, even a formalized treaty will yield an extremely porous ceiling. Significantly, in the minds of most officials, the MIRV ceiling was desirable not for the purpose of abolishing nuclear arms, but for maintaining the utility of the land-based ICBM force of the United States. By using an arms control agreement to protect Minuteman missiles from a preemptive Soviet attack, U.S. officials have demonstrated their desire to retain these weapons as ends in themselves, rather than as a means to enhance security. They are no longer an essential part of a credible deterrent. With Soviet satellites pinpointing U.S. land-based missiles as targets, and with the MIRVing of Soviet missiles (stimulated by earlier U.S. deployment of MIRVs), U.S. stationary missiles are becoming obsolete. Thus, even with all of the new enthusiasm generated for arms control by Carter and Paul Warnke, the potential agreement legitimizes the continuation of a nuclear force far in excess of what is required for deterrence. The agreement does much more to protect and increase war-fighting capability than to reduce or abolish it.

Similarly unpromising policies were carried out by the Carter administration on military expenditures and international arms

113

sales. Although in 1976 and early 1977 Carter promised to cut the defense budget, by 1978 he called for a $56 billion increase in military expenditures over a five-year period. The increase, after accounting for inflation, would mean a growth of 2.7 percent a year. The president sought a 3 percent real increase for the 1978-79 fiscal year.[188]

The president also made firm promises to reduce international arms transfers, declaring that the United States could not be "both the world's leading champion of peace and the world's leading supplier of weapons of war."[189] In a statement promising restraint, he said arms sales would be "an exceptional foreign policy implement, to be used only in instances where it can be clearly demonstrated that the transfer contributes to our national security interests." Yet the preliminary figures for FY 1977 and FY 1978 showed a rise in arms sales, with total sales for 1978 likely to reach a record $13 billion.[190] The United States remained by far the world's leading exporter of arms. A lengthy study prepared for the Senate Foreign Relations Committee by the Library of Congress concluded that "rather than being used as an 'exceptional foreign policy implement,' United States arms transfers continue to occur on a rather routine basis."[191] In sum, Carter's rhetoric seemed more enlightened than that of his predecessors. He and his official appointees generated new activity and enthusiasm for arms control. But there was not the slightest evidence that the arms buildup—even the strategic arms buildup—was being reversed.

The record of arms control negotiations since 1945 demonstrated that, at best, the United States has tailored arms control policy to restrict weapons in areas of relative unimportance, while allowing the arms competition to continue earnestly in areas where new research and development lead toward more sophisticated weapons. The United States offered either proposals that were designed to produce such one-sided advantages for the United States that the Soviet Union could not be expected to accept them, or else proposals that covered such limited areas of the weapons buildup as to make a consummated agreement largely inconsequential for the arms race. For example, after World War II, the Baruch proposals to establish international control over nuclear testing would have given the United States a monopoly on the technology to produce nuclear weapons—a result obviously unacceptable to the Soviet Union.

114

The proposal of the mid-1950s to stop further production of fissionable materials for weapons purposes came only after the U.S. had stockpiled so much material that the plan would have had no significant restrictive effect on the United States nuclear arsenal, but would have handicapped all other potential or actual nuclear powers, which had much smaller stockpiles. Even though an agreement banning atmospheric nuclear testing was concluded in 1963, officials earlier had opposed a test ban until the United States reached the point at which any further testing would probably have contributed little to arms innovation. Moreover, officials agreed to end atmospheric tests only after legalizing the further testing of weapons underground. In any case, the 1963 treaty did not decrease the intensity of testing. During the eighteen years between 1945 and 1963, nuclear powers tested 477 devices (including 98 underground). During the ten years between 1963 and 1973, nuclear powers exploded 456 devices (including 48 French and Chinese tests in the atmosphere).[192] Officials recognized in the 1950s that a ban on the first test-firing of ICBMs was the easiest way to prevent deployment of ICBMs, but serious pursuit of such a plan was delayed until after the missiles had been tested, making control much more difficult. The Threshold Nuclear Test Ban Treaty of 1974 prohibited test explosions exceeding 150 kilotons, but this limit was the size of ten Hiroshima bombs, and test devices exceeding that amount represented no more than 10 percent of the Soviet and American tests during the years immediately preceding the new accord.[193] Similarly, the superpowers discussed ceilings on delivery vehicles only after the number of vehicles had become less important than developing MIRVs and precision guidance systems. A detailed analysis of postwar arms talks would confirm the idea that arms control proposals bore fruit only in areas of weapons development that were peripheral to the principal dimensions of the arms buildup, while new areas for arms competition remained unrestricted.

To conclude: Because of important domestic pressures for an arms buildup, bolstered by United States-Soviet competition, new destructive capability was being added to the arsenals of both sides during every year in which the two superpowers discussed arms control accords. The arms buildup continued despite widely acclaimed arms control agreements and despite evidence that the buildup decreased humanity's overall security. In the absence of radically different policies, there is good reason to expect that the future world will contain even more potential for violent cataclysm than the past.

An Alternative Framework

A policy approach based on the values of global humanism would take initiatives to (1) halt the testing and deployment of new weapons;[194] (2) reduce military budgets by a regular percentage each year; (3) reduce and eventually abolish national military arsenals; (4) prohibit the production of military equipment; (5) establish a global monitoring agency to inspect and verify all agreements limiting and reducing arms; (6) study the use of civilian resistance and nonviolent techniques for defense and social change; (7) establish a transnational peace force to help protect security during the transition to a new peace system; and (8) make plans for converting domestic industries to peaceful purposes.

This approach would shun prolonged arms control negotiations that are used to legitimize armaments and to justify unneeded weapons. Many national initiatives to reverse the arms buildup can be taken by either superpower without jeopardizing its security during the first one or two years, even if there were no immediate reciprocation. Acts of self-restraint or initial arms reductions should probably precede negotiations in order to avoid the following negative consequences that frequently accompany diplomatic efforts:

—Arms control negotiations often focus attention on inequalities in weapons deployed by two sides, so that the inferior side steps up its efforts to become equal, while the superior side tries to move farther ahead in order to be able to negotiate from a position of strength.

—Weapons that might never have been deployed, or that might not have been deployed so soon, are quickly developed to serve as bargaining chips to "negotiate away" during arms control talks. However, weapons developed as bargaining chips often are later deployed in expanded arsenals.

—The domestic vested interests that favor military expenditures are so powerful that often only cosmetic agreements, formalizing what would have been done without any agreement, are possible.

—If an agreement is eventually reached, the Department of Defense often can be moved to accept a treaty only if it is prom-

116

ised something in return, such as the right to develop a more advanced and more destructive weapon.

—Continuing arms control negotiations encourage the public to believe, mistakenly, that the government is doing all that can be done to end the arms buildup.

Because the arms competition is driven mainly by international political conflicts or by domestic pressures for weapons expenditures, it is not likely that arms can be reduced by focusing mainly on negotiations for arms reductions. Substantial reductions will occur only when a sufficient number of people press their governments for decreased expenditures and a transformation of the present international system in which military power plays a key role in settling disputes. Negotiations will not bring this shift in citizens' attitudes and values.

If negotiations for disarmament were preceded by wide public education for planetary citizenship and diplomatic efforts at system transformation, then they would be very useful. But they would then become a process for registering and facilitating a fundamental shift in the priorities of the superpowers, rather than a diplomatic exercise aimed at discovering a rare formula that both sides can agree upon without significantly decreasing their military weapons or abolishing the existing war system.

Reorientation of U.S. policies can be aided by a government decision to devote substantial bureaucratic resources to developing models of a disarming and of a disarmed world. In the long run, of course, global agencies will be required to monitor and enforce disarmament and facilitate peaceful change. The focus of global humanists is therefore on *system* change, not on incremental arms control measures that set high ceilings on equipment and fail to treat the fundamental causes of arms buildups and collective violence.

None of the major forces propelling the world toward more and more arms can be dependably halted or disarmament achieved without some fundamental changes in the existing nation-state structure of political organization. At this stage of history, that structure is both unacceptably dangerous (because war could be suicidal for an entire civilization) and totally unnecessary (because modern communication, technology, and values could, if properly applied, support a system that allowed only peaceful settlement and enforcement of political decisions). The "only" barriers to disarmament and a preferred system of world order are political. Thus a life-sustaining shift in the beliefs and values of U.S. citizens could replace the contemporary neo-Westphalian political leadership with a leadership less alienated from reality and better equipped for the fulfillment of human needs, including security, in the twenty-first century.

For skeptics who doubt that such shifts are possible, it is instructive to note the rapid expansion in the size of the group with whom people identified during the rise of European nationalism in the seventeenth and eighteenth centuries. Dramatic changes are possible in a relatively short time. A growth of global community and modern breakthroughs in information technology permit dependable policy coordination without heavy-handed, hierarchical political structure.[195] Moreover, global economic and technological currents are running so strong that the issue probably is no longer whether a global political tapestry is now being woven. Instead, it is concern that the new creation be artfully conceived, harmoniously constructed, and vividly colored by humane values, instead of being tailored for the benefit of the world's few and erected to cover up the overt and covert violence of global society.

Indicators of World Order Progress

The following questions provide convenient points of departure for assessing the performance of the United States (or another great power) in minimizing collective violence in the subject covered by this case study:

1. Has the government made a firm commitment—in terms of behavior as well as rhetoric—to global system change that will eventually make disarmament feasible?

2. Has the government devoted substantial resources to developing models of a disarming world?

3. Has the government increasingly sought impartial non-military means for dispute settlement, such as accepting without reservation the compulsory jurisdiction of the International Court of Justice?

4. Has the government sought to subject its foreign arms sales to international inspection and regulation?

5. Has the government supported educational efforts aimed at developing citizens' loyalties to reach beyond the nation-state to the global human community?

6. Has the government halted the deployment of new strategic weapons?

7. Is destructive capability in national arsenals decreasing?

8. Is military spending for strategic weapons decreasing, both absolutely and as a percentage of the national budget?

9. Are international arms sales decreasing?

10. Has the government passed legislation that dampens or prohibits the accumulation of profit as a stimulus to the production and sale of military equipment?

11. Are the combined financial, educational, institutional, and communications resources of the domestic proponents of disarmament increasing in comparison to the same resources possessed by the military-industrial-scientific complex that favors arms production?

I. *Interim Agreement Between the United States of America and the Union of Soviet Socialist Republics on Certain Measures With Respect to the Limitation of Strategic Offensive Arms*

The United States of America and the Union of Soviet Socialist Republics, hereinafter referred to as the Parties,

Convinced that the Treaty on the Limitation of Anti-Ballistic Missile Systems and this Interim Agreement on Certain Measures with Respect to the Limitation of Strategic Offensive Arms will contribute to the creation of more favorable conditions for active negotiations and limiting strategic arms as well as the relaxation of international tension and the strengthening of trust between States,

Taking into account the relationship between strategic offensive and defensive arms,

Mindful of their obligations under Article VI of the Treaty on the Non-Proliferation of Nuclear Weapons,

Have agreed as follows:

Article I

The Parties undertake not to start construction of additional fixed land-based intercontinental ballistic missile (ICBM) launchers after July 1, 1972.

Article II

The Parties undertake not to convert land-based launchers for light ICBMs, or for ICBMs of older types deployed prior to 1964, into land-based launchers for heavy ICBMs of types deployed after that time.

Article III

The Parties undertake to limit submarine-launched ballistic missile (SLBM) launchers and modern ballistic missile submarines to the numbers operational and under construction on the date of signature of this Interim Agreement, and in addition to launchers and submarines constructed under procedures established by the Parties as replacements for an equal number of ICBM launchers of older types deployed prior to 1964 or for launchers on older submarines.

Article IV

Subject to the provisions of this Interim Agreement, modernization and replacement of strategic offensive ballistic

120

missiles and launchers covered by this Interim Agreement may be undertaken.

Article V

1. For the purpose of providing assurance of compliance with the provisions of this Interim Agreement, each Party shall use national technical means of verification at its disposal in a manner consistent with generally recognized principles of international law.

2. Each Party undertakes not to interfere with the national technical means of verification of the other Party operating in accordance with paragraph 1 of this Article.

3. Each Party undertakes not to use deliberate concealment measures which impede verification by national technical means of compliance with the provisions of this Interim Agreement. This obligation shall not require changes in current construction, assembly, conversion, or overhaul practices.

Article VI

To promote the objectives and implementation of the provisions of this Interim Agreement, the Parties shall use the Standing Consultative Commission established under Article XIII of the Treaty on the Limitation of Anti-Ballistic Missile Systems in accordance with the provisions of that Article.

Article VII

The Parties undertake to continue active negotiations for limitations on strategic offensive arms. The obligations provided for in this Interim Agreement shall not prejudice the scope or terms of the limitations on strategic offensive arms which may be worked out in the course of further negotiations.

Article VIII

1. This Interim Agreement shall enter into force upon exchange of written notices of acceptance by each Party, which exchange shall take place simultaneously with the exchange of instruments of ratification of the Treaty on the Limitation of Anti-Ballistic Missile Systems.

2. This Interim Agreement shall remain in force for a period of five years unless replaced earlier by an agreement on more complete measures limiting strategic offensive arms. It

is the objective of the Parties to conduct active follow-on negotiations with the aim of concluding such an agreement as soon as possible.

3. Each Party shall, in exercising its national sovereignty, have the right to withdraw from this Interim Agreement if it decides that extraordinary events related to the subject matter of this Interim Agreement have jeopardized its supreme interests. It shall give notice of its decision to the other Party six months prior to withdrawal from this Interim Agreement. Such notice shall include a statement of the extraordinary events the notifying Party regards as having jeopardized its supreme interests.

Done at Moscow on May 26, 1972, in two copies, each in the English and Russian languages, both texts being equally authentic.

II. *Protocol to the Interim Agreement Between the United States of America and the Union of Soviet Socialist Republics on Certain Measures With Respect to the Limitation of Strategic Offensive Arms*

The United States of America and the Union of Soviet Socialist Republics, hereinafter referred to as the Parties,

Having agreed on certain limitations relating to submarine-launched ballistic missile launchers and modern ballistic missile submarines, and to replacement procedures, in the Interim Agreement,

Have agreed as follows:

The Parties understand that, under Article III of the Interim Agreement, for the period during which that Agreement remains in force:

The U.S. may have no more than 710 ballistic missile launchers on submarines (SLBMs) and no more than 44 modern ballistic missile submarines. The Soviet Union may have no more than 950 ballistic missile launchers on submarines and no more than 62 modern ballistic missile submarines.

Additional ballistic missile launchers on submarines up to the above-mentioned levels, in the U.S.—over 656 ballistic missile launchers on nuclear-powered submarines, and in the U.S.S.R.—over 740 ballistic missile launchers on nuclear-powered submarines, operational and under construction, may become operational as replacements for equal numbers of ballistic missile launchers on older types deployed prior to 1964 or of ballistic missile launchers on older submarines.

The deployment of modern slbms on any submarine, regardless of type, will be counted against the total level of slbms permitted for the U.S. and the U.S.S.R.

This Protocol shall be considered an integral part of the Interim Agreement.

Done at Moscow this 26th day of May, 1972.

Source: U.S. Arms Control and Disarmament Agency, *Arms Control and Disarmament Agreements* (Washington, D.C.: Government Printing Office, 1975), pp. 139-142.

II. *Joint U.S.-Soviet Statement on Strategic Offensive Arms Issued at Vladivostok*

During their working meeting in the area of Vladivostok on November 23-24, 1974, the President of the U.S.A. Gerald R. Ford and General Secretary of the Central Committee of the CPSU, L. I. Brezhnev discussed in detail the question of further limitations of strategic offensive arms.

They reaffirmed the great significance that both the United States and the U.S.S.R. attach to the limitation of strategic offensive arms. They are convinced that a long-term agreement on this question would be a significant contribution to improving relations between the U.S. and U.S.S.R., to reducing the danger of war and to enhancing world peace. Having noted the value of previous agreements on this question, including the Interim Agreement of May 26, 1972, they reaffirm the intention to conclude a new agreement on the limitation of strategic offensive arms, to last through 1985.

As a result of the exchange of views on the substance of such a new agreement, the President of the United States of America and the General Secretary of the Central Committee of the CPSU concluded that favorable prospects exist for completing the work on this agreement in 1975.

Agreement was reached that further negotiations will be based on the following provisions.

1. The new agreement will incorporate the relevant provisions of the Interim Agreement of May 26, 1972, which will remain in force until October 1977.

2. The new agreement will cover the period from October 1977 through December 31, 1985.

3. Based on the principle of equality and equal security, the new agreement will include the following limitations:

a. Both sides will be entitled to have a certain agreed aggregate number of strategic delivery vehicles;

b. Both sides will be entitled to have a certain agreed aggregate number of ICBMs and SLBMs [intercontinental ballistic missiles; submarine-launched ballistic missiles] equipped with multiple independently targetable warheads (MIRVs).

4. The new agreement will include a provision for further negotiations beginning no later than 1980-1981 on the question of further limitations and possible reductions of strategic arms in the period after 1985.

5. Negotiations between the delegations of the U.S. and U.S.S.R. to work out the new agreement incorporating the foregoing points will resume in Geneva in January 1975.

November 24, 1974.

SOURCE: *Department of State Bulletin*, 71 (December 23, 1974), 879.

IV. *Excerpt from President Ford's News Conference of December 2, 1974*

We agreed on the general framework for a new agreement that will last through 1985. We agreed it is realistic to aim at completing this agreement next year. This is possible because we made major breakthroughs on two critical issues:

—Number one, we agreed to put a ceiling of 2,400 each on the total number of intercontinental ballistic missiles, submarine-launched missiles, and heavy bombers.

—Two, we agreed to limit the number of missiles that can be armed with multiple warheads, MIRVs. Of each side's total of 2,400, 1,320 can be so armed.

These ceilings are well below the force levels which would otherwise have been expected over the next 10 years and very substantially below the forces which would result from an all-out arms race over that same period.

What we have done is to set firm and equal limits on the strategic forces of each side, thus preventing an arms race with all its terror, instability, war-breeding tension, and economic waste.

We have, in addition, created the solid basis from which future arms reductions can be made and, hopefully, will be negotiated.

It will take more detailed negotiations to convert this agreed framework into a comprehensive accord, but we have made a long step toward peace on a basis of equality, the only basis on which an agreement was possible.

Source: *Department of State Bulletin*, 71 (December 23, 1974), 861.

THREE · *United States Foreign Aid to India*

CHRONIC, pervasive poverty is the most distressing and persistent obstacle to humanizing life for two-thirds of the world's population. Few needs press so urgently or present opportunities so potentially fruitful for advocates of world order reform as maximizing economic well-being for all people. The principal immediate purpose of the second value of global humanism (V_2) is, at the least, to insure that no person lacks the minimal amounts of food, shelter, clothing, medical care, and education necessary to live a healthy life with reasonable fulfillment and dignity. A more complete expression of this second value is the achievement of economic justice on a planetary scale.[1]

Because the United States is the wealthiest nation in the world, it bears the heaviest moral responsibility for assisting in the promotion of universal human welfare. Thus it is instructive to investigate the impact of United States policy upon the realization of V_2 and thereby to assess this second dimension of the U.S. role in achieving general world order reform. To provide focus for this analysis, I have chosen to examine United States development assistance to India.

The selection of the Indian case study is appropriate for several reasons. India is a significant country because of its geographical area, location, and enormous population. Its 600 million people constitute a major segment of the population of Asia and even of the world. India is by far the most important political power in south Asia. During all but two years of the period examined in this study, India enjoyed a democratic, parliamentary system. India's commercial records have been relatively good, and important data for economic planning have been available. The Indian strategy for development has been often contrasted, wisely or unwisely, with the Chinese approach as an instructive example for others to follow. Finally, the economic needs of India have been great. India's enormous population presses heavily upon the available land, food, jobs, housing, and other vital welfare services.

Given India's attributes, United States policy toward that country should be a fair test of United States performance on

126

V_2. India has been too large to be overlooked inadvertently, too important politically to be dismissed as of no concern to the future of Asian or worldwide international relations, too open and communicative to be accidentally misunderstood, too democratic and too close to the British parliamentary tradition to be incomprehensible, and too needy to be cast aside as unworthy of United States help. How, then, have American policies influenced the realization of V_2 in the Indian context? Has aid been designed to fulfill basic human needs, to reduce worldwide economic inequity, and to restructure global commercial relations and political authority in order to increase the influence of the weak and poor in planetary economic decisions that affect their lives? Or have national advantages in U.S. military and economic relations been the major motivation for development assistance?

This chapter will proceed by (1) describing the amount and mode of U.S. development assistance; (2) assessing whether this empirical statement of aid policies confirms or negates the official rationale for the aid; and (3) contrasting the values implicit in U.S. policy with the values of global humanism.

DESCRIPTION OF U.S. AID POLICIES

For several years after the Indians won their independence in 1947, the United States gave no development assistance to India, in part because foreign aid had not yet become an established part of United States foreign policy and in part because the United States' first concern was European postwar recovery. Perhaps a humanitarian motive was present in the U.S. Marshall Plan aid for reconstruction of Europe, but no such humanitarianism aroused the United States to undertake the enormous, obvious opportunities to help India.

The aid program for India and other less developed countries was rooted in President Harry Truman's perception of a world communist movement that threatened U.S. interests. This perception encouraged him in January 1949, to include an item in his inaugural address that was to become the well-known Point Four Program: "We must embark on a bold new program for making the benefits of our scientific advances and industrial progress available for the improvement and growth of underdeveloped areas." The United States should help "peace-loving peoples," he continued, in order "to help them realize their aspirations for a better life."[2] Still, no actual disbursements were

127

forthcoming for India until fiscal year 1951, when a grant of $4.5 million was extended to help India overcome food shortages resulting from poor weather conditions.

Total Assistance

Total development assistance in the form of loans and grants rose in succeeding years to a high in 1962. Commitments that year came to a total of $465.5 million, or the equivalent of $2.49 for every U.S. citizen, as indicated in Table 3-1. For the entire period from 1950 through 1976, the average yearly grant and loan development assistance to India per United States capita was $.74. This amounted to $.30 per Indian per year.[3]

Table 3-1
Total Grant and Loan Commitments[a] to India
for Economic Development from U.S. Agency for International
Development and Predecessor Agencies[b]

Fiscal Year	Total grants and loans in millions of U.S. dollars	Total grants and loans per U.S. capita, in dollars	Total grants and loans per Indian capita, in dollars
1950	0.0	0.00	0.00
1951	4.5	0.03	0.01
1952	52.8	0.34	0.14
1953	44.3	0.28	0.12
1954	87.2	0.53	0.23
1955	85.7	0.52	0.22
1956	60.0	0.36	0.15
1957	65.3	0.38	0.16
1958	89.8	0.51	0.22
1959	137.0	0.77	0.33
1960	194.6	1.08	0.45
1961	200.8	1.09	0.46
1962	465.5	2.49	1.04
1963	397.2	2.10	0.86
1964	336.5	1.75	0.71
1965	264.6	1.36	0.55
1966	308.8	1.57	0.62
1967	202.5	1.02	0.40
1968	241.5	1.20	0.47
1969	167.2	0.82	0.32
1970	159.0	0.78	0.29

Table 3-1 (cont.)

Fiscal Year	Total grants and loans in millions of U.S. dollars	Total grants and loans per U.S. capita, in dollars	Total grants and loans per Indian capita, in dollars
1971	202.1	0.97	0.37
1972	2.5	0.01	0.00
1973	12.0	−.06	−.02
1974	13.6	.06	.02
1975	19.7	.09	.03
1976	−1.5	−.01	.00
Total net obligations	3,789.2		

SOURCES: Up to 1971, U.S. Agency for International Development, Office of Statistics and Reports, *U.S. Economic Assistance Programs Administered by the Agency for International Development and Predecessor Agencies, April 3, 1948 to June 30, 1971*. After 1971, U.S. Agency for International Development, Statistics and Reports Division, Office of Financial Management, *U.S. Overseas Loans and Grants and Assistance from International Organizations, July 1, 1945-June 30, 1973*, and subsequent years. Population figures for computing per capita amounts were taken from United Nations, *Demographic Yearbook*.

NOTES [a] Commitments may be defined as development loans authorized and obligations of other AID funds. Annual commitment data are on a "net" basis, that is, new obligations from funds appropriated for that fiscal year, plus reobligations and minus deobligations of prior years' funds. Negative figures represent deobligations in excess of new commitments during one fiscal year.

[b] Predecessor agencies dealing with economic assistance programs during the Marshall Plan period and the Mutual Security Act period were, successively: The Economic Cooperation Administration (1948-1951); the Mutual Security Agency (1951-1953); the Foreign Operations Administration (1953-1955); the International Cooperation Administration (1955-1971); and the Development Loan Fund (1957-1961).

Although fluctuations have occurred, there was a gradual decline from 1962 until 1971, when the U.S. aid program was cut back sharply because of United States hostility toward Indian military intervention in the war beween West Pakistan and what was to become Bangladesh. These figures should be considered in light of a recognition that in the 1970s the United States GNP per capita exceeded that of India by approximately 57 times.

A loan or grant to India of $.74 per United States citizen may seem low in comparison to India's needs and to United States wealth, but this figure in fact gives an exaggerated picture of aid to India. In the first place, less than 14 percent of the economic assistance was in the form of grants. Loans, representing by far

129

the largest portion, are being repaid with interest. To be sure, if given at below commercial rates, loans themselves contain a "grant element." The extent to which loan aid was genuinely concessional depended on what the capital might have yielded from possible alternative uses, minus the rate of return received from Indian interest payments on the loans. Many economists estimate that the concessional element is from 15 to 30 percent of the nominal value of loans.[4]

The need to repay indebtedness has created new shortages of foreign exchange for India and a sense of resentment about the political leverage wielded by the lending state. India's service payments on external public debt as a percentage of its income from exports of goods and services have been gradually increasing.[5] As of June 30, 1973, India's external debt totalled an estimated $9 billion, excluding debts owed to the Soviet Union. In 1974, the effort to repay former debts cost India over $500 million a year, or nearly one-third of its total income from exports.[6] From 1969 to 1974, India's inflow of new grants and loans from all sources averaged $980 million per year; this amounted to $400 million per year after meeting service charges on outstanding debt. The International Bank for Reconstruction and Development projected a deficit in India's international payments of $12 billion for 1975-80.[7]

The requirements for debt repayment meant that in order to prevent net foreign assistance from declining, assistance to India would have to grow higher each year to offset increased repayments to suppliers of assistance. Decreases in utilizable funds actually resulted if there was a failure to offset the annual back flow of capital to repay previous loans. In recent years, for example, United States net grant and loan assistance averaged less than $5 million annually. At the same time, India sent over a quarter billion dollars to the United States for debt repayment, and thus became a net exporter of capital to the United States.[8]

Second, in addition to the repayment problem, 90 percent of U.S. loans and grants have been tied to purchases in the United States, so that Indians have had no choice but to use the credit to purchase equipment or materials from U.S. corporations, sometimes at inflated prices. When aid has been tied to the United States and also to a proposed project, suppliers sometimes have enjoyed near monopoly conditions. The excess cost of goods imported from the United States over the cost from alternative sources represented an export subsidy which India paid to U.S.

130

exporters to secure the aid-financed contracts. Aid-tying amounted roughly to a 20-25 percent savings for the United States (and cost to India) over the nominal value of the aid.[9] In effect, tied loans have been a type of "foreign aid" that created jobs for Americans, stimulated demand for products of United States corporations, and provided a United States-financed, Indian subsidy for the corporations benefiting from aid allocations.

The Agency for International Development (AID) has not, as a general rule, spent money overseas to assist in Indian development. As William S. Gaud, former administrator of AID has reported, "The biggest single misconception about the foreign aid program is that we send money abroad. We don't."[10]

Jagdish N. Bhagwati has attempted to estimate the real cost of total aid programs by using data including grants, loans, and commodity assistance. After adjusting these combined aid flows for aid-tying, loan repayment, and the lower opportunity costs of commodity assistance, he concluded that the *real* cost "may well be somewhere between 55 and 70 percent *below* their nominal values."[11] Where in that range the cost of aid might fall, of course, would depend heavily on the percentage of the aid which was extended in the form of grants.

One final caveat must be noted. The costs of aid for the United States and the benefits of aid to India were not necessarily symmetrical. A costless U.S. disposal of agricultural surplus may have been valuable to India. Likewise, an expensive capital transfer for the United States may have had little value to India. A study conducted by the Secretariat of the United Nations Conference on Trade and Development (UNCTAD) for 1964 and 1965 suggested that the real worth of aid may have been 30 to 35 percent of the nominal aid values (grants and loans combined).[12] Thus the overall real worth of aid may not be far out of line with the real cost of aid, but both are far below the nominal figures for aid.

Grants

A somewhat oversimplified but nonetheless useful picture of the burden of aid-giving on the American taxpayer comes from examination of the grant portion of the aid program.[13] Like loans, grants have not been payments of cash to India. They have been donations of goods and services to India, valued at prevailing U.S. prices, with the Federal government paying U.S.

131

producers. The highwater mark for grant commitments to India came long ago, in 1954, at the conclusion of the Korean War, as shown in Table 3-2. The quantity of grants has generally declined ever since, in spite of the fact that India's needs, ability to utilize aid, and United States wealth have all increased. Since 1950, the average yearly grant commitment to India per United States capita has been $.10. On an Indian per capita basis, it has been $.04.[14] In the last decade, U.S. citizens each spent an average of three pennies a year for Indian development grants at a time when the average per capita income of United States citizens was forty-five times greater than the per capita income of Indians.[15]

Before attempting to assess the impact of this level of assistance upon the realization of economic well-being for all, it is necessary to clarify both the professed and implicit values of U.S. aid policy.

Official Rationale Compared to The Values Implicit in U.S. Policy

The values explicitly professed as motivations for granting foreign assistance to India have been expressed in various rationales for foreign aid over the years since the Point Four Program began in 1949. U.S. officials have publicly advocated foreign aid (1) to enhance United States security, (2) to promote United States economic growth and prosperity, and (3) to express humanitarian concern for others. Although these three objectives have been expressed in different ways by various officials, they have been remarkably constant since 1949, as the following elaboration demonstrates.

Professed Value 1: To Serve U.S. Security Interests

In surveying policy statements, whether originating from the legislative or the executive branch, five themes constantly recur, although with different emphasis, as explanations of how foreign assistance contributes to United States security. Officials said that foreign aid could help: (1) to dampen conflict anywhere on the globe and to discourage threats to stability in the international system;[16] (2) to create and strengthen allies among the nonindustrialized states in the U.S. struggle against communism; (3) to prevent nonallies from becoming communist or friendly toward communist states; (4) to discourage internal instability in nonindustrialized countries and thereby to avert

132

Table 3-2
Total Grant Commitments[a] to India for Economic Development from
U.S. Agency for International Development and Predecessor Agencies

Fiscal year	Grants in millions of U.S. dollars	Grants per U.S. capita in U.S. dollars	Grants per Indian capita in U.S. dollars	Ratio of U.S. GNP per capita to Indian GNP per capita
1950	0.0	0.00	0.00	50
1951	4.5	0.03	0.01	52
1952	52.8	0.34	0.14	51
1953	44.3	0.28	0.12	50
1954	87.2	0.53	0.23	48
1955	40.7	0.25	0.11	50
1956	22.5	0.13	0.06	49
1957	17.8	0.10	0.04	49
1958	14.8	0.08	0.04	46
1959	17.0	0.10	0.04	48
1960	23.3	0.13	0.05	45
1961	20.7	0.11	0.05	45
1962	19.6	0.10	0.04	47
1963	4.9	0.03	0.01	47
1964	5.9	0.03	0.01	46
1965	8.8	0.05	0.02	51
1966	9.5	0.05	0.02	54
1967	7.7	0.04	0.02	52
1968	12.8	0.06	0.02	53
1969	8.6	0.04	0.02	52
1970	27.6	0.13	0.05	51
1971	9.5	0.05	0.02	52
1972	4.2	0.02	0.01	56
1973	−3.2	−.02	−.01	57
1974	3.2	.02	.01	b
1975	.1	.00	.00	b
1976	−.1	.00	.00	b

Total net obligations, 464.5

SOURCES: Up to 1971, U.S. Agency for International Development, Office of Statistics and Reports, *U.S. Economic Assistance Programs Administered by the Agency for International Development and Predecessor Agencies, April 3, 1948 to June 30, 1971*. After 1971, U.S. Agency for International Development, Statistics and Reports Division, Office of Financial Management, *U.S. Overseas Loans and Grants and Assistance from International Organizations, July 1, 1945-June 30, 1973*, and subsequent years. GNP data are from United Nations Department of Economic and Social Affairs, Statistical Office, *Yearbook of National Accounts Statistics*.

NOTES: [a] Commitments are defined in Table 3-1. All aid figures are net.

[b] Not available.

133

spreading instability to the international system; (5) to encourage a "demonstration effect" in order to prove that economic growth, capitalism, and democratic, or at least anticommunist, political institutions go hand in hand. Let us examine these in turn.

TO DAMPEN INTERNATIONAL CONFLICT AND DISCOURAGE THREATS TO STABILITY

Defending the international status quo meant protecting United States hegemony and prosperity and moderating the harsher conditions of foreign poverty in order to decrease threats to the international status quo. President Nixon's rationale for U.S. policy was typical:

> . . . as long as millions of people lack food, housing, and jobs; starvation, social unrest and economic turmoil will threaten our common future. . . . Peace and poverty cannot easily endure side by side. All that we have worked, and fought, and sacrificed to achieve will be in jeopardy as long as hunger, illiteracy, disease, and poverty are the permanent condition of forty percent of the populace in developing nations of the world.[17]

> We must respond to the needs of those [less developed] countries if our own country and its values are to remain secure. . . . No more abroad than at home can peace be achieved and maintained without vigorous efforts to meet the needs of the less fortunate. . . . Political stability is unlikely to occur without sound economic development.[18]

The hallmark of aid policy was the use of U.S. money to promote political stability in less developed countries in order to enhance U.S. security. In a candid statement of United States foreign assistance objectives, John Hannah, a former director of AID, explained:

> It is unrealistic to think that thirty years from now 300 million Americans can live comfortably here while across the continents of Asia, Africa, and Latin America in the LDCs [less developed countries] more than twice the present population, some seven billions of people, struggle to eke out an existence. There can be no assured peace for Americans unless we join the other developed nations of the world in a continuing effort to develop a stable world order.[19]

Earlier, President Johnson had spoken of a similar goal: "The foreign aid program . . . is designed to foster our fundamental American purpose: to help root out the causes of conflict and thus ensure our own security."[20] Dollars spent for foreign assistance, the argument went, decreased the likelihood of conflict and social upheaval, thus increasing United States security. "Dollar for dollar," said President Johnson, "no United States expenditures contributed more to United States security and world peace than dollars spent in foreign aid."[21]

The use of aid to promote stability in the international environment also meant, of course, discouraging any increase in the influence of United States rivals overseas. President Nixon warned that "the unmet needs of South Asia, and its unresolved enmities, could make the area vulnerable to an undesirable level of foreign influence."[22]

As an intended guarantor of national security, aid was based on the idea that peace was indivisible, that worldwide stability was a virtue, and that a threat to peace and stability anywhere in the world was a threat to world peace and U.S. interests. In justifying aid requests to less developed countries in 1964, President Johnson had explained: "Our own security rests on the security of others."[23] Secretary of State Dean Rusk later said that both United States safety and economic well-being "require a safe world environment; for America cannot find security apart from the rest of the world. And we can be neither prosperous nor safe in the long run if most other people live in squalor or if violence consumes the world around us."[24] In reflecting upon the many years of American foreign assistance, Undersecretary of State Nicholas Katzenbach commented that "our policy toward the less developed world has been based on the assumption that these countries are, on the whole, important to United States national security."[25] Secretary of State Henry Kissinger declared that foreign assistance requests "are the resources required to carry America's role in building a more secure and stable world."[26]

During 1974 and 1975, Kissinger began to express the desire for stability in a somewhat new form by stressing the management of global interdependence.[27] Earlier, officials had emphasized a threat to United States security that was one step removed from the present. The United States would be threatened by newly independent states only if they became communist or friendly toward the Soviet Union and China. By

135

1974, the threat was perceived as more immediate, simple, and direct: if the world order were disrupted, regardless of whether communists were behind it, it was a threat to the privileged position of the United States. Kissinger explained, "Economics, technology, and the sweep of human values impose a recognition of global interdependence and the necessity of American participaton in its management."[28] Furthermore, "If we fail to manage the growing pains of an interdependent world, we risk a return to the autarkic policies of the thirties—policies which led to a collapse of world order." Thus, Kissinger said, aid programs should be seen "not as 'do good' programs, but as the vital tools through which we help build an international climate conducive to American interests."[29]

When India failed to support Kissinger's definition of U.S. interests, the impact on aid expenditures was sometimes swift. India's support for Bangladesh in seeking independence from Pakistan so angered Kissinger that U.S. aid programs were, for all practical purposes, suspended. Eighty-seven million dollars of previously promised aid was withheld after the Indian-Pakistan war in December 1971.[30]

A list of the twenty states (Table 3-3) receiving the largest quantities of grants for economic development from 1949 to 1974 confirms the security-dominated design of even "economic" development assistance. Among the largest recipients almost all were important military allies or military client states. India, which refused to become an ally, ranked eighteenth, even though its needs and population vastly exceeded those of every state that was accorded higher United States priority. Thailand, for example, with one-sixteenth the population of India, received $54 million more in grants. Spain received more grants than did India. Tiny Laos, with 1/200 the population of India, and relatively wealthy Austria, both preceded India on the list.[31]

TO CREATE AND TO STRENGTHEN ALLIES IN THE STRUGGLE
AGAINST COMMUNISM

Since the Mutual Security Act of 1953, officials often have expressed a direct relationship between foreign assistance and a perceived communist threat. In AID's first annual report summarizing past mutual security activities and explaining future "working concepts" for AID, the agency clarified the basis for assistance: "Aid programs will be tailored to the capacity of a

Table 3-3
The Twenty Largest Recipients of Grant Assistance from the United
States Agency for International Development and Predecessor
Agencies, 1949-1974

	Millions of dollars
1. South Vietnam	$4930.1
2. United Kingdom	3450.1
3. France	2964.7
4. South Korea	2556.6
5. Italy	1554.7
6. Fed. Rep. of Germany	1255.5
7. Republic of China	1154.8
8. Turkey	984.9
9. Greece	962.3
10. Netherlands	839.1
11. Laos	827.1
12. Austria	726.0
13. Pakistan	685.4
14. Jordan	585.2
15. Thailand	517.4
16. Belgium-Luxembourg	492.0
17. Spain	480.6
18. India	461.3
19. Cambodia	426.0
20. Yugoslavia	386.3

SOURCE: Data are taken from U.S. Agency for International Development, Statistics and Reports Division, *U.S. Overseas Loans and Grants and Assistance from International Organizations July 1, 1945-June 30, 1973* and subsequent years.

country to use assistance effectively, as well as to the varied needs of different countries with respect to the threat of Communism."[32]

Three principal United States objectives in Asia were typically articulated by the House Committee on Foreign Affairs:

(a) To develop sufficient military power where needed to maintain internal security and discourage Communist military aggression.

(b) To assure, in cooperation with the present free governments, that the forces of nationalism are associated with the rest of the free world instead of with Communism.

(c) To assist in the creation of social and economic conditions that will permit the growth and survival of non-communist

137

political institutions under which the people can feel that the fulfillment of their basic needs and aspirations is being effectively sought by their own free governments.[33]

In a report on foreign aid to India, Pakistan, Thailand, and Indochina, a subcommittee of the House Foreign Affairs Committee explained:

(a) That it is in our interest to help the free nations of Asia in resisting Soviet dominance;
(b) That United States military aid is required to enable certain countries in the area to maintain internal security and discourage Communist encroachment from without;
(c) That economic and political stability are interdependent and together increase the capacity and the will to resist internal and external Communist aggression.[34]

In noting the crucial relationship between foreign aid and the struggle against a perceived communist threat, Secretary of State John Foster Dulles warned: "The present world situation demands, as a first priority, the maintenance of unity and cooperation among the non-communist nations. None of us alone could face with assurance an all-out struggle with the Communist empire." The safety of the United States, he said, "no longer depends merely upon our own Armed Forces . . . but upon the combined military power and political and economic stability of the free world as a whole. For this reason, I . . . say with complete assurance that every dollar in this mutual security program is designed to protect and advance the security and well-being of the United States."[35] Dulles' successor, Christian Herter, reaffirmed the anticommunist security motivation for foreign economic assistance. The foreign economic aid program, he said, was "essential" in the U.S. effort to construct a barrier of strength against "the threat of communist expansion."[36] In 1964, Secretary of Defense Robert McNamara declared: "This [military assistance] program, and the foreign aid program generally, has now become the most critical element of our overall national security effort."[37]

TO DISCOURAGE NONALLIES FROM ESTABLISHING FRIENDLY
RELATIONS WITH COMMUNIST GOVERNMENTS

If the cold war with communism and the creation of allies were prime motivating forces behind foreign assistance, Washington officials were willing to settle for half a loaf, merely to create friends unwilling to become allies, if alliances could not be established. The purpose was simply to avert the building of friendly relations between newly independent states and the Soviet Union, a distinct possibility given the serious grievances of recent colonies against the former imperial powers. In addition, the United States feared the effects of the flexible diplomacy of Nikita Khrushchev, begun in the mid-1950s. Therefore, the militant anticommunism of U.S. foreign policy expressed in Dulles' earlier condemnation of Indian neutralism required some modification.[38] Although nonalignment was not appreciated, it was still a preferable alternative to communism.

Congressional reluctance to accept nonalignment was expressed in a House report on a special study mission to India: "Many Indians aspire to have their country play the sort of role in Asia that Sweden plays in Europe. Others, more realistic, recognize that India's geography and economy and hope of retaining her independence inevitably place her in the Western World. In the opinion of the study mission such a position of neutrality is neither tenable nor desirable."[39] The report also explained that many influential Indians agreed that neutrality was not desirable and that India should be more closely associated with the United States. The House study then suggested a foreign assistance strategy to strengthen the political influence of those Indians who were sympathetic to a pro-American position.

Secretary of State Christian Herter pointedly discussed the reason for United States interest in the development of societies that were nonaligned: "Ignoring their problems and their needs would inevitably leave them no alternative but recourse to the Communists. It is true that their absorption into the Communist fold would confront us with a grim if not hopeless security position." The secretary of state explained aid policy as a quasi-military holding action, to retain United States influence around the world. Although the military defense of the United States was the first preoccupation, "it is very dangerous to assume merely because we have military security that we are going to be able to hold these large areas of the world that are in ferment and wanting a higher standard of living on our side of the free world, unless we continue with the economic program." Herter concluded, "We have a tremendous selfish stake in having the uncommitted . . . nations of the world . . . not succumb to the Soviet bloc."[40]

TO INSURE INTERNAL POLITICAL STABILITY
IN NEWLY INDEPENDENT NATIONS

Washington's fear of and opposition to threats to the political stability of the international system were matched by opposition to internal political instability in most of the less developed countries, including India. Officials assumed that internal stability would contribute to maintaining the status quo in the international system. Foreign assistance, therefore, was useful insofar as it dampened the expression of internal grievances that might break out into open rejection of existing governments by domestic reformers. The latter claimed that the Congress party in India, for example, was too much an agent of the status quo, defending the residues of colonialism and privilege for a few within India. U.S. officials assumed that dissatisfied Indians would become agitators for change, if not outright communists. Aid was designed to decrease the level of domestic economic dissatisfaction.

The intention to use economic aid as an instrument of political influence in the internal affairs of other states was usually expressed as an effort at peacekeeping. For example, AID administrator Daniel Parker explained: "The central theme of our request is that U.S. foreign assistance programs are essential components of our foreign policy strategy for strengthening world peace and for expanding international economic cooperation in a rapidly changing world environment."[41] The utility of aid for enhancing international stability depended upon insuring definite internal political consequences. The United States discouraged structural reforms demanded by political radicals in less developed countries.[42] Former White House National Security Adviser and M.I.T. economist, Walt Rostow, wrote that

We alone in all the world have the resources to make steady and substantial economic growth an active possibility for the underdeveloped nations of the Free World. *But our basic objectives are political rather than economic.* They are political in the sense that our most pressing interest is to help the societies of the world develop in ways that will not menace our security— either as a result of their own internal dynamics or because they are weak enough to be used as tools by others. But our ability to influence political development by direct argument or intervention is very slight. Indeed, direct political intervention is almost certain to set up resentments and resistances which will produce the exact reverse of the result we seek. Economic programs . . . can be effective instruments of political influence.[43]

Thus foreign aid programs, in his judgment, were perhaps the only way "around the impasse which confronts us when we try to use our political influence directly. . . . [E]conomic programs are one of our few potentially effective levers of influence upon political developments in the underdeveloped areas."[44]

Like most U.S. officials, Rostow sought to circumvent rather than respect the desire of foreign governments to exclude foreign interference:

There is no point in evading the fact that these [U.S. policy goals in the Third World] . . . involve an attempt to interfere in the evolution of other societies. . . . The task of American policy is not to delude yourself that we are, in fact, respecting other people's sovereignty. In a world as intimately interacting as ours you cannot respect sovereignty in the old purist sense, notably if you are the major power.[45]

In short, the use of economic assistance to influence political events in recipient nations was "the key relation which underlies American foreign aid programs. Since the end of the Second World War, almost without exception, the ultimate objective of these programs, from UNRRA to the Indian surplus food deal, has not been economic but political."[46]

Harold E. Stassen, as director of the United States aid program in 1954, explained that it was necessary to extend economic assistance to India so "that it not fall into the chaotic conditions that could lead to Communist domination of that country."[47] Secretary Dulles declared many times in similar language: "The Communists move into every situation in the world where there is some ingredient of injustice." Dulles frankly admitted that "India's foreign policy . . . is not one which measures up to what we think are the best standards." Nevertheless, he favored foreign aid to India because "Nehru is conducting a very strong campaign against communism within India; the Communists are his bitter enemies domestically."[48]

President Johnson declared that, in order to ease domestic unrest in the less industrialized countries, the foreign assistance programs were "as important and as essential to the security of

141

this nation as our military defenses. . . . If most men can look forward to nothing more than a lifetime of backbreaking toil which only preserves their misery, violence will always beckon, freedom will ever be under siege."[49] President Nixon also commented that "the prospects for a peaceful world will be greatly enhanced if the two-thirds of humanity who live in [poor] countries see hope for adequate food, shelter, education and employment in peaceful progress rather than in revolution."[50]

TO ENCOURAGE A POSITIVE DEMONSTRATION EFFECT FOR NONCOMMUNIST SYSTEMS

In the background of most discussions of aid to India was the desire of officials to prove that India would not be outdone by the communist government of China, with which it so frequently has been compared because of some obvious similarities in development needs. As the Foreign Assistance Act establishing AID and an early AID report explained, the purpose of United States foreign aid was "to help make a historic demonstration that economic growth and political democracy can go hand in hand."[51] Secretary Dulles expressed the notion more pointedly: "There is no doubt in my mind that the people of Asia will be much influenced by their comparison of the economic progress made under the democratic system of India and the Communist dictatorship system in China."[52] Dulles' summation was typical of other official statements: "[United States aid] . . . does contribute quite an essential element in helping India to win this particular contest with communism which, from our standpoint, it is very important that India should win."[53]

In summary, an important part of the foreign aid strategy was to insure stability in the international system. Stability meant preserving an economic and political structure in which the United States enjoyed a per capita income more than forty times that of many less developed countries, and an unequaled worldwide political influence that protected its preeminence. It also meant the United States had the freedom to improve its position if possible. For the poor states, stability meant the perpetuation of a grossly unjust structure of wealth that kept them in poverty.

In the quest for protecting the existing global structure of power and wealth, the United States used aid to create allies, to promote internal stability, to discourage domestic dissatisfaction in less developed countries and the resulting reform movements that might be unfavorable to U.S. interests, to promote anticommunist political and economic institutions, and to demonstrate that pro-Western governments held more promise for economic development than anti-Western governments or socialist institutions.

Professed Value 2: To Protect or Improve Economic Benefits from International Trade and Investment

Since 1950 officials have repeatedly used three principal, interrelated arguments in their economic rationale for foreign assistance: (1) to increase foreign demand for U.S. goods and services; (2) to maintain open commercial relations with countries supplying raw materials to the United States; and (3) to expand United States overseas commercial influence and benefits by encouraging private enterprise both as an economic system and as an ideology. Each of these ideas deserves elaboration.

TO INCREASE FOREIGN SALES OF UNITED STATES GOODS AND SERVICES

President Kennedy was one of many officials who noted that foreign aid gave U.S. business access to otherwise closed markets, encouraged foreign consumers to develop lasting preferences for U.S. exports: "Too little attention . . . has been paid to the part which an early exposure to American goods, American skills, and the American way of doing things can play in forming the tastes and desires and customs of these newly emerging nations which must be our markets for the future."[54] Without U.S. foreign assistance to less developed countries, "their traditional ties are in Europe and Europe will be the beneficiary." With aid-inspired exports from the United States, Kennedy explained, business and industry in these countries would become acquainted with United States goods, and a tradition would be laid for growing future markets for U.S. products long after the developing economies no longer required foreign aid.

Soon after World War II ended, many U.S. officials believed that the United States would need foreign outlets to absorb the surplus of U.S. postwar production. They recognized that a regulated United States economy would not need to induce foreign purchases of excess U.S. goods resulting from economic expansion, but they did not consider such an economy to be a desirable alternative.[55] As John Hannah, former administrator of AID, explained: "The United States cannot achieve our aspira-

143

tions for . . . an expanding economy in isolation from the [less developed countries]."[56] He noted that developing countries that experienced a substantial measure of economic growth also substantially increased their imports of U.S. products.[57]

Officials frequently used empirical data to make their point. In 1972, the less industrialized countries provided a $14.6 billion market for United States goods and services, a market larger than U.S. exports to the European community. These countries bought about a third of all United States exports. As a group, they have purchased more from the United States than the United States has from them.[58] William J. Casey, under secretary of state for economic affairs, noted the importance of promoting exports to developing countries: "The United States needs the foreign exchange from expanded exports and from investment earnings to pay for our growing raw material requirements."[59] In recent years, "the less developed part of the world was the only area in which we had any kind of a significant trade surplus."[60] Another former administrator of AID, William Gaud, pointed out that in the late 1960s, for example, more than 4,000 United States firms in all fifty states received well over a billion dollars a year in AID funds for products supplied as part of the foreign aid program.[61] As George D. Woods, the president of the World Bank Group, told the UN Conference on Trade and Development in New Delhi in 1968: "Bilateral programs of assistance have had as one of their primary objectives helping the high-income countries themselves; they have looked toward financing export sales."[62]

TO MAINTAIN OPEN COMMERCIAL RELATIONS WITH COUNTRIES PROVIDING RAW MATERIALS

Secretary Kissinger believed that foreign aid was an important device to "place us in a better position to enlist the developing nations' cooperation in sustaining an open global economy."[63] In using foreign aid to establish commercial relations with aid recipients, trade is also encouraged in both directions. Aid-inspired personal contacts among bankers and business people across national boundaries facilitate business outside the realm of foreign aid programs. It is good business to be a customer for one's own customer whenever possible.

Foreign assistance programs have helped maintain access to raw materials imported from the less developed countries, which have accounted for over one-third of United States raw

144

material imports.[64] As the dependency of the United States on foreign raw materials has increased, a higher percentage of foreign goods has come from these developing countries. For example, of essential industrial raw materials purchased abroad, the United States imported approximately 65 percent from the developing countries and only 35 percent from the developed countries.[65]

Although the United States historically has had only limited interest in direct purchase of raw materials from India itself,[66] the United States has had an intense interest in access to raw materials from the less developed countries in general. Since Indian development strategy might influence other societies, the United States sought to pull India, and thereby India's Asian neighbors, toward the private enterprise system in order to keep the global as well as the Indian economy more open to U.S. investment and trade.[67]

Douglas Dillon, under secretary of state in the 1950s, once candidly remarked: "I am an investment banker by trade, and I speak as an investment banker when I say that today's less developed nations are tomorrow's richest economic and political asset."[68] Secretary of State William Rogers noted that, with only 6 percent of the world's population, the United States consumed 40 percent of the world's annual output of raw materials and energy. "Increasingly, we depend on the developing countries for these supplies."[69]

William Casey, the under secretary of economic affairs, explained how the need for foreign resources was matched by a need for earnings from foreign investments in order to purchase materials, and how both of these needs were served by aiding developing nations: "Our increasing dependence on foreign sources of energy and raw materials brings with it a need for greater access to foreign markets and a need for investment income to pay for the larger volume of imports. . . . We invest more when the investment climate is best, and this normally is in stable countries."[70]

TO ENCOURAGE PRIVATE ENTERPRISE IN OTHER COUNTRIES AND TO EXPAND U.S. COMMERCIAL INFLUENCE OVERSEAS

A recurring theme during the policy discussions about economic assistance was that it should be used to foster private enterprise. It is difficult to separate the diverse sources of support for private enterprise as a matter of American ideology, as an

145

intentional effort to encourage U.S. economic and political expansion abroad, as an expression of the vested interests of financiers with capital to invest abroad at high rates of profit, and as a genuine belief that economic development proceeded most efficiently when left to private enterprise. These various motivations, of course, were mutually reinforcing. Washington officials assumed that development of a private enterprise system in India, as opposed to a socialist system, would encourage commercial intercourse with the United States instead of, say, the Soviet Union. Sales and investments abroad by United States nationals would enhance the economic power of the United States in southern Asia.

This did not mean that the United States government made a major effort to encourage the economic penetration of India in order to gain political influence there, but instead that the foreign assistance program was intended to tilt the Indian economic structure in favor of a private enterprise system that would be open to United States investors, that would facilitate the sale of American goods in India, and that would produce secondary effects throughout Asia. U.S. Ambassador to India, Daniel P. Moynihan, explained that the United States effort to remove some of the Indian irritation caused by the food assistance program of the 1960s, which produced enormous rupee credits for the United States, was based on the hope that the debt settlement would create "an improving investment climate for U.S. firms seeking opportunities to manufacture in India and search for and develop oil deposits off its coast."[71]

The mutually reinforcing dimensions of the preference for promoting private enterprise were ubiquitous and sometimes surprisingly straightforward in official rationales for aid policy. A typical position was expressed in a Senate Foreign Relations Committee Report: "Development achieved under State direction . . . cements fewer strong ties with the United States than development achieved largely by way of the activation of latent private resources in the less developed countries."[72] Harold Stassen, as administrator of the Foreign Operations Administration, explained, "We encourage private enterprise, private investment, strengthened stability, and anti-Communist development."[73] The AID statement of goals typically declared: "It is a major objective of AID to encourage increased United States private investment in the developing countries and to strengthen the growth of strong, vigorous private sectors in these economies."

146

Under Secretary Casey reported that in 1972 the United States had offset a $6 billion trade deficit with a $7 billion net inflow in dividends and interest from United States investment abroad. "As a country which faces increasing needs for resources of energy and raw materials from abroad, we will have to invest abroad and increase the inflow of investment earnings to justify that investment."[74] Secretary Rogers pointed out that whereas United States foreign investment is concentrated in industrial countries, 50 percent of the U.S. income from foreign investment has come from the less developed countries.[75]

The preference for promoting private enterprise was not simply a product of Soviet-American rivalry. With the waning of the cold war in the 1960s and 1970s, loans and grants have been continuously channeled to encourage private enterprise abroad.[76] This has been done by often loaning money to private investors instead of to public corporations, by having the United States government guarantee the foreign investments of U.S. investors, and by providing credit for private foreign purchases from United States corporations.

As might be expected, the strongest political support in the United States has been for programs that would bring potential profits for United States corporations. The development of foreign industries which might compete with U.S. corporations has not been encouraged. Instead, U.S. corporations have supported the construction of infrastructure, such as roads and electric power, which the corporations need to market their goods but do not want to construct themselves. They also have favored "concentrating aid in priority problem areas, such as rural development, food production, population and disease control, and education."[77] They have expressed a decided preference for assistance measures that will encourage Indians to become consumers of U.S. manufactured goods. As the president of the National Association of Manufacturers explained, his organization "supports the concept of helping low-income countries in the development process, since it reduces human suffering and raises the world standard of living which, in the long run, means new and expanded markets for American products."[78] David Rockefeller, president of Chase Manhattan and founder of the Trilateral Commission, once noted that United States exports to the lowest income countries were "doing poorly." This was, he explained, because of foreign exchange problems and financing on terms that made U.S. exports uncompetitive. Thus he urged extending credit to the less

147

developed countries as "a necessary and useful instrument for American exports to become competitive in this neglected market."[79]

In 1973 Edward Hood, vice-president of General Electric, assessed future markets in the developing countries of the Far East and Africa with a GNP per capita of $200 or less, and projected a market there in the next five years of $4.1 billion for electrical equipment. He told the House Committee on Foreign Affairs that this was a potential of about 16,000 additional jobs on an average annual basis. This estimate was on the conservative side since it did not include the potential increase in demand for allied equipment in related fields.[80]

In summary, from the early 1950s until the present, one of the objectives uppermost in the minds of officials was that private enterprise should be encouraged by foreign aid. Concrete aid programs were tailored to increase foreign demand for U.S. goods; to insure profits—through the tying of aid—for U.S. corporations; to protect opportunities for United States investment abroad; to facilitate continued access to foreign raw materials; and to promote the establishment of capitalist enterprises in the less developed countries in order to protect and expand the rewards of the United States economic system for Americans.

Professed Value 3: To Express Humanitarian
Concern for Helping People in Need

In the public rationales for foreign aid to India, most advocates expressed a humanitarian motive. Officials occasionally spoke simply about a moral obligation to people in need. For example, Undersecretary of State Nicholas Katzenbach explained: "Our people want to help their less fortunate fellow man. They want this because it is right. To do otherwise would be to deny an essential part of our national heritage."[81] A director of AID put it bluntly: "We . . . seek to help the poor two-thirds of the world because it is right. Hunger is wrong. Ignorance, disease, and hopelessness are wrong. . . . Indifference to poverty and despair is wrong."[82] Henry Kissinger once declared, "The economic assistance program of the United States is a faithful expression of our moral values." For Cyrus Vance, "Foreign assistance efforts demonstrate America's humanitarian compassion for the world's poor."[83]

Yet for most officials the humanitarian motive was almost inseparable from the security motive. From their perspective, the world would be more humane if it were secured behind a benevolent U.S. military shield. Such a secure world system would avoid the suffering of revolutions and social dislocation concomitant with rapid changes in the structures of power and wealth, whether on the domestic or global level.

In 1964 President Johnson typically expressed the convenient marriage of practical concern for security with principled expression of compassion: "There is no conflict between 'humanitarian' goals and 'national' goals. Our own security rests on the security of others. Their good health is our good health. As they prosper we prosper. Our concern must—and does— transcend national borders."[84] Several years later he continued to repeat the familiar theme of convergence between prudence and ethical prescription: "Foreign aid serves our national interest. It expresses our basic humanity. It may not always be popular but it is right. Foreign aid . . . is a commitment to conscience as well as to country."[85] Johnson said that "the pages of history can be searched in vain for another power whose pursuit of that self-interest was so infused with grandeur of spirit and morality of purpose."[86]

Beginning in the 1970s, the humanitarian-security motif occasionally was expressed as a global, rather than strictly national, bilateral concern: "Our economic assistance is designed to reinforce developing nations' efforts to bring a better life to their citizens, increasing their stake in a cooperative global economy at a time when events threaten to divide the world anew— between North and South, developed and developing, consumer and producer."[87] The most dramatic rhetorical expression of a new global perspective came from Secretary of State Cyrus Vance at the Conference on International Economic Cooperation and Development. He sought to counter the idea "that we, as a rich and powerful nation, can only be addressed as though we were an adversary." He declared: "I want the policy of the U.S. to be understood. There should be a new international economic system. In that system, there must be equity; there must be growth; but above all, there must be justice. We are prepared to help build that new system."[88]

Despite this rhetoric, the Carter administration has not made any substantial departure in practice from the implicit values of previous Republican and Democratic administrations. The percent of U.S. GNP going into development assistance failed to increase. Less than half of bilateral development assistance went to countries with per capita incomes of less than $200 per year. On the one hand, the president promised before the UN that the United States was ready to "promote a new system of international economic progress and cooperation."[89] On the other hand, the Department of State directly rebuffed the desire of the less developed countries for a restructuring of the global economy in a new international economic order: "The United States believes that the best way for LDC's [less developed countries] to attain development objectives is within the existing international economic system."[90] U.S. officials, in effect, would continue to seek first their own political and economic advantages in the face of an overwhelming need for a new structure of commercial relations and global economic decision making that would place more emphasis on serving human needs and less on producing unessential consumer items.

Comparison of Professed Values, Implicit Values,
and the Maximization of Economic Well-Being

We turn now from a discussion of the rationale for aid that was articulated by political leaders to a delineation of the values implicit in the aid policy itself. The implicit values, which were actually expressed in concrete governmental behavior, can then be compared with the values expressed in official rhetoric. Such a comparison will clarify the extent to which rhetoric has been an accurate indicator of the normative basis for United States policy. In the final portion of this chapter, the values that have guided United States aid policy will be compared to the guidelines for foreign assistance that are derived from the values of global humanism.

The discussion of values to this point has focused primarily on what officials said, which may of course have been different from what they believed. Regardless of individual beliefs, however, widespread agreement among official policy statements does provide an indication of the prevailing norms guiding foreign aid policy. We may assume that it has been politically useful for officials to discuss foreign aid in terms of its contributions to United States security, prosperity, and humanitarian concern. In contrast, officials have not customarily spoken in favor of redistributing the world's wealth, nor proclaimed that the United States should equitably share the power to decide how the world's resources should be used. Nothing has been said about

THREE · *Values Implicit in Policy*

establishing a minimum standard of living for all persons on the globe. When these generally ignored values are juxtaposed against the recurring public statements of policymakers, it is possible to discern the rough outlines of official consciousness and intentions.

AID AS AN INSTRUMENT OF SECURITY

The mode and amount of U.S. aid given to India leave little doubt that *enhancing U.S. power and strategic advantages was a major reason for U.S. economic assistance* (implicit value A). Aid began after the United States took a new interest in helping Asian countries during the Korean War. The largest amount of grants came in 1954, at the conclusion of the war, and at the height of Dulles' efforts to encircle the Soviet Union and China with military alliances. At that time, the United States attempted unsuccessfully to enroll India as a member of SEATO. During the 1960s, as the cold war diminished, United States grant and loan economic assistance to India (as to most other countries) gradually declined. Pakistan, a staunch Asian ally in the sense of being willing to join SEATO and CENTO, received larger amounts of aid after SEATO was formed than did India, in spite of India's vastly greater population and needs. Indeed, grants to Pakistan from 1948 to 1976 exceeded those to India by $732 to $464 million. This was in spite of an additional $712 million in military aid going to Pakistan during these years as opposed to $144 for India, given largely because of India's border war with China. In short, India received limited amounts of aid to encourage internal stability, discourage communism, and insure some degree of progress in its competition with China. But its nonaligned status and professed intention to build a socialist society served as constraints upon the amount of aid the United States was willing to extend. The most compelling and consistent explanation for aid was its usefulness as a tool to produce military and political benefits for U.S. security policies.

AID AS AN INSTRUMENT FOR U.S. ECONOMIC BENEFIT

There is no significant evidence to suggest that the values implicit in United States aid policy were inconsistent with the professed value of bringing economic rewards to the United States. U.S. dollars channeled through the foreign assistance program ended up in U.S. pockets. Hundreds of thousands of jobs in the United States resulted from the aid programs.[91]

Perhaps the best example of United States efforts to use aid specifically for United States benefit has been the requirement that aid be used to purchase goods from the United States. Between 1960 and 1964, when tying was begun in earnest, a number of aid-financed exports were affected: sale of United States fertilizers quadrupled; chemical products more than doubled; textiles and industrial machinery increased five times over. As AID reported in 1964: "One result of these increased exports is that new markets are being opened up for American products in parts of the world where they have never before been seen."[92]

When some officials once proposed discontinuing tied aid,[93] they faced corporate protest that to do so would "undermine American opportunities to develop long-range trade relationships with these nations. Experience shows that as emerging nations grow into a viable economy, they tend to do business with the commercial ties developed under AID programs."[94] Those ties also encouraged investment. By 1975 about 60 percent of all new U.S. investment went to developing countries.[95]

The percentage of tied aid has generally increased since 1950. By the late 1960s, 93 percent of AID funds were spent directly in the United States. Ninety-eight percent of AID's commodity requirements were procured in the United States.[96] All grants were normally spent in the United States. The shipment of U.S. goods abroad was restricted to American ships, and no AID funds could be paid to foreign flag vessels.[97] Even replenishment capital that the United States gave to the Asian Development Bank for concessional loans was tied to procurement of United States goods and services.[98]

The 1968 AID report proudly announced the creation of an "Additionality Working Group" whose purpose was to insure that United States commercial exports were not adversely affected by AID-financed exports. In short, this group required that a country like India continue importing goods from the United States at a level constant with past purchases before AID credits could be used to finance similar goods, thus insuring that any AID purchases would be in addition to what might have been bought without any aid.[99]

As a result of these policies, aid has stimulated the exports and profits of developed countries. Meanwhile, the share of world total exports for the less developed countries has dropped from 30 percent in 1948 to 23 percent in 1958 to 18 percent in 1969.[100] Exports from developed countries increased 156 percent during the decade of largest assistance from 1959 to 1969, while exports from the less developed countries rose only 87 percent.[101] By 1976, 27 percent of U.S. exports—more than the amount going to the members of the European communities, Eastern Europe, and the Soviet Union combined—went to non-OPEC developing countries. Altogether, the less developed countries bought 40 percent of total U.S. exports. If the United States retains with developing countries the same trade patterns established by foreign aid during the decade of the 1960s, by 1985 U.S. exports to developing countries would account for two million additional jobs in U.S. export industries.[102]

Implicit value B is synonymous with professed value 2: Aid was valued as an instrument *to promote economic benefits for the United States derived from international trade and investment.*

AID AS HUMANITARIAN CONCERN

In assessing the impact of humanitarianism upon American foreign aid policy, the professed humanitarian value is contradicted by several values implicit in the aid policies themselves. To be sure, if one views various AID projects as isolated cases, they often produced local humanitarian benefits. But if one examines the cumulative effects of the overall aid policy in the context of world geopolitics, the policy looks far different. The important questions in this examination are: To what extent did U.S. policy contribute to genuine internal or global structural change that helped decrease economic injustice and eliminate poverty? Did officials aim at structural change, or simply at moderating some of the worst economic conditions enough to perpetuate a roughly similar planetary distribution of wealth?[103] Did aid—insofar as it had a humanitarian element at all— express a charity mentality that offered relief to the poverty-stricken, or instead a concern with economic justice that promised eradication of poverty for millions of inhabitants of the globe? For aid to be considered humanitarian, it would need to be extended as a matter of right to persons, regardless of their race, ideology, or strategic importance, who lacked minimal requirements for physical existence and a life of dignity. Humanitarian assistance also would decrease the recipient's dependency on the donor and promote structural change empowering the weak to achieve greater equity in global decision making on economic affairs.

The values implicit in U.S. behavior contradicted the pro-

153

fessed value of humanitarianism. Officials consistently negated humanitarianism by shaping aid to promote military and political advantages for their own government. Official statements themselves frequently revealed U.S. priorities. The United States should give humanitarian aid to developing countries, most officials argued, because (1) aid would bind recipients to the service of U.S. economic and security needs and (2) without aid, the entire existing structure of world order, upon which U.S. wealth and power depended, would collapse in disorder, violence, and revolution. Officials feared that if the United States did not help the developing countries, their governments or reformers within their societies, would try to upset the prevailing allocation of power and wealth in the world, to the great disadvantage of the United States. In a typical speech entitled "Reform of the U.S. Foreign Assistance Program," President Nixon noted that the United States had built a "world order which insures peace and prosperity for ourselves and for other nations. . . . This world order cannot be sustained if . . . two-thirds of the world's people see the richer third as indifferent to their needs and insensitive to their aspirations." The purpose of aid was to enable the two-thirds of humanity who live in poor countries to "see hope . . . in peaceful progress rather than in revolution."[104] Kissinger believed that "economic assistance programs are essential instruments as we seek to shape a cooperative international order that reflects our interests." Vance warned that failure to undertake substantial aid obligations would mean the United States could not protect its security interests "in a hungry, angry, and bitter world."[105] Similarly, President Johnson on one occasion explained: "The forces of human need still stalk this globe. Ten thousand people a day . . . die from malnutrition. Diseases long conquered by science cut down life in villages still trapped in the past. In many vast areas, four out of every five persons cannot write their names." With understandable concern, he continued, "These are tragedies which summon our compassion." But, somewhat surprisingly, "More urgently, they threaten our security. They create the conditions of despair in which the fires of violence smoulder."[106] The president's conviction that mass starvation or widespread illiteracy were conditions that "more urgently" threaten United States security than call forth compassion demonstrated the secondary importance of U.S. compassion.

There was, perhaps, one possible exception to the generalization that humanitarianism failed to guide U.S. aid policy. When

India faced severe food shortages, the United States did sell large quantities of grain to India, financed from credit extended by the United States under P.L. 480. The program known as "Food for Peace" or "Food for Freedom" enabled the United States to make foreign concessionary sales of its unwanted agricultural surpluses. The government had these on hand as a result of its vast purchases from American farmers in its domestic farm price-support program.

There is considerable disagreement about the costs of P.L. 480 aid to the United States and its benefits to India. India received more feed grain through the program than any other country in the postwar period, as indicated in Table 3-4. The commodities

Table 3-4
The Twenty Largest Recipients of Total P.L. 480 Assistance

	Millions of Dollars
India	$4718
Pakistan	1714
South Korea	1677
South Vietnam	1281
Yugoslavia	1133
Indonesia	888
Brazil	844
Egypt	700
Israel	635
Turkey	553
Italy	465
Morocco	444
Spain	438
Tunisia	398
Taiwan	338
Colombia	269
Philippines	265
Greece	247
Chile	246
Algeria	177

SOURCE: Data are taken from U.S. Agency for International Development, Statistics and Reports Division, *U.S. Overseas Loans and Grants and Assistance from International Organizations, July 1, 1945-June 30, 1973.*

obviously benefited thousands of Indians who suffered from malnutrition. On the other hand, the program has been the object of several serious criticisms. First, it often provided insufficient assistance, arriving too late to prevent physical and mental impairments that result from malnutrition, especially among children. Second, some Indians feared that the aid—and the threat to withhold it—gave the United States political leverage in Indian affairs. AID officials have privately acknowledged that occasionally the United States delayed food shipments until the Indian government shifted some of its economic policies, such as to deflate its currency or raise its agricultural prices, in directions the United States favored. Third, the provision of aid may have enabled the Indian government to postpone painful but apparently necessary economic and agricultural reforms, thus actually slowing the movement toward economic autonomy and self-sufficiency in agriculture.[107] Finally, the particular arrangements in which most of the grain was sold rather than given to India produced a separate set of new problems. These were caused by the "blocked rupees" which the United States accumulated as India repaid the loans extended for the purchase of the grain. The loans were to be repaid in rupees that could not be converted to dollars or taken out of the country. Thus new rupees were deposited on U.S. accounts in India with each additional grain shipment. The United States used a portion of the money (roughly 15 percent) for paying the cost of running its embassy in India and similar overhead expenses. In addition, approximately 5 percent of the money went into so-called "Cooley loans," which were made to U.S. businesses for expenses in India, as a strategy for encouraging private investment there.[108] The remainder of the funds were to be granted or loaned to the Indian government for purposes that both governments agreed upon. Of this portion, 50 to 80 percent was usually restricted to loans.

Blocked rupee sales caused several problems.[109] The United States-owned rupees promised to grow indefinitely, since the United States was unable to spend them all or to take them out of India. U.S. agreements also restricted interest on loans to making future loans to India. By 1974, 3.3 billion dollars' worth of rupees were credited to the U.S. account for repayment of loans to finance the purchase of U.S. farm surpluses. The United States technically possessed about 20 percent of all Indian currency. Interest alone amounted to over $100 million per year,[110] a figure that exceeded by $80 million the average annual total U.S. grants to India for economic development.

U.S. Ambassador to India, Daniel P. Moynihan, said "We could never spend this amount of money. Twice as much is now coming in as going out. There is no possible escape from indebtedness for India. It could go on into the twenty-second century." Even without further grain purchases, the interest would have accrued to produce a total of $6 billion by the end of the century.[111]

U.S. ownership of so much Indian currency became an embarrassment for both governments and, in Moynihan's judgment, poisoned relations between the two societies.[112] Indian political resentment about the accumulation of these funds grew, even though the United States could not use most of the funds without the approval of the Indian government. Some Indians feared United States manipulation of the Indian economy, where the United States could, through reloaning of rupees, create money, aggravate inflation, or otherwise distort the economy.[113] The large rupee balance led the United States to build up an aid and diplomatic establishment twice as big as any other country, in part just to spend the money. Canada, in contrast, had provided large-scale food aid in the form of grants.[114] Some believed the United States should have erased all of the rupee indebtedness acquired as a result of United States disposal of its surpluses. However, the United States refused.

Instead, Moynihan succeeded in making a less sweeping arrangement in which rupees worth $2.03 billion were forgiven. The one third of indebtedness not forgiven would continue to be used by the United States for operating its embassy and for other educational and cultural programs. In addition, India agreed to pay $64 million to the United States in dollars over a ten-year period.[115] Fifty-one million dollars over a forty-year period had been due before the new agreement.[116]

Assessing the costs of the aid program to the United States is no easier than comprehending its political and economic impact upon India. Since the United States had to pay the costs of storing new U.S. grain if it remained unsold, some have argued that P.L. 480 disposal of agricultural surplus actually incurred savings.[117] The United States also augmented its economic benefit from P.L. 480 aid by occasionally imposing the requirement that the recipient buy a certain quantity of grain at commercial rates as part of the agreement to receive the P.L. 480 grains at a concessionary price.[118]

The element of humanitarianism in P.L. 480 aid must be viewed in the light of these qualifications:

(1) Although the gross figures in Table 3-4 show that India was the beneficiary of enormous food aid, it is not clear that the aid program was aimed solely or even mainly at serving human needs. Among the countries needing and receiving food assistance, on a per capita basis Indians ranked *forty-fifth*. Seldom was the aid swift or massive enough to avert starvation or malnutrition for many persons. A majority of the states that received more food assistance than India (shown in Table 3-5) also had significantly higher average per capita incomes. P.L. 480 programs in general were not focused on the poorest of the poor. Of the twenty top recipients, only two—South Vietnam and Burundi—were among the forty poorest states in the world (listed in Table 3-9).

Table 3-5
Largest Per Capita Recipients of P.L. 480 Aid

1.	Israel	$212	24.	Jamaica	$17
2.	Iceland	110	25.	Pakistan and Bangladesh	16
3.	South Vietnam	80	26.	Lesotho	16
4.	Tunisia	80	27.	Colombia	15
5.	Jordan	64	28.	Sri Lanka	15
6.	South Korea	60	29.	Botswana	15
7.	Yugoslavia	60	30.	Guinea	15
8.	Ryukyu	56	31.	Spain	14
9.	Burundi	46	32.	Panama	14
10.	Cyprus	44	33.	Ecuador	12
11.	Dominican Republic	38	34.	Hong Kong	12
12.	Morocco	34	35.	Portugal	12
13.	Chile	31	36.	Austria	12
14.	Malta	30	37.	Ghana	11
15.	Bolivia	28	38.	Nepal	11
16.	Taiwan	28	39.	Syria	11
17.	Greece	27	40.	Gambia	11
18.	Lebanon	26	41.	Liberia	11
19.	Egypt	23	42.	Peru	11
20.	Uruguay	22	43.	Afghanistan	11
21.	Libya	22	44.	Brazil	10
22.	Paraguay	18	45.	India	10
23.	Turkey	18			

SOURCE: Data were taken from U.S. Agency for International Development, Office of Statistics and Reports, *U.S. Economic Assistance Programs Administered by the Agency for International Development and Predecessor Agencies, April 3, 1948 to June 30, 1971*; U.S. Agency for International Development, Statistics and Reports Division, *U.S. Overseas Loans and Grants and Assistance from International Organizations, July 1, 1945-June 30, 1973*; United Nations, *Demographic Yearbook*.

THREE · *Values Implicit in Policy*

(2) The original intention of the Title I P.L. 480 aid was not to make the grain an outright gift, but to enable food importers to buy U.S. farm surplus. Although this preference for loans rather than grants no doubt owed more to U.S. domestic political reasons than to economic selfishness, it nonetheless demonstrates that the prevailing values did not sanction an act so "generous" as giving away wheat and corn held by the U.S. government in such quantity that officials paid U.S. farmers to remove fertile land from production. Moreover, once commodity surpluses began to decline in 1966, the United States required a transition from sales in Indian currency to sales in U.S. dollars.[119] Food aid dwindled when wheat could be sold for a sizable profit to nations less needy but richer than India. P.L. 480 aid did not increase Indian agricultural self-sufficiency nor decrease dependency on U.S. commodities nearly as much as would have grant assistance to upgrade Indian agricultural and fertilizer production.

(3) The relatively late decision to forgive two-thirds of the loans stopped short of completely abolishing Indian indebtedness under P.L. 480. Of the remaining one-third, Moynihan said, "we would retain control over our use of these rupees for the full ranges of purposes and programs we previously funded with rupees." Thus, "what we have granted India costs us very little."[120]

(4) The rupee agreement was intended not merely to end "a period of massive U.S. assistance and involvement in Indian economic policy decision-making." The United States also sought, according to Ambassador Moynihan, to improve sales opportunities for U.S. manufacturers in the country with the tenth largest GNP in the world. Moreover, officials hoped, as noted above, that the agreement would lead to a more receptive climate for U.S. investors in India and for corporations interested in exploring for oil off India's coast.[121]

(5) The most compelling arguments—hardly humanitarian—for the Moynihan arrangement were that the United States could never use the Indian currency it possessed, and that to continue the soft currency indebtedness would exacerbate India's difficult economic position so much as to make repayment of $3.4 billion in U.S. hard currency loans almost impossible.[122] Moreover, the World Bank's estimate that India would have a shortfall of foreign exchange of $12 billion from 1974-80 also impressed U.S. officials as having such serious economic implications for India's poor that it would produce political unrest and

159

instability within India, which the United States sought to prevent.

Therefore, in the framework of this analysis, the decision to eliminate two-thirds of the P.L. 480 debt was done more in the service of the first and second professed values—to serve the strategic and economic interests of the United States—than to achieve structural reform of the global economy, and thereby eliminate the gap between rich and poor. Upon close examination, even programs as apparently humanitarian as food aid fail to be a serious or unequivocal expression of the second value of global humanism.

To the extent that aid *was* humanitarian, it was rooted in a charity mentality, and not in a sense of global justice or a belief that no society had the right to withhold the "excess" fruit of its soil while others on the planet starved. Emergency food aid kept the Indians and Americans in their accustomed relative positions in the geopolitical structure. Apparently United States officials believed that the Indians were worthy of charity in moments of desperation, but the same officials did little to facilitate Indian equality in terms of standard of living or participation in decisions about allocating the world's wealth. The United States sent emergency food aid when it was easy to give in the form of loans to Indians so they could purchase U.S. surplus. But at the same time, the United States opposed structural change for a more equitable distribution of wealth and an increase, even to the level of one percent of GNP, in the burden of United States assistance to all countries.

Returning to our wider assessment of the humanitarian element in United States aid policy, the pattern of assistance shows that aid was, to a significant extent, a function of anticommunism. During the late 1950s, United States officials began to understand that what they perceived as a communist threat could not be handled exclusively by military equipment and alliances. Thus Secretary of State Dulles' harsh criticism of India's neutralism was moderated as Washington officials began to see nonaligned countries as potential outposts of stability in a world of flux. The subsequently increased aid program for India reflected the American change of mood, but the motivation remained tied to national security.

The United States shifted tactics to counter new Soviet diplomatic flexibility toward the less developed countries during the mid and late 1950s. As James H. Smith, the director of the

International Cooperation Administration (ICA) explained before the House Committee on Foreign Affairs: "The Soviet economic program . . . must be given due weight in the formulation of our policies. The Soviets have revealed a large and apparently highly effective apparatus. The administration of Soviet aid is of particular significance to the operations of ICA."[123]

The strategy of using aid as an instrument for buying influence was publicly denied. As Nicholas Katzenbach reported, "faithful conformity to our foreign policy views has not been, and should not be, the criterion for eligibility."[124] In practice United States aid carried political strings insofar as it was aimed at resisting socialism. With the exception of Yugoslavia, a "deviant" from the Warsaw Pact, aid was limited to noncommunist states. For a nation as rich as the United States, simply the power to withhold aid from the poor constituted significant political influence. Even the well-known liberal administrator of the Foreign Operations Administration, Harold Stassen, said: "We should, and we do take a more generous attitude toward Pakistan, particularly . . . as they join with us in the defense arrangements, than we do toward India."[125] Because of the linkage between economic aid and building military alliances, from 1950 through 1973 Pakistan received three times as much economic aid per inhabitant as did India. Countries neither allied to nor sympathetic with U.S. strategic interests were unlikely to receive substantial economic assistance.[126] In surveying the pattern of U.S. aid on a per capita basis for all countries (with populations in excess of two million) from 1946 through 1973, of the twelve states receiving the most grant assistance for *economic* development, eleven were also among the largest recipients of *military* aid.[127]

Furthermore, the professed value of humanitarian concern is negated by the glaring inequities between the aid levels extended to India and to relatively more wealthy countries. Other things being equal, if humanitarian values had been paramount, a country with a smaller population and higher standard of living would not have received more assistance than India. As Table 3-6 shows, aid followed a radically different pattern. Relatively wealthy Iran, for example, received six times as much grant and loan assistance per capita as did India. Laos received almost four hundred times as much per capita grant aid as did India. The Laotian aid was high, of course, because of U.S. military involvement there, not because of an enormous effort to

161

fulfill human needs. Similarly, military activity or alliance-building was responsible for the higher levels of aid in all the other cases in Table 3-6.

If one examines per capita grant and loan economic assistance to other U.S. aid recipients worldwide (Table 3-7), India ranks sixtieth. The top two dozen states in the U.S. aid program received eight to forty times as much per capita assistance as Indians. The Indian case was not atypical of many poor states. Of the forty largest per capita recipients of U.S. economic assistance from 1946 to 1974, only three states—Cambodia, Laos, and South Vietnam—were among the forty poorest countries of the world.[128]

Table 3-6

Economic Assistance to Selected Asian Countries:
Average Annual Per Capita Grant and Loan Net Commitments
from AID and Predecessor Agencies, in Dollars

Country	Years Covered	Loan and Grant Assistance	Grant Assistance
Laos	1955-73	$19.74	$19.74
South Vietnam	1955-73	16.83	16.52
Taiwan	1949-63	10.67	9.19
South Korea	1952-73	5.61	4.91
Cambodia	1955-73	4.05	4.05
Turkey	1949-73	3.10	1.53
Iran	1952-66	2.08	1.34
Pakistan	1952-73	1.19	.35
Thailand	1951-73	.93	.82
India	1951-73	.35	.05

SOURCES: Data were taken from U.S. Agency for International Development, Office of Statistics and Reports, *U.S. Economic Assistance Programs Administered by the Agency for International Development and Predecessor Agencies, April 3, 1948 to June 30, 1971*; U.S. Agency for International Development, Statistics and Reports Division, *U.S. Overseas Loans and Grants and Assistance from International Organizations, July 1, 1945- June 30, 1973*; United Nations, *Demographic Yearbook*.

If loans are separated from total assistance, the remaining figures for grant assistance substantiate the conclusion that U.S. aid was not designed to help those most in need. (See Table 3-8.) Among per capita grants for all U.S. aid recipients in the world, India ranks ninety-third. Of the thirty-five states receiving the largest per capita grant assistance, again only three were among the forty poorest countries of the world—the same three in

Table 3-7
Total Loan and Grant Commitments from U.S. AID and Predecessor
Agencies to 60 Largest Recipients on a Per Capita Basis, 1946-1973

1.	South Vietnam	$314	31. Honduras	$49
2.	Jordan	304	32. Ireland	49
3.	Iceland	301	33. Paraguay	47
4.	Laos	276	34. Trinidad-Tobago	39
5.	Israel	204	35. Ecuador	34
6.	Panama	191	36. Italy	32
7.	Liberia	169	37. Yugoslavia	30
8.	Guyana	123	38. El Salvador	30
9.	Greece	118	39. Lebanon	29
10.	Taiwan	114	40. Morocco	27
11.	South Korea	107	41. Ghana	26
12.	Bolivia	105	42. Venezuela	26
13.	Austria	104	43. Fed. Rep. of Germany	25
14.	Dominican Republic	91	44. Iran	24
15.	Nicaragua	90	45. Pakistan-Bangladesh	24
16.	Libya	86	46. Uruguay	22
17.	Netherlands	83	47. Somalia	21
18.	Malta	80	48. Haiti	20
19.	Chile	77	49. Thailand	19
20.	United Kingdom	71	50. Afghanistan	19
21.	Cambodia	71	51. Spain	18
22.	Costa Rica	70	52. Peru	18
23.	Norway	69	53. Brazil	18
24.	Turkey	69	54. Zaire	16
25.	Tunisia	66	55. Philippines	14
26.	France	65	56. Sweden	13
27.	Denmark	56	57. Guinea	13
28.	Belgium-Luxembourg	56	58. Ethiopia	10
29.	Colombia	52	59. Venezuela	8
30.	Guatemala	50	60. India	8

SOURCES: Data are taken from U.S. Agency for International Development, Statistics and Reports Divisions, *U.S. Overseas Loans and Grants and Assistance from International Organizations, July 1, 1945-June 30, 1973*; United Nations, *Demographic Yearbook*.

which the U.S. had been pressing military objectives for years: South Vietnam, Laos, and Cambodia. The total assistance to India also has been below that which went to richer states many years ago. Countries that received forty to three hundred times as much aid per capita as India included, among others: Denmark, Norway, France, United Kingdom, Netherlands, Israel, Greece, Austria, Taiwan, Cambodia, and South Vietnam.

163

Table 3-8

Total Grant Commitments from U.S. AID and Predecessor Agencies on a Per Capita Basis, 1946-1973

1. South Vietnam	$308	34. Costa Rica	$21	67. Dahomey	$3
2. Jordan	293	35. Yugoslavia	20	68. Togo	3
3. Laos	276	36. Haiti	18	69. Central African Rep.	3
4. Iceland	178	37. Thailand	17	70. Senegal	3
5. Israel	126	38. Somalia	15	71. Cyprus	3
6. Greece	107	39. Iran	15	72. Malawi	3
7. Austria	104	40. Spain	15	73. Indonesia	2
8. Taiwan	96	41. Afghanistan	14	74. Brazil	2
9. Liberia	93	42. Ecuador	13	75. Iraq	2
10. Korea	91	43. El Salvador	12	76. Morocco	2
11. Libya	81	44. Zaire	11	77. Mali	2
12. Cambodia	71	45. Sweden	11	78. Egypt	2
13. Netherlands	70	46. Guinea	10	79. Cameroon	2
14. United Kingdom	64	47. Philippines	10	80. Tanzania	2
15. Malta	63	48. Chile	10	81. Niger	2
16. France	61	49. Pakistan	9	82. Congo (Brazzaville)	2
17. Bolivia	60	50. Peru	7	83. Venezuela	2
18. Norway	59	51. Gabon	7	84. Gambia	2

19.	Panama	59	52.	Yemen Arab Republic	7	
20.	Denmark	50	53.	Jamaica	7	
21.	Belgium-Luxembourg	49	54.	Ireland	6	
22.	Dominican Republic	41	55.	Nepal	6	
23.	Trinidad, Tobago	39	56.	Sierra Leone	6	
24.	Guyana	33	57.	Bangladesh	5	
25.	Turkey	32	58.	Uruguay	5	
26.	Italy	30	59.	Ethiopia	5	
27.	Guatemala	28	60.	Nigeria	4	
28.	Tunisia	27	61.	Sudan	4	
29.	Lebanon	26	62.	Saudi Arabia	4	
30.	Nicaragua	22	63.	Colombia	4	
31.	Honduras	22	64.	Ghana	4	
32.	Paraguay	22	65.	Kenya	3	
33.	Fed. Rep. of Germany	21	66.	Uganda	3	

85.	Portugal	2
86.	Chad	2
87.	Ivory Coast	2
88.	Sri Lanka	1
89.	Zambia	1
90.	Upper Volta	1
91.	Burma	1
92.	Rwanda	1
93.	India	1
94.	Argentina	1
95.	Malagasy Republic	1
96.	Botswana	1
97.	Lesotho	1
98.	Mauritania	1

SOURCES: Data are taken from U.S. Agency for International Development, Statistics and Reports Division, *U.S. Overseas Loans and Grants and Assistance from International Organizations, July 1, 1945–June 30, 1973*; United Nations, *Demographic Yearbook*.

Table 3-9
The Forty Countries with Lowest Gross Domestic Product Per Capita

Afghanistan	60
Botswana	150
Burma	97
Burundi	55
Cambodia	124
Cameroon	188
Central African Republic	127
Chad	67
Dahomey	81
Ethiopia	66
Gambia	123
Guinea	80
Haiti	88
India	94
Indonesia	92
Kenya	134
Laos	65
Lesotho	64
Madagascar	131
Malawi	68
Mali	54
Mauritania	170
Nepal	78
Niger	97
Nigeria	99
Pakistan	128
Rwanda	53
Sierra Leone	176
Somalia	65
South Vietnam	194
Sri Lanka	162
Sudan	110
Tanzania	93
Thailand	178
Togo	148
Uganda	123
Upper Volta	67
Yemen, Dem. Rep. of	56
Yemen, Dem.	97
Zaire	85

SOURCES: Data are taken from *UN Yearbook of National Accounts Statistics* (New York: United Nations, various years), and *Statesman's Yearbook* (New York: St. Martin's Press, 1978). Data are estimated in U.S. dollars for fiscal or calendar year 1969, a representative year for the period covered in this study.

Table 3-10
U.S. Loans and Grants for Military Assistance on a Per Capita Basis,
1946-1973

1. South Vietnam	$914
2. Israel	477
3. Laos	437
4. Taiwan	284
5. Greece	260
6. Norway	229
7. South Korea	216
8. Belgium-Luxembourg	126
9. Denmark	125
10. Turkey	120
11. Jordan	119
12. Netherlands	105
13. Cambodia	101
14. France	89
15. Iran	55
16. Italy	46
17. Saudi Arabia	42
18. Thailand	38
19. Portugal	38
20. Yugoslavia	37
21. Spain	26
22. Chile	23
23. Philippines	22
24. Uruguay	20
25. United Kingdom	20
26. Lebanon	17
27. Austria	17
28. Fed. Rep. of Germany	16
29. Venezuela	15
30. Ecuador	13

SOURCES: Data are taken from U.S. Agency for International Development, Statistics and Reports Division, *U.S. Overseas Loans and Grants and Assistance from International Organizations, July 1, 1945-June 30, 1973*; United Nations, *Demographic Yearbook*.

These trends were also evident in a simple country-by-country analysis, on a *non*-per capita basis. Of the states receiving the most bilateral development grants from AID and predecessor agencies from 1949 to 1974, India ranked eighteenth, even though India's needs exceeded those of each of the states receiving higher United States priority.[129] Why should the national governments of Thailand, Spain, Austria, the United Kingdom, or Laos, for example, have received more grant aid than India?

These data also demonstrate no correspondence between the ability of a country to repay aid and the inclination of United States officials to extend grants as opposed to loans. The fact that the United Kingdom received nearly seven and a half times as much grant assistance as India demonstrated the racial, national, and cultural limits of United States generosity.[130] In sharp contrast, total development loans to India ($3,296 million) by 1974 were roughly comparable in amount to grants to the United Kingdom ($3,450 million), whereas grants to India ($461 million) were somewhat similar in amount to loans to Britain ($385 million).[131]

Many other European countries, which were better able than India to repay loans, received grants greatly in excess of those going to India. To be sure, much of the aid for European countries helped reconstruction after World War II. (None of the figures in this analysis include postwar relief, in contrast to reconstruction.) Yet the needs of India following its struggle for independence and the civil strife and partition with Pakistan were not less than those of postwar Europe. Any determination of aid policy that was based on ability to repay loans—ignoring, for the moment, humanitarian concern—would never have resulted in the allocation of more grants to the rich than the poor.

Clearly, those countries receiving more aid than India—even on a non-per capita basis—represented client states of the United States, such as Taiwan, Thailand, South Korea, and South Vietnam, or military allies, such as the Federal Republic of Germany, France, the United Kingdom, Pakistan, Turkey, and Greece (Table 3-3). The one exception was neutral Austria, which received its assistance during the Marshall Plan and while Austria was still a bone of contention between the United States and the Soviet Union.

The high levels of economic aid received by South Vietnam, South Korea, and other client states casts doubt on the extent to which most economic aid is categorically different from military aid, even though it is spent on nonmilitary items.[132] From 1954 to 1958, South Korea received more economic aid (in addition to enormous military aid) than all of India, Pakistan, the Philippines, Burma, and Ceylon combined.[133] During the same period, even before the more direct United States military involvement in Laos and the southern segment of Vietnam, those governments received grants and loans almost equal in sum to those received by India and Pakistan, which had populations exceeding Laos and South Vietnam by over 450 million, or more than twice the total population of the United States. In 1966 alone, Vietnam received almost twice as much AID assistance as any other country of the world.[134] In the first two years following the January 1973 ceasefire in Vietnam, U.S. aid in all forms (military and economic) to Indochina was $8.2 billion,[135] or more than twice the total loan and grant commitments to India from AID and predecessor agencies for the entire period from 1949 to 1974.

Just as building military power dominated the humanitarian motive for aid, when a conflict arose between serving humanitarian interests and U.S. economic interests, the humanitarian concern again had lower priority. Despite U.S. wealth, the amount of development aid supplied by the United States has fallen short of the capital flows asked by the United Nations,[136] and compares unfavorably with the aid records of other industrialized states in the Organization for Economic Cooperation and Development (OECD).[137] Of sixteen members of OECD, the United States ranked twelfth. On the basis of aid commitments as percentage of GNP, only Japan, Switzerland, Italy, and Austria performed more poorly than the United States.[138]

In contrast, the newly rich grantors of aid, members of OPEC (Organization of Petroleum Exporting Countries), did much better than the United States. Aid-giving oil exporters contributed 1.8 percent of their gross national product in 1974. In 1975, the major OPEC donors were giving 2 percent of their GNP, and Kuwait, the oldest Arab donor, contributed 6 percent of its GNP. The United States was among only four Western countries that rejected, as too high, an international aid target of 0.7 percent of their GNP for official development assistance.[139] Moreover, nearly 40 percent of OPEC aid went to what the United Nations called "the most seriously affected countries," the poorest of the poor. Only 28 percent of Western aid went to that group.[140]

When United States official development assistance of all kinds to all countries is added together, the amount in constant dollars has declined by 50 percent over the last 15 years. During this period, U.S. GNP climbed by more than 20 percent. In 1977, for each dollar of GNP, the United States committed itself to spend .24 percent, or about one-fourth of one cent to help all the developing countries.[141] Even this tiny figure exaggerates

169

Table 3-11

Official Development Assistance in Relation to Gross National Product, 1962-1975

Countries	1962	1963	1964	1965	1966	1967	1968	1969	1970	1971	1972	1973	1974	1975
Australia	0.43	0.51	0.48	0.53	0.53	0.60	0.57	0.56	0.59	0.53	0.61	0.44	0.55	0.61
Austria	0.03	0.05	0.08	0.11	0.12	0.14	0.14	0.11	0.07	0.07	0.09	0.14	0.18	0.17
Belgium	0.54	0.57	0.46	0.60	0.42	0.45	0.42	0.50	0.46	0.50	0.55	0.51	0.51	0.59
Canada	0.09	0.15	0.17	0.19	0.33	0.32	0.26	0.33	0.42	0.42	0.47	0.43	0.50	0.58
Denmark	0.10	0.11	0.11	0.13	0.19	0.21	0.23	0.38	0.38	0.43	0.45	0.47	0.55	0.58
France	1.27	0.98	0.90	0.76	0.69	0.71	0.67	0.67	0.66	0.66	0.67	0.58	0.59	0.62
Germany	0.45	0.41	0.44	0.40	0.34	0.41	0.41	0.38	0.32	0.34	0.31	0.32	0.37	0.40
Italy	0.18	0.14	0.09	0.10	0.12	0.22	0.19	0.16	0.16	0.18	0.08	0.14	0.14	0.11
Japan	0.14	0.20	0.14	0.27	0.28	0.31	0.25	0.26	0.23	0.23	0.21	0.25	0.25	0.24
Netherlands	0.49	0.26	0.29	0.36	0.45	0.49	0.49	0.50	0.61	0.58	0.67	0.54	0.63	0.75
Norway	0.14	0.17	0.15	0.16	0.18	0.17	0.29	0.30	0.32	0.33	0.41	0.46	0.57	0.66
Portugal	1.26	1.46	1.48	0.59	0.54	0.54	0.54	1.29	0.67	1.42	1.91	0.59	a	a
Sweden	0.12	0.14	0.18	0.19	0.25	0.25	0.28	0.43	0.38	0.44	0.48	0.56	0.72	0.82
Switzerland	0.05	0.05	0.07	0.09	0.09	0.08	0.14	0.16	0.15	0.12	0.22	0.16	0.15	0.18
United Kingdom	0.52	0.48	0.53	0.47	0.45	0.44	0.40	0.39	0.37	0.41	0.40	0.35	0.38	0.37
United States	0.56	0.59	0.56	0.49	0.44	0.43	0.37	0.33	0.31	0.32	0.29	0.23	0.24	0.26
Total DAC Countries	0.52	0.51	0.48	0.44	0.41	0.42	0.37	0.36	0.34	0.35	0.34	0.30		

SOURCE: OECD, *Development Assistance Efforts and Policies, 1973 Review*, p. 189; *1974 Review*, p. 116; *1976 Review*, p. 206.
NOTE: a Not available.

American generosity. As noted earlier, when aid is properly adjusted for factors such as the repayment of loans and the tying of aid by source, the real cost of aid to the United States is reduced by 55 to 70 percent of the nominal figures. With or without the adjustment that economists suggest,[142] the amount of aid is so small a portion of the GNP that it can hardly be called a "burden" at all.

The United States contributed aid in a more generous and genuinely humanitarian spirit (2 percent of GNP) during the Marshall Plan when the sharing of wealth was among the relatively rich, than after the Marshall Plan when the sharing (.2 percent of GNP) was with the poor, who were also nonwhite and culturally different from U.S. officials. For example, in 1949, when United States gross national product was $257 billion, the United States committed $5.5 billion to foreign assistance for the Marshall Plan. After twenty-five years, the gross national product had quintupled, but foreign aid, then going to the relatively poor, had shrunk by more than one-third.

An accurate picture of the relationship between United States wealth and its effort to help the poor is portrayed by constructing an aid burden index in which yearly total grant and loan commitments for development assistance are divided by the gross national product per capita, as shown in Table 3-12. The aid burden index in 1974 was only one-twelfth of its level in 1949, even though during that same period the gross national product increased by five times. (See Figure 3-1.) These data include, one should recall, AID economic assistance to military client states, such as South Vietnam, South Korea, Laos, and Cambodia. If the index were to account only for aid going into economic development more narrowly defined, it would be substantially lower.

When sharing more than 2 percent of its GNP with Europe, the United States asked European states to decide their own plans for development and the United States pledged to support them. When sharing .24 of 1 percent of its GNP with less developed countries, the United States hedged its support with self-serving restrictions. After World War II, the United States government permitted Europe to discriminate against its exports, overcoming strong business pressures at home to avoid excessive profit-taking on European problems.[143] In India, the United States government has insisted that aid serve the profit motive of U.S. exporters.[144] The United States has refused to forego even

171

Table 3-12
Aid Burden Index[a] for Total Commitments to All Countries
By AID and Predecessor Agencies

Fiscal Year	Aid Burden Index[a]	U.S. GNP	Loans	Grants
		millions of dollars		
1949	3.22	256500	1165	4352
1950	1.93	284800	163	3451
1951	1.24	328400	45	2577
1952	0.91	345500	201	1784
1953	0.86	364600	26	1934
1954	1.00	364800	114	2114
1955	0.76	398000	197	1624
1956	0.61	419200	208	1298
1957	0.63	441100	322	1305
1958	0.63	447300	417	1202
1959	0.70	483700	626	1291
1960	0.67	503700	564	1302
1961	0.71	520100	707	1315
1962	0.84	560300	1330	1180
1963	0.74	590500	1346	954
1964	0.65	632400	1333	808
1965	0.58	684900	1129	904
1966	0.67	749900	1228	1326
1967	0.56	793900	1091	1162
1968	0.44	864200	929	963
1969	0.32	930300	570	879
1970	0.35	977100	680	988
1971	0.33	1055500	608	1091
1972	0.37	1155200	625	1446
1973	0.33	1294900	664	1338
1974	0.27	1397400	519	1290
1975	0.35	1516000	809	1710
1976	0.30	1692000	857	1476

SOURCES: GNP data were taken from *Economic Report of the President* (Washington, D.C.: Government Printing Office, 1974, 1976). Population data are from United Nations, *Demographic Yearbook*, various years. Data for total loan and grant commitments for development assistance were taken from U.S. Agency for International Development, *U.S. Economic Assistance Programs Administered by the Agency for International Development and Predecessor Agencies, April 3, 1948-June 30, 1971*; after 1971, U.S. Agency for International Development, *U.S. Overseas Loans and Grants and Assistance from International Organizations*, various years.
NOTES: [a] Aid Burden Index = (total annual commitments for grants and loans to all countries from AID and predecessor agencies)/(U.S. GNP per capita).

relatively minor trade advantages in commercial intercourse with India, even though this stance doubtless harms Indian economic planning and development. Two-thirds of the aid to Europe was in outright grants; less than one-seventh of development aid to India was in grants. During the aid program to Europe, U.S. officials were inclined to ask: what do recipients need? For aid to less developed countries, officials have tended to ask: what return will the United States receive? When the United States was most generous in giving aid, its programs were also less selfish in their techniques of execution.

Perhaps a Senate study on technical assistance best sums up the normative foundation upon which United States development aid has been based:

> . . . the sole test of technical assistance is the national interest of the United States. Technical assistance is not something to be done, as a Government enterprise, for its own sake or for the sake of others. The United States Government is not a charitable institution, nor is it an appropriate outlet for the charitable spirit of the American people. . . . the cost of any foreign activity of the United States becomes significant only when it is related to the benefits which the United States receives from that activity.[145]

Were it not for U.S. military activity, fear of political instability, or a perceived threat of a disliked ideology, there would have been little, if any, reallocation of wealth to the developing countries at all. The amount of aid has been determined more by assumed military needs and economic self-interest than by a humanitarian desire to reform the global economic and political structures that perpetuate poverty.[146]

While the average per capita income in the United States has been more than 40 times that of India, while the annual increase in the goods and services produced in the United States during some years equalled *all* the goods and services produced annually in India,[147] while the number of Indians living below the rock-bottom Indian poverty line of $60 per year has exceeded the total population of the United States, while the United States annually has absorbed 40 percent of the world's annual energy output and nonrenewable resources,[148] and while a substantial portion of this wealth has originated from the less developed countries, the United States in the last decade has granted to India about three cents a year for each U.S. citizen. Surely it

173

Figure 3-1
Total U.S. Grant and Loan Commitments to All Countries as Ratio of U.S.
GNP per Capita

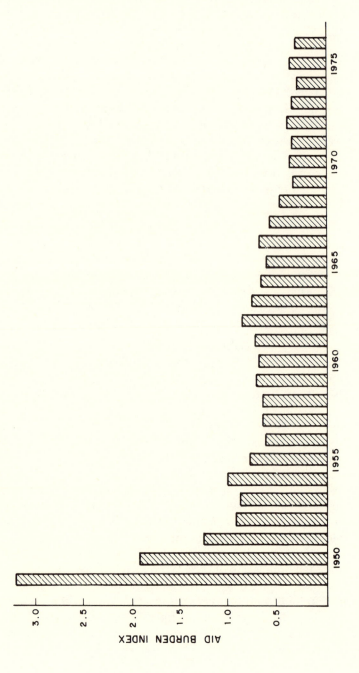

Figure 3-2
Comparison of U.S. and Indian GNP per Capita in Constant 1972 Dollars

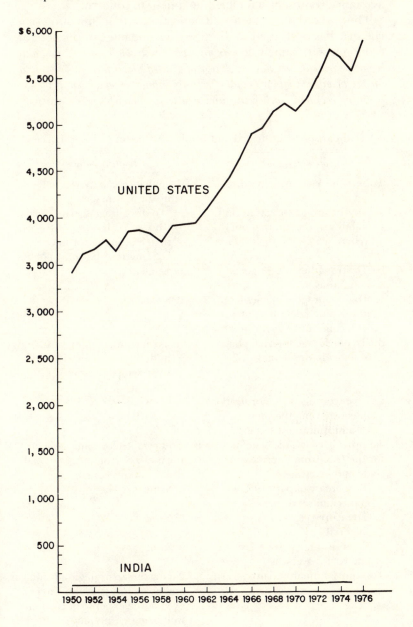

stretches the bounds of credibility to suggest that such a level of assistance represents tangible humanitarian concern.[149]

The preceding evidence demonstrates that humanitarian rhetoric has been used to disguise the fundamental purpose of economic aid: namely, *to maximize power, strategic advantages, and economic benefits for those in charge of United States foreign policy and for the privileged minority that effectively supports them, even at the expense of economic well-being and equity for other societies* (implicit

Table 3-13
A Comparison of Professed and Implicit Values in U.S. Aid Policies

Professed Values	Implicit Values
1. To serve U.S. security interests.	A. To enhance U.S. power and strategic advantages.
a. To discourage threats to the stability of the international system.	a. To discourage social reformers who would be less sympathetic than existing governments to U.S. interests in world politics.
b. To strengthen allies against communism.	b. Same.
c. To discourage nonallies from developing friendly relations with communist governments.	c. Same.
d. To encourage internal political stability in developing countries.	d. To encourage internal stability in developing countries that were sympathetic to U.S. interests.
e. To encourage a demonstration effect showing the superiority of noncommunist systems.	e. Same.
2. To provide economic benefits for the U.S. from international trade and investment.	B. To promote economic benefits for the U.S. from international trade and investment.
a. To increase exports of U.S. goods and services.	a. Same.
b. To insure access to raw materials.	b. Same.
c. To encourage private enterprise overseas.	c. Same.
3. To express humanitarian concern.	C. To maximize strategic advantages and economic gains for the U.S. even at the expense of economic well-being, equity, and compassion for other societies.

176

value C). To be sure, some sincere persons had humanitarian motives in favoring foreign assistance. But there can be no doubt that the values cumulatively expressed in actual aid programs failed to include both a sense of urgency about structural change and a meaningful concern by the relatively rich, U.S. segment of the world's population for meeting the basic human needs of the world's poor.

A GLOBAL HUMANIST APPROACH

The final portion of this chapter will compare the values implicitly expressed in United States foreign assistance policy with the second value of global humanism, namely the maximization of economic well-being for all persons on the planet. If one assumes this value position, it is evident that substantial redistribution of wealth throughout the globe is imperative. Regardless of how one figures personal incomes and basic costs for a decent livelihood, there is no persuasive normative justification for the vast income and consumption differentials that exist between the people of the United States and the people of India.

Universal Minimum Standard of Living

All human beings deserve an equitable opportunity to acquire the basic essentials for physical existence. These include sufficient food, shelter, clothing, medical care, and educational opportunities to achieve some degree of human fulfillment without chronic anxiety about continuing existence. Until all persons of the globe are fed, there can be no compelling justification for color television sets, conspicuous consumption, or other luxuries that absorb scarce energies and resources which, from a global standpoint, are in short supply. Although controversy may surround the debate about whether one person's luxury is another's necessity, there need be little debate about the glaring inequity of enormous expenditures by the wealthy minority of the world's population that lives in the United States and other industrialized nations and the inability of a majority of people on earth to buy the minimum requirements for a healthy physical existence. Such requirements can, to a satisfactory degree, be objectively defined.

Attention also should be given to the more difficult issue of what constitutes an equitable sharing of resources globally, over and above a minimum for existence, but that troublesome ques-

177

tion need not detain us much at present. Current efforts should be aimed at the less controversial goal of insuring that every person on the globe has a minimum standard of living to meet the necessities for survival. During the second stage of transition toward realizing the values of global humanism, the emphasis should shift from building an income floor for overcoming poverty and establishing minimal human decency, toward constructing greater economic equity and human justice.

Critics of the relatively modest proposal presented here for a universal minimum standard of living will argue with some justification that resources should not be sent abroad while some Americans still suffer from malnutrition. The strength of this argument and the presence of widespread poverty in the United States reveal further, of course, the extent to which humanitarianism is absent from the United States political process even domestically. For millions of Americans to be living in poverty—not as a temporary phenomenon, but as a permanent subculture—is morally outrageous in a society as rich and wasteful as the United States.

The opponents of a universal minimum standard of living are likely to be the same people who oppose elimination of poverty and income equalization within the United States. The importance of this understanding is to illustrate the genuine, common interests between advocates in this country of the universal minimum standard of living and people in the less developed countries who together can work against the political forces that seek to perpetuate the political and economic status quo. There is, in short, a potentially strong moral and practical bond between advocates of global humanism, regardless of nationality, and the dispossessed people of the world, whether in the United States or India. It is this commonality which could provide the basis for a genuinely multinational movement for world order reform.

Empowering the Dispossessed

The values of global humanism suggest another major departure from past aid programs. It is important not merely to share wealth equitably enough to achieve a universal minimum standard of living, but also to share participation in decision making about how the resources of the world should be utilized. On the one hand, it is economically intolerable for 6 percent of the world's population living in the United States to consume 40 percent of the world's raw materials and energy resources, because such disproportionate consumption deprives others of reaching the universal minimum standard of living; on the other hand, it is politically intolerable to allow a small number of the world's people to make the decisive determination of how to use the resources that belong to many more. The existing political structure of the world is unjust in failing to allow all persons to participate fairly in the decisions that affect the use of the resources of the planet. That structure is presently tipped far in the direction of giving the United States more influence on decisions than equity dictates.

A second reason for sharing decision-making authority more widely is that wealth redistribution is politically infeasible without wide sharing of power. Historically, whether in the nineteenth century extension of the franchise in Britain or in the recent civil rights movement in the United States, poor people have sought greater participation in the political process as a means for achieving more economic egalitarianism. The dispossessed could not achieve redistribution of wealth without extension of the franchise. To equalize the distribution of wealth in the world, it is necessary to equalize the distribution of power. Conversely, when wealth is to some extent redistributed, as it was after the oil-exporting states raised the price of oil, power begins to shift as well. In short, substantial foreign aid is unlikely to come merely by cajoling the American electorate to "give" more to others. Equalization of wealth will come when the "others" become a part of the decision-making process for allocating wealth.

The above changes, of course, cannot occur without the spread in the United States of a political consciousness that emphasizes the solidarity of all human beings, not just of United States citizens; that seeks to promote the well-being of all humans, not just the security and wealth of the privileged in the United States; that aims at the service of human needs, not the maximizing of profit through production of goods that fail to contribute to human health, safety, or welfare.

Contrasting Value Orientations

IMPLICIT VALUES AND FUTURE TRENDS

By rejecting policies aimed at realization of global socioeconomic welfare, U.S. officials have also impeded the implementation of the other three world order values. If past U.S. policies continue, one can expect these consequences in the various value areas:

(V_1) Social unrest and both repressive and revolutionary uses of violence will doubtless accompany the conflict between rich and poor societies, as well as between rich and poor classes within a given society. Terrorism will increase. Military power will be used to protect the nonsharing wealthy from change and to keep the poor powerless.

(V_2) Structural changes leading to the elimination of poverty will not occur. The gap between rich and poor will grow.

(V_3) Economic inequities defended through repression will perpetuate injustice and unequal opportunity for human fulfillment. Many persons will starve; many others will live without dignity and without being able to use their creative abilities.

(V_4) Overconsumption and wasting of nonrenewable resources by wealthy, overdeveloped, and misdeveloped countries will prevent the reasoned diminishing of pollution, the conservation of resources, and the concentration of productive capacity upon necessities (such as food) for human survival. In short, there are striking contrasts between the values expressed in United States foreign aid policy and the four values of global humanism. (See Table 3-14.)

WORLD ORDER RHETORIC

One difficulty in reforming U.S. aid policies is that occasionally official rhetoric, unlike official practice, closely resembles the values of global humanism. Governmental and corporate spokesmen have used enough language of global concern to convince some constituencies that the United States acts with unusual magnanimity in its development assistance. This inaccurate perception undermines efforts to bring about fundamental change in aid programs. Meanwhile, officials engage in little follow-through to implement their lofty rhetoric.

In recent years, officials of both the Nixon-Ford and Carter administrations have occasionally spoken of the need to take account of a global interest. Secretary Kissinger stressed the need for global cooperation to prevent the breakdown of the international order. Jimmy Carter declared that "we must replace balance-of-power politics with world-order politics." Secretary Vance said that the United States was ready to help build a new economic system that was, above all, just.[150]

Table 3-14 (cont.)

Global Humanism	*U.S. Policy*

Ecological Balance

1. Past and present policies have pro-
ced ecologically dangerous world pri-
ties. Industrial states are over-
veloped or misdeveloped. Continued
planned economic growth poses
eats to survival from unnecessary pol-
ion and resource depletion. Con-
ued poverty and illiteracy in the less
veloped countries make population
nning difficult.

1. Global economic priorities are not
viewed as a major contributor to environmental problems. While growing
attention is paid to environmental questions, there is a reluctance to take international action based on the assumption
that the industrial nations are consum-
ing too much, or endangering human
life by failing to regulate their economic
growth in the interest of serving first the
human needs of all.

Yet, regardless of rhetoric, the United States has not gone far
toward helping create a more just and economically rational
economic order. Officials have made no statement that the
amount of resources consumed by the United States has been
disproportionate, unfair, or has contributed to human misery in
other parts of the world. Also, proposals for fairer pricing and
decision making in global economic relations have been repeatedly rejected. The United States has shown no embarrassment in its desire to take resources from both the less developed
countries and the high seas—once declared the "common heritage" of humankind—to enhance its own wealth.

After examining United States aid to India for a quarter of a
century, one must also be skeptical about government intentions
to engage in any genuine redistribution of the world's wealth.
Public opinion about foreign assistance over the long run has
been roughly balanced between favorable and unfavorable attitudes toward aid among the general public. One recent survey
showed that 79 percent of U.S. citizens favored development assistance when they believed that the aid actually reached the
people for whom it is intended.[151] Thus, the leadership could
have provided much more aid, presumably, if it had chosen to
do so.

Finally, the expression of concern for global, as distinct from
strictly national well-being, usually has rested upon an implicit
assumption that what is good for the United States is good for
the world. The United States government is concerned about

183

maintaining a system of global order and stability in order to protect its own presently privileged position.[152] As a result, "despite high-minded rhetoric," says Senator Mark Hatfield, "our Government has sat on its bureaucratic hands while millions eke out a malnourished existence or starve."[153] In fact, past aid programs and the official rhetoric of global concern mask a policy that seeks to enlist the rest of the globe in the service of United States special privilege.

Since the maintenance of a privileged share of the world's wealth and decision-making power by the United States is a major obstacle to the realization of V_2, one must consider the possibility that continuing past aid policies may be less progressive than abolishing the aid program altogether. Full consideration of that possibility is beyond the scope of this study, and such a conclusion is likely to be more accurate for some aid recipients than others. Nonetheless, it is instructive to examine several arguments against foreign aid in general.

RADICAL PERSPECTIVES

First, radical critics point out that aid may encourage economic and political stability when the imperative is for change. Aid has on occasion fortified elitist governments in the underdeveloped countries against the mobilizing lower classes intent upon major reform.

Aid to some countries has made them dependent upon continued U.S. assistance and subjected them to U.S. political influence. This dependency has enabled the United States to influence internal politics sufficiently to serve U.S. interests and prevent the radical socioeconomic change necessary for realization of V_2. To be sure, in subtle and complicated ways, the United States has sought to influence Indian affairs. AID officials point out that their efforts usually were designed to encourage Indian development, but their vision of development always encompassed a largely United States-dominated world of capitalist enterprises. Even when U.S. AID officials' suggestions may have been economically rational from the Indian point of view, they were irritating to Indians because of Indian self-consciousness about being economically vulnerable to pressures by capital exporting nations.[154] The net result of this relationship among unequals has not encouraged generous assistance nor greater economic equity. Paternalism, even when well-intentioned and well-received, leads to results that are qualitatively different from the results that arise from equal participation in decisions about how to use the world's wealth.

In the mid-1960s, for example, the United States directly, as well as through the World Bank and International Monetary Fund (IMF), pressed the Indian government to devalue the rupee. U.S. AID officials believed that devaluation plus increased aid would help solve India's economic difficulties. However, after Indian compliance with U.S. requests, U.S. aid decreased, in part because so much money was spent for the war in Vietnam.[155] As former AID official John Lewis commented, U.S. aid to India seemed inversely correlated with the worthiness of the recipient.[156] Devaluing the rupee, of course, lowered the price of Indian goods for U.S. purchasers, and it provided a more profitable field for U.S. investment.

The United States has, through multilateral financial institutions and bilateral aid negotiations, persuaded many less developed countries at various times to devalue their currencies to combat inflation and to facilitate foreign private investment. By improving the climate for U.S. investment and increasing the dollar's buying power abroad, such policies have effectively foreclosed some alternatives for autonomous national development, thus slowing the achievement of economic independence in the long run. And, some critics point out, economic dependency has contributed to the perpetuation of an international economic system featuring U.S. wealth and the poverty of the less developed nations.[157]

Furthermore, aid opponents argue that as long as U.S. capital goes primarily to nonsocialist economic structures, it will inevitably be used for the production of goods that maximize profits. That means producing goods for which there is a demand generated by those with money to buy goods. Other persons too poor to create demand will continue, under such an economic system, to have many of their most fundamental needs ignored. As Herbert Feldman has observed, in some poverty-ridden cities on the Asian subcontinent, more time, money, and effort have been expended in providing popular (and profitable) brands of fizzy drinks than in providing a hygienic milk supply.[158] The wealthy can buy Coke, but the poor lack means to generate demand for milk. In short, if maximizing profits determines what will be produced, then even with the influx of new foreign capi-

185

tal, the poor will doubtless remain poor. Historically, the aid program has demonstrated a fundamental contradiction between maximizing private profit and serving human needs.[159]

The U.S. desire for profitability has slowed autonomous economic development in India to some degree. In the early years of foreign aid, the United States resisted the idea that Indians should manufacture items such as machinery or chemicals because that would have deprived U.S. producers of markets in India and brought new competition in other world markets.[160] U.S. aid also skewed some economic decisions in the direction of capital intensive industries[161] when labor intensive projects might have been wiser. The latter form of Indian self-sufficiency, however, would have been less profitable for U.S. producers.

It was, perhaps, a sign of the arrogance of wealth to assume without any question that the less developed countries were better off with U.S. aid than without it. The Chinese model provides a unique but instructive exception to aid recipients, insofar as it has had no substantial outside assistance, and thus is not burdened with heavy loan repayments. Yet, the Chinese government has done far better than many less developed countries in serving human needs of food, clothing, housing, and medical care. Radical political economists note that instead of investing where the rate of return was greatest, as occurs in capitalist development, the Chinese sought to eradicate poverty. They focused on what to produce and for whom, not on how quickly they could produce goods to earn foreign exchange.[162]

To the extent that U.S. foreign assistance has discouraged internal and global structural change, influenced Indian politics toward serving U.S. present and future economic interests at the expense of domestic equity, inhibited the growth of either genuine economic self-sufficiency or interdependency among equals, to that degree it has been imperialistic. So many difficulties attend the bilateral transfer of capital from rich societies to economically less powerful societies that some critics believe that the process is often damaging to the recipient.[163] If humanity is one, then any unilaterally determined, disproportionate use of the world's resources by one society can be viewed as imperialistic. In a world of scarcity, for some to consume more than they need while others have less than they need means one society enjoys privilege at the other's expense, sacrifice, and misery.

Elements of an imperialistic mentality have been present even among some well-intentioned liberal advocates of foreign assistance. They have often overlooked structural origins of poverty. For example, the Pearson Commission concluded that "the major external constraint [for economic development] may be summed up as the availability of foreign exchange."[164] Yet, the reason Indians need foreign exchange is that the prices paid for their exports are too low in comparison to the prices paid for their imports, chiefly manufactured goods and food. There is nothing inherently virtuous about the setting of those prices. They are a product of the configuration of political and economic power in the world, not of any conception of justice. If global political self-determination could suddenly be realized, no doubt the world's people would change the pricing structure. But the United States, as the largest producer of manufactured goods and food for export, has refused to alter those prices in the interest of the poor at the same time that it has used its military strength and covert CIA activities to inhibit a more influential exercise of power by the world's poor.[165]

The imperialistic element in aid policies springs from the assumption that what Americans have is in fact their possession. Yet the sources of wealth (or poverty) are somewhat arbitrary, and historical accidents often determine whether one society is richer than another. To the extent that economic affairs are not arbitrary and are under human control, the wealth of rich societies often has been—whether intentionally or unintentionally—deprived from the poor because the poor were less powerful.

This idea was illustrated by U.S. officials' response to the explosion of an Indian nuclear device. They expressed dismay, and accused the Indians of wasting their scarce resources.[166] Some officials urged a reevaluation of U.S. aid to India as an expression of displeasure, but aid was at the time almost nonexistent, so that potential political lever was absent. Meanwhile, the U.S. government saw nothing wrong with continued United States explosion of nuclear devices. However, if a sense of human solidarity had motivated U.S. officials, they would have understood that the scarcity of Indian resources should impinge as much on the conscience of U.S. officials as they argued it should have on Indian officials. From a planetary perspective, the wasting of global resources on United States nuclear development hurt the Indian poor as much as a similar Indian use of resources.

187

THREE · *Foreign Aid to India*

One might even argue that the Indian effort, unlike U.S. nuclear development, could possibly give India more political power through which to achieve greater global economic equity. Insofar as the acquisition of power by the weak has been a key to more equitable distribution of wealth, the Indian nuclear explosion—deplorable though it was in terms of V_1—seemed a symbolic statement that V_1 could hardly be realized if V_2 were ignored. Significantly, the United States has objected to other states acquiring equality in nuclear power as much as it has refused to share its wealth globally as a matter of human right. By opposing economic justice and nuclear proliferation, U.S. officials have sought to perpetuate both their economic and military advantages. In pursuing this policy, however, officials have actually encouraged nuclear proliferation. The governments of the less developed countries can recognize that U.S. political and economic preeminence have been mutually reinforcing. Thus, in the effort to overturn U.S.-sponsored global economic inequities, poor states will be inclined to erode, through partial imitation of U.S. military might, the expensive military capabilities by which the United States retains its economic position, wasteful though such expenditures might otherwise be.

In short, radical critiques of U.S. foreign aid policies alert us to the counterproductive consequences of many past aid programs. One need not fully agree with these critiques to understand that, in the Indian case, even if the aid program had been allowed to develop according to the direction featured in its best years, it would have had little redistributive content meaningful for world order reform. Aid tended to be limited philanthropy, largely irrelevant to structural economic transformation.

The well-known liberal Under Secretary of State, George Ball, accurately reported that the goal of U.S. foreign aid policies was neither to remove nor even to narrow the gap between the rich "North" of the planet and the poor "South." "[I]n spite of the hyperbole of political speeches, we are not going to reduce the disparity in wealth between North and South. In the face of all our foreign efforts, that disparity has been growing and it will continue to grow. . . . With luck the poor will get richer, but the rich will, in absolute terms, get richer much faster."[167]

Redistribution of Wealth

A foreign policy truly aimed at achieving V_2 should consider discontinuing all programs designed to serve short-range national security and economic interests of the United States as these have been traditionally defined. These interests are worthy of support only if they are redefined to give priority to long-term considerations of human security and global economic needs. Such redefinition would free policymakers from the past chronic tension between national security and human compassion; it would allow political prudence to converge with moral principle.

Policymakers should consider replacing all existing aid programs with an alternative program based upon the frank assumption that a universal minimum standard of living is a human right. In the absence of its achievement, existing income inequities of forty or fifty to one are morally and politically wrong. If a universal minimum standard of living is a matter of right, aid should not be considered a gift. Income redistribution is required because the resources of the world belong to the people of the world.

If one proceeds from this assumption, income redistribution should not be curtailed or halted if India criticizes United States foreign policy, if India refuses to be a military ally, or if Indian ideologies are dissimilar to American. What matters is that Indians are human beings every bit as much as Americans. When, in a world of scarcity, there is insufficient food to nourish everyone, then all nationalities should bear equally the burden of insufficiency and any requisite decrease in life expectancy.

From this vantage point, aid should not be tailored to buy friends, to stimulate demand for United States goods, nor to alleviate a United States balance of payments problem. Income redistribution aimed at global equity can be justified both for friend and "enemy" simply to achieve minimal essentials of life for all human beings. If aid were justified on these grounds, debate would not focus on "who are our friends?" but instead on "what are the minimum requirements for life which are a matter of responsibility for all members of the world community?"

Larger amounts of aid might be forthcoming if the government refused to justify aid in terms of contributing to United States security and instead made a frank, humanitarian appeal for global justice. Past programs have been intellectually deceptive and politically self-defeating in their claim to aid development and at the same time serve the strategic interests of the United States. If a program failed to produce strategic dividends, then aid was curtailed.[168]

To grasp the philosophical underpinnings of the approach proposed here, it is useful to distinguish three general orientations toward aid. U.S. policy has been a combination of the first two. The advocate of a conservative policy generally has opposed foreign aid on the grounds that the rich deserve their wealth and the poor deserve their poverty. From this perspective, the main U.S. interest in assistance for India was strategic, and since aid failed to produce dividends, it should be terminated. The liberal view has favored limited aid to help persons less fortunate. Desiring "change within the system," liberals have sought to remodel it enough to perpetuate it and retain economic and political control largely in the same national hands. This has been a "charity mentality" based upon the trickle down theory of assistance, in which it was assumed that as the rich nations got richer, the poor would also improve their lot, but little attention was given to diminishing the gap between the two as an end in itself. In a world of scarcity and finite growth, however, the liberal vision is seriously challenged, because the rich can maintain their pace of material accumulation only if they refuse to divert needed resources to eliminating poverty.

A third perspective, represented by V_2, calls for a strategy in which the purpose of political and economic activity should be to help first those people in the worst conditions. This view bases the argument for aid not only on a sense of moral obligation to help the poor survive, but more firmly on a concept of justice that affirms a humane existence based upon equal opportunity as a matter of right. Adherents advocate structural change, not only to eliminate economic inequities, but also to share power widely so that the presently dispossessed may participate in decisions about allocation of planetary resources.

The difference between what I have called the liberal, charity mentality and the idea of structural reform can perhaps be best understood by drawing an analogy from the United States civil rights movement in the 1960s. Liberals espoused civil rights as long as the goal was congenial-sounding "integration," which often meant in practice that blacks would join white society. Some of the same liberals experienced deep, negative, emotional reactions when the goal of civil rights groups became "black power." Already we have forgotten how serious were the debates among liberals about the extent to which black power was tinged with tones of black supremacy and intimidation of whites. Whites were threatened when blacks asked for power because then blacks asked not merely to join white society, but to exercise power in determining what that society would be and how it should be structured.

Similarly, liberal advocates of foreign aid have been willing to share a relatively small amount of surplus wealth with the poor states who were willing to "join," in effect, the U.S. model of international society and capitalist values. But many liberals have resisted the idea that Indians (and others) actually have a right to determine what to do with that part of "United States wealth" that exceeds the rightful share of the people who happen to live in the United States. Like liberals uneasy about black power in the 1960s, foreign aid liberals react to the idea of equal Indian power with emotional arguments of incredulity. For Indians to ask for an equal share of the world's pie, when the pie is finite, is viewed as dangerously destabilizing.

Given the dominance of the conservative and liberal perspectives in U.S. politics, is realization of economic well-being for all really feasible? It is not feasible given the prevailing attitudes and political forces in the United States today. Nevertheless, this alternative image is useful in the urgent effort to change attitudes and realign political forces so that its implementation may become feasible in the near future. Compared with past programs, the alternative suggested above certainly is no less "realistic" or effective even in serving some of the traditionally defined national interests; it is much more promising than current programs in serving the values of global humanism.

For example, past efforts to use aid to buy friendship and strategic advantage have worked poorly because these programs have not maximized development potential. Moreover, in retrospect it is clear that strategic goals have been shortsighted and counterproductive in some cases, due to the unpredictability of political forces. Often the United States has put its money on the wrong political horses. Much aid has contributed to dictatorships and military takeovers instead of to the service of human needs.[169]

In contrast, the aid approach suggested here would free policymakers from any necessity to make uncertain assessments about which potential pro-American political leaders might be the best future bets. Aid severed from the desire for strategic advantage makes it unnecesary to support domestic repression even in the short run in return for alliances. Aid would be designed to alleviate human suffering universally, instead of to

191

create political fortunes for clients of the United States. The United States could thus avoid making enemies or offending potential, yet-to-emerge foreign leaders by a discriminatory aid policy that can never fully predict nor control events.

Aid would not insult the governments of less developed countries by seeming to compromise their independence or their possible preference for non-American systems and ideologies. Such an aid perspective need not view all radical reformers as hostile to the United States, because the overriding goal would be to serve human needs instead of maintaining alliances or existing economic arrangements. Aid would not need to serve as a quasi-military holding action against social change, as it so often has in the past. Under this proposed approach, assistance could go much further in producing development, since investments could be spent for purchases from the economically most rational sources instead of from only the donating country's corporations. This approach, in addition, would decrease the likelihood of violent conflicts between rich and poor nations that may occur if the present distribution of wealth is perpetuated indefinitely. Thus, this alternative program holds substantial promise even in terms of contributing to global security.

Furthermore, the global humanist approach would, in the long run, enhance global prosperity insofar as it would greatly increase the productivity of human societies and eliminate the drag upon economic and social services of millions of persons living in poverty with resulting physical, educational, and mental impairments. It would help rich nations, such as the United States, (1) correct present misperceptions of the poor as undeserving of an equal share of wealth and power and (2) decrease the self-serving exploitation of the poor. Both of these problems, however unintentional, seem to be almost inevitable whenever wealth is seriously maldistributed in human societies.

An alternative aid program underscores the need for more policy coordination at the global level. The rich would be more willing to help implement income redistribution if in turn a central guidance network would facilitate meaningful efforts to relate population size to scarce resources. In addition, it is necessary to insure that wealth redistribution would be used to serve human needs rather than the repressive inclinations of some totalitarian systems. It seems reasonable that a degree of measurable performance in serving human needs should be a condition of income redistribution. In this sense, strings would be attached to aid, but the strings would be community-established, and would not be tied to serving the economic or strategic interests of the United States, as in current aid programs. The norms governing both income redistribution and population planning would be a product of global political processes.

Despite many warnings during the 1960s that the longer development problems were put off the more difficult would be their solution, the United States did not transform its assistance programs. They were "falling short at the very time when some of the most important, most promising, and hardest pressed of the developing nations are doing what they most need to do and when they can use far more aid than they are getting."[170] The decade of the 1960s was a crucial period in India's development plan because of the particular convergence of economic conditions, potential for unwanted population growth, and political moderation. One of the most knowledgeable aid officials in India, John P. Lewis, wrote in the early 1960s: "The massive expansion program to which India now is deeply committed is one whose momentum cannot be slowed much below its designed pace without grievously disrupting the economy."[171] Failure to achieve a minimal level of growth would place protracted and debilitating drains on India's foreign exchange, as well as waste psychological resources built during the first decade of independence.

Moreover, Lewis argued, political instability after the sixties and early seventies would doubtless be a growing problem if development did not progress at a pace that exceeded population growth. In the absence of rapid economic development during the sixties, Lewis warned, traditional subnational divisions would be increasingly expressed, disappointment and frustration might result in irreparable political breakdown. "India's still-novel constitutional habit would be broken, and there would be no assurance that she would find her way back to it from whatever pattern of authoritarianism intervened."[172] In little more than a decade after Lewis wrote, events confirmed his fears. By mid-1975, Indira Gandhi suspended civil liberties, silenced the press, and jailed the political opposition. The trickle of U.S. aid and Indian economic policies had failed to satisfy the internal demands for fairness and decency. Thus the Indian government—in a manner not unlike British responses to Mohandas Gandhi's call for civil disobedience—suppressed advocates of structural change in order to preserve stability.

193

The return to constitutional government in 1977 demonstrated the miscalculations of an authoritarian government as well as the resiliency of Indian democracy. But new elections did not solve any of India's economic problems nor change the uncongeniality of the present global economic and political structure to their solution.

Despite the warning signs, the United States has not made any real sacrifices in shouldering obligations for achieving economic equity and a life of decency throughout the world. Nor has the United States been willing to take substantial steps "to counteract the market forces that in the field of trade and capital movements have continuously been holding the underdeveloped countries down in poverty since colonial times."[173] The sharing with Indians by U.S. citizens of an average of less than ten cents per person per year over a twenty-seven year period reveals the need for a radical reversal of current policies.[174]

Indicators of World Order Progress

How can citizens assess progress or regress by their own government in constructing policies for redistribution of wealth? From our examination of United States foreign assistance to India and our discussion of an alternative approach, it is possible to suggest some indicators of the extent to which a rich country's aid policy is conducive to implementing the values of global humanism.

1. How firm are officials' commitments to establishing and implementing a universal minimum standard of living? What concrete steps have been taken in this direction?

2. How firm are officials' commitments to increasing participation of other societies in decisions about how to use the world's resources?

3. How firm are officials' commitments to decreasing a globally disproportionate share of resource usage by the rich nations? What concrete steps have been taken to decrease overconsumption, for example, of food and energy by the rich nations?

4. Is aid officially justified on grounds of, and in fact designed to serve, national security? Or to serve universal human needs?

a. Are political strings attached to recipients of aid in order to encourage them to become military allies? Or, is aid given as a matter of right to those below a minimum standard of living, regardless of their strategic alignment?

194

b. Does the commitment to a universal minimum standard of living include reasonable precautions to insure that aid in fact reaches the needy, instead of the rich elite in the less developed countries?

5. Is aid justified on grounds of, and designed to serve, the national economic benefit of the donor? Or to serve universal human needs?

a. Is aid tied to purchases from the donating country or instead freed for use where it is economically most rational?

b. To what extent is aid concessional?

c. Is aid designed to encourage inequitable economic systems that will allow further economic advantage for the foreign donor and possible exploitation of the less developed country? Or, is it designed to encourage the economically most rational division of labor globally?

6. To what extent does the level of aid represent a fair share of the global burden of wealth redistribution?[175]

a. Is official development assistance at least one percent of GNP?

b. Is aid per dollar of GNP increasing every year?

7. Are aid programs viewed as charity for helpless, somewhat less worthy people, or are they aimed at structural reform of the socioeconomic order and designed to realize the human right of equality of opportunity?

FOUR · *The United States and Human Rights in Chile*

THE value of laws and political institutions, as of society itself, may be judged largely by the extent to which they protect and facilitate the fulfillment of human rights and dignity. Most people in the United States are proud of what they perceive as the unusual degree to which human rights are practiced within their society and honored in their external relations with other countries. A long-standing, positive human rights image has been tarnished recently by a growing awareness of past violations of human rights. These have been illustrated at home by mistreatment of American Indians, women, blacks, and political dissidents; and overseas by brutality in Vietnam, support for repressive military governments, and a plethora of secret interventions by the CIA in less wealthy and powerful societies.

The purpose of this chapter is to clarify the overseas performance of the United States in implementing the human rights and principles of social justice that are represented by the third value of global humanism.[1] The main objective of this value is to assure conditions that will facilitate the realization of individual and group dignity.[2] Its principal dimensions include the prevention of genocide; the elimination of colonial regimes or imperialistic policies; the drastic modification of racist regimes; the elimination of torture and cruelty; progress toward equality of treatment for different races, sexes, ages, religions, tribes, and political groups; and realization of the rights of self-expression and equitable political participation, both globally and domestically.

In particular, the present chapter will examine U.S. respect for procedural and normative restraints against arbitrary governmental interference in people's lives and in the exercise of their rightful decision-making authority. In foreign relations, the question of respect for this kind of right most frequently arises in the context of supporting or resisting the exercise of self-determination by other societies. Self-determination is defined as the right of a nation to make political decisions and to choose its form of government without illegal or unjust inter-

196

vention by outside governments and powerful private organizations.[3] For our purposes, self-determination can be viewed in conjunction with the principle of nonintervention by one state in another state's domestic affairs. The principal focus will be upon the legally binding obligation not to intervene, especially in a subversive way, in another state's internal exercise of self-determination. In addition, the impact of U.S. policies upon other human rights, such as the conduct of open elections and the exercise of a free press will be discussed where relevant. Special attention will be paid to the attitude of U.S. officials toward the protection of human rights in the conduct of their foreign policies.[4]

Self-determination will be treated as an important illustrative component of a more comprehensive cluster of human rights. To be sure, self-determination does not touch all other rights, but it offers a reasonable focal point for assessing official attitudes toward human rights in general. Although firm U.S. support for self-determination might not mean similarly strong support for other human rights (such as elimination of racism or sexism), the failure to respect self-determination is likely to be accompanied by similar indifference to most other human rights. This indifference is not unlike the callousness that historically has characterized imperialism, the classic violation of the right of self-determination.

The modern drive for self-determination is one of the most powerful political forces in contemporary societies. To be free of unwarranted external interference, whether in the form of imperial control or less visible external manipulation, is widely recognized as an important human right in our era. One of the purposes of the United Nations, stated in Article 1 of the Charter, is to "develop friendly relations among nations based on respect for the principle of equal rights and self-determination of peoples." Even before the influx into the UN of newly-independent states that led the struggle against colonialism, the General Assembly formally recognized self-determination as a fundamental human right and asked the Economic and Social Council and the Commission of Human Rights to suggest means to "ensure the right of peoples and nations to self-determination."[5] The UN Covenant on Human Rights declares: "All peoples have the right of self-determination. By virtue of that right they freely determine their political status and freely pursue their economic, social, and cultural development." Parties to the covenant are required to "promote the realization of the right of self-determination."[6]

In the "Declaration on the Granting of Independence to Colonial Countries and Peoples," the Assembly adopted—with the United States abstaining—the proclamation that "subjection to alien . . . domination and exploitation constitutes a denial of fundamental human rights, [and] is contrary to the Charter of the United Nations." It asked all governments to respect the principle of "noninterference in the internal affairs of all states."[7] U.S. officials have endorsed the "inherent and inalienable right of self-determination"[8] and the "duty" of states "to respect the principle of self-determination."[9] In short, governments generally endorse the right of self-determination defined as freedom from external intervention.[10] No states explicitly claim a right to intervene in the domestic affairs of other states.

Yet the world's most powerful national governments and multinational corporations frequently yield to the temptation to violate self-determination. As people in the developing countries exercise greater influence over decisions that affect their lives, the influence of major external governments diminishes in areas where these governments have served their own strategic and economic interests at the expense of the less developed countries. The prospect of an unwanted relative decline in the globally disproportionate privileges of the United States, especially if accompanied by the growth of radical movements overseas, will probably tempt U.S. officials to violate self-determination through covert interventions or to condone repression by reactionary governments. Thus self-determination and other human rights issues are likely to be of central importance for U.S. policies in coming decades. Insofar as the fuller expression of self-determination contributes to a more equitable distribution of power among nations, it aids the achievement of V_3. Any effort to impede this shifting of power and authority prevents the achievement of the third global humanist value. Because self-determination is a necessary (though not sufficient) condition to satisfy the aspiration for human liberation and yet is frequently under attack in the political arena, self-determination provides an instructive focus for studying the realization of worldwide human rights and justice.

Self-determination is also a useful focus because it lies at the center of foreign policy debates that profoundly affect the prospects for world order reform. Present and future generations must address the question: What political units shall decide what range of issues? What degree and kind of influence in other societies' political processes constitute a violation of human rights? When does such action amount to "manipulation without representation," a twentieth-century equivalent of King George's eighteenth-century taxation without representation?

U.S. performance on the self-determination question will be examined in the context of U.S. policy toward Chile from 1970 to 1974. This case has been selected for these reasons:

1. The often-noted problem of deciding who deserves the right of determination does not arise in this case. Chile clearly constituted a nation deserving self-determination.

2. The human rights issue of self-determination was clearly tested. A government existed which was democratically elected but not favored by the United States.

3. Chile was small and distant enough to constitute no security threat to the United States, thus enabling the investigator to avoid entangling the human rights question in a security issue.

4. The political process in Chilean politics was sufficiently similar to other European and Latin American political systems to be easily understood by United States officials.

5. The Chilean example presented a case where the economic interests of large corporations were present. Thus it is possible to examine the idea, anticipated in Chapter One, that multinational corporations will play a salient role in the future of foreign policy decision making.

6. Issues posed within Chile, especially for a radical internal alteration of the distribution of wealth, are likely to be repeated in coming decades in other contexts.

7. Policy toward Chile was typical of U.S. policy elsewhere insofar as it was not an aberration or a fluke based on faulty information or official actions lacking in proper authority. United States behavior resulted from deliberate, repeated, informed discussion by officials at the highest level of the government.

8. A focus on U.S. policy towards a Latin American country provides a case study in the geographic area where the United States has had the greatest historical experience and the most conscious, long-standing discussion of self-determination. In Latin America, one could most reasonably expect a seasoned, well-informed sensitivity on the part of U.S. officials to the right of self-determination.

United States interest in self-determination for Latin American countries goes back, at the least, to the early nineteenth-century recognition of independent Latin American governments and the Monroe Doctrine of 1823, in which the United States warned European states against seeking to impose control over any states in the Western Hemisphere. Of course, the principle of prohibiting extrahemispheric intervention was later transformed, with the help of the Roosevelt Corollary, the Platt Amendment, and similar actions, into a self-proclaimed right for the United States to intervene and establish virtual de facto control over the governments of some Latin American societies. That is a familiar story to students of history.

At the same time, there has been a fairly constant repetition, sometimes voiced by only a few, of a genuine intention to restrain the United States from violating the political independence of Latin American countries. This voice of restraint often has been honored in the rhetoric of officials, if not always in their practice. Nonetheless, the point remains that the principle has been frequently discussed, and the United States has had numerous opportunities to learn from its mistakes and hone its policy to a sharper recognition of self-determination during the many years of foreign relations with Latin America.

Precisely because of the greater power and interventionist policies exercised by the United States in inter-American relations, Latin American states have been particularly sensitive to the prohibition of outside intervention. In the Charter of the Organization of American States (OAS), the principle of self-determination is given prominent attention: "No state . . . has the right to intervene, directly or indirectly, for any reason whatever, in the internal or external affairs of any other state. The foregoing principle prohibits not only armed force but also any other form of interference."[11]

The governments of Chile and the United States, among others, in the Puente del Este Declaration, declared their adherence to "the principles of self-determination and non-intervention as guiding standards of coexistence among the American nations." They pledged support for "the principle of non-intervention and the right of peoples to organize their way of life freely in the political, economic, and cultural spheres expressing their will through free elections, without foreign interference."[12]

The relevant treaties, such as the OAS Charter, were duly ratified by the United States Senate, and thus their provisions carry the constitutionally-defined status of "the supreme law of the land."[13] The principles of self-determination and noninterference are firmly and unequivocally established as legal obligations for the United States and its officials.

DESCRIPTION OF U.S. POLICY TOWARD CHILE

The Problem of Secrecy

A question of whether to respect the right of self-determination in Chile arose in U.S. policy because of the strong opposition of U.S. officials and the executives of several multinational corporations to the political success of Salvador Allende Gossens, a physician and leader of a socialist party in Chile. In a three-way race for president on September 4, 1970, Allende won a national popular election by a narrow margin, receiving 36.3 percent of the total vote. In cases where the highest candidate had a plurality but not a majority of the votes, the Chilean Constitution required that the selection of a president from among the two highest candidates be decided by the Congress. This was normally a formality: Congress had always elected the front-runner in the popular vote. On October 24, following their constitutional tradition, the Congress did overwhelmingly elect Allende president of Chile.

From the moment that Allende won the popular election for the presidency of Chile, Washington officials showed their displeasure. They publicly promised, however, not to interfere in the affairs of another people who had expressed themselves freely at the ballot box. Three years later, in September 1973, Allende died during a violent military takeover of his government. U.S. officials, denying any United States complicity in supporting anti-Allende forces, showed their pleasure that the Allende administration had collapsed by quickly extending recognition and financial assistance to a new military dictatorship.

Between the election and the death of Allende, rumors flourished about United States intervention in Chile. All rumors were officially denied. In truth—or as much truth as investigators have with difficulty ferreted out—the CIA and Department of Defense played a substantial role in creating conditions designed to achieve a speedy overthrow of the elected government. For example, when in October 1970, the Chilean Congress ratified Allende's electoral victory, the Department of State

201

solemnly told the American people that the United States had "firmly rejected" any attempt to block his inauguration. But already $350,000 had been secretly authorized for an unsuccessful effort to bribe members of the Chilean Congress to prevent Allende's inauguration.[14]

In attempting to reconstruct the actions of the United States government in this case, we must assume that the story remains partially hidden. What is known has been revealed in successive waves, after each of which government officials have claimed that the "whole story" was then known. Syndicated columnist Jack Anderson first reported intervention involving the effort of International Telephone and Telegraph (ITT), which had substantial holdings in Chile, to urge the CIA to prevent an Allende victory. Lengthy congressional hearings were conducted on that incident, and investigations were closed. Months later, a largely new story developed about separate CIA authorization of money supposedly to help save a free press in Chile. Later still, it was disclosed that the money went not merely to help threatened news media but also to disrupt Chilean society in order to make it impossible for the Allende administration to govern. After the CIA came under criticism for illegal activities within the United States, yet another series of investigations revealed that the United States had been involved in planning the abduction of a high Chilean military official (who was eventually assassinated) in order to pave the way for a military coup d'état that would have prevented Allende from taking the oath of office in 1970.[15]

At every stage of investigations, the executive branch refused to provide the evidence in its hands that was sought by legitimate investigators. In the final report of the Senate Subcommittee on Multinational Corporations,[16] which examined the role of ITT, the committee expressly criticized "the refusal of the State Department to cooperate" in making available documentary evidence that would have established more clearly the substance of United States policy during the time of the Chilean elections.[17] After the second wave of revelations, several senators on the subcommittee said they earlier had been deceived.[18] The committee staff reported that several high-level officials testifying before the subcommittee were possibly in contempt of Congress.[19]

Despite the reluctance of officials to divulge information that might subject them to criticism, substantial evidence is available that reveals the behavior of United States officials in the Chilean case.

U.S. Policy Toward Self-Determination

PREINAUGURAL CLANDESTINE INTERVENTION

According to the staff report of the Senate Select Committee to Study Governmental Operations with Respect to Intelligence Activities, covert U.S. involvement in Chile between 1963 and 1973 was "extensive and continuous."[20] Secret U.S. efforts influenced "almost every major election in Chile in the decade between 1963 and 1973. In several instances the United States intervention was massive."[21] In the 1964 presidential election, for example, the CIA spent three million dollars to manipulate the Chilean electoral process and prevent Allende from winning the presidental election. The United States secretly financed more than half the total cost of his opponent's campaign, carried out under the banner of the Christian Democratic party. According to the Senate Select Committee, the propaganda campaign in the 1964 election was "enormous." During the first week of intensive propaganda activity, a CIA-sponsored propaganda group produced twenty radio spots per day in Santiago and on 44 provincial stations; twelve-minute news broadcasts five times daily on 27 radio stations throughout Chile; thousands of cartoons; and numerous paid advertisements in newspapers and magazines. Later the CIA group produced 24 daily newscasts in Santiago and the provinces, all colored by an "anti-communist scare campaign."[22]

The United States also intervened in Chilean congressional elections, and according to CIA internal memoranda, the U.S. manipulation of the electoral process had substantial impact, including the defeat of a number of leftist reform candidates who might otherwise have won congressional seats. The CIA also spent money for bribery and supported and helped organize student, women's, professional, and peasant groups for political activity.[23]

One year before the election in which Allende finally won the presidency despite U.S. efforts, the CIA spent $500,000 to mobilize anti-Allende forces.[24] This money was authorized by the then top secret 40 Committee in the White House, which included the secretary of state, chairman of the Joint Chiefs of Staff, deputy secretary of defense, under secretary of state for political affairs, and director of the CIA. President Ford later reported that the 40 Committee "reviews every covert operation undertaken by our Government."[25]

Beginning in May 1970, discussions about the elections occurred between officials of International Telephone and Telegraph and the U.S. government. John McCone, an ITT director, held several meetings with Richard Helms, then CIA director. McCone was a former director of the CIA and he remained a consultant to the CIA after joining ITT. (Helms had been McCone's former subordinate.) At least two conversations between Helms and McCone took place in CIA headquarters in Langley, Virginia. At least one was at McCone's home in California. In these conversations McCone told Helms that ITT expected Allende to win the election and that Allende was running on a platform calling for expropriation of foreign businesses, including ITT's properties. McCone said that the United States national interest, as well as business interests, were at stake. McCone asked if the CIA needed funds to intervene in the election to encourage the support of "one of the candidates who stood for the principles that are basic in this country." Helms said that the 40 Committee had considered intervention and that a decision had been made that "nothing of consequence should be done." Helms did indicate that "some minimal effort was authorized" which "could be managed within the flexibility of their [the CIA's] own budget."[26]

More than two months before the general elections, the 40 Committee authorized the CIA to spend $400,000 to $500,000 secretly in Chile in opposition to the Allende candidacy.[27] In July, the National Security Council Staff was also at work on its top secret Study Memorandum 97, which outlined policy options toward Chile.[28]

On July 16, 1970, as a result of directives from McCone and Helms, a meeting occurred between William V. Broe, the chief of the CIA's Clandestine Services Western Hemisphere Division (also known as the Directorate of Plans) and Harold Geneen, ITT's chief executive officer and chairman of the board, at ITT's Sheraton-Carlton Hotel in Washington. Geneen offered to provide an election fund for Jorge Alessandri Rodriguez, the conservative candidate running against Allende. Geneen said the fund would be "substantial" and that he wanted the fund controlled and channeled through the CIA. The amount discussed was reportedly "up to seven figures." Broe reported that he refused the offer.[29]

The CIA did, however, offer advice about "reliable" individuals who might serve as a conduit for ITT funds to the Alessandri campaign. The CIA also advised ITT about a secure funding mechanism for making secret payments to the National party, which opposed Allende. This procedure utilized two CIA contacts in Chile who were also channeling United States government money to the CIA operation to defeat Allende. ITT and other U.S. private corporations secretly paid at least $700,000 to anti-Allende efforts during the electoral campaign.[30]

After Allende's victory in the national election but before the congressional confirmation vote making the results final, there was a flurry of activity in Washington. McCone met with Henry Kissinger and Richard Helms and offered to give a million dollars "in support of any plan that was adopted by the government for the purpose of bringing about a coalition of the opposition to Allende [in the Chilean Congress] so that when confirmation was up . . . this coalition would be united and deprive Allende of his position." Mr. Geneen testified that "even if the plan did not block Allende's election, he hoped it would create a situation in which Allende would go slowly on the nationalization of American property in Chile.[31] Significantly, ITT offered these large-scale financial inducements to officials to encourage a more widespread effort of CIA subversion, even though ITT's chief executive knew Helms had already told McCone that CIA plans could be handled within the existing CIA budget.

At the same time, the 40 Committee, in response to Kissinger's request, authorized the expenditure of $250,000 to $350,000 to overturn the results of the popular election by bribing Chilean congressmen to vote for Allende's campaign opponent, Alessandri Rodriguez.[32] He was the candidate of the right-wing National party, a fusion of the Conservative and Liberal parties. According to those involved, the money was not used because United States operatives in Chile feared such a plan would not work. Not enough Chilean congressmen could be bribed to swing the elections. Also, some CIA officials feared that a strategy of bribes could not be kept secret. The reason for failing to use the authorized money for bribes did not include official restraint based on a belief that bribery would be wrong.[33] Restraint was based on fear of ineffectiveness and exposure.

During the interval between the general and congressional elections, ITT officials kept in close touch with the CIA. On one occasion, William R. Merriam, vice-president and head of the Washington office of ITT, showed some suggestions from ITT operatives in Chile to William Broe. The recommendations, which Broe said were good, included the following:

1. We and other U.S. firms in Chile pump some advertising into *Mercurio* [the leading conservative newspaper]. (This has been started.)

2. We help with getting some propagandists working again on radio and television.

3. Assist in support of a "family relocation" center in Mendoza or Baires [Buenos Aires] for wives and children of key persons involved in the fight. This will involve about 50 families for a period of a month to six weeks, maybe two months.

4. Bring what pressure we can on USIS [United States Information Service] in Washington to instruct the Santiago USIS to start moving the *Mercurio* editorials around Latin America and into Europe.

5. Urge the key European press, through our contacts there, to get the story of what disaster could fall on Chile if Allende & Co. win this country.

These are immediate suggestions and there will be others between now and October 24 as pressure mounts on [President] Frei and the Christian Democrats [to help in averting a congressional confirmation of the general election].[34]

On September 29, 1970, Broe met with E. J. Gerrity, ITT senior vice-president. Under instructions from Helms, Broe proposed a plan "to accelerate economic chaos in Chile as a means of putting pressure on Christian Democratic Congressmen to vote against Dr. Allende or in any event to weaken Dr. Allende's position in case he was elected." Broe's suggestions were based upon ideas that originated from ITT operatives in Chile. These suggestions included the following:

1. Banks should not renew credits or should delay in doing so.

2. Companies should drag their feet in sending money, in making deliveries, in shipping spare parts, etc.

3. Savings and loan companies there are in trouble. If pressures were applied they would have to shut their doors, thereby creating stronger pressure.

4. We should withdraw all technical help and should not promise any technical assistance in the future. Companies in a position to do so should close their doors.

5. A list of companies was provided [to contact and enlist their support].[35]

Broe said the plan to create economic chaos had been developed after determining the points of vulnerability in Chilean society. Since some middle-class Chileans were uneasy about the future of the economy and were withdrawing their money from banks, the CIA thought that if additional pressure were placed on the Chilean economy, "the deterioration would be accelerated and Christian Democratic Congressmen who were planning to vote for Allende would be shocked into changing their minds and [voting for] Alessandri."[36]

In short, the Senate Subcommittee on Multinational Corporations reported "the CIA suggestion to ITT was that they work to create economic chaos in Chile by causing a run on financial institutions." ITT rejected the plan, company officials said, because ITT concluded that it was unworkable in the limited time before the congressional vote, but not because they thought it was wrong.[37]

At the same time, ITT asked its employee in Santiago, Bob Berrellez, to contact Alessandri's brother-in-law, Dr. Arturo Matte, and offer support, financial or otherwise, if that would help implement what was known as the "Alessandri formula."[38] This was a maneuver in which Alessandri promised that, if the Congress would elect him president on October 24, 1970, he would immediately resign, thus paving the way for a new general election in which Frei (the then current president) would be eligible to run against Allende. Frei had been unable to run against Allende in the September election because the Chilean Constitution forbade any president to succeed himself. ITT and the CIA hoped that in a two-man race, Frei would beat Allende. The U.S. ambassador to Chile, Edward Korry, told the Senate subcommittee that the United States "obviously" was against Allende and that Frei, his associates, the Chilean military, and all political observers in Chile knew that the United States sympathized with the Alessandri formula.[39]

On September 17, 1970, Hal Hendrix (another ITT reporter in Chile) and Berrellez cabled Gerrity: "We know that the Chilean army has been assured full material and financial assistance by the U.S. military establishment." However, they also reported that the military was unwilling to move unilaterally to prevent Allende from taking office as this would be a clear violation of the Constitution.[40] Hendrix also reported that at this time Korry was maneuvering with the Christian Democrats and the Radical and National parties to implement the Alessandri formula. Korry denied all such activity,[41] but later hearings confirmed that it did take place.

In spite of these plans and surreptitious activities, sufficient

Christian Democratic votes could not be turned against Allende (even to give their own leader, Frei, a chance to run again), the Alessandri formula could not be implemented, and on October 24, Allende won the congressional election by a vote of 153 to 42.

During the interval between the general and congressional elections, ITT reporters in Chile informed their company's headquarters that on September 15, Edward Korry "finally received a message from [the] State Department giving him the green light . . . to do all possible—short of a Dominican Republic-type action—to keep Allende from taking power."[42]

Significantly, Korry, who received the cable from the State Department, refused to divulge what his instructions were. Assistant Secretary of State for Inter-American Affairs, Charles Meyer, who sent the message, also refused to testify about the contents of cables at that time. Both denied requests to testify before the Senate Foreign Relations Committee even in executive session. The State Department refused to furnish copies of the cable in question. Later hearings in 1975 confirmed the general accuracy of the report by Hendrix about the "green light" cable.[43] Korry cabled Washington immediately after Allende's victory in the popular election saying that an Allende presidency would not be in the best interests of the United States.[44] Korry was immensely displeased with the results of the general election.[45]

In a background briefing to a group of newspaper editors in Chicago on September 16, 1970, Kissinger said an Allende presidency would cause substantial problems for the United States as well as for Latin American countries bordering on Chile. Kissinger suggested that the Congress of Chile should break with tradition, refuse to ratify the winner of the popular vote, and instead install the runner-up, the conservative candidate for president. Kissinger expressed certainty that Allende had little respect for constitutional processes: "I have yet to meet somebody who firmly believes that if Allende wins there is likely to be another free election in Chile. . . . So I don't think we should delude ourselves that an Allende takeover in Chile would not present massive problems for us, and for democratic forces and for pro-U.S. forces in Latin America, and indeed to the whole Western Hemisphere."[46]

In June 1970, Kissinger chaired the 40 Committee that authorized the CIA to use $400,000 secretly to oppose Allende's candidacy. And in July, the National Security Council prepared plans for U.S. intervention. Two days after the off-the-record briefing for reporters, Kissinger reportedly advocated allocating $350,000 in the effort to bribe Chilean congressmen.[47] In October, Kissinger supported a military coup. There can be no doubt, concluded the Senate Subcommittee on Multinational Corporations in its final report, "that both the U.S. Embassy in Santiago and high levels of the U.S. Government in Washington viewed with hostility the prospect of an Allende Government."[48]

When it seemed apparent that economic pressure and bribery would not work to stop Allende's election, "President Nixon informed CIA Director Richard Helms that an Allende regime in Chile would not be acceptable to the United States and instructed the CIA to play a direct role in organizing a military coup d'état in Chile to prevent Allende's accession to the Presidency."[49] The CIA then attempted, directly, to foment a military coup.[50] During October the CIA made more than twenty contacts with key military and police officials in Chile. The United States threatened to cut off U.S. military aid and sales if Chilean officers refused to carry out a coup before the October 24 congressional vote. The United States also promised those plotting a coup that they would receive U.S. support, both before and after a coup, with all means possible short of direct U.S. military intervention.[51] Washington cabled Ambassador Korry in Santiago: "If any steps the [Chilean] military should take should result in civil disorder, we would also be prepared to deliver support and material that might be immediately required."[52]

One of the main obstacles to a coup was the firm, constitutionalist stance of the Chilean Army Commander-in-Chief, René Schneider. At the request of the CIA, pro-United States Chilean officers attempted to persuade Schneider to go along with a coup, but he flatly refused to move illegally against the Allende election. Thus Schneider himself became a target for the CIA. If he were removed, it was assumed that Allende's inauguration could be more easily prevented. The CIA's mission was to overcome "the apolitical, constitutional-oriented inertia of the Chilean military."[53]

A group of Chilean military officers, whom the CIA actively supported, unsuccessfully attempted to abduct Schneider on October 19, 1970. A second unsuccessful attempt was made the following day. Two days later the CIA gave nontraceable machine guns and ammunition to the group that had failed in the first abduction. Later that day General Schneider was mortally wounded in a third kidnapping attempt. The Senate report concluded that the shooting was "apparently conducted by conspirators other than those to whom the CIA had provided weapons earlier in the day." The report acknowledged, however, that the Senate committee "has not been able to determine whether or not the machine gun at the scene of the Schneider killing was one . . . supplied by the CIA."[54]

There is really no point in debating whether Schneider's death was at the muzzle of a particular CIA-supplied gun. The United States government attempted to foment a coup,[55] it discussed coup plans with the Chileans later convicted of Schneider's abduction, it advocated his removal as a step toward overturning the results of a free election, it offered payment of $50,000 for Schneider's kidnapping, and it supplied weapons for this strategy—acts that clearly signaled disrespect for human rights and involved significant probability of his death.[56]

In short, the United States government did not merely hope for a coup; the White House applied "intense pressure" to get CIA operatives to execute one. Thomas Karamessines, the CIA deputy director for plans, said that Kissinger "left no doubt in my mind that he was under the heaviest pressure to get this accomplished, and he in turn was placing us under the heaviest pressures to get it accomplished." The deputy chief of the Western Hemisphere Division of the CIA testified that the pressure was "as tough as I ever saw it in my time there, extreme." William Broe testified that "I have never gone through a period as we did on the Chilean thing. I mean it was just constant, constant . . . just continual pressure . . . from the White House."[57]

POSTINAUGURAL POLICY

After Allende took office, U.S. pressure against him intensified. The contacts between U.S. intelligence agents and Chilean military officers were maintained and, where possible, tightened. The Department of Defense played a less well-known but in the end no less decisive role than the CIA in overthrowing Allende. Significantly, the Senate Select Committee on Intelligence concentrated on CIA activities, not the role of the Pentagon's Defense Intelligence Agency. Armando Uribe, counselor to the Chilean embassy in Washington from 1968 to 1970 and later a consultant to the Allende administration on U.S.-Chilean military relations, reports that the Department of Defense played the central role in developing plans for a coup d'état in 1970 and again in communicating support to Chilean military officers for the 1973 implementation of parts of the original plan.[58]

After CIA efforts at destabilization caused internal dissatisfaction and economic panic, the Pentagon was surprised when the Allende coalition of parties gained strength in the congressional elections of 1973. At that time, according to Uribe, the Defense Intelligence Agency decided upon resurrecting the 1970 plans for a coup by dissident officers.[59] The plan called for working mainly through Naval Intelligence because the Chilean Navy was more conservative than the rest of the armed forces. Also, the plan was to be carried out in conjunction with Chile-U.S. naval maneuvers that were scheduled for September of each year.

Among the many Chilean officers who had been trained and indoctrinated by U.S. military personnel, some had maintained close contact with U.S. officers over many years. Chilean armed forces were equipped and, to some extent, dependent upon the United States for replacement parts, maintenance, and technological innovations. Some Chilean officers doubtless felt more comfortable collaborating with longtime friends in the U.S. military than with a Chilean Marxist president, even if democratically elected.

According to Gabriel Garcia Marquez, in several meetings in Washington and Santiago before Allende's election, U.S. military officials had discussed and agreed upon contingency plans in which "those Chilean military men who were bound most closely, heart and soul, to United States interests would seize power in the event of Allende's Popular Unity Party victory in the election."[60]

Chilean officers in those discussions included General Ernesto Baeze, who led the attack on the presidential palace, gave the order to burn it, and became director of national security in Chile. Two of his subordinates at the time of the meetings with Pentagon officials were General Augusto Pinochet, who became president of the military government, and General Javier Palacios. Also present at some meetings were Air Force Brigadier General Sergio Figueroa Gutierrez, who became minister of public works and was an intimate friend of another member of the military junta, Air Force General Gustavo Leigh, who ordered the rocket bombing of the presidential palace. Another participant was Admiral Arturo Troncoso, later named naval governor of Valparaiso; he was instrumental in carrying out the bloody purge of progressive naval officers.[61]

U.S. congressional hearings established that, from 1970 until the coup, the CIA instructed its agents to develop additional contacts with Chilean military officials plotting a coup against Allende. CIA officials acknowledged the difficulty of drawing a firm line between monitoring coup plotting and becoming involved in it. They also realized that their desire to be in clandestine contact with those plotting a violent takeover could easily be interpreted as U.S. support for a coup. The CIA subsidized an antigovernment news pamphlet aimed at the armed services, compiled arrest lists and other data useful in a coup, and engaged in at least one "deception operation" which included a fabricated letter designed to turn the military against Allende.

U.S. agents had frequent communication with the group that carried out the successful coup against Allende on September 11, 1973.[62] In addition to the promotion of an outright, violent overthrow of the Chilean government, after Allende's election the 40 Committee authorized the CIA to spend at least seven million dollars to "destabilize" Chilean society.[63] The CIA exchanged U.S. currency on the black market, thus magnifying its purchasing power in Chile by as much as 500 to 800 percent.[64] The purpose of this program was both to discredit a socialist government and to encourage domestic discontent useful for making the population receptive to a coup d'état. Those persons authorizing the money sought to make it impossible for elected Chilean officials to govern.[65]

In seeking to "destabilize" Chile and to create "economic chaos," as officials described it, the CIA secretly financed opposition groups from before Allende's inauguration until after his violent removal from office. The CIA gave money to the Christian Democratic party, the National party, and several splinter groups. These funds strengthened antigovernment activity and enabled the Christian Democratic party and the National party to purchase their own radio stations and newspapers. Additional CIA money and intrigue were aimed at breaking up Allende's Popular Unity coalition. Although United States officials professed a desire to distinguish between support for opposition parties and support for groups trying to bring about a military coup, this distinction was impossible to make in practice. There were many connections among CIA-supported political parties, the militant trade associations, and paramilitary groups prone to terrorism and violent overthrow of the government. The 40 Committee was aware of these links. The *Patria y Libertad* (Fatherland and Liberty) was a prominent right-wing paramilitary group which formed before Allende's inauguration during the period the CIA was attempting to organize a coup. The CIA helped finance this group's efforts in order to create tension and to provoke intervention by the Chilean military. The group received some additional funding in 1971, and it is possible that it received still further CIA money which was channeled through political parties with close ties to *Patria y Libertad*. Two months before the successful coup against Allende, the *Patria y Libertad* claimed responsibility for an abortive coup (June 29), and later announced its intention to unleash a total armed offensive to overthrow the government.[66]

Considerable controversy has arisen about whether the CIA directly helped a truck owners' strike that led to disorders and eventually precipitated the final coup. William Colby denied the CIA was *directly* involved in the last prolonged strike by Chilean truckers that preceded the coup. Nevertheless, the United States passed money to private sector groups which supported various strikes during the Allende administration. Some intelligence officials reported substantial funds went directly to various unions and strikers.[67] The money provided strike benefits and other means of support for strikers, thus prolonging work stoppages by truckers, middle-class shopkeepers and taxi drivers who together disrupted the capital city of Santiago immediately before Allende was overthrown.

The staff report of the Senate Select Committee noted: "All observers agree that the two lengthy strikes (the second lasted from July 13, 1973 until the September 11 *coup*) could not have been maintained on the basis of union funds. . . . It is clear that anti-government strikers were actively supported by several of the private sector groups which received CIA funds." The CIA continued to pass money to at least one group that it knew gave money directly to strikers.[68] Thus the 40 Committee's claim that it did not approve money for direct support of the truck strike may be technically accurate but politically misleading in view of indirect U.S. support.

Because of Chile's peculiar geography and general transportation network, trucking was absolutely necessary to maintain an adequate supply of food and other materials for a healthy economy. The country depended far more heavily on trucks than on the state-owned railways for movement of goods. Thus the truck strikes seriously crippled Chile's economy, stimulated inflation and black marketeering, and provoked a chain reaction of discontent. Shortly before the military moved against Allende, strikes involved a total of 250,000 truck and taxi drivers, shopkeepers, and professionals, making a violent overthrow of the government more likely. The CIA's support of strikes was only one part of a "broad effort to infiltrate all areas of Chile's governmental and political life." One official with direct knowledge of the decision making on Chile explained, "What we really were doing was supporting a civilian resistance movement against an arbitrary Government. Our target was the middle-class groups who were working against Allende."[69]

It is difficult to know precisely the effect of Chilean public opinion on the level of United States involvement, but some evidence shows that Allende's continuing popularity surprised the CIA and worried the Pentagon. U.S. intervention increased after Allende's party coalition continued to enjoy popular support and showed electoral strength. Allende retained a substantial base of support throughout his tenure—though not a majority—in spite of the economic dislocation caused by his economic policies and the United States credit squeeze. Although the results of the municipal elections of 1971 were doubtless influenced by local issues, they were also viewed by many as a test of Allende's popularity. Thus the CIA secretly helped fund all opposition parties in those elections. Nonetheless, Allende's Popular Unity coalition received 50 percent of the votes.[70]

Following this disappointment for Kissinger's interventionist policy, the CIA poured more money into strengthening the National party, the Christian Democratic party, and splinter groups. U.S. funds also aimed at manipulating four congressional by-elections in 1971 and 1972. The money passed to political parties not only supported opposition candidates in various elections, but also encouraged the parties to maintain strong antigovernment campaigns throughout the Allende years, including demonstrations of opposition to the government.[71] During the legislative elections of March 1973, which came almost at midpoint of the presidential term, the CIA contributed at least $1.5 million to opposition candidates who hoped to gain a two-thirds congressional majority that would have enabled them to impeach Allende. Surprisingly, despite all U.S. efforts, the Marxist Popular Unity coalition received 43.4 percent of the popular vote, compared with the 36.3 percent that Allende had received in the presidential race in 1970. Thus Allende supporters picked up two Senate seats and six seats in the Chamber of Deputies.[72]

Soon after these elections, money in new amounts suddenly began to arrive from businesses in neighboring countries for the purpose of helping to finance the Chilean strikes that, along with intervention by Chilean military forces, eventually brought down the Allende government. The funds for strikers came from companies based in Mexico, Venezuela, and Peru. Businessmen there said they had personally channeled funds to strikers amounting to $200,000 in the weeks preceding the fall of Allende.[73] It is probable, although not certain, that much of this money originated from CIA funds. In discussing the August 1973 truck strike, one intelligence official reported: "If we give it [money] to A, and then A gives it to B and C and D, in a sense it's true that D got it but the question is—did we give it to A knowing that D would get it?"[74]

In addition to funding political opposition groups, the 40 Committee spent enormous amounts to buy or influence media in order to launch what the Senate report called a "hard-hitting propaganda campaign." Chile's largest newspaper, *El Mercurio*, alone received $1.5 million. CIA-inspired editorials were published "almost daily" in *El Mercurio*, and after 1968 the CIA exerted substantial control over the content of the paper's international news section.[75] The CIA intervention included producing several magazines with national circulations; publishing a large number of antigovernment books and special "studies"; placing its own material in the *El Mercurio* chain, which amounted to a total daily circulation of over 300,000; financing opposition party newspapers; and getting anti-Allende propaganda played on all radio stations controlled by opposition parties and on several regular television shows on three different channels. The CIA also funded over 75 percent of an opposition "research" organization. A constant stream of economic and technical material—all slanted against Allende—flowed from this organization to opposition parties and other private groups. Many of the bills introduced in the legislature by opposition politicians were in fact drafted by CIA personnel working in the CIA's own Chilean research organization.[76]

Within two weeks of Allende's electoral victory, the CIA brought journalists, who were CIA agents, to Chile from at least

215

ten different foreign countries. These journalist-agents and other foreign correspondents were directed by high-level CIA agents who held managerial posts in the media field.[77] The journalist-agents wrote slanted reports which were published in foreign newspapers as genuine on-the-scene reporting. The published articles were then circulated to President Frei, military and political leaders, and the Chilean domestic press in order to create the impression that unbiased foreign press comment was highly unfavorable to Allende.

The CIA also gave special intelligence and "inside" briefings to U.S. journalists. Although the impact of these efforts at influencing the press can hardly be assessed, one example illustrates the possibilities. According to CIA documents, a *Time* correspondent in Chile was writing what later became a cover story about Allende. This correspondent reported that Allende intended to uphold the Chilean Constitution. Briefings by the CIA for *Time* in Washington changed the basic thrust of the *Time* story on Allende.[78]

By spreading "black" propaganda—material falsely purporting to be the product of a particular individual or group—the CIA attempted to sow discord among the parties in Allende's Popular Unity coalition. Moreover, the CIA paid teams of Chileans to erect signs and paint posters that depicted Allende as a Stalinist dictator, complete with firing squads for innocent people. The scare campaign used large photographs of Soviet tanks in Prague alongside of tanks in Santiago. Some CIA posters warned that an Allende victory would "mean the end of religion and family life in Chile."[79]

While no statistics are available for the size of the propaganda activity during Allende's administration, during the six-week period between his election and inauguration the scope of the activity was revealed by Senate investigators. According to CIA records, which admittedly were only partly reported, 726 articles, broadcasts, and editorials in the Latin American and European media directly resulted from agency activity. The CIA concluded that this work produced "substantial and significant" impact.[80] According to internal CIA documents, the propaganda efforts "played a significant role in setting the stage for the military coup of September 11, 1973."[81]

In addition to support for opposition groups and propaganda activity, U.S. officials deliberately designed both overt and covert U.S. economic policies to wreck the Chilean economy. Economic hardship, U.S. officials calculated, would insure Allende's demise and discredit socialism as well. Although the precise effect of U.S. actions remains controversial, there is little doubt that in general U.S. policies succeeded in encouraging economic panic among many Chileans. The Chilean economy was vulnerable to abuse by U.S. governmental and private economic pressures because it was so dependent upon commercial intercourse with the United States. The Chilean economy depended on the uninterrupted importation of 30 percent of its goods, including food, machinery, and machine parts which could not be produced in Chile. About 40 percent of these came from the United States.

More importantly, Chile had a record of dependency on U.S. credit to finance its day-to-day life. Chile had been the largest per capita recipient of U.S. aid in Latin America. This dependency had been encouraged by past United States efforts to increase exports of U.S. goods and to maintain a buoyant Chilean economy to prevent the growth of electoral support for left-wing parties. Because previous Chilean administrations had made large-scale credit purchases from the United States, the Allende administration inherited the second highest per capita foreign debt in the world when it took office.[82] This debt presented no insurmountable problem if the United States continued to offer generous credit to finance the importation of United States goods and to ease the repayment of previous loans. On the other hand, a restriction of credit would cause severe hardship, exacerbated by falling prices on the world markets for copper, Chile's single basic export. The latter event, of course, curtailed scarce foreign exchange earnings necessary to finance imports.

Like the United States government, many private corporations publicly assumed a correct posture toward Santiago while secretly attempting to overthrow the Chilean government. Following Allende's inauguration, ITT sought to protect its assets in Chile by simultaneously pursuing two different strategies. First, ITT tried to insure the overthrow of Allende by pressing the United States government, through Kissinger's office, to oust the new president. Second, ITT wanted to secure, through guarantees from Allende, the payment of full book value for any ITT property that might eventually be nationalized.

In January 1971, ITT sought help from other companies with investments in Chile to persuade Kissinger to block loans to Chile by institutions such as the World Bank and the Inter-

217

American Development Bank. By confronting the Chilean government with economic collapse, William Merriam, head of ITT's Washington office, said ITT would more easily gain concessions from Allende.[83] Allende had not, at that time, taken any expropriatory action against any United States company.

At the same time that it secretly promoted economic chaos, ITT prepared for negotiations with Allende on its primary investment in Chile, the ownership of 70 percent of the Chilean telephone company, Chiltelco. ITT's holdings in Chile, including Chiltelco, totaled approximately $160 million. During the first negotiations, Allende personally told ITT representatives that he had not decided what course of action to follow with Chiltelco. He had, however, mentioned the possibility of nationalizing Chiltelco in a campaign speech of September 2, 1970. On May 26, 1971, Allende informed ITT that Chiltelco would be nationalized. ITT asked for compensation at the full book value of $153 million. The Chilean government offered $24 million for ITT's interest. Allende then proposed valuation by international arbitration, with the government managing the company pending the arbitration. ITT opposed this arrangement allegedly because of fears that the value of the property would deteriorate under Chilean management.[84] Thus they reached no agreement.

During the negotiations, ITT attempted to convince Allende that by making a satisfactory deal with ITT, he could then confiscate with impunity other U.S. companies without creating an image of being totally hostile to foreign investments. ITT used this negotiating technique successfully in Peru, when faced with expropriation there.[85]

Through Nixon's White House confidant, John Ehrlichman, Merriam arranged for a meeting with Kissinger's deputy, General Alexander Haig, and Peter Peterson, assistant to the president for international economic affairs. Following the meeting, under instructions from ITT Chairman Geneen, Merriam forwarded an 18-point action plan to the White House to insure that Allende would not "make it through the next six months."[86] The plan included these suggestions:

> Continue loan restrictions in the international banks such as those the Export/Import Bank has already exhibited.
> Quietly have large U.S. private banks do the same.
> Confer with foreign banking sources with the same thing in mind.

Delay buying from Chile over the next six months. Use U.S. copper stockpile instead of buying from Chile.

Bring about a scarcity of U.S. dollars in Chile.

Discuss with CIA how it can assist the six-month squeeze.

Get to reliable sources within the Chilean Military. Delay fuel delivery to Navy and gasoline to Air Force. . . . A false delay could build up their planned discontent against Allende, thus bring about necessity of his removal.

Help disrupt Allende's UNCTAD plans.

As many U.S. markets as possible should be closed to Chile.[87]

Thus, one year after the CIA proposed a plan to accelerate economic chaos in Chile, ITT was proposing to the president's assistant for international economic policy a more comprehensive plan to exacerbate the economic situation. Peterson denied that government action was taken to implement the plan.[88] But, as Colby later revealed, by that time the CIA had a twelve-month start in implementing its own seven million dollar plan to destabilize Chilean society. And Peterson's testimony to the contrary notwithstanding, ample evidence demonstrates that many parts of the plan were implemented and caused a serious shortage of credit in Chile.

Negotiations between ITT and the Allende government resumed in December 1971, through Chile's ambassador in Washington, Orlando Letelier. Until March 20, 1972, Letelier focused discussions on arranging for international appraisal of the company's assets, an approach that Chile favored. On that date Jack Anderson published his first column explaining ITT's secret efforts in September and October 1970 to avert congressional ratification of the Chilean national election. A previously scheduled meeting with ITT was canceled by the Chilean embassy after Anderson's revelations. Negotiations were never resumed.[89]

As indicated earlier, both governmental and corporate officials hoped that either the Alessandri formula or a military coup would prevent Allende from taking office, and that if inaugurated, he would be ousted. These officials initiated plans to destabilize Chile even before Allende took office, and long before anyone could know the extent to which nationalization of United States companies would include adequate compensation. Five weeks before Allende was sworn in as president, Richard Helms met with President Nixon and recorded his instructions:

"Make the economy scream." A week after that meeting Ambassador Korry reported telling the Frei administration that "not a nut or a bolt would be allowed to reach Chile under Allende."[90]

The later inability of U.S. companies to reach agreement with Chile on compensation for expropriated copper interests served as a convenient rationale for a restrictive United States economic policy already underway. Thus it is inappropriate to focus exclusively on the expropriation issue, or to see United States economic policy as a response to expropriation without compensation. Nevertheless, the hostility toward Allende was based to a significant degree on a widely held belief that private investors would not fare well with a socialist president. The point is that United States policies to destabilize Chilean society were at first based on general dislike for socialism and fear of future expropriation, not on a specific or empirical finding that U.S. investors were being mistreated by Allende's government. But in the arena of public debate, officials reversed the chronology: They sought to document their presuppositions against Allende on the basis of later expropriations of United States corporations by Chile.

Nurtured by statements from Washington, the idea also spread in the United States that the U.S. copper corporations enjoyed substantial support in Chile, except for the Allende coalition. That was not true. By the end of the Frei administration there was little or no domestic support within Chile for the large copper companies. Support had dwindled to such an extent that, when the Frei administration asked for a joint ownership arrangement between the Chilean government and Anaconda, the company preferred to get out completely and asked for nationalization rather than accept joint ownership. Thus some copper interests were nationalized during the Frei term of office, even before Allende assumed the presidency.

The deep feeling against the copper companies was due to the extent to which Chile had been affected by these giant foreign interests. All the *Fortune* 500 companies combined do not play a role in the economy of the United States equivalent to the role of Anaconda and Kennecott in Chile. U.S. corporations controlled the production of 80 percent of Chile's copper, which accounted for four-fifths of Chile's foreign exchange earnings. Compared to the strength and past profits of the companies, the Chilean response was muted and cautious.[91]

Chilean support for nationalizing the foreign copper com-

220

panies was overwhelming. Ten months after Allende's electoral victory, the Chilean Congress, although controlled by the non-Marxist opposition Christian Democrat and National parties, unanimously passed a constitutional amendment nationalizing the copper mines. Even the head of Chile's Roman Catholic bishops, Raúl Cardinal Silva Henríquez, said that the nationalization was right and that "the process . . . had been constitutionally impeccable."[92] The congressional vote "reflected widespread popular sentiment that the country had been plundered" by U.S. copper corporations over the previous sixty years.[93] These companies included among their largest stockholders the Rockefeller and Morgan financial groups. The nationalization legislation called for compensating the companies at full book value, less excess profits.

The determination of "excess profits," which became an extremely controversial doctrine, was carried out by the comptroller general's office, the members of which had been appointed before Allende took office. This autonomous body weighed the facts of each corporation in light of the 10 percent annual return considered normal in Chile. The comptroller's office determined that compensation should be for full book value for two new mines, but found that in the other mines, the excess profits of Kennecott and Anaconda already exceeded the total book values. In the eyes of United States investors and officials, who denied the legitimacy of the excess profits doctrine, this was tantamount to expropriation without compensation. The excess profits doctrine looked much more reasonable, of course, in the eyes of people whose wealth had been extracted for many years by foreign corporations without concern for economic justice.

The Chilean action, based upon the excess profits doctrine, intensified the determination of Washington officials already intent upon Allende's ouster. This doctrine was reasonable and likely to spread to other countries if not opposed by the United States. Any reservations about U.S. policy among lower echelons in the State Department were ignored as the initiative for policy making moved to the Treasury Department and White House.[94] This occurred in large part because the curtailment of United States commercial benefits in Chile was an economic issue and a central irritant in White House and corporate hostility to Allende.

Faced with the prospect of further expropriations of United States companies in Chile or elsewhere, plagued by growing

221

economic difficulties within the United States, and spurred by the secretary of the treasury's extreme hostility toward socialism and the decline in United States overseas commercial influence, the Treasury Department, under the direction of Secretary John Connally, set the tone for U.S. policy and coordinated economic sanctions against Chile. The goal was to protect over $1 billion of U.S. private investment in Chile, as well as to insure no default on the additional $1 billion of indebtedness to the U.S. government which was incurred by Allende's predecessors.[95] "Once policy had been defined through Connally's initiative, the State Department moved toward the more extreme position, shedding its reservations."[96]

Connally, Nixon, and Kissinger shaped an extremely hard, vengeful policy line against the Chilean government. Connally acted on behalf of the vested interests of the United States business community. He was angry over nationalizations of private holdings in countries such as Chile, Peru, and Bolivia. He said it was time to "get tough" with Latin American countries that expropriated U.S. property.[97] *Business Week* reported that "Connally is forcing the reopening of debate at top levels on what U.S. policy should be. He is particularly bitter about Latin American hostility toward U.S. investment."[98]

Treasury officials, most of whom were drawn from the business world, reflected the attitudes and interests of large business and financial institutions. As Collins concluded after his extensive study of U.S. economic policy toward Chile: "When Chile dared to try to gain a modicum of freedom from foreign financial domination, it came up against . . . financial giants working out of the Executive branch and dictating U.S. foreign policy."[99] Some key officials designing U.S. economic policy toward Chile were: Assistant Secretary of the Treasury for International Affairs, John M. Hennessey, formerly general manager of the First National City Bank in Lima and La Paz; Assistant Treasury Secretary John R. Petty, formerly a vice-president of Chase Manhattan Bank and later a partner of Lehman Brothers; Under Secretary of the Treasury for Monetary Affairs, Paul A. Volcker, a vice-president and director of planning for the Chase Manhattan Bank and on the board of directors of the Overseas Private Investment Corporation; Deputy Secretary of the Treasury, Charles E. Walker, formerly special assistant to the president of the Republic National Bank of Dallas and former executive vice-president and chief lobbyist of the American Bankers Association; and the Assistant to the President for International Economic Policy, Peter Peterson, a director of the First National Bank of Chicago and former chairman of Bell and Howell.

Just as governmental officials making policy toward Chile were dominated by businessmen, U.S. businesses utilized people from government to work for their interests in Chile. For example, prior to becoming secretary of the treasury, John Connally had been hired as legal counsel by ITT.[100] And for thirty-five years before he became ITT's International Relations Director, Jack Neal had been an influential official at the Department of State. McCone, of course, was former director of the CIA; later he was a consultant to the CIA and simultaneously a director of ITT.

These officials harbored professional hatred for the excess profits doctrine because its spread would mean that other countries might expropriate companies and deduct past excess profits of a corporation from payment for nationalization. Assistant Secretary of the Treasury for International Affairs, John M. Hennessey, termed the effort to establish an excess profits doctrine "a very dangerous precedent."[101]

In order to avert future expropriations, the White House and Treasury Department undertook several studies and set forth, in an executive statement of January 19, 1972, the following guidelines: "When a country expropriates a significant U.S. interest without making reasonable provision for . . . compensation to U.S. citizens, we will presume that the U.S. will not extend new bilateral economic benefits to the expropriating country. . . . We will presume that the United States government will withhold its support from loans under consideration in multilateral development banks."[102] Assistant Treasury Secretary John Petty indicated that in the future "you'll find the U.S. less prepared to turn the other cheek. It's a new ball game with new rules."[103] The "new rules" were a more explicit intention to strangle the economy of any country that expropriated United States business without compensation satisfactory to the United States.

The response to the Chilean case was thus part of a general policy to prevent the decline of United States commercial—and political—influence in countries where a quasi-colonial relationship has existed for years. It was not really a new policy; it had been used in Cuba, Bolivia, Peru, and elsewhere in Latin America. Benjamin Welles reported that Connally's strategy was

223

"a business version of a military domino theory. . . . Mr. Connally is said to believe that his policy of deterrence—cracking down on Chile—may frighten off other possible expropriating countries."[104]

The above attitudes and policies produced these concrete results:

1. The Treasury Department's Export-Import Bank denied all the Allende administration's requests for credit, which normally had been generously extended to Chile for purchases from the United States. (The Export-Import Bank gives short-term credit to facilitate sales of United States goods to foreign purchasers.) Chile traditionally had purchased about 40 percent of its total imports from the United States, and in the 25 years preceding Allende's election, Chile received $600 million worth of direct credits from the bank.[105] Its credits dropped to zero after Allende entered office.[106]

The first Chilean request for credit came early in 1971, before the nationalization of copper mines. It was from the Chilean airline, which had a flawless repayment record. At that time, United States officials acknowledged that Chile had been scrupulous in paying debts, and the Commerce Department admitted that Chile's "credit worthiness" was not the central issue.[107] The decision to block loans to Chile was political, made on the White House level and under pressure from corporation executives.

2. The Export-Import Bank also terminated its long-standing policy of guaranteeing and insuring commercial transactions of United States banks and other companies with Chile. This insurance program, carried out through the Foreign Credit Insurance Association, normally made it possible for U.S. commercial interests to engage in foreign transactions with the United States government undertaking most of the extra risks involved in foreign trade. This cutoff not only directly discouraged private commercial relations with Chile, but also signaled private banks and suppliers to follow the Treasury Department's example of general economic hostility. At the same time that the Export-Import Bank denied Chile new loans, it extended new loans to economically unstable countries such as Haiti and Bangladesh. This communicated a message of importance to other governments and private banks. As Henry Kearns, former president of the Export-Import Bank explained, "Eximbank credit ratings have an enormous influence on other bankers. If we are not willing to loan to a country, few others will."[108]

For a dozen years before Allende's administration, Chile normally had available about $300 million in short-term private commercial credits, mainly from United States banks. Such loans from U.S. banks dropped to about $30 million by 1972. The drop "seriously affected the Allende government's ability to purchase replacement parts and machinery for the most critical sectors of the economy: copper, steel, electricity, petroleum, and transport."[109]

3. Economic assistance to Chile from the Agency for International Development was dramatically reversed in 1970 because of United States hostility toward the Chilean government. Table 4-1 shows the annual net quantities of aid Chile received from the Agency for International Development and its predecessor agencies.

Three major discontinuities in United States assistance reveal the political use of aid. During the first new U.S. fiscal year (1960) following the 1958 Chilean election—the point at which the United States became seriously concerned with the growing electoral strength of Allende's party—United States assistance to Chile suddenly increased. The increase was designed to dampen popular support for left-wing parties. Aid rose more than sixfold over previous years, the single earlier exception being the year before the election itself. During this period of generally rising AID budgets, the assistance to Chile by 1961 climbed tenfold over 1959, and by 1962 jumped to forty-seven times the 1959 level. [110]

Aid was also curtailed after the electoral success of the Popular Unity coalition. Although $5.5 million had been authorized to go to Chile in 1971 and 1972 under previously negotiated AID programs, no new assistance agreements were made with the Allende government.[111] During the entire nineteen-year period (1952-70) of economic assistance to Chile prior to Allende's election, aid amounted to an average of $33.7 million per year. During the three U.S. fiscal years that overlapped Allende's administration (1971-73), United States net aid, due to cancellation of previous obligations, amounted to a *negative* figure of $26.7 million.

The third reversal in AID policies coincided with the overthrow of Allende and the installation of the military dictatorship. As Table 4-1 shows, as soon as the antisocialist generals were in power, aid was quickly resumed.

4. The Nixon administration also used its enormous economic power to prevent the extension of credit to Chile by multilateral

Table 4-1
Loan and Grant Commitments[a] to Chile from the United States
Agency for International Development and Predecessor Agencies

Fiscal Year	Net Obligations, Millions of Dollars
1952	1.1
1953	1.3
1954	1.4
1955	2.0
1956	2.1
1957	3.0
1958	12.8
1959	3.1
1960	18.3
1961	31.1
1962	142.4
1963	40.4
1964	78.5
1965	99.0
1966	85.6
1967	12.0
1968	53.9
1969	34.6
1970	17.2
1971	−25.1
1972	.4
1973	−2.0
1974	5.1
1975	25.5
1976	20.5

SOURCES: U.S. Agency for International Development, *U.S. Economic Assistance Programs Administered by the Agency for International Development and Predecessor Agencies, April 3, 1948-June 30, 1971* (Washington, D.C.: U.S. Agency for International Development, 1972); U.S. Agency for International Development, Statistics and Reports Division, *U.S. Overseas Loans and Grants and Assistance from International Organizations*.

NOTE: [a] Commitments are given in net terms. That is, the figures include total new obligations entered into during each year, less deobligations of prior years' funds. Negative figures mean that canceled obligations exceed new obligations.

lending institutions. The Inter-American Development Bank (IDB), in which the United States held what amounted to a veto, had extended 59 loans to Chile since 1959, totaling over $310 million. But with two very limited exceptions, the IDB denied all new loans to Chile during the Allende administration. The exceptions were two small loans of $7 and $4.6 million for private universities. These had been tentatively promised to the previous Chilean government.[112]

The first requests by the Allende government were for development of electric power, natural gas, and a petrochemical complex. These had already undergone favorable preliminary examination by the IDB before Allende's election. They were denied, however, after Allende took office. Similarly, the IDB even refused relief to victims of the earthquake of 1971. Chile faithfully repaid its pre-Allende obligations to the bank, and thus it became an exporter of capital to a multilateral development bank that would not even lend it aid for emergency humanitarian needs.

The United States pursued a similar policy in the World Bank. Before Allende's election, Chile had received loans of $234,650,000 from the bank. After the election, the bank refused to act upon all Chilean loan requests. No new loans went to Chile between 1970 and 1973. Among other projects, the bank refused to finance the second stage of a cattle breeding program, even though the first stage was begun with bank assistance. A request for continued support for an ongoing electrification program was rejected, although for the previous twenty years the bank had provided similar assistance.[113]

The International Monetary Fund (IMF), where the United States had less decisive influence, provided a sharp contrast. The Allende government continued normal drawing rights there and received $148 million in partial compensation for falling copper prices. The action of IMF suggests that the reason given by the United States for denying credit, namely that Chile was a poor credit risk, was largely a ploy to deceive the public.[114] To be sure, Chile's exchange position was weakened by declining copper prices and internal economic difficulties, but a major influence upon Chile's credit scarcity was the United States' concerted effort to deny Chile the credit upon which it had grown dependent over the years before Allende's election. During previous economic crises, as well as after the Allende government fell, both the United States and the IDB did not hesitate to provide generous assistance.

U.S. economic policies had a devastating effect upon Chile. Washington policymakers had correctly calculated that denying Chile credit would encourage economic chaos. In the absence of additional credit from the United States, the Chilean government needed to reschedule its previous timetable for debt re-

227

tirement and institute an internal program of austerity to cut imports and curtail the need for foreign currency. But the United States resisted efforts to reschedule debt repayment.[115] Moreover, lacking the strong support of the middle class, and faced with a mobilizing right wing and a military prejudiced against socialism, an austerity program was a political impossibility for Allende. This was especially true because of his intention to avoid repressive measures. The politically sensitive and influential middle class was accustomed to imported U.S. goods, and thus would be irritated by any cutoff of those goods.

Within two years, Chile's imports from the United States declined from 40 to 15 percent of total imports. In addition, total imports declined. While the large lower class improved its access to basic goods as a result of Allende's economic reforms, the middle class suffered dislocation of their usual consumption patterns. Many goods were simply unavailable. Perhaps most important politically, a severe shortage of replacement parts developed for all machinery previously purchased from the United States. Production suffered as a result of machines left idle. Since a large percentage of all buses and trucks were of U.S. origin, by 1972, 30 percent of privately owned city buses, 21 percent of taxibuses, 33 percent of state-owned buses, and about 33 percent of the diesel trucks at Chuquicamata Copper Mine were immobilized because of lack of parts.[116] Private owners of vehicles, who participated in the prolonged strike that led to the military takeover, often gave lack of replacement parts as a reason for their striking. On the one hand, United States government and businesses withheld credit and slowed shipment of goods in order to stimulate parts shortages that encouraged potential strikers to halt work. On the other hand, the United States secretly spent money to sustain strikers and increase the economic agony. The U.S. Treasury Department worked hand in hand with the CIA to promote conditions that would mean the ruin of Chile's constitutional government.

Two more points will complete this description of United States policy toward the Allende government: the first includes some events that were omitted from policymakers' considerations; the second shows the reversal of United States policy after the violent end to Allende's government.

The severe policies of United States officials gave no deference whatever to the Chilean Congress, controlled by opposition parties, which passed expropriation legislation unanimously. U.S. officials spoke disparagingly of Allende as a "minority" president, but contemptuously sought to reverse the sweeping mandate for nationalization expressed by Chilean voters who freely elected a Congress two-thirds of which had campaigned for expropriation. U.S. officials failed to acknowledge that some United States businesses received satisfactory compensation. Additional corporations might have received payment if the United States had showed willingness to terminate its credit squeeze. The Bank of America, for example, received in compensation "precisely the amount that we originally invested."[117] Other companies, such as Bethlehem Steel and North Indiana Brass Company, also negotiated satisfactory settlements.[118]

As indicated earlier, negotiations with ITT were in progress until the Jack Anderson columns showed that ITT was trying to stimulate an illegal overthrow of Allende at the same time that it was demanding full book value compensation for its properties.[119] According to ITT officials, Allende said that "he did not want to expropriate or nationalize fully, emphasizing he would prefer a partnership arrangement of some sort."[120] Despite this, ITT enlisted the support of other corporations, Kissinger's office, and the CIA to force Allende's hand. Even ITT's legal department expressed concern about the surreptitious activities of ITT in Chile, fearing that they might make null and void the U.S. government-sponsored insurance to pay companies expropriated without compensation. But ITT officials were convinced that the potential benefits of promoting economic chaos would outweigh any negative repercussions that might result should their secret activities be discovered. Significantly, the first ITT discussions with government officials to prevent Allende from governing were made over a year before the Chilean government's decision to administer the telephone company.[121]

The nature and intention of United States policy were starkly revealed when U.S. officials terminated the economic squeeze. Immediately upon seizing power from Allende, the Chilean military dictatorship promised to wash away any vestige of socialism, to compensate U.S. copper interests, and to return to private hands "the vast majority" of the foreign and domestic concerns that were nationalized by the Allende government.[122] In turn, the United States reversed all economic policies carried out against the previous constitutional government. Post-Allende

United States efforts aimed at assisting the economy and helping the new dictatorship remain in power. As the United States increased aid, Britain, Sweden, and other states ended assistance to the new regime because of its ruthlessness.

The United States had maintained contact with the Chilean military during the Allende administration. At the same time that the United States denied Allende credit for hydroelectric projects and even for 300,000 tons of wheat during a foreign currency shortage, the United States had ample funds to give to the professional military in Chile. The United States sought to perpetuate its influence with the Chilean military through authorizations of $45.5 million in military aid from 1970 to 1974.[123] The single largest disbursement was $10 million during 1972.[124]

In contrast to the AID *de*obligations that produced a net loss of $25 million in assistance during the Allende years, AID programs quickly resumed after the coup.[125] During fiscal 1974, United States aid to Chile was $21 million, of which $16.5 million was for the armed forces. In 1975, the United States gave $85 million in aid, including $22 million for the armed forces.[126] U.S. officials underscored the point of their policy only a few weeks after rejecting Allende's request for credit to buy wheat: as soon as the generals seized power, the United States granted $24.5 million for wheat purchases.[127]

Soon the Export-Import Bank reopened its program for Chile. Private banks began lending again, and by mid-1974, Chile's short-term credits were nearly at pre-Allende levels. The IDB granted Chile several very large loans for hydroelectric and agricultural projects similar to those that went unfunded under Allende. The United States renegotiated Chile's debt repayments. The World Bank announced a $5.25 million loan for "preinvestment studies."[128]

The National Foreign Trade Council estimated in March 1974 that the credit granted the new Chilean regime from the United States, Brazil, Argentina, the IMF, the World Bank, the IDB, and the Andean Development Corporation amounted to $468.8 million. Private banks had given credit worth another $250 million. As Elizabeth Farnsworth has concluded: "The loans granted since the coup represented phase two of the U.S. counterinsurgency program in Chile—they prop up a brutal dictatorship which rules through terror but promises good investment opportunities for American businesses. Questions of credit worthiness are not even raised. As Secretary of Agriculture Earl L. Butz said in justifying the Department of Agriculture [wheat] credits, 'they were made in the interest of national security.' The Allende government 'was not friendly. It was essentially a diplomatic decision.' "[129].

In summary, United States officials from the White House, Treasury Department, State Department, and CIA developed policies in cooperation with United States investors in Chile. At the same time, the Department of Defense maintained close ties with friendly military officers in the Chilean armed forces. Together, U.S. officials implemented a policy to cut off Chile's customary sources of private and public financing from the United States and other nations at the same time they fed money and support to Allende's internal opponents and the Chilean military. The staff report of the Senate Select Committee concluded that, as a result of the 40 Committee's actions, "a major financial panic ensued."[130] To be sure, the decline of the Chilean economy should not be attributed exclusively to U.S. harassment. Some responsibility for the economic dislocation must be placed upon Allende's policies and the response from powerful internal economic forces resisting Allende's initiatives. However, even though Allende's nationalization and income redistribution policies may be subject to criticism, the shortages that were so irritating to middle-class Chileans would have been much less severe if Allende had not been prevented by the United States from receiving normal credit and purchases from the United States. U.S. policy reinforced the polarization of Chilean society, as well as directly contributed to economic hardship.

When considered in both economic and psychological terms, U.S. economic policies had a devastating effect upon Chile. According to Laurence Birns, a former economist for the United Nations Economic Commission for Latin America in Santiago: "The U.S. bears major responsibility for what happened in Chile. Its systematic policy of economic strangulation created a momentum which led to the death of constitutional democracy. This policy reflected the demands of the American corporations that had been nationalized or controlled in Chile."[131] In the context of strikes, political disruption, and economic distress, the stage was set for the intervention of dissatisfied Chilean military officers whom the U.S. had urged to intervene in 1970, and with whom the U.S. had maintained close ties during Allende's tenure in office.

OFFICIAL RATIONALE COMPARED TO THE VALUES
IMPLICIT IN U.S. POLICY

The foregoing survey of United States behavior toward Chile raises several questions: To what extent did U.S. officials violate the right of self-determination and the treaties that constituted part of the supreme law of the land? What justification have officials given for their policy? Were the values they professed to serve consistent with the values implicit in actual governmental behavior?

The principal official justification for U.S. intervention was to protect democracy in Chile. In a nationwide televised statement, President Ford elaborated upon this central purpose by adding these other broad dimensions: "I think this [policy of intervention] is in the best interest of the people in Chile." The activity was designed "to help implement [U.S.] foreign policy and protect national security." The CIA policy of intervention "is . . . certainly in our best interest."[132] These explicit public justifications of United States policy should be examined in light of the values implicit in the means used to implement policy.

Professed Value 1: To Sustain Democratic Parties and Maintain Political Pluralism in Chile

Before United States intervention was publicly acknowledged, President Nixon assured the American people that the United States was willing to live happily with a "community of diversity" among Latin American governments. "Our relations depend not on their internal structures or social systems, but on actions which affect us in the inter-American system."[133] In another speech commenting on Latin America, the president said, "We therefore deal with governments as they are—right and left . . . we respect the hemispheric principle of non-intervention."[134] In affirming support for this principle, the president proclaimed, "Our relations with Chile are an example. . . . Our relations will hinge not on their ideology but on their conduct toward the outside world. As I have said many times, we are prepared to have the kind of relationship with the Chilean Government that it is prepared to have with us."[135]

In September 1974, after a *New York Times* story by Seymour Hersh made it impossible for officials to maintain the lie that the United States had undertaken no clandestine political activity in Chile, Secretary Kissinger and President Ford justified the CIA involvement by saying its purpose was solely to keep alive supposedly threatened opposition political parties and news media. Kissinger said that the "very minor" role of the CIA was aimed at strengthening the "democratic political parties."[136]

In an effort professedly to clear the political air and tell the "whole story," Kissinger gave separate briefings to congressional leaders and the Ford Cabinet at the White House. In both meetings persons present reported that, according to Kissinger, "All we did was support newspapers and political opponents of Allende who were under siege."[137] Kissinger repeated this to the Senate Foreign Relations Committee, meeting in secret session. According to sources present during the briefing, at no time did Kissinger mention the financing of labor unions or trade groups. He denied that any efforts were aimed at subverting the Chilean government.[138]

A similarly misleading description of the U.S. role was given by Ford on nationwide TV. He said that U.S. intervention was a response to attacks by Allende on a free press and opposition parties: "There was an effort being made by the Allende Government to destroy opposition news media, both the writing press as well as the electronic press. And to destroy opposition political parties. And the [CIA] effort that was made in this case was to help and assist the preservation of opposition newspapers and electronic media and to preserve opposition political parties."[139]

This principal justification of United States policy becomes unbelievable after consideration of available evidence. First of all, both United States purposes and policies directly violated—rather than protected—the democratic process itself. The United States sent secret money and agents into Chile over a period of at least ten years to prevent the Popular Unity parties from receiving the support at the polls that they would have received in the absence of a United States covert effort against them. The United States sought to use illegal means to prevent Allende from being elected by Congress after he won the national election. The United States infiltrated the Chilean government and created civil strife and economic chaos to discredit the Allende government and to encourage a coup by the U.S.-trained and supplied Chilean military officers. The United States, through the CIA, penetrated labor unions, trade groups, and all areas of Chile's government. The CIA had agents in every major party making up Allende's Popular Unity coalition.[140]

Second, United States policies could not have been, as officials publicly claimed, primarily a response to alleged offenses of the Allende administration. Three U.S. presidents and their close advisers authorized secretly spending millions of dollars to manipulate Chilean elections before Allende came to power. The United States promoted a coup d'état to abort the results of a free election. Former CIA Director Richard Helms reported that "the Nixon administration would like to have had President Allende overthrown," and made an effort to determine whether it could be done, even before the Allende government had taken office.[141] Surely those actions could not have been inspired as a result of the policies of an Allende administration which had not then taken office.

Some persons might justify United States policy as "anticipatory intervention," based on a calculation (mistaken, as it turned out) about Allende's attitude toward civil liberties. Yet, to argue that officials acted before Allende was inaugurated in anticipation that, if elected, Allende would be antidemocratic, even if true, in no way negates the conclusion that the United States purpose was to prevent Chileans from freely expressing at the polls their right of self-determination.

Moreover, the argument that some officials genuinely feared that Allende would establish a one-party government insensitive to civil liberties is uncompelling, given U.S. intelligence reports confirming Allende's commitment to democratic freedom and the willingness of U.S. officials to acquiesce in gross violations of civil liberties in countries such as Brazil and post-Allende Chile. The real meaning of the decisions by the 40 Committee, as well as the constancy and unambiguous intention of both Republican and Democrat administrations, becomes clear when viewed in the context of earlier policy.

U.S. efforts had been designed to prevent the electoral success of the coalition of Chilean socialist parties ever since the 1958 election in which Allende's coalition lost to Jorge Alessandri by only 35,000 votes. Thereafter, the United States gave Chile more economic assistance per capita than any other country in Latin America.[142] In the months just before the 1964 election, the United States Agency for International Development gave Chile a grant of $40 million to buoy up the economy and lower unemployment in order to decrease popular support for the parties of the Left.[143] For at least a dozen years, Chile had been regarded as a pivotal country in Latin America. Allende and the forces supporting him, according to Latin American specialist

Richard R. Fagen, "had been considered the chief threats to American interests. Directly and indirectly, perhaps a billion dollars in public funds had been committed by the United States during this period to the 'battle to preserve democracy in Chile,' largely defined as a battle to prevent the Left from coming to power."[144]

When Allende ran against Eduardo Frei in 1964, according to William Colby, at least three million dollars of CIA funds went into covert efforts to prevent an Allende victory.[145] *Washington Post* reporter Laurence Stern, on the basis of interviews with intelligence officers at the time, estimated as much as $29 million in funds were involved. As one strategically placed intelligence officer told Stern: "U.S. Government intervention in Chile in 1964 was blatant and almost obscene. We were shipping off people right and left, mainly State Department but also CIA with all sorts of covers."[146]

Immediately after the socialist government of Chile was overthrown by the pro-U.S. military dictatorship, the United States made no serious efforts to protect democratic pluralism or a free press. When the new regime shut down the legislature, banned political parties, and shackled the free press, the United States used its secret agents "to assist the junta in gaining a more positive image, both at home and abroad, and to maintain access to command levels of the Chilean government." The CIA retained its penetration of Chilean media outlets in order "to help build Chilean public support for the new government." The CIA efforts aimed "to present the junta in the most positive light for the Chilean public." The CIA also helped the new military government organize and implement policy. CIA collaborators helped prepare an initial overall economic plan that served as the basis for the junta's most important economic decisions, decisions which have proved as disastrous for the lower classes as they were rewarding for U.S. investments in Chile.[147] Two CIA collaborators assisted the junta in writing the *White Book of the Change of Government in Chile*. This book, widely distributed in Washington and other foreign capitals, was written to justify the overthrow of Allende. The CIA also developed new contacts with Chilean police and internal security forces.[148]

The nature, duration, and timing of U.S. covert actions in Chile clearly demonstrate that U.S. policy was not aimed primarily at rescuing newspapers or political parties from a repressive Chilean government. On the contrary, when many civil liberties

235

were vigorously practiced by diverse groups during the Allende period, the United States sought to overthrow the democratically elected government. When the same civil liberties were extinguished by a military dictatorship, the United States assisted the military officials in securing power. The United States helped organize and support those who wrote and distributed propaganda to improve the dictatorship's image at home and abroad. By violating the Chilean electoral process, the United States helped destroy—rather than protect—political pluralism and self-government in Chile. For more than a decade, Washington officials opposed the expression of self-determination and then actively worked to overturn the results of a legal election after it had occurred. Thus the United States violated self-determination in both of its conventional usages, whether defined as freedom from external interference or as internal democratic government. In direct conflict with the U.S. officials' professed value of protecting Chilean democracy, an alternative value was embedded in United States behavior: *to undermine and prevent the exercise of the right of self-determination* (implicit value A).

In order to implement this value, the United States violated its pledge, solemnly given in duly ratified treaties, to refrain from intervening or encouraging conditions likely to produce violence in other Latin American countries. The United States directly promoted a coup in 1970. The staff report of the Select Committee on Intelligence Activities concluded that the CIA's propaganda " 'scare campaign' contributed to the political polarization and financial panic of the period."[149] In 1973 the United States nurtured conditions designed to provoke a coup. The second U.S.-encouraged coup brought widespread, arbitrary arrests, imprisonments, torture, and executions. The new, harsh dictatorship extinguished the free press, prohibited activity by political parties, forced the Chilean Congress to close, and deliberately violated civil liberties.[150]

In spite of public statements by Kissinger and Ford to the contrary, the majority of secret money sent into Chile by the CIA during Allende's administration went to finance clandestine, disruptive activity in Chile—not to protect civil liberties. "Broadly speaking, U.S. policy sought to maximize pressures on the Allende government."[151] To the extent that money did go to friendly media, one high official explained that this support was necessary not because the United States wanted opposition media in themselves—the CIA usually has not encouraged opposition media in pro-United States authoritarian governments—but because "it wouldn't have been good to have strikes if nobody knows about it."[152] Moreover, money that appeared as if it was designed to help a beleagured press was designed in fact to play "an important role in setting the stage for the . . . military coup which overthrew Allende."[153]

The CIA willingly supported specific parties, movements, and policies that were unequivocally antagonistic to legal and democratic political processes. This support went in some cases to those promoting violence and an end to civilian politics altogether. As late as July 25, 1973, the CIA sought authorization to spend $200,000 for clandestine support of the National party, which had urged Chileans to reject the Allende administration by violence if necessary. During the twelve months before Allende's overthrow, it had close ties with the *Patria y Libertad*, which openly boasted of its involvement in military efforts to overthrow the Allende government.[154] The CIA's "rule of thumb apparently was to throw its weight behind the strongest source of opposition to the Allende Government."[155]

The tone of United States policy was vividly captured by one United States diplomat who served in Chile. He said that officials at the U.S. embassy in Santiago felt that "they were engaged in a kind of warfare. People either were with you or against you when it came to Allende. There were a lot of people in Santiago on the far right who were essentially dedicating their lives to the overthrow of Allende—it was like a holy war. These people were increasingly seen at the Embassy in 1972 and 1973. Just putting some resources at their disposal alone would be enough."[156] In sum, U.S. behavior *encouraged conditions likely to produce civil strife and violence* (implicit value B).

The accuracy of the analysis underlying implicit values A and B is confirmed by a series of National Intelligence Estimates (NIEs). These were joint assessments by all U.S. intelligence agencies. An NIE issued on Chile in August 1971, nine months after Allende came to power, suggested that Allende was not the threat to democracy that some officials had originally expected. The NIE said that the consolidation of a Marxist political leadership was *not* inevitable. The report acknowledged that Allende preferred to adhere to constitutional means, although it also speculated that he might be impelled to circumvent the Constitution to stay in power. It noted that Allende had taken great

237

care to observe all constitutional requirements, and that he enjoyed substantial popularity in Chile. An NIE of June 1972 stated that the democratic political system of Chile possessed remarkable resiliency and that the prospects for the continuation of democracy in Chile were higher than at any time since Allende's inauguration. Legislative, student, and trade union elections continued to take place in normal democratic fashion. Pro-Allende forces willingly accepted election results when they were adverse. The NIE stressed that the Christian Democratic party and the National party were using their control of both houses of Congress to stall government legislation and to pass their own legislation designed to curtail Allende's powers. The news media continued to criticize the government. This NIE concluded that Allende would probably slow the pace of his program for change in the next year in order to accommodate the opposition and to preserve the gains he had made.

U.S. intelligence agencies issued another NIE shortly before Allende's overthrow in September 1973. This one stated clearly that Allende was unlikely to establish an Eastern European style Marxist regime. The NIE reported that the majority of low-income Chileans knew that Allende had improved their conditions and represented their interests. The NIE noted that support for the Popular Unity coalition had grown because of Allende's political ability and the popularity of his measures. The NIE also warned that growing polarization of Chilean society was harming the Chilean predilection for political compromise.[157]

These NIEs initially carried a predictable governmental hostility toward Allende and the expectation that he would impose a heavy-handed dictatorship of the Eastern European variety. But as Allende proved himself to be serious about protecting both civil liberties and the Chilean Constitution, the NIEs reported that dictatorship was unlikely and that Allende was indeed popular among the segments of the electorate most in need of governmental action to promote their personal, economic, and political liberty. Despite these reports, the United States opposition to Allende became more intense as he succeeded in upholding democratic practices. At the same time as the NIEs became more certain that Allende would not impose a dictatorship, the 40 Committee authorized more and more money for covert operations to promote his downfall.[158]

238

Professed Value 2: To Protect the Interests of the Chilean People

Whose interests were served by U.S. policy? Economically, the Chileans who benefited most from United States intervention were those who needed help the least. Upper-class people, who collaborated with United States corporate interests in Chile, could, after 1973, once again control a disproportionate share of Chilean income. The military, who were trained and equipped by the United States, were in complete control. And middle-class people, who clung to a moderately satisfactory yet somewhat precarious social position, could, by acquiescing in the repression of the poor, once again enjoy the importation of goods from the United States. The large lower class, whose interests were historically ignored and whom Allende sought to raise above second-class citizenship, were hurt most by United States intervention.

Politically, the beneficiaries of U.S. policy that President Ford apparently had in mind were anti-Allende political parties and newspapers. However, even in the alleged effort to protect political pluralism, once again those who needed help the most—the dispossessed people lacking political resources—were harmed by United States intervention. Far from benefiting most Chileans, the military government that replaced Allende's administration executed profoundly vengeful and inhumane policies. Upon taking power, the junta controlled the people by military force. The military government seized the universities, abolished labor organizations, and suspended political parties.[159] Ten to fifteen thousand persons were killed. Over a million were ejected from their jobs and blacklisted so they could not obtain employment elsewhere. Over twenty thousand were driven into exile.[160] Tens of thousands were imprisoned, often without specific charges against them, and many of the imprisoned were tortured. According to the International Commission of Jurists, torture was widely practiced and included "electric shock, burning with acid or cigarettes, extraction of nails, crushing of testicles, sexual assault, and hanging."[161] Approximately one million Chileans moved outside their homeland in order to escape the repressive government.

In contrast, Laurence Birns, a former UN employee for the Economic Commission for Latin America in Santiago, reported that there was "far less intentional police brutality under Al-

239

lende than existed under the previous Christian Democratic regime. There were hardly any cases of imprisonment on political grounds. The universities were entirely free although some faculties became heavily politicized. Political life was almost entirely free of secret police surveillance."[162] According to Birns, "Not a single newspaper was censored by the civilian authorities, and opposition political parties could rage at will against the government. . . . Allende was scrupulously correct in maintaining unimpaired, under unrelieved internal and external pressure, all the nation's institutions."[163] Paul Sigmund, a U.S. critic of the Allende government, admitted that until the junta took power away from Allende in September 1973, Chile "had a more open political structure than our own."[164]

Kissinger's disregard for the Chileans' right of self-determination was paralleled by his lack of concern for the loss of individual human rights within Chile after the pro-United States military government deposed Allende. Richard Holbrooke, editor of *Foreign Policy*, reported that Kissinger was "wholly free of any constraint based on a set of moral beliefs [and] without feeling for human suffering." He did not let "human beings interfere with policy."[165] When the United Nations General Assembly passed a resolution urging Chile to restore human rights and free political prisoners, the United States abstained. Only seven other Latin American countries voted with Chile against the resolution.[166]

Kissinger also reportedly rebuked David H. Popper, the new United States ambassador to Chile, after Popper had attempted to discuss torture and other human rights issues with Chilean officials in the context of negotiations about military aid to Chile. As a result of a Kissinger directive, a formally drafted State Department letter of complaint went to Popper. Some State Department officials indicated that Popper's rebuke was a demonstration of the administration's unwillingness to press human rights issues with the junta. Kissinger's aides defended the action by arguing that Kissinger's objection was based on Popper's efforts to link "unrelated" issues such as human rights with United States military aid to the junta.[167]

This Kissinger action took place in spite of legislation passed by Congress in 1973 calling on the Nixon administration to request that the Chilean government "protect the human rights of all individuals." Congress also declared that any military or economic assistance should be conditional upon Chilean guarantees of safe conduct for refugees, humane treatment of prisoners, and no imprisonment of people for political purposes.[168]

One might attempt to defend United States interventionist policy by arguing that United States officials may not have wanted such a vengeful regime to take the place of Allende's. Nevertheless, United States policies did promote civil strife. Assistance was not limited to democratic opponents of Allende. It was widely assumed in the United States government that any political alternative in Chile was preferable to a Marxist government. For example, even after the brutality of the military government was convincingly documented, Ray S. Cline, director of the State Department's Bureau of Intelligence and participant in the 40 Committee's deliberations from 1970-73, said that the Chilean people were better off under the military government than when governed by Allende.[169] Throughout the Allende administration, the United States maintained separate, direct contact with the Chilean military, and discussed plans for a coup d'état. Therefore, even if United States officials preferred a less vengeful regime, the nature of their intervention makes it clear that the United States never seriously sought to avoid promoting conditions likely to bring a brutal regime into power.

In addition, the United States government and at least some corporation officials made a concerted effort to encourage the corruption of Chilean political leaders through the use of money for bribery of candidates or members of Congress and the Chilean executive branch. Although bribery is a constitutionally defined cause for impeachment in the United States, officials of the United States and of U.S. corporations developed a policy in Chile to bribe political leaders and then to enthrone those successfully bribed.

Finally, U.S. intervention lent support to the notion, of significance to reformers around the world, that a program of fundamental change could succeed only if accompanied by widespread force and repression. By helping eliminate a democratic road to reform in Chile, U.S. officials mocked moderate reformers who genuinely believed that the United States would not subvert their legal processes. As a result of the destruction of the Allende government by U.S.-supported Chilean militarists, Allende was more likely to be viewed by observers either as a naive social democrat or as a revolutionary failure because he tried to make changes without a Leninist hold on the apparatus of state power. U.S. policy vindicated the proponents of more authoritarian models of change. Within Chile, the United States encouraged the polarization of citizens toward two irreconcilable camps: those of the authoritarian right, who believed that their government should repress social reformers and cooperate with United States economic and strategic interests, and those of the authoritarian left, who believed that achieving economic equity would be possible only through a violent, centrally-directed movement to oust the United States and its indigenous collaborators.

In sum, U.S. policy served those Chileans most willing to collaborate with the perpetuation of U.S. interests in Chile, rather than the wider Chilean public. William Colby stated U.S. intentions more accurately than President Ford when he explained that covert operations were taken in Chile to serve "the best interests of our country, and friendly elements in another one."[170] For several U.S. administrations to help violent, militaristic, and antidemocratic groups meant that officials preferred the retention of economic inequities and the promotion of authoritarian government to the acceptance of an elected government committed to radical socioeconomic change aimed at greater equity in Chile. U.S. actions meant Washington officials believed they knew what was good for Chileans even better than Chileans expressing themselves at the polls. U.S. policies meant a Latin American country would not be allowed to choose a different economic system, less subject to United States investment, profit-taking, and commercial and political influence, without suffering United States reprisals. In its policies of overt economic pressure and covert support of Allende's opponents, the United States helped set in motion and sustain forces that led to the eventual death of the Allende government.

Thus, rather than protecting the interests of the Chilean people, as officials professed, United States behavior expressed an alternative value cluster: *to encourage disrespect for individual human rights and the rule of law, to promote the corruption of Chilean officials, and to discourage nonviolent, humane processes of social change* (implicit value C).

In support of the implicit values noted above, United States policy carried other implications which were generally applicable to many less developed countries. U.S. policy tended *to discourage overseas elites from solving their real domestic problems of injustice and human suffering* (implicit value D). United States policy

242

invited foreign officials, such as the Chilean dictatorship, to focus on developing pro-United States relations and at the same time to enrich a small Chilean group of collaborators with U.S. economic interests, to cater to middle-class consumers of U.S. exports, and to ignore the grievances of the lower classes. For an elite to stay in power in Chile, after all, depended as much on retaining friendly relations with the United States as with meeting the needs of their own dispossessed people.

U.S. policy also served *to discourage overseas elites from dealing with underlying international dimensions of their internal problems* (implicit value E). U.S. officials induced foreign political leaders to overlook the extent to which the poverty of their suppressed classes was due to the wealth-extracting role of capital-exporting states and of indigenous collaborators with the latter. The preoccupation of many Latin American governments with bilateral relations with the United States has deterred them from recognizing the need to transform the international economic structure for greater fulfillment of human needs. They have failed to press for global systemic change that would facilitate political self-determination, redistribute the world's wealth more equitably, and yield a greater degree of economic justice internally. They have remained happy with their privileged positions within their national structures, often propped up by United States-based multinational corporations, overt U.S. aid, and covert CIA activity.

Professed Value 3: To Protect United States National Security

Objectively, the existence of the Allende government in itself could hardly have threatened United States security. Chile was thousands of miles away, with 5 percent of the population and one half of one percent of the GNP of the United States. Allende made no plans to attack the United States nor to harm any neighboring states. Why, then, did the United States fear Allende enough to violate self-determination and to spend millions of dollars for his demise?

The security rationale for United States intervention contained two dimensions, one ideological and the other economic, neither of which constituted a direct strategic threat. First of all, many officials continued to view the spread of socialism, especially to the Western Hemisphere, as a threat to United States security. This was an ideologically determined assumption, not an empirically rooted conclusion. These ideological beliefs, al-

243

though unfounded, guided policy just as surely as if they were rooted in reality.

The earlier cold war belief that the spread of communism threatened United States security continued to influence officials. In mentioning security as a rationale for United States policy, Ford fell back upon the standard cold war strategy that CIA operations were a necessary part of a policy of opposing communism. Since the United States was anticommunist, the argument went, any Marxist government must be part of an anti-United States communist coalition. But this line of argument was unpersuasive for at least two reasons. In the first place, Allende was in no sense an agent of the Soviet Union or China or even of the Communist party of Chile, with which he had occasionally been at odds during his career as leader of Chilean socialists. Second, if the United States could normalize relations with the communist giants—China and the Soviet Union—it made little sense, from a strategic viewpoint, to disrupt relations with a small power like Chile. As the cold war had waned, officials learned to accept existing communist governments, but still retained the belief that the spread of Marxism was a danger. Thus United States officials promoted détente with the Soviet Union and China at the same time they sought to overturn the relatively weak Chilean government's more moderate Marxism.

The hold of cold war rhetoric upon the minds of officials was echoed by the president himself in condoning the superpowers' practice of maintaining client states. In justifying the United States clandestine intervention, Ford revealed how much even in his own mind the guiding principle—if not the dollar amount—of United States foreign policy was similar to Soviet policy: "Communist nations spend vastly more money than we do for the same kind of purposes."[171] The common purpose, apparently, was to maintain in power foreign elites more sympathetic to a superpower's interests than would have existed without clandestine superpower intervention.[172]

United States officials were angry about Allende because his government represented the expansion of socialism in the Western Hemisphere, but more importantly because he represented something that the ideologically molded worldviews of officials could not tolerate: a Marxist who was elected through a fair, democratic process. In this sense, a constitutional Marxism, respecting many civil liberties, was more of a threat to U.S. officials than Fidel Castro's more authoritarian version of communism.

As a Marxist and a democrat, Allende existed in two mutually exclusive categories. To make Allende fit their presuppositions, U.S. officials constantly distorted his position on civil liberties, and discussed him in nearly Stalinist terms. Rather than bring their ideology into conformity with reality, they sought to change reality to fit their ideology. Thus the longer Allende continued in office without abolishing civil liberties, the more money Washingtonians spent to hasten his demise.[173] The long tradition of anticommunist thinking and the constraints of personal ideology upon policymaking prevented a realistic foundation upon which to build policy.

The Allende government was feared and hated because it represented radical economic change and could stimulate a chain of events—falling economic dominoes—that would be disorderly and costly for the U.S. Allende's vision of radical change encouraged a fundamental altering of the status quo in which the United States enjoyed vastly disproportionate wealth and power. In spite of the economic difficulties of Allende's government, we should recall that he "attempted to undo a system in which 5 percent of the families controlled some 35 percent of the agricultural land, in which the banks worked only for the established rich and industries underproduced products that were overpriced. He attempted, and with significant success, to bring health, housing, a better diet, and education to the poor, and a sense of dignity and of national participation to those for whom Chile's constitutional system had previously been unreal and fraudulent."[174]

The main objection of U.S. officials to democratic socialism was that it meant less opportunity for foreign investment of U.S. capital, less opportunity for profit for U.S. corporations, and less influence by the United States over the affairs of other countries. Thus the fear of corporation executives and U.S. government officials that private enterprise would be nationalized without compensation was only one part of a much larger fear that future investment and profit opportunities in Chile would be foreclosed. (They had, in previous years, been steadily growing.)

U.S. policymakers would not have been happy to have accepted expropriation even if it were carried out with fair compensation. The United States declined Allende's request to submit the disputed offers for compensation to international arbitration. Since 1916 a treaty had been in force between Chile and the United States which established a commission of five

245

persons to solve disputes between the two countries. Chile proposed that its interpretation of the nationalization proceedings be studied by the international commission according to the provisions of the treaty. The United States recognized that the treaty was valid, but refused.[175]

The fear of diminished profits for investors explains why officials were promoting more credit and trade with the Soviet Union at the same time they curtailed them with Chile: in the Soviet case, where there were no large U.S. private investments, détente promised new economic benefits for U.S. businesses; in the Chilean case, where profitable investments had long paid dividends, the advent of socialism promised loss of profits. With Allende in power, U.S. corporations, which had not benefited the lower classes in Chile, would be required to participate in distributing wealth more equitably. Thus officials opposed Chilean economic nationalism and control of U.S. corporations more than they opposed Marxism itself in China or the Soviet Union.

Thus the ideological rigidity toward Chile was buttressed by a larger design in world politics. As indicated above, Ambassador Korry and others feared that a successful Allende government would aid the rising electoral strength of communist parties in Italy and France.[176] When Kissinger briefed congressional leaders about Chile, he also said that CIA activity was necessary in other contexts, such as to prevent the Italian government from becoming communist.[177] Within the hemisphere, the demonstration-effect or domino theory had a different variation. Rather than expect other socialist parties to win election, United States officials worried—as Connally openly admitted—about the likelihood that simply having a Chilean government strongly opposed to continued United States profit-taking in Latin America would encourage reformist tendencies in Bolivia, Peru, and elsewhere. As Fagen has reported, Washington officials feared that the Popular Unity government "would profoundly affect the correlation of political forces on the landmass of South America, link economic nationalism more directly to socialist forms and solutions, and give a new and difficult-to-counter legitimacy to anti-Americanism and the nationalization of banks, large industries, and subsoil resources."[178]

Ideological hostility toward radical Latin Americans, who were skeptical about the utility of the profit motive of United States corporations for serving the human needs of their lower classes, reinforced the desire to protect the present and potential profits of U.S. investors, who were often important architects of U.S. policy in Washington. By helping discredit Allende, U.S. leaders could in a single act, reestablish their ideology overseas, reduce the cognitive dissonance caused by the incompatibility of their ideology with reality, promote their own personal and institutional wealth, and protect their national power.

It would be erroneous to suggest that there were no differences among United States policymakers about the specific policies to pursue toward Chile. There were differences of opinion within the Department of State, as well as between members of the State and Treasury Departments, between ITT and the State Department, between the CIA and the State Department. Kissinger reportedly took over the direction of the covert action of Chile because he felt that Charles Meyer, assistant secretary of state for Latin America, might be unenthusiastic about a hard-line policy. Nevertheless, these disagreements seldom reflected significant differences in policy goals. In general, the entire bureaucratic apparatus was cooperating in the implementation of policies designed to make it impossible for the Popular Unity coalition to govern.[179]

After examining the security considerations in United States policy, it is clear that the professed value of serving national security was hardly reflected in actual practice. U.S. behavior would be more accurately characterized by implicit value F: *to maintain United States overseas economic and political influence in the face of a radical movement to realize greater self-determination and economic equity.*

In several ways, United States policy negatively affected national security. In the first place, the intervention contributed to a United States image throughout the world of a manipulative, unfair, dishonest, ruthless giant resisting the rights of the weak and poor. At the time of the Chilean revelations, Ambassador Daniel P. Moynihan noted this effect in India.[180] Washington's posture meant the United States exposed itself to blame even for some subversion of which it was innocent. In the long run this image could hardly serve the legitimate security needs of any United States citizen.

The policy of secret intervention also violated United States security interests because it encouraged other states to employ "dirty tricks" more widely. Such policies victimize small societies, subject them to great power machinations, and make orderly,

247

humane change less likely. Reformers in the less developed countries are taught to accept the status quo or else become violent revolutionaries.

Thirdly, the policy of secret intervention violated United States security interests because it lowered the expectations in the international community for legal behavior. It would be foolish, of course, to believe that if the CIA avoided interventions that the Soviet KGB would immediately stop them also, but it would be equally foolish to ignore that norms for behavior do influence decision makers to some extent, and that the norms themselves are strengthened or weakened by United States behavior. When Ford justified U.S. intervention on the grounds that the USSR engaged in similar action, he encouraged a worldview which, if generalized, would result in a gradually deteriorating expectation about what constituted conventional, legitimate international behavior. That jeopardized the security not simply of all U.S. citizens, but of all citizens on the planet.

Moreover, interventionism violated United States security interests because, when repeated, it distracted U.S. decision makers from constructing foreign policies to deal with root causes of social conflict throughout the world. The CIA intervention in Chile was only one of a long list of examples that showed the United States opposed to self-determination if it brought radical reallocation of wealth and power. Other examples of United States intervention included: the overthrow of the reform government of President Jacobo Arbenz Guzman of Guatemala (1954); the engineering of economic and political agitation against Cheddi Jagen, the socialist premier of British Guiana (1961-62); the training, transport and air support for the invasion of Cuba to overthrow Fidel Castro (1961); intervention in the Dominican Republic by 18,000 U.S. marines to oppose the return to power of reform-minded President Juan Bosch, who was earlier deposed by a military takeover; infiltration and establishment of political and economic control of the Ecuadorian labor movement in the early 1960s leading to the overthrow of the civilian government by a military dictatorship; the use for more than two years of a Bolivian cabinet official as a CIA operative; and the overthrow of Iranian Premier Mohammed Mossadegh (1953) who had nationalized the Iranian oil industry. According to the findings of the Senate Select Committee, the United States instigated assassination plots against at least two foreign leaders and became embroiled in plotting that led to the

248

deaths of three others. CIA officials gave orders to assassinate Patrice Lumumba in 1960 although his death may not have been due to CIA activity. Eight unsuccessful schemes were planned against Fidel Castro's life between 1961 and 1965. Three other high officials who were targets for removal, kidnapping, or assassination were Rafael Trujillo of the Dominican Republic, Ngo Dinh Diem of South Vietnam, and General René Schneider of Chile, all of whom eventually were killed, although apparently not directly by the CIA. The CIA also supplied arms to dissidents planning the overthrow of President Sukarno of Indonesia.[181]

In addition, many less dramatic interventions have occurred in recruiting and paying money to foreign officials willing to collaborate with the CIA. For example, Jose Figueres, the former president of Costa Rica, admitted he had worked for the CIA in "twenty thousand ways" since it was founded. He said other Latin American presidents had done the same.[182] Philip Agee asserted that Mexican President Luis Echeverria worked as a "collaborator" with the CIA while he was Minister of the Interior.[183]

In the hope that secret financing of strikers, bribing officials, stuffing ballot boxes, or assassinating politicians would produce pro-U.S. governments, U.S. officials have ignored more basic issues. of self-determination and social justice in developing societies, as well as issues of human survival on the planet. Addressing these basic issues could have done far more, in the long run, to serve United States security. Thus, surprising though it might have seemed to the leadership, it was true that insensitivity to human rights actually harmed efforts to achieve genuine security for United States citizens.

Finally, a policy of intervention discouraged a long-run approach to transform the present nation-state structure to a more fully global structure of world order. The CIA provided a crutch for a limping international political system, and sought to prolong the system's life through more crafty use of national sovereignty, when in fact without the covert, interventionist crutch officials would have seen more clearly that competitive sovereignty and excessive unregulated power at the national level were part of the infirmity. In sum, the cumulative impact of U.S. policy in Chile directly contradicted professed value 3. Rather than safeguard U.S. citizens, Washington's policies served *to undermine U.S. security in the long run* (implicit value G).

Professed Value 4: To Protect the Interests of U.S. Citizens

Kissinger, Nixon, Ford, and others claimed that U.S. policy served the interests of the people of the United States. Although these officials never specified precisely whose interests they had in mind, the most obvious beneficiaries were the owners of United States corporations in Chile. Companies such as ITT, Anaconda, and Kennecott were promised compensation by Allende's successors.

Although some United States corporations did benefit economically from the collapse of constitutional government in Chile, this did not mean that intervention benefited the U.S. public in general. Not even all businesses agreed that U.S. intervention served their interests.[184] Except for the average citizen's predilection for private enterprise systems, there is little evidence of any benefits to the U.S. public from the subversion of self-determination. At the same time, citizens' interests in protection of constitutional government and human rights, and elimination of poverty in Chile all were damaged by United States policy.

As revealed in the foregoing examination of professed values, the best explanation for U.S. policy was the desire on the part of U.S. officials *to oppose the political and economic success of a newly established socialist government as a strategy to advance economic benefits for large U.S. investors* (implicit value H).[185]

By rhetorically wedding the economic interests of some United States-based multinational corporations with the public interest, the U.S. government—intentionally or unintentionally—encouraged the public to believe that overseas reformers, especially socialists, pursued policies that were contrary to the interests of the U.S. public because they were contrary to the profit maximizing desires of multinational corporations. In many cases, of course, this was untrue. Because these corporations decided what to produce on the basis of profitability, they frequently reduced productive capacity for less profitable goods that could have fulfilled the human needs of large sections of the public in the United States as well as in Chile. But because the poor lacked money to generate demand for such products, multinational corporations had no interest in producing them. By using patriotic appeals to induce public support for United States foreign policy, by drawing upon the traditional preference of the public for private enterprise, by combining antiradical inclinations and dislike for foreign "disorder" with the as-

250

sumption that what was good for big corporations was good for all United States citizens and all Chileans as well, the U.S. government has slowed the growth of public support for overseas social reform movements.

In the Chilean case, the U.S. government's actions misled the public about the nature of social problems and political activity in Chile. United States leaders encouraged their constituents to believe that Allende's goals were alien to the people of Chile and to the Western Hemisphere. Yet, however strongly one may accuse Allende of economic misjudgment in his conduct of public affairs, many of his goals enjoyed the support of a majority of Chilean citizens, as the unanimous passage of expropriation legislation indicated. Tomic, the presidential candidate of the centrist Christian Democrat party, ran on a platform that resembled Allende's in many respects, and which included nationalization of the major industries. Thus in the long run, only indefinite United States manipulation of Chilean politics or a right-wing Chilean dictatorship could have prevented growing Chilean control over United States corporations, regardless of what happened to Allende. The new military government was an oligarchic force, representing the coalition of big business and big landowners that had opposed the reforms of President Frei as well.[186] Both Republican and Democratic administrations discouraged the U.S. public from understanding these political realities. Officials sought *to prevent the growth of public support in the United States for overseas radical movements aiming at more equitable distribution of economic and political resources globally and within their own societies* (implicit value I).

U.S. officials justified their policies in terms of widely held humanitarian values, but perverted those values in executing specific policies. In the words of the Senate Select Committee on Intelligence, official deceptiveness sustained covert actions that were "inconsistent with our basic traditions and values."[187] The inconsistencies were demonstrated in several ways.

In the first place, for more than three years U.S. leaders continually denied taking either overt or covert action to harm the Allende administration. They did this because they feared that their policies would not be supported by the general public if the truth were known. After the *New York Times* story first reported major CIA involvement, officials continued to cover up as much of the activity as possible, rather than give a full accounting.[188] The further those in power moved beyond the publicly-defined

251

limits of generally acceptable behavior, the more they hid their acts under a blanket of secrecy.

Second, rather than tolerate a diversity of views on issues of overseas social reform, the United States government harrassed even U.S. citizens, living in Santiago, who were neutral or pro-Allende. The U.S. embassy in Santiago spied on the activities of U.S. citizens and perhaps even communicated their findings to Chilean military officials.[189]

Finally, even if by some disjointed logic one might argue that the CIA intervention served the interests of the United States public, that would not have justified overthrowing the constitutional government chosen by the Chilean public. Surely most U.S. citizens would have agreed that no errors of political judgment and no peculiarities of ideology on the part of an elected U.S. president would justify intervention by a foreign power in the affairs of the United States.

In sum, U.S. officials designed policies *to utilize the public preference for private enterprise systems in a strategy that, on a concrete level, contradicted the public's humanitarian sympathies, ideas of political rectitude, and sense of fair play* (implicit value J).

Secret CIA activity abroad spilled over into illegal governmental behavior at home. The *Pentagon Papers*, the Watergate scandals, and a twenty-year record of illegal CIA domestic activities[190] provide ample evidence that decision makers who develop strategies to subvert self-determination abroad are irresistibly tempted to subvert it at home. As Daniel Ellsberg said after the first Watergate revelations, the logic of Watergate was the same as the logic of Vietnamese policy documented in the *Pentagon Papers*: for United States officials, the law stopped at the White House fence. In making policy for Chile, the members of the 40 Committee saw themselves as above the law. Some of the same people who covered up Watergate misdeeds similarly claimed that they were circumscribing investigations in order to protect national security and CIA secrets. Typically, when some of Kissinger's covert policies began to be discussed in public, he approved the wiretapping of his own advisers and staff in order to prevent public scrutiny of United States policies.[191] Rather than confine their conduct to the legally-defined limits, officials in several administrations preferred *to risk undermining the legitimacy of the United States government within U.S. society* (implicit value K).

CIA operations like the Chilean intervention lowered the expectations of citizens that their government would be honest and open. After all, if "dirty tricks" were performed, officials could be expected to lie about them. They would publicly deny what they privately did. In Henry Kissinger's own words, the CIA was used for covert actions "because it was less accountable."[192] When accurate information about public affairs is no longer available or highly valued in a society, the practice of democracy becomes impossible. When U.S. leaders insisted upon the widespread need for secrecy, they indicated that they did not welcome participation in decisions. They did not favor self-government. In this sense, Washington national security managers made themselves enemies of the people.

Executive officials deliberately deceived members of Congress, who were duty-bound to carry the preferences of the people into the policymaking process. During the Allende campaign, the State Department maintained a public facade of nonintervention and proclaimed it repeatedly. Long after the United States had spent millions of dollars to create economic chaos, manipulate elections, and foment a coup, the president told Congress: "We respect the hemispheric principle of nonintervention. . . . We recognize that [Chile's leaders] . . . are serious men whose ideological principles are, to some extent, frankly in conflict with ours. Nevertheless, our relations will hinge not on their ideology but on their conduct toward the outside world."[193]

After the coup in 1973, the State Department formally denied any financial involvement in opposition protests and strikes, declaring "such suggestions are absurd."[194] Edward Korry, former ambassador to Chile, testified under oath to a subcommittee of the Senate Foreign Relations Committee that it was true and "obvious from the historical record that . . . the United States gave no support to any electoral candidate; that the United States had maintained the most total hands-off the military policy from 1969 to 1971 conceivable; that the United States did not get involved in the so-called Alessandri formula; that the United States did not seek to pressure, subvert, influence a single member of the Congress at any time in the entire 4 years of my stay."[195] Again and again, Charles A. Meyer, former assistant secretary of state for Latin American affairs, assured senators:

The policy of the Government . . . was that there would be no intervention in the political affairs of Chile. . . . We financed

253

no candidates, no political parties. . . . The policy of the United States was that Chile's problem was a Chilean problem to be settled by Chile. As the President stated in October of 1969, "We deal with governments as they are."

The policy of the U.S. government . . . remained non-interventionist. We neither financed candidates nor financed parties nor financed Alessandri gambits. Nor tried to precipitate economic chaos, and promoted neither civil nor military nor any other coup. The policy of Chile's future was Chile's.

We bought no votes, we funded no candidates, we promoted no coups. . . . We were religiously and scrupulously adhering to the policy of the Government of the United States . . . of nonintervention.[196]

Assistant Secretary of State Jack Kubisch told the House Subcommittee for Inter-American Affairs on September 20, 1973:

The United States had no desire to provoke a confrontation with the Allende Government. On the contrary, strong efforts were repeatedly made to seek ways to resolve our differences. . . . The position of the United States was quite correct. . . . We were not involved in the coup in any way. . . . It is untrue to say that the United States government was responsible—either directly or indirectly—for the overthrow of the Allende regime. We were not responsible for the difficulties in which Chile found itself, and it is not for us to judge what would have been best or will now be best for the Chilean people. That is for the Chileans themselves to decide, and we respect their right to do this.[197]

Corporate officials were equally blind or deceptive in describing their own role. For example, ITT senior vice-president E. J. Gerrity testified, "We did everything possible to build good faith with Mr. Allende."[198]

CIA Director William Colby's later testimony demonstrated that officials from the Department of State, the Treasury Department, the CIA, and the White House repeatedly, intentionally misled the public and Congress. Jerome Levinson, chief counsel for the subcommittee investigating the ITT role in Chile, reportedly said the subcommittee had been "deliberately deceived."[199] The White House described what later was revealed to have been a highly misleading briefing by Kissinger as a "full and frank discussion of the full range of CIA activities."[200]

Because of executive deception and congressional inaction, the public was deprived of any effective role in policymaking during the years of the Allende government. For example, a confidential staff report of the Senate Foreign Relations Subcommittee on Multinational Corporations reportedly charged that misleading testimony under oath had been given by Henry Kissinger; Charles Meyer, assistant secretary of state for Latin America; Edward M. Korry, ambassador to Chile from 1967 to 1971; Nathaniel Davis, Korry's successor as ambassador; Richard Helms, CIA head; William Broe, director of CIA clandestine activities for Latin America; and John Hennessy, assistant secretary of the treasury for international affairs. The staff memorandum reportedly urged contempt of Congress charges for at least some of the officials, and said that Helms, Meyer, and Hennessy might have committed perjury.[201] Senators Church, Symington, Muskie, Case, and Percy, the members of the subcommittee, failed to implement the staff report. As Laurence Birns correctly concluded, the available evidence about United States policymaking reveals "the staggering immorality of the policy's architects and the ineffectuality and irrelevance of most scholars, journalists and Congressional leaders, whose professional obligation it was to oversee executive policies toward Chile."[202]

Instead of promoting public participation, based on truthful information about U.S. behavior, Washington officials preferred *to undermine the conditions essential for democracy in the United States* (implicit value L). As Table 4-2 shows, the values implicit in U.S. policy differed widely from the professed values of the Washington leadership.

A GLOBAL HUMANIST APPROACH

Comparison of Professed Values, Implicit Values,
and the Promotion of Human Rights

The preceding appraisal of United States policy toward Chile has revealed a cluster of implicit values expressed in official behavior. They represent U.S. performance on the particular issue of self-determination and will be compared, in this concluding section of the chapter, with the third value of global humanism:

255

Table 4-2
A Comparison of Professed and Implicit Values
in U.S. Policy on Self-determination

Professed Values	*Implicit Values*
1. To sustain democratic parties and maintain political pluralism in Chile.	A. To undermine and prevent the exercise of the right of self-determination and democratic government.
	B. To encourage conditions likely to produce political polarization, civil strife, and violence.
2. To protect the interests of the Chilean people.	C. To encourage disrespect for individual human rights and the rule of law within Chile, to promote the corruption of Chilean officials, and to discourage nonviolent, humane processes of social change.
	D. To discourage overseas elites from solving their real domestic problems of injustice and human suffering.
	E. To discourage overseas elites from dealing with underlying international dimensions of their internal problems.
	F. To maintain U.S. overseas economic and political influence in the face of a radical movement to realize greater self-determination and economic equity.
3. To protect U.S. national security.	G. To undermine U.S. security in the long run.
4. To protect the interests of U.S. citizens.	H. To oppose a newly established socialist government as a strategy to advance economic benefits for U.S. investors with property in Chile.
	I. To prevent the growth of public support in the U.S. for overseas radical movements aiming at more equitable distribution of economic and political resources globally and within their own societies.

Table 4-2 (cont.)

Professed Values	Implicit Values
	J. To utilize the U.S. public's preference for private enterprise systems in a strategy that, on a concrete level, contradicted the public's humanitarian sympathies, ideas of political rectitude, and sense of fair play.
	K. To risk undermining the legitimacy of the U.S. government within U.S. society.
	L. To undermine the conditions essential for democracy in the U.S.

the promotion of universal human rights and justice (V_3).

The articulated goals of United States policy were frequently in harmony with V_3. To support democratic constitutional government in Chile, and to serve the common interests of Chileans and U.S. citizens were goals obviously compatible with V_3. However, if one moves from the abstract level of policy goals as expressed in official rhetoric to the concrete level of government behavior, United States policy directly violated fundamental human rights.

In particular, U.S. policy aimed at preventing the exercise of self-determination by a people who had, in a constitutional election, favored substantial socioeconomic change. The covert intervention of officials in itself violated the solemn commitment, given in several duly ratified treaties, to respect the principles of self-determination and noninterference in the affairs of other states. Moreover, subverting self-determination was not an incidental or accidental consequence of official behavior; it was a deliberate intention. Officials aimed at perpetuating the disproportionate power of the United States in Chile through covert manipulations, rather than expanding the perimeters of participation in decision making to include Chileans affected by United States government and corporate actions. In defense of United States policy, many have argued that Allende would have fallen somewhat later, due to internal opposition, even without United States intervention. That may perhaps have been true, although

257

if Allende had been actively assisted by the United States in the way that pre- and post-Allende governments were, the conclusion would hardly have followed. Nevertheless, this argument is largely irrelevant to the main point here. Regardless of what would have happened to Allende if left on his own, the fact remains that the United States deliberately intervened numerous times at decisive moments, and for more than a decade, to subvert the practice of self-determination.

Moreover, even if indigenous right-wing forces could have ousted the Allende government, these forces expressed the same elitist, profit-motivated political interests and hostility to human rights and needs that were expressed by U.S. officials. Regardless of the array of internal forces against Allende, an important conclusion is that, in practice, the United States threw its weight against the forces of political and economic reform.

The issue of human rights had a very low priority in policy-making, ranking below capitalist ideological sympathies; human rights were unimportant to strategic advantages and irrelevant to the protection of investment and profit advantages for U.S. corporations. The United States weakened the movement for human rights both internationally and internally in Chile.

The Chilean case study also shows that the ideologically-skewed perception of U.S. officials made them ill-equipped to understand the value impact of U.S. policy and to promote human rights. U.S. leaders operated with a false consciousness[203] from which they made decisions that served their apparent interests, but which overlooked the general public's long-range interests—interests that were partially expressed in the professed values of those in power.

The gap between professed values and behavior suggests the existence of a bureaucratic version of truth that includes a deeply entrenched distortion of reality. Those in power confirmed one another's distortions of reality as policy was set in motion. Bureaucratic disagreements, which might have given opportunity for reality-testing, were confined to the best tactics to follow. Instead, there should have been a debate about whether United States goals were wrong.

Several examples illustrate this faulty comprehension of the real world. Kissinger believed that Allende lacked legitimacy because he had not won a clear majority of the popular vote in the national election. Yet only once in this century had a Chilean president won a majority in a popular election. The Constitution fully anticipated this possibility and defined the procedures, which were followed, for a congressional election of the president. Moreover, Kissinger never questioned the legitimacy of United States presidents, including Nixon in his first term, who were elected by a minority of those voting. The former director of the CIA also misperceived the meaning of the Chilean elections: "I have a difficult time feeling that the Chileans, who are very superior people . . . really wanted that [socialist] type of a government imposed on them, and it was only through the unfortunate division of the opposition that the situation turned out the way it did. Without such a division the results would have been as they were in 1964."[204] In fact, no government was "imposed" on Chile until the U.S.-supported military junta came to power. Allende did not take office primarily because of a split in the opposition. Many Christian Democrats were closer ideologically to the Popular Unity coalition than to Alessandri. Every member of the Christian Democratic party, which McCone described as part of the "opposition" and which won the 1964 election to which McCone referred, freely voted in the Congress to elect Allende to the presidency. They voted for him precisely because the national mandate expressed in the combined vote for the Christian Democrats and the Popular Unity coalition—well over a simple majority—had been in support of major social reform, rather than the reactionary policies of the right-wing candidate.

This faulty hold on reality extended to the corporate world as well. The chief executive officer and chairman of the board of ITT, Harold Geneen, said that the United States would naturally oppose Allende because the United States supported democratic regimes.[205] Ignoring the naiveté of the belief that the United States had guided its policies by opposition to dictatorships and by support for democracies, Geneen failed to comprehend that a socialist system was also democratic if it was chosen as a result of democratic processes and continued to respect those processes. Likewise, ITT's Director of Public Relations for Latin America, Hal Hendrix, reported from Santiago with certainty: "There is no doubt among trained professional observers with experience in the United States, Europe and Latin America that if Allende and the UP [Popular Unity coalition] take power, Chile will be transformed quickly into a harsh and tightly-controlled Communist state, like Cuba or Czechoslovakia today. The transition would be much more rapid than Cuba's.[206] This prediction ignored Allende's lifetime of support for democracy, his opposition to Marxist totalitarianism and to a violent road to socialism, and the assessments of many "trained professional observers."

Government officials also justified United States violation of self-determination because Allende expropriated United States property without compensation. Yet, intervention began long before any expropriation occurred. Officials implied that Allende's government was behaving unconstitutionally in expropriating United States property. Yet, in the general election, the population overwhelmingly voted for candidates espousing policies of nationalization.

Another justification for United States action came from a high intelligence official: "As long as you don't make it sound like we were trying to start a coup, it [intervention] will be all right. You've got to understand that he [Allende] was taxing them [the middle-class] to death."[207] Yet surely Chile's tax laws could not justify United States interference with Chilean self-determination.

United States officials continuously distorted Allende's position on civil liberties and elections. In fact, free elections were held as scheduled. Allende's Christian Democratic opponent, Radmiro Tomic, attested to Allende's faithful adherence to democratic principles until he paid with his life for honoring them.[208]

The ideological blindness of United States officials was summed up well in Kissinger's reported comment: "I don't see why we need to stand by and watch a country go Communist due to the irresponsibility of its own people."[209] If Kissinger had possessed an accurate grasp of reality, he would have understood that the expression of people at the polls was the essence of "responsible" government, and that to overturn the mandate of the people was the true irresponsibility. Officials ignored both the right of Chileans to self-determination, and the legal prohibitions that, if applied, doubtless would have shown U.S. officials to be in violation of the law.

U.S. leaders reinforced one another's comforting deception that, from a moral and legal standpoint, as long as their activity was covert, it did not occur. Thus Korry and Meyer could say that it was the policy of the United States not to intervene, because they did not consider the work of the CIA as part of the policy of the United States. Those in power felt a deep need for

260

secrecy to protect their operative ideology from open scrutiny and to manipulate the public more effectively. That United States interference with self-determination could go unchecked for a decade demonstrated the pervasive acceptance of secrecy among Washington officials and their willingness to collaborate in self-justifying deceptions. This widespread code of behavior not only prevented democratic policymaking, it also made the realization of human rights impossible.

The Chilean case shows that the most highly respected U.S. officials of both political parties consistently deceived their constituents about their own human rights policies. They lied not to protect U.S. security, as they eventually claimed, but to disguise the true intent and value impact of their actions. U.S. leaders continued the coverup even after the alleged security threat had been killed and his government overthrown.

The main constraint upon policymakers was the fear of public exposure. Breach of the curtain of secrecy would have revealed the subordination of human rights to corporate-government desires for profit and power. Investigative reporters, such as Seymour Hersh and Jack Anderson, did as much to penetrate government secrecy and to enable the public to comprehend the gap between reality and the bureaucratic version of it as did the internal governmental system of checks and balances. Some CIA and ITT plans were aborted because of fear of publicity or the knowledge that the plans would be counterproductive if discovered. Fear of public reaction forced the government to rule out gunboat diplomacy and substitute two techniques, consistent with a "low profile": (1) covert intervention and (2) overt, politically unsensational but economically damaging credit curtailment. In brief, respect for human rights was inversely related to the degree of government secrecy.

The substance of policy and the process of policymaking were heavily influenced by multinational corporations like ITT, Anaconda, and Kennecott. Profit took priority over human rights. In examining the enormous, detailed hearings and studies on the policymaking process, one of the most striking features is the frequency with which corporate officials, advocating Allende's overthrow, had meetings with government officials. At least weekly contact occurred between ITT officials and William Broe, the CIA's chief of clandestine activity for Latin America. Daily reports were dispatched between the two offices. Occasionally, ITT officials would talk with Kissinger or his chief

261

aides Alexander Haig and Viron Vakey. Other private meetings were arranged with White House advisers John Ehrlichman and Charles Colson; Assistant to the President for International Economic Policy, Peter Peterson; Secretary of State William Rogers; Secretary of the Treasury John Connally; Attorney General John Mitchell; Secretary of Commerce Maurice Stans. Frequently, ITT Director John McCone met or talked with CIA Director Richard Helms.

The policy process was tilted radically against any balanced consideration of viewpoints. There was no opportunity for those sympathetic to Allende to have similar meetings with high-level officials. No spokespersons were invited to argue for defense of humanitarian values. Not only were advocates of an alternative view unable to gain frequent access to key officials, they were also continuously deceived about the content of policy by those officials denying them access.

Even in the post-Vietnam era of "new awareness," Congress failed to exercise an effective human rights check on United States policy. In analyzing U.S. performance on the self-determination issue, it is instructive to examine the impact upon policy of those who opposed intervention in Chile.[210] The most apparently influential opposition came from members of Congress, especially from some members of the Senate Foreign Relations Committee and the Subcommittee on Civilian and Refugee Problems, plus the individual work of Representative Michael Harrington. Legislators' public speeches were useful in informing the public on some issues, usually long after the policy in question had been implemented. Congressional hearings collected evidence that otherwise may not have become known. However, there was little effective follow-through to insure that United States policy would be any different on human rights issues in the future.

Members of Congress generally lacked sufficient time, dedication, energy, persistence, and imagination to redirect U.S. human rights policy. In the first place, Congress was relatively slow and inactive. The rise and fall of the Allende government had occurred before Congress began to conduct rigorous investigations to learn the real nature of U.S. policy. The House and Senate subcommittees charged with CIA oversight were inactive. For example, the Senate Armed Services Subcommittee met a total of only 26 times between January 1966 and December 1975 to watch over, among other things, all CIA activities. During the years of the most intense pressures on Allende, the subcommittee met not at all in 1971 and only once each year in 1972 and 1973.[211]

Full disclosure hardly ever occurred even when the subcommittees did meet. Of the 33 covert action projects which the 40 Committee approved to undermine the electoral process in Chile, Congress was briefed in some fashion on only eight. Often briefings were after the fact. Among the projects on which Congress was not briefed at all were authorizations to purchase Chilean radio stations and newspapers, to support candidates in anti-Allende parties, and to support opposition parties themselves. Moreover, Congress was not consulted or informed about projects which were not reviewed by the full 40 Committee. One of these was the attempt by the CIA, at the instruction of the president, to prevent Allende from taking office in 1970 by instigating a coup d'état.[212]

Second, to the extent that the ITT hearings conducted before the 1973 coup did expose the tip of the iceberg, leads were not persistently pursued. After the more complete story was known, the Subcommittee on Multinational Corporations could have acted to improve the reliability of its information in future cases, but it did not. In spite of misleading testimony by officials, Congress did almost nothing to call the officials to account or to reaffirm and specify the norms that should insure that accurate information would be forthcoming to Congress in the future. In the legislation passed by the Senate in response to investigations of the ITT role,[213] U.S. citizens were prohibited from contributing to a U.S. governmental agency in an effort to influence the outcome of a foreign election. Also, United States officials were prohibited from soliciting or accepting contributions from any United States citizen for the purpose of influencing foreign elections. But these matters were not central to the Chilean intervention. In contrast, there was no legislative effort by the Subcommittee on Multinational Corporations to restrict direct foreign efforts by United States corporations to influence the outcome of foreign elections so long as they did not attempt to work through the U.S. government. Nor was interest shown in effectively preventing the United States government itself from directly intervening or hiring local agents to influence foreign elections. Yet these possibilities were the most likely future strategies for preventing self-determination abroad.[214]

Finally, like the executive participants who disagreed somewhat with Kissinger-Nixon-Connally tactics, up to 1974 Congress failed to raise questions about policy goals. Throughout

263

the hearings by the Subcommittee on Multinational Corporations, Senators paid enormous deference to the interests of U.S. corporations in Chile, and only suggested that corporate officials may have gone too far in using questionable tactics to protect their interests. There was no expression of general support for the Chileans seeking economic and political self-determination.[215] During the ITT hearings, no Senator pressed the idea that the United States should respect self-determination, even at the cost of diminishing the profits of some multinational corporations. Corporate values, not humane values, dominated the practice of Congress as much as of executive participants.

Specifically, a striking omission from the final report of the Subcommittee on Multinational Corporations was its failure flatly to condemn the then known interventions of ITT and the CIA as violations of the right of self-determination and the principle of noninterference in the internal affairs of another state. Instead, the committee report based its criticism on the argument that such tactless policy might jeopardize the future investments of other corporations.

> What is not to be condoned is that the highest officials of the ITT sought to engage the CIA in a plan covertly to manipulate the outcome of the Chilean presidential election. In so doing the company overstepped the line of acceptable corporate behavior. If ITT's actions in seeking to enlist the CIA for its purposes with respect to Chile were to be sanctioned as normal and acceptable, no country would welcome the presence of multinational corporations. Over every dispute or potential dispute between a company and a host government in connection with a corporation's investment interests, there would hang the spectre of foreign intervention. No sovereign nation would be willing to accept that possibility as the price of permitting foreign corporations to invest in its territory. The pressures which the company sought to bring to bear on the United States Government for CIA intervention are thus incompatible with the long-term existence of multinational corporations; they are also incompatible with the formulation of U.S. foreign policy in accordance with U.S. national, rather than private interests.[216]

The final report did not conclude that the ITT role constituted a violation of human rights in Chile.

In assessing the significance of the then known United States governmental intervention in Chilean affairs, there was even less inclination to assess the illegality or immorality of United States manipulation of Chilean politics. Instead, CIA policy, like ITT activity, was primarily assessed in terms of its impact on United States corporate interests: "It is clear from this case that there were significant adverse consequences for U.S. corporations which arose out of the decision to use ITT in the way it was used—willing as ITT may have been—and that it was not in the best interests of the U.S. business community for the CIA to attempt to use a U.S. corporation to influence the political situation in Chile."[217]

The emphasis of the main Senate staff study on covert action in Chile stressed the self-defeating nature of clandestine activity. CIA support for overseas politicians could become the kiss of death if the support became known. For example, the report concluded that "it would be the final irony of a decade of covert action in Chile if that action destroyed the credibility of the Chilean Christian Democrats."[218]

The shallowness of the report was partially revealed in its own closing paragraphs: "This report does not attempt to offer a final judgment on the political propriety, the morality, or even the effectiveness of American covert activity in Chile." The report stopped short of saying that U.S. intervention violated the obligation of nonintervention. It concluded by explaining: "Given the costs of covert action, it should be resorted to only to counter severe threats to the national security of the United States. It is far from clear that that was the case in Chile."[219]

Yet the point that needed to be made was not merely that the costs involved may have been too great for the benefits desired, but that the benefits sought were themselves wrong. The United States had no right—and it had said so in legally binding documents—to intervene to overthrow a democratically elected Chilean government in order to secure political, economic, or even security benefits for the United States.

Congress became more forthright in its criticism of the CIA's overseas operations only after being confronted by undeniable evidence of illegal CIA actions within the United States. A desire to examine the CIA's domestic role, more than concern for universal human rights, prompted new congressional investigations.

The final report of the Senate Select Committee to Study Governmental Operations with Respect to Intelligence Activities was clearly unique in calling attention to the undesirability of overthrowing democratically-elected governments: "It is the Committee's view that the standards to acceptable covert activity should . . . exclude covert operations in an attempt to subvert democratic governments or provide support for police or other internal security forces which engage in the systematic violation of human rights."[220] Legislation strictly to prohibit such activity, however, seemed unlikely. If the committee had sought to end the subversion of human rights by the CIA, it could have supported legislation to terminate covert activity. However, it left the door open by saying that covert action should "be undertaken only when the national security requires it and when overt means will not suffice."[221]

The loopholes provided by such language were illustrated in an action unrelated to the work of the Senate Select Committee. Congress in 1974 passed a provision, known as the Hughes-Ryan Amendment, to the Foreign Assistance Act. This amendment prohibited CIA use of funds for operations not intended solely for obtaining intelligence, unless "the President finds that each such operation is important to the national security of the United States." As a result of this legislation, the CIA took the position that the amendment "clearly implies that the CIA is authorized to plan and conduct covert action."[222] The Senate Select Committee concluded that as a result of the passage of the amendment and subsequent developments, "there is little doubt that Congress is now on notice that the CIA claims to have the authority to conduct, and does engage in, covert action. Given that knowledge, congressional failure to prohibit covert action in the future can be interpreted as congressional authorization for it."[223]

Throughout the ten-year period studied by the Select Committee, Congress displayed a notable "hesitancy . . . to use its powers to oversee covert action by the CIA." Part of the hesitancy "flowed from the fact that congressional oversight committees are almost totally dependent on the Executive for information on covert operations. The secrecy needed for these operations allows the Executive to justify the limited provision of information to the Congress."[224] In addition, many members of Congress were reluctant to learn about "dirty tricks" that would bother their consciences if they knew about them and were unable or unwilling to prevent them. Given this congressional atmosphere, to sanction further covert action in the interest of national security was not an effective barrier to further violation of the right of self-determination. Finally, even in the unlikely event that the CIA would be prohibited from covert activity, coups and similar action could continue to be promoted without any legal restrictions if the operations were carried out by contacts between U.S. military officials—rather than CIA personnel—and foreign military or civilian leaders. In this area, the Select Committee sought no limits at all.

As the preceding analysis shows, to realize human rights more fully, the most critical need was not for better control and oversight of the CIA, but for a fundamental revision of officials' values and objectives.[225] The bureaucracy was not acting without deliberation or instructions from the highest authorities. The leadership was not tactically foolish. It pursued goals antagonistic to human rights.

This conclusion takes on deeper importance when one understands that the Chilean case, while unusually dramatic in its reportage to the public, is typical of much U.S. foreign policy. Soon after the Central Intelligence Agency was established, covert action became "a routine program of influencing governments and covertly exercising power." This effort involved literally hundreds of projects each year. By 1953 there were major covert operations underway in forty-eight countries. Several thousand individual covert action projects have been undertaken since 1961.[226] As the staff report of the Senate Select Committee on Intelligence concluded: "The pattern of United States covert action in Chile is striking but not unique. It arose in the context not only of American foreign policy, but also of covert U.S. involvement in other countries within and outside Latin America. The scale of CIA involvement in Chile was unusual but by no means unprecedented."[227]

The Carter Administration

This analysis has focused on a distinct case study that preceded the Carter presidency and its highly visible emphasis on human rights. Although at the time of this writing it is too early to assess Carter policies conclusively, it is instructive to examine the first evidence of Carter's human rights policies. On the positive side, the Carter administration

—gave strong rhetorical support to human rights in several presidential news conferences and major speeches;

—indicated its intention to sign the UN covenants on human rights and to ratify the Genocide Convention;

—took the unprecedented step of ending military aid to

267

Uruguay and of cutting it to Argentina and Ethiopia on human rights grounds;

—halted military aid to Chile, as required by congressional action barring military aid to countries that consistently violated human rights;

—published, as required by the 1976 military aid law, a critique of human rights practices in aid-receiving countries; as a result of this, Brazil, Guatemala, Uruguay, Argentina, El Salvador, and Chile all took offense and withdrew from the U.S. military aid program; and

—supported a UN embargo on arms for South Africa.

On the negative side, the administration

—contributed to multilateral aid (through World Bank loans) to Argentina, Chile, Uruguay, and Ethiopia, even though Congress sought to ban bilateral military aid to these states because of rights violations;

—requested increases in military aid to several repressive governments for fiscal year 1978: for example, a 77 percent increment for South Korea ($280 million total) and a 40 percent increment for Indonesia ($58 million total);

—opposed congressional legislation requesting the United States to vote in multilateral lending agencies against extending loans to countries violating human rights; the administration's counter proposal, favored by the White House and Treasury and State Departments, would have allowed U.S. representatives to vote for loans to governments grossly violating human rights, including even loans for purposes unrelated to direct meeting of human needs;

—opposed a UN resolution for comprehensive economic sanctions against South Africa;

—opposed congressional efforts to terminate military training programs for Argentina;

—continued high levels of aid to Thailand, the Philippines, Brazil, Nicaragua, and other countries with poor records on human rights;

—continued major arms sales to countries, such as Iran, with a record of serious violations of human rights;

—made public statements in support of secret CIA payments to overseas officials;

—supported restrictive executive branch procedures to insure greater secrecy in execution of U.S. covert policies; and

—justified CIA covert political intervention on national security grounds.

This evidence presents a decidedly mixed, and at first glance, confusing picture. The Carter administration has used human rights advocacy to recapture the spirit of a highly moral foreign policy—a spirit lost during the long years of the Vietnamese war and Watergate. Especially the treatment of the human rights issue with the Soviet Union seems colored by a desire to show the superiority of the United States in this area. To threaten to withhold aid from less developed countries for human rights violations is a step forward, even if not a giant step. Aid recipients either may comply with the Carter request for respect for human rights, or they may—as some did—get angry and tell the United States to keep its aid. Either way, self-determination is likely to benefit, at least slightly.

On the other hand, Carter has not moved far enough to make substantial or comprehensive policy changes. Consistent with the posture of his predecessors, Carter has frequently subordinated the promotion of human rights to economic and strategic advantages for the United States.

The public support for human rights, especially as evidenced in congressional action to compel the president to curtail aid to brutal regimes, is a sign of a more enlightened world order struggling to be born. Resisting this new potential is a deep governmental reluctance to apply its lofty rhetoric in cases where U.S. security benefits are jeopardized. Government refusal to establish a global political order more congenial to human rights is a frank admission by officials that when it matters most human rights will be sacrificed for national advantage.

This does not mean that Carter's intentions are fundamentally hostile to human rights, but that powerful vested interests and the apparent requirements for functioning effectively within the international system force human rights into a subordinate position. Structural impediments—such as discrimination against others because of territorial location—and the traditional attitude toward human rights were evident early in the policies of President Carter, even though he prided himself on a willingness to break from the past and respect moral values. Only one month after taking office, for example, Carter, Vance, and CIA Director Stansfield Turner all publicly argued that it was proper for the CIA to pass money secretly to officials of other governments. After reviewing some newly revealed CIA payments to various heads of governments over the past twenty years, Carter concluded, "I have not found anything illegal or improper."[228] Turner euphemistically called clandestine CIA payments "foreign aid, in secrecy," and described such aid as "a very common and a very legitimate tool of foreign policy."[229]

The Carter administration behaved on this issue similarly to the 40 Committee in its earlier dismissal of the self-determination question. The Carter administration said that violation of the noninterventionist principle was legitimate if the purpose would benefit the United States. As Turner explained, the propriety of secret payments "depends on the purpose of that money." If the government thinks the money should be sent, then it "does not involve things that are improper."[230]

Time and again during his campaign the president said he wanted a government as decent as the American people. Such decency surely includes respect for the U.S. Constitution. Yet bribery is explicitly mentioned there as grounds for impeachment of a U.S. president. How can Carter publicly endorse undercover payments, which could easily be construed as bribes, to other presidents and prime ministers? He can do that only by traveling down the road of secrecy, by invoking national security justifications, by discouraging wide disclosure of such acts in Congress, and by preaching a double standard of human rights to the world's publics.

Consistent with the preceding argument, Carter expressed, as did Nixon, Ford, and Kissinger before him, deep concern about the secret payments being revealed to the public. It could be "extremely damaging" to national security, he said, "for these kinds of operations which are legitimate and proper to be revealed." To prevent disclosures in the future, he initiated measures to reduce the number of persons in the executive branch and Congress who would know about such actions. He said also that knowledge of these policies "makes it hard for us to lay a groundwork" for meeting future threats to national security, when similar payments might be used in future policy.[231]

The Carter administration's attitude was also similar to that of preceding administrations in protecting official secrecy rather than the public's right to know. For example, when Richard Helms was finally brought under investigation for dishonesty during hearings on his confirmation as ambassador to Iran, Carter authorized the Attorney General to arrange a plea bargain with Helms.[232] Helms pleaded *nolo contendere* (no contest) and in return escaped a trial. The Carter administration justified this failure to pursue fully a case of prosecutable perjury on familiar national security grounds. It seemed apparent that the administration's policy was designed to protect the system of secrecy and the reputations of officials more than the security of the U.S. people.

Like preceding administrations, the Carter leadership also invoked the national security justification for continuing foreign aid to South Korea and the Philippines even while reducing it to Argentina, Uruguay, and Ethiopia because of the latter's repressive policies. In using the security argument to justify U.S. aid to repressive governments, Carter seemed to endorse human rights violations, because all regimes rationalize their repression on national security grounds. If national security is a good reason to overlook human rights violations, then human rights are no longer inviolable rights but mere privileges that governments may extend or deny at their pleasure. In the absence of any global authority to render impartial assessments of such national security claims, every government of the world defines its own security needs. Carter himself therefore has provided a rationale for rights violations. For example, if Carter argues that the world's security is so precarious that the South Korean ally of the United States must have U.S. aid despite Seoul's brutality, then the South Korean government might similarly argue that its security is precarious enough to justify its own ruthlessness.

Secretary Vance also made it clear that where "the strategic situation is of critical importance," the U.S. would not allow human rights questions to curtail arms transfers.[233] Although there were no obvious security interests at stake, Carter used this argument to continue selling sophisticated arms to the Shah of Iran at an unprecedented rate, despite Amnesty International's report that Iran had the highest rate of death penalties in the world, no valid system of civilian courts, and a long history of torture. Moreover, "freedom of speech and association are non-existent."[234] When the Shah visited Washington in November 1977, Carter praised the Shah for his leadership in maintaining a "strong, stable and progressive Iran."[235]

In brief, it appears that Carter policies have not gone as far to bolster some repressive regimes, like the one in Chile, as those of his predecessors. Carter draws the line at a different point in answering the question: "How many human rights violations must we accept in order to maintain friendship with repressive regimes?" However, on a more fundamental level, the Carter administration is not substantially different from its predecessors:

271

officials still in principle condone violating self-determination and other rights in the name of U.S. security; they view covert activity as legitimate; they protect pervasive secrecy for intelligence operations. Carter's rhetoric and his withholding of aid for rights violations may be viewed as a slight change toward global humanist values. But the domination of these progressive policy elements by the traditional policies is correctly seen as the resistance of the present system to necessary change. The Carterian human rights ambivalence—if not schizophrenia—indicates an inherent inability to fulfill human rights within the present structure of interests and institutions. The pursuit of advantages for national governments continues to overwhelm the achievement of universal human rights.

An Alternative Framework

If United States policies toward human rights were to become responsive to the values of global humanism, these policies would depart sharply from past governmental behavior as illustrated in the Chilean case. The global humanist approach would seriously seek to move toward the following goals.

1. Terminate all covert intervention.[236] Because such intervention inherently violates self-determination, respect for legal processes, and the fulfillment of democracy in the United States and abroad, it should be prohibited as an instrument of policy. Critics of this view postulate that in a few cases, at least, covert intervention is necessary. However, if a certain foreign policy is of such vital and overriding importance that some form of intervention is generally recognized as legitimate, then it can be carried out publicly. Clandestine intervention is not consistent with the values of global humanism.

2. Terminate all covert intelligence gathering. Many persons who have acknowledged the need to end all secret CIA political operations still have insisted that the CIA needs to gather intelligence through secret means. But one must ask: Can not any information required by the United States be learned openly? Newspaper reporters, business people, scholars, and the United States embassy all supply information about a country. U.S. citizens are likely to justify the open gathering of any necessary information. It is not easy to find legitimate reasons for secret intelligence work in Chile.

The implementation of 1 and 2, of course, would eliminate

most of the need for the CIA. If CIA work had been terminated before 1970, this would have vitally served the cause of human rights in Chile.[237] There would have been far less temptation to violate self-determination, no concern about oversight to control CIA foreign or domestic activities, a substantial economic saving, and an enhanced reputation for the United States that would have made its conventional, legitimate diplomacy no less effective.

Additional benefits might accrue from the absence of secret intelligence. The president might actually develop a more accurate picture of reality. Without the availability of what he believes are "inside" or "secret" reports, the president would not so easily assume that his view was singularly correct. Nicholas Katzenbach, who has worked closely with two administrations, described the effect of secret intelligence on the policy process: "Unfortunately, Presidents are inclined to think . . . [that] blind trust in their wisdom is wholly justified. . . . Having almost sole access to the full range of classified information and expert opinion, Presidents are tempted to think that the opinions of Congressmen, academics, journalists and the public at large are, almost unavoidably, inadequately informed."[238]

More openness would increase the accuracy of information available to the outsider. It would also encourage wider utilization of existing information by scholars, journalists, and the public and enable them to render more autonomous judgments, which would serve as checks on official perceptions of reality. Outsiders would be less intimidated by the usual official response to policy suggestions: "If only you knew what I know but cannot say because it is classified." Finally, more openness would encourage the president to consider the advice of persons outside the White House, whose views would be of enhanced value because of their exposure to all available information. Not only would this approach produce greater wisdom and generate opportunities for social unity based on discussions among people using the same information pool, it is also far more consistent with democratic principles than is current practice.

Moreover, less dependency on secret information would at last open the door to understanding that value questions are more important in major decisions than technical details contained in intelligence reports. The latter encourage presidents erroneously to assume that the irrelevancy of outsider's views on

273

technical questions is matched by the irrelevancy of the outsider's discussion of value questions. In the Chilean case, for example, officials considered technical issues such as: How many Christian Democrats could be bribed to vote for Alessandri, or how much economic chaos would result from credit curtailment? They gave almost no attention to the much more important value question: Who will do more to fulfill human needs and serve humanitarian values in Chile—Allende or the leaders of a military coup? To answer the latter question, one had no need for secret intelligence. The very availability of secret intelligence narrowed official vision on human rights questions.

3. Extend credit and aid on the basis of objective determination of human needs, not according to the extent to which the ideology of the recipient's government is sympathetic to the interests of multinational corporations. In order to discourage the tendency to serve the profit and power of a few at the expense of universal human rights, financial assistance should be restricted to nonmilitary purposes and channeled through multilateral organizations that include equitable representation of the poor.

4. Prohibit United States-based multinational corporations from undertaking clandestine political activities. These activities usually are aimed at securing advantages for corporations in preference to securing human rights for the most needy and victimized members of societies. Indeed, even public activities, such as making campaign contributions, should be strictly regulated. Toward this end, where multinational corporations are not expropriated, consideration should be given to establishing supranational regulatory agencies, with heavy representation on the part of less developed countries, to govern the multinational corporations. Such agencies could restrict the political activity of these corporations, and prevent their economic activity from exceeding a mutually agreed upon amount of return on investment. Even more important, such regulatory agencies could insure the production of goods for meeting human needs, rather than for returning a profit regardless of the usefulness of the goods.

If relatively poor and militarily weak societies were brought into the decision-making process of large multinational corporations, which often possess more economic power than their host governments, these underdeveloped societies would be more likely to appreciate the positive contributions that such corporations can make. This would encourage the less developed countries to deal fairly with multinational corporations. Likewise, an increase of citizen control would make these corporations more responsive to human needs.

5. Use the influence of political leadership positions in the United States to educate the public to accept and even support rapid socioeconomic change abroad where an indigenous demand is expressed for it. Radical change may help achieve the values of human dignity even though such change may seem contrary to the short-run interests of U.S. investment and political influence.

6. Agree in advance to submit any disputes over nationalization to an existing judicial tribunal or to an ad hoc board of arbitration selected by both parties. An impartial judicial procedure would defuse the compensation issue. The United States business-government elite could not so easily use the issue to justify intervention. On the other hand, radical governments of developing countries could agree to provide some compensation, impartially determined, without feeling embarrassed by their more radical critics who may want to avoid any compensation that appears to submit directly to United States pressure.

7. Use principles of human rights to restrict policy means as well as to guide policy ends. Officials should first clarify policy goals by giving explicit attention to value questions such as these:

—Should the United States accept self-determination when it is expressed as support for socialism, or use covert means to maintain U.S. economic and political benefits in other societies at the expense of the politically weak and poor?

—Should the United States seek to distribute global wealth more equitably in order to help the poor achieve dignity, or continue to protect the current U.S. income advantage compared to other societies?

—Should U.S. corporations refuse to conduct business in, say, South Africa until they can implement racial equality in corporate life?

The Chilean case demonstrates the insufficiency of merely comparing policy ends with professed, terminal values without also scrutinizing policy means. Too often, rhetoric about goals in Chile sounded sympathetic to human rights. At the same time, the means used, as expressed in the preceding discussion of implicit values, clearly violated almost all human rights related to the rhetorical goals. Many who accept the need to select policy goals in light of human rights often reject the selection of means

275

on the same basis. They ask: Is not some violation of self-determination justifiable in the present in order to achieve greater fulfillment of human rights in the future? Is it not appropriate to use covert means to speed the demise of an unwanted government?

In the Chilean case, even if covert intervention would have produced more moderate results, it would have still carried with it some serious obstacles to realizing V_3. Suppose, for example, that as a result of United States-supported internal unrest, President Allende had resigned and the Christian Democrats were victorious in a special election. Still, covert intervention would have encouraged disrespect for due legal process in Chile; eroded international norms against intervention by other nations; instilled an unhealthy dependency in the new government on the CIA and its potential for future intervention; postponed social reforms that served the needs of the lower class of Chile; reinforced the attitude of United States officials that they may, with impunity, violate reciprocity in international relations, thus encouraging repetition of covert activity and perhaps precipitating a major conflict in a context where reciprocity was expected by another great power; signaled United States corporations that the government would protect their investments and profits with little regard for the overseas domestic implications of their investments; disenfranchised Chileans who in the future might be, as a result of past United States intervention, more violent and authoritarian; and encouraged officials to depend in the future on unilateral manipulation of foreign governments in order to salvage threatened United States interests, thus postponing the realization of systemic changes in the global political structure. If intervention is justified to advance human rights, it should be undertaken openly, as a result of multilateral decision making, and only on behalf of the world community.

Even granting that the global humanist approach would facilitate the realization of human rights, some critics still reject such policies because of fear that they would jeopardize United States security. However, in spite of short-run detriment to some investments and to United States overseas political control, honoring self-determination could, in the long run, enhance prospects for world peace. The traditional effort to throw United States weight against radical social reform movements probably postpones present "disorder" by making likely the more violent expression of discontent at some point in the future. Counter-

276

revolutionary policies that deny equity will doubtless encourage some dispossessed nations to acquire nuclear weapons and some dispossessed people dominated by their own repressive government to seek outside help for sustaining a revolutionary movement. By opposing the right of self-determination in the short run, the United States dehumanizes the process of change in the long run. An alternative approach could help realize V_1 by reducing the violence that results from the postponement of demands for equity and from the prospect of frequent U.S. covert actions that might precipitate counterintervention.

This approach is based on the notion that the best way to avoid violent upheavals is to invite those parties with grievances to share in decision making instead of repressing them and denying them a legitimate role in the political processes. It is also rooted in the assumption that, in general, governments more responsive to human needs will be created in Third World societies as a result of the unimpeded interplay of indigenous forces than as a result of United States intervention and military assistance. This is a policy of political and military noninterference, not a policy of isolationism. It promises substantial international assistance for redistribution of wealth and the inclusion of all societies in decision making.

Such an alternative approach finds the traditional arguments for CIA action uncompelling. The most common justification is that the United States must have and use a secret intelligence agency because the Soviet Union or some other political rival has one. To be sure, it would be unrealistic to conclude that other governments would refrain from foreign interventions simply because the United States did. However, an awareness of the United States' absolute rejection of covert intervention, coupled with support for self-determination, would have some healthy effects in the less powerful countries. First of all, it would encourage governments to develop more equitable domestic programs and popular support or else to face the prospect of falling from power. Thus, being more responsive governments, they would not be such easy prey for covert intervention by U.S. rivals. Moreover, this policy would encourage other states to aid in establishing regional or global processes for protecting self-determination and averting outside intervention against self-determination. The success of such efforts would promote human rights by complicating the task of other great powers who sought to retain quasi-colonial relationships of their own.

277

Although the approach I propose is far from a panacea and contains many explicit risks, it promises a future that is at least as secure for humanity as the present approach. In addition, it contains much greater potential for realizing human rights and the other values of global humanism. If 1 and 2 above were implemented, they would remove the most important political instruments that operated against human rights in the context of the present case study. The third and fourth suggestions would eliminate the economic instrumentalities and incentives for opposing human rights. Building public support for global reform, which will be painful for some U.S. citizens, would be facilitated by 5 and 6. And 7 would provide a general normative guideline for the formulation of future policy. The extent to which policy makers implement these suggestions can be used as a measure of U.S. performance on V_3.

In sum, United States officials ignored human rights in formulating the goals and means of United States foreign policy whenever human rights came into sharp conflict with the vested economic and hegemonic interests of government and corporate officials. As Table 4-3 indicates, stark contrasts separate the picture of the world painted by U.S. officials from the picture envisaged by advocates of global humanism.

Indicators of World Order Progress

The following questions can be used to assess the extent to which governmental behavior helps realize V_3 in the areas examined in this case study:

1. Has the government terminated all clandestine political operations in foreign countries? Has it dismantled institutions designed for such operations?

2. Has the government supported legislation prohibiting U.S. corporations from making secret contributions to political parties, candidates, or other persons seeking to influence political activity in other countries?

3. Has Congress terminated all revenue for covert political activity abroad? Has Congress passed legislation making it a criminal act to use public revenues for such purposes?

4. Has Congress declared and enforced the principle that any occupant of public office must be barred from holding further office if it is determined, after due process, that the official lied during congressional testimony?

5. Has the government demonstrated its respect for human

rights by curtailing overseas programs that deliver weapons and training more useful for repressive police or military operations than for exercising self-determination?

6. Has the government consistently supported multilateral aid programs that promote self-determination and other human rights? Or, has the government instead curtailed aid as a political reprisal against governments seeking greater autonomy from U.S. economic and military influence?

7. Has the government applied equal human rights standards in its relations with allies and opponents alike—for example in Iran or South Africa, as well as the Soviet Union—and thereby demonstrated that human rights will not be subordinated to advancing the special interests of U.S. economic and political leadership?

8. Has the government supported the presence and investigatory work of respected private or UN agencies whose purpose is to expose violations of human rights?

9. Has the political leadership made reasonable efforts to inform the U.S. public of the need in many less developed countries for internal, radical (structural) change to eliminate poverty and political repression?

Table 4-3

Selected Values of Global Humanism Compared to U.S. Policy Toward the Exercise of Self-Determination by the Chilean Electorate and Congress in 1970

Global Humanism	U.S. Policy
Peace	
1. Although in the short run the exercise of self-determination may lead to civil strife in some cases, in the long run self-determination is valued because it increases the likelihood for peace by facilitating the participation of all groups in the determination of their own affairs. Opposing self-determination will prolong and increase the suffering that may accompany radical change.	1. Self-determination in less developed countries is valued as conducive to peace where its exercise serves the strategic and economic interests of the United States; it is viewed as dangerously destabilizing where its exercise would not benefit U.S. investors or increase the influence of U.S. national security managers.
2. Covert intervention should not be used to inhibit self-determination, even if the latter affects U.S. property or overseas influence.	2. Covert intervention to prevent severe economic or hegemonic losses to the U.S. is preferable to allowing the exercise of self-determination.
Economic Well-Being	
1. By increasing the effective participation of politically and militarily weaker societies in planetary decision making, self-determination facilitates a more equitable sharing of the economic resources of the globe.	1. Insofar as respect for self-determination and other human rights might bring more equitable sharing of global economic and political resources of which the U.S. now enjoys a privileged portion, these rights are commonly opposed.
2. Economic and political self-determination should apply internally to all people within a society as well as externally between societies.	2. There is a tendency to favor control by the middle and upper classes within nonsocialist foreign societies, rather than extend internal self-determination to the poor. A similar attitude applies between rich and poor nations.
3. Collective responsibility and human equality are emphasized more than the privilege of wealthy individuals to pursue unregulated profits.	3. The liberty of those with capital to an unhindered right to accumulate more capital is emphasized rather than the right of the poor to an equal share in decision making or an equal opportunity to accumulate wealth.

Human Rights and Social Justice

1. Human rights are profoundly important guidelines for policymaking.

2. Self-determination is a fundamental human right that should be universally nurtured. It is valued because it facilitates a more just participation in planetary decision making and contributes to spiritual and psychological well-being.

3. The exercise of self-determination is desirable because in the long run it encourages the achievement not only of V_3, but also V_1, V_2, and even to some extent, V_4.

1. Human rights for citizens of the less developed countries are insignificant considerations as ends in themselves. Their rights should be subordinated to U.S. strategic and economic interests. Rhetorical support for human rights is useful primarily to disguise an interventionist strategy for opposing the decline of the privileged position of the U.S.

2. Self-determination is useful primarily as a means to achieve other ends. It is favored for developing countries only insofar as its exercise does not impinge upon the wealth and influence of the U.S.

3. The exercise of self-determination in many less developed countries, while honored in rhetoric, is in fact feared as a stimulus to instability and to the alteration of existing global structures of wealth and power.

Ecological Balance

1. By respecting the rights of other societies and encouraging their participation in global decision making, productivity in the long run will conform more closely to meeting universal human needs, rather than to serving the military hegemony of a superpower and the profitability and growth of multinational corporations. More widespread participation in global decision making will encourage the conversion of existing productive capacity from the provision of unessential goods into production of food and other essential items. This in turn will increase the feasibility of more enlightened disposal of pollutants and conservation of resources.

1. Respecting the rights of other societies and encouraging their participation in decision making are not favored as techniques for shifting productive capacities away from careless resource depletion and unnecessary consumption. Little weight is given to the idea that popular local control or global coordination of U.S.-based multinational corporations would establish a more rational response to ecological limits and basic human needs than occurs under present systems of entrepreneurship and decision making.

FIVE · U.S. Policy for International Control of Marine Pollution

No problem better demonstrates the need and potential for global cooperation than the improvement of ecological quality, where "everything is related to everything else." Atmospheric nuclear tests in China may, depending on where the winds blow, affect unborn babies in the United States. The use of DDT to protect dairy cattle from flies in Wisconsin a decade ago will increase the quantity of DDT in a tuna fish sandwich in Copenhagen today. Radioactive emissions from nuclear reactors in the Federal Republic of Germany affect residents in Switzerland and France. The sewage dumped into New York Bight adds to the decay of the oceans that affects vacationers in the Bahamas. In many parts of the world, humanity fails to conserve scarce living and nonliving resources of the planet; disposes harmful quantities of toxic chemicals and other wastes into the soil, oceans, and atmosphere; and refuses to relate global resource usage and productive capacity to fulfillment of basic human needs. Separate national groups, each maximizing its own immediate gains, violate the common good and decrease the global commons' productivity.

Environmental protection requires global cooperation on a variety of problems: ecological disasters of a sudden character (e.g., oil tanker collision); gradual deterioration of environmental quality through cumulative processes (e.g., ozone depletion); the disposal of ultrahazardous materials (e.g., radioactive wastes); destruction of endangered species or historically, archeologically, or scientifically valuable sites; depletion of resources required for a life of dignity; consumption of resources for unproductive or wasteful purposes (e.g., luxury items or military spending); and employment of environmental warfare (e.g., inducement of floods or poisoning of rice crops).[1]

In promoting ecological balance, global humanists seek to contain pollution, to control population, and to use resources for the most rational service of human needs, for both present and future generations. Furthermore, the fourth world order value encourages aesthetic appreciation of nature and the pro-

282

tection of diverse forms of plant and animal life. Both qualitative (e.g., the preservation of endangered species) and quantitative (e.g., the promotion of agricultural production and family planning to provide food for all people) considerations are part of V_4. Pollution control in the oceans, for example, contributes quantitatively to the protection of marine food resources and qualitatively to the aesthetic appreciation of beaches, both now and in the future.

The promotion of environmental quality is complicated by the delicacy of ecological balances, the inadequacy of knowledge about tolerable pollution limits, and the shortsightedness and selfishness of political actors. Many environmental problems at present are politically unmanageable because they defy national boundaries and literally encompass the globe. Environmental action also poses difficult choices among conflicting values. A society may seek to maximize food production by using chemical fertilizers and pesticides, but residues of these chemicals impede the effort to avoid pollution.

Recent international discussions regarding the use and protection of the marine ecosystem have touched upon many areas of concern within V_4. First of all, no issue holds more serious long-range consequences for the human race than the problem of maintaining a healthy marine ecosystem. Climate, rainfall, ultraviolet radiation, cloud cover, the oxygen-carbon dioxide balance essential to life, and the movements of winds and tides are all affected by the seas. They could be unpredictably disrupted if careless human activity changes the marine ecosystem.[2] If the oceans die, so will humanity. As Russell Train, administrator of the U.S. Environmental Protection Agency commented, "Not only are resources and nourishment essential to billions of human beings increasingly threatened by pollution of the seas, but our very survival on this planet is dependent upon the healthy functioning of the natural systems of the seas."[3] Former UN Secretary-General U Thant similarly reported: "For the first time in the history of mankind there is arising a crisis of worldwide proportions involving developed and developing countries alike—the crisis of the human environment. . . . If current trends continue, the future of life on earth could be endangered."[4] While there is disagreement among marine biologists on the precise extent of the harm in present patterns of pollution, most agree that the seas are in decline.[5]

Second, the marine environment provides a unique arena in

which to observe the rise or fall of the modern age's tide of national prerogatives. The seas represent the two-thirds of the planet's surface over which national sovereignty has not been exercised in the past. This global commons has presented an extraordinary, historic opportunity to establish a new regime based on global policy coordination. The oceans cannot be protected or rationally exploited by nations acting separately. Yet the traditional demands of the global system of national sovereignty keep transnational collaboration in a state of anemic, chronic infancy.

In preparing U.S. positions for international negotiations on marine pollution, policymakers have debated a variety of political arrangements to govern future uses of the oceans. They have clearly understood, for example, that in a decentralized, international legal system the rational maximization of self-interest, such as increasing one's harvest of "free" fish on the high seas, will lead, like the demise of the English commons, to the destruction of the resource for all concerned.

Third, the United States has long diplomatic, commercial, and military experience as a great sea power. For more than twenty years the United States has participated in various international negotiations to prevent pollution of the oceans. As citizens of a scientifically advanced nation, U.S. officials have had opportunity to inform themselves about the dangers of pollution. As a wealthy country, the U.S. has possessed ample resources for pollution control. As an industrialized nation, the United States has been a major polluter. As a geographically large country with the most coastal waters of any state in the world and as a great trading nation, harvester of fish, and sea power, much is at stake for the United States. U.S. ocean policy provides a fair test of U.S. performance in implementing V_4.

This chapter will examine U.S. policies to control marine pollution within the three major contexts where the issue has been addressed: the International Maritime Consultative Organization (IMCO) to control discharges from vessels at sea; in negotiations to control ocean dumping; and in the effort to control marine pollution at the Third UN Law of the Sea Conference. Although marine pollution was not a central issue at the Law of the Sea Conference, it was an explicit agenda item and its treatment within that conference is instructive. Because the negotiations covered many difficult issues, there was a constant need to consider trading off one value against another in order to reach a compromise agreement with approximately 150 other nations. As a result, value preferences became clear as officials set policy priorities.

DESCRIPTION OF U.S. POLICIES TO CONTROL MARINE POLLUTION

In the past two decades, humanity has revolutionized the uses of the ocean by building giant oil tankers, harvesting more fish, submerging nuclear submarines beneath the waves, extracting oil from the continental shelf, mining valuable metals from the deep seabed, and depositing millions of tons of wastes annually in the oceans. Traditional international law has failed to protect the marine environment. No state or international organization acts on behalf of the global community to protect environmental quality in the unowned, high seas. No organization manages marine activity to maximize the often competing benefits of mining, fishing, oil recovery, recreation, and navigation.

Before considering the impact of U.S. pollution control policies, we must examine briefly the main ocean pollutants in order to assess the need for environmental action. We are here concerned with the introduction by human activity of substances on a scale which threatens the marine environment, "resulting in such deleterious effects as harm to living resources, hazards to human health, hindrance to marine activities including fishing, impairment of quality for use of sea water and reduction of amenities."[6] This task is complicated by the variety of pollutants, their different sources and pathways to the ocean, the nature and extent of their effects, and the degree to which they pose a threat in the future. Some pollutants persist for centuries, others become harmless in hours or days. Some threaten the environment and human health immediately, others do so only because of long-term cumulative effects. The full danger of most pollutants, and the point at which damage may reach a self-generating, rapid deterioration is still unknown.[7]

Pollutants

PETROLEUM

Of all the serious known pollutants in the sea, oil is present in the largest quantities. Scientists disagree on the exact amount that enters the oceans directly from various human activities, but most estimates range from 6 to 11 million tons per year.[8] If one includes all land-based vaporization of petroleum which moves eventually to the seas, the annual rate of petroleum products entering the ocean may be nearer 100 million tons annually.[9] Most petroleum pollutants enter the oceans from land-based activity. Of these, approximately 90 percent come from vaporization of petroleum products used on land, transmitted through the atmosphere, and dropped into the ocean by rain and wind.[10] Additional land-based pollution enters the oceans through rivers and coastal waste disposal. Pouring dirty motor oil into municipal sewers is one example.

Seagoing vessels and offshore wells discharge roughly 1.5 to 2 million tons yearly.[11] Captains of oil tankers deliberately pump oil into the oceans as part of the process of flushing tanks and draining ballast water. Ocean water is pumped into empty tankers on return voyages to increase seaworthiness. During the voyage, the seawater mixes with the oil sticking to the inside walls of the "empty" tanker, forming an oily emulsion that vessels discharge into the sea before reloading.

The lightest fractions of petroleum hydrocarbons on the sea surface evaporate quickly when exposed to the atmosphere. The remainder form slicks which float on the ocean surface until absorbed by solid particles which may sink. Oil remaining on the surface undergoes a process of oxidation which consumes dissolved oxygen from the water. This means that oil-polluted waters suffer serious decreases in oxygen which is vital to all high-order marine life. In areas of the oceans where temperatures remain below ten degrees centigrade, the oxidation process is inhibited, and Arctic oil spills may remain as long as fifty years.[12] Similarly, in deep waters, bacterial degradation may be very slow because of less light and oxygen.[13] Oil that remains on the sea forms balls of tar. These have been found throughout the Atlantic, affecting hundreds of thousands of square miles of surface water.[14]

The effects of pollution vary greatly depending on the nature of the petroleum and the conditions of the area where it is present.[15] Especially in coastal waters where most marine life is concentrated oil is present in seriously harmful amounts. Some marine life retains hydrocarbons, which then become protein-bound and concentrated in organisms that feed upon previously contaminated lower forms of life in the food chain.[16] Thus low-level contamination may have long-range consequences caused by the concentration of hydrocarbons moving up the food chain. Fish that do not themselves receive lethal doses of crude oil may nevertheless contain too much oil to be palatable.[17]

Petroleum also injures plant life such as the tiny phytoplankton, which is the basic material in the ocean's food chain and an important source of oxygen. This plant life is heavily affected by oil pollution throughout the Atlantic.[18] A chronic film of oil on the ocean surface interrupts cellular division of phytoplankton, retards the photosynthetic cycle that maintains oxygen-carbon dioxide balance, and could lead to other secondary effects.[19]

Recovery of coastal areas suffering from oil spills can be very slow, and chronically polluted areas comprehensively destroy marine life. When the oxidation process causes the dissolved oxygen supply to fall too low, marine animals suffocate. The growth of phytoplankton, necessary to replenish the oxygen supply, is inhibited. Some coastal areas are presently threatened with ecological collapse,[20] and a few have passed beyond the point of recovery without drastic and monumental international efforts.

Virtually nothing is known about the long-range consequences of widespread low-level oil pollution.[21] Yet the subtle effects of such pollution on marine life are likely to be the most serious in the long run.[22] No one knows, for example, the long-term effects of oil which has sunk to the deep ocean floor where the supply of dissolved oxygen is very limited. Nearer the surface of the sea, an increase in the incidence of cancerous lesions, leukemia, skin ulcerations, tail deformities, and genetic changes among marine animals indicates serious long-term problems.[23] An international group of ecologists, collaborating in a study sponsored by the Food and Agricultural Organization (FAO) concluded, "There is inadequate information on the . . . effects of oil discharges. . . . There is no doubt, however, that the quantities of oil discharged to the oceans must be markedly reduced."[24]

Because of increased drilling, transportation, and consumption of oil, the amount discharged into the seas will probably increase several times during the next decade.[25] The percentage of oil production coming from offshore wells will also rise rapidly, thus increasing the probability of accidents per million tons produced. Drilling will occur in deeper waters, making blowouts harder to plug and accidents more likely. Moreover, the number and size of supertankers will increase. The largest ones are extremely difficult to navigate. With emergency "crash stop" procedures and engines in full reverse, a 200,000 ton tanker cannot stop in less than approximately two and a half miles. During engine reversal, steering is impossible.[26] The largest tankers ride so deeply in the water that they are in "shallows" when they move over the continental shelf. Between 1960 and 1973 the transport of oil by sea tripled. Between 1973 and 1980 it will double, making a sixfold increase in twenty years.[27] Giving additional attention to vessel and drilling safety is unlikely to compensate for the increased probability of accidents and deliberate discharges of oil at sea. In any case, because of rising consumption and consequent vaporization of oil in land-based activities, even if deliberate and accidental vessel-source pollution and drilling risks could be magically and completely eliminated by 1980, the oceans would still receive a larger volume of petroleum pollutants than in 1970.[28]

CHLORINATED HYDROCARBONS

Chlorinated hydrocarbons that are known to be harmful to the marine environment include the insecticides DDT, dieldrin and endrin; polychlorinated byphenyls (PCBs); and polyvinyl chloride by-products. No one knows precisely how much DDT is in the oceans, but by 1970 there were approximately one billion pounds of DDT in the biosphere.[29] Insecticides are sprayed into the atmosphere for agricultural and public health purposes, and thus the atmosphere contributes a majority of the chlorinated hydrocarbons in the oceans. Since DDT persists for many years, probably 40 to 60 percent of the total amount produced will eventually enter the oceans from the atmosphere or as runoff from the land.[30] DDT is widely distributed through the world's oceans and is even found in penguins in Antarctica. In one research study, twenty whales born and bred in the East Greenland current coming from the North Pole were found to contain six identifiable pesticides, including DDT.[31] The global distribution is roughly what might be expected if the sprays were spread by prevailing winds.[32]

DDT affects the growth, reproduction, and mortality of marine animals at levels currently existing in coastal ocean waters.[33] DDT is dangerous even in concentrations of only a few parts per trillion, because it, too, accumulates in the food chain. Phytoplankton at the base of the food chain acts as a concentrator of DDT. Oysters alone have amplified small concentrations of DDT 70,000 times in a month.[34] Concentrations as low as three parts per trillion have been lethal to shrimp.[35] DDT prevents the hatching of fish larvae and oyster and mussel eggs.[36] It causes death of some fish in concentrations of five parts per trillion. Rain water falling on the ocean often contains eighty parts per trillion.[37] DDT currently in some marine fish approaches levels associated with the collapse of fisheries in fresh-water areas. Thus many experts believe some species of fish life in the oceans will be destroyed.[38]

DDT has caused deaths of bald eagles, common loons, peregrine falcons, and other birds which eat fish. In the Channel Islands Wilderness area, the bald eagle and peregrine falcon have completely disappeared because of DDT.[39]

DDT harms plant life also. Algae reproduction is altered by minor doses of DDT, dieldrin, or endrin.[40] At concentrations of four parts per billion, it inhibits photosynthetic activity in phytoplankton, which supply nearly one third of the world's oxygen. Most scientists do not expect the atmospheric oxygen supply to be adversely affected in the foreseeable future, but since plankton are at the base of many marine food chains, any change in the rate of primary photosynthesis is certainly critical to humanity's food resources.[41]

There are over 45,000 registered pesticidal formulations in the United States alone. These highly toxic and carcinogenic substances have been released in such large quantities and so broadly that they are among the most widely distributed chemicals on this planet. Scientists at a recent FAO technical conference agreed that pesticides "have the ability to exert biological effects on all living organisms." Thus international regulation "must be devised" to curtail the use of persistent pesticides.[42]

The DDT that in the past has been released into the atmosphere will continue to enter the seas in the years to come; thus the polluting effects of DDT will, for some time, become more severe even if it were completely banned now on a worldwide scale.[43] The amount of DDT compounds in marine life is estimated to be less than 0.1 percent of total production, yet this amount has produced a demonstrable negative impact upon the marine environment. Perhaps as much as 25 percent of the DDT compounds produced to date have been transferred to the sea.[44] Further concentration of DDT in marine life will continue to occur from both the DDT already present in the sea as well as from DDT yet to enter the water.

The rate at which DDT degrades to harmless products is unknown, but the National Academy of Sciences report on chlorinated hydrocarbons estimated that the half-lives of some of the more persistent materials "are certainly of the order of years, and perhaps even of decades or centuries." The report continued: "If these compounds degrade with half-lives of decades or longer, there will be no opportunity to redress the consequences. The more the problems are studied, the more unexpected effects are identified. In view of the findings of the past decade, our prediction of the potential hazards . . . may be vastly underestimated."[45]

Other chlorinated hydrocarbons, such as PCBs, have been available since 1929, but they were not identified in the ocean until 1966. They are used in the plastics, electronics, paint, and rubber industries. Like DDT, they have been disbursed all over the world. PCBs enter the oceans through sewage effluents, runoff, and atmospheric transport following incineration. Their properties are similar to DDT but even more toxic and persistent.[46]

The long-term effects of these materials are not fully known, nor are the quantities being introduced annually to the sea. Some corporations, such as Monsanto Chemical Company, have refused to release production figures for PCBs although requested to do so by many scientists and government officials.[47] Sufficient evidence is available, however, to demonstrate that the anticipated industrial growth and continued production of hazardous chlorinated hydrocarbons will decrease the marine protein supply and affect the total ecosystem; it already constitutes "a serious hazard to human health."[48]

HEAVY METALS

At least 4,000 to 5,000 tons of mercury per year enter the oceans from the mercury compounds that humans release to the rivers and atmosphere.[49] Industrial wastes are the largest source of this pollutant, but mercury has also been used as a fungicide in dressing seeds for agricultural purposes.[50] In the early 1970s, people in the Northern Hemisphere alone injected 350,000 tons of lead, a second heavy metal, annually into the atmosphere by burning antiknock automobile fuels.[51] These metals are widely dispersed and fall in the oceans remote from the areas of their origin and use. More of these metals enter the oceans through the atmosphere than through any other source.[52]

Mercury's toxicity is permanent. Like the pollutants previously discussed, marine organisms concentrate mercury in the food chain. The amount of mercury in fish may be 10,000 times

290

that found in seawater itself.[53] Mercury has toxic and genetic effects on marine life and upon those who feed on that life. As a result, extensive shellfish grounds have been closed in Canada, the United States, Spain, France, Germany, Japan, and elsewhere because of metal pollution. Additional shellfish grounds will be closed if the present rate of pollution continues. Mercury killed the swordfish industry in the United States and temporarily forced mackerel and tuna off the market.[54] The toxicity of mercury to human beings is well-documented.[55] In Minimata and Niigata, Japan, 168 people suffered mercury poisoning and 52 people died from mercury-contaminated fish and shellfish. Because there is no means of treatment, prenatal poisoning causes permanent disability.[56] Mercurialism, a chronic form of poisoning, affects the nervous system in a way in which the patient may exhibit no well-defined symptoms for months or years after exposure.

Because the industrial uses of mercury and other metals are likely to increase in the future, in the absence of international pollution control, their levels in the oceans will continue to rise.[57] In the United States alone, the quantity of industrial wastes is expected to increase sevenfold within a decade.[58] UN experts concluded that measures "must be devised" for international control of mercury.[59] In brief, mercury is highly toxic to most forms of life, a nearly permanent poison once introduced into the environment, biologically accumulated in organisms including human beings, and utilized in increasing quantities throughout the world. It "threatens to become critical in the world environment."[60] Moreover, although mercury and lead are generally considered to be the most threatening inorganic pollutants, approximately two dozen additional metals are highly toxic to plants and animals.

NATURAL ORGANIC WASTES AND INORGANIC NUTRIENTS

Natural organic pollutants (such as human fecal matter from municipal sewage) and inorganic nutrients (such as nitrogen fertilizer runoff) are a mixed blessing, because they can enrich the marine environment if they are diluted in proper degree. In this sense, they are unlike the pesticides and heavy metals, which are poisonous to living organisms. Natural organic pollutants, even though biodegradable, are harmful when they are so concentrated that bacteria, which help decompose the pollutants, use up much of the oxygen dissolved in the water, thus leading to

291

eutrophication. This process decreases the capacity of the marine ecosystem to sustain and renew life in the sea. When eutrophication progresses to extreme stages, all useful marine species die. Even if not all oxygen in the water is exhausted at first, extreme enrichment may lead to "blooms" of plants which cut down the water's productivity because dense phytoplankton at the surface decrease the penetration of light and hence the total amount of oxygen-producing photosynthesis in the water column. In Europe, for example, the oxygen content of the Baltic has fallen severely since 1900, to a point where it is almost exhausted in a substantial area.[61]

Eutrophication of estuaries and adjacent coastal areas has occurred in some areas through overfertilization of waters by phosphorus and nitrogen. Approximately 60 percent of phosphorus in North American coastal waters comes from disposal of municipal waste. The remaining portion comes from urban and agricultural runoff.[62]

Even slight eutrophication in estuaries is extremely costly, because estuaries are the permanent residence, passage zone, or nursery area for about 90 percent of commercially important fish. Over 20 percent of the world's minimal protein needs could come from the sea by the year 2000, if estuaries remained healthy.[63] Precise figures on the decline of fish populations in coastal areas are unavailable, but there are many instances of estuarine harvesting being terminated because of pollution. Most of the world's large urban centers are located on estuaries and discharge wastes into coastal waters. Industrialization, urbanization, and population are all increasing. Agricultural uses of nitrogen fertilizer can also be expected to increase. Thus without major efforts to cut down nutrient pollutants, coastal pollution will become more serious.

RADIOACTIVE WASTES

Radioactive wastes released by humans to the marine environment probably amount to less than 3 percent of the background radiation from natural sources. Nevertheless, human activity has injected sufficient radionuclides in all of the oceans to present a potential health hazard as well as a disruption of the marine environment.[64] The principal sources of contamination are: fallout from atmospheric nuclear weapons tests, direct or indirect wastes from nuclear power reactors and fuel processing plants, wastes from medical, scientific, and industrial uses, and accidents involving reactor malfunctions, the transport of nuclear materials, or mobile power units in nuclear submarines or artificial earth satellites.

"Transuranics"—elements with atomic numbers greater than that of uranium—are highly dangerous materials some of which must be isolated from the environment as long as a *half-million years*.[65] A National Academy of Sciences panel studying ocean pollutants estimated that by 1970, the release of over 20,000,000 kilocuries[66] of alpha-emitting plutonium into the oceans as fallout had resulted in plutonium contamination of marine organisms throughout the world. Of this total, 200,000 curies were plutonium 239.[67] It has a half-life[68] of 24,000 years. (See Table 5-1.) It cannot be retrieved once dispersed, and thus it will continue to affect the environment for more than 100,000 years.

Table 5-1
Half-Lives of Plutonium Isotopes

Plutonium Isotope	Half-life in years
236	3
238	88
239	24,400
240	6,540
241	15
242	387,000

SOURCE: National Research Council, Study Panel on Assessing Potential Ocean Pollutants, *Assessing Potential Ocean Pollutants*, p. 31.

Fallout from nuclear weapons tests has been the largest source of marine contamination in the past. However, since the United States and Soviet Union have banned atmospheric nuclear tests, and because the demand for nuclear power plants is increasing, the wastes from nuclear power reactors and the fuel processing plants that prepare nuclear materials are likely to become the greatest radioactive pollutants in the future.[69] This picture could change suddenly if several nonnuclear countries or nonsignatories of the test ban treaty, such as China and France, should undertake major testing programs. Use of any weapons in war would also completely change all predictions of modest pollution from fallout.

Radioactive wastes are generated in nearly all stages of the nuclear fuel cycle, including the process of uranium enrichment,

293

the use of fissionable material in a reactor for generating electricity, and the reprocessing of the spent fuel from reactors. Wastes may accumulate as liquids, solids, or gases, and at enormously varying radiation levels. High-level wastes, characterized by extremely hazardous and persistent radioactivity, are produced in greatest quantities during the purification stage of a reprocessing plant. Low-level wastes have shorter half-lives and are generated at nuclear power plants and by industrial operations. Liquid wastes are held or released under controlled conditions; solids are packaged and shipped to regulated burial sites.[70] The United States Atomic Energy Commission (AEC) predicted sizable increases in the future quantities of low-level solid wastes from U.S. commercial activity alone:[71]

Year	Cubic feet
1968	666,570
1970	1,000,000
1975	3,000,000
1980	6,000,000

The AEC expected that high-level wastes would increase as follows:

Year	Gallons
1970	17,000
1980	4,400,000
2000	46,000,000

As far back as 1946, the United States dumped hazardous radioactive wastes into the Atlantic in steel drums. Before this practice was terminated, the United States had deposited 86,758 containers on the ocean floor.[72] Later, Europeans followed the same practice. In 1967-68, the European Nuclear Energy Agency sank approximately 60,000 containers with approximately 30,000 curies of beta/gamma radiation into the North Atlantic.[73] Japan has also dumped wastes into the oceans off its coast. In 1976, traces of plutonium and cesium contaminating the ocean floor were discovered off the east and west coasts of the United States. The radioactive materials appeared to have leaked from the drums of low-level wastes dumped there between 1946 and 1970. In the Pacific dumping site, the level of plutonium contamination ranged from two to twenty-five times higher than the maximum expected concentration that would have resulted from weapons testing fallout. In the Atlantic site, plutonium contamination was up to seventy times higher than weapons testing fallout.[74] Throughout the world, hundreds of millions of gallons of high-level wastes are now in storage. They will remain highly active for hundreds of years, but the tanks will last only decades.[75]

Because nuclear power reactors generate enormous amounts of heat in the process of making electricity, they are usually constructed close to rivers or oceans so that water may be used as a coolant. Tritium is emitted as tritiated water, has a half-life of about twelve years, and thus has potential for affecting other countries.[76] Most reactor owners, such as the United Kingdom, France, Italy, and India discharge low-level radioactive wastes directly or indirectly into the oceans.[77] Standards defining tolerable limits are not universal. British policy permits greater release of radioactivity in the oceans than U.S. policy, and Soviet policy is more restrictive than the United States.[78] Reactors also release gaseous wastes to the atmosphere, including xenon, tritium, krypton 85, iodine 129, and carbon 14. These have half-lives sufficiently long to affect populations outside the country of release.[79] Nuclear-powered ships, and submarines also discharge contaminated wastes into the sea.[80]

Accidents contribute sporadic but significant amounts of radioactivity to the environment. Some scientists estimate that the accidental release of plutonium 238 had almost tripled the global deposit of this isotope by 1970. An accident at the Windscale (United Kingdom) plant in 1957 released more radioactivity into the atmosphere than fell on Hiroshima in 1945.[81] In 1964, the disintegration of a United States earth satellite spread plutonium 238, which was aboard for power generation, into the atmosphere. It behaved much as fallout from weapons tests.[82] Nuclear bombs may cause local contamination as a result of accidents even though the bombs do not explode. Similarly, the loss of nuclear submarines at sea may present danger to the ocean environment, both from their reactors and nuclear warheads.[83]

Small doses of radioactivity probably harm, even if imperceptibly, nearly all forms of plant and animal life. Although low levels of radioactivity may produce no obviously harmful effects in the short run, any increase in the amount of radiation absorbed by a population will increase the incidence of cancer or genetic damage in the population.[84]

The most serious threat to human life and health from transuranic elements in the sea comes from their extreme toxicity, their persistence, their potentially harmful effects to marine plants and animals, and their subsequent danger to humans through ingestion of seafood.[85] Like chemical toxins, marine organisms may concentrate radioactive elements throughout the food chain. Thus oysters 250 miles from any nuclear source have contained 200,000 times more radioactive zinc than the surrounding ocean. River plankton of the Columbia River downstream from U.S. nuclear production facilities in Washington have had concentrations of radioactivity 2,000 times higher than the water. Fish and ducks feeding on plankton had concentrations 15,000 and 40,000 times greater, and radioactivity in egg yolks of water birds was more than a million times greater.[86] Strontium 90 in the oceans already may have accumulated in some fish to levels which contribute to high mortality rates.[87] The presence of small amounts of radioactivity in algae that are often used to fertilize potato fields in coastal areas also constitute a hazard for human beings.[88]

Experiments have shown that continuous discharge of low-level wastes can cause damage to hereditary material of all kinds of organisms and cause abnormal growth and fatalities.[89] Radioactivity causes cancer, liver and kidney failure, and genetic defects in marine life, but often defects are unnoticeable at low dosages. Radioactivity also affects the life-sustaining photosynthetic process, although the precise consequences and long-term effects are unknown.[90]

Despite the relatively low levels of radioactive pollution of the marine environment and the absence of scientific knowledge about some of the potentially most dangerous long-term hazards, the National Academy of Sciences study of ocean pollutants cautioned that all releases of transuranic elements to the environment should be carefully regulated. Both accidental and planned releases "should be kept to an absolute minimum." The experts warned: "The rapidly increasing production of transuranic elements, combined with the present and potential leakages to the environment, could lead to concentrations in the environment that, because of the toxicity of these elements, would jeopardize the health of man and the integrity of ecosystems."[91] The Federal Radiation Council, the National Council on Radiation Protection and Measurements, and the International Commission on Radiological Protection have all recommended restricting exposure to the lowest practicable level.[92] Because radiation hazards are cumulative and irreversible, the International Atomic Emergency Agency (IAEA) warned that even small increments could spell disaster for future generations.[93]

Despite the gravity of increasing levels of radioactive pollution, more transuranic elements will inevitably enter the ocean. Some of the radioactivity released into the atmosphere by weapons tests has yet to fall into the lower atmosphere and into the oceans. The leaching activity of fresh water to propel land-based contamination to the oceans also takes time. Perhaps, as one study speculated, radioactive materials from underground nuclear tests, such as on Amchitka Island in 1970, may reach the ocean years after a test.[94] The containers dumped by the United States and European nations into the oceans may begin to disintegrate with age or become damaged by fishing trawlers or earthquakes. Some nations may conduct atmospheric tests of nuclear weapons.

Demand for more nuclear power reactors is likely to rise. Some experts have predicted that commercial nuclear reactors are "bound to multiply three- or four-fold even over the next 10 to 15 years."[95] A 1,000 megawatt nuclear power reactor has an annual output of radioactive materials equal to a 23 megaton bomb.[96] There may be 400 large nuclear plants around the world by 1985, perhaps 2,000 by the year 2000.[97] Because of the growth of nuclear power, the storage of liquid wastes and fission materials could be multiplied more than a hundredfold by 2000.[98] While such an increase of fissionable materials is being mined, enriched, transported, stored, used, and reprocessed, the risks of leakage or accident will increase enormously, in spite of the closest attention to safety. Reactors malfunction, transportation vehicles have accidents, storage tanks leak.[99] The intentional discharge of radioactive waste products will also increase.

It is possible that a discontented party may engage in environmental war using highly toxic materials. Even a few grams of plutonium dispersed in a city or a major river as a finely divided powder would produce lethal consequences for millions of people. Contamination could last for thousands of years.

The future thus promises increased risks of radioactive pollution. One must add to this ominous trend the possibility that some pollutants already discharged may cause damage presently unanticipated. Automobiles were driven for fifty years before

297

the injurious qualities of exhaust fumes were recognized. It took a quarter century of spraying DDT before scientists understood DDT's most dangerous characteristics.

SYNERGISTIC EFFECTS

We are largely ignorant of the synergistic effects pollutants may produce when several are present in the same ocean space.[100] Nonetheless, "it is a serious oversimplification to consider the effects of materials separately."[101] Some substances produce unforeseen combinations which may have a wholly unanticipated and more powerful effect than the sum of the substances taken separately. Smog, for example, is a familiar example of the combination of smoke, exhaust fumes, and atmospheric conditions.

In the marine environment, one serious synergistic consequence of oil pollution could arise from the property of chlorinated hydrocarbons, such as DDT and dieldrin, to be highly soluble in oil films floating on the ocean's surface. Some measurements in a slick in Biscayne Bay, Florida, showed that the concentration of dieldrin in the top one millimeter of water was over ten thousand times higher than in the underlying water. Since the small larval stages of fishes and both plant and animal plankton tend to spend some of the night hours near the surface, it is highly probable that they will extract, and concentrate further, the pesticides present in the surface layer. This could have "seriously detrimental effects on these organisms,"[102] which form the basis for the food chains of most marine life.

Oil, DDT, plastics, heavy metals, radioactive wastes, and concentrated sewage from growing coastal cities are likely to have synergistic effects. Roughly a thousand new and untested materials are added each year to modern chemical manufacturing. Most are not biodegradable. In all of the general categories of pollutants discussed here, the quantities in the oceans are increasing.[103]

Even if all synergistic effects were understood, we would still be ignorant of the permissible threshold of pollutants that the ocean can accommodate before irreversible, snowballing consequences occur.[104] The sea obviously has enormous capacity for renewal and regeneration, but as an organic system, it is vulnerable to death at some point. It is not known when the dangerous threshold for some marine plants and animals may be crossed, thereby causing imbalances elsewhere in the ocean ecosystem. The dissolved oxygen levels of the Caspian, Baltic, and Mediterranean seas, for example, are extremely low in many parts. To be sure, these are enclosed waters but so, ultimately, are all the oceans.

Moreover, the bulk of plankton and other marine life dependent on photosynthesis is concentrated in an upper layer of ocean water no deeper than the Great Lakes. The surface waters do not mix rapidly with deep waters. About 80 percent of the world's fish catch is derived from waters less than 200 meters deep, which is half the depth of Lake Superior. About 90 percent of all marine animal life is concentrated above the continental shelves in coastal waters which are the most polluted.[105] The Great Lakes are vulnerable to ecological collapse, even though located between two—only two—wealthy and scientifically advanced nations of the world. If these governments have found it impossible to prevent acute ecological decay in the Great Lakes, where they "own" the marine environment, how much more difficult it will be to prevent ecological disaster in the oceans, where jurisdiction belongs to no one and where political rivalries and ideological rigidities will make cooperation less likely. Yet, if one conclusion is clear from the preceding discussion of pollutants, it is that the oceans cannot be protected by national action alone. Standards for tolerable pollution must encompass the globe.

International Efforts to Control Marine Pollution

Most ocean pollutants originate within the national jurisdiction of states, but the pollutants affect distant populations and the global environment. Thus, serious efforts to reduce pollution naturally require some international cooperation. This requirement was recognized in the 1958 Geneva Convention on the High Seas, which asked all parties to "draw up regulations to prevent pollution of the seas by the discharge of oil from ships . . . or resulting from the exploitation . . . of the sea-bed and its subsoil."[106] In addition, states agreed "to prevent pollution of the seas from the dumping of radioactive waste."[107] Similarly, the 1958 Continental Shelf Convention specified that all coastal states were obliged to take "all appropriate measures for the protection of the living resources of the sea from harmful agents."[108] These vague obligations have been neither specifi-

299

cally defined nor effectively enforced. Although legally binding upon parties to the treaties, in practice they have been statements of intention rather than standards for behavior.

In three areas, however, the United States and other countries have discussed more concrete environmental standards: to regulate petroleum discharges by ships at sea; to control the dumping of wastes into the seas; and to define international standards for environmental protection. We will examine these in turn.

POLLUTION BY SHIPS AT SEA

The United States and other nations slowly have established more exact standards for marine protection in several conventions negotiated within the Inter-Governmental Maritime Consultative Organization (IMCO). Through this specialized agency of the United Nations, U.S. officials have aimed at reducing the discharge of oil and other hazardous substances from ships at sea. A brief survey of the important treaties will clarify the results of IMCO negotiations.

The first IMCO action regulated the discharge of oil, primarily from tankers. The International Convention for the Prevention of Pollution of the Sea by Oil was completed in 1954 but not ratified by the United States until 1961. It specified that tankers could not discharge any waste or ballast with more than one hundred parts of oil per million and closer than fifty miles from the nearest land. This measure helped protect coastlines but not the oceans in general. Dirty ballast of any amount could be discharged beyond the fifty-mile limit. Nontankers had even less stringent standards for oily discharges. The seven-year delay for United States ratification reflected official indifference to protecting the environment. Moreover, the United States refused to ratify two provisions of the treaty: the requirement that signatories provide adequate port reception facilities for receiving waste materials that should not be dumped in the prohibited zones; and the obligation for ships to carry oily-water separation equipment for bilge discharges.[109]

During negotiations in 1962, the 1954 agreement was modified to expand the prohibited discharge zones to one hundred miles in some cases. In 1969 it was amended to institute modest standards for all discharges even outside the prohibited zones. In 1971 limits were established on compartment size within tankers. The 1969 amendments took effect in 1978, but the 1971 amendments have yet to come into force.

Table 5-2
IMCO Treaties to Control Oil Pollution from Ships

	Text Completed	Date in Force	U.S. Ratification
1. International Convention for the Prevention of Pollution of the Sea by Oil			
London	1954	1958	1961
2. Amendment to #1 (expands zones to 100 miles)			
London	1962	1967	1966
3. Amendment to #1 (sets standards *outside* zones)			
London	1969	1978	1973
4. Amendment to #1 (sets compartment size in tankers)			
London	1971		
5. International Convention Relating to Intervention on the High Seas in Cases of Oil Pollution Casualties			
Brussels	1969	1975	1974
6. International Convention on Civil Liability for Oil Pollution Damage			
Brussels	1969	1975	
7. International Convention on the Establishment of an International Fund for Compensation for Oil Pollution Damage			
Brussels	1971		
8. International Convention for the Prevention of Pollution from Ships			
London	1973		

In 1973, important negotiations performed a major overhaul of the 1954 treaty[110] and resulted in the International Convention for the Prevention of Pollution from Ships. If ratified by enough states, the new treaty will replace the 1954 agreement. The new convention expands coverage to include discharges of refined petroleum products.[111] In addition to repeating previous restrictions on oily wastes close to shore, the 1973 treaty prohibits all discharges in five special areas—the Red, Black, Baltic, and Mediterranean seas, and the Persian Gulf. "Clean ballast," however, is not regulated. It is defined as containing no

301

more than fifteen parts of oil per million. Total discharges in one voyage must not exceed one fifteen-thousandth of the vessel's cargo-carrying capacity. Existing ships will have to be fitted with "load on top" equipment which enables ballast water to be drained out from the bottom of tanks after oil residue has separated on top. The new load is then added on top, thus making it unnecessary to discharge oily ballast into the sea. Finally, for new tankers which are over 70,000 deadweight tons and placed under contract after December 31, 1975, the convention requires segregated ballast tanks. Total discharges for new ships may not exceed 1/30,000 of the vessels cargo capacity.

The treaty requires that port facilities be provided to receive oil residues from ships, the provision rejected by the United States in 1961. Moreover, new regulations were introduced to set international standards for size limitation and arrangement of cargo tanks, tank subdivision, and ship stability. In a major improvement over the 1954 convention, the negotiators expanded the scope of the treaty to include the bulk transport of noxious liquid substances other than oil.

In three areas, the United States advocated environmentally more progressive positions than were accepted by other governments. First, the United States and the Soviet Union sought to require double bottoms in ships over 70,000 deadweight tons. U.S. officials believed that such bottoms would decrease oil spills in case of grounding. Second, the United States wanted to make visible discharges in a ship's wake presumptive evidence of violation. The burden of proof would then have been imposed on the suspect ship to show that it was adhering to the regulations. Third, the United States and Canada wanted to give port states the right to punish owners of ships coming into their ports if the ships violated regulations when outside territorial waters.[112] This provision, if included, would have closed some of the loopholes in previous treaties, which allowed flag states to regulate their own delinquent ships. Similar port state prerogatives have been used successfully to enforce regulations against slave trading and skyjacking. In these cases a government has jurisdiction beyond its territory, thus making enforcement possible even if an offense is not committed in its territory and the ship is not owned by its nationals.

Three more international treaties, if ratified by a sufficient number of states, will regulate the transport of oil at sea. The International Convention Relating to Intervention on the High

Seas in Cases of Oil Pollution Casualties specifies that parties may take action on the high seas to protect their coastlines after a maritime casualty has occurred.[113] The International Convention on Civil Liability for Oil Pollution requires shipowners to compensate persons, up to a ceiling of $14 million, for damage from a maritime casualty involving petroleum-carrying ships.[114] The International Convention for the Establishment of an International Fund for Compensation for Oil Pollution Damage[115] insures that injured parties will receive compensation for pollution damage even if they are unable to obtain it from the owner of the ship concerned. It also attempts to give relief to shipowners for the additional financial burden imposed on them by the Liability Convention. The Fund will receive contributions from persons that transport more than 150,000 tons of crude oil annually.

The regulations established in these conventions to control the discharge of oil and other substances from vessels at sea are significant departures from past practice. The United States favored most of the provisions strengthening the original 1954 agreement.[116] Still, when the conventions are compared with the threats to the marine environment, they are little more than a drop of prevention in an ocean of need.

First of all, except for the 1954 oil pollution convention as amended in 1962 and 1969, none of the standard-setting IMCO conventions was in force by the end of 1978. The slow record of ratification reveals governments' unresponsiveness to the need for environmental protection. Even if all the conventions eventually come into force, they will provide inadequate protection of the environment. Some states may choose not to join in order to avoid the restrictions that the more conscientious states implement. In addition, most tankers are not "new" according to the treaty's definition. They can escape the stricter standards, such as the segregated ballast requirement.[117] All military ships and other government-owned vessels employed in noncommercial service escape international regulation. Seeking to avoid any international intrusion into military affairs, the United States favored allowing military vessels to discharge toxic wastes without any international control whatsoever. Parties will, however, accept the vague obligation that such ships behave in a manner consistent with the treaty "so far as is reasonable and practicable."[118]

For the regulated vessels, the legal discharges—"clean

ballast"—may prove ecologically disastrous to the ocean because the limits are high and are defined as a percentage of the total tonnage transported.[119] As tonnage increases each year, the absolute amount of legal pollution increases. To protect the oceans, maximum acceptable levels must decrease to prevent total pollution from growing, even assuming that all conventions will be widely implemented and honored.

Although the strengthened IMCO treaty allows the discharge of only a small percentage of the cargo hauled, for a 200,000 ton tanker 13 metric tons of oil could be discharged legally during each voyage. In 1974, tankers carried 1,800,000,000 metric tons of oil.[120] Given that total tonnage, the new treaty, if in force, would have allowed legal discharge of 120,000 metric tons. These amounts will probably double by 1985. Yet in practice, the quantity of oil pollution is likely to be much higher than these legally allowed deballasting ceilings. If tanker spills increase at rates proportional to those projected for world petroleum production and for tanker transport, Robert Citron, director of the Smithsonian Institution's Center for Short-Lived Phenomena, estimates that by 1985, 4 to 5 million tons of oil will enter the oceans annually from tanker operations and accidents.[121] Moreover, additional oil is discharged each year by nontankers from bilge-pumping operations, which account for a substantial portion of ship-generated oil pollution.[122] The IMCO treaties lack strong measures to prevent oil discharges before they occur.[123] For example, provisions emphasize compensating victims of damages after spills occur, rather than establishing international inspection to prevent damage in the first place. Furthermore, international cooperation is arranged to ease the payment of casualties by owners of tankers, but no international procedures were established for citizens to sue for damages to the high seas.

Most importantly, enforcement of the treaties depends mainly on the goodwill and conscientiousness of a contracting government to apply the provisions to ships flying its flag. Yet states like Panama and Liberia, which offer flags of convenience to substandard vessels, are interested in the fees paid by shipowners, not in necessary safety improvements in construction and navigational procedure. Should their registration requirements be as strict as other states, these flag-of-convenience states would lose many of their ships (and fees) to other countries. Tankers fly flags of convenience precisely because they seek to evade rigorous standards for safety. The ill-fated *Argo Merchant* and *Torrey Canyon* for example, were Liberian tankers. Flag-of-convenience vessels comprise 23 percent of the world's merchant fleet, but account for more than half of all tonnage lost.[124] Since the effectiveness of the IMCO treaties depends largely upon the voluntary cooperation of governments in imposing standards on their citizens or customers, the temptation is to cut corners and costs in order to gain advantage. Safer ships, higher insurance, and sophisticated navigational aids all cost more money. The results are clear: After a twenty-year effort to regulate oil emissions, two million tons of oil are still poured into the sea each year.[125]

Protection of the oceans can hardly depend upon the willingness of governmental collaborators with profit-motivated shippers to replace cheap waste disposal with more expensive discharge of wastes. Even assuming more conscientious attitudes by flag-of-convenience states, most lack the necessary equipment for effective policing. Many of their vessels never rest in their own ports. A major difficulty is simply identifying the source of pollution at sea. To enforce IMCO treaties, states would need inspection forces all over the globe. In the absence of these on the high seas, self-policing by shippers is the only enforcement.[126] When asked by a Senate committee whether the discharge standards of the potential IMCO treaty could be enforced, U.S. Coast Guard officials reported that "there is no known means of determining the oil content of a discharge once it has entered the sea."[127] Except in cases of blatant violations, enforcing agents would be unable to know whether the rules had been honored.

One of the most serious deficiencies of the oil conventions is that they ignore the hydrocarbons that enter the ocean from non-vessel sources. A study by the National Academy of Sciences estimates that more than 95 percent of the petroleum polluting the oceans each year comes not from tanker breakups on deballasting, but from using petroleum products ashore.[128] By themselves the IMCO treaties will not protect the sea. They even allow a state to receive oily ballast from a tanker in an onshore reception point and then pump it directly into the sea from a land-based source. Although the state would be polluting the ocean close to its own shores, the past record of coastal pollution suggests that such an event is within the realm of possibility.

In general, during negotiations for the 1973 IMCO treaty

305

(still not in force) the United States favored almost all of the provisions specifying standards for vessel-source pollution. In addition, the United States sought to implement some construction standards and port state enforcement which other states would not accept. These represented desirable steps toward recognizing an international obligation to protect the oceans. Yet, the IMCO treaties are a bit like closing the chicken house door after the fox has walked inside. The IMCO treaties give the appearance of protection, and do protect against a few problems, but the treaties do not offer a response at all proportional to the dimensions of the threat.

IMCO, like some national regulatory agencies, has been a club of maritime nations, and it has served rather than regulated the interests of shippers. Many provisions of the conventions have done little more than codify existing commercial practices among the major maritime nations.[129] The willingness to establish slightly more stringent standards in the 1973 conference was encouraged by a fear that continued IMCO delinquency might prod coastal states like Canada to act unilaterally or nonseapowers to press for action at the Law of the Sea Conference where the maritime nations had proportionately less influence.[130] According to a representative of the U.S. Environmental Protection Agency at the 1973 IMCO conference, none of the new treaty provisions were due to the participants' concern for the global environment.[131] Instead, states pressed for stricter controls to protect their own shippers from cut-rate competitors and their own territory from foreign polluters. That falls far short of a policy aimed at protecting the commons.

United States policy was determined less by ecological concern than by a desire to protect navigational freedom for its warships and merchant marine, the commercial value of its own coasts, and economic benefits for oil companies and shippers. During the late 1960s and early 1970s, domestic environmentalists had pressed Congress and the executive branch to take national pollution control measures.[132] Domestic pressures and the costs of heavy coastal pollution, plus the comparatively wealthy position of the United States, encouraged the United States to enact domestic environmental legislation before most other countries. Since environmental protection costs money, domestic legislation placed U.S. shippers, oil companies, and consumers of oil at a competitive disadvantage unless the United States could extend its domestic control regulations to the rest of the world.[133]

Thus, the domestic U.S. legislation of 1970 and 1972 led directly to the international treaty of 1973.

Trying to eliminate competitive disadvantage, Congress directed the president, in the Water Pollution Control Act, to reach agreements with other nations to upgrade international standards. Members of Congress had noted that if foreign vessels were not forced to comply with the domestic standards imposed on U.S. flag ships, the foreign shippers "obviously . . . have a subsidy."[134] Spokesmen for the executive branch viewed the 1973 convention as "an agreement which fulfills that Congressional mandate to a substantial degree."[135] Russell Train, the director of the Environmental Protection Agency, reported that avoiding competitive disadvantages for U.S. commercial interests was "one of the reasons for the U.S. interest in a convention of this sort. . . . We have been concerned over the competitive problem. It is our desire or interest in achieving . . . uniformity of standards and operating rules around the world that has led us to push for this convention."[136] Similarly, Admiral Chester R. Bender, commandant of the Coast Guard, which was charged with enforcing environmental protection legislation on the ocean, warned: "If standards are imposed on only U.S.-flag vessels stricter than those standards adopted internationally, serious inequities could arise when U.S. vessels call in U.S. ports alongside foreign vessels engaged in the same trade but not subject to the same regulatory constraints."[137]

Because of concern for competitive disadvantage rather than for global environmental protection, Coast Guard officials cautioned Congress against requiring stricter standards or more vigorous enforcement of standards for U.S. ships than for foreign vessels, even if such action was suggested in the Ports and Waterways Safety Act of 1972: "In adjudging the sufficiency of the Convention in respect to the Ports and Waterways Safety Act, it must be recognized that unilateral action presents intrinsic dangers. We should avoid unilateral action which would result unnecessarily in economic disadvantage to the U.S. Merchant Marine."[138]

If the United States established standards more strict than IMCO's, other states might similarly introduce requirements that U.S. shippers would not want to meet in, say, Canadian ports or territorial seas. Thus the United States opposed any treaty provision that would allow states to set standards above the lowest common denominator established at the IMCO conference. Interest in relatively unrestricted navigation thus took priority over restrictive measures for environmental protection.[139]

If the United States genuinely sought to implement rigorous standards and still avoid competitive disadvantage, Washington could have advocated strong international enforcement. However, the United States did not favor international regulation of private commercial affairs. Thus U.S. policy stopped far short of supporting international inspection and enforcement of standards for the offshore extraction or transport of oil. Neither did the United States favor a global regime to prevent unlimited extraction, refinement, and shipping of oil from threatening the environment.

In sum, U.S. officials gave highest priority to maintaining navigational freedom and to gaining international sanction for the minimum vessel discharge and construction standards necessary to avoid competitive disadvantages for U.S. commercial interests.

POLLUTION FROM DUMPING

In the second major field of international activity for protecting the seas, eighty governments in 1972 negotiated the Convention on the Prevention of Marine Pollution by Dumping of Wastes and Other Matter. It took effect in 1975 and regulates the deliberate disposal of most materials at sea. It does not cover the discharges of ships from their operations, such as oily ballast, nor pollution caused by fishing, deep sea mining, oil drilling, or other exploitation of oceanic resources.[140]

The treaty prohibits dumping of extremely hazardous materials including mercury, cadmium, high-level radioactive wastes (the definition of which was left to the International Atomic Energy Agency), and organohalogen compounds (such as DDT and PCBs), persistent plastics, petroleum, and agents of biological and chemical warfare. Second, it allows the licensed dumping of arsenic, lead, zinc, fluorides, certain pesticides, and non-high-level radioactive wastes, if permitted by a designated national authority. Each contracting party governs the disposal of all waste material loaded in its ports for the purpose of ocean dumping, regardless of the ship's flag. In addition, each government is required to regulate the activity of its own flag ships anywhere in the world if they load waste material in the port of a state not a party to the treaty.[141] This treaty to establish international controls for dumping many hazardous substances is a departure from previous practice, and should slow the anticipated increases of these materials in the sea. Yet, when examined carefully, the treaty falls far short of providing effective guarantees against further environmental deterioration.

In the first place, although the treaty was opened for ratification in 1972, many states had not yet ratified it by 1979, including the industrial countries of Japan, West Germany, Italy, and Belgium. The states that do not ratify the treaty are free to ignore its provisions.

Even with the treaty in force for the ratifying parties, many loopholes remain. For example, United States officials insisted on exempting military ships and aircraft from all international regulations.[142] In addition, the convention does not apply to all ships and aircraft entitled to "sovereign immunity," which means all state-owned vessels. In an age when an increasing proportion of the world's ships and aircraft are owned by states, to exempt such vessels—even if used for commercial ends—is a significant omission. Moreover, the prohibition against dumping biological and chemical agents of warfare could be a somewhat meaningless provision, since parties would be free to assign such dumping to military vessels. States are, however, expected to require their own vessels to operate in a manner consistent with the convention. Yet, as one critic observed, "the restrictive effect of this watered-down version of the provision is virtually nil."[143] The treaty will do little to compel states to behave any more responsibly than they would have without it.

Another loophole in the dumping convention is the "emergency clause." This allows dumping of prohibited substances "in emergencies, posing unacceptable risk relating to human health and admitting no other feasible solution." On this particular provision, the United States said that "emergencies" included situations "requiring action with a marked degree of urgency, but . . . not limited in its application to circumstances requiring immediate action."[144]

In addition to these problems, universal adherence to treaty provisions will be difficult to insure. There will be at least three general problems. First of all, noncontracting parties are unaffected. Even a state ratifying the treaty may terminate the limited restrictions of the treaty by withdrawing whenever convenient. Second, the familiar weaknesses of flag-state enforcement are present. A government that ratifies the treaty may fail to enforce the provisions if dumping occurs far from the flag state's shores. Competitive advantages, after all, would accrue to the states and corporations that violate the treaty if other states honor it. Some governments may want to violate the convention to dispose of hazardous chemicals, such as nerve gas.[145] Not even well-intentioned governments will know if their ships have loaded materials in distant foreign ports for dumping beyond territorial waters. Jurisdiction on the high seas is limited to the flag states, so a nonflag state or an international organization cannot seek to enforce the treaty on another state's ships.[146]

Third, the prospect that states will leniently grant licenses to their own ships for dumping designated substances provides an easy way to circumvent treaty guidelines. Given the economic savings derived from ocean dumping, to give states the right to license their own dumping is hardly an effective restraint. If nations pollute their own rivers and lakes, they will not refrain from contaminating the high seas far from their own coasts. As the U.S. Council on Environmental Quality concluded, the treaty has no protection against nonimplementation.[147]

Furthermore, approximately 90 percent of all the pollutants in the ocean come from polluted rivers or atmospheric fallout.[148] Thus even an extremely restrictive dumping treaty would not affect most ocean pollution. States and corporations seeking to avoid the treaty prohibitions could simply allow disposal of wastes in rivers where many of the substances would eventually flow to the ocean anyway.

In examining the interests served by U.S. policy on ocean dumping, one finds many parallels with the IMCO treaties. The United States supported a treaty on ocean dumping primarily to encourage other nations to pass national environmental legislation similar to the domestic regulations established for United States industries. If foreign governments would not establish standards similar to those contained in U.S. domestic law, their industries could gain a competitive edge, because the price of their products would not reflect the costs of pollution abatement.[149]

In the late 1960s, the U.S. Environmental Protection Agency became concerned about environmental danger caused by U.S. dumping in coastal areas such as the New York Bight. As a result, in 1970 the Council on Environmental Quality published a lengthy study containing strong recommendations to curtail ocean dumping.[150] The president proposed and Congress passed the Marine Protection, Research and Sanctuaries Act of 1972, which prohibited dumping material in territorial and contiguous waters without a permit. The act laid the basis for most of the provisions later included in the international treaty. Thus domestic legislative activity encouraged U.S. officials to negotiate an international convention that would, in effect, solicit other national governments to help implement similar regulations worldwide.[151]

During the international negotiations, the United States strongly resisted attempts by some nations to establish state responsibility for extraterritorial environmental damage caused by dumping. This resistance demonstrated that officials were less concerned about enhancing global ecological quality than about avoiding competitive disadvantage for U.S. corporations that were prohibited by domestic legislation from dumping in U.S. coastal areas. The United States did not want to assume responsibility for damage to the environment committed by its nationals. U.S. official rhetoric endorsed the Stockholm Declaration of Principles which said in Article 21: "States have . . . the responsibility to ensure that activities within their jurisdiction or control do not cause damage to the environment of other states or of areas beyond the limits of national jurisdiction."[152] U.S. official behavior entailed advocating an amendment to prevent Principle 21 from being included in the treaty on dumping. A U.S. substitute proposal (Article 10) took the place of Principle 21 in the treaty. The contrast was clear: Principle 21 said states were responsible for damage to the environment; Article 10 merely said states should consult about establishing procedures for settling disputes over dumping.[153]

In summary, as in the IMCO case, officials gave global environmental protection low priority in the dumping convention. The treaty provided no international enforcement. Nor did it offer international inspection, which should have been less objectionable than enforcement to states jealous of sovereignty. The United States also refused to place state-owned vessels under any international obligation even though the United States government would be the only enforcement agent overseeing U.S. ships under the treaty.[154] To be sure, the United States did support some environmental measures to avoid competitive disadvantages. But rather than bring about more effective implementation of standards—even for the sake of prohibiting competitive disadvantage more fully—by advocating a

311

strong central authority, U.S. officials preferred to have no international interference with U.S. ships and aircraft. Officials were unwilling to pay even a small price in restricting their sovereignty in order to protect the marine environment.

THE THIRD UN LAW OF THE SEA CONFERENCE

A third field of international activity to protect the marine environment existed within the Third UN Law of the Sea Conference. This conference, spanning several years, grew out of a 1967 proposal by Malta's ambassador, Arvid Pardo. He said that the UN should establish international control over the vast mineral wealth of the seabed and ocean floor in order to avoid conflicts arising from competing national claims to those resources. In addition, ocean resources should be regarded as the "common heritage of mankind" and should serve global human needs. His proposal provided an opportunity to implement a new, genuinely international regime with broad powers to administer the more than two-thirds of the earth's surface covered with oceans. The new international agency should, in Pardo's view, use the financial benefits derived from the exploitation of seabed resources for promoting the development of the poor countries.[155]

In response to the Maltese proposal, the General Assembly created a seabed committee to discuss issues raised by Pardo. By 1970, the Assembly decided to convene a Third UN Law of the Sea Conference to consider not only seabed resources but also the width of the territorial sea, freedom of movement through international straits, management of fishing on the high seas, regulation of marine scientific research, and protection of the marine environment.[156]

The first substantive session of the Third Law of the Sea Conference, upon which this analysis focuses, was held in Caracas, Venezuela in 1974. It was followed by a second in Geneva in 1975, the original target year for concluding an agreement. None was achieved, and three more series of sessions were held in New York during 1976 and 1977. Clearly, the global sweep of discussions and the nearly universal governmental participation made the Law of the Sea Conference an appropriate arena for United States action to guarantee international protection of the ocean ecosystem.

Pollution abatement, however, was not a major concern of the United States at Caracas or at subsequent conferences.[157] In-

312

stead, officials worked hard to establish international guarantees (1) for unimpeded passage of military (and commercial) vessels through international straits falling within other states' territorial waters; (2) for maximum freedom of the seas to allow movement as close as possible to the land masses of all countries; and (3) for maximum national access, through U.S. corporations, to hard minerals on the ocean floor and to the oil and natural gas resources in the U.S. continental shelf. The pollution issue was pushed far down the ladder of priorities. Because U.S. officials pressed other delegates hard on the strategic and mineral issues, they thereby constricted the range of feasible political compromise on the pollution question. To understand U.S. priorities, we must begin by examining briefly the competing national claims on the strategic and economic issues.

From the beginning, U.S. ocean policy gave highest priority to strategic interests.[158] The Department of Defense held the strongest hand during bureaucratic infighting over ocean policy, and it aimed to achieve unimpeded transit by U.S. military vessels over as large an area of the oceans as possible. This goal required limiting the territorial seas to the widely agreed upon 12-mile limit. Such a limit, if generally accepted in a treaty, would roll back the 200-mile limit that some states claimed. The Department of Defense preferred a territorial sea even narrower than 12 miles, but in order to gain international consensus on a limit that clearly would prevent the wider claims from becoming law, the 12-mile limit was accepted with one condition. There must be "unimpeded transit" through straits used for international shipping, including the more than 100 straits that would fall within territorial waters if the territorial limit were increased from the traditional 3 to the proposed 12 miles.

Without unimpeded transit, United States military vessels would have been subject to the right of "innocent passage," which provided that vessels had the right of transit if their passage was innocent. That is, passage must not be "prejudicial to the peace, good order and security" of the coastal country through whose territorial sea the ships are transiting. Under this doctrine, submarines would be required to surface and show their flags when passing through a strait that forms part of a foreign nation's territorial sea.

U.S. negotiators attempted, with considerable success, to build support for a "free transit" rule to replace "innocent passage" through straits. The U.S. proposal, supported by the USSR,

313

would enable all kinds of surface ships, submarines, and aircraft to travel in the air, on the surface of the sea, or under water through international straits without coastal state control. "The failure of a vessel to act 'innocently,' that is, in a manner which complies with the long recognized doctrine of innocent passage, would not be a bar to . . . [the vessel's] right to transit straits under the U.S. proposal." In short, U.S. military vessels would enjoy even broader legal protection for navigational freedom through straits than they had in the past under innocent passage.[159]

Some states argued that large petroleum tankers and all nuclear-powered vessels "are inherently non-innocent."[160] The United States, however, maintained that free transit, even for the most dangerous vessels afloat, was of vital strategic and economic importance.[161] In Senate hearings, John R. Stevenson, chief of the U.S. delegation and special representative of the president for the Law of the Sea Conference, was asked why the U.S. delegation devoted so much of their energy and political leverage at Caracas to gain even freer navigation than existed under innocent passage. He replied: "Mobility . . . in one word is the most important single factor, the ability of our Navy and our Air Force to navigate the seas without interference." He cautioned that the need for U.S. submarines "to navigate without surfacing is very, very critical. . . . The ability to get through important straits such as the Strait of Gibraltar has been very critical. . . . The whole question of being able to transport oil without interference is very critical for [national security]. I think these are critical U.S. interests and our whole effort has been to advance the whole complex of U.S. interests."[162] Stevenson flatly told the international conference that the United States could accept no treaty that did not insure unrestricted transit of ships up to the 12-mile limit and within that limit through international straits.[163]

Defense officials, in short, sought to minimize other states' national jurisdiction over the oceans in order to retain maximum opportunity for themselves, as operators of the largest military force in the world, to send ships, submarines, and aircraft where they chose. The weak and poor states, in contrast, wanted to circumscribe the behavior of the maritime powers by claiming sovereignty over straits and wider areas of the oceans. Claims by smaller states for a 200-mile territorial sea aimed at insuring national control over fisheries and offshore oil, as well as keeping foreign military vessels farther from shore.

314

U.S. officials at first (1970) based their negotiating strategy upon gaining international support for narrow territorial waters by generously offering other coastal states control over minerals and fish in their coastal waters and continental shelves. The control would be exclusively national to a distance from shore where the water reached a depth of 200 meters. Beyond that depth, coastal states would exercise jurisdiction over exploitation of living and nonliving resources up to 200 miles or to the edge of the continental margin, but only as "trustees" for the international community. Revenues from minerals beyond the 200-meter isobath would go to an international agency to be used for economic development of poor states.[164] The Pentagon wanted the coastal waters beyond the 200-meter depth to be formally part

Figure 5-1
Profile of the Continental Terrace (vertical scale exaggerated)

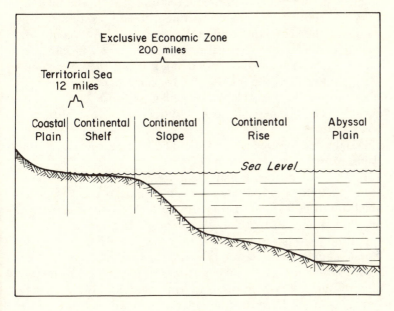

of an international regime because defense officials feared "creeping jurisdiction" in an expanding exclusive *national* resource or economic zone. The Nixon administration asked that all nations adopt as soon as possible a treaty renouncing national claims over seabed resources beyond the 200-meter isobath and agree to regard those resources as the common heritage of humanity. Thus some offshore oil would be placed under the authority of an international regime.

U.S. oil companies bitterly opposed the 1970 proposals advanced by the Department of Defense. Their political power, expressed through the National Petroleum Council and the Department of the Interior, soon proved irresistible.[165] U.S. officials shifted their position toward support of a broader economic zone 200 miles in width.[166] This assured the oil companies exclusive access to oil under the U.S. continental shelf. The shift was possible only with the assurance to the Pentagon that navigation must be unimpeded throughout the coastal economic zone beyond the 12-mile territorial sea.[167] The oil companies forced the Defense Department to compromise slightly insofar as the economic zone in the new proposals was not formally part of an international regime as defense officials originally wanted. To achieve their political goals, the oil corporations "combined an ingenious early version of a national 'energy crisis' argument with elaborate geological and legal reasoning."[168] They claimed offshore resources were vital to the nation's security. The oil industry was clearly the single most influential force in moving the United States to extend territorial claims over minerals to 200 miles.

The U.S. government offered a more generous and somewhat more powerful international seabed regime to the less developed countries in 1970 than in 1974, after the oil industries had mobilized their strength in Washington. Defense officials favored the 1970 position because they calculated that an international regime would never be strong enough to restrict their navigation. They urged oil companies to gain access to foreign underwater reserves through an international authority. The Department of Defense pointed out that 92 percent of the world's continental margins were off foreign, not United States, shores. The Pentagon was willing to risk oil resource interests in U.S. coastal areas in return for internationally agreed rights of transit.[169]

Oil companies, on the other hand, were willing to risk the un-

316

likely encroachment of "creeping jurisdiction" upon navigation in order to secure national control of the U.S. continental shelf. In addition to wanting assured access to U.S. coastal waters, oil companies assumed that they could achieve better access to and higher profits from oil deposits in foreign coastal waters by dealing bilaterally with other national governments than by operating through an international regime. In addition, if an international authority were established in an intermediate zone between the 200-meter isobath and the end of the shelf, the less developed countries in such an authority might have power to extract large royalties. The oil companies were calculating from past experience that national governments, handled separately, were more amenable to allowing corporate profits and could be more easily influenced by oil companies than an unfamiliar international regime.[170]

Although defense officials favored and oil executives opposed an international regime over the coastal and deep seabed beyond 200 meters' depth, both groups had the same goal of minimizing interference by other governments or international organizations in their own affairs. Neither side sought to create a genuinely transnational regime to govern navigation, pollution, and resource usage of the oceans. The defense officials' position appeared more generous, but their generosity was the assumed necessary price to gain internationally-sanctioned freedom of transit for military craft. Officials hoped to sail nuclear submarines secretly, to implant submarine listening posts, and to gather intelligence with ships and aircraft close to the shores of other nations. In the final U.S. proposals for the Caracas conference, strategic considerations were accorded priority over resource interests, but resource interests received priority over environmental protection.[171]

Mining corporations also eventually exerted enormous impact upon the U.S. negotiating position, but their influence developed more slowly than that of the Pentagon and National Petroleum Council. Whereas the Defense Department promoted its interests throughout all the sea, and the oil companies sought access to hydrocarbon reserves under the continental shelves, the mining companies were concerned instead with scooping up potato-shaped "manganese" nodules that lay on the ocean floor in the deepest parts of the sea. In addition to manganese, the nodules contained copper, nickel, cobalt, and iron. No politically feasible extension of the territorial seas or of a wide economic

317

zone for resources could bring the nodules within the mining corporations' control. Thus the mining companies had a simple goal: to establish a modest international authority that would register companies' claims to mine in designated areas of their choice and protect them against claim jumping by other companies. Beyond this, the less international control of mining and the less onerous the royalties or profit-sharing requirements, the better the corporation officials liked it. Most advocated making the international regime only a registration agency.[172] The debate between the National Petroleum Council and the Defense Department was not central to the concerns of miners, but the latter did not view favorably any international regime that promised significant revenue for the less developed countries or international regulation of mining activities.[173]

Mining officials faced formidable opposition to their goals, however, from the less developed nations who wanted to maximize their own economic benefits from the common heritage on the ocean floor. At first the mining companies believed that the executive branch pressed their corporate position with insufficient vigor during international negotiations.[174] Although the Interior Department was sympathetic to the miners' interests, its personnel seemed occupied with forwarding the position of the oil industries on the issue of the 200-mile zone.

Fearful that the Nixon administration's proposals of 1970 were too generous in offering the common heritage to other countries, the mining corporations turned to congressional allies to influence the United States position. One of the most receptive groups was the Senate Committee on Interior and Insular Affairs, chaired by Senator Henry Jackson. Senator Lee Metcalf presided over this committee's Special Subcommittee on the Outer Continental Shelf and spoke boldly in behalf of mining interests. The Senate Committee on Commerce was also sympathetic to the mining corporations.[175]

Senator Jackson sent staff members to attend the 1971 sessions of the UN Seabed Committee and to report their findings. Their report expressed a belief that the U.S. delegation placed too much emphasis on military objectives and too little on securing seabed resources: "We fear that the Defense Department might urge the administration to abandon its deep seabed mining objectives and support the creation of an international seabed mining monopoly controlled by less developed nations as a trade-off for the votes of such less developed nations in favor of the Defense Department-sponsored free transit proposal."[176] Through congressional pressure and increasing effort by the Interior Department, the Administration did, at the least, honor the mining corporations' demand that national access to the nodules be internationally guaranteed. From the beginning the Nixon proposals called for nothing less.

The less developed nations wanted to create an international authority with exclusive right to exploit minerals of the seabed beyond the economic zones of coastal states. The authority would either directly or through contracts explore the seabed, and mine and market the nodules. The international machinery should have broad, general powers, including the right to set prices and production levels for the nodules. The developing nations argued that the poorest countries should be the principal recipients of the benefits derived from the exploitation of the deep sea minerals.[177]

In sharp contrast, the United States and other industrial states, which were leading in deep sea mining technology, wanted an international authority that would merely issue licenses to national or private companies and receive small royalties. The industrial countries, led by the United States, sought an international guarantee to right of access to the materials. Guaranteed access included a requirement that mining rights be granted automatically to any qualified applicant.[178] The United States also opposed any international controls on profit or production.[179]

The debate between the United States and the less developed countries on the seabed regime helps explain various national positions on pollution abatement. Thus this debate deserves some elaboration here. Insisting upon national access to the minerals, U.S. officials at Caracas and Geneva astonishingly denied that the international community could "own" the "common heritage of mankind." Leigh S. Ratiner, the U.S. representative, said the idea of international ownership "is completely unacceptable to us." The proposed authority should not "have title in a legal sense to the Common Heritage of Mankind." The common heritage should be kept out of any international hands. "This [authority] is not a sovereign State but a regulatory body for the Common Heritage of Mankind."[180] According to U.S. officials, national governments and private mining corporations possessed the right to exploit the common heritage. The international community lacked the right to own and control it. U.S.

officials clung tenaciously to this view, because if the international community owned the resources of the high seas, then it
would have the right to exploit the minerals on its own behalf if
it so decided. Such a decision could have decreased potential
profits for U.S. corporations from the vast ocean wealth.

The U.S. delegation devoted enormous energy at the Caracas
conference to promoting the idea that an international authority
should not be allowed directly to exploit the resources of the
common heritage. This promotional effort described the issue as
one of "non-discrimination." U.S. officials said that for an international authority to mine nodules would be "discrimination"
against the "right" of states with advanced mining technology to
take the nodules. Less developed countries wanted to build an
international authority to prevent industrial states from dis-
criminating against nonindustrial states by mining the choicest
areas before the poor countries developed the necessary
technology.

With consistency inspired by selfish interest, the United States
insisted that, if the nonindustrial states agreed to an international licensing agency, the treaty establishing it must prohibit
the agency from choosing among applicants for mining rights.
The United States demanded that the international authority be
required to grant licenses to all applicants satisfying one condition: they must begin mining within a reasonable number of
months after the license was granted. Since the less developed
countries lacked the technical skills and capital required for
exploitation, the United States in effect was proposing a "non-
discriminatory" system that discriminated against the technically
less advanced. Lacking the capability to mine, the less developed
states could not even secure licenses to mine in the distant
future.[181]

The United States also insisted that no limit could be set on
the number of claims it could request and be granted. Stevenson
declared: "If the authority has the power to restrict the number
of areas available for commercial development and to select
among applicants, my government would not be satisfied that
our access was secure and free of potential discrimination."[182]
Ratiner warned: "It is not reasonable or proper to impose restrictions on the area available for exploitation or the number of
such areas which a particular country or company may be permitted to mine."[183] Thus United States officials asked for conditions in which corporations would be guaranteed the right to

320

exploit as many areas as they were able to mine at once. There would be no limits on their production or profits. The United States informed the other delegates that without such arrangements the United States would not ratify any law of the sea treaty.[184]

Stevenson emphasized that the right that "most critically" must be guaranteed was the "right to nondiscriminatory access . . . to the seabed's resources."[185] Ratiner explained: "Industrialized countries . . . cannot be expected to agree that . . . they will surrender rights or access to the abundant raw materials of the seabed by agreeing to a system in which an international Authority could limit or exclude their access."[186]

Because the United States also feared that an international authority might provide subsidies to poor countries for exploiting the nodules, U.S. officials insisted that detailed provisions be included in the treaty to govern conditions of exploitation. Ratiner told the conference that agreement on "fundamental conditions of exploitation is essential if we are to have a successful treaty on the Law of the Sea. . . . For my delegation it is essential that fundamental conditions of exploitation be included in the treaty." Ratiner said that "the principal United States interest in that part of the treaty which Committee I is responsible for is to guarantee to ourselves and to all other countries a right to a secure supply of the minerals which the United Nations said were the Common Heritage of Mankind."[187]

The United States proposals for a seabed regime were largely determined by a desire to maximize U.S. national economic benefits and corporate profits from ocean wealth. Officials sought to recover previous U.S. corporate investment in deep-sea mining technology by securing international recognition of the claims of U.S. companies to mine specific seabed areas and to reap unregulated profits.[188] "Non-discriminatory access" facilitated the opportunity for the states and corporations leading in mining technology to accumulate the largest economic benefits. The American Mining Congress stressed in congressional testimony that any delay in seabed mining would erode the existing U.S. technical lead and competitive advantages.[189] The United States wanted to define the conditions for exploitation in the treaty to insure that "the private enterprise system will produce nodules from the sea [and] . . . will have an opportunity to make profits."[190]

Except for maximizing U.S. profits, there was no reason why

the nodules could not be exploited by an international authority, if the majority in the world community preferred that approach. The authority would no doubt arrange contracts with some U.S. companies to do the mining, since these companies had the most advanced technology to do it. No company could be forced to sign a contract against its will. If companies from Japan, the Soviet Union, or other countries could offer better terms to the international authority for exploitation, that would not harm the international community, nor would it deprive the world of the use of the minerals. But the U.S. refused such an arrangement precisely because an international authority might not guarantee U.S. companies all the minerals they wanted. As Stevenson explained, the United States "has sought in the deep seabed negotiation to protect its principal national interest in access to these mineral resources."[191] The economic conditions for exploitation were, according to Ratiner, "the most important subject in this part of the Law of the Sea negotiation."[192]

The United States opposed socializing the distribution of ore taken from the sea, even though this practice might stabilize the price of raw materials, and greatly benefit less developed countries. Ratiner informed the other delegates that, even though the nodules were part of the common heritage, "My delegation is not prepared to see the Authority control processing and marketing."[193] Moreover, U.S. advantages might be compromised if the world community had knowledge about where the richest source of nodules in the common heritage was located. Thus, even though the nodules supposedly were part of a common heritage, U.S. companies, with the backing of the U.S. government, would not divulge their knowledge about where the richest ore deposits lay: "A blanket provision that the exploiter turn over to the authority all data is a death warrant to manganese nodule production and to the realization of benefits for mankind. Companies will not do it. We know they do it in sovereign States, but the Authority is not a sovereign State." Until the international authority had been tested, Ratiner said "no company will be willing to give the Authority its most basic and valuable information."[194] Of course, if an international authority owned, mined, processed, and marketed the nodules, and distributed the proceeds equally to all people, there would have been no need for keeping knowledge secret about the richest sites.

The United States also wanted national access to the nodules in order to insure an increasing abundance of copper, nickel, manganese, and cobalt for the U.S. at lower prices. The U.S. trade deficit from imports of these minerals totaled over $1.1 billion in 1972 and was steadily increasing. T. S. Ary, representing the American Mining Congress, claimed that without the nodules the balance of payments deficit for primary minerals would reach $64 billion by the year 2000, assuming only 1970 prices.[195] Moreover, the United States wanted to eliminate the possibility of any future OPEC-like actions by producer cartels in metals such as copper. This desire buttressed the mining companies position, despite a State Department study which concluded that price-raising metal cartels were unlikely and hardly feasible, regardless of the nature of a new seabed regime and U.S. access to ocean floor minerals.[196]

Officials felt a general responsibility to make the United States less dependent upon foreign sources of materials.[197] Rather than seek to conserve minerals and arrange a dependable supply of metals at stable prices through an international agreement for resource allocation keyed to meeting human needs, the United States chose unilateral action that would not constrain U.S. consumption. Because a majority of the governments at Caracas seemed intent on establishing international control over the nodules, congressional sentiment grew for allowing U.S. mining operations to begin without any international agreement on the subject.[198] Many members of Congress, reflecting the position of the mining corporations, preferred risking investment capital without international protection for their claims rather than allowing the international community to regulate the mining operation and limit their profits.

To protect future access to resources and profits for U.S. corporations, the United States refused to support a UN resolution declaring a moratorium on all exploitation of the seabed resources pending the establishment of an international seabed regime.[199] The Department of State wanted to protect the right of U.S. corporations to proceed with unilateral action in the absence of a treaty.[200]

The year after the Caracas session, the Law of the Sea Conference at Geneva produced a single negotiating text for future consideration. It was written by chairmen of the committees and reflected the discussions of the delegates, but it was not a negotiated document. Because it did not fulfill U.S. goals, it was widely denounced in Congress. Senator Lee Metcalf said the part of the single negotiating text which described the mining regime was "an unmitigated disaster."[201] "It would appear that we're in bad trouble. As I read it [the single negotiating text], the international community owns, and runs, everything beyond 200 miles. . . . The international agency is going to adopt budgets, make rules, decide on benefit sharing, determine compensation, borrow money, and be exempt from taxes and customs. . . . It may itself conduct research. It regulates fixed installations. It may do its own developing, processing, transportation and marketing."[202]

The chairman of the Oceanography Committee in the House of Representatives expressed similar fears that the international community would take control of the common heritage. He said that "of highest priority before my Oceanography Committee is legislation dealing with how Americans can gather a part of the three trillion dollars worth of nickel, manganese, copper, and cobalt concentrated in tomato-sized nodules on the deep ocean floor." He concluded that "the interests of the American people will best be served by speedy Congressional action in the above areas on a unilateral basis."[203]

Both the legislative and executive branches opposed an international authority that could allocate seabed minerals among competing purposes and potential recipients. U.S. officials wanted to allow the United States to continue using the most resources per capita of any country in the world. An international decision-making process might favor moving toward equity. Such a process, in the words of the U.S. spokesman, "breeds discrimination. Sovereign States have the right to discriminate, the Authority does not. A Sovereign State does not administer the Common Heritage of Mankind, the Authority does."[204] U.S. officials favored discrimination once the materials were in national hands—since United States hands were fullest—but not when the materials were in the hands of the world community.[205] The United States preferred the discrimination of unregulated inequity to the discrimination of regulated equity.

Because the United States wanted a treaty to protect its interests, during 1976 and 1977 it shifted its negotiating position in important respects to accommodate the less industrialized nations. In brief, the new U.S. posture favored (1) establishing an International Seabed Resource Authority (ISRA) that would be allowed to conduct its own mining in addition to that of private or government corporations; (2) diverting some revenues from the ISRA to assist less developed countries, especially those affected by seabed mining; (3) reserving some mining sites for exclusive exploitation by the ISRA; (4) sharing mineral revenues, derived from a system of royalties or profit-sharing, with the international community; (5) providing some technical assistance to the less industrialized nations to upgrade their capabilities in deep-sea mining; (6) creating a permanent seabed tribunal with compulsory jurisdiction to adjudicate disputes; and (7) accepting a temporary limitation, for a fixed period of time, on production of seabed minerals so that total seabed extraction would not exceed the growth in the world demand for nickel, anticipated to be about 6 percent a year.

These concessions, although significant, were designed to sweeten the bargain so that developing countries would accept an international regime that still fell far short of furthering a genuinely new economic order. "Sweeteners" were offered, because, as Kissinger explained, "no one recognizes more clearly than American industry that investment, access and profit can best be protected in an established and predictable environment"[206] which only a treaty could provide. Modest concessions by the United States to achieve international legitimacy for long-range U.S. access to rich minerals were a good bargain. Because the United States sought stability within a favorable legal framework, it also supported compulsory adjudication of disputes.

Kissinger stressed the importance of reaching a binding agreement: "There is no alternative to chaos but a new global regime defining an agreed set of rules and procedures. The problem of the oceans is inherently international. No unilateral or national solution is likely to prevail without continual conflict." He argued that "a cooperative international regime to govern the use of the oceans and their resources is . . . an urgent necessity. . . . Only rarely does mankind comprehend the significance of change in the world as we so clearly do today." The Law of the Sea meetings were "an unprecedented opportunity for the nations of the world to devise the first truly global solution to a global problem."[207]

U.S. policies hardly matched these words of realism and promise. Despite Kissinger's self-proclaimed comprehension of the unique opportunities for global community-building, many of the old U.S. reservations about a treaty remained. Even though he said that the alternative to agreement was chaos, he insisted that the United States "cannot delay in its efforts to develop an assured supply of critical resources through our [national] deep seabed mining projects." Unilateral action, he argued on the one hand, would lead to "continual conflict"; yet "if agreement is not reached this year [1976] it will be increasingly difficult to resist pressure to proceed unilaterally." Indeed, "the United States can and will proceed to explore and mine on its own."[208]

Would the United States concede that the common heritage of humanity should be reserved for common usage in order to achieve a "truly global solution to a global problem"? Once again, national greed dominated global humanitarianism. The United States threatened not to sign any treaty that contained "restrictive limitations on the number of mine sites which any nation might exploit." Kissinger declared: "What the United States *cannot* accept is that the right of access to seabed minerals be given exclusively to an international authority."[209] As Robert Vastine of the Treasury Department put it, U.S. officials "are inalterably opposed to attempts to impose any system which would arbitrarily limit the number of sites that firms of any one signatory can exploit."[210]

The apparent concession to limit seabed production to about 6 percent a year of the existing nickel market for a fixed period was inconsequential. The chief U.S. negotiator in 1976, Ambassador T. Vincent Learson, said that that provision would not affect the anticipated level of operation by U.S. private industry anyway. The reason for including it, he explained, was that such a provision "was essential to bring the developing world along to agree to access by nations and States and their contractors."[211]

The voting procedure in the council of the ISRA was a matter of severe dispute. U.S. officials favored weighted voting as in the World Bank, whereas the less developed countries favored an equal vote for each member. Technologically advanced countries were already given weighted membership within the 36-member body.[212] The Ford Administration also sought to exercise future influence on the proposed ISRA through direct governmental control of revenue going to it. Less industrialized nations and some U.S. companies favored revenue collection for the ISRA through a system of company payments that could be taken as a foreign tax credit. Since such monies would not require the ISRA funds from U.S. corporations to go through Washington, the United States opposed this approach.[213] In sum, despite the admitted profound importance of the Law of the Sea deliberations for the future of humanity, the Nixon and Ford administrations objected to placing the seabed under the general control of a global authority.

The Carter administration, represented by Elliot Richardson as head of the U.S. delegation, seemed much more enthusiastic about achieving progress at the conference. During informal negotiations in 1977, many of the developing countries moved closer to accepting U.S. positions, so that for the first time an agreement seemed a serious possibility. According to Richardson, the compromise proposals "were by no means acceptable from our standpoint," but they provided the basis for further negotiation.[214]

Then at the last minute in the 1977 session, the chairman of Committee I, Paul Barnela Engo of Cameroon, changed some articles to reflect once again a regime more favorable to the less developed countries.[215] Richardson reacted strongly, recommending publicly that "the United States undertake a most serious and searching review of both the substance and procedures of the conference." He denounced the provisions on exploiting seabed minerals as "fundamentally unacceptable." He even said the United States should consider withdrawing from the conference, despite good progress in all subject areas except mining.

His complaints about the negotiating text included the following points:

—mining companies might not have automatic access to seabed minerals;

—a condition for access by such companies might be the transfer of mining technology to the international enterprise conducting mining for the ISRA;

—the international community might set unwanted limits on the quantities of minerals to be exploited;

—the industrialized states, being a minority in the international organs to govern the seabed, might be unable to defend their interests in its deliberations;

—the provision calling for an international review conference after twenty years might mean that parallel exploitation by both private companies and the ISRA might be terminated, with exploitation thereafter being exclusively in the hands of an international enterprise.[216]

The U.S. position, as reflected in Richardson's press conference, represented a strong bias, characteristic of previous

327

administrations, in favor of exploiting the common heritage through national means. Although the Carter administration offered concessions that were slightly more favorable to the less developed countries, officials still tailored their proposals to fit familiar national and corporate economic interests. Without substantial progress in achieving a more equitable economic order, there probably was little prospect of achieving a new international environmental order. We turn now to an examination of environmental issues at the conference.

Despite the growing public appeal of ecological protection, marine pollution did not even appear as a subject of United States policy in the first two years of preliminary meetings. The United States preferred to handle pollution questions on a piecemeal basis in IMCO and other organizations. Even after the item became part of the Law of the Sea Conference, United States activity on the issue was minimal. The environmental subcommittee of the U.S. advisory committee on the Law of the Sea contained only two members until 1973, and it remained one of the smallest subcommittees. The Environmental Protection Agency and the Council on Environmental Quality did not even participate in the law of the sea negotiations from 1970 until the summer of 1973.[217]

Although the Caracas conference possessed the authority to negotiate specific measures for pollution control in all of ocean space, the United States sought to avoid setting standards in that forum. As Ambassador Stevenson explained, in the area of environmental protection, "detailed rule making may best be left to the future."[218] The United States saw little purpose in Subcommittee III (which was charged with pollution control) other than general discussion of issues. Despite United States support for general statements obliging national governments to prevent pollution, both the decision to omit specific provisions that would give meaning to the generalities and the desire to transfer issues to a not-yet-established international authority demonstrated the modest extent of U.S. concern with marine pollution. Ratiner explained: "We take this [environmental protection] matter seriously, but we are not in a position at this time to recommend conditions on preservation of the environment—too little is known. So this task must be done by the Authority, and done well. . . . We are sure that we have a good idea of what will encourage investment [for exploiting nodules] but on this [environmental] one we are not so sure what the rules should be."[219] Thus, the United States asked for no specific standards for environmental protection, while it demanded that guarantees be entrenched in the treaty for free navigation and the opportunity to extract profits from mining nodules.

Although the UN Conference on the Law of the Sea was responsible for considering all forms of marine pollution, the United States limited its modest negotiating activities in this area mainly to pollution produced (1) by seabed activities, such as recovery of oil and nodules, and (2) by vessels at sea.[220] In the first area, the United States favored an International Seabed Resource Authority that could prescribe rules limited to guarding against pollution arising from activity on the seabeds.[221] The Authority would have the duty to grant licenses for mineral exploitation, to set pollution standards related to mineral extraction, to monitor the results, and to impose penalties for noncompliance. Yet the Authority was also vested with an exploitation mandate. It would suffer from a conflict of interest. Furthermore, the provisions were vague about the scope of the Authority's standard-setting and enforcement functions.

Within the entire subject area of pollution control, U.S. officials devoted by far their most attention at Caracas to vessel-source pollution. But here their purpose was not to enforce stricter international standards. Instead, it was to prevent the proposed international authority from taking control of this source of pollution. Officials reserved the exclusive right for IMCO to set such standards. They opposed the setting and enforcing of restrictions either by a unified international environmental protection agency or by national governments seeking to regulate commerce passing through their own coastal waters. If non-flag-state inspection and enforcement were allowed, it might interfere with U.S. vessels.[222]

In a seven-page special report entitled, "U.N. Law of the Sea Conference 1975," the State Department summarized U.S. positions on all issues during the Caracas and Geneva sessions. The complete summary of the "U.S. Position" on marine environmental protection was a single sentence: "We have strongly urged that standards for vessel-source pollution should only be set internationally through IMCO, by flag states for their own vessels, or by port states for vessels using their ports."[223] This report accurately summarized U.S. activity. The central environmental thrust was to retain most of the inadequate standards and enforcement procedures that had not protected the

329

oceans in the past, rather than to launch a bold, new protection program.

Some environmentalists concluded that a coastal state authority to enforce stricter standards in the economic zone would provide "the most effective means for controlling vessel-source pollution and protecting vulnerable coastal zones."[224] Thus in continuing to resist the requests of coastal states to set non-emergency pollution standards, U.S. officials opposed the single most promising measure for upgrading standards against vessel-source pollution. In effect, the effort of coastal states to get stronger pollution standards was "the principal problem" for the United States in the committee discussing pollution in the economic zone.[225] According to Stevenson, "the most troublesome problem in the pollution area is the extent of coastal state control of vessel source pollution in the economic zone."[226]

As a leading specialist on U.S. ocean policies concluded after her study of the Law of the Sea Conference, "The overriding concern was to accommodate coastal state concerns while avoiding pollution [control] zones and other potential restrictions on maritime transit."[227] The Senators on the U.S. delegation at Caracas reported that "the basic goal of the U.S. pollution articles is to protect U.S. navigational interests by preventing coastal nations from asserting and enforcing vessel pollution standards in their economic zones."[228] Thus, the small amount of official U.S. activity devoted to marine pollution was largely aimed against coastal state protection of the environment in order to maintain a greater navigational freedom. Since the United States required the exemption of all military vessels from such provisions anyway,[229] the U.S. opposition seemed particularly aimed at protecting vested oil and shipping interests at the expense of the environment.

Within the 200-mile economic zone, the United States did support the principle that international standards should be set for pollution arising from seabed activity, such as extracting oil and natural gas.[230] In addition, the United States favored the idea that states were obliged to conserve fish that lived or spawned in the various national economic zones.[231] Yet no specific standards were proposed. The most serious problems were left to the future. States were not obliged to establish international regulations within any specific length of time. No provisions explained how the international obligations would be defined and enforced. Although the United States supported international inspection to insure that coastal states followed international pollution guidelines for seabed activities in their own economic zones,[232] there was no procedure for enforcing the requirement that national standards at least equal the internationally prescribed guidelines. Without an enforcement procedure, coastal states would be tempted to ignore international standards in order to give their own oil corporations a competitive advantage or to finance development at lowest cost.

In another departure from past practice, the United States asked for compulsory settlement of disputes arising under the proposed treaty.[233] This was desirable from an environmental point of view. Yet until there were compulsory standards to enforce, compulsory judicial settlement would be of limited value. Nonetheless, the widespread agreement at the conference that compulsory judicial settlement should be a part of the treaty did appear to be a significant step toward a preferred global system.

With regard to land-based pollution of the oceans, U.S. negotiators argued that an international convention suggesting guidelines for national pollution legislation would be "universally beneficial in preserving the marine environment, especially in the inshore regions of the world where excessive pollution is beginning to have an adverse effect upon the marine environment."[234] Despite such a promising statement, U.S. officials made no effort to establish international restrictions on marine pollution originating from territorial waters, the atmosphere, or land-based sources. "Control of such pollution must come largely from national legislation and local action."[235] The proposals for a new international authority were restricted to pollution caused by seabed exploration and exploitation.[236] Thus even if all U.S. draft articles had been accepted and fully successful in stopping ocean pollution from ships at sea, from mining and extracting oil from the seabed, and from dumping, the largest sources of damage to the ocean environment, which are land-based, would remain unregulated.

As is clear from the preceding survey, U.S. policies were neither overtly hostile to nor vigorously supportive of environmental protection. Strategic and economic self-interest in the short run clearly dominated the development of U.S. policies. Pursuing short-range self-interest prevented the United States from responding sensitively to the requests of the less developed

331

countries for greater economic equity. For several reasons, this posture virtually foreclosed progress in environmental protection.

First of all, many developing countries were unenthusiastic about pollution control. The industrialized countries had partially financed their industrialization during the past century by contaminating the environment. Only after becoming relatively affluent did the rich consider environmental quality. Some poor nations also were willing to finance their development in the cheapest way possible. Restrictions upon industrial growth and diversion of capital to environmental protection would slow the development of the poorer nations.[237] Among private enterprise systems, capital moves to regions where profits may be maximized. Thus capital could be encouraged to move from rich to poor societies by creating pollution havens in the less developed countries.

Furthermore, many less industrialized nations were concerned that costs for sea transportation, energy, fertilizer, herbicides, and insecticides would rise if high safety standards were imposed upon tankers and drilling operations, and if the cheapest chemical substances, such as DDT, were banned. Some countries exporting raw materials feared that export earnings would decline because of pollution abatement measures. Products from the poorer nations might even be discriminated against on environmental grounds, with consequences similar to protectionist tariff walls erected against them. Retrieval of deep-sea nodules would affect the cobalt exports of Zaire, Morocco, and Zambia; the nickel exports of Indonesia and Cuba; the manganese exports of Ghana and Gabon; and the copper exports of Chile and Zambia.[238]

Brazil and India both pressed the idea that a lower standard should be allowed for pollution by developing countries in the 200-mile economic zone. Brazil argued that all seabed activities within the economic zone should be under exclusive national jurisdiction, thus enabling Brazilians to extract minerals more cheaply from their seabed if they were willing to pollute more freely. India opposed a binding obligation to accept international standards for dumping in its zone, reserving the right to apply less stringent standards.[239] Many of the developing countries supported the provision that in considering whether a country has discharged its obligations under the treaty "due regard must be paid to . . . the economic and financial ability of a

State to provide the resources necessary for the discharge of such obligations and the stage of economic development of the State."[240] Most less industrialized countries wanted the industrialized states to pay for cleaning up the environment and to provide assistance equivalent to any financial costs that developing countries might incur from environmental action,[241] including declines in export earnings that resulted from ecological concern.[242]

U.S. negotiators said that the level of economic development was irrelevant to the performance of obligations by developing countries.[243] Equal standards must be applied to industrialized and developing nations alike. Going beyond this, the United States opposed resolutions asking for foreign aid to soften any decrease in earnings from export of raw materials as a result of environmental protection. "As a matter of principle, [the United States government] opposes compensating countries for declines in their export earnings for whatever cause and believes that a commitment to pay such compensation would serve as a disincentive to environmental controls."[244] The United States also opposed an effort on the part of the less developed countries to increase assistance to meet the additional environmental requirements of developed countries. U.S. officials argued that there was no rationale for singling out environmental protection costs from among other costs for special accounting in giving aid.[245] The United States refusal to grant a double standard for performing pollution control obligations was environmentally sound. But the reluctance of the United States to help the poor states perform their responsibilities was politically self-defeating and environmentally dangerous.

The debate over who should pay for clean oceans was merely one issue of the broader question: What is a just distribution of global resources? No one denied that there could be better protection of the marine environment. But almost all improvements required more capital, more skills, and more reasonable allocation of resources among competing needs. If, for example, tighter regulation of oil discharges and strengthened safety standards increased the price of petroleum products, who should pay for the increase? The rich nations answered "the consumer should pay." But many poor nations argued that the cost of environmental cleanup should be borne by the users of unnecessary consumer goods and luxury items. The point here is not that all virtue lies on one side of the question, but that legitimate issues of pollution abatement bear directly upon global resource allocation and use.

U.S. officials ignored the environmentally crucial issue of economic equity. Equity could not be achieved by stressing the freedom of states to have unrestricted access to seabed resources. That produced a decided advantage for those with technology and capital. Equity could be achieved only by allowing nations fair participation in a global political process that would preside over the exploitation and marketing of the minerals. United States resistance to that option doomed the cause of environmental protection. If the governments of the less industrialized states had to choose between allowing people to starve or rivers to be polluted, pollution would be the preferable alternative. When people worry about their next meal, they can hardly be expected to be concerned about amenities for the next generation of vacationers at a distant beach.

U.S. proposals contributed to environmentally-threatening, economic inequity. The United States opposed efforts to link world strategies for marine protection with strategies to adjust resource allocation. No development assistance was offered for raising environmental standards. Officials made no effort to enable the developing countries to pay for the increased costs of pollution abatement without increasing the gap between rich and poor.[246] In assessing the accomplishments of the Law of the Sea conference, Ann Hollick concluded: "From the perspective of international equity the likely outcome is a worsening of the already monumental gap between the poorest nations and the rest of the world."[247] F. H. Knelman commented: "A minority of people controls the majority of the world's resources from calories to capital. This fact is perhaps the most urgent threat to global survival."[248]

At present the industrial nations are by far the greatest polluters of the oceans. The rich also most rapidly deplete scarce resources. Some critics have labeled industrial countries like the United States "pollution imperialists" because the global burden of pollution that they impose on others is roughly equal to the proportion of their consumption. Thus the rich now bear the major responsibility for the stresses on the global ecosphere.[249] But as the rich gain environmental sensitivity—if they do—and as the developing countries industrialize and increase the size of their urban populations, pollution will no longer be a product primarily of the presently rich countries.

334

Rather than build upon the common heritage idea, nations at the Third Law of the Sea Conference scrambled for more resources and for extending national control over ocean space. The United States began this process after World War II with the first Truman Proclamation. In this statement, the president informed the world that the United States would unilaterally extend national control over its continental shelf beyond the limits of the territorial seas.[250] The purpose was to extract offshore oil. Within a few years, one coastal state after another made similar claims for various reasons.

Three decades after the United States exploitation of minerals outside its territorial jurisdiction, the less developed countries made a concerted effort to improve their own economic well-being and prevent further extension of the economic advantages of the rich. They imitated but went beyond the Truman Proclamation by claiming a 200-mile economic zone. This was a means of countering the advantages of the maritime powers in a regime based on freedom of the seas.[251] Less developed countries sought to overcome their powerlessness through extension of national sovereignty over more ocean territory, formerly a part of the commons. Given the legacy of colonialism and territorial expansion, this reaction was not surprising. Poorer nations did not want to compete with large factory fishing ships of the great powers; nor did they want supertankers spilling oil close to their shores since they lacked technology to clean up spills. The history of colonialism, economic exploitation, and CIA interventions also conditioned many of these countries to be suspicious of what the United States favored; hence, the early support for the Pardo proposals, which maximized the dimensions of the common heritage, evaporated in part because the less developed countries later learned that the United States—especially the Pentagon—favored a narrow continental shelf as Pardo recommended.[252]

The less wealthy countries could support a narrow shelf approach only with apprehensiveness about the intentions of the industrial states. If the latter continued to oppose a strong international agency, then the narrow shelf thesis would work greatly toward the economic vulnerability of the poorer countries. A maximum area of the high seas would be open to exploitation by the technically advanced states without any obligations being incurred to the developing world. The less advanced states reasoned that if they could not jointly gain a distributable income from the exploitation of the high seas, then they should individually maximize their opportunities for sharing in the wealth of the ocean by extending their claims as far seaward as possible.[253]

The poorer countries may, however, have pursued a strategy that violated their own best interests. Only a small percentage of them will benefit from the 200-mile resource zone. The biggest losers will be the landlocked, shelflocked, short coastal states, and states with comparatively few resources off their coasts, a group of nations which includes among its numbers some of the poorest countries of the world. By letting the offshore oil and natural gas reserves come under coastal state control, over 90 percent of those minerals were transferred outside the common heritage. If the smallest islands of mid-ocean are given a 200-mile economic zone or if their colonial parents may declare them archipelagoes with base lines drawn to their outermost points, and if coastal states with major bights can connect them within their zones, then as much as half of the world's mine-grade nodules could also fall under national jurisdiction.[254] The United States would gain more square miles of exclusive economic zone than any other country in the world. The proposed treaty provisions, if ratified, will produce consequences opposite to the proclaimed intentions of those favoring a new international economic order.

Because the less developed countries sought to overcome their disadvantages by staying within a territorial system of national sovereignty, they could not achieve their objectives. Pardo's original idea was a collective global regime for the benefit of all. This was rejected as states sought to maximize individual gain through the sovereign territorial state. A more equitable division of resources would have been ensured by enlarging, not narrowing, the domain of the common heritage. By increasing the dimensions of the common heritage and asserting the right to an equitable portion of the petroleum, fish, and nodules within the 200-mile economic zones of the industrialized nations, the poorer countries could more fully have redressed the imbalance of resource allocation. However, the political difficulties of accomplishing this goal and the fear that the rich states would control any new global regime encouraged the poor states to fall back upon the more familiar territorial principle and anti-imperialist strategy of maximizing their sovereign control wherever they could.

The more pronounced and persistent the gap between rich

and poor nations, the more impossible it will be to protect the marine environment. Poor nations will feel justified in passing weak environmental legislation. The absence of international consensus on pollution standards will encourage the industrialized nations to be satisfied with inadequate safeguards in order to avoid competitive disadvantages for their industries.

The failure of the United States to exercise farsighted leadership for pollution control at Caracas and Geneva portends a grim future for the ocean. The United States could have agreed that costs of environmental protection reasonably should be charged to states according to their ability to pay. The United States could have advocated rules prohibiting the transfer of capital to pollution havens. The United States could have proposed that benefits from deep-sea mining should be granted to poor countries on a scale proportional with the pollution standards achieved in the recipient nation. The United States could have insisted upon an international commitment to transfer annually one percent of the GNP of the richest nations to international efforts to protect the environment in poorer nations only now acquiring industries. Such measures would be easier to institute when industries were developing than after they acquired vested interests in polluting the environment. But the United States rejected all these ideas for environmental protection.

OFFICIAL RATIONALE COMPARED TO THE VALUES IMPLICIT
IN U.S. POLICY

By describing the environmental policies of the United States in the three principal international proceedings for marine protection, the basis is laid for comparing the values expressed in official behavior with the values expressed in the rhetoric of U.S. officials. In public statements and at international conferences U.S. officials articulated a deep concern about ocean pollution and spoke with pride about United States actions for environmental protection. Most statements contained professions of one or more of the following three values.

Professed Value 1: To Undertake All Measures Necessary to
Protect the Marine Environment

The United States government publicly committed itself to "take all possible steps to prevent pollution of the seas by substances that are liable to create hazards to human health, to harm living resources and marine life, to damage amenities or to interfere with other legitimate uses of the sea."[255] Moreover, officials formally assumed the responsibility "to ensure that activities within their jurisdiction or control do not cause damage to the environment of other states or of areas beyond the limits of national jurisdiction."[256] A further U.S. profession of intent is contained in Article 1 of the convention on dumping: "Contracting parties shall individually and collectively promote the effective control of all sources of pollution of the marine environment."[257] In President Nixon's 1972 State of the Union Message on Natural Resources and the Environment, he informed Congress that the United States attacked the pollution problem "with all the power at our command. There is encouraging evidence that the United States has moved away from the environmental crisis that could have been and toward a new era of restoration and renewal."[258]

The preceding examination of the U.S. role at the conferences on the Law of the Sea, ocean dumping, and vessel discharges calls professed value 1 into serious question. Surely the optimism that the United States "has moved away from the environmental crisis" was unwarranted. In the proceedings for the dumping and IMCO conventions, as well as at the Law of the Sea Conference, the protection of the environment was consistently subordinated both to the Defense Department's insistence upon sweeping navigational freedom and to the oil, mining, and shipping industries' requests for protection of their economic interests. To be sure, the United States did favor minimum international standards for pollution in the exclusive economic zones. This posture reflected the interests of U.S. oil companies, which were subject to U.S. domestic legislation governing their operations in U.S. coastal waters. U.S. officials wanted similar restrictions applied to other nations. Thus the United States favored modest international standards that would help protect the environment while, as the U.S. representative said, "assuring coastal states that they will not suffer competitive economic disadvantage by applying such standards."[259] As a result of the general desire to enhance U.S. prosperity, Edward Wenk, the former presidential adviser and executive secretary of the U.S. National Council on Marine Resources and Engineering Development, reported that environmental issues were "grasped as chips in the international poker game without regard for long-term implications."[260]

U.S. policies expressed laxity in establishing pollution stand-

338

ards and enforcement measures in each of the three areas examined. Officials made no effort to set any international standards for by far the largest source of marine pollution, namely land-based activity. In brief, these analyses of U.S. ocean policies suggest that U.S. behavior reflected implicit values quite different from professed value 1. The United States sought *to subordinate environmental protection to U.S. military, navigational, and economic interests* (implicit value A).

On a more concrete level, the most obvious failure to attack pollution vigorously was the U.S. opposition to establishing an international regime that could effectively implement even modest international standards. The United States favored a fragmentary, haphazard approach to environmental protection. Guidelines for use of the seabed would be set by a proposed seabed authority, for vessels by IMCO, for radioactive materials by a third agency; for pollution originating from other sources, there would be no international control at all. The United States never sought to establish a general environmental protection authority that could coordinate pollution abatement measures, set universal standards, reduce unfair competitive advantages, and take account of synergistic effects throughout all the sea.

Enforcement procedures were even weaker than pollution standards. In the three general areas of pollution control examined above, with the exception of the limited area of seabed mining, the United States did not even attempt to establish an organization for global enforcement of environmental standards.[261] The United States advocated non-flag state enforcement—far different from enforcement by an international organization—only in a few narrowly limited cases where such enforcement protected U.S. companies against competitive disadvantages, but not in other cases where it "merely" could have protected the environment. At Caracas and Geneva the United States moved to port state enforcement only under some pressure, and never accepted coastal state enforcement except in emergency situations. In sum, the United States chose *to avoid creating effective international enforcement procedures for protection of marine ecology* (implicit value B).

Professed Value 2: To Protect and Share Equitably the Common Heritage for All Humanity

At various times in the late 1960s and early 1970s the United States renounced national claims to the common heritage. In 1966 President Lyndon Johnson promised that throughout the

339

oceans: "Under no circumstances . . . must we ever allow the prospects of rich harvests and mineral wealth to create a new form of colonial competition among the maritime nations. We must be careful to avoid a race to grab and to hold the lands under the high seas. We must ensure that the deep seas and the ocean bottoms are, and remain, the legacy of all human beings."[262] In 1970 the United States supported a General Assembly resolution, entitled "Declaration of Legal Principles," which stated: "The seabed and ocean floor, and the subsoil thereof, beyond the limits of national jurisdiction . . . as well as the resources of the area, are the common heritage of mankind."[263] In the proposals developed by the United States for the Law of the Sea Conference, the government declared in Article 1: "The international Seabed Area shall be the common heritage of all mankind."[264] The Nixon administration proposed that "all nations adopt as soon as possible a treaty under which they would renounce all national claims over the natural resources of the seabed beyond the point where the high seas reach a depth of 200 meters and would agree to regard these resources as the common heritage of mankind."[265]

In addition U.S. officials professed a desire to share the benefits of the oceans equally with all people. In the first report to Congress under the Marine Resources and Engineering Development Act of 1967, President Johnson promised: "We shall bring to the challenge of the ocean depths . . . a determination to work with all nations to develop the seas for the benefit of mankind." He pledged that "the wealth of the ocean floor must be freed for the benefit of all people."[266] Three years later President Nixon said that the central issue of ocean policy was whether the seas would be used "rationally and equitably and for the benefit of mankind or whether they will become an arena of unrestrained exploitation." He assured Congress and the public that the U.S. proposals for the Law of the Sea Conference would utilize the sea "for the benefit of all."[267]

Among the very first principles U.S. officials introduced for negotiation at the United Nations Conference on the Law of the Sea was the idea that "there should be no discrimination in the availability of the area for exploration, scientific research [and] . . . the exploitation of resources." The U.S. representative said the Law of the Sea negotiations were "the first clear opportunity to begin to manage in common resources of great value, to create situations of equality with respect to resources which have not previously existed but should exist in the future."[268] In contrast to this rhetoric, the United States in practice transformed steps toward "equality" into a strategy for maximizing U.S. access to the richest supplies of minerals. Equal opportunity to exploit meant those countries best able to exploit in the near future could exploit the most. "Equality" did not mean establishing global coordination for the exploitation and sale of the nodules.

The same set of priorities determined the evolution of U.S. policy on the continental shelf. The U.S. position in 1970 placed more shelf resources in the common heritage than the 1973 position, which bore the imprint of oil interests within Washington.[269] The extension of national jurisdiction from the 200-meter isobath to the 200-mile limit contributed to national wealth at the expense of universal environmental protection and resource conservation. Undersecretary of State Russell Train had argued that by extending the national claim over marine resources to 200 miles, oil companies would reap greater profits. The president later appointed him chairman of the Council on Environmental Quality. Congress, the Interior Department, and the State Department all opposed an expansion of the common heritage, even though it could have aided the poor states as well as provided a more universal context for pollution abatement.[270] As time passed, U.S. negotiators spoke less and less about ocean resources belonging to the people of the world.

Thus, rather than implement the second professed value, the United States sought *to maximize national access to the common heritage* (implicit value C).

Furthermore, U.S. officials worked vigorously to insure U.S. opportunities for profit from the common heritage. At Caracas, officials rejected all controls on profits, refused limits on the number of claims the United States would be granted, opposed high royalties, favored guarantees against loss of capital investment, and made no proposals for specific environmental standards related to mining. At the same time, the United States sought to avoid any general international financial commitments to help poor states implement international standards, or to transfer mineral consumption from luxury use in rich countries to, say, food production in poor countries. Similarly, global equalization of wealth was never a goal of U.S. policy. Royalties from mining or "transfer payments" to the less developed countries were acceptable primarily as political lubricants to move the UN machinery toward sanctioning the right of unrestricted

341

navigation and national access to the ocean wealth. Knowledge-able U.S. observers calculated that if U.S. proposals were implemented, the gap between the rich and poor states would widen. The second professed value was subordinated to an alternative preference: *to maximize U.S. economic benefits from mining, with little regard for international equity* (implicit value D).

In addition to securing national economic advantages, U.S. officials opposed international coordination of resource usage. This policy exacerbated two serious environmental problems. First, increased urbanization and industrialization clearly endangered the ocean environment if pollution abatement measures did not accompany socioeconomic changes. Thus one measure for slowing the pace of pollution would have been for the industrialized nations to restrict their economic growth to production for serving basic human needs, especially of the poorest nations. Such a cooperative effort would also have helped minimize the desire of the less developed countries, nurtured by an international variation of keeping up with the Joneses, for some forms of industrialization that might harm the environment yet remain a relatively inefficient means for serving human health and welfare.

Second, in a world where states sought national competitive advantage, environmental deterioration was inevitable. As long as the industrialized states consumed an inequitable share of the world's output, the developing states hesitated to slacken their development in order to pay for environmental protection. Yet the rich states were reluctant to limit their prosperity for environmental protection of areas beyond their national jurisdiction. The United States refused to limit its consumption of minerals and energy, to tailor its consumption and profits to help serve non-U.S. needs, or to consider environmental protection equal in importance to rapid national access to seabed resources.

The U.S. president had warned in 1970: "The stark fact is that the law of the sea is inadequate to meet the needs of modern technology and the concerns of the international community. If it is not modernized multilaterally, unilateral action and international conflict are inevitable."[271] Despite this warning, U.S. corporate and military interests mobilized and exerted enormous pressure upon the executive branch and Congress. They shaped U.S. policy so that modernizing the law multilaterally, according to U.S. guidelines, meant enlisting the rest of the world in the service of U.S. interests. Official behavior expressed implicit value E: *to refuse global coordination of resources for the purpose of maximizing environmental protection and the service of global human needs*.

In failing to support some global coordination of resource usage and in refusing to charge pollution abatement to those with the most ability to pay, the United States subordinated environmental protection to increasing its already high standard of living. Never did United States officials acknowledge a need to decrease the U.S. share of the global consumption of resources. This omission occurred in the face of statements by environmentalists that the planet was literally incapable of supporting the world's existing population at the level of U.S. consumption.[272]

Global guidelines for resource usage and pollution control were even more objectionable to U.S. officials than competitive disadvantages for U.S. companies. In many instances, protection against competitive disadvantage could have been increased by replacing flag-state or national enforcement with enforcement by an international authority. Yet if an international authority were created to set pollution ceilings and conservation standards for various nations, the consequences would be serious for the United States as the biggest industrial economy with high per capita consumption and as one of the worst polluters of the world. (The United States, for example, injected into the sea one-third to one-half of the waste products resulting from the burning of fossil fuels.)[273] Thus a further qualification to the second professed value is required: U.S. officials sought *to protect the U.S. position as a disproportionately large consumer of resources and energy, despite the negative ecological consequences* (implicit value F).

Professed Value 3: To Provide Environmental Leadership Among Other Nations

The U.S. president informed the citizenry that the United States has attacked the environmental problem "with all the power at our command." The environmental crisis, the president reassured Congress in 1973, was diminishing in the face of a "new era of restoration and renewal. . . . We are well on the way to winning the war against environmental degradation—well on the way to making our peace with nature."[274] The president said that international concern for the environment "is en-

343

couraging. Many significant international actions have been taken in recent years, and the United States can be proud of its leadership."[275]

U.S. Ambassador John Stevenson often stressed the importance of international cooperation that transcended narrow national interests. The Law of the Sea Conference, he said, "may well determine whether we have the will and the institutional structure to achieve cooperative solutions for important global problems."[276] Stevenson warned that if the international community "cannot deal effectively with the problems of lawmaking in this area, in which a large measure of mutual accommodation appears feasible and in which there is a very broad common interest in minimum rules of order on which all can rely, thus giving negotiation a dimension going beyond the mere maximization of particular national interests, the prospects for dealing with other more intensely political disputes is bleak indeed."[277] Congressional legislation also acknowledged that a U.S. program for ocean space could not be effective unless it worked "for the benefit of mankind."[278] All parties in Washington seemed aware that unbridled nationalism would destroy the marine environment.

Thus it was an ominous sign when, in all the proceedings examined, the United States government did not exercise creative leadership for environmental protection. The main trade-off among policymakers within Washington between 1970 and 1977 was between strategic and economic interests.[279] Environmental protection was not even an important stake in the bargaining process. At the Law of the Sea Conference, officials used their important political capital to win enlarged freedom of transit for aircraft and seagoing vessels and insured access to nodules and petroleum for U.S. corporations. Except for limited provisions in the IMCO and dumping conventions, U.S. officials did not work for preventive measures against pollution. Instead, arrangements were suggested to recover damages after injury. In contrast, when it came to protecting the mining companies against loss of profit, the United States insisted that the international authority for dispute settlement must be empowered "to give interlocutory decrees, and injunctive relief. In an operation where the Authority's orders can cause losses that amount to thousands of dollars per day, the exploiter can't wait to learn whether he must comply. That is no way to run a business." For mineral exploitation, "it is essential that fundamental conditions of exploitation be included in the treaty."[280] For the environment, "detailed rule making may best be left to the future."[281] Thus the optimistic 1967 observation of the U.S. Commission on Marine Science proved untrue: "In these vast areas of untold riches few, if any, national economic interests have been vested, nor have the nations of the world as yet any fixed political positions. . . . There is opportunity, therefore, to design a framework that will eliminate international conflict from this area of human endeavor."[282] Vested interests of U.S. corporations and the power of Pentagon officials made 1970 already too late to respond rationally to the common heritage idea. Strategic and economic interests violated environmental needs. After the Geneva session of the Law of the Sea Conference, the environmental provisions in the Single Negotiating Text, which were not greatly dissimilar from United States preferences, promised sufficient future damage to the oceans that many environmental groups opposed the treaty. The Environmental Defense Fund, the Friends of the Earth, the National Audubon Society, the Natural Resources Defense Council, and the Sierra Club informed the Senate Commerce Committee that if a treaty including such provisions came before the Senate for advice and consent to ratification, they would recommend that the Senate *reject* the treaty.[283]

United States officials doubtlessly would have preferred to increase U.S. strategic strength and economic prosperity and at the same time to encourage the rest of the world to participate in modest environmental protection. But if that were not possible, officials sought material prosperity—even inequitable prosperity—at the price of marine deterioration.

As indicated above, U.S. officials opposed limits on national sovereignty even more than loss of potential national wealth. This was most evident in the failure to press for enforcement by a global environmental authority. Officials feared the latter might somehow encroach upon U.S. military activity. National security led the list of considerations on ocean policy, followed closely by oil and mining interests.[284] If, as argued in implicit value F, officials preferred to protect national advantages through self-help rather than to achieve greater equity through international organizations representing more of a planetary interest, then Washington required a military presence around the world. Characteristically, official behavior expressed a desire *to be more responsive to military and corporate interests than to the needs of the international community for environmental leadership* (implicit value G).

To gain a few billion dollars more in mineral wealth, to retain a degree of unregulated navigational freedom more appropriate for the nineteenth century, and to guard its vast military power located in and above the sea, the United States risked the deterioration of the marine ecosystem. Policies of the United States and most other nations were narrowly nationalistic and of fleeting insignificance in terms of humanity's existence on the globe. It is impossible to know whether the Law of the Sea Con-

Table 5-3

A Comparison of Professed and Implicit Values
in U.S. Policy for Reducing Marine Pollution

Professed Values	*Implicit Values*
1. To undertake all measures necessary to protect the marine environment.	A. To subordinate environmental protection to U.S. military, navigational, and economic interests.
	B. To avoid creating effective international enforcement procedures for protection of marine ecology.
2. To protect and share equitably the common heritage for all humanity.	C. To maximize U.S. access to the common heritage.
	D. To maximize U.S. economic benefits from deep-sea mining, with little regard for international equity.
	E. To refuse global coordination of resources for the purpose of maximizing both environmental protection and the service of global human needs.
	F. To protect the U.S. position as a disproportionately large consumer of resources and energy, despite the negative ecological consequences.
3. To provide environmental leadership among other nations.	G. To be more responsive to military and corporate interests than to the needs of the international community for environmental leadership.

ference was the last, best hope for securing environmental protection, or whether another opportunity may appear before the oceans reach a stage of irreparable harm. However, the health of the oceans will decline as long as U.S. officials continue each year to give highest priority to acquiring, through shrewdly-waged competition with other states, a little more national wealth and power.

A GLOBAL HUMANIST APPROACH

Implicit Values and Environmental Protection

Compared to other states, the various U.S. positions on marine pollution were among neither the most nor the least enlightened in the three contexts examined here. If behavior had conformed with official rhetoric, the implementation of ecological balance would have been an integral part of U.S. foreign policy. However, the values implicit in U.S. policy differed significantly from professed values.

Predictable interests determined the various U.S. positions during complex negotiations to control pollutants. To gain the right for a nuclear submarine to remain submerged in straits or to prevent non-United States jurisdiction over U.S. ships at sea, the United States sacrificed international regulation of hazardous vessels. To gain national access to oil under the U.S. continental shelf and minerals on the deep seabed, the United States eroded the common heritage and undermined economic incentives for developing countries to join the effort for environmental protection. To protect U.S. companies from competitive disadvantage, the United States sought to apply universally the standards established in its domestic legislation, but without helping to achieve the worldwide equity that made equal environmental standards politically feasible and morally justifiable.

Inadequacies of Past International Action

Understanding the following inadequacies of the U.S. approach to pollution abatement helps define a contrasting, global humanist perspective for harmonizing humanity's relationship to nature.

THE PIECEMEAL PROBLEM

In the absence of a global environmental authority,[285] various international organizations might set modest pollution control standards in isolated areas, but wide gaps would probably remain between areas. For all of the most toxic substances, such as heavy metals, PCBs, pesticides, oil, and radioactive wastes, there remain absolutely no international ceilings for the total amounts that can be transferred to the oceans each year. Haphazard regulations apply to dumping or discharging these substances from ships—but here enforcement usually is to be carried out by governments now allowing pollution of the seas. Even this restriction applies only to ships of states voluntarily agreeing to sign the various conventions. All substances may be disposed freely, in any quantities, from within territorial waters if they do not directly harm a neighboring state. Moreover, the piecemeal approach has failed to prevent cumulative and synergistic effects of pollution. These cannot be managed successfully with a collection of uncoordinated international organizations such as IMCO, IAEA, and others. International organizations can hardly be blamed for the haphazard approach to pollution control. They accomplish what national governments expect of them. The absence of coordination and effective follow-through reveal "the lack of political will and the inability of the sovereign nation-state system to adapt to today's needs."[286]

THE COMMON POOL PROBLEM AND THE TERRITORIAL PRINCIPLE

The most serious criticism of the probable Law of the Sea treaty is its shortsighted response to population increases, industrial growth, and resource scarcity. At Caracas, national governments sought to manage the consequences of these forces by extending the principle of territorial control to coastal waters and parts of the deep seabed. However, even if the extension of national sovereignty may work for the management of fixed mineral resources, it cannot successfully regulate marine pollution or nurture certain forms of marine life.[287] The past record of destroying habitats for fish within territorial seas where individual nations have had control for decades makes this clear. As a result, the potential world fish harvest will probably fall to a level far below the maximum possible sustainable yield.

Moreover, expanding the territorial principle of national control over ocean resources will exacerbate existing international inequities and probably generate more conflicts than it resolves.[288] At points where the line between two states' coastal waters meet above a subterranean oil field, there will no doubt be rapid efforts by each party to pump oil before the other can. Not only are many competing wells along a given boundary inefficient, they are environmentally harmful because each well has attendant risks of leaks, blowouts, or other accidents. Rivalry will encourage cutting corners on safety. Oil slicks may appear with each state blaming the other, and neither accepting responsibility for damages or expensive cleanup. A similar set of problems arises for protecting fish that live in waters covering two or more states' jurisdictions. Each state may seek to harvest the fish before the other side does. Fear that the stocks are in decline motivates states seeking national advantage to maximize the harvest before it is gone.

Judging by the results of the Caracas, Geneva, and New York meetings, the Law of the Sea Conference will accentuate the state system. The territorial principle will be extended, not transcended. The global environmental interest will not be protected by officials who view the central issue as one of resolving conflicts between those who want to maximize territorial prerogatives over the sea's bounty and those who want to maximize national prerogatives for unregulated navigation. The negotiations seem headed toward an outcome that will render humanity's future ability to protect the sea as ineffectual as its past inability to protect against irresponsible national activities that injured lakes, streams, and territorial waters.[289]

Particularly discouraging for advocates of both equity and ecological protection was the failure of the most natural governmental allies of a new economic order to support a strong common heritage position at the Law of the Sea Conference. The small and poor countries, who presumably would have had the most to gain from maximizing the common heritage, feared that any new global regime would be controlled by the major powers. Thus many disadvantaged states sought to protect their interests through following the traditional habit of the major powers, i.e., by expanding their sovereign claims rather than by implementing a vision of a cooperative world order.

This stance illustrates how difficult it is to move into a new political framework while still operating within the intellectual and attitudinal parameters of the old order. The nonindustrialized powers seemed frozen in their response to the common heritage idea. Understandably, they reacted as if trying to gain control of their own land, still held by an imperialist power. Just

349

as the imperialist legacy made it unlikely that formerly exploited governments would opt for a new, untried vision of global cooperation, so the legacy of competing sovereignties among both the former imperial powers and the newly independent states make movement into an ecologically secure age extremely difficult. Such an age cannot be founded upon the existing system's attributes of unregulated growth, wasteful competition, and the pursuit of national advantages over rivals. Operating within the patterns of the present system, neither the rich nor the poor favored an ecologically sound global framework.

Indeed, the gap of wealth and power between the most and the least privileged nations will continue to be an obstacle to wise environmental policies. The side inferior in wealth and technology refuses to accept an environmental treaty that might lengthen its period of economic inferiority because of environmental standards that are difficult to implement. On the other hand, the side that is superior in wealth refuses to accept an environmental treaty that seems to require it to pay for the pollution of others, to restrict its consumption for the benefit of competing societies, or in general to concede more than its opponents in negotiations.

The aforementioned dilemma is so profound that it is difficult to believe that ecological decay can be halted before greater economic equity is achieved.

THE NONSIGNATORY PROBLEM

Enlightened national efforts by themselves—like separate acts of self-restraint on the English commons—can hardly be effective.[290] The U.S. ban on the use of DDT could be offset by increased spraying of it elsewhere. Even international control efforts could not succeed if states were allowed to exclude themselves from the standards. As persistent poisons pile up, one or two offending states could contaminate a major region of the oceans, and unalterably affect the environment. A handful of nuclear powers have already done this by increasing radioactivity in every corner of the globe. As our earlier discussions showed, even the positive examples of environmental progress—the IMCO and dumping conventions—apply only to those agreeing to the conditions. With many economic incentives for desperately poor or selfishly acquisitive societies to create pollution havens, such an approach cannot provide assurance of achieving ecological balance.

350

ENFORCEMENT

As long as sovereign states oppose worldwide enforcement measures, many environmental goals will remain impossible to achieve. Weak enforcement of regulations that do exist produces a practical effect no different from the absence of regulations. Flags of convenience must some day disappear from the sea. Probably a single global regime will need to register all vessels of large size, of hazardous nature, or of questionable purpose. Because of ineffective enforcement, for example, the International Whaling Commission has been unable to save the blue whale from near extinction because of overhunting by only two countries: the Soviet Union and Japan. Protecting this whale encroaches very little upon any state's sovereignty and threatens no state economically. Moreover, the national governments of the world have voted overwhelmingly for a moritorium on hunting this whale. Yet enforcement has been ineffective.[291] Similarly, the bilateral International Joint Commission for regulating United States and Canadian fresh waters reportedly has enforcement problems and lacks powers to compel obedience to its decisions.[292] Global regulation will be far more difficult to achieve than enforcement between two friendly, wealthy states. Nowhere is the inadequacy of enforcement better illustrated than in the handling of radioactive materials. Even obligatory standards for waste disposal would hardly be sufficient, since discovery of a violation after it occurred could not avert irretrievable damage to the environment. No procedure would be adequate for after-the-fact enforcement, once materials with a contamination life of centuries or millennia have entered the ocean. Effective regulation within the existing decentralized legal order is simply not possible.[293]

LAND-BASED POLLUTION

Because more than three-fourths of the contaminants in the oceans come from land-based sources,[294] an environmentally healthy ocean must eventually be protected by world regulation of land-based polluting activity. Without a global regime, pollutants will probably accumulate in the high seas for one of two reasons: (1) states will pollute the commons to save their own land and territorial waters from contamination, or (2) states will contaminate their own land, waters, and atmosphere with pollutants, many of which eventually will find their way to the oceans, because of intersocietal economic competition.

351

FINANCING POLLUTION ABATEMENT

Just as the absence of a global environmental authority will enable nonsignatories or delinquent signatories to escape environmental obligations, so it also will allow industrial states to escape their financial responsibilities to protect marine ecology. Few states on the planet possess sufficient expertise or resources to prevent and clean up major environmental problems, like oil spills or blowouts. Indeed, it would be wasteful if all oil-producing states individually acquired the capacity to take comprehensive measures against pollution. Continued IMCO efforts to place the burden of environmental responsibility on separate states are economically inefficient, politically divisive, and environmentally hazardous. Moreover, outright bans on persistent herbicides and pesticides without internationally subsidized substitutes could, some developing countries claim, bring disaster to their peoples from disease and famine.[295] Only some variation of global authority would be capable of systematically subsidizing nonpolluting alternatives to hazardous substances and expensive measures for enforcement and cleanup.

COORDINATING POLLUTION CONTROL

Global coordination of pollution does not require an absolute ban on waste discharges. Nature can provide for some waste treatment of substances such as oil and municipal sewage. The problem is one of overloading. The solution is to insure that permissible levels are not exceeded and that the tolerable quantity of pollution results from producing the goods most useful to enhancing the quality of human life, as opposed to enhancing profit or national power as ends in themselves. The need is to coordinate pollution abatement in one area with "acceptable pollution" in another area. For example, if the oceans can withstand only a severely limited quantity of a given pesticide, then a global decision-making process is required to insure that the allowable amount is used to protect humans against malaria, not to serve another less life-preserving function.[296] Global coordination is also needed to insure that waste disposal prohibited in one area is not simply transferred to another. In the long run, it is environmentally useless to prohibit oil discharges in coastal waters if the oil is simply discharged from land-based reception tanks into internal or territorial waters; to prohibit dumping plastics if they are then incinerated on land and the hazardous substances are later transferred through the atmosphere to the sea; or to ban nuclear tests in one state if others continue them.

COORDINATING RESOURCE USAGE

If tolerable pollution must be globally coordinated, the use of certain resources cannot be left uncoordinated. In the cases examined, the question of equity was never far removed from ecological issues. Global environmental control without a redistribution of power and resources was unacceptable to many have-not nations because they viewed such control as likely to freeze fundamental inequalities.[297] In addition, if restrictions are imposed on use of hazardous substances, the determination of allowable national quotas would be extremely controversial. For example, if the environment can withstand only 5,000 tons of mercury per year, some authority must resolve how much may be used as a fungicide for dressing seeds to increase agricultural productivity and how much may be used for industrial processes to manufacture military equipment. Often one state might prefer to accomplish the former goal and a different state the latter. If production of any substance is limited either to advance conservation or avert environmental overload, choices will inevitably need to be made among competing national claims for diverse purposes. Only a system global in its reach can rationally accomplish these tasks.

There would, of course, be ecological benefits resulting from planetary resource coordination. For example, arrangements guaranteeing purchases from a developing country for a ten-year period at designated prices could help poor states plan for the recovery of some costs of pollution abatement measures. In order to insure that stable commodity prices on trade "concessions" be used to avert the potential pollution attending industrialization, some agency would need to link such arrangements directly to environmental protection measures. Because of the need to set global standards for waste disposal and to avoid competitive disadvantages within industries, this linkage could most conveniently be established through a global organization with compulsory jurisdiction.

THE COMMONS IN A DECENTRALIZED COMPETITIVE
INTERNATIONAL SYSTEM

The problem of the English commons could have been solved by distributing the land to the herdsmen using it. Each herdsman might have enclosed his or her share of the commons and increased the herd size up to but not beyond the limit the enclosed pasture would bear. Regulating marine pollution is more difficult. Distributing ownership of all the oceans to various coastal "herdsmen" will not suffice. One country's use of its waters would influence adjoining sections of "enclosed" oceans belonging to other states. Eventually all the oceans are affected by such things as the use of DDT or the atmospheric explosion of nuclear devices. National control over segments of the oceans divides the planet, while ecological protection requires managing the planet as a single entity. Governments serving traditional national interests, even if expressed and mediated in an international organization, will not protect the environment. Under such conditions, no powerful actor speaks for the general (ecological) interest; all speak for separate, particularized interests.

On a concrete level, it is neither rational nor likely that one state will spend its resources to protect the high seas—which it does not own—if other states fail to assume a fair share of the burden of restrictions on national behavior. Even worse, as long as the goods are "free" and the oceans held in common, each state will gladly harvest nodules or fish without even assuming the responsibility for the pollution generated by its own harvesting. Within the existing, competitive international system, governments seek to increase the relative share of wealth enjoyed by their national subjects. Each state seeks to maximize its gross national product and to expand its share of the gross world product. Uncoordinated economic growth and unrestrained national economic competition are the rule. Both forms of self-assertion are contrary to ecological rationality and to the collective good.[298]

Planetary welfare can only be pursued through transnational cooperation. Yet the present structures for restraint and coordination are inadequate both at the national and international levels. This case study suggests that states may use positive rhetoric for protecting the oceans, but they will not produce the structures of regulation and control that are necessary for fulfilling their professed goals. Richard Falk notes that even among developed nations, where "interests . . . are convergent in relation to environmental quality, the prospect of an implementing (as distinct from a pious) consensus on action remains poor. Just as with disarmament . . . the dynamics of competition lead to an endless search for relative advantage, to distrust of rival proposals, and to a self-interested set of perceptions that induce contradictory assessments of what constitutes a reasonable adjustment [of interests]."[299] Events at the Caracas, Geneva, and New York Sessions of the Law of the Sea Conference confirm this view. The intense conflicts between industrial and poor states diverted the attention of many observers from the failure of the industrial powers to agree upon international standards for pollution or to establish concrete measures for international enforcement.

POLITICAL FEASIBILITY

The extent to which environmental policy changes are probable depends greatly on how the environmental question is perceived by those persons able to influence the vested interests resisting change. These interests have established a strong hold upon our institutions and behavior because previous generations living in the industrialized countries thought little about future inhabitants when they promoted their own prosperity at the expense of the environment and nonindustrialized societies. The legacy of uneven global development has produced severe political problems today in terms of ecological and egalitarian imperatives which call for industrial states to pay to clean up their own wastes, and in addition, to subsidize the cost of environmental protection in the poor states. Most citizens in the rich states are not prepared to do this now. Certainly governments will not do this in the absence of citizen pressure.

The resistance of those with vested economic interests was voiced quite honestly by the Kennecott Copper Company's Director of Ocean Resources, in commenting on the seabed negotiations: "As long as we face the rhetoric and aspirations of the new economic order, real progress is not possible." Rather than trying to build the best possible international regime to serve human needs, Kennecott Copper's executives concluded: "The time has come for all to face these facts [that progress is impossible] and to take the necessary alternative [unilateral] steps to foster the needs and well-being of the United States."[300] Similarly, Exxon Corporation opposed any agreement that treated the richest states differently from the poorest states. Despite the enormous inequality in income levels and per capita resource usage between the industrial states and less developed countries, to give the latter a bigger share of revenues from oil under the high seas "is surely unjustified."[301]

When—if ever—the United States and other industrial states will be willing to make economic sacrifices for environmental protection of the commons remains uncertain. But it is quite clear that they will not assume the responsibility to pay for international efforts unless there are some reciprocal guarantees of

355

Table 5-4

Selected Values of Global Humanism Compared to U.S. Policy for Reducing Marine Pollution

Global Humanism	U.S. Policy
Peace	
1. Protecting the future of the global ecosystem is more important than preserving the military superiority of one state over another.	1. Protecting U.S. strategic advantages is more important than long-range problems of environmental deterioration.
2. Uneven global economic development is undesirable because it (1) perpetuates disharmony within and among nations, and (2) wastes resources in military production and unnecessary consumption.	2. Officials have not seen uneven global economic development as a significant cause of the strains placed on the environment, whether in the form of ecocide in warfare, environmental overload, depletion of scarce resources, or population pressure upon resources. In any case, ecologically sound cooperation among nations is less important than perpetuating U.S. strategic and economic advantages.
3. The desire of maritime states for unregulated navigation and the interest of their military officials in unimpeded transit should be restrained in order to achieve world environmental protection.	3. The desire of U.S. officials for sweeping navigational freedom, including unimpeded transit for military and intelligence work, takes priority over measures for world environmental protection.
Economic Well-being	
1. Maldistribution of the world's resources, both intra- and internationally, is undesirable because it produces ecologically damaging relationships between the world's population and resources. If all people followed the consumption and pollution patterns of the rich, the earth's eco-system would be overloaded. Resources should be reallocated to reflect concern for ecology and equity.	1. Official behavior has denied that unequal distribution of the world's resources is a cause of damage to the environment. The poverty of the less developed countries and the overconsumption of the industrial states are not central concerns for U.S. officials.

2. Evironmental protection should be financed by those most able to pay.

3. Per capita consumption of the rich states should not be increased until the gap between rich and poor is substantially narrowed and protection of the world's ecosystem is more nearly secured.

4. Economic growth is not desirable as an end in itself; it should be tailored to maximize fulfillment of human needs and minimize environmental overload. Conservation of resources and endangered species is highly valued.

Human Rights and Social Justice

1. Respect for human rights and elemental justice requires that the benefits of the common heritage be used for overcoming poverty in the poorest societies.

2. The poor states should pay the costs they incur for environmental protection, without substantial aid from the U.S.

3. Increasing per capita consumption and corporate growth are primary goals, even if these goals widen the gap between rich and poor societies.

4. Economic growth is desirable in itself because it promises greater prosperity for U.S. citizens. U.S. officials have resisted establishing international guidelines to focus resource use on maximizing fulfillment of human needs, because this focus could constrain U.S. consumption. The impulse to exploit has taken precedence over the need to conserve and to avoid environmental overload.

1. "Nondiscriminatory access" to the common heritage means that the international community should allow nearly unlimited access to ocean wealth by those corporations presently best able to extract it.

Table 5-4 (cont.)

Global Humanism	U.S. Policy
2. The right of the poor to have basic needs satisfied should influence decisively the allocation of world resources when a balance must be struck between exploitation of resources and conservation of the environment.	2. The right of the rich to invest, exploit, profit, and consume need not be compromised in order to alleviate their effect on poor societies. U.S. officials did not tailor resource use to the need for environmental balance, conservation, or equity.

Ecological Balance

Global Humanism	U.S. Policy
1. Many industrial states are "misdeveloped" and should reorient priorities so they no longer unnecessarily deplete scarce resources by using them for wasteful forms of consumerism and for the prosperity of a small minority of the world's population.	1. Policy is based on the unexamined assumption that the United States is not "misdeveloped." U.S. citizens do not waste or consume too many resources.
2. Securing long-range survival of the species and harmonizing the relationship between humanity and nature (e.g., relating food to population) are more important than achieving national competitive advantages.	2. Securing the survival of the species in the long run and improving the quality of life for non-U.S. people are less important goals than the short-range enhancement of U.S. strategic and economic interests.
3. Some qualification of national sovereignty should occur to facilitate global coordination of resource policies and environmental standards.	3. International environmental regulation is undesirable if it encroaches on U.S national sovereignty or decreases U.S. political advantages. Officials envisage a world with largely voluntary standards and without supranational universal enforcement.

support from the poor nations.[302] That cannot be achieved unless the developing nations participate in major planetary decisions about resource usage—decisions which are now made in the capitals of industrial states and the boardrooms of multinational corporations. The less developed countries will not want and should not agree to become part of a strengthened global political and commercial system without having genuinely equitable participation in its decision making. Anything less would be a new variety of imperialism. In short, to insure the health of the marine ecosystem and the human species, a reasonable portion of the existing structures of authority, power, and wealth must be placed in the hands of developing countries.

An Alternative Framework

The preceding analysis suggests that following past national priorities holds little promise for environmental protection. A planetary—not national or class—focus is necessary for environmental protection. Despite the inadequacies of U.S. policies when compared to the need for fundamental change, these policies do contain some indications of the direction in which future policy must move to become more effective. The following are examples:

1. Construction standards for tankers, regulations for dumping, and international guidelines for seabed mining and mineral extraction on the continental shelf lead toward the idea that universal standards must eventually be used to protect the oceans.

2. U.S. acceptance of port state enforcement of pollution and construction standards for non-U.S. ships entering U.S. harbors illustrates the need to establish enforcement that will penetrate the exclusive jurisdiction of sovereign states over their own nationals and flag ships. This is a small recognition that eventually there must be nonterritorial jurisdiction applying to all actors, regardless of geographic location or nationality.

3. The U.S. concession to allow some transfer of revenues from seabed minerals to the less developed countries, as well as its acceptance in principle that new mineral exploitation should not exceed the growth of demand in key mineral markets, is a small recognition of the idea that greater economic equity will be required to achieve even minimal international cooperation, to say nothing of a new global regime.

4. Allowing the International Seabed Resource Authority, if created, to set some standards for pollution control during the mining of hard minerals represents a tacit admission that a

global agency must handle the setting of some standards for environmental protection. Insofar as the members, especially the industrialized states, seek what will in effect amount to a collective veto in the Authority, it would be a mistake to characterize the ISRA as a supranational organization. Instead, it will operate more as familiar UN organizations, acting on behalf of a collection of national interests, rather than on behalf of the global interest. It would, however, move beyond the UN General Assembly in being able to take decisions that are legally binding, and beyond the UN Security Council in allowing no single nation a veto. In these regards, it could be one institutional step closer to the necessary global authority.

5. Finally, the U.S. acceptance of compulsory judicial settlement in disputes arising out of the obligations of the treaty is a more genuine step toward a supranational organization.

Although some of these innovations were taken to enable the traditional sovereign state system to better serve national interests rather than to advance global coordination, they illustrate the extent to which technological progress and the fledgling environmental movement have moved even national policies toward a planetary orientation. Strengthening these trends would be the most productive activity for advocates of a new policy based on global humanism. A genuinely global environmental authority would be even less restricted by commercial, navigational, and national economic interests than the authority contemplated in the Law of the Sea Conference. Its potential utility can be illustrated by considering the possibilities for controlling a common pollutant, such as petroleum.

A global authority could assume a commitment to insure ecological quality of all the oceans, instead of merely enabling states to act for recovery of damages suffered within the seas under their national jurisdiction. The proposed approach would attempt to establish state, corporate, and individual responsibility for injuries to the marine environment anywhere on the seas. A new authority could set an annual global maximum of permissible oil pollution from all vessels, and then allocate specific allowable maximums for every state or shipper. It could also establish international safety inspection of tankers as a prerequisite to annual international licensing for all ocean transport.

A global environmental authority could base enforcement upon the idea that the right to use any part of the sea depended upon honoring the obligation not to abuse it. The authority could dispatch aircraft with sophisticated photographic equipment to detect even at night the sheen of ship discharges on the surface waters below. Such an enforcement agency could have authority to obtain other kinds of evidence, to board and inspect ships at any point on their voyages, and to initiate prosecution, regardless of the location of the discharge and the registry of the vessel. A universal public authority to regulate oil transport could initiate plans to move oil from tankers to internationally organized and maintained pipelines in some parts of the world, especially across isthmuses or through shallow and narrow waters.

Moreover, a global authority could institutionalize cooperative efforts for cleanup of spills on the high seas. In the past, such spills were not cared for because they would involve expense by one state for the common good. Furthermore, a universal antipollution organization could help to clean up spills adjacent to countries which lack the necessary technology or finances to protect their own coasts.

Finally, many complex political issues could be better handled in a global system for environmental protection. For example, at some point in history it may become necessary to set an annual world maximum for pesticide or petroleum consumption to prevent the oceans from deteriorating. If an average of 0.2 percent of the oil transported enters the oceans through accidents or intentional discharge, and if another given percentage of oil consumed enters the oceans through the atmosphere and rivers, then the world's people may be forced to conclude that in the interest of environmental protection, only a certain maximum of petroleum can be carried by ships and consumed each year. How will that difficult decision be made? Will the rich decide that they need more oil to drive heavy cars or travel frequently by jetliner while the poor have inadequate petroleum for fertilizer? Until a transnational environmental movement and a global authority are established, such decisions will continue to be made with no effective voice for the planetary interest in protecting the commons.

In general a global humanist approach to the control of marine pollution would aim to fulfill these needs:

(1) to create a global environmental authority whose principal task would be to protect the planetary environment;

(2) to create and enforce community-established standards for total annual permissible marine pollution of the most hazardous substances; in addition, to set national, regional, or per capita quotas as components of the general maximum allowed;

361

(3) to provide incentives for compliance with standards and to establish sanctions for violators, including such measures as deprivation of navigational rights and the privilege to use marine resources;

(4) to place the economic burden for environmental protection upon those most able to pay the costs;

(5) to establish global guidelines for national consumption of nonrenewable resources;

(6) to establish global guidelines for long-range national economic policies in order to encourage economic growth that serves human needs, meanwhile discouraging economic expansion for other purposes.[303]

Efforts to strengthen environmental legislation domestically may be the most potent political lever to encourage a more progressive posture internationally. On the basis of the cases examined here, a reliable rule of thumb would seem to be that any success in strengthening domestic legislation will both benefit the environment and increase the likelihood for establishing improved global standards. National governments will be likely to support international environmental action in order to avoid competitive disadvantages, for shippers or manufacturers, imposed by domestic legislation. Some corporations may not be concerned about uneven enforcement of environmental standards if they are free to move operations to pollution havens. Global enforcement, of course, should discourage such possibilities.[304] A global authority could be useful to support and stiffen efforts of governments to prevail against antiecological vested interests within their own societies.

The proposed approach would seek to overturn the prevailing idea that marine pollution is acceptable until widespread damage has occurred. Large segments of the oceans have already been endangered and only one-third of humanity has entered the industrial era. Extrapolations of comparable industrial output and waste disposal to match rising world industrial activity show massive increases of toxic substances in the oceans by 2000.[305]

Most importantly, an alternative approach could yield many presently unrealized fruits. For example, some scientists believe that appropriate pollution abatement, fertilization, and conservation practices could provide ten times the already bountiful harvest of protein obtained from the sea.[306] This food, as well as the windfall hard minerals of the common heritage, could provide enormous assistance in eliminating poverty. The industrial states could avoid costly duplication of efforts to test, monitor, and clean up the hundreds of new substances being introduced into the environment each year. This might partially compensate them for their "losses" in sharing resources with the developing countries. Finally, the aesthetic and recreational uses of the sea—hardly mentioned in this study—are an unmeasurable treasure that can be retained with more enlightened policies.

Indicators of World Order Progress

The following questions can be used to assess the extent to which a major industrial power, such as the United States, is helping to realize a more harmonious balance between humanity and nature within the range of issues covered by this case study:

1. Has the government favored a mode of exploiting the common heritage that leads to global equity and protection of the marine environment?

2. Has the government committed at least 1 percent of its annual GNP to international efforts for subsidizing pollution abatement in the developing countries?

3. Has the government established guidelines for curtailment of its own excessive economic growth in areas unsuitable to fulfilling human needs or contrary to conservation of scarce resources and endangered species?

4. Has the government committed itself to strong domestic environmental legislation?

5. Has the government given all useful data to international agencies monitoring known pollutants, including information about disposal of toxic substances such as chemical warfare agents and radioactive wastes produced in the course of weapons procurement?

6. Is the disposal of hazardous substances decreasing, whether measured on a per capita or total basis?

7. Has the government extended invitations to international agencies, such as the IAEA, to inspect all (not just nonmilitary) production and waste disposal facilities of extremely hazardous materials, such as nuclear fuel processing plants, to encourage institutional and attitudinal movement toward eventual regulation by a global environmental authority?

8. In concrete cases, has the government given higher priority to protecting the planetary environment or to advancing national economic and strategic benefits?

SIX · *Building a Just World Order*

EACH of the four case studies illustrates a different value of global humanism and provides the basis for assessing the impact of U.S. foreign policy on the prospects for achieving a more humane and secure system of world order. In each case, the values implicit in U.S. political behavior differed sharply from the values of global humanism. The juxtaposition of professed values and implicit values defined the policy gap between rhetoric and reality. A realistic understanding of the values served by U.S. policy leads inescapably to pessimistic conclusions about the prospects of that policy for transforming the present international system into one better able to provide a secure and humane life for all people. The conflicts between the values implicit in U.S. policy and the values of global humanism will not be repeated here because summaries of these differences have already been presented in separate chapters on the case studies. It will be useful for readers to refer to the summaries again while considering this concluding chapter.[1]

The remaining pages will describe the value foundation for U.S. policy, the domestic constraints on policy innovation, and the world view that undergirded official thinking. The discussion then turns to the impact of the existing international system upon efforts for world order reform. The chapter closes with an analysis of the implications of this study for political action by persons interested in promoting system change.

The Normative Orientation of U.S. Policy

As the previous analysis has shown, behavior was a more reliable guide than rhetoric to the normative content of U.S. policy. In the following description of the value foundation for U.S. policy, generalizations about the values of officials will, like all generalizations, simplify reality. The nuances of some positions cannot be included in a brief summary. At the same time, U.S. policies contained sufficient consistency to make possible a description of a composite official perspective encompassing the four value areas examined above.[2]

364

PEACE

Three decades of arms control negotiations have produced nine major bilateral treaties between the United States and the Soviet Union and seven multilateral agreements among many states. But these have not significantly reduced the nuclear threat to humanity.[3] Throughout the long years of negotiations, officials have believed that accepting the risks of the arms build-up and the proliferation of nuclear weapons was wiser than undertaking minimal risks for arms reductions. Policymakers sought neither to decrease the capacity of the superpowers for inflicting violence nor to change the international system to one less violence-prone. By perpetuating the existing international system and the attitudinal base upon which this system rested, officials made disarmament virtually impossible. In general, they did not seek to decrease the role of military power in human affairs. Neither Republican nor Democratic leadership used bureaucratic resources to devleop models of a disarming world.

ECONOMIC WELL-BEING

Just as officials sought in the first value area to protect the U.S. power position through deploying advanced military technology rather than halting the arms competition, so within the scope of the second value they shaped economic relations with other states to enhance U.S. prosperity and to nurture strategic collaboration rather than to contribute generously to the fulfillment of human needs beyond U.S. territory. The single most influential determinant of aid policy was the desire to maximize U.S. strategic advantages. Within the policy boundaries of U.S. strategic desires, officials further shaped aid programs to enhance the interests of U.S. investors and producers. One of the least significant determinants of aid policy was the unmet human needs of other societies.

Officials intended no substantial redistribution of global wealth. Only once in the thirty years studied did the United States contribute as much as 1 percent of its GNP to foreign assistance. That was when aid went to Europe after World War II. Never did the United States extend such generosity toward the poorer, darker-skinned peoples of the world. At the very best, officials saw aid as charity, not as an instrument of systemic change in which the poor would eventually be on an equal footing with the rich.

Among the serious shortcomings of U.S. aid policies, one

365

stands out. The aid "burden" of the U.S. has declined sharply during the last decade, while U.S. per capita wealth has grown. Recently the United States has contributed less than a third of a penny for each dollar of its GNP to the fulfillment of non-U.S. human needs. For the richest and most powerful national society on earth to do so little to relieve human misery provides a bleak portent for achieving a life of decency for much of the world's population. In brief, the United States gave low priority both to abolishing the suffering of poverty-stricken people and to creating a new economic order that would distribute wealth more equitably and concentrate productive capacity on serving human needs.

HUMAN RIGHTS AND SOCIAL JUSTICE

The tradition of respect for civil liberties within the United States and the revolutionary, anticolonial origins of the U.S. government have provided a long-standing foundation for widespread support of self-determination and other human rights elsewhere in the world. But this foundation has been undermined by policies subordinating human rights to what officials perceived or professed as national security needs.

Despite rhetoric to the contrary, United States violation of Chilean self-determination did not enhance human dignity. Instead, officials intervened to satisfy ideological hostility toward socialism in the Western Hemisphere, to protect U.S. private investments in Chile and other countries potentially influenced by the Chilean example, and to maintain U.S. political influence in Latin America. U.S. leaders in fact feared self-determination as a stimulus to instability in the existing international structure of wealth and power. Rhetorical support for human rights justified and disguised intervention against human rights. This was part of a political strategy, which included the denial of human rights when their exercise came into conflict with U.S. policies, to manipulate Chilean political groups that aimed at decreasing U.S. economic or political control of and benefits from Chile.

ECOLOGICAL BALANCE

On ecological questions, officials served the same value priorities as in the three areas already discussed. The government gave environmental protection only slight weight compared to that given military, navigational, and economic interests. U.S. officials placed highest value upon enhancing the

366

opportunities for U.S. military aircraft, ships, and submarines to navigate without restriction. Preserving economic opportunities for corporate interests, such as expressed by shipping, oil, and mining companies, received slightly less emphasis, but still ranked well above environmental protection in priority.

The United States more fully recognized the need for global collaboration in the environmental area than in the other value areas. This was due to the obvious impossibility of administering environmental standards through national action alone or even through multilateral action that permitted a few major actors to remain outside of environmental norms that others followed. However, the awareness of the need for global coordination was not matched by a willingness to organize the relationship between humanity and nature in a way to provide equal benefits for all people, to respect the needs of future generations, or to protect important natural resources. Environmental collaboration was aimed at protecting the interests of what might be called the global upper class—the industrialized as opposed to the poor societies, and the owners and managers of private corporations and public bureaucracies as opposed to the less powerful.

Domestic Constraints on U.S. Policy

It is easy but in itself not very useful to criticize officials for failing to implement preferred world order values. Decisions were the result of politics, not logic about world order imperatives. In addition to international constraints, domestic political forces heavily influenced the government's decisions. Table 6-1 shows that powerful domestic interests in each case study expressed themselves against global humanism in all four value areas. (The various domestic influences included in the table were not, of course, of equal intensity or effect.) For example, large military expenditures not only inhibited realization of V_1, but also discouraged implementation of V_2 because money spent for arms could not help fertilize rice fields in India; of V_3 because reinforcing the role of military power in human affairs made political repression more likely; and of V_4 because unproductive use of resources for weapons caused pollution and resource depletion that exceeded what was necessary if productive capacity were rationally focused upon meeting human needs.

The domestic constituency for each of the global humanist values was weak and uncoordinated. Military and industrial forces pressed for a further military buildup. The Vladivostok

Table 6-1

Illustrative U.S. Domestic Pressures Against the Realization of Preferred World Order Values

Value area	Vladivostok Accord	Aid to India	Self-determination in Chile	Marine Pollution
Peace	The military-industrial complex pressed for deployment of more weapons.	The drive for U.S. security and economic benefits—not human needs—determined most aid programs.	Corporate and governmental leadership wanted a pro-U.S. government in power to secure U.S. influence, even if establishing a pro-U.S. government produced violence and repression	The desire for unimpeded military transit and the jealous protection of sovereignty made international pollution control unfeasible.
Economic Well-being	Money for military equipment detracted from resources available for increasing food production.	Money allocated to buy influence with allies and to open opportunities for U.S. investors did not maximize the service of human needs.	Corporate and governmental leadership opposed a Chilean government that advocated radical change, even though it was designed to help abolish poverty for the lower classes.	Giving the United States greater national access to oil and nodules did not serve the needs of the planet's poor. U.S. proposals if implemented, would widen the gap between rich and poor.

Human Rights	Perpetuating the role of military power in world affairs encouraged the militarization of the entire planet and the denial of human rights by military governments.	The right of the rich to invest and to make profit was stressed, while the right of equity was rejected.	Corporate and governmental leadership opposed radical socioeconomic change aimed at achieving human rights for the dispossessed.	Governmental and corporate leadership gave higher priority to the right of unregulated transit and of access to nodules than to the right of poor people to economic equity.
Ecological Balance	The Vladivostok Accord demonstrated no concern for ecocide in event of nuclear war or for environmental hazards of nuclear proliferation. The ecological strains caused by continued production and operation of military equipment were ignored.	The "trickle-down" approach to development meant that pollution and resource depletion would exceed the minimum necessary to achieve a standard of decency for all. Without official objection, the rich continued to overconsume while the poor had inadequate resources for a life of dignity.	Corporate greed focused resources and productive capacity upon maximizing profit rather than fulfilling human needs. Unnecessary pollution and resource depletion continued without official objection.	The corporate and government impulse to exploit resources for private profit and lavish national consumption took precedence over the need to conserve or to share resources with the world's population. This exacerbated the imbalance between humanity and nature.

case corroborated many other observers' conclusions that domestic pressures, rather than security needs arising from competition with the Soviet Union, often stimulated U.S. weapons innovations.[4] Development assistance also had no substantial domestic constituency, unless the aid was designed to benefit U.S. producers or alliance policy. But under those conditions U.S. policy could not lead toward V_2. Similarly ITT, Kennecott, and the CIA cared far more about protecting their investments and influence than about human rights. The environment issue seemed, on the surface, to be the least highly politicized of the four value areas. Yet the development of the U.S. position for the Law of the Sea Conference illustrated the regressive power of military and corporate influences on decision makers. To be sure, officials at first constructed a policy that seemed to grow out of some genuine desire to avoid destruction of the oceans (with the exception of seeking unreasonable navigational freedom for military planes and ships). But as the political and economic costs of a generous common heritage and strong environmental program became clear, and as oil and mining interests mobilized, officials retreated from their relatively enlightened 1970 position. Even ignoring the direct expression of corporate and military hostility to V_4, few U.S. citizens wanted to decrease their consumption or raise tax revenues to aid developing countries in curtailing global pollution.

In sum, bureacratic, economic, military, and ideological forces reinforced the inclination of those in power to give low priority to the values of global humanism. The presence of these forces meant that officials would hesitate to implement global humanist values, even if they privately favored them, because such efforts would cost them political support essential for preventing their being displaced by political opponents who were even more opposed to preferred world order values. A progressive official thus often was forced to choose between two unpleasant alternatives. The official could do little to advance global humanism against hostile domestic forces and thereby advance his or her own political career. Or, he or she could embrace global values vigorously and soon be replaced by a member of Congress or another bureaucrat more sympathetic to nationalistic, military, oil, and mining interests. As a result of such a dilemma, even those leaders with private sympathies for the values of global humanism would often implement values consistent with the generally accepted, less humanitarian operational code.

370

The Operational Code of Officials

The political leadership's fundamental assumptions about the nature of international relations, the motivation for human behavior, and the possibility of human influence on history provided the background against which the decisions analyzed in the case studies were made. These fundamental beliefs constituted an "operational code"[5] which provided the guidelines that influenced the weighing of alternative courses of action and the choice of strategy and tactics for action. The values implicit in U.S. policy and delineated in each case study give shape to the U.S. operational code that was the spring from which policies flowed.

THE PERVASIVE POWER GAME

Washington officials seemed heavily influenced by a bureaucratic model of reality—a model which often did not correspond to reality more objectively perceived. Adopting the bureaucratic model of truth seemed the key to prestige and influence in Washington. The basic premise of this model was that international politics was a game, the object of which was to avoid losing influence and if possible to gain more. Power was measured in terms of the capacity to dominate or exercise influence over the decision of other governments. Toughness was a positive attribute. For officials exhilarated by the game of nations, "the whole field of international relations is a confrontation."[6] As we have seen, the desire to maintain power heavily influenced U.S. policies at the Vladivostok and Caracas meetings, and determined the stance taken toward the governments in New Delhi and Santiago.

Officials pictured Western civilization as threatened by the demands of the developing countries, perhaps backed by major industrialized rivals of the United States, for a redistribution of the world's wealth, power, and authority. Despite recognition of a new global interdependency and rhetorical support for equity, U.S. officials expected other states to continue allowing the United States to maintain a preeminent position in global economic and political structures. Instead of shouldering responsibilities commensurate with its resources in order to realize a humane structure of interdependency, the United States developed policies to maintain the U.S. global position. Officials assumed that what was good for the United States would also benefit the rest of the world. As Henry Kissinger explained in a reflective interview with James Reston: "When we talk interdependence, we are not just talking [about] an American desire to exploit the resources of other nations. What we are saying is for our own benefit, of course. But it is also for the benefit of everybody else." Kissinger warned nations pressing for change that if they ignored U.S. interests "the Western civilization that we now have is almost certain to disintegrate because it will first lead to a series of rivalries in which each region will try to maximize its own special advantages. That inevitably will lead to tests of strength of one sort or another. These will magnify domestic crises in many countries, and they will then move more and more to authoritarian models. I would expect then that we will certainly have crises which no leadership is able to deal with."[7] In spite of these dire warnings, Kissinger himself demonstrated little inclination—as the case studies showed—to implement policy that put global interests above national advantages.

HUMAN MOTIVATION

A second tenet of the bureaucratic model of reality was that the international system functioned best as a threat system. The premium placed on toughness dictated that negative reinforcements and deprivations were used more often than positive inducements to influence behavior. To offer positive inducements in the form of concessions meant losing points in the competition for power.

The officials in the above case studies viewed intergroup human relations as basically conflictual rather than cooperative. For example, in the Vladivostok case study, U.S. political leaders thought self-restraint in weapon deployments was tantamount to diplomatic or military retreat. They assumed that the only way of encouraging the Soviet Union to negotiate seriously was to amass superior weaponry in order to force Soviet officials to the bargaining table. Even in environmental affairs, U.S. policies were based upon the assumption that national conflict rather than transnational cooperation would be the bedrock for future human transactions. That assumption made compromise on the nodule issue—relatively unrelated to the sensitive security area—so difficult.

To the extent that the struggle for power was waged through psychological means, symbolic actions became important. Thus officials destabilized Chilean society not only to save their influence in Chile, but also to demonstrate that socialism and programs for nationalization of U.S. capital could not work else-where. This would be a lesson to any countries contemplating Chilean-like expropriation. To respect self-determination as a human right was alien to the prevailing diplomatic approach of punishing those countries that pursued unwanted policies. Thus such respect was unimportant in policymaking. Consistent with a carrot-stick diplomacy, enough aid might be sent to India to retain some influence there, but aid programs were never de-signed to produce structural change in India or in the interna-tional system. The United States curtailed aid when it failed to buy political support.

If officials used tough, shock tactics in the psychological com-petition for power and wealth, they largely ignored world opin-ion that supported the preferred world order values. An unusu-ally blunt but typical expression of this approach came from John McCloy, a frequent White House consultant. When once recommending that the United States resume nuclear testing, he told President Kennedy: "World opinion? I don't believe in world opinion. The only thing that matters is power."[8] As the arms control case study revealed, it mattered little that many na-tions had explicitly called, through various resolutions at the UN, for disarmament. It mattered little that the nuclear powers had formally bound themselves to negotiate arrangements for nuclear disarmament. In the case of foreign aid, it mattered lit-tle that world opinion favored transferring a minimum of .7 percent of GNP from the rich to the poor each year. In the Chil-ean case, it mattered little that the United States had legally committed itself not to intervene in any Latin American state for any reason. Officials assumed they could win few points by act-ing generously, graciously, or even legally.[9]

INEFFECTIVENESS OF LEGAL AND MORAL RESTRAINTS

The four case studies showed that legal restraints and global humanist values were not an important determinant of official behavior. The United States' violation of human rights in Chile concerned officials only because they feared public disclosure of their acts. They were unmoved by legally binding treaties which had been duly approved by the Senate and were thus part of "the supreme law of the land." Similarly, oil and nodules for U.S. citizens were sought without much regard for equity or ecology. Those in power pursued the national advantages of un-regulated navigation even if this helped kill the prospects for international enforcement of pollution control. Within this bureaucratic understanding of human motivation, the U.S. leadership judged humanitarian arguments to be irresponsible as a guide to policy, although excellent for rhetorical purposes.

VIEW OF HISTORY

Just as U.S. leaders advanced the interests of only a small segment—rather than all—of humanity, they also designed policies for only a short span—rather than a long term—of history. A short-range view of history meant that marine resources could be exploited or a pro-United States government could be kept in Chile. Pollution or longer-range structural change in Chile could be dealt with by some later administration. However, a continuous series of administrations thinking in four-year spans would never consider how to make long-range structural changes in international society.

As long as officials were unconcerned about the more distant future, a policy influenced heavily by global equity and compassion seemed to contradict a policy determined by self-interest. Yet in the long run, moral principles and pragmatic imperatives are not contradictory. Respect for nature may seem a desirable moral principle but an impractical restraint on profits and prosperity in the immediate future. However, in the more distant future, environmental protection is prudent as well as moral. Similarly, many people in the 1970s might believe that war would be prudent to stop communist advances and that the political conflict between U.S. capitalism and Soviet communism justified nuclear deterrence. But by 2080, someone looking back might well think that the differences between United States and Soviet societies in the 1970s, while significant, were small compared to the imprudence of risking nuclear war. Thus governmental preoccupation with maximizing power and wealth in the present and immediate future turned policy away from realizing global humanist values in the long run.

U.S. officials displayed a curiously ambivalent set of assumptions about their own ability to influence history. On the one hand, they were optimistic that they could avoid eventual ecological catastrophe, even though there was little empirical basis in past performance for this notion. Likewise, they thought they could partially control Chilean society, or avert nuclear destruction during moments of crisis. This reflected a strong belief that they could influence the direction of historical events. On the other hand, they assumed that they were powerless to change the structure of the international system in order to increase human cooperation and global equity. This ambivalence once again grew out of their own vested interests. Both their optimism about averting crises and manipulating political events and their pessimism about system change to curb Darwinian national appetites justified the acquisition of further power and wealth by the United States.

NATIONAL PARTISANSHIP

Rather than recognize the positive links among all human beings, officials practiced national partisanship. The government rewarded friends and punished enemies. Thus it was "natural" to give much more aid to authoritarian Pakistan, an ally, than to more populous and democratic India, a nonally. A radical Chilean government should be punished, but a pro-U.S. Chilean dictatorship which abolished civil liberties while compensating U.S. corporate owners should receive aid. The equity-seeking countries at the Caracas conference were viewed as ideological, rigid, and unreasonable. Equity-denying proposals for harvesting nodules were nonideological and reasonable.

The U.S. government failed to practice reciprocity. "Equal access" to the common heritage for U.S. officials meant those states with the most technology got the most nodules. It did not mean equal benefits for all. The United States insisted on unlimited nuclear capability for itself, but it sought to discourage other nations from acquiring equal power. Within their distorted model of reality, U.S. officials could condone deployment of thousands of nuclear warheads by the United States and simultaneously condemn India for one test explosion. U.S. corporations and the CIA could intervene in Chile, but reciprocal intervention by foreign powers in the United States would outrage the governmental elite. Because the United States had excess capital to export to India, the United States could influence Indian economic decisions, but because India had "excess population" it gained no opportunity to influence U.S. economic affairs.

Because those in power lacked both a sense of human solidarity extending beyond national territory and a long-range view of history, their worldview excluded two dimensions that were crucial to human survival. Without these, policies failed to tran-

375

scend the parochialism and narrow selfishness of the leadership's own vested interests, ethnicity, and historical era. National partisanship flourished in such a congenial environment.

COMPREHENSION OF REALITY

The leadership resisted the examination of opposing views.[10] To entertain perspectives that differed substantially from the official version of reality would open one to the charge of sympathizing with the adversary. Kissinger and Helms did not listen to those who believed that Allende's reforms were desirable, but they repeatedly heard those who saw Allende as the embodiment of evil. To take a second example, advocates of sharing the common heritage on the basis of population and need were unheard among senior officials in Washington. It did not matter that such resource allocation would have advanced equity, been reasonable, and reflected the highest ideals in the United States own value tradition. Such allocation would have been a softhearted giveaway.

Because they refused to consider alternative views seriously, those in high office lacked objectivity. They characteristically expressed support for a lofty world order principle, and then carried out a policy that denied the principle in practice. What in reality were targets for new deployments of more advanced weapons, officials called ceilings for arms control. Strategically motivated foreign aid was labeled "humanitarian." Several administrations described intervention to undermine self-government as protection of democracy. Weak pollution standards with no international enforcement became environmental protection.

Officials lacked objectivity also because they derived their self-identity and prestige from the organizations they served. Loss of national power eroded self-importance. Enhancing national power was exhilarating. Similarly, within the nation, such officials fought against decreased budgets for their governmental department or corporation because that signalled a demise of their own importance. If they thought about the global interest at all, they equated it with the national interest, and the national interest with their organization's or department's interest.[11] Defense officials wanted to build redundant weapons, which they justified as being vital to U.S. security, in order to maintain a powerful self-image for themselves and their own department. ITT officials fought to protect their investments in

Chile by arguing that Allende posed a threat to the security of the United States. The National Petroleum Council and American Mining Congress advanced their interests in the Law of the Sea debate by saying that undersea soft and hard minerals were essential to the strategic position of the United States. The Pentagon advanced the same justification for its pleas to let nuclear submarines sail through narrow waters without surfacing.

The need to serve vested economic and political interests distorted the perceptions of the most astute officials. For example, Secretary Kissinger several times explained why the U.S. government had been so slow to understand the world food problem. "Until 1972," he said, "we thought we had inexhaustible food surpluses, and the fact that we have to shape our policy deliberately to relate ourselves to the rest of the world did not really arise until 1973."[12] Of course, starvation had been a problem for many years in some parts of the world, and for more than a decade well-known demographers had specifically predicted a world food shortage in the 1970s.[13] That a person as intelligent as Henry Kissinger could believe up until 1972 that the world had "inexhaustible food surpluses" and that the United States did not need to shape its policies "deliberately to relate . . . to the rest of the world" demonstrated the resistance of official minds to unpleasant truths.

This bureaucratically-reinforced, nationalist version of reality produced psychological and material incentives to seek further U.S. advantages through competition with other nations. These incentives drowned out any inclination toward recognizing a global human interest. Unable to look beyond the statist, Westphalian image of the world, U.S. leaders were ill-equipped to guide the international system toward the twenty-first century.[14]

The official operational code violated both reason[15] and preferred moral values. In their actions on behalf of the United States, officials developed new weapons of mass destruction aimed at extinguishing life in scores of cities, trampled the rights of Chilean social reformers, squandered vital opportunities to advance international environmental protection, and designed aid policies that caused untold persons to starve who might have lived and others to suffer needlessly. Yet these same officials did not see themselves as insensitive, self-serving, or shortsighted. Instead, they saw themselves as responsive to the call of duty as they perceived its demands within the nation-state system.

Some simple defense mechanisms enabled those in power to profess one value while implementing a contrary one. Reason and consciousness were isolated from action to escape the potential pain attending unreasonable and unconscionable acts. There were several modes of absolution. The unconscious lie was a belief that one should know to be false but has come to believe is true.[16] Many examples exist in the four case studies. Officials at the Caracas conference believed that their proposals for equal access to the common heritage would produce a fair share of the harvest. Some CIA officials believed that clandestine intervention to overturn the results of a free election would protect democracy. Aid officials believed that assistance in behalf of strategic advantage or against socialism was genuinely humanitarian.

The "need not to know" also freed officials of responsibility that they should have taken seriously. Congress for months deliberately avoided ferreting out the facts about the Chilean intervention. Once investigations were begun, members of Congress failed to press most witnesses on crucial issues. When evidence of perjury arose, Congress quickly closed the issue and chose not to investigate further in order to avoid ruining the reputations of some longtime friends and acquaintances in the executive branch.

By taking a narrow view of issues and by denying information that did not fit their limited image of reality, officials decreased the scope of their felt responsibilities. In each of the case studies, they refused to analyze their policy preferences within a larger value context that might reveal the moral bankruptcy of their actions. They chose not to articulate the concrete consequences of their behavior viewed as a process of value realization. At the Law of the Sea Conference, U.S. leaders chose not to tailor policy to a calculation of what would maximize benefits for humanity and the environment. Instead, they began by articulating the goals of oil, mining, and naval interests. From there they moved to an explanation of what concessions the rest of the world must make to accommodate U.S. interests. Similar criticisms could be made of the Vladivostok-legitimized deployment of MIRVs as a measure of arms control, the use of foreign aid to bolster strategic interests instead of serve human needs, and the secret intervention to oppose self-determination. In each case, global humanist values, which would have served universal human needs instead of national advantages, were turned on their heads by isolating and narrowing the context for analysis.

Thus more weapons for war became "an historic step forward" in arms control; aid to buy friends for strategic advantages became humanitarian assistance; reversal of self-determination became protection of democracy; and self-serving exploitation of marine resources by the already resource-wasteful United States became respect for the common heritage. Only when seen in the wider value context were official claims visibly untrue.

Those in power lacked empathy for the poor. They seemed to fear that policy based on identity with the poor would make the United States less prosperous or a weak participant in the power-seeking international arena. Clearly, U.S. officials would have advocated different behavior if they had been born in sub-Saharan Africa or a peasant village of southern Asia. They avoided the psychologically troublesome consequences of information that did not dovetail with personally and nationally self-seeking behavior. By believing that they did not need to understand the views of those with whom they differed, they could overlook the advice of those sympathetic to disarmament, global equity, Allende reforms, or radical measures for environmental protection. Through the processes of unconscious, selective perception and deliberate decision about what they needed to know and understand, it was possible for highly respected officials who were good parents and neighbors to commit acts with profoundly inhumane consequences. Their reasonable behavior in some areas of life was not matched by reasonable behavior in other areas.

As we have seen, the manipulation of language was one of the most effective means of deception. Although official behavior had a generally negative or regressive impact on the prospects for world order reform, official rhetoric often supported the four preferred world order values. This disarmed governmental critics and blurred the distinction in the public's minds between the genuine reformer and the rhetorically progressive but politically reactionary leader. For example, to support the "management of global interdependence" may have meant structural reform in conformity with global humanism, or—as it did for U.S. officials—enlistment of the rest of the world's cooperation to protect existing trade, energy, consumption, political, and military arrangements in which the United States enjoyed preeminence.

On the other hand, to embrace global humanist values, even if only rhetorically, was probably a favorable portent. During the last three decades rhetoric seemed increasingly supportive of some global humanist values. This reflects a changing mythology that eventually may provide the basis for system change. A fundamental gap between behavior and rhetoric is an attribute of a transition period between different systems of social order.[17] Rhetoric may begin to take into account present realities, even though policy substance remains patterned on past habits rather than present needs. Rhetoric in support of preferred values is better than no support at all, because it provides a new standard by which to judge behavior. Milton Rokeach, the well-known student of human values, has reported that humans possess a psychic need to believe that their behavior conforms with their professed values.[18] Thus by noting the gap between rhetoric and behavior, eventually officials may be encouraged to move behavior toward rhetoric.

Perhaps more importantly, frequent repetition of preferred values encourages the public to believe that the values should be honored. This may in the long run have a political impact. Historic repetition of the idea that all people are created equal eventually eased social acceptance of belated changes for sexual and racial equality. The decades of inequality, however, suggest that favorable rhetoric means little without accompanying political struggle to stimulate behavioral change.

Many of the ideas that U.S. officials advanced did indeed disguise reality for the public and inhibit and deflect genuine efforts to reform the international system. Government spokespersons told the public that the United States was making all possible efforts to disarm, to help the poor, to encourage human rights, and to protect the environment. The preceding case studies show that this picture was false. Because many persons erroneously believed government reports were true, they failed to support genuine change. They vented their indignation for the arms race primarily upon the Soviet Union. They viewed poverty as a hopeless tragedy rather than as an unnecessary condition resulting from unfair economic structures. They blamed denial of human rights on military dictatorships instead of recognizing United States complicity in the militarization of the planet. They tempered their disappointment about polluted oceans with the wistful hope that some day a UN agency might do more. Posturing and professions by members of Congress facilitated the executive branch's obfuscation of issues. When questionable executive policies were first reported by the press, chairmen of congressional committees frequently announced they would hold hearings on relevant issues. But usually the congressional action died without producing substantial change. Congressional committees made only weak recommendations after the Chilean intervention. Congress allowed those officials responsible for human rights violations to continue in public office. Useful hearings by Senator Edmund Muskie and Thomas McIntyre on armaments later proved to little avail as the military buildup continued. In the area of marine pollution many of the hearings advanced the interests of oil, mining, and shipping companies rather than environmental protection. And most hearings on foreign aid were relatively unconcerned about achieving a minimum standard of living for all. Thus congressional checks on the executive branch's shortsightedness or abuse of power were so limited that they often simply nurtured the process of misinforming the public. Congressional activity was sufficiently visible to give an air of rationality and legitimacy to policy, but insufficiently penetrating and purposeful to justify the rationality and legitimacy widely attributed to U.S. policy. Congressional efforts were useful for making incremental policy changes within the existing international system, but not for generating support to change the system itself.

The failure of Congress to open debate on a global humanist platform suggests that, while the constitutionally prescribed sharing of powers in the U.S. federal system may work satisfactorily for writing domestic legislation, it does not work well for serving global needs. Too many interests within the United States executive branch, Congress, and the judicial system are all on the same (national) side of the global issues. Instead of the threefold separation of powers extant on domestic questions, there is a threefold concentration of mutually reinforcing powers on global issues.[19] The president, Congress, and even the Supreme Court often agree on policies that are· antagonistic to universal human and environmental needs. Although the authors of the U.S. Constitution successfully averted the abuse of power that might have resulted from monolithic U.S. national government, there is no similar system of global checks and balances against excessive national power abusing the global commonweal.[20]

The work of official mythmakers is well-received by citizens who understandably want or psychologically need to believe in the righteousness of their own government. To favor the pre-

381

ferred structural changes, after all, means recognizing that the existing global structure is neither fair nor life-enhancing. When one is at the top of the existing structure, that conclusion does not come easily or pleasantly. It requires a tacit admission, at least to a limited degree, of one's own past involvement in perpetuating and reaping rewards from the obsolescent system.

HIERARCHY OF VALUES

The four case studies demonstrate that officials gave highest priority to two values: maintenance of the U.S. power position in world affairs, and promotion of economic benefits for U.S. corporations. All other values were subordinated to these two. Officials in practice gave very low priority to the human interest as expressed in the world order values. (See Table 6-2.) The government aimed policies toward preservation of the international status quo in which the United States enjoyed preeminence, whereas the preferred world of global humanism required restructuring the international system. The U.S. government actively resisted progressive steps in each value area.

Table 6-2
Official Priorities on Selected Issues

World Order Value	Issue	Value Priority High	Medium	Low
Peace (V₁)	Strategic arms reductions			X
Economic Well-being (V₂)	Redistribution of wealth to serve human needs			X
Human Rights and Social Justice (V₃)	Respect for self-determination			X
Ecological Balance (V₄)	International control of marine pollution			X

To be sure, peace, economic well-being, human rights, and environmental protection were rhetorically supported. It is possible, as Table 6-3 shows, to formulate isolated value statements in which officials *appeared* to support world order values. But where officials gave a high or medium level of priority to a certain isolated value, their support carried conditions that were disallowable if one genuinely wanted to implement all four preferred values. The positions in lines 1 and 2, 4 and 5, 7 and 8, and 10 and 11 (Table 6-3) sacrifice other values and fall short of a worldview consistent with global humanism. In line 1, for example, peace without diminishing U.S. power would retain national nuclear arsenals (V_1-denying), perpetuate inequity of wealth (V_2-denying), maintain disproportionate U.S. influence over global political and economic issues (V_3-denying), and preserve ecologically hazardous military weapons and patterns of consumption and resource depletion (V_4-denying). A similar set of criticisms could be made about each of the other seven areas in which officials might appear to be giving high or medium support to preferred world order values. In fact, the statements in lines 3, 6, 9, and 12 were more fully compatible with global humanism. Officials shunned those value positions.

The accuracy of this appraisal is borne out by the low priority given to systemic change, regardless of how intensely an official might support a value like peace or human rights. Officials did not endorse positions 3, 6, 9, and 12 because they did not welcome structural change.[21] The general opposition to structural change meant leaders often gave high priority to one of the four world order values while opposing progress in one or more of the other three areas. In effect, this nullified the apparent support for the rhetorically embraced value. For example, self-determination or peace would be supported only if there were no danger of decreasing U.S. power or wealth. Likewise, elimination of poverty would be supported only if its elimination did not unfavorably alter the U.S. position in the overall geopolitical structure.

The introduction or omission of crucial but hidden assumptions during policy debates made many people perceptually confused and politically ineffective. By taking a narrow view of different value questions and by deemphasizing implicit assumptions such as contained in statements 1, 4, 7, and 10, one could plausibly argue that the United States favored peace, universal human welfare, social justice, or environmental protection. But by examining policy on a less abstract level and by emphasizing implicit values, one began to understand that the United States favored these goals under conditions that simultaneously negated one or more world order values. This normative approach reveals the hidden value compensations that officials sought in adopting a posture that appeared to favor the four values of global humanism.

Table 6-3
U.S. Value Priorities Viewed in the Context of Implicit Value Assumptions

Value Area	Illustrative value statements with implicit assumptions made explicit	Official value priority		
		Strongly favor	Modestly favor	Strongly oppose
Peace V_1	1. Pursue peace without erosion of present U.S. power and prosperity	X		
	2. Pursue peace with slightly more equitable global distribution of political power and economic advantages		X	
	3. Pursue peace by taking steps toward abolition of the war system and creation of effective central guidance in a world security agency			X
Economic Well-being V_2	4. Fulfill human needs at no political or economic cost to the U.S.	X		
	5. Fulfill human needs by transferring some U.S. wealth to other societies in return for potential pro-U.S. sentiment		X	
	6. Fulfill human needs through redistribution of wealth aimed at global equity and by creation of a world tax and development agency based upon balanced representation of weak and poor			X
Human Rights and Social Justice V_3	7. Implement human rights by demanding self-determination in states not presently pro-U.S.	X		
	8. Implement human rights even if supporting self-determination meant a few pro-U.S. states may move toward less deferential relations with the U.S.		X	
	9. Implement human rights by supporting international			

Table 6-3 (cont.)

Value Area	Illustrative value statements with implicit assumptions made explicit	Official value priority		
		Strongly favor	Modestly favor	Strongly oppose
	structural changes that encourage internal and international justice and provide transnational monitoring of violations of rights, thus penetrating traditional sovereignty			X
	10. Achieve environmental protection without additional costs to U.S.	X		
Ecological Balance V_4	11. Achieve environmental protection without suffering major competitive disadvantages, but with some alteration of global consumption patterns and the use of U.S revenue to help less developed countries in environmental protection		X	
	12. Achieve environmental protection through creation of a world environmental authority with power to create and enforce guidelines to protect against worldwide environmental hazards			X

MUTUALLY REINFORCING VALUE POSITIONS

Officials carried out a remarkably consistent foreign policy. They did not serve a particular value in one context and an opposing value in another. On the contrary, their positions in the four value areas were mutually reinforcing. For example, restrictive foreign aid policies (V_2-denying) in Chile dovetailed with covert intervention to undermine self-determination (V_3-denying). These in turn perpetuated the international status quo which augmented United States political and military influence in Latin America (V_3- and V_1-denying). Maintenance of the status quo in the first three value areas enabled the United States to use scarce resources for its own excessive consumption, thus producing an inefficient global relationship between population and resources (V_4-denying).

The reinforcing quality of U.S. positions can be stated more generally. Large military budgets (1) enabled the United States to resist reformist challenges to an inequitable international system; (2) decreased the funds available for realizing V_2; (3) encouraged the militarization of many societies and thereby discouraged respect for V_3; and (4) made implementation of V_4 less feasible because the United States military, corporate elites, and the less developed countries would resist universal standards and supranational enforcement as uncongenial, respectively, to their hegemonial and developmental interests. In addition, these policies would not respect nature or allocate resources for optimum fulfillment of the necessities of life for all people.

In general, officials designed V_1 policies to prevent major rivals or guerrilla movements from modifying the status quo through use of force. U.S. policies in the areas of V_2 and V_3 aimed at aborting nonviolent reform movements for radical change. For example, the government tailored V_2 policies to create Third World allies that would buttress U.S. V_1 policies, to shore up unpopular but pro-U.S. regimes, and to defuse or to repress potential "disorder" from internal social reformers. In the V_3 area, policies were developed which utilized the CIA for manipulation of foreign polities to protect U.S. strategic and economic advantages. Finally, the regressive stance on V_4 to maximize U.S. navigational freedom and access to resources was conditioned by and contributed to U.S. strategic (V_1-denying), economic (V_2-denying), and manipulatory or managerial (V_3-denying) preferences.

The Normative Deficiency of U.S. Policy

The global meaning of U.S. policy was clear: the United States stood firmly and sometimes ruthlessly as a major impediment to the fulfillment of the values of global humanism in a new world order. Officials served a state-centered version of vested interests rather than a new image of order aimed at meeting global human needs. Where global humanist goals only modestly threatened the status quo, as in short-range steps for pollution abatement, U.S. policies protected national interests and at the same time accommodated some imperatives for international cooperation. Where a proponent of global humanism would seek fundamental shifts in the planetary distribution of wealth, power, and authority in order to facilitate disarmament, equitable distribution of wealth, self-determination, and environmental protection, U.S. officials launched counterhumanitarian attacks. Their purpose was to maintain the privileged U.S. geopolitical position in world society. Never, one is forced to conclude, did the United States government vigorously pursue implementation of any of the four world order values in the cases examined here.

The seriousness of this conclusion raises the question: have the selected case studies fairly represented the normative content of U.S. policy? To be sure, some differences inevitably existed among different policies. Nonetheless, by focusing on the fundamental values and structural impact of U.S. policies rather than the idiosyncratic nature of specific issues or the policymaking processes, typical behavior patterns serving a recurrent structure of interests have become clear. An investigation of any phase of arms control policy since World War II would reveal essentially the same value patterns evinced in the Vladivostok accord. Similarly, the findings about implicit values embedded in the aid policy to India could be duplicated by studies of numerous other recipients. The brief discussion of U.S. economic aid to all countries in comparison to the Indian case has confirmed this notion. The study of foreign aid covered all administrations over a twenty-five year period. Likewise, a student of human rights would doubtless find a structure of interests being served similar to the Chilean case, whether one studied U.S. policies toward South Africa, Brazil, the Dominican Republic, Portugal, Indonesia, Iran, South Korea, or South Vietnam. Where the United States more genuinely supported self-determination, the exercise of it frequently meant the demise of another colonial power or a U.S. strategic rival, thus providing potential advantages to U.S. strategic and economic interests. As noted earlier, the Senate Select Committee called the U.S. role in Chile "typical" of other U.S. interventions around the world from the Truman years to the present. Finally, U.S. officials have treated land-based and atmospheric pollution in general in the same manner as marine deterioration. On the related question of resource usage, U.S. food and energy policies also have shown no sense of urgency to abolish hunger.

In short, among the various cases one might select, the instrumentalities for carrying out U.S. policy may differ some-

387

what, but the hierarchy of values and the interests served were conspicuously constant. The constancy applies both to issues and to the two major political parties. The studies show no significant differences among various administrations from 1945 to the present on the issue of structural transformation. Variations are inconsequential when measured against overriding world order issues and the need for system change.

THE CONSTRAINTS OF THE PRESENT INTERNATIONAL SYSTEM

Protecting the preeminent position of the United States was, of course, precisely what officials were expected to do, if one accepted the dynamics of present international relations. The prevailing operational code assumed the perpetuation of a system of sovereign states competing for national advantages. According to the widely accepted "realist" paradigm—whether one preferred the nuances of Niccolo Machiavelli, Otto von Bismarck, Hans Morgenthau, or Henry Kissinger—governments do and should seek to enhance their power positions. The United States, one might argue, constructed a deceptively congenial international structure for implementing Machiavellianism of a most selfish nature. The United States pursued narrow, short-range interests at the expense of others, as many great powers have done in the past. Officials were hypocritical when they claimed that their policies adhered to preferred values more closely than did comparable policies of other states, especially when their respective resources and opportunities are taken into account.

Since other major powers were not vigorously pursuing the values of global humanism, can it fairly be argued that U.S. leaders should have adopted a global humanist operational code in the absence of any global authority? Would that not have been foolish? As the parable of the commons illustrates, it is not rational for one actor to behave as if an overarching authority administers the commons when in fact none exists. The greed of other actors will nullify the self-restraint of the morally most scrupulous. My point here is *not* that U.S. officials should have based their policies on the faulty assumption that a system of global policy coordination already existed. On the contrary, the point is that they should have stopped basing their policies on quite different but similarly faulty assumptions. These were the ideas that (1) a more equitable global system of policy coordination was impossible to create, or (2) if such a system were possible, steps toward its creation should be actively resisted. More positively, officials should have recognized the compatability of the global human interest with their own professed values and then have taken preliminary steps toward the establishment of a just and nonviolent system. These steps might have included, for example, a public announcement that the United States would not be the first country to test or deploy any new generations of weapons, like the maneuvering reentry vehicle, a mobile ICBM, or the cruise missile. Other steps, such as annually transferring 1 or 2 percent of GNP to poor societies, could have been taken to move toward economic equity, probably a prerequisite for establishing global cooperation for a new international economic order, enforcement of international norms for human rights, for war prevention, and for ecological protection. These and similar innovations could have improved the prospects for global policy coordination and structural change without sacrificing any of the professed values of the leadership.

The innovations were not taken because the material interests and psychological orientation of those in power made their worldview or operational code extremely resistant to change. The rigidity of the official outlook was illustrated throughout the case studies and revealed again in a reflective assessment by Henry Kissinger of his own achievements as the president's national security advisor and the secretary of state: "What will probably give me satisfaction in the longer term are structural achievements: the attempt to create a foreign policy based on permanent values and interests."[22] "Structural achievements" were aimed at preserving "permanent" U.S. interests. Kissinger did not favor a new international structure. Nor did he, during his service to two administrations, reassess U.S. interests. For him, they were unchanging. Implicit assumptions about the permanency of U.S. interests and of the state system made Kissinger and his colleagues ineffective and inefficient servants of even traditional U.S. interests, as evidenced in Kissinger's Vietnamese policies, because they did not take into account changing global realities.

U.S. policies produced disastrous consequences aside from the unnecessary human suffering that directly resulted from the policies themselves. Many potential supporters of a movement for a just world order have become disillusioned because they have erroneously believed that humanity's last, best hope (the

389

United States) has been unable to bring a better system into being. The failure to usher in the new age has forced many people back into a self-defeating political posture shaped by the belief that the world is such a hard and cruel place that the way things are now is the way they have to be. Such people acquiesce in an unsatisfactory status quo because they have been discouraged from rising above national parochialism to build institutions capable of furthering a sense of human solidarity.

In practice, the U.S. policy approach has ignored the certainty that when self-seeking national behavior is added up on a planetary scale, the aggregate of many separate pursuits for national advantage will work to the disadvantage of all. The U.S. government designed policies that served its separate (national) interests and took a laissez-faire approach to fulfilling planetary interests. In a system devoid of central guidance, when states compete with one another to achieve national economic and political advantages, officials will not disarm, wealth will not be used rationally to maximize fulfillment of human needs, the drive for overseas political influence and economic exploitation will ride roughshod over respect for human rights, and nationally selfish exploitation of resources plus environmentally hazardous (though economically cheap) waste disposal will occur. A competitive situation encourages those governments with the most economic and political resources to protect and increase their advantages without much regard for the plight of those with fewer resources. Only a planetary political process which opens itself to the politically effective expression of grievances by the have-nots can prevent the imbalances in wealth and power from remaining intolerably unjust. Only by constructing a global umbrella of central guidance to protect humanity's common interest in averting nuclear war and in decreasing poverty, injustice, and ecological imbalance will it become rational for separate actors to cooperate and exercise self-restraint for the good of all.

Justice cannot be achieved without empowering the people who presently lack political and economic resources in order to enable them to express their needs in the political process. This principle U.S. officials flatly rejected in the global area, even though it was precisely the same principle upon which Jeffersonian democracy was based: fair representation is the key to avoiding tyranny, whether by a king, by a distant Parliament imposing an unwanted tax on tea, or by an economic superpower taking advantage of its leverage in the marketplace. Because the human species faces threats that extend beyond national boundaries in their scope, the political process in which these threats can be successfully challenged must necessarily be global.

In examining the complexities of controlling marine pollution, for example, it became clear that the concept of sovereignty and the idea that governments should exercise exclusive control over "their" land or sea divided the planet in a way that made environmental protection hopeless. Separate governments ruling separate territories violated the ecological imperative of planetary unity. Similarly, disarmament will not occur until national arsenals are superfluous for protecting security, and this result will not occur within the existing nation-state system. Wealth will not be redistributed and productive capacity sharply focused on helping the world's poorest people without empowering the weak to influence the allocation of the world's resources. Concomitantly, the rich and strong will be most likely to support reallocation of wealth only when they receive guarantees that the poor are behaving "responsibly," and this cannot be politically and psychologically assured within the existing international system, short of imposing some modern variety of imperialism. Human rights can better be advanced and dependably respected with a transnational authority to arbitrate disputes, to detect violations reliably, and to discourage rights-denying mutual counterinterventions by groups like the CIA and the KGB. Each of the four case studies revealed strong arguments for supplementing sovereign states as prime centers of international decision making with supra- and sub-national centers of new strength and vitality. Some kind of world authority eventually must monitor planetary pollution, ration scarce resources and the right to pollute, enforce pollution standards, and react quickly to disasters in the commons. Other world agencies would be useful to enforce disarmament, to create a tax authority for redistribution of wealth, and to realize human rights.

Therefore, either the national interest, which fashionably clothes even the most unfashionable implicit values and modes of conduct, must be stripped of its prevailing virtuous disguise, or else redefined to make it consistent with the global human interest. If, as I have argued above, there is a growing planetary unity to the functions vital to meeting human needs, then the national interest begins to converge with the global interest, insofar as any threat to the species as a whole threatens every part

391

of it. During periods of growing scarcity, however, the temptation will be to secure resources and power for one national or regional segment of the species, while letting other segments of the species suffer or die. (This is, to a large extent, the operational definition given to the national interest by the superpowers.) Thus the global human interest differs radically from traditional national interests insofar as the former protects the resources of the world for the people of the world, whereas the latter seeks to serve the people of one nation. The contrast between the two interests is as clear as the difference between species solidarity and subspecies solidarity.

We have come to the point in history when even the wisest practitioners of statecraft operating with traditional operational codes based on Westphalian logic are themselves a serious threat to the human species. They frustrate opportunities for improving the quality of our lives. No political leader, however enlightened, who rationally pursues the traditionally defined national interest of his or her own state can realize the preferred world order values. Policymakers serving traditional national interests are agents of the past and subverters of a more humane future.

It is time to discard the idea that an enlightened pursuit of competitive national interests is consistent with the global or human interest. As we have seen, in the world of competing sovereignties it did not seem rational or in the national self-interest for industrial states to give up the deep-sea nodules. Only if acts were inspired by some notion of human solidarity would the use of deep-sea minerals fulfill the most pressing human and environmental needs. It is possible, of course, to argue that the long-range national interest takes into account the good of all. But that is true only if one chooses to take into account the human misery and suffering in the weak and poor societies of the earth. Such extranational concern is frequently resisted by dominant national institutions. Increased understanding may be gained by stating frankly the obsolescence of the national worldview. I have little doubt that current expressions of great power nationalism and the self-seeking policies of sovereign states will eventually be understood to be as morally outrageous as racism is viewed today. None of us, after all, chose the race or the nation into which he or she was born. Privileges that automatically accrue to one's nationality (or race) because of economic and political structures cannot be justified either by reason or the most widely professed moral philosophies of the world.

In summary, the preceding case studies point toward two general conclusions. United States policies were normatively defective because they either failed to advance or actively resisted realization of the four world values. Second, the existing international system severely inhibited the implementation of the same values. One can rightly criticize U.S. officials for short-sightedness and for hypocritical indifference to pressing human needs and aspirations. There was no leadership offered on world order questions and often progressive initiatives by others were opposed. At the same time, the structure of both the domestic and international economic-political orders pressed and to some extent seduced officials to serve the implicit values delineated in preceding chapters. In other words, domestic and international political environments determined policy sufficiently that global concerns were subordinated to narrower, self-serving goals. The political leadership failed to point out to the citizenry that the international system itself inhibited the realization of the values everyone professed to be serving. The dysfunctional nature of the international system and the implicit values of U.S. policy together offered little promise that the future would hold substantially more peace, economic equity, social justice, or environmental harmony than the past.

THE IMPLEMENTATION OF WORLD ORDER VALUES

Organizing for System Change

What can be done to implement the preferred world order values? First, it is wise to acknowledge the obstacles to change. Left to its own pursuits, the U.S. government probably will not lead the way toward a system characterized by more equal distribution of wealth and power. U.S. officials are privileged persons within a national society that is, in global terms, also highly privileged. Unless vigorously pressed, officials are unlikely to favor structural change that would to some extent decrease their preeminent positions. The world's strongest military state is unlikely to be enthusiastic about building a world system in which military power would play no role. The world's richest society is reluctant to promote genuine redistribution of wealth. To wait for the United States government, which enjoys so many advantages in the existing system, to initiate steps toward a new, demilitarized, more equitable system is almost as unreasonable as centuries ago to expect a divine-right king to lead a democratic revolution to abolish his throne and establish majority rule. One of the most important conclusions to draw from this analysis is that citizens who favor the four preferred values should not wait for the governments of the major powers to take the first measures to implement the values. Citizen action will have to precede progressive government policies.

Although the small states benefit far less than the great powers from the present international system, even the elites in the less powerful states enjoy their seats of national power. Thus they are frequently indifferent or hostile to creating more humane global governance. The four case studies show that political change is most needed precisely at the points where power is most concentrated in the existing political order. That is why incremental shifts of policy, not aimed at fundamental systemic change, will do little to realize global humanism.

Existing international organizations, at least for the present, provide only slightly more hope for world order reform because they are designed to serve the interests of the member states. An organization such as the United Nations, however, does contribute symbolic importance and some institutional innovations useful for bringing about systemic change. It symbolizes the idea of universal human solidarity so vital to world order reforms. In addition, some international organizations are doubtless likely to create an authority-accumulating momentum that will increase the degree of global policy coordination, even though it may be unwanted by member states who unsuccessfully resist the historical trend.

A third group of international actors, the multinational corporations, offer less certain results. Although they are more interested than nation-states in peace and functional reorganization of the planet on a nonterritorial basis, they seek a new order to enlarge their markets and profits. Realization of their preferred world might encourage peace between national governments, but it also would concentrate capital and maximize profit for a few instead of promote human rights, protect the environment, or guide productive capacity to focus first on eliminating poverty. In such a world, war between states might be replaced by conflict between transnational classes of poor and rich. Repression of the poor would be likely. One may hope that at

394

some point the U.S. national government and multinational corporations will become allies in the movement toward the preferred world of global humanism, but it would be foolish to expect widespread governmental and corporate sympathy before substantial attitudinal changes have occurred in the United States electorate.

As in the antimonarchical movements of years ago, the large majority of citizens have a long-range interest in developing a global system better able to realize the values of global humanism. Yet U.S. officials have not advanced a system based on those values. Thus in this regard the political leadership has not represented or served the long-range interests of most citizens. Insofar as Washington policymakers violate the interests of U.S. citizens and of humanity as a whole, to that degree the government lacks moral legitimacy, even though it may continue to enjoy political legitimacy which people, acting out of habit or misunderstanding, give to it.

Citizens commonly look to their government for leadership, especially on foreign policy issues. Most people allow the government with its complicated military strategies and intelligence networks to carry out the policy it chooses. This posture flows partly from choice and partly from a feeling of resignation that citizens cannot affect policy even if they try. In any case, most people have been politically and psychologically conditioned to accept a generally passive role toward determining governmental policy that affects their own destiny. They are obedient to a national authority that is now becoming obsolete, and they are socialized to violate their own and the species' long-range interests. No matter how sensible such a citizen response may have been in the past, to continue it will have disastrous results because we live now in an era when *systems*, not simply policies, must be changed. The existing political system and its prime actors lack the flexibility, imagination, and freedom from vested interests to generate the imperative transformation to a new, more humane order. The drive to change the prevailing operational code and thereby the international system will require energy from outside the existing political institutions. Whether one describes the process of transformation as consciousness-raising, fundamental attitudinal change, spiritual rebirth, or revolution, the passive relationship of citizens to authority must be broken in order to implement the preferred values.

A remodeled international system might be engineered with-

395

out the mobilization of citizens working on behalf of global humanist values. However, such a system would probably be an intergovernmental global hierarchy dominated by a concert of great powers and regional hegemonies that served many of the same people and values as the present system. Such a system would serve, with greater efficiency than ever before, the implicit values that were revealed in the case studies. In short, it would deny the values of global humanism.

The desired change to a preferred world will occur probably only after a globally minded minority educates and organizes an increasingly larger group of citizens to exert pressure for structural change. As Richard Falk once commented: "The renewal of America and more generally the reform of world society will depend on a kind of populism arising among people who lose faith in the capacity of their governments to be the repository of legitimacy and to serve as the valid expression and agency of national interests."[23] Like Ulysses who ordered himself tied to the mast when his ship passed the island of the sirens, citizens must bind themselves to their view of a preferred world future and develop a consensus-building yet nondoctrinaire global belief system, lest they be seduced by governmental rhetoric, the attractiveness of power, or the lure of wealth in the existing order to adopt a posture of subspecific solidarity and to defer to a species-endangering, national authority.[24] Guided by global humanist values and strengthened by a transnational network of local support groups, citizens would detect the deceptiveness of officials who speak of humanitarian concern while they protect a 45 to 1 superiority in national per capita income, or who speak of disarmament while tailoring agreements to legitimize arms deployment in new areas. Without skepticism of the old order, citizens will be misled by officials seeking to pacify and co-opt advocates of change. As each case study showed, officials produced enough policy results to give the appearance of serious efforts to implement rhetorical support for world order values, even though there was no intent to implement structural change.

Even small-scale efforts at local education and political organization for structural change is probably of greater usefulness than more glamorous lobbying in Washington for incremental improvements in current pieces of legislation. It is more important to educate citizens about the fundamental threat the arms buildup poses to humanity than to work to decrease the defense budget by, say, one billion dollars in any given year. (Of course, working at the latter issue may advance the former idea if the issue is posed in structural terms.) Similarly, it is of dubious utility to lobby strenuously for Senate support of an agreement based on revised Vladivostok ceilings, even though it may have some desirable elements, when one instead could emphasize that retaining 1,320 MIRVs or 2,250 launch vehicles is an illegitimate enterprise in the sense that no foreseeable political objective could justify using such weapons in combat. Intellectuals should probably spend less time in cynical complaints about governmental mistakes or in status-seeking cultivation of contacts with current decision makers as a professed technique for change, and more time in developing strategies and organizations to encourage new value consensus and to nurture a world social movement that would eventually bring irresistible pressure to bear on existing structures to move them toward the values of human dignity.

The aim of political activity should be to make fundamental alterations in both the domestic and world geopolitical orders. Disarmament most likely cannot occur without a world security system of some sort, but effective strides toward it depend upon first curtailing the excessive influence of the military-industrial complex within our own national decision-making processes. The creation of a world environmental authority will be needed to save the oceans, but it cannot be established until the National Petroleum Council and American Mining Congress have been bridled and their headlong rush to maximize profit is redirected toward fulfillment of human needs.

One technique for stimulating Washington officials to act more in the global interest is to pass domestic legislation that places the United States at a competitive economic or political disadvantage unless the government negotiates with other states to implement universally the principles that U.S. legislation established nationally. Especially in the area of environmental protection, relatively progressive standards for U.S. producers and shippers in coastal waters encouraged action on both the IMCO and dumping conventions in order to avoid competitive disadvantages. Thus to get international environmental action, one might first pass protective environmental legislation domestically. To stimulate action for disarmament, the U.S. military budget might be cut. To advance the right of self-determination, one might pass restrictive legislation for the CIA and U.S. cor-

397

porations with foreign investments. To move the United States toward using its diplomatic leverage in OECD to encourage all industrial states to give 1 percent of their GNP to less developed countries, citizens could press for congressional action to set the same target immediately for the United States.

The main drawback in the approach of the preceding paragraph is that the same domestic forces oppose national legislation as obstruct more progressive international action. Pressing for such legislation, however, does give concerned citizens a focus for mobilization and an immediate opportunity to attempt to advance national institutions toward respect for preferred values.

International politics is a value-realizing process. The advocate of global humanism stresses the need for value clarification in the selection of U.S. foreign policy goals. Officials could be required to demonstrate that their arms control proposals will lead to disarmament rather than to a further buildup, that foreign aid will lead to a new structure of economic relationships, that human rights are honored in deed as well as word, that environmental protection will not be sacrificed to military and shipping interests. Rather than uncritically accepting the statement that the government will do what is "required" to serve the national interest, one might ask: Who benefits from this policy? Does it increase the likelihood of peace, equity, justice, and ecological protection?

A movement for global humanism may at times create coalitions of unlikely allies. For example, multinational corporations may eventually provide a powerful restraint on national ambitions that threaten to violate the peace. Thus they could help to realize V_1. In the quest for V_2 and V_3, groups in the less developed countries should forge an alliance with world order activists in the industrial states to help restrain both the power-seeking desires of the superpowers and the profit-maximizing motives of multinational corporations. If domestic environmentalists gain sufficient influence in Washington, then the national government can become an ally in persuading multinational corporations and reluctant foreign governments to respect the environment.

The Selection of Means

Consensus on the values and goals of global humanism is imperative among those seeking to develop a successful transnational social movement. On the selection of means, however, wisdom requires one to remain experimental. Knowledge about political effectiveness is presently too limited to select any single approach to system change. A counterculture life-style in an intentional community may in certain contexts be as useful in transforming society as an academician's scholarship or a candidate's campaign on a global platform.

The values of global humanism do define certain limits for means that may be considered acceptable. For example, if global humanists were able to gain influence in a national government somewhere, it would be inappropriate for them to threaten nuclear war in order to compel disarmament. Because the preferred world is a humane world, respectful of life and nature, and based on human solidarity of all on the planet, the means for change should be nonviolent. Nonviolent action underscores the basic humaneness of the ends sought. It is a powerful force, yet at the same time less threatening to the elites that must relinquish some of their unfair control over power and wealth. Nonviolence facilitates a degree of psychological openness to considering alternative images of world order.[25] Nonviolent means also take into account the allies of global humanism who are within the national bureaucracy, even though reticent and politically outnumbered. Their support will be valuable in the movement for fundamental change.

The consistency between ends and means of global humanists will sharpen the contrast between themselves and governmental spokespersons for the obsolete social order. Many of the contradictions between the present leadership's implicit and professed values in the four case studies could be viewed as the use of means that were inconsistent with the ends professed. Officials said they wanted peace, but they sought to achieve it through threats and the buildup of more weapons of war. The president and secretary of state claimed to want civil liberties for Chileans but they used means that denied human rights and were consistent with authoritarian dictatorships. By requiring that means be more consistent with ends, the movement for change can avoid the kinds of hierarchical command structures, organizations, and actions that so frequently corrupt the existing actors in international politics.

To advocate nonviolent change does not mean that the process will occur without great personal sacrifice by many people. When the world order movement becomes more successful, it

399

will become more threatening to those who resist it.[26] As in the U.S. civil rights movement, people may have to risk their jobs and even their lives to correct past prejudices. Deep political conflict may accompany the decision about whether policies will serve the old interests or the movement toward a new, more humane system of governance. These decisions will not, of course, come all at once. Except in retrospect, it may not even be evident when the tide was turning. The pain of systemic change will be serious. But that pain doubtless will be less severe than the agony of nuclear war, the death of the sea, or the continuation of poverty for one billion people. The pain of change can be no greater than the suffering of the 10,000 persons who died each week as these chapters were written. Those were the people who succumbed from lack of adequate nutrition even though other humans had more food than they needed but did not share it with their poorer coinhabitants of the planet because the latter happened to live on the other side of an economic or political boundary.[27]

Many persons argue that the fundamental changes described above can be brought about only through violent revolution. There are strong historical arguments to support the view that people in positions of political and economic privilege will not relinquish their preeminence voluntarily. Yet the loss of life and the political and military obstacles to such a revolution in the United States would yield an unacceptable cost and uncertain results. Precisely because the political debate and conflict may be attended by bitterness and hostility, it is especially important to make explicit the nonviolent character of the movement for change.

Of course, it is a mistake to focus only upon the negative, conflictual side of social change. More important is the attractiveness of the unifying and mobilizing potential of a vision of human liberation and positive innovation. This vision will become politically more powerful as people from religious organizations, environmental groups, labor unions, the peace movement and many other professional and interest groups build coalitions to abolish war and poverty and to create new institutions for security, social justice, and ecological health.[28]

Indicators of World Order Progress

The indicators of world order progress, which are included at the end of each case study, suggest landmarks which can be used

400

to survey the position of the United States within the world order landscape. These indicators are not the only dimensions of performance that should be examined in appraising U.S. positions on world order values, but they are a starting point. The political activist can use them as criteria for assessing U.S. policies and for questioning candidates running for office.

Most of the indicators also can be used to assess the performance of other great powers. The percentages of GNP devoted to foreign aid or military spending, for example, suggest fairly clear directions when examined over several years. Such figures may be summed for regions or for the entire world to indicate rough movement toward or away from the preferred world order system.

The Transition Process

There is probably an inverse relationship between the interval of time available for system transformation and the likelihood of violence and coercion accompanying the process of change.[29] Moreover, the later that the consciousness-raising process begins, the lower the odds that the emerging global system—if and when it comes into existence—will nurture preferred humanist values instead of new institutional expressions of the old values that now undergird hegemonic structures based upon class and nationality. The longer people wait to act for system change, the more desperate will be the conditions under which change must occur. Ecological problems mount, armaments expand, the gap between rich and poor widens. From the vantage point of global humanism, the years since World War II have largely been lost opportunities. Rather than set long-range goals and plan a strategy for implementing fundamental changes based on a rational appraisal of human needs and respect for nature, U.S. policies have been deliberately designed to maintain and strengthen the structural status quo.

From at least the inception of the Truman Doctrine, U.S. policy was set on an anticommunist course that eventually resisted many radical movements, rather than on a course aimed at eliminating human suffering and injustice. No one can know with certainty whether opportunities like those symbolized by meetings at Vladivostok and Caracas, by AID policy in India, and by Allende reforms will reappear in future policy decisions. But many opportunities that arose since 1945 cannot be repeated. Some opportunities that were missed have already

401

caused untold misery for many people. The coming generation faces unnecessary malnutrition, injustice, and violence because U.S. and other national officials served the values of statism rather than the needs of humanity. For many people, change is already too late. For others it will not come in time to save their desperate lives. For the human species, we can only hope that sufficient time remains to change the course upon which national governments and economic enterprises are now headed.

Our fate is uncertain because irreversible political or ecological trends may be set in motion before their seriousness is recognized. As reported above, for example, we have yet to discover the ecological effects of some hazardous chemicals already set loose in the planet's environment. We will probably have no last chance to vote against nuclear war if a crisis takes us to the brink of violence. The desires of many national governments and corporations for prestige, profit, and energy are so strong that the increase of nuclear power plants and the spread of nuclear fuels around the world pose threats both to the environment and to the effort to avoid proliferation of nuclear weapons. The frightening consequences of human and ecological damage from the use of nuclear weapons in war, in terrorist acts, or from nuclear accidents will produce consequences that will last hundreds of years. It is highly probable that, during the years in which the superpowers discussed the decision to allow 2,400 strategic launchers, they squandered the last relatively easy opportunity to limit and dismantle nuclear arms in time to prevent additional nations from acquiring plutonium and enriched uranium.

U.S. policymakers failed to take seriously the possibility that the United States might some day find itself no longer the most wealthy and powerful society on earth—regardless of what officials now do. Historical experience suggests that a relative decline of United States preeminence, as of Roman grandeur and the British Empire, eventually is likely. A wise diplomacy would create global institutions now to protect humane values long after the United States will lack the power to protect itself by itself. One might expect officials to establish global guidance procedures for peaceful change, for assuring equitable sharing of resources, for respecting human rights and nature so that the descendents of Washingtonians will not suffer a plight similar to the one that the West inflicted on the rest of the world when imperialism flourished and industrial prosperity turned its back on overseas poverty.

It is unclear whether the opportunities for establishing those humane and just institutions for future generations will increase in the future. Our children will doubtless long regret the more than three decades wasted since 1945, during which so many energies were needlessly devoted to building massive armaments, to waging ideological warfare, and to isolating admittedly imperfect but nonetheless understandable revolutions in China, Indochina, Cuba, Chile, and elsewhere. Those were years in which the United States could have advanced global equity and human rights without jeopardizing its own security. The United States could have avoided reaping the whirlwind of justifiable resentment that the poor may increasingly focus on the industrial states. From the standpoint of structural change, those were the years of opportunity to achieve great progress without great cost.

Citizens should no longer retain in public office persons who act as if it is certain that the United States should and always will be the greatest military power in the world, the consumer of the most resources per capita, and the owner of the most advanced technology. To say this is not to wish failure upon the United States, but simply to recognize that the tides of wealth, power, science, and organizational skills ebb and flow. We cannot now foresee when U.S. advantages may recede or in what areas of endeavor the lead may pass to other hands. But to assume that the United States will remain number one in so many fields for the indefinite future will prove a regretable form of self-indulgent presumptuousness. Yet the foundation upon which United States foreign policies are based is precisely this erroneous, ethnocentric presumption.

If one contemplates the future with a mind less bound by national culture and historical era than the official mind, one sees more clearly that the United States should now move generously to establish new world and local agencies designed to implement the values of global humanism. To try to preserve such values only within the shell of the United States and its allies will be self-defeating and ultimately impossible. The time may come—indeed is at hand—when the United States will need unprecedented help and cooperation from other parts of the world. Such cooperation cannot be secured and is actively discouraged within the existing international system.

Is there any likelihood that officials will really implement the values of global humanism if they seem to conflict with acquiring

403

further power and wealth? Judging from the investigation of policies that showed the destruction of democracy in Chile, the deployment of additional nuclear weapons that did not increase human security, the lack of enthusiasm for a universal minimum standard of living, and the opposition to international control for environmental protection, it may already be too late to reconstruct the self-serving models of reality that flourish in government offices.

If officials base decisions on a system of values that deny the primacy of global human needs, then it is likely that the future will include more violence, inequity, repression, and ecological damage than the past. Poverty and the debilitating consequences of malnutrition often encourage a high birthrate. Consumerism and materialism of the industrialized states deplete resources and pollute the environment. Therefore, the postponement of economic well-being and equity will continue to increase the pressures upon available resources and systems of waste disposal. If industrialization proceeds with growing populations, the prospects for environmental overload will also increase. The continuation of gross inequalities of wealth is likely to polarize political forces within and between societies as well as encourage the creation of a world system designed for the benefit of the rich and maintained by repressing the poor through psychological, political, and military means. Proliferation of nuclear materials makes it more difficult to avert nuclear war or serious environmental damage.

Realism demands that we note the negative trends evinced in the case studies. Awareness of such trends will help citizens understand that the implicit values served by those presently in power and reflected in the general public are values that threaten the well-being of the species. Thus morally sensitive citizens should take their political future into their own hands. Happily, people are capable of extraordinary attitudinal change and social adjustment when they feel that all persons will share the necessary sacrifices equally, when they are convinced that change is imperative because of external circumstances (such as a diminishing supply of oil), and when the need for change is related directly to the pursuit of higher values. U.S. citizens could, with graciousness and even good spirits, make the sacrifices necessary to implement the values of global humanism if they knew that the purpose was to create a more just global order, to relieve human misery, and to build the foundation for transnational cooperation on other issues.

404

Milton Rokeach has persuasively argued that the political implications of our existing knowledge about value change has not been taken seriously by most social scientists. His studies show that major changes in values, attitudes, and behavior are possible when a person becomes aware of contradictions that exist among his or her fundamental values.[30] Change could be rapid when people eventually become conscious of the contradiction between ranking compassion and peace highly in their system of values, on the one hand, and ranking loyalty and unreflective obedience to the nation-state highly, on the other. Political values represent basic ideological predispositions that are related to many different kinds of attitudes and behaviors. A value change would affect one's positions on specific political issues and one's willingness to take political action.[31]

The values of global humanism provide the foundation for developing a positive vision which can help to mobilize people for establishing more humane governance on a planetary scale. This vision includes dependable nonviolent means to settle disputes, a prohibition against the deployment of nuclear weapons, and the reduction of national military arsenals because they will be superfluous for providing security. It is a world where careful planning and fair distribution can eliminate starvation. By increasing economic coordination and cooperation, poverty and unemployment can be abolished. Human rights might be transnationally monitored and encouraged. The common heritage could be shared equitably according to a formula that recognized the needs of all societies.

Peace, economic well-being, justice, and ecological balance will not be permanently guaranteed by any system, but they can become the goals for action to establish a new system in which their realization would be a reasonable possibility. Economic and political decisions *can* be based upon a genuine feeling of human solidarity. Conflicts will remain in any transformed system, but it is possible to build a wide consensus that decisions ought to serve universal human needs rather than to maximize the power or profit of institutions seeking competitive advantages without regard for human or environmental consequences.

Such a backdrop for political decisions would produce significantly different political results. The bonds that unite humanity need not be envisaged as a sentimental feeling of the people of Chicago for the people of Shanghai. The necessary sort of identity is the far more limited and possible sense of solidarity felt by the people in Florida for those in California. It

405

should not be impossible for the people in Florida to care about the people in Cuba as much as they care about those in California.[32]

Critics will perhaps argue that I have been ungenerous in evaluating governmental actions. Have U.S. officials not done their best to implement the values of world order, but been rebuffed by a hostile world? To be sure, most officials would like to see world peace, food for all, respect for certain human rights, and a clean ocean. However, their behavior reveals that they usually wanted to achieve these global goals only under conditions that did not erode their vested interests or special privileges that attended their leadership position in the world's most privileged society. These narrower interests, especially in the short run, often conflicted with global interests, which remained unrealized because they were not given a high priority. The government and its citizenry have spent more money for achieving a killing capacity that exceeds Hitler's most extreme military hope than for initiating a disarmament process. We have curtailed U.S. food production to keep food prices high rather than feed malnourished children. We have violated self-determination and destabilized another society rather than allow the changes that would be brought about by democratic socialism. We have satisfied a self-indulgent appetite for minerals, profits, and unimpeded military navigation rather than safeguard the marine ecosystem. This painful assessment of U.S. priorities is not mine alone. It is not the result of some ingenious interpretation of events. It is evident from any careful analysis of the impact of U.S. political behavior, as opposed to the rhetoric of U.S. officials. Were it not so, the Vladivostok agreement would not have been called an "historic breakthrough"; children in southern Asia would have been fed; Latin Americans would not suffer today, after years of the Good Neighbor policy, from pervasive, structurally perpetuated injustice and poverty; and at least a few effective measures for global enforcement of pollution abatement would have been initiated.

For U.S. citizens and public officials to want peace only if we can be number one is not to want peace. To want universal economic well-being only if we can continue a wasteful materialism is not to want an end to poverty. To want human rights only if we can protect our dominant power position is not to want justice. To want pollution abatement only if we can have unregulated navigation and continue to consume a disproportionate share of the world's resources is not to want genuine harmony between humanity and nature.

In summary, U.S. behavior failed to support the values of global humanism. Although officials could have helped realize the preferred values, which they often supported rhetorically, the structure of both the domestic and international economic-political systems made supportive behavior unlikely. It will remain unlikely until political values, attitudes, and institutions begin to reflect a genuine sense of human—as opposed to national—solidarity. Pending fundamental changes, the existing array of governmental and internal forces against global humanism will probably either perpetuate the nation-state system until a major trauma occurs, or, in a severely limited way, adjust present institutions to the need for some global organization of economic and political power. Such minor adjustment, however, will not substantially reduce the unfair privileges of the presently well-off, abolish the war system and the weapons of mass destruction, liberate the poor and oppressed, or respect environmental limits.

In a world where system change is desirable and necessary but where dominant institutions resist change, an extraordinary responsibility falls upon the individual citizen, religious communities, and other nongovernmental agencies to bring about the required changes. These groups should make themselves more genuinely transnational and then provide the bridge between the present and the future systems, while pressing institutions with a vested interest in the prevailing structures of power and wealth to join the forces for a humane transformation. Realizing the four values of global humanism will indeed be difficult. But failing to realize them will be disastrous for millions of coinhabitants of our planet, if not eventually for all of human civilization. The road leading to destruction is easy because it is familiar. The road toward achieving peace, economic well-being, justice, and ecological balance is difficult and unfamiliar but promises some hope. Traveling down that road during the remainder of the twentieth century depends upon a popular movement fueled by our own imagination and willingness to act.

Notes

ONE. THE ELUSIVENESS OF A HUMANE WORLD COMMUNITY

1. These ideas both support and are reinforced by the present international system. Its roots extend back to the fundamental political changes that accompanied the transformation from feudalism to modern nationalism more than four centuries ago.

2. See, for example, Louis Beres and Harry Targ, *Reordering the Planet*; Barry Commoner, *The Closing Circle*; Richard A. Falk, *A Study of Future Worlds* and *This Endangered Planet*; Garrett Hardin, *Exploring New Ethics for Survival*; Robert L. Heilbroner, *An Inquiry into the Human Prospect*; Ervin Laszlo, *A Strategy for the Future*; Mihajlo D. Mesarovic and Eduard Pestel, *Mankind at the Turning Point*; Dennis C. Pirages and Paul R. Ehrlich, *Ark II*; Jan Tinbergen, *Reshaping the International Order*; Van Rensellaer Potter, *Bioethics*; Warren Wagar, *Building the City of Man*.

3. Exhaustive treatments of the contemporary challenges to the human race are available elsewhere. The reader seeking further substantiation of the assertion that there is a planetary crisis should consult the sources cited in note 2.

4. The discussion that follows is not a critique of the theory of deterrence itself but a statement of several of the instabilities inherent within such a strategy. For a somewhat dated but still useful examination of deterrence, see Philip Green, *Deadly Logic*. Falk has discussed the dangers of the war system itself, and has included a brief critique of deterrence in *This Endangered Planet*, pp. 105-132. For some frequently overlooked criticisms of deterrence logic, see Jonathan Knight, "Risks of War and Deterrence Logic," *Canadian Journal of Political Science*, 6 (1973), 22-36.

5. Paul Doty, Richard Garwin, George Kistiakowsky, George Rathjens, and Thomas Schelling, "Nuclear War by 1999?," pp. 19-25; reprinted in *Current*, January 1976, pp. 32-43.

6. Frank Barnaby, "The Mounting Prospects of Nuclear War," p. 11, and "The Technological Explosion in Armaments," *Bulletin of Peace Proposals*, 8 (1977), 347.

7. The illegal, deep penetration of Soviet airspace by a U.S. spy plane during the height of the tension over the United States "quarantine" of Cuba in 1962 is an example of how easily dangerous mistakes can occur. On this occasion, a number of Soviet fighters quickly took off in response to the U.S. plane. President Kennedy "wondered if Khrushchev would speculate that we were surveying targets for a preemptive nuclear strike." Theodore Sorensen, *Kennedy*, p. 804

409

8. Ibid., p. 795.
9. Ibid., p. 767.
10. Robert Kennedy, *Thirteen Days*, p. 109. Emphasis added.
11. Ibid., p. 93.
12. Ibid., p. 97.
13. Ibid., p. 98.
14. Sorensen, *Kennedy*, p. 807. Emphasis added. The "deterioration" mentioned here was the shooting down of a United States U-2 plane illegally overflying Cuban airspace to photograph the construction of missile sites.
15. Ibid.
16. Ibid., p. 808.
17. Herbert F. York, "Deterrence Gone M.A.D.," pp. 5, 7.
18. For Iklé's statement, see the *New York Times*, September 6, 1974; Fred Iklé, "Nuclear Disarmament without Secrecy," speech before the Council on Foreign Relations, Chicago, September 5, 1974 (Washington, D.C.: United States Arms Control and Disarmament Agency, n.d., mimeo.), p. 5. For other discussions of atmospheric pollution and the ozone problem, see Steven C. Wofsy and Michael McElroy, "HO_x, NO_x, and ClO_x: Their Role in Atmospheric Photochemistry," *Canadian Journal of Chemistry*, 52 (April 15, 1974), 1582-1591; Richard S. Stolarski and Ralph J. Cicerone, "Stratospheric Chlorine," ibid., pp. 1610-1615; and Paul Crutzen, "A Review of Upper Atmospheric Photochemistry," ibid., pp. 1569-1581; Ralph Cicerone, Richard Stolarski, and Stacy Walters, "Stratospheric Ozone Destruction by Man-Made Chlorofluoromethanes," *Science*, 185 (September 27, 1974), 1165-1166; *New York Times*, September 26, 1974, and November 23, 1975.
19. Study of Critical Environmental Problems, *Man's Impact on the Global Environment*, pp. 127-136; Bostwick Ketchum, "Biological Implications of Global Marine Pollution," in Fred Singer, ed., *Global Effects of Environmental Pollution*, pp. 190-194; Frank Graham, *Since Silent Spring*, p. 113; Georg Borgstrom, *The Hungry Planet* (New York: Macmillan, 1965), pp. 352, 382-383, Commoner, *The Closing Circle*, p. 227; C. F. Wurster, "DDT Reduces Photosynthesis by Marine Phytoplankton," pp. 1474-1475; D. W. Menzel, J. Anderson, and A. Randtke, "Marine Phytoplankton Vary in their Response to Chlorinated Hydro-carbons," *Science*, 1970, p. 167.
20. Of course, U.S. citizens usually are better represented than citizens of smaller nations whose governments lack the economic and diplomatic power to express their views forcefully in other capitals.
21. Jimmy Carter, "Remarks by President Jimmy Carter Videotaped for Delivery to People of Other Nations," p. 1.
22. Lester R. Brown, *By Bread Alone*, pp. 4-7.
23. Harold M. Schmeck, *New York Times*, October 7, 1974.

24. Bernard Weinraub, *New York Times*, February 2, 1975; see also Catherine Lerza and Michael Jacobson, eds., *Food for People—Not for Profit*, p. 3.

25. James P. Grant, "U.S. Policy and the Food Parley," *New York Times*, November 3, 1974; Jean Mayer, "By Bread Alone," *New York Times Book Review*, December 15, 1974, p. 19.

26. *New York Times*, November 5, 1974.

27. Ibid.

28. Martin M. McLaughlin, "Feeding the Unfed," *Commonweal*, July 12, 1974, p. 376. Average American consumption was about twice that of Western Europe. See also Brown, *By Bread Alone*; *New York Times*, October 25, 1974.

29. *New York Times*, March 17, 1975; Lerza and Jacobson, *Food for People*, p. 1.

30. *New York Times*, March 17, 1975. The CIA report was based in part on speculation about climatic changes. Although most climatologists doubt that the assumption of climatic changes is presently warranted, the political consequences of food shortages, regardless of cause, could be similar to those described in the CIA report.

31. For a more comprehensive treatment of these themes, see Richard A. Falk, "The Interplay of Westphalia and Charter Conceptions of the International Legal Order," in Richard A. Falk and Cyril E. Black, eds., *The Future of the International Legal Order*, 1, 32-70. See also Richard A. Falk, "A New Paradigm for International Legal Studies," 978-987.

32. John Herz discussed the demise of the territorial state in *International Politics in the Atomic Age*. He revised his assessment of the end of territoriality in "The Territorial State Revisited," pp. 11-34.

33. Garrett Hardin, *Exploring New Ethics for Survival*, p. 254.

34. "On the Origin and Foundation of the Inequality of Mankind," translated by G.D.H. Cole, *The Social Contract and Discourses* (London: J. M. Dent, 1913), p. 194. Kenneth Waltz discusses this passage in *Man, the State and War* (New York: Columbia University Press, 1954), pp. 167-168.

35. Waltz in part suggests this reasoning, *Man, the State and War*, p. 169.

36. This fourfold value framework was first suggested by a transnational group of scholars representing all major regions of the world and participating in the World Order Models Project. Their purpose has been to develop models of a preferred world order for the 1990s. In the early stages of their efforts, they agreed to focus upon these four value areas to provide a basis for studying strategies of world order reform. For an early statement of the objectives of this project, see Ian Baldwin, "Thinking About a New World Order for the Decade 1990," *War/Peace Report*, 2 (January 1970), 3-7. For a more recent statement, see Saul H. Mendlovitz and Thomas G. Weiss, "Towards Consensus: The World Order Models Project of

411

the Institute for World Order," in Grenville Clark and Louis B. Sohn, eds., *Introduction to World Peace Through World Law*, pp. 74-97. The important products of this project to date are a series of books on "Preferred Worlds for the 1990s." See Falk, *A Study of Future Worlds*; Johan Galtung, *The True Worlds*; Rajni Kothari, *Footsteps Into the Future*; Gustavo Lagos and Horacio H. Godoy, *Revolution of Being*; Ali A. Mazrui, *A World Federation of Cultures*; Saul H. Mendlovitz, *On the Creation of a Just World Order*.

37. The values of global humanism could, of course, be used as yard-sticks to measure the foreign policy behavior of any government at various points in time. Such indicators could also be used to judge the relative merit of differing policies advocated by competing sets of leadership within a single country at the same time.

38. For the role of values as guides for decision making, see Milton Rokeach, *The Nature of Human Values*, p. 12.

39. The text of this speech of November 15, 1961 was reprinted in United States Arms Control and Disarmament Agency, *Disarmament*, p. 18.

40. The typology and following analysis of alternative models of world order are drawn in part from the ground-breaking scholarship of Richard A. Falk, especially "A New Paradigm," pp. 999-1017.

41. The political structures of each type of system could vary some-what. A range of normative orientations is also possible in the first three models, although their structures limit the extent to which they could realize the preferred values. The prospects are most se-verely limited in the first two examples. The models are described in what the author calculates are their most likely manifestations.

42. See Richard Barnet and Ronald Mueller, *Global Reach*.

43. Clark and Sohn, *World Peace Through World Law*, p. xv. (Italics in original.)

44. Falk, *A Study of Future Worlds*, pp. 224-276.

45. In some cases, development of socially destructive values has corre-lated more closely with a person's expectation for future conflicts than with the subject's background and experience. For example, Arthur L. Stinchombe found that different images of the future in part determined whether young people rebelled: "the future, not the past, explains adolescent rebellion, contrary to the hypothesis that deviant attitudes are the result of distinctly rebel biographies." *Rebellion in High School* (Chicago: Quadrangle Books, 1964), p. 6, noted in Wendell Bell and James A. Mau, eds., *The Sociology of the Future*, p. 33.

46. Bell and Mau, *Sociology of the Future*, p. 18; Harold Lasswell, *The Analysis of Political Behavior: An Empirical Approach* (London: Rout-ledge and Kegan Paul, 1948), and "The Changing Image of Human Nature: The Socio-cultural Aspect, Future-oriented Man," *American Journal of Psycho-Analysis*, 26 (1966), 157-166; Heinz

Eulau, "H. D. Laswell's Developmental Analysis," *Western Political Quarterly*, 2 (1958), 229-242.

47. Bell and Mau, *Sociology of the Future*, p. 14.

Two. The Vladivostok Accord

1. Stockholm International Peace Research Institute, *World Armaments and Disarmament: SIPRI Yearbook 1974*, p. 123. Hereafter cited as *SIPRI Yearbook*, various years.

2. See Alan Newcombe, Gernot Koehler, and Maire A. Dugan, "The Inter-Nation Tensiometer for the Prediction of War," paper presented at the International Studies Association Annual Meeting, Washington, D.C., February 21, 1975.

3. This approach assumes that nuclear deterrence does not satisfy minimum long-range essentials for security. The failure of deterrence would produce irreversible disaster for perhaps the entire human race, or at least large segments of it. Even the secondary consequences of radioactive fallout, such as the weakening of the ozone shield, could inflict severe suffering upon humanity. A quarter-century of deterrence has not substantially increased human security; instead, it has increased destructive capacity far beyond the minimum necessary even for deterrence.

    Problems posed by deterrence as a guarantor of security are discussed in Richard A. Falk, *A Study of Future Worlds*, pp. 13-17. For a criticism of the war system, see ibid., pp. 96-103 and Richard A. Falk, *This Endangered Planet*, pp. 105-132. An early but still useful criticism of deterrence is Philip Green, *Deadly Logic*. For comments on counterforce strategy, see G. W. Rathjens, "Flexible Response Options," pp. 677-688 and Robert C. Johansen, "Countercombatant Strategy: A New Balance of Terror?," pp. 47-53.

4. "Equality" is used here to mean rough equivalence in military power rather than an identical matching of capabilities at every point along the force spectrum.

    "Disarmament" refers to measures aimed at major arms reductions and the eventual abolition of nuclear and conventional forces used for war. Usually disarmament measures mean large reductions, but they may also refer to small reductions if they are part of a process leading toward general and complete disarmament. Disarmament, as used here, does not include the abolition of equipment used by police for maintaining domestic tranquility.

    "Arms control" is used to refer to policies aimed at stabilizing levels of armaments. Such policies may specify that arms be modestly reduced, increased, or maintained at existing levels.

5. The representative nature of the Vladivostok accord and its appropriateness for assessing U.S. performance on the minimization of collective violence are amplified in the concluding section.

6. In a later agreement, the two parties restricted ABMS to one site, since neither country had shown interest in deploying ABMS at more than one site. The agreement entered into force on October 3, 1972. The text for the ABM agreement may be found in *SIPRI Yearbook 1973*.

7. For an analysis of this agreement, see *SIPRI Yearbook 1973*, pp. 1-28. The text for the Interim Agreement is reprinted in Appendix 1.

8. U.S. Arms Control and Disarmament Agency, *SALT Lexicon*, No. 71 (Washington, D.C.: Government Printing Office, 1974), p. 1.

9. The text is in the *New York Times*, December 3, 1974. Hereafter, all direct quotations from officials' speeches or news conferences which are cited from the *New York Times* refer to the texts of official statements.

10. *New York Times*, November 25, 1974; see also Kissinger's statement in *New York Times*, December 1, 1974.

11. "Interview for 'Bill Moyers' Journal.' " *Department of State Bulletin*, 72 (February 10, 1975), 176.

12. *New York Times*, November 25, 1974; for corroborating statements, see *New York Times*, December 1, 1974, and *Department of State Bulletin*, 71 (December 23, 1974), 899.

13. "Secretary Kissinger's News Conference of December 7," *Department of State Bulletin*, 71 (December 30, 1974), 910.

14. *New York Times*, December 3, 1974; see also "Secretary Kissinger's News Conference of December 7," p. 910.

15. *New York Times*, December 7, 1974. Malcolm Currie, director of defense research and engineering, called it a "major breakthrough." See also U.S. Congress, Senate, Committee on Armed Services, *Fiscal Year 1976 and July-September 1976 Transition Period Authorization for Military Procurement, Research and Development, and Active Duty, Selected Reserve, and Civilian Personnel Strengths, Hearings*, p. 2693. Hereafter cited as *FY 1976 Authorizations*.

16. The Soviet Union had 2,031 warheads on missiles and a total of 2,500 warheads on bombers and missiles combined. The United States possessed 7,086 and 7,650 warheads, respectively. Stockholm International Peace Research Institute, *Armaments and Disarmament in the Nuclear Age*, p. 49.

17. Ibid.

18. A .7-megaton warhead is fifty times the size of the Hiroshima bomb.

19. *Department of State Bulletin*, 71 (December 30, 1974), 911. See also Ford, *Department of State Bulletin*, 71 (December 23, 1974), 863-864.

20. E. C. Aldridge, deputy assistant secretary of defense for strategic programs, noted that the Vladivostok agreement had no effect on reloading but only on the number of silos. See *FY 1976 Authorizations*, p. 1741.

21. James R. Schlesinger, *Annual Defense Department Report FY 1976 and FY 197T* (Washington, D.C.: Government Printing Office, 1975), p. 11-21. Hereafter cited as *Defense Department Report FY 1976*.
22. Paul H. Nitze, "The Vladivostok Accord and SALT II," p. 160.
23. *New York Times*, November 26, 1974, p. 6.
24. *FY 1976 Authorizations*, p. 469.
25. U.S. Congress, Senate, Committee on Appropriations, *Department of Defense Appropriations, Fiscal Year 1975*, p. 487. Hereafter cited as *Appropriations Hearings FY 1975*. Kissinger's advocacy of a high MIRV ceiling would allow the Joint Chiefs of Staff to complete their existing modernization programs. Leslie Gelb, *New York Times*, December 3, 1974; December 10, 1974.
26. *New York Times*, December 7, 1974; December 10, 1974; February 12, 1975.
27. See Secretary Schlesinger's advocacy of advanced research in all of these areas, *Defense Department Report FY 1976*, pp. 11-10, 11, 20-54; Currie, *FY 1976 Authorizations*, pp. 2644, 2694-2709; George J. Brown, chairman of the Joint Chiefs of Staff, ibid., p. 212.
28. U.S. Congress, Senate, Committee on Foreign Relations, *ACDA* [Arms Control and Disarmament Agency] *Authorization*, p. 20. Hereafter cited as *ACDA Authorization*.
29. *Department of State Bulletin*, 71 (December 23, 1974), 862-863.
30. *Defense Department Report FY 1976*, pp. 1-9, 11-8.
31. *FY 1976 Authorizations*, p. 502.
32. Gerard C. Smith, "SALT After Vladivostok" p. 8. Emphasis added.
33. *New York Times*, November 29, 1974.
34. *FY 1976 Authorizations*, pp. 2640, 2644, 3998. Emphasis added.
35. Ibid., p. 489. Emphasis added.
36. Ibid., p. 2154. Emphasis added. See also statement by John L. McLucas, ibid., p. 468.
37. This point was confirmed by frequent references to the Vladivostok agreement in justifying the need to develop a new M-X missile to replace the Minuteman, and to develop the Trident missile to supplement the Polaris and Poseidon. In each case, officials sought to replace existing weapons with weapons of higher performance per unit. They argued that these should not be subject to the normal fiscal constraints, since new weapons could not readily meet past standards, in terms of increased firepower per dollar spent, if only a limited number of each weapon would be deployed. See statements, ibid., by David C. Jones, p. 489; John L. McLucas, p. 468; Malcolm Currie, p. 2644; James R. Schlesinger, p. 2154.
38. E. C. Aldridge, ibid., p. 2141.
39. In the secretary of defense's classified statement on the FY 1975

415

defense budget, he said: "Strategic programs . . . affect the prospects for arms control. And specific weapons systems are the coin of this particular realm. Not only are such systems the mediums of exchange; they are also the basis for expanding or contracting the forces. As a consequence, arms control objectives must have a major impact on our planning." For differing interpretations of this statement, see the brief exchange between Senator Symington and Secretary Schlesinger, *Appropriations Hearings FY 1975*, pp. 35-36.

40. Federation of American Scientists, "Scientists Comment on SALT Agreement" (press release of December 12, 1974).

41. Carl Kaysen, former deputy special assistant to the president for national security affairs and consultant to the weapons systems evaluation group of the Department of Defense, told the Senate Arms Control Subcommittee that "if there is no substantial ABM, the only excuse for MIRV then is a counterforce or first strike weapon." United States Congress, Senate, Committee on Foreign Relations, Subcommittee on Arms Control, International Law and Organization, *Arms Control Implications of Current Defense Budget*, p. 75. Hereafter cited as *Arms Control Implications*.

42. See the statement by David Packard, deputy secretary of defense, ibid., pp. 181-183.

43. For example, Senator Edmund Muskie, chairman of the Arms Control Subcommittee, argued that by developing and deploying MIRV "we reduce the possibility of a MIRV limitation." Ibid., p. 183.

44. *SIPRI Yearbook 1974*, pp. 105, 107.

45. *Arms Control Implications*, p. 100. The Limited Nuclear Test Ban Treaty of 1963 was another example of arms control efforts' increasing the pace and extent of military innovation. The United States conducted more tests than it would likely have carried out if the treaty had not been negotiated. See George W. Rathjens, "Future Limitations of Strategic Arms," in Mason Willrich and John Rhinelander, eds., *SALT: The Moscow Agreements and Beyond*, p. 236.

46. Marshall D. Shulman, "SALT and the Soviet Union," in Willrich and Rhinelander, *SALT*, p. 120.

47. Written response from the Joint Chiefs, reprinted in *Arms Control Implications*, p. 43.

48. For discussion of a view contrary to the ideas expressed in this paragraph, see Smith, "SALT After Vladivostok," p. 13. He argued that the prolonged SALT negotiations produced some benefits even if no agreements were reached in the end.

49. *New York Times*, December 1, 1974. Emphasis added.

50. *Arms Control Implications*, p. 25.

51. In assessing the consequences of SALT I, the authors of the *SIPRI Yearbook 1973* came to the conclusion that "the technological arms

race is encouraged and even legitimized" (p. 17). George Rathjens concluded, "I believe that efforts to negotiate a treaty based on the Vladivostok Agreement are more likely to facilitate than to inhibit the acquisition of superfluous strategic arms. The effects on Soviet-American relations are likely therefore to be adverse in the medium and long term if not immediately. . . . Perhaps most serious of all, these efforts are likely to be a stimulus to nuclear proliferation." "Scientists Comment on SALT Agreement," p. 6.

52. See statement by James Schlesinger, United States Congress, Senate, Committee on Foreign Relations, Subcommittee on Arms Control, International Law and Organization, *U.S.-U.S.S.R. Strategic Policies*, p. 18. Hereafter cited as *Strategic Policies Hearings*. See also *Defense Department Report FY 1976*, pp. 1-15, 16; II-9, 10; *FY 1976 Authorizations*, p. 2101.

53. *Defense Department Report FY 1976*, p. II-18.

54. See, for example, *Strategic Policies Hearings*, p. 18; *Defense Department Report FY 1976*, p. II-90; *FY 1976 Authorizations*, p. 19.

55. *SIPRI Yearbook 1974*, p. 110.

56. Counterforce capability for hard targets was proportional to the square of the accuracy of the warhead (doubling accuracy increased capability fourfold), whereas it was proportional to the 2/3 power of the yield of the warhead (increasing megatonnage by a factor of eight would increase counterforce capability only four times). See Robert L. Leggett, "Two Legs Do Not a Centipede Make," p. 30.

57. Ibid., pp. 30-32.

58. *SIPRI Yearbook 1974*, pp. 110-111; *New York Times*, March 21, 1971; A. B. Martin, "The Land-Based ICBM," paper presented at the American Institute of Aeronautics and Astronautics, 10th Annual Meeting, Washington, D.C., 1974.

59. *SIPRI Yearbook 1974*, p. 111.

60. *SIPRI Yearbook 1974*, p. 117.

61. Herbert Scoville, "A Leap Forward in Verification," in Willrich and Rhinelander, *SALT*, p. 176.

62. Senator Thomas McIntyre called it a "radical revision of our strategic policy from one of mutual deterrence to one of nuclear warfighting." "Security Through Détente: Limits and Possibilities," speech before the International Studies Council, University of New Hampshire, May 5, 1975.

63. Bernard Feld, "Doves of the World Unite," *New Scientist*, December 26, 1974, p. 912.

64. J. P. Ruina, "U.S. and Soviet Strategic Arsenals," in Willrich and Rhinelander, *SALT*, p. 41. For an appraisal of objections to flexible options see Rathjens, "Flexible Response Options," pp. 677-688.

65. See the secretary of defense's vague justifications for more U.S. weapons, based on the assumed need to equal potential Soviet de-

ployments, *Defense Department Report FY 1976*, p. 1-13; *FY 1976 Authorizations*, p. 19; *Strategic Policies Hearings*, p. 18; *Appropriations Hearings Fiscal 1975*, p. 97. See also the statement of Paul C. Warnke, former assistant secretary of defense, in the United States Congress, Senate, Committee on Foreign Relations, Subcommittee on United States Security Agreements and Commitments Abroad and Subcommittee on Arms Control, International Law and Organization, *Nuclear Weapons and Foreign Policy*, p. 55. Hereafter cited as *Nuclear Weapons Hearings*. See also Schlesinger's statement in *Strategic Policies Hearings*, pp. 2, 7, 29, that sufficient targeting flexibility could be achieved with existing weapons and guidance systems.

As early as 1964, Secretary of the Navy Paul Nitze testified that eight on-station Polaris submarines could destroy 25-35 million Soviet people and most of the industrial war-making potential of the Soviet Union; *Arms Control Implications*, p. 42. That was a tiny fraction of the total U.S. force by 1974. Even one-tenth of the U.S. bomber force could inflict damage equivalent to about a thousand Hiroshima bombs; Ruina, "U.S. and Soviet Strategic Arsenals," p. 58. Senator Symington reported that "we have the capacity to destroy the Soviets hundreds if not thousands of times." *Arms Control Implications*, p. 40. Many knowledgeable, independent observers believed that slbms alone (which even a new Soviet counterforce strategy could not destroy), were "sufficient to meet our overall needs." See the statement by Carl Kaysen, *Arms Control Implications*, p. 59. If, out of the entire U.S. arsenal, only several Poseidons were to escape a Soviet first strike, they could inflict destruction on the Soviet Union sufficient to make a first-strike strategy unworkable. Thus any alleged threat posed to land-based icbms by increased Soviet throw weight could not in itself justify an enlarged buildup of U.S. counterforce. On the absence of need for the new weapons sought, see Rathjens, "Flexible Response Options," p. 681; Kaysen, *Arms Control Implications*, p. 62. On Soviet inability to launch a successful first-strike attack against the United States, either in 1974 or by 1985, see Schlesinger's statements in *Defense Report FY 1976*, p. 1-15; *Nuclear Weapons Hearings*, p. 193; and United States Congress, Senate, Committee on Foreign Relations, Subcommittee on Arms Control, International Law and Organization, *Briefing on Counterforce Attacks*, p. 9. Hereafter cited as *Counterforce Hearings*.

66. *Strategic Policies Hearings*, p. 38. See also p. 19.

67. *Defense Department Report FY 1976*, pp. 1-15, 16.

68. See, for example, *Nuclear Weapons Hearings*, pp. 161-192.

69. Military planners were far ahead of the arms controllers in planning for the future. Even before the Vladivostok accord became a treaty, new weapons were being prepared for deployment after

the potential treaty was scheduled to expire. See, for example, the statement of E. C. Aldridge, *FY 1976 Authorizations*, p. 2119.

70. Schlesinger, *Defense Department Report FY 1976*, p. I-14. *Appropriations Hearings FY 1975*, p. 89.

71. *FY 1976 Authorizations*, pp. 2079, 2089-2095. See also Schlesinger's statement in *Counterforce Hearings*, p. 8; McIntyre, "Security Through Détente," p. 8; Admiral Thomas Moorer, *Arms Control Implications*, p. 19.

72. McIntyre, "Security Through Détente," p. 8.

73. For a discussion of this point, see Rathjens, "Flexible Response Options"; Johansen, "Countercombatant Strategy," pp. 47-53; McIntyre, "Security Through Détente"; Warnke, *Nuclear Weapons Hearings*, pp. 55, 139; and Muskie, *Arms Control Implications*, p. 145.

74. See Schlesinger, *Strategic Policies Hearings*, p. 35; *Defense Department Report FY 1976*, p. I-11.

75. *New York Times*, December 3, 1974.

76. Kissinger, "*Newsweek* Interview," *Department of State Bulletin*, 72 (January 21, 1975), 58.

77. *SIPRI Yearbook 1974*, p. 123.

78. Ibid., pp. 159-160.

79. *New York Times*, December 3, 1974.

80. *New York Times*, December 8, 1974.

81. *New York Times*, December 18, 1974.

82. Outlays are funds actually spent, whether authorized in the current or previous years. Budget authority suggests the trend of future outlays.

83. *Defense Department Report FY 1976*, Appendices A, B, and C.

84. John W. Finney, *New York Times*, February 9, 1975. Pentagon calculations showed that 1974 defense spending was 18 percent below the level of 1964, before the Vietnam buildup. In taking account of inflation to arrive at this figure, however, officials not only compensated for price increases because of inflation but also for military pay increases. This questionable accounting procedure ignored that most of the pay increases were made not to offset inflation, but because of a political decision in 1968 that the military should receive higher pay, comparable to that of civilians.

85. *New York Times*, February 4, 1975; *Defense Department Report FY 1976*, Table 2, Appendix B.

86. *New York Times*, November 19, 1975.

87. *FY 1976 Authorizations*, p. 28; Donald H. Rumsfeld, *Annual Defense Department Report FY 1977*, pp. 28-30.

88. *Defense Department Report FY 1976*, p. I-26, Appendix A, p. A-1.

89. *New York Times*, February 7, 1975.

90. *New York Times*, December 4, 1974.

91. *FY 1976 Authorizations*, pp. 2001-2003.

92. U.S. Congress, House, Committee on Armed Services, *Hearings on Military Posture and H.R. 3689, Department of Defense Authorization for Appropriations for Fiscal Year 1976 and 197T*, p. 985. Hereafter cited as *Military Posture Hearings*.

93. *FY 1976 Authorizations*, pp. 2773, 2789, 3995; *Military Posture Hearings*, p. 237.

94. *Appropriations Hearings Fiscal 1975*, pp. 483-484.

95. *FY 1976 Authorizations*, p. 2775.

96. "Remarks by Hon. James R. Schlesinger, Secretary of Defense, at Rollout Ceremony for B-1 Bomber," ibid., p. 2115.

97. " 'Bill Moyers' Journal,' " p. 176.

98. *New York Times*, December 3, 1974.

99. " 'Bill Moyers' Journal,' " p. 176.

100. *Department of State Bulletin*, 71 (December 23, 1974), 863, 865; *New York Times*, November 25, 1974.

101. *Department of State Bulletin*, 71 (December 30, 1974), 910. See also " 'Bill Moyers' Journal,' " p. 176.

102. *New York Times*, December 23, 1974.

103. *Department of State Bulletin*, 71 (December 30, 1974), 912. Emphasis added.

104. Ibid., p. 913.

105. Ibid. Emphasis added.

106. Editorial, *New York Times*, December 26, 1974; see also the editorial of November 29, 1974.

107. Frye, "U.S. Decision Making for SALT," in Willrich and Rhinelander, *SALT*, p. 76; see also Donald R. Westervelt, "The Essence of Armed Futility," p. 703.

108. Kissinger, "*Newsweek* Interview," p. 58.

109. "In essence, both sides have agreed not to challenge the effectiveness of each other's deterrent missile forces." "Current Negotiations on Arms Limitations," *U.S. Arms Control and Disarmament Agency*, No. 72 (April 1974), p. 1.

110. See *SIPRI Yearbook 1973*, p. 18.

111. For the text of the treaty, see U.S. Arms Control and Disarmament Agency, *International Negotiations on the Treaty on the Nonproliferation of Nuclear Weapons* (Washington, D.C., 1969).

112. See Alva Myrdal, "The High Price of Nuclear Arms Monopoly," p. 30.

113. The text is in U.S. Arms Control and Disarmament Agency, *Arms Control and Disarmament Agreements* (Washington, D.C.: Government Printing Office, 1975), pp. 40-42. For comprehensive and penetrating analysis of the failure of the superpowers to work seriously for arms reductions, see William Epstein, *The Last Chance*, and Alva Myrdal, *The Game of Disarmament*.

114. Myrdal, "High Price," p. 36.

115. *New York Times*, June 26, 1975.

116. U.S. Arms Control and Disarmament Agency, *World Military Expenditures and Arms Trade 1963-1973*, p. 72. Hereafter cited as *World Military Expenditures*.

117. U.S. Congress, Senate, Committee on Foreign Relations, *Foreign Assistance Authorization 1974*, p. 245.

118. U.S. Congress, House, Committee on Foreign Affairs, *Fiscal Year 1975 Foreign Assistance Request*, p. 74. Hereafter cited as *FY 1975 Foreign Assistance Request*.

119. *New York Times*, April 14, 1975.

120. Ibid. The United States' share of total world exports was 54.5 percent; the Soviet share was 27.5 percent.

121. *Foreign Assistance Authorization 1974*, p. 69.

122. An analysis of the State Department study is in the *New York Times*, October 21, 1975.

123. The secretary of defense has used financial and political inducements to expand U.S. arms sales abroad. For example, see inducements to Belgium in 1975 to purchase F-16s, *New York Times*, June 5, 1975.

124. *Foreign Assistance Authorization 1974*, p. 248. This statement was the written response of the Department of Defense to questions raised in the Senate Foreign Relations Committee.

125. *The Baltimore Sun*, February 26, 1975. The Arabian American Oil Company (owned 60 percent by Saudi Arabia and 40 percent by Exxon), as well as Texaco, Standard Oil of California, and Mobil Oil have exported from the United States "firearms, ammunitions, explosives, aircraft and related articles, military electronics, auxiliary military equipment and miscellaneous articles." From the report of the State Department's Office of Munitions Control, quoted in the *New York Times*, October 21, 1975.

126. *FY 1975 Foreign Assistance Request*, p. 80. Schlesinger also said the export of arms was used to continue "an uninterrupted access to [foreign] bases." Ibid., p. 44.

127. *New York Times*, April 14, 1975.

128. *New York Times*, February 20, 1975.

129. Schlesinger, *FY 1975 Foreign Assistance Request*, p. 44.

130. *FY 1976 Authorizations*, p. 433.

131. Charles R. Gellner, senior specialist in international relations, Foreign Affairs Division, Congressional Research Service, in U.S. Arms Control and Disarmament Agency, *The International Transfer of Conventional Arms: Report to Congress*, p. CRS-11. Hereafter cited as *Transfer of Arms*. This point is confirmed by Vice Admiral Ray Peet, director of Defense Security Assistance Agency, in *FY 1975 Foreign Assistance Request*, pp. 321-322, and by ACDA in *Transfer of Arms*, p. 94.

132. *Transfer of Arms*, p. 88.

133. Cf. Herbert York, who served on the president's Scientific Advi-

421

sory Committee during two administrations: "Over the last 30 years we have repeatedly taken unilateral actions that have unnecessarily accelerated the race. Our unilateral decisions have set the rate and scale for most of the individual steps in the strategic-arms race." *Race to Oblivion*, p. 230. See also Richard J. Barnet, *The Economy of Death*, especially chap. 11, and *Who Wants Disarmament?*; Jerome H. Spingarn, "The Cosmetics of Disarmament," *War/Peace Report*, 13 (June 1974), 11-13; Robert C. Johansen, "Arms Control Chicanery," *War/Peace Report*, 13 (June 1974), 16-19.

134. Rathjens, "Future Limitations of Strategic Arms," p. 231.

135. See Barnet, *The Economy of Death*; York, *Race to Oblivion*; Ralph E. Lapp, *The Weapons Culture*; John M. Swomley, *The Military Establishment*; Clark Mollenhoff, *The Pentagon*; Seymour Melman, *Pentagon Capitalism*; Fred J. Cook, *The Warfare State*; Tristram Coffin, *The Armed Society*; George Thayer, *The War Business*.

136. For comment on the need to remain number one, see the statements by Nixon, quoted in *Arms Control Implications*, p. 44; in Chalmers Roberts, "The Road to Moscow," Willrich and Rhinelander, *SALT*, p. 32; Schlesinger, *Defense Department Report FY 1976*, p. 11-1; *Appropriations Hearings FY 1975*, p. 65; *Military Posture Hearings*, pp. 92, 238; *Nuclear Weapons Hearings*, p. 173; Malcolm Currie, in *FY 1976 Authorizations*, p. 2639.

137. Press conference of December 6, 1974, Department of Defense, mimeo.

138. *Arms Control Implications*, p. 8.

139. *Defense Department Report FY 1976*, p. 11-7.

140. *Department of State Bulletin*, 71 (December 30, 1974), 913.

141. Ted Greenwood and Michael L. Nacht, "New Nuclear Debate," p. 778.

142. *FY 1976 Authorizations*, p. 2639.

143. *Military Posture Hearings*, pp. 238, 246.

144. See Rathjens, "Future Limitations of Strategic Arms," p. 230; Herbert York, *Arms Control Implications*, p. 99.

145. He made this claim in *Department of State Bulletin*, 71 (December 30, 1974), 910.

146. Ibid.

147. Ibid.

148. Gerard Smith, former director of the Arms Control and Disarmament Agency, has noted that the 1972 ABM Treaty "bans deployment of a defensive system not based on the type of ABM existing in 1972, thus banning exotic future systems. . . . The ABM Treaty proved that qualitative restrictions can be negotiated." See Gerard C. Smith, "SALT After Vladivostok," p. 11.

149. Leslie H. Gelb, "Our Arms Offer Rejected by U.S.," *New York Times*, January 18, 1976.

150. *Department of State Bulletin*, 71 (December 30, 1974), 910.

151. *Appropriations Hearings FY 1975*, p. 293.
152. *New York Times*, June 16, 1975.
153. *New York Times*, December 6, 1974.
154. The following brief discussion of technocratic pressures for weapons innovation is based in part on *SIPRI Yearbook 1974*, pp. 125-128.
155. Ibid., p. 127.
156. Herbert York, in *Arms Control Implications*, pp. 83, 99; Rathjens, "Future Limitations of Strategic Arms," p. 228; Alton Frye, in Willrich and Rhinelander, *SALT*, p. 97.
157. *Nuclear Weapons Hearings*, p. 140. Emphasis added. Schlesinger confirmed this description, ibid., p. 197.
158. General William J. Evans, deputy chief of staff for research and development, for example, argued that the United States needed to build additional B-1 prototypes to keep Rockwell plants operating. *Fiscal Year 1976 Authorizations*, p. 1962.
159. See *SIPRI Yearbook 1974*, p. 126.
160. *Nuclear Weapons Hearings*, p. 190.
161. *FY 1976 Authorizations*, p. 205.
162. *New York Times*, December 3, 1974.
163. *New York Times*, April 11, 1975.
164. *New York Times*, December 18, 1974.
165. *New York Times*, December 4, 1974.
166. This debate included the following articles in *Foreign Policy*: Albert Wohlstetter, "Is There a Strategic Arms Race?" pp. 3-20 and "Rivals, But No 'Race,'" pp. 48-81; Philip Odeen, "In Defense of the Defense Budget," pp. 93-108; Paul H. Nitze, Joseph Alsop, Morton H. Halperin, and Jeremy Stone, "Comments," No. 16, pp. 82-92; Paul H. Nitze, "The Strategic Balance Between Hope and Skepticism," pp. 136-156; David Aaron, "SALT: A New Concept," pp. 157-165; Paul C. Warnke, "Apes on a Treadmill," pp. 12-29; Johan Jorgen Holst, "A Strategic Arms Race? What is Really Going On?", pp. 152-162; Michael L. Nacht, "The Delicate Balance of Error," pp. 163-177; Albert Wohlstetter, "How to Confuse Ourselves," pp. 170-198.
167. Wohlstetter, "How to Confuse Ourselves," p. 179.
168. Ibid., p. 198.
169. Wohlstetter, "Rivals, But No 'Race,'" p. 57. The same point is made in Wohlstetter, "How to Confuse Ourselves," p. 176.
170. Wohlstetter, "Rivals, But No 'Race,'" pp. 79-80.
171. Wohlstetter, "How to Confuse Ourselves," p. 178. Emphasis added.
172. Of course, if spending decreased every year until it was less than required for weapons maintenance, then a genuine change in direction—toward disarmament—would occur through the decay of existing weapons.

423

173. See the discussion of the data in Nacht, "The Delicate Balance of Error," p. 172; also, Alton H. Quanbeck and Barry M. Blechman, *Strategic Forces*, pp. 91-94.
174. Wohlstetter, "How to Confuse Ourselves," pp. 176-177.
175. For example, see the statement of Senator Clifford Case in *Arms Control Implications*, p. 179.
176. Ibid., p. 167.
177. For discussion of the idea that recent innovations have impaired security, see Schlesinger, *Nuclear Weapons Hearings*, pp. 167-168; Edmund Muskie, *Arms Control Implications*, p. 23; Paul Warnke, *Nuclear Weapons Hearings*, pp. 206-207; Carl Kaysen, *Arms Control Implications*, pp. 66-67.

   There was no widespread public debate about the real possibility that the citizens of both the Soviet Union and the United States, to say nothing of the rest of the world, would all have been better off if only one side had such a substantial counterforce capability, regardless of whether it was Soviet or American. Even if a partial first-strike capability could not have been altogether prohibited, the security of the people of the United States could probably have been enhanced by letting the Soviet Union go ahead with such a capacity but preventing the U.S. government from matching it. If only one side had such a capability, "crisis instability" could have been avoided.

178. *New York Times*, December 4, 1974.
179. *New York Times*, December 1, 1974.
180. Immediately after the Vladivostok meeting, Secretary Kissinger said that the "Backfire" and the FB-111 were not considered strategic weapons and therefore did not come within the overall ceilings. Since the Soviet Union had deployed only 25 planes within a year after the Vladivostok meeting, their impact on the Soviet strategic force was not large. The dispute, however, posed a threat to the consummation of the entire agreement. For an analysis of the shifting Kissinger and Schlesinger positions, see John W. Finney's article in the *New York Times*, October 10, 1975. See also *New York Times*, October 14, 1975, and October 15, 1975.
181. At Vladivostok, the participants specified that airplane-launched missiles with a range of more than 360 miles were to be considered as strategic delivery vehicles. Later, the United States maintained that this understanding included only ballistic missiles which follow a high trajectory after being launched. The Soviet Union contended that the agreement also covered airbreathing missiles which follow a low trajectory and may be guided constantly during their flights. See John W. Finney, "The Soviet Backfire Bomber and the U.S. Cruise Missile," *New York Times*, December 3, 1975.
182. *New York Times*, June 16, 1975; October 15, 1975.
183. *New York Times*, December 3, 1975.

184. Address at the United Nations, March 17, 1977, text in *New York Times*, March 18, 1977; commencement address at Notre Dame University, text in *New York Times*, May 23, 1977.

185. Text in *New York Times*, January 21, 1977.

186. The Carter administration approved the first stage of development for a more accurate and powerful warhead, the Mark 12 A, which would sharply increase the ability of the United States to attack Soviet missiles in their silos. Improved guidance systems were to be installed on Minutemen in 1977, with the new warhead itself planned for completion in 1979. *New York Times*, June 1, 1977.

187. *New York Times*, October 23, 1977.

188. *New York Times*, February 13, 1978.

189. *New York Times*, January 30, 1977. See also his comments in *New York Times*, October 11, 1977; address at Notre Dame University, *New York Times*, May 23, 1977.

190. *New York Times*, February 13, 1978.

191. *New York Times*, October 11, 1977.

192. *SIPRI Yearbook 1974*, pp. 508-509. The data for 1973 are preliminary.

193. Marek Thee, "The Nuclear Momentum: Arms Race and Disarmament," *Internasjonal Politikk* (Oslo), No. 1 (1975), reprinted in part in *Bulletin of Peace Proposals*, 6, No. 2 (1975), 133.

194. Many advocates of nuclear deterrence have informed Congress that deployment of additional weapons was wasteful and unnecessary for protecting security. Carl Kaysen, a former consultant to the Defense Department's Weapons Systems Evaluation Group, and deputy assistant to the president for national security affairs, testified: "It is my judgment that we would be making no compromise with our security and sustaining no deterioration of the effectiveness of our deterrent posture if we forewent all new developments and deployments of land-based ICBMs and long-range aircraft. . . . [T]here are no reasons that can justify planning the deployment of new systems." *Arms Control Implications*, p. 62.

195. For discussion of this point, see Falk, *A Study of Future Worlds*, pp. 50-52, 224-276, and "Arms Control, Foreign Policy, and Global Reform," p. 52, n. 36; W. Michael Reisman, "Sanctions and Enforcements," in Cyril E. Black and Richard A. Falk, eds., *The Future of the International Legal Order*, III, 273-335.

THREE. UNITED STATES FOREIGN AID TO INDIA

1. The justness of the current distribution of wealth is considered here, as well as the provision of necessities for physical existence, although the distributive issue could as well be viewed as part of worldwide human rights (V_3).

2. *New York Times*, January 21, 1949.

425

3. Data for these computations are taken from U.S. Agency for International Development, Office of Statistics and Reports, *U.S. Economic Assistance Programs Administered by the Agency for International Development and Predecessor Agencies, April 3, 1948 to June 30, 1971*; after 1971, U.S. Agency for International Development, Statistics and Reports Division, Office of Financial Management, *U.S. Overseas Loans and Grants and Assistance from International Organizations: Obligations and Loan Authorizations, 1945-73, 1945-74, 1945-75, 1945-76.*

4. See Jagdish N. Bhagwati, *Amount and Sharing of Aid*, pp. 14-15. Some Marxist writers, in contrast, assume that the aid is "excess capital" and that the various returns derived from loans to India could be interpreted as producing net returns for the donating country. This would be true if the opportunity cost were zero.

5. United States Congress, Senate, Committee on Foreign Relations, *United States Participation in ADB* [Asian Development Bank] *and IDA* [International Development Association], p. 45. Hereafter cited as *ADB Hearings*.

6. See Willard L. Thorp, *The Reality of Foreign Aid*, p. 210; *The Economist*, March 30, 1974, p. 127.

7. *The Economist*, March 30, 1974, p. 127.

8. U.S. Congress, House of Representatives, Committee on Foreign Affairs, Subcommittee on the Near East and South Asia, *Indian Rupee Settlement Agreement*, p. 2. Hereafter cited as *Rupee Settlement Hearings*. See also, *New York Times*, April 27, 1974.

9. Bhagwati, *Amount and Sharing*, p. 17.

10. William S. Gaud, "Foreign Aid: What It Is; How It Works; Why We Provide It," p. 603.

11. Bhagwati, *Amount and Sharing*, p. 18. Emphasis added. Swedish economist Gunnar Myrdal estimates that "considerably less than half of the appropriations and disbursements . . . would remain as genuine aid" after making necessary adjustments to nominal values. Gunnar Myrdal, *The Challenge of World Poverty*, p. 352.

12. Bhagwati, *Amount and Sharing*, p. 18. See also UNCTAD Conference, New Delhi, Second Session, *Problems and Policies of Financing*, IV (New York: United Nations, 1968), 45-110; John Pincus, "The Cost of Foreign Aid," *The Review of Economics and Statistics*, 45 (November 1963), 360-367.

13. In order to satisfy its own desire to avoid "charity" and to demonstrate its self-reliance, the Indian government itself has, on occasion, preferred loans to grants. Nevertheless, the point remains that loans constitute a substantially lighter form of wealth redistribution than do grants.

14. The data for these computations are taken from sources cited in note 3.

15. See the national income figures in United Nations Department of Economic and Social Affairs, Statistical Office, *Yearbook of National Accounts Statistics*.

16. "Stability" in fact meant preserving an international structure that enabled the United States to protect or increase its preeminence in the global distribution of power and wealth.

17. Richard Nixon, "President's Message Transmitting Draft of Proposed Legislation to Amend the Foreign Assistance Act of 1961," U.S. Congress, House of Representatives, Committee on Foreign Affairs, *Fiscal Year 1975 Foreign Assistance Request*, pp. 717, 720. Hereafter cited as *FY 1975 Hearings*.

18. Richard Nixon, "Foreign Assistance for the 'Seventies,' " pp. 372-378.

19. John A. Hannah, "Institutional Problems in the Developing Countries," p. 301. See also William J. Casey, "A Comprehensive Development Policy for the United States," p. 692.

20. Lyndon Johnson, "To Build the Peace—The Foreign Aid Program for Fiscal 1969," p. 322.

21. Lyndon Johnson, "The Importance of Foreign Aid to U.S. Security and World Peace," p. 178.

22. Richard Nixon, "U.S. Foreign Policy for the 1970's: Building for Peace," p. 385.

23. Lyndon Johnson, "Letter of Transmittal," U.S. Agency for International Development, *The Foreign Assistance Program: Annual Report to the Congress, 1964*, p. iii. Hereafter cited as *AID Report*, various years.

24. Dean Rusk, "Testimony Before the Senate Committee on Appropriations," *Department of State Bulletin*, 59 (October 21, 1968), 419. See also U.S. Agency for International Development, *Principles of Foreign Economic Assistance*, p. 1.

25. Nicholas Katzenbach, "United States Policy Toward the Developing World," p. 209. See also the statement of G. Lewis Jones, assistant secretary of state for Near Eastern and South Asian affairs, United States Congress, Senate, Committee on Foreign Relations, *Mutual Security Act of 1960*, p. 266. Hereafter cited as *Mutual Security Act of 1960*.

For other examples of the theme that peace is indivisible and stability in the newly independent countries is essential for American security, see the following statements: John Foster Dulles, United States Congress, Senate, Committee on Foreign Relations, *Mutual Security Act of 1954*, pp. 8-9; Harold E. Stassen, director of Foreign Operations Administration, ibid., p. 42; G. Lewis Jones, *Mutual Security Act of 1960*, p. 273; Secretary of State Christian Herter, ibid., pp. 5-11; Cyrus Vance, "Secretary Testifies on Administration's Approach to Foreign Assistance," p. 237.

26. Henry Kissinger, "The Foreign Assistance Program and Global Stability," p. 290. Hereafter cited as "The Foreign Assistance Program."

27. See, for example, Kissinger's emphasis on stability in *FY 1975 Hearings*, p. 2.

28. Kissinger, "The Foreign Assistance Program," p. 290.

29. Henry Kissinger, "The Foreign Assistance Program: A Vital Tool in Building a More Cooperative World," p. 50. Hereafter cited as "A Vital Tool."

30. *New York Times*, July 17, 1973.

31. Although much of the aid to European governments was given for the purpose of rebuilding Europe after World War II, it should be noted that these figures from 1949 through 1973 do not include postwar relief to Europe, which began in 1945.

32. *AID Report*, 1962, p. 4.

33. United States Congress, House, Committee on Foreign Affairs, *Report of Special Study Mission to Pakistan, India, Thailand, and Indochina*, p. 21. Hereafter cited as *Study Mission Report*.

34. Ibid., p. 1.

35. *Mutual Security Act of 1954*, pp. 8-9.

36. *Mutual Security Act of 1960*, p. 7.

37. U.S. Congress, House of Representatives, Committee on Foreign Affairs, *Foreign Assistance Act of 1964*, pp. 83-85. Also quoted in Michael Hudson, *Super Imperialism*, pp. 156-157.

38. Dulles had denounced neutralism several times during his career. He once explained that in a world where there are aggressors "neutrality is no protection, rather it encourages aggression. [A] . . . policy of neutrality means in fact 'conniving at aggression.' " See Dulles, "Peace Without Fear," p. 729. On another occasion, Dulles said that "neutrality . . . except under exceptional circumstances . . . is an immoral conception." Quoted by Emmet John Hughes, *America the Vincible* (Harmondsworth, Middlesex: Penguin, 1960), p. 241; also, E. I. Brodkin, "United States Aid to India and Pakistan," p. 665.

39. *Study Mission Report*, p. 21. The curious sentence referring to the Western world must have meant to the authors that allies of the United States were part of the Western world. In conventional usage, of course, Sweden could not leave the Western world by being a nonally, nor India become part of the Western world by becoming an ally. This demonstrates the extent to which human affairs were viewed through the distorting lenses of military alliances.

40. *Mutual Security Act of 1960*, pp. 8, 10-11.

41. Daniel Parker, *FY 1975 Hearings*, p. 92.

42. The long-range consequences, of course, may be socially explosive. After two decades of development in India, the problems of

428

the very poor had not decreased. "There is a consensus that the discontent of the disadvantaged is nearing some kind of ignition point." John P. Lewis, *Wanted in India*, p. 27.

43. Max F. Millikan and Walt W. Rostow, *A Proposal*, p. 39. Emphasis added.

44. Ibid., p. 33.

45. W. W. Rostow, *The Relation Between Political and Economic Development*, speech before the Foreign Service Institute, October 31, 1956, Massachusetts Institute of Technology, Center for International Studies, Economic Development Program, General Project Pamphlets, 1, 10; see also Walt W. Rostow, *The United States in the World Arena*, p. 252.

46. Rostow, *Relation Between Political and Economic Development*, p. 1.

47. *Mutual Security Act of 1954*, p. 67.

48. Ibid., pp. 14-15, 20.

49. Johnson, "To Build the Peace," p. 322. Rusk believed that insufficient aid would result in violent revolutions, "Testimony," pp. 421-422. See also Thorp, *Reality of Foreign Aid*, p. 30; John P. Lewis, *Wanted in India*, p. 27.

50. Richard Nixon, "Reform of the U.S. Foreign Assistance Program," p. 614. Zbigniew Brzezinski argued in 1956 that rapid industrialization might encourage totalitarian regimes in the less developed countries. But, in his view, the great tragedy was that "any effort to slow down the development of these areas will immediately play into the hands of the extremists, particularly the Communists, who are waiting on the sidelines." "The Politics of Underdevelopment," p. 73.

51. *Foreign Assistance Act of 1961*, p. 424; *AID Report, 1962*, p. 2.

52. *Mutual Security Act of 1954*, p. 5. The sentiment regarding competition with China was echoed by Henry Byroade, assistant secretary of state for Near Eastern, South Asian and African affairs, ibid., p. 282, as well as by Senators J. W. Fulbright, ibid., p. 72 and Alexander Smith, ibid., p. 14. See also the statement of Vice-President Richard Nixon in *India and the United States*, ed. Selig S. Harrison, p. 144; Henry Kissinger's press conference of December 27, 1973, quoted by Daniel Moynihan in *Rupee Settlement Hearings*, p. 7; Katzenbach, "United States Policy," p. 210.

53. *Mutual Security Act of 1954*, p. 15.

54. John Kennedy, address before the White House Conference on Export Expansion, *Department of State Bulletin*, 49 (October 14, 1960), 597-598.

55. Bruce Nissen, "Building the World Bank," in Steve Weissman, ed., *The Trojan Horse*, p. 39.

56. United States Congress, House, Committee on Foreign Affairs, *Mutual Development and Cooperation Act of 1973*, pp. 47-48. Hereafter cited as *Mutual Development and Cooperation Act of 1973*.

57. Hannah, "Institutional Problems," p. 300.
58. Secretary of the Treasury, George P. Shultz, *ADB Hearings*, p. 11. Also, Hannah, *Mutual Development and Cooperation Act of 1973*, p. 51.
59. William J. Casey, "A Comprehensive Development Policy," pp. 692-693. See also Cyrus Vance, "Secretary Vance Emphasizes Importance of Foreign Assistance Programs," p. 336.
60. Casey, *ADB Hearings*, pp. 55-56.
61. Gaud, "Foreign Aid," p. 603. See also, Myrdal, *Challenge of World Poverty*, p. 355.
62. Quoted from a speech by George D. Woods of February 9, 1968, in Myrdal, *Challenge of World Poverty*, p. 359. See also William J. Casey, "A Comprehensive Development Policy," pp. 692-693.
63. Kissinger, *FY 1975 Hearings*, p. 4.
64. Rusk, "Testimony," p. 419. See also, Casey, "A Comprehensive Development Policy," p. 692.
65. Charles O. Sethness, U.S. Congress, House, Committee on Appropriations, Subcommittee on Foreign Operations and Related Agencies, *Foreign Assistance and Related Agencies Appropriations for 1975*, p. 844. The source of the study quoted in testimony is: *Mining and Minerals 1973*, Second Annual Report of the Secretary of the Interior Under the Mining and Minerals Policy Act of 1970 (Washington, D.C.: Government Printing Office, 1974).
66. India's main exports are jute products, tea, and cotton textiles. The United States is one of India's principal trading partners, but imports from India are a small part of total U.S. imports. In 1972, the United States exported goods worth $349.9 million and imported goods valued at $426.5 million. *ADB Hearings*, p. 58. India is a major supplier of sheet mica, the U.S. supply of which is 100 percent imported. *FY 1975 Hearings*, p. 734. In 1974, Ambassador Moynihan noted U.S. interest in offshore oil.
67. The desire for United States investment and sales in India, noted earlier, was probably a stronger motive for determining the mode of assistance to India than India's raw materials.
68. Douglas Dillon, "The Contribution of Trade to the Cause of Peace," p. 881.
69. *Mutual Development and Cooperation Act of 1973*, p. 255.
70. *ADB Hearings*, pp. 55-56.
71. *Rupee Settlement Hearings*, p. 7.
72. United States Congress, Senate, Committee on Foreign Relations, *American Private Enterprise, Foreign Economic Development and the AID Program* (Washington, D.C.: Government Printing Office, 1957), p. xiii. Emphasis added. Quoted in Leo Tansky, *U.S. and U.S.S.R. Aid to Developing Countries*, p. 6.
73. *Mutual Security Act of 1954*, p. 50.
74. William J. Casey, "The Rule of Law in International Economic Affairs," p. 326.

75. *Mutual Development and Cooperation Act of 1973,* p. 255; Casey, "The Rule of Law," p. 326.
76. See Richard Nixon, *AID Report, 1969*, p. iii.
77. Letter from E. D. Kenna, president of the National Association of Manufacturers, to Thomas E. Morgan, chairman of the House Committee on Foreign Affairs, *Mutual Development and Cooperation Act of 1973,* p. 647.

    David Rockefeller, president of Chase Manhattan Bank, expressed a similar hope that development aid would concentrate "particularly on those problems so basic to the broad modernization of the developing countries, including food production, rural development, education, health, and family planning." Ibid., p. 497.
78. Kenna, ibid., p. 647.
79. Ibid., p. 497.
80. Ibid., p. 495.
81. Katzenbach, "United States Policy," p. 210. See also Herter, *Mutual Security Act of 1960*, p. 8.
82. Gaud, "Foreign Aid," p. 605.
83. See Kissinger, *FY 1975 Hearings*, p. 10; Cyrus Vance, "Secretary Vance Gives Overview of Foreign Assistance Programs" (statement made before the Subcommittee on Foreign Operations of the House Committee on Appropriations on March 2, 1977), p. 284.
84. *AID Report, 1964*, p. iii.
85. Johnson, "To Build the Peace," p. 322.
86. Quoted by Lloyd Black, *The Strategy of Foreign Aid*, p. 20.
87. Kissinger, "A Vital Tool," p. 50. An earlier expression of the global dimension was made by William Rogers: "The world remains divided politically, but it is being drawn together functionally. U.S. foreign relations increasingly reflect the need to deal with issues—many of them new ones—which are global, not bilateral, in nature." William Rogers, "United States Foreign Policy 1969-70," p. 474.
88. Cyrus Vance, "Secretary Vance Attends Ministerial Meeting of the Conference on International Economic Cooperation," p. 645.
89. Jimmy Carter, "Peace, Arms Control, World Economic Progress, Human Rights," p. 333.
90. U.S. Department of State, "North-South Dialogue," pp. 235-236. Confirmation of the intention not to restructure the global economy is found in the March 22, 1977 statement of the Deputy Assistant Secretary for Near East and South Asia, Adolph Dubs, before the House Committee on International Relations, "Department Discusses South Asia and U.S. Assistance Programs," pp. 344-346.
91. Douglas Dillon, *Mutual Security Act of 1960*, p. 51.
92. *AID Report, 1964*, p. 19.
93. Such a proposal was made because tied aid was (1) economically

431

costly to the recipient; (2) politically irritating to U.S. relations with the less developed countries; and (3) not so important for growing U.S.-based multinational corporations, which could often sell goods at a profit from one of their foreign subsidiaries.

94. "Fertilizer Group Raps AID Program Change as Harmful to Industry," *Journal of Commerce*, November 9, 1970. Quoted in Michael Hudson, *Super Imperialism*, p. 147.

95. U.S. Agency for International Development, *AID's Challenge in an Interdependent World* (Washington, D.C.: AID, 1977), p. 6. Hereafter cited as *AID's Challenge*.

96. Gaud, "Foreign Aid," p. 603. Secretary Dulles testified that all dollars of the Mutual Security program directly or indirectly go into the payroll of American workers. *Mutual Security Act of 1954*, p. 14.

97. *AID Report, 1965*, p. 8.

98. George P. Shultz, "Administration Stresses Importance of U.S. Action on Funding for IDA and ADB Replenishment," p. 735.

99. *AID Report, 1968*, p. 2.

100. Thorp, *Reality of Foreign Aid*, p. 273.

101. Another indication of the self-serving nature of foreign aid is found in the return on investment that often is a companion of foreign assistance and a result of perpetuating stability in the less developed countries. Senator Charles Mathias noted in 1969 that "capital flows from Latin America and into the United States are now over four times as great as the flow south. The countries of Latin America, in a way, are actually giving foreign aid to the United States, the wealthiest country in the world." Quoted by Myrdal, *Challenge of World Poverty*, pp. 322-323, from a mimeographed speech delivered at the University of Maryland, July 22, 1969.

102. John W. Sewell, *The United States and World Development*, p. 2.

103. The extent to which U.S. aid may have prevented internal economic structural change in India is beyond the scope of this essay. There was, however, no doubt that some U.S. officials hoped aid would prevent radical change.

104. Nixon, "Reform of the U.S. Foreign Assistance Program," pp. 614, 624. According to W. W. Rostow, "In the Administration's initial strategic dispositions economic aid had only one clear purpose—to assist the nation's Eurasian allies to maintain deterrent forces on a scale sufficient for the United States to cut down its own ground forces and concentrate on weapons of mass destruction, their means of delivery, and the means of defense against them." See *The United States in the World Arena*, p. 364.

105. Kissinger, *FY 1975 Hearings*, p. 7; Cyrus Vance, "Secretary Testifies on Administration's Approach to Foreign Assistance."

106. *AID Report, 1967*, p. 1.

107. *New York Times*, April 27, 1974; Baldev Raj Nayar, "Treat India Seriously," p. 142.

108. Indian rupee payments for U.S. surpluses in effect helped finance U.S. private enterprise in India to the extent of 1,250,701,337 rupees from 1960 to 1972. *Rupee Settlement Hearings*, pp. 111-113.

109. For a more complete treatment, see John P. Lewis, *Quiet Crisis in India*, pp. 315-332; *Rupee Settlement Hearings*.

110. *New York Times*, June 18, 1974; January 30, 1975.

111. *New York Times*, June 18, 1974; February 19, 1975.

112. *New York Times*, June 18, 1974; *Rupee Settlement Hearings*, p. 3.

113. *Rupee Settlement Hearings*, p. 7.

114. *New York Times*, June 18, 1974; April 27, 1974.

115. *New York Times*, January 20, 1975; February 19, 1975.

116. *Rupee Settlement Hearings*, pp. 26-27.

117. Bhagwati, *Amount and Sharing*, p. 17.

118. Hudson, *Super Imperialism*, p. 145.

119. Thorp, *Reality of Foreign Aid*, p. 55.

120. These purposes included: "All USG expenditures in India, including Congressional travel, payment of official and personal obligations, international transportation, procurement for overseas use, payments to USG annuitants, contributions to international organizations." In addition, the Cooley loan portfolio for U.S. businesses was not transferred to the Indian government. *Rupee Settlement Hearings*, pp. 5-6, 15.

121. Ibid., pp. 7, 12.

122. According to the General Accounting Office and Ambassador Moynihan, "we could expect to spend only a small portion of these claims." The chairman of the subcommittee, Lee Hamilton, wrote that "rupees were coming into the account twice as quickly as we were able to spend them. . . . We would never be able to spend all the rupees we had." Ibid., pp. v, 2-6.

123. United States Congress, House, Committee on Foreign Affairs, *Mutual Security Act of 1958*, p. 388. Also cited in Tansky, *U.S. and U.S.S.R. Aid*, p. 5.

124. Katzenbach, "United States Policy," p. 211.

125. U.S. Congress, House, Committee on Foreign Affairs, *Mutual Security Act of 1955*, p. 99. Hereafter cited as *Mutual Security Act of 1955*.

126. See Lewis, *Quiet Crisis in India*, p. 253.

127. The single exception was Austria, unable to receive military aid because of its internationally guaranteed neutral status. The largest recipients of grant aid are listed in Table 3-8. For this comparison Iceland, Liberia, Libya, and Malta were omitted as their populations were each less than two million. The largest recipients of military aid are listed in Table 3-10.

128. In making comparisons of this sort, the specific rankings should not be given undue weight, as possible adjustments of data or differing approximations for missing data might make a difference of several places in rank. However, the enormous variations in the

amounts of aid between the top and the bottom of the list are profoundly significant.

129. See Table 3-3 above.

130. The differences have nothing to do with "ability to absorb aid." India could have easily utilized much more assistance. See Jagdish N. Bhagwati, ed., *Economics and World Order*, pp. 11-12.

131. In addition, these figures do not account for the inflationary trend of the dollar since 1949. Because the UK received the bulk of its aid earlier in time than India, and because the figures are given in current dollars, the UK received even more, compared to India, in actual purchasing power than the figures indicate. I have made these comparisons using data from the U.S. Agency for International Development, Statistics and Reports Division, *U.S. Overseas Loans and Grants*.

132. AID administrator Parker explained that economic assistance could have a military function. It served this end in Cambodia, for example, "by enabling the Cambodian Republic to remain in place and to resist the attacks of the Khmer Communists." Some AID funds also went to such "private" agencies as Air America, which carried out military functions for the CIA and Department of Defense. See *FY 1975 Hearings*, pp. 102, 122.

133. Myrdal, *Challenge of World Poverty*, p. 343.

134. *AID Report, 1967*, p. 5.

135. *New York Times*, January 9, 1975.

136. The General Assembly of the United Nations established a goal for capital transfers of one percent of national income for industrialized nations as early as 1960 [Resolution 1522 (xv)]. Before then, this figure was widely accepted among liberal writers and political parties, such as the British Labor party, which included it in its party platform in the 1950s. The original conception of one percent of national income referred only to official aid [Jagdish Bhagwati, *Amount and Sharing*, p. 45], but the UN discussions referred to both official capital flows and to private capital transfers. This goal was restated in 1961 in Assembly Resolution 1711 (xvi), at the beginning of the First United Nations Development Decade. It was later adopted at numerous other forums, including the UNCTAD Conferences in 1962 and 1968, and by the DAC. The inclusion of private capital flows, which are transferred at commercial rates and with the intent of profit-taking, makes the goal in effect lower than it should be, as well as misleading insofar as aid is viewed as a concessional flow of capital. Consequently, there is increasing awareness of the need to define a goal in terms of official flows alone. In 1968, at the New Delhi UNCTAD Conference, the less developed countries attempted to formulate a subsidiary target of .75 percent of GNP for official flows, but several donor countries opposed this move. The Pearson Commission

Report stated a target for official aid transfers at the level of .70 percent of GNP. See Bhagwati, *Amount and Sharing*, pp. 45, 47.

137. The Development Assistance Committee of the OECD includes major noncommunist industrial countries: Australia, Austria, Belgium, Canada, Denmark, France, Germany, Italy, Japan, Netherlands, Norway, Portugal, Sweden, Switzerland, United Kingdom, United States.

138. Organization for Economic Co-operation and Development, *Development Co-operation Efforts and Policies of the Members of the Development Assistance Committee*, 1973, p. 188. Hereafter cited as OECD *Development Co-operation*, various years.

139. *New York Times*, April 19, 1975. The others were Austria, Italy, and Switzerland.

140. Jonathan Power, "Cranking Up Oil Producers' Aid-Giving Machines," *New York Times*, April 15, 1975.

141. See Sewell, *United States and World Development*, p. 127.

142. See Bhagwati, *Amount and Sharing*, p. 117; David Wall, *The Charity of Nations*, p. 21.

143. Myrdal, *Challenge of World Poverty*, p. 337.

144. In addition, during some recent years the United States has extended less aid than it received in payment from earlier aid programs. Michael Hudson reported that in 1970, the United States earned $1.3 billion on its foreign aid programs, the amount by which its hard currency interest and principal repayments exceeded the balance of payments cost of its new aid extensions (*Super Imperialism*, p. 166).

145. United States Congress, Senate, Committee on Foreign Relations, *Technical Assistance*, 1957, pp. 18-19. Also cited in Hudson, *Super Imperialism*, p. 131.

146. If aid sprang more from strategic than humanitarian interests, one must ask: why was not more assistance given? Why was the program almost phased out in the early 1970s? There are many explanations for this, but only two need be mentioned here. First of all, Washington officials began to doubt that aid produced sufficient strategic dividends in countries like India—which refused to become client states—to justify it. India, as members of Congress never tired of pointing out, had refused to become a U.S. ally and in fact had improved relations with the Soviet Union (long before détente was fashionable in the United States). The absence of any important humanitarian concern for India in the extension of aid facilitated its decline after the strategic argument had been discredited.

Second, there was growing congressional dislike for bilateral aid that might result in new military involvements like Vietnam. Thus liberal critics joined the traditional conservative opponents of aid, who had seldom pretended that aid should be humanitarian.

435

The per capita data also show that officials' state-centric view of reality leads them to ignore the number of people living inside the legal shell of the state; aid is given to state entities instead of to people. Thus states with small populations, sometimes by legislative "accident," may receive higher aid per capita than larger, more populous societies. This state-centric perception of the world, therefore, adds to the propensity to deny the realization of V_2.

147. Leonard Woodcock, *Mutual Development and Cooperation Act of 1973*, p. 652.

148. William Rogers, "United States Foreign Policy," p. 724.

149. Although conclusions about U.S. aid policies to all countries can only be tentatively advanced from this limited study, the evidence collected here is typical of the entire aid program and is corroborated by the work of several other students of aid policies. See, for example, John G. Sommer, *Beyond Charity*; Bhagwati, *Amount and Sharing*; Bhagwati, ed., *Economics and World Order*, pp. 1-15; Myrdal, *Challenge of World Poverty*, pp. 3-29, 275-385; Thorp, *Reality of Foreign Aid*, pp. 128-148, 215-216, 234-244, 266-267, 324; Wall, *Charity of Nations*, pp. 32-49; Hudson, *Super Imperialism*; Denis Goulet and Michael Hudson, *The Myth of Aid*; Weissman, *The Trojan Horse*.

150. The text of Henry Kissinger's revealing interview with James Reston is in the *New York Times*, October 13, 1974. The new Carter perspective was discussed in the *New York Times*, July 7, 1976; see also Carter, "Basic Priorities"; Vance, "Secretary Vance Attends Ministerial Meeting," pp. 645-648.

151. *AID's Challenge*, p. 4; see also Michael Kent O'Leary, *The Politics of American Foreign Aid*, pp. 77, 112.

152. See Henry Kissinger, "A Vital Tool," p. 49.

153. Senator Mark Hatfield, *New York Times*, December 19, 1974.

154. Lewis reported that Indians were most vulnerable to foreign influence when suffering shortages of foreign exchange, *Wanted in India*, pp. 18-19.

155. William J. Barnds, "India and America at Odds," pp. 379-380.

156. Lewis, *Wanted in India*, pp. 20-21.

157. Cheryl Payer, "The IMF and the Third World," in Weissman, *The Trojan Horse*, p. 68; Nissen, "Building the World Bank," ibid., p. 55.

158. Herbert Feldman, "Aid as Imperialism?," p. 229.

159. One example is the aid-tying which insured U.S. corporate profits but gave lower priority to serving human needs in India.

160. Harrison, *India and the United States*, p. 143.

161. Speech by John Lewis at Princeton University, Woodrow Wilson School of Public and International Affairs, April 23, 1975.

162. Steve Weissman, "Inside the Trojan Horse," in *The Trojan Horse*, p. 13.

163. Ibid.

164. Lester Pearson, *The Crisis of Development*, p. 69; Goulet and Hudson, *Myth of Aid*, p. 18.

165. Henry Kissinger's opposition to a new global economic order in which prices offered for raw materials would be adjusted according to prices charged for manufactured goods was explicitly expressed in his speech on raw materials reported in *New York Times*, May 14, 1975.

166. *New York Times*, June 15, 1974.

167. George Ball, *The Discipline of Power*, pp. 222-223.

168. See Myrdal, *Challenge of World Poverty*, p. 347. Sweden perhaps provides the best evidence up to the present for realistic assessment of prospects for implementing some features of this approach. In Sweden, Myrdal reports, the only reason given for aid to the less developed countries "is the moral one of solidarity with people in distress." That is the same principle upon which Swedes have built their domestic welfare state (*Challenge of World Poverty*, p. 363). Sweden has rapidly increased its assistance, aid is not tied to purchases from Sweden, and about half of its aid is given through international organizations.

169. See Richard Barnet, *Intervention and Revolution* (New York: World Publishing Company, 1968).

170. William S. Gaud, "Development—A Balance Sheet," p. 705. See also Hannah, "Institutional Problems," p. 297, and John N. Irwin, "A Strengthened and Revitalized Foreign Aid Program," p. 659.

    In India in 1975, 65 percent of all deaths were under age five. Malnutrition was a direct or associated cause for at least 57 percent of all these deaths. See Parker's statement about the effects of poverty in *FY 1975 Hearings*, p. 161.

171. Lewis, *Quiet Crisis in India*, p. 11.

172. Ibid., p. 19.

173. Myrdal, *Challenge of World Poverty*, p. 313. See also Roger D. Hansen, "The Political Economy of North-South Relations," p. 927.

174. The annual spending of Americans on tobacco and alcohol is several times larger than the total foreign economic assistance program to all countries.

175. A useful guide is an aid burden index where burden index = total aid in millions of dollars/GNP per capita.

FOUR. THE UNITED STATES AND HUMAN RIGHTS IN CHILE

1. In the realm of international relations, human rights might be separated into individual and collective rights. The European

Convention of Human Rights contains some of the best examples of individual rights that are given an international status. Signatories to this agreement recognize an international legal obligation to respect the right to life; the right to liberty and security of person; the right to a fair trial; the right to an effective remedy if one's rights are violated; freedom from torture and from inhuman treatment; freedom of thought, conscience, and religion; freedom of expression and freedom of assembly and association. In these examples, individuals are treated as subjects of international law with specifically guaranteed rights. Other, historically older examples of individual rights under international law include the prohibition of slavery, the protection of innocents during war, and the obligation to insure humane treatment of prisoners of war.

On the other hand, collective human rights might include the following: the international protection of minority rights, such as required of the successor states of the Austro-Hungarian Empire after World War I; the prohibition of racial discrimination, such as expressed in frequent UN resolutions condemning apartheid; the prohibition of genocide; the obligation of colonial governments to protect the rights of non-self-governing peoples; and the right of all nations to self-determination.

Although the international community has recognized both individual and collective human rights, individual human rights have not played as important a part in foreign policy as have collective rights.

2. For discussion of this value, see Richard A. Falk, *A Study of Future Worlds*, pp. 23-26.

3. This chapter will not seek to resolve the debate over the degree of economic self-determination that must occur to achieve meaningful political self-determination. The analysis will focus on the exercise of political self-determination and U.S. policies—whether political or economic—relevant to that exercise.

4. One particular virtue of a normative approach to foreign policy analysis is illustrated here. The "level of analysis problem" is overcome insofar as a normative framework transcends the more traditional nation-state focus of inquiry. The Chilean case reveals official attitudes toward human rights in at least these three loci of human transactions: within Chile, between Chile and the United States, and within the United States.

5. General Assembly Resolution 420 (v), December 4, 1950. The United States and Britain cast votes against the resolution. See Louis K. Hyde, *The United States and the United Nations: Promoting the Public Welfare* (New York: Manhattan Publishing Company, 1960), p. 176.

6. In the crucial vote in 1955 on including the first article in the Cov-

enants, the United States, United Kingdom, and France voted "no." See Vernon Van Dyke, *Human Rights, the United States, and World Community*, p. 78; Arthur Henry Robertson, *Human Rights in the World*, p. 95.

7. United Nations General Assembly, Resolution 1514 (xv), December 14, 1960.

8. Harlan Cleveland, "Reflections on the Pacific Community," *Department of State Bulletin*, 48 (August 19, 1963), 286; Van Dyke, *Human Rights*, p. 79.

9. General Assembly *Official Records*, xxi, 1966. Annexes, Vol. iii, Agenda item 87, p. 91, quoted in Van Dyke, *Human Rights*, p. 79. A survey of UN practice led Rosalyn Higgins to the "inescapable" conclusion that self-determination "has developed into an international legal right." *The Development of International Law Through the Political Organs of the United Nations* (New York: Oxford University Press, 1963), p. 103.

10. Van Dyke, *Human Rights*, p. 80.

11. Article 15. Text is in Inter-American Institute of International Legal Studies, *The Inter-American System*, p. 133.

12. "Punta del Este Declaration," *American Journal of International Law* (December 1962), pp. 605, 607.

13. Article 6 of the U.S. Constitution.

14. United States Congress, Senate, Committee on Foreign Relations, *CIA Foreign and Domestic Activities*, pp. 13, 24. Hereafter cited as *CIA Hearings*. See also *New York Times*, September 8, 1974. Officials have reported that although the money was authorized it was not used because United States operatives in Chile thought the plan would backfire. The point remains that United States officials did authorize the use of money to reverse the results of an election.

15. *New York Times*, November 21, 1975.

16. This committee, headed by Senator Frank Church, was a subcommittee of the Senate Foreign Relations Committee. Other members included Stuart Symington, Edmund Muskie, Clifford Case, and Charles Percy. Chief counsel was Jerome Levinson.

17. United States Congress, Senate, Committee on Foreign Relations, Subcommittee on Multinational Corporations, *The International Telephone and Telegraph Company and Chile, 1970-71*, pp. 1, 7. Hereafter cited as *ITT and Chile*.

18. *New York Times*, September 8, 1974.

19. Richard R. Fagen, "The United States and Chile," pp. 309-310. None of these witnesses was recalled before the subcommittee, nor charged with contempt of Congress. Helms was later asked about CIA activity in Chile by the full Senate Foreign Relations Committee (*CIA Hearings*), but many of the questions raised were never fully answered.

20. U.S. Congress, Senate, Select Committee to Study Governmental

Operations with Respect to Intelligence Activities, *Covert Action in Chile 1963-73*, p. 1. Hereafter cited as *Covert Action in Chile*.

21. Ibid., p. 9.
22. Ibid., pp. 15-16.
23. Ibid., pp. 1, 9.
24. *CIA Hearings*, p. 8.
25. *New York Times*, January 19, 1975.
26. United States Congress, Senate, Committee on Foreign Relations, Subcommittee on Multinational Corporations, *Multinational Corporations and United States Foreign Policy*, Part 1, p. 96. Hereafter cited as *MNC Hearings*, with designation of whether source is Part I or Part II. See also *ITT and Chile*, p. 3.
27. *CIA Hearings*, p. 8.
28. Fagen, "United States and Chile," p. 298.
29. *ITT and Chile*, p. 4.
30. *Covert Action in Chile*, pp. 12-13.
31. *ITT and Chile*, p. 5.
32. *New York Times*, September 8, 1974; *CIA Hearings*, p. 8; *Covert Action in Chile*, p. 24. The latter sets the figure at $250,000.
33. *Covert Action in Chile*, p. 24; *CIA Hearings*, p. 8.
34. *ITT and Chile*, p. 7.
35. Ibid., p. 10.
36. Ibid.
37. Ibid., pp. 10-11.
38. Ibid., pp. 8, 16; *MNC Hearings*, Pt. II, p. 610. The Hendrix cable read: "The anti-Allende effort more than likely will require some outside financial support. The degree of this assistance will be known better around October 1. We have pledged our support, if needed." Hendrix denied in the hearings that he meant financial support (*MNC Hearings*, Pt. I, p. 136); text of message to Gerrity is in ibid., Pt. II, p. 610. In addition, ITT sought to support *El Mercurio*, the leading conservative paper in Chile (ibid., Pt. I, pp. 2-30).
39. Ibid., Pt. I, pp. 282, 313, 315.
40. Ibid., Pt. II, p. 610.
41. Ibid., Pt. I, p. 134.
42. *ITT and Chile*, pp. 6, 7; *MNC Hearings*, Pt. II, p. 608.
43. See *Covert Action in Chile*, pp. 1-40.
44. *ITT and Chile*, p. 9.
45. For example, see the Hendrix report to Gerrity (*MNC Hearings*, Pt. II, p. 610) about Korry's brusque, cold treatment of Allende's emissary sent to the U.S. embassy to pay respects and to say that the "Allende government wanted to have good relations with the Ambassador and the United States."
46. *MNC Hearings*, Pt. II, pp. 452-453; *ITT and Chile*, p. 9.

47. Fagen, "United States and Chile," p. 289; *New York Times*, September 8, 1974.

48. *ITT and Chile*, p. 9.

49. *Covert Action in Chile*, p. 23.

50. Ibid., p. 2.

51. The chief of the CIA operation in Chile told a high-ranking Chilean police official that "The U.S. Government favors a military solution and is willing to support it in any manner short of outright military intervention." U.S. Congress, Senate, Select Committee to Study Governmental Operations with Respect to Intelligence Activities, *Alleged Assassination Plots Involving Foreign Leaders*, p. 240. Hereafter cited as *Assassination Plots*. See also p. 232 and *Covert Action in Chile*, p. 26. In fact, military assistance was not cut off after Allende became president. Ibid., p. 37.

52. *Assassination Plots*, p. 232.

53. Ibid., p. 240.

54. Ibid., pp. 225-226.

55. After a meeting at the White House on October 15, 1970, the CIA headquarters cabled the results of the meeting to its mission in Santiago: "It is firm and continuing policy that Allende be overthrown by a *coup*. . . . We are to continue to generate maximum pressure toward this end utilizing every appropriate resource." Ibid., p. 243.

56. Ibid., pp. 239-246.

57. Ibid., p. 235.

58. Armando Uribe, *The Black Book of American Intervention in Chile*, pp. 43, 125-150.

59. Ibid., p. 125. Uribe provides a detailed description of the Pentagon plan for a takeover by Chilean armed forces (pp. 126-133).

60. Gabriel Garcia Marquez, "Why Allende Had to Die," *New Statesman*, 87 (March 15, 1974), 356.

61. Ibid.

62. *Covert Action in Chile*, pp. 38-39.

63. *CIA Hearings*, pp. 23-24; *Covert Action in Chile*, p. 27.

64. *New York Times*, September 20, 1974, and October 16, 1974. Fagen estimated the purchasing power of the 8 million was about 40 or 50 million ("United States and Chile," p. 298).

65. *New York Times*, September 8, 1974. This article by Seymour Hersh was based on the secret testimony of CIA Director William Colby.

66. Ibid., pp. 28, 31.

67. *New York Times*, September 20 and October 16, 1974; *Covert Action in Chile*, p. 2; Tad Szulc, "The CIA and Chile," *Washington Post*, October 21, 1973, reprinted in Laurence Birns, ed., *The End of Chilean Democracy*, p. 157. Many of the direct strike subsidies were

441

initiated in 1972 after Nathaniel Davis, a specialist on Eastern Europe, was assigned as ambassador to Chile.

68. *Covert Action in Chile*, p. 31.
69. *New York Times*, September 20, 1974.
70. Paul E. Sigmund, "Chile: What Was the U.S. Role? Less Than Charged," p. 148; *Covert Action in Chile*, p. 28. Two observers suggest that the abortive rightist coup leading to the assassination of the commander in chief of the Chilean army, General Schneider, may have contributed to the increase of leftist support from 36 to 50 percent in 1971. James F. Petras and Robert LaPorte, "Can We Do Business with Radical Nationalists? Chile: No," p. 132.
71. *Covert Action in Chile*, pp. 28-29.
72. *New York Times*, October 16, 1974.
73. Ibid.
74. *New York Times*, September 20, 1974.
75. *Covert Action in Chile*, p. 19.
76. Ibid., pp. 8, 29-30.
77. Ibid., p. 24.
78. Ibid., p. 25.
79. Ibid., pp. 7, 22.
80. Ibid., p. 25.
81. Ibid., p. 29.
82. Only Israel had a larger per capita debt. Pierre Kalfon, *Le Monde*, June 20 and 21, 1973, reprinted in Birns, *End of Chilean Democracy*, p. 11.
83. *ITT and Chile*, p. 13.
84. Ibid., pp. 13-14.
85. Ibid.
86. Ibid., p. 15.
87. Ibid.; also *MNC Hearings*, Pt. II, Appendix III.
88. *ITT and Chile*, p. 15.
89. Ibid., p. 16.
90. *Covert Action in Chile*, p. 33.
91. The discussion of the copper expropriation is based largely on Theodore Moran, *Multinational Corporations and the Politics of Dependence*, pp. 7, 120, 146, 150, 213-215; *Covert Action in Chile*, p. 33.
92. *New York Times*, Oct. 24, 1971.
93. Joseph Collins, "Tightening the Financial Knot," in Birns, *End of Chilean Democracy*, p. 179.
94. *New York Times*, August 15, 1971; Fagen, "United States and Chile," p. 305.
95. *MNC Hearings*, Pt. I, p. 334.
96. Petras and LaPorte, "Can We Do Business," pp. 141-142. After conducting extensive interviews with State Department officials, Petras and LaPorte concluded that the State Department had not

been frequently consulted about events after the copper nationalization crisis.

97. *New York Times*, August 15, 1971.

98. *Business Week*, July 10, 1971; quoted in Collins, "Tightening the Financial Knot," p. 183.

99. Collins, "Tightening the Financial Knot," p. 182.

100. *MNC Hearings*, Pt. I, p. 40.

101. Ibid., Pt. I, p. 332.

102. Collins, "Tightening the Financial Knot," p. 183.

103. Mark L. Chadwin, "Foreign Policy Report: Nixon Administration Debates New Position Paper on Latin America," *National Journal* (January 15, 1972), p. 97, quoted in Collins, "Tightening the Financial Knot," p. 180.

104. *New York Times*, August 15, 1971.

105. Collins, "Tightening the Financial Knot," p. 184.

106. *Covert Action in Chile*, p. 33.

107. *Wall Street Journal*, June 4, 1971; Collins, "Tightening the Financial Knot," p. 189.

108. Elizabeth Farnsworth, "Chile: What Was the U.S. Role? More Than Admitted," p. 131. This is part of an important exchange with Sigmund, "Chile."

109. *Covert Action in Chile*, p. 32; Jonathan Kandell, "Private U.S. Loan in Chile Up Sharply," *New York Times*, November 12, 1973, reprinted in Birns, *End of Chilean Democracy*, p. 194. For slightly different comparisons, see Farnsworth, "Chile," p. 132 and Sigmund, "Chile," p. 146.

110. Assistance in 1958 was higher than the average for 1952-59 because of the election that year. Thus 1959 is most useful as a base from which to measure.

111. Sigmund, "Chile," p. 144.

112. *MNC Hearings*, Pt. I, pp. 327, 335.

113. Collins, "Tightening the Financial Knot," p. 187; *Covert Action in Chile*, p. 33.

114. The Staff Report of the Senate Select Committee on Intelligence declared: "It seems clear from the pattern of U.S. economic actions and from the nature of debates within the Executive Branch that American economic policy was driven more by political opposition to an Allende regime than by purely technical judgments about Chile's finances." *Covert Action in Chile*, p. 35.

115. In the negotiations with Chile's principal foreign creditor nations, the United States alone refused to consider rescheduling Chile's foreign debt payments. Ibid., p. 35.

116. Collins, "Tightening the Financial Knot," p. 185; *Covert Action in Chile*, p. 33.

117. *MNC Hearings*, Pt. I, p. 389. William Bolin, senior vice-president, testified before the subcommittee.

118. *New York Times*, August 15, 1971.
119. *MNC Hearings*, Pt. I, pp. 48-49.
120. Ibid., Pt. I, p. 48.
121. Ibid., Pt. I, pp. 37, 75-76.
122. Kandell, "Private U.S. Loan," p. 195.
123. Farnsworth, "Chile," p. 139.
124. *MNC Hearings*, Pt. I, p. 338.
125. In resuming the assistance program, AID reported: "Given the willingness of outstanding bilateral problems of debt and compensation, the efforts underway to regularize Chile's international financial obligations, and the serious Chilean stabilization effort, reactivation of the AID loan program is proposed." See "U.S. Response to the Chilean Coup," *Inter-American Economic Affairs*, 28 (Summer 1974), 89.
126. Gary MacEoin, "The U.S. Government and Chile," p. 222.
127. Szulc, "CIA and Chile," p. 156.
128. Farnsworth, "Chile," p. 140.
129. Ibid., p. 141. Butz was quoted by the *Miami Herald*, November 26, 1973.
130. *Covert Action in Chile*, p. 25.
131. Laurence Birns, "The Demise of a Constitutional Society," in Birns, *End of Chilean Democracy*, p. 26.
132. *New York Times*, September 17, 1974.
133. "Second Annual Report to the Congress on United States Foreign Policy," February 25, 1971, in Richard Nixon, *Public Papers of the Presidents of the United States* (Washington, D.C.: Government Printing Office, 1972), pp. 246-247; *ITT and Chile*, p. 19.
134. "Message From the President of the United States Transmitting His Annual Report on the State of U.S. Foreign Policy," February 1972. Text is reprinted in U.S. Congress, House, Committee on Foreign Affairs, Subcommittee on Inter-American Affairs, *United States and Chile During the Allende Years, 1970-1973* (Washington, D.C.: Government Printing Office, 1975), p. 453. Hereafter cited as *United States and Chile*.
135. Ibid. Identical wording was used in Nixon's "Second Annual Report," pp. 246-247. Charles Meyer, assistant secretary of state for inter-American affairs attested to the accuracy of the president's assertion that U.S. policy in fact followed the principle of nonintervention and was based on the president's statement, which he quoted, that " 'We will deal with governments as they are.' The policy of the United States was that Chile's problem was a Chilean problem, to be settled by Chile." *MNC Hearings*, Pt. I, p. 402.
136. Kissinger's statements are in *New York Times*, September 20 and 21, 1974; for Ford's statement, see ibid., September 17, 1974.
137. *New York Times*, September 21, 1974.
138. *New York Times*, September 20 and 21, 1974.

139. *New York Times*, September 17, 1974. House Speaker Carl Albert said that the Kissinger-Ford private briefing for congressional leaders at the White House contained the same information as the president gave in his TV appearance. *New York Times*, September 21, 1974.

140. *New York Times*, September 20, 1974.

141. *CIA Hearings*, pp. 6, 24.

142. Fagen, p. 303.

143. *Washington Post*, April 6, 1973.

144. Fagen, "United States and Chile," p. 304.

145. *CIA Hearings*, p. 3; Fagen, "United States and Chile," p. 303.

146. *Washington Post*, April 6, 1973.

147. *Covert Action in Chile*, p. 40.

148. Ibid.

149. Ibid., p. 23.

150. *New York Times*, September 13 and 23, 1974.

151. *Covert Action in Chile*, p. 29.

152. *New York Times*, September 20, 1974.

153. *Covert Action in Chile*, p. 8.

154. *New York Times*, October 21, 1974.

155. *New York Times*, October 16, 1974.

156. *New York Times*, September 20, 1974.

157. *Covert Action in Chile*, p. 45.

158. Ibid., p. 48.

159. Ramsey Clark, "The Law and Human Rights in Chile," p. 164.

160. MacEoin, "U.S. Government and Chile," p. 221.

161. Ibid., p. 222; Clark, "Law and Human Rights," p. 163; *New York Times*, September 23, 1974. Covey Oliver, former assistant secretary of state for Latin America, was a member of the fact-finding mission. A special five-nation investigating team of the Organization of American States and an independent study by Amnesty International confirmed the reports of widespread torture and repression. The findings of the OAS's Inter-American Committee on Human Rights were described in the *New York Times*, December 10, 1974. Studies by Amnesty International were reported in the *New York Times*, January 20, May 30, and September 11, 1974.

162. Birns, *End of Chilean Democracy*, p. 24.

163. Laurence Birns, "Allende's Fall, Washington's Push," *New York Times*, September 15, 1974.

164. Paul Sigmund, "Correspondence," *Foreign Affairs*, 53 (January 1975), 376.

165. *The Boston Globe Magazine*, September 15, 1974; also MacEoin, "U.S. Government and Chile," p. 223.

166. *New York Times*, January 10, 1975.

167. Ibid., September 27, 1974.

168. Ibid.; MacEoin, "U.S. Government and Chile," p. 222.

445

169. Statement in panel discussion, Princeton University, October 21, 1974.
170. "Interview with William E. Colby, Director of Central Intelligence," *U.S. News and World Report*, 77 (December 2, 1974), 29.
171. The text of President Ford's statement about national security is in *New York Times*, September 17, 1974.
172. The similarity of United States policies to Soviet interventionist policies was ironically highlighted in the 1962 statement of foreign ministers at Punta del Este. At the urging of the United States, the foreign ministers adopted a statement warning governments against the deceptiveness and spread of communism in Latin America: "With the pretext of defending popular interests, freedom is suppressed, democratic institutions are destroyed, human rights are violated." "Punta Del Este Declaration," *American Journal of International Law*, 56 (April 1962), 604. One could accurately use the same language to describe U.S. intervention in Chile.
173. *Covert Action in Chile*, pp. 43-49. A similarly distorted perception afflicted officials before the Bay of Pigs invasion to overthrow Castro in 1961. Then officials held the mistaken belief that a large popular uprising would occur in Cuba if only the CIA would help set it in motion. In both cases, U.S. officials seemed reluctant to believe that a Marxist could have a substantial degree of popular support.
174. Birns, "Demise of a Constitutional Society," in Birns, *End of Chilean Democracy*, p. 25.
175. See Project for Awareness and Action, "Chile's Foreign Debt," Birns, *End of Chilean Democracy*, p. 192; Uribe, *Black Book*, p. 107.
176. *MNC Hearings*, Pt. 1, p. 298; Fagen, "United States and Chile," p. 301.
177. *New York Times*, September 27, 1974.
178. Fagen, "United States and Chile," p. 303.
179. Ibid., p. 305.
180. *New York Times*, September 13, 1974.
181. For discussion of various assassination plots, see U.S. Congress, Senate, Select Committee to Study Governmental Operations With Respect to Intelligence Activities, *Alleged Assassination Plots Involving Foreign Leaders, An Interim Report*, pp. 4-5; *New York Times*, November 21, 1975 and March 12, 1976; Richard Barnet, *Intervention and Revolution*.
182. *New York Times*, March 10, 1975.
183. See *New York Times*, March 18, 1975.
184. Although many banking institutions did cut off credit to Allende's government [*New York Times*, November 12, 1973], they seemed less enthusiastic than ITT about covert intervention. Many United States banks pursued a strategy of keeping their capital at home until the political climate stabilized in Chile. If the resulting government was socialist, they believed there would still be future op-

portunities to do business in Chile. The Allende government, after all, continued to need credit. One U.S. business in Chile, Ralston Purina, refused to take part in the ITT-sponsored meetings to press Kissinger to intervene in Chilean affairs.

185. Petras and LaPorte, "Can We Do Business," p. 135. After a detailed study of U.S. policy in Chile, James Petras and Robert LaPorte came to a similar conclusion: "Policy tends to follow the line favored by a single interest—the U.S. investor community. U.S. economic interests appear to be the only concrete, specific, and visible reference point to which policy-makers refer."

186. Birns, "Demise of a Constitutional Society," *End of Chilean Democracy*, p. 22.

187. U.S. Congress, Senate, Select Committee to Study Governmental Operations with Respect to Intelligence Activities, *Foreign and Military Intelligence, Final Report*, Book I, p. 445. Hereafter cited as *Select Committee Final Report*.

188. Even the Select Senate Committee to investigate the CIA failed to get good cooperation from the executive branch. *New York Times*, March 6, 1975.

189. Fagen detailed the evidence in a lengthy letter to J. W. Fulbright, reprinted in Birns, *End of Chilean Democracy*, pp. 166-167. A career foreign service officer told Fagen that Frederick Purdy, chief consul of the embassy, was a CIA agent. Charges against Purdy were corroborated by the *New York Times*, November 20, 1973. In one case, it appears as if embassy officials were inactive in protecting a young U.S. citizen working in Santiago, and may even have condoned his arbitrary arrest, detention, and killing by the newly-formed junta.

190. See the *New York Times*, March 6, 1975.

191. After examining U.S. policy in Chile, Gary MacEoin concluded: "What is now overwhelmingly clear is that government by deceit, treachery, and perjury is firmly entrenched in Washington and that the liquidation of Watergate has been strictly cosmetic." See MacEoin, "U.S. Government and Chile," p. 223.

192. *Select Committee Final Report*, p. 157.

193. "President's Annual Report on Foreign Policy," p. 453.

194. *New York Times*, September 20, 1974; *Washington Post*, April 6, 1973.

195. *MNC Hearings*, Pt. I, pp. 281, 301.

196. Ibid., p. 402; pp. 414, 426; p. 406.

197. Jack Kubisch, "The United States is Innocent of Complicity," statement of September 20, 1973, before House Subcommittee for Inter-American Affairs, in Birns, *End of Chilean Democracy*, pp. 151-153.

198. *MNC Hearings*, Pt. I, p. 189.

199. *New York Times*, September 8, 1974.

200. *New York Times*, September 21, 1974.

201. MacEoin, "U.S. Government and Chile," p. 221; Fagen, "United States and Chile," pp. 309-310.
202. Birns, "Allende's Fall, Washington's Push."
203. "False consciousness" is discussed in Richard A. Falk, *This Endangered Planet*, pp. 84-85. According to Falk, "Alienation involves false consciousness, an estrangement so extreme that a person loses the ability to discern his own interests, the conditions of his own fulfillment, or the actuality of his role as a victim or perpetrator of exploitation."
204. *MNC Hearings*, Pt. I, p. 121.
205. Ibid., p. 478.
206. Memo of September 17, 1970, ibid., Pt. II, p. 611.
207. *New York Times*, September 20, 1974.
208. Address at Princeton University, March 11, 1975. Professor Laurence Birns, a former UN economic affairs officer in Santiago, has written: "Allende was scrupulously correct in maintaining unimpaired, under unrelieved internal and external pressure, all the nation's institutions. . . . Not a single newspaper was censored by the civilian authorities and opposition political parties could rage at will against the Government." See Birns, "Allende's Fall, Washington's Push." Sigmund confirmed the openness of Chilean society in "Correspondence," p. 376.
209. MacEoin, "U.S. Government and Chile," pp. 220-221; Fagen, "United States and Chile," p. 304; *New York Times*, September 26, 1974.
210. As Petras and LaPorte, "Can We Do Business," have concluded: "Congress serves as a forum for airing dissident and critical opinions, but has been of little importance except where the position of Congress coincides with that of the executive branch and the business community," p. 136.
211. *Select Committee Final Report*, p. 150.
212. Ibid., pp. 150-151.
213. See S. 2239, 93rd Cong., 1st Sess.
214. Subsequent legislation attached to foreign assistance appropriations did ask that foreign CIA covert political activity be limited to national security questions and that Congress be informed of covert activities. However, provisions for implementation of this idea were weak, and the legislation itself fell far short of prohibiting covert intervention, even intervention undertaken for the purpose of overturning free elections.
215. The report said: "We hold no brief for President Allende's decision, in effect, to expropriate the property of U.S. owned corporations without adequate compensation. On the contrary, we condemn it." *ITT and Chile*, p. 18.
216. Ibid.
217. Ibid., p. 20.
218. *Covert Action in Chile*, p. 55.

219. Ibid., p. 56.
220. *Select Committee Final Report*, pp. 159, 160, 448.
221. Ibid., pp. 160, 446.
222. Ibid., p. 507. The act is quoted on p. 506.
223. Ibid.
224. Ibid., p. 157.
225. On this point, see Stephen D. Krasner, "Are Bureaucracies Important? (Or Allison Wonderland)," p. 178.
226. *Select Committee Final Report*, pp. 153, 445.
227. *Covert Action in Chile*, p. 2.
228. Text in *New York Times*, February 24, 1977.
229. Printed transcript of interview on "Face the Nation," CBS Television, March 20, 1977, mimeographed, p. 3.
230. Ibid., p. 4.
231. Text in *New York Times*, February 24, 1977.
232. *New York Times*, November 4, 1977.
233. Press conference text, *Department of State Bulletin*, 76 (February 28, 1977), 164.
234. Amnesty International, "Iran," *Amnesty International Briefing*, November 1976, p. 10.
235. *New York Times*, November 16, 1977.
236. Former Attorney General and Under Secretary of State Nicholas Katzenbach has come to a similar conclusion: "We should abandon publicly all covert operations designed to influence political results in foreign countries. Specifically, there should be no secret subsidies of police or counterinsurgency forces, no efforts to influence elections, no secret monetary subsidies of groups sympathetic to the United States, whether governmental, nongovernmental, or revolutionary." See Nicholas deB. Katzenbach, "Foreign Policy, Public Opinion, and Secrecy," p. 15.
237. In contemplating the abolition of the CIA, one immediately thinks of the effort to learn the size of the Soviet missile arsenal as a more troublesome problem. However, artificial earth satellites currently gather such information regularly, and this work can be done openly. Likewise, the effort to detect any possible Soviet violations of future arms control agreements, such as a comprehensive test ban, can best be carried out through open, public means.
238. Katzenbach, "Foreign Policy, Public Opinion, and Secrecy," p. 8.

Five. U.S. Policy for International Control of Marine Pollution

1. For a discussion of these environmental problems as world order issues, see Richard A. Falk, *A Study of Future Worlds*, pp. 27-28.
2. Robert M. Hallman, *Towards an Environmentally Sound Law of the Sea*, p. 6.
3. "Statement of the Honorable Russell E. Train, Chairman, (U.S.)

Council on Environmental Quality, Executive Office of the President of the United States, Before the Council of the Inter-Governmental Maritime Consultative Organization," London, June 5, 1973, mimeographed, p. 3. See also Robert A. Shinn, *The International Politics of Marine Pollution Control*, p. 183; Colin Moorecraft, *Must the Seas Die?*, p. 2.

4. Quoted in George Kennan, "To Prevent a World Wasteland," p. 401.

5. Moorecraft, *Must the Seas Die?*, p. 3.

6. This most widely used definition of marine pollution was developed by the United Nations Group of Experts on the Scientific Aspects of Marine Pollution (GESAMP), a group of experts drawn from the Inter-Governmental Maritime Consultative Organization (IMCO), the Food and Agricultural Organization (FAO), the United Nations Educational, Scientific and Cultural Organization (UNESCO), the World Meteorological Organization (WMO), the World Health Organization (WHO), and the International Atomic Energy Agency (IAEA). See "Comprehensive Outline of the Scope of the Long-Term and Expanded Programme of Oceanic Exploration and Research," UN Doc. A/7750 (November 1969), Annex 1, section 3.

7. Shinn, *International Politics*, p. 1.

8. National Academy of Sciences, *Petroleum in the Marine Environment* (Washington, D.C.: National Academy of Sciences, 1975), p. 6; Swadesh S. Kalsi, "Oil in Neptune's Kingdom," p. 79; National Academy of Sciences, Ocean Science Committee of the NAS (National Academy of Sciences)-NRC (National Research Council) Ocean Affairs Board, *Marine Environmental Quality*, p. 7 (hereafter cited as *NAS Study on Marine Environmental Quality*); Oscar Schachter and Daniel Serwer, "Marine Pollution Problems and Remedies," p. 89; Workshop on Global Ecological Problems, *Man in the Living Environment*, p. 256.

9. See *NAS Study on Marine Environmental Quality*, pp. 7-8; Hallman, *Towards an Environmentally Sound Law*, p. 5; E. W. Seabrook Hull and Albert W. Koers, "A Regime for World Ocean Pollution Control," *International Relations and the Future of Ocean Space*, Symposium on International Relations and the Future of Ocean Space, University of South Carolina, 1972, ed. Robert G. Wirsing (Columbia, South Carolina: University of South Carolina Press, 1974), p. 93.

10. Study of Critical Environmental Problems, *Man's Impact on the Global Environment*, pp. 139-141; Kalsi, "Oil in Neptune's Kingdom," p. 81; U.S. Council on Environmental Quality, *Environmental Quality, Annual Report*, 1972, p. 86. Hereafter cited as *Environmental Quality, Annual Report*. The *NAS Study on Marine Environmental Quality* estimated that "over 95 percent . . . [of the pollutants from petroleum products] is air-borne." See pp. 7-8.

11. FAO Technical Conference on Marine Pollution and Its Effect on Living Resources and Fishing (Rome, 1970), *Marine Pollution and Sea Life* (London: Fishing News Books, 1972), p. 451 (hereafter cited as *FAO Technical Conference*); see also Schachter and Serwer, "Marine Pollution Problems," p. 89; Shinn, *International Politics*, p. 8.

12. Schachter and Serwer, "Marine Pollution Problems," p. 89.

13. *FAO Technical Conference*, p. 114.

14. Richard Bernstein, "Poisoning the Seas," p. 15.

15. M. Blumer, for example, has stated categorically that "all crude oils and all oil fractions except highly purified and pure materials are poisonous to all marine organisms." Workshop on Global Ecological Problems, *Man in the Living Environment*, p. 256.

16. *FAO Technical Conference*, p. 534.

17. Schachter and Serwer, "Marine Pollution Problems," p. 92; *FAO Technical Conference*, p. 534.

18. Bernstein, "Poisoning the Seas," p. 15.

19. *FAO Technical Conference*, pp. 2, 192.

20. Barbara Ward Jackson and René Dubos, *Only One Earth*, p. 201. *FAO Technical Conference*, p. 534.

21. Richard Sandbrook and Anita Yurchyshyn, "Marine Pollution from Vessels," in *Critical Environmental Issues on the Law of the Sea*, ed. Robert E. Stein, p. 19.

22. Schachter and Serwer, "Marine Pollution Problems," p. 90.

23. Bruce Halstead, "Toxicological Aspects of Marine Pollution," mimeographed, quoted by Shinn, *International Politics*, p. 10.

24. *FAO Technical Conference*, pp. 452-453. The UN Secretary-General drew a similar conclusion in "Marine Pollution and Other Hazardous and Harmful Effects Which Might Arise From the Exploration and Exploitation of the Seabed and the Ocean Floor, and the Subsoil Thereof, Beyond the Limits of National Jurisdiction," *Report of the Secretary-General*, UN Doc. A/7924 (June 11, 1970), p. 4. Hereafter cited by document number only.

25. Kalsi, "Oil in Neptune's Kingdom," pp. 79-80; Study of Critical Environment Problems, *Man's Impact*, p. 139; Schachter and Serwer, "Marine Pollution Problems," p. 91; Robert W. Holcomb, "Oil in the Ecosystem," *Science*, No. 166 (October 10, 1969), p. 204; The Study of Critical Environmental Problems estimated that production will roughly double during the 1970s (*Man's Impact*, p. 266).

26. Kalsi, "Oil in Neptune's Kingdom," p. 93; E. Gold, "Pollution of the Sea and International Law," *Journal of Marine Law Command*, 3 (1970), 42.

27. "Statement of the Honorable Russell E. Train," p. 2. See also Robert J. McManus, "New Treaty on Vessel Pollution," p. 59; J. Porricelli et al., "Tankers and the Ecology," *Transactions of the Society of Naval Architects and Marine Engineers*, 79 (1971), 169-170.

451

28. Michael Hardy, "International Control of Marine Pollution," *International Organization*, ed. James E.S. Fawcett and Rosalyn Higgins, p. 162.

29. Wallace S. Broecker, "Man's Oxygen Reserve," *Science*, 168 (June 26, 1970), 1538.

30. IMCO/FAO/WMO/WHO/IAEA/UN Joint Group of Experts on the Scientific Aspects of Marine Pollution, "Report of the Third Session" (Rome: FAO, 1971), UN Doc. GESAMP III/19, Annex IV, p. 6. Hereafter cited by document number only.

31. Jackson and Dubos, *Only One Earth*, p. 199.

32. UN Doc. GESAMP III/19, Annex IV; Schachter and Serwer, "Marine Pollution Problems," p. 96; Bernstein, "Poisoning the Seas," p. 16.

33. Study of Critical Environmental Problems, *Man's Impact*, p. 127.

34. Tony J. Peterle, "Pyramiding Damage," *Environment*, 11 (July-August 1969), 34.

35. Shinn, *International Politics*, p. 33.

36. *FAO Technical Conference*, p. 193.

37. Study of Critical Environment Problems, *Man's Impact*, p. 128.

38. See Schachter and Serwer, "Marine Pollution Problems," p. 97.

39. Study of Critical Environmental Problems, *Man's Impact*, p. 129.

40. *FAO Technical Conference*, pp. 191-192.

41. Broecker, "Man's Oxygen Reserve," p. 1538; quoted in Schachter and Serwer, "Marine Pollution Problems," p. 96.

42. *FAO Technical Conference*, pp. 534, 602.

43. Workshop on Global Ecological Problems, *Man in the Living Environment*, p. 253.

44. National Research Council, Panel on Monitoring Persistent Pesticides in the Marine Environment, Committee on Oceanography, *Chlorinated Hydrocarbons in the Marine Environment*, pp. 1-2.

45. National Research Council, ibid., pp. 1-2. See the identical conclusion of the MIT Study of Critical Environmental Problems, *Man's Impact*, p. 136.

46. Workshop on Global Ecological Problems, *Man in the Living Environment*, p. 254.

47. National Research Council, *Chlorinated Hydrocarbons in the Marine Environment*, p. 17.

48. IMCO/FAO/UNESCO/WMO/WHO/IAEA/UN Joint Group of Experts on the Scientific Aspects of Marine Pollution, "Report of the Fourth Session" (Geneva, September 1972), text reprinted in United States Congress, Senate, Committee on Commerce, *1973 IMCO Conference on Marine Pollution from Ships, Hearings*, p. 66. Hereafter cited as *1973 IMCO Hearings*.

49. Edward D. Goldberg, "Chemical Invasion of Ocean by Man," *Man's Impact on Terrestrial and Ocean Ecosystems*, ed. William H. Matthews, Frederick E. Smith, and Edward D. Goldberg, p. 262.

50. Workshop on Global Ecological Problems, *Man in the Living Environment*, p. 257.

51. Goldberg, "Chemical Invasion," p. 264.

52. Coastal Zone Workshop, *The Water's Edge*, ed. Bostwich H. Ketchum, p. 152.

53. Workshop on Global Ecological Problems, *Man in the Living Environment*, p. 257.

54. Douglas M. Johnston, "Marine Pollution Control," p. 72.

55. See Workshop on Global Ecological Problems, *Man in the Living Environment*, p. 257.

56. Study of Critical Environmental Problems, *Man's Impact*, p. 137. Two major incidents occurred in 1953 and 1964. See also T. Nitta, "Marine Pollution in Japan," *FAO Technical Conference*, pp. 77-81.

57. Organization for Economic Cooperation and Development, *Mercury and the Environment*, p. 30. One exception to the general increase anticipated is the substitution of unleaded gasoline for leaded gasoline, thus eliminating one major source of lead pollution.

58. Schachter and Serwer, "Marine Pollution Problems," p. 102.

59. *FAO Technical Conference,* p. 602.

60. Study of Critical Environmental Problems, *Man's Impact*, p. 138.

61. Jackson and Dubos, *Only One Earth*, p. 66. Sharp declines were measured at Landsort Deep.

62. Study of Critical Environmental Problems, *Man's Impact*, p. 146; Johnston, "Marine Pollution Control," p. 71.

63. Study of Critical Environmental Problems, *Man's Impact*, p. 148.

64. A. H. Seymour, "Introduction," in National Research Council, *Radioactivity in the Marine Environment*, p. 1.

65. *Environmental Quality, Annual Report*, 1974, p. 166.

66. A curie is a unit of radioactivity equal to 3.7×10^{10} disintegrations per second.

67. National Research Council, Study Panel on Assessing Potential Ocean Pollutants, *Assessing Potential Ocean Pollutants*, pp. 27, 35. Hereafter cited as *Assessing Ocean Pollutants*.

68. Half-life is a measure of the time it takes for half of the radioactivity to dissipate from a given source. This should not be misunderstood as half of the amount of time the material is dangerous. Plutonium 239, for example, has a half-life of 24,400 years, which means that its radioactivity will be decreased by half after the first period of 24,400 years, but only half of the remaining emissions will be dissipated after the second period of 24,400 years. Thus one-fourth of the original radioactivity would still remain after 48,800 years, one-eighth after 73,200 years, and so on.

69. Seymour, "Introduction," *Radioactivity in the Marine Environment*, p. 2; Herbert Volchok, Chemist for the Environmental Studies Division, Atomic Energy Commission, in U.S. Congress, Senate,

Committee on Commerce, Subcommittee on Oceans and Atmosphere, *Ocean Pollution,* p. 56. Hereafter cited as *Ocean Pollution.*

70. U.S. Atomic Energy Commission, *The Nuclear Industry, 1973,* pp. 57, 59, text reprinted in U.S. Congress, Joint Committee on Atomic Energy, *Development, Growth, and State of the Nuclear Industry,* pp. 328, 330.

71. Ibid., p. 330; Harold P. Green, "Radioactive Waste and the Environment," p. 284.

72. Jack W. Hodges, "International Law and Radioactive Pollution By Ocean Dumping: 'With All Their Genius and With All Their Skill . . . . ,' " *San Diego Law Review,* 2 (May 1974), 760; U.S. Congress, House, Committee on Merchant Marine and Fisheries, Subcommittee on Fisheries and Wildlife Conservation and Subcommittee on Oceanography, *Hearings on H.R. 285,* 92nd Cong., 1st Sess. (Washington, D.C.: Government Printing Office, 1971), p. 235.

73. The European Nuclear Energy Organization for Economic Cooperation and Development, *Radioactive Waste Disposal Operations in the Atlantic, 1967* (Paris: OECD, 1968), quoted in Shinn, *International Politics,* p. 30.

74. *New York Times,* May 21, 1976.

75. Richard H. Wagner, *Environment and Man,* pp. 194-195.

76. Study of Critical Environmental Problems, *Man's Impact,* p. 76.

77. *Assessing Ocean Pollutants,* pp. 42-43.

78. Shinn, *International Politics,* p. 28.

79. International Atomic Energy Agency, *Nuclear Power and the Environment,* p. 76.

80. Shinn, *International Politics,* p. 44; Edward Wenk, *The Politics of the Ocean,* p. 185.

81. Moorecraft, *Must the Seas Die?,* p. 107.

82. *Assessing Ocean Pollutants,* p. 44.

83. Two United States nuclear submarines, the Thresher and Scorpion, and at least one Soviet submarine carrying nuclear warheads have sunk.

84. Jackson and Dubos, *Only One Earth,* p. 133. In 1963, the Atomic Energy Commission asked John W. Gofman and Arthur R. Tamplin to conduct a study of the effects of contamination due to the release of radioactivity. They concluded that if the radiation dosage "acceptable" under AEC standards were in fact received by the total United States population, the result would be 32,000 deaths each year from cancer and leukemia. The expected expansion of the nuclear power industry might move radiation exposures beyond even the present permissible standard by the year 2000. See Barry Commoner, *The Closing Circle,* p. 58.

85. *Assessing Ocean Pollutants,* p. 27.

86. Moorecraft, *Must the Seas Die?,* p. 109.

87. J. W. Hedgpeth, "The Oceans: World Sump," *Environment*, 12 (April 1970), 44.

88. *Assessing Ocean Pollutants*, p. 51.

89. Moorecraft, *Must the Seas Die?*, p. 109.

90. *Assessing Ocean Pollutants*, pp. 37-38, 51.

91. Ibid., pp. 10, 12, 53.

92. R. F. Foster, I. L. Ophel, and A. Preston, "Evaluation of Human Radiation Exposure," in National Research Council, *Radioactivity in the Marine Environment*, p. 258; International Atomic Energy Agency, *Nuclear Power and the Environment*, p. 76.

93. International Atomic Energy Agency, *Nuclear Power and the Environment*, p. 76.

94. Moorecraft, *Must the Seas Die?*, pp. 104, 108.

95. William O. Doub and Joseph M. Dukert, "Making Nuclear Energy Safe and Secure," p. 756.

96. See Hallman, *Towards an Environmentally Sound Law*, p. 7.

97. *New York Times*, September 11, 1975.

98. Jackson and Dubos, *Only One Earth*, p. 133.

99. Even low-level storage facilities in Kentucky leaked plutonium into the surrounding soil. Although no humans were directly harmed by the leakage, the radioactive results will be in the Kentucky soil for thousands of years. *New York Times*, September 8, 1977.

100. The group of UN experts concluded: "There is an almost complete lack of data on the synergistic effects of these poisons on both marine organisms and man." *FAO Technical Conference*, p. 535.

101. *Assessing Ocean Pollutants*, p. 9; Workshop on Global Ecological Problems, *Man in the Living Environment*, pp. 257-259; *FAO Technical Conference*, p. 114.

102. Study of Critical Environmental Problems, *Man's Impact*, pp. 142-143.

103. Hallman, *Towards an Environmentally Sound Law*, pp. 5, 7. See also, *Identification and Control of Pollutants of Broad International Significance*, report prepared for Stockholm Conference, UN Doc. A/CONF. 48/8 (January 7, 1972); *The Sea: Prevention and Control of Marine Pollution*, Report of the Secretary-General, UN Doc. E/5003 (May 7, 1971).

104. *FAO Technical Conference*, p. 113; Kalsi, "Oil in Neptune's Kingdom," p. 79.

105. See Jackson and Dubos, *Only One Earth*, pp. 197-198.

106. Article 24.

107. Article 25.

108. Article 5 (7).

109. McManus, "New Treaty," p. 59. The text of the 1954 treaty as amended in 1969 is in *International Legal Materials*, 9 (1970), 1-24.

455

110. For a brief comparison of the 1973 and 1954 treaties, see the *1973 IMCO Hearings*, pp. 20-21. The text of the treaty is in ibid., pp. 101-177.
111. McManus, "New Treaty," p. 61.
112. Statement of Russell Train, *1973 IMCO Hearings*, pp. 5, 13, 18.
113. Text in *International Legal Materials*, 9 (1970), 22-44.
114. Text in ibid., 9 (1970), 45-67.
115. Text in ibid., 11 (1972), 284-302.
116. *Environmental Quality, Annual Report*, 1973, p. 333.
117. Ibid., p. 61. The definition of new ships is contained in Annex I.
118. Article 3.
119. Kalsi, "Oil in Neptune's Kingdom," p. 86.
120. Statement by Robert Citron in U.S. Congress, Senate, Committee on Commerce, National Ocean Policy Study, *Tankers and the Marine Environment, Hearings*, p. 39. Hereafter cited as *Tankers and Marine Environment Hearings*. McManus reported that in 1970 tankers hauled about 1,300,000,000 metric tons of oil. Of this amount shippers lost roughly 2,500,000 or about 0.2 percent of their cargo. McManus, "New Treaty," p. 59; Porricelli, "Tankers and the Ecology," pp. 169-170. John M. Hunt, vice chairman of the National Academy of Sciences Workshop on Inputs, Fates, and Effects of Petroleum in the Marine Environment, reported that 0.4 percent of the cargo is, on the average, retained on the inside wall of the "empty" tanker. *Tankers and Marine Environment Hearings*, p. 36.
121. Robert Citron in *Tankers and Marine Environment Hearings*, p. 39.
122. McManus, "New Treaty," has reported that only about 40 percent of the ship-generated oil pollution is attributable to tank washing and deballasting operations (p. 59). Six percent is due to accidents.
123. *Environmental Quality, Annual Report*, 1973, pp. 332-333.
124. *Marine Week*, September 13, 1974, reprinted in *Tankers and Marine Environment Hearings*, p. 142.
125. Jackson and Dubos, *Only One Earth*, p. 204.
126. Kalsi, "Oil in Neptune's Kingdom," pp. 86, 98.
127. *Ocean Pollution*, p. 190.
128. *NAS Study of Marine Environmental Quality*, pp. 7-8. See also *Environmental Quality, Annual Report*, 1972, p. 86.
129. A spokesman testifying before the Senate Commerce Committee for five well-known environmental groups commented upon the IMCO proceedings that preceded negotiation of the treaty: "As presently proposed . . . the Convention appears to do little more than codify existing commercial standards among the major maritime nations, provides no incentive to *improve* such standards, and offers insufficient environmental protection." Eldon Greenberg on behalf of the Environmental Defense Fund, Friends of

456

the Earth, Natural Resources Defense Council, National Parks and Conservation Association, and Sierra Club. *Ocean Pollution*, p. 201.

130. McManus, "New Treaty," p. 60; Russell Train, *Ocean Pollution*, p. 171.

131. McManus, "New Treaty," p. 64.

132. For example, the Water Quality Improvement Act of 1970; the Marine Protection, Research and Sanctuaries Act of 1972; the Water Pollution Control Act Amendments of 1972; the Ports and Waterways Safety Act of 1972.

133. See *Environmental Quality, Annual Report*, 1973, p. 334.

134. Senator Ted Stevens (Alaska), *1973 IMCO Hearings*, p. 12.

135. Statement of Admiral Chester R. Bender, commandant, U.S. Coast Guard, ibid., p. 22.

136. Ibid., p. 12. See also statements by Russell Train, Senator Ted Stevens, and James Reynolds of the American Institute of Merchant Shipping, *Ocean Pollution*, pp. 169-186.

137. *1973 IMCO Hearings*, p. 23.

138. Bender, ibid., p. 23.

139. Said Bender: "We should avoid any unilateral action which would encourage the proliferation of differing regulatory schemes imposed by individual nations." Ibid.

140. Article III. Text in *International Legal Materials*, 11 (1972), 1291.

141. Article VI.

142. Article VII (4). Robert J. McManus, "The New Law on Ocean Dumping," p. 31.

143. Johnston, "Marine Pollution Control," p. 92.

144. McManus, "New Law," p. 31.

145. Two years before the treaty was signed, the U.S. sank nerve gas in the Atlantic. Some experts have judged that this action violated international law. See the discussion by E. D. Brown, "International Law and Marine Pollution," pp. 249-255.

146. The single exception is where the foreign flag ship has loaded material for dumping from a port of the state seeking to enforce the law on the high seas. Such loading requires a license from the port state.

147. *Environmental Quality, Annual Report*, 1973, p. 335.

148. McManus, "New Law," p. 26; *Clean Air and Water News*, 5 (January 25, 1973), 1.

149. See McManus, "New Law," p. 26.

150. U.S. Council on Environmental Quality, *Ocean Dumping*.

151. *Environmental Quality, Annual Report*, 1973, p. 335.

152. *Stockholm Declaration on the Human Environment*, adopted by consensus at the United Nations Conference on the Human Environment held at Stockholm in June 1972, text in James Barros

and Douglas M. Johnston, *The International Law of Pollution*, p. 301. See also United Nations Conference on the Human Environment, Report of the UN Conference on the Human Environment, UN Doc. A/CONF.48/14/Rev.1.

153. On this point, see also Johnston, "Marine Pollution Control," p. 96.

154. The only exception was that foreign states would need to grant a license for U.S. ships in foreign ports to load waste material for ocean dumping.

155. United Nations, General Assembly, *Declaration and Treaty Concerning the Reservation Exclusively for Peaceful Purposes of the Sea-Bed and of the Ocean Floor Underlying the Seas Beyond the Limits of Present National Jurisdiction, and the Use of Their Resources in the Interests of Mankind*, A/6695, August 18, 1967 (xxii). See also U.S. Congress, House, Committee on Foreign Affairs, Subcommittee on International Organizations and Movements, *The United Nations and the Issue of Deep Ocean Resources*, 90th Cong., 1st Sess. (Washington, D.C.: Government Printing Office, 1967), pp. 267-286; U.S. Congress, Senate, Committee on Commerce, *The Third UN Law of the Sea Conference*, p. 9. Hereafter cited as *Third UN Law of the Sea Conference*, p. 9.

156. United Nations, General Assembly, Resolution 2750 (xxv).

157. Ann L. Hollick, "Bureaucrats at Sea," in Ann L. Hollick and Robert E. Osgood, *New Era of Ocean Politics*; Ann L. Hollick, "What to Expect from a Sea Treaty," pp. 68-78; *Third UN Law of the Sea Conference*; U.S. Congress, Senate, Committee on Foreign Relations, *The Third UN Law of the Sea Conference, Report to the Senate*, 94th Cong., 1st Sess. (Washington, D.C.: Government Printing Office, 1975). Hereafter cited as *Senate Report on the Caracas Conference*. The texts of all important statements by Ratiner and Stevenson before the Caracas Conference are reprinted in this report.

158. U.S. Congress, Senate, Committee on Interior and Insular Affairs, *Ocean Manganese Nodules*, p. 90. Hereafter cited as *Senate Report on Ocean Nodules*.

159. U.S. Congress, Senate, Committee on Interior and Insular Affairs, *The Law of the Sea Crisis*, pp. 9-10. Hereafter cited as *Law of the Sea Crisis*.

160. John Norton Moore, "U.S. Position on Law of the Sea Reviewed," p. 398.

161. *Third UN Law of the Sea Conference*, p. 28.

162. U.S. Congress, House, Committee on Merchant Marine and Fisheries, Subcommittee on Oceanography, *Oceanography Miscellaneous*, p. 55. Hereafter cited as *Oceanography Hearings*.

163. *Third UN Law of the Sea Conference*, pp. 25, 28, 29. See also the ad-

dress of John Stevenson to the conference on July 11, 1974, reprinted in *Senate Report on the Caracas Conference*, pp. 8-9.

164. United Nations, General Assembly, *Draft United Nations Convention on the International Seabed Area*. UN Doc. A/AC.138/25 (1970); United Nations, ECOSOC, *Uses of the Sea*, UN Doc. E/5120 (1972), p. 5; Hollick, "Bureaucrats at Sea," p. 3 and "What to Expect," p. 76.

165. Wenk, *Politics of the Ocean*, describes the conflict between the Department of Defense and the National Petroleum Council, pp. 268-278.

166. *Third UN Law of the Sea Conference*, p. 26. See also United Nations, Third Conference on the Law of the Sea, *United States of America: Draft Articles for a Chapter on the Economic Zone and the Continental Shelf*, UN Doc. A/CONF.62/L.47 (1974).

167. Stevenson address of July 11, 1974 in *Senate Report on the Caracas Conference*, p. 8.

168. Hollick, "Bureaucrats at Sea," pp. 18, 57-58. The first publication of the oil industry's argument was July 1968 in *Petroleum Resources Under the Ocean Floor*.

169. Hollick, "Bureaucrats at Sea," p. 20.

170. Ibid., pp. 19, 32.

171. Ibid., pp. 40-41.

172. See the statement of T. S. Ary, speaking on behalf of the American Mining Congress, *Senate Report on Ocean Nodules*, p. 62.

173. Hollick, "Bureaucrats at Sea," p. 25.

174. Ibid., pp. 57-58.

175. Other committees that held hearings on law of the sea issues included: Senate Committee on Interior and Insular Affairs, Subcommittee on Minerals, Materials, and Fuels; Senate Committee on Foreign Relations, Subcommittee on Ocean Space; Senate Committee on Commerce, Subcommittee on Oceans and Atmosphere; House Committee on Foreign Affairs, Subcommittee on International Organizations and Movements; House Committee on Merchant Marine and Fisheries, Subcommittee on Oceanography.

176. *Law of the Sea Crisis*, p. 10; *Senate Report on Ocean Nodules*, pp. 63-64.

177. See *Senate Report on the Caracas Conference*, p. 5; Stevenson's statement in *Oceanography Hearings*, p. 15; *New York Times*, May 9, 1975.

178. *Senate Report on Ocean Nodules*, p. 93.

179. Stevenson, *Oceanography Hearings*, p. 15.

180. Leigh Ratiner address of August 9, 1974 in *Senate Report on the Caracas Conference*, pp. 34, 44-45.

181. By 1975, sustained, vigorous pressure from the less developed countries encouraged the United States to shift its position. The

459

United States agreed to set aside, or to "bank," areas for later exploration if the less developed countries would agree to let U.S. companies begin mining immediately.

182. Stevenson address of July 17, 1974 in *Senate Report on the Caracas Convention*, p. 17.

183. Ratiner address of August 9, 1974, ibid., p. 54.

184. Ratiner address of August 9, 1974, ibid., pp. 30, 39. Under strong international pressure, the United States in 1975 agreed to allow some joint ventures and profit-sharing, but retained the demand that no limits be set on number of claims, total production, or overall profits. See the statement by Moore in U.S. Congress, Senate, Committee on Commerce, *Geneva Session of the Third United Nations Law of the Sea Conference*, p. 5. Hereafter cited as *Geneva Session Hearings*. See also *Senate Report on Ocean Nodules*, p. 96.

185. Stevenson address of July 11, 1974 in *Senate Report on the Caracas Convention*, p. 10.

186. Ratiner address of June 4, 1975, text reprinted in U.S. Congress, Senate, Committee on Interior and Insular Affairs, Subcommittee on Minerals, Materials, and Fuels, *Status Report on the Law of the Sea Conference*, pp. 1198-1199. Hereafter cited as *Senate Status Report on the Law of the Sea Conference*.

187. Ratiner address of August 9, 1974 in *Senate Report on the Caracas Convention*, pp. 30-31. Committee I discussed all matters related to the deep seabed.

188. See *Senate Report on Ocean Nodules*, p. 97.

189. Statement of T. S. Ary, ibid., p. 72. Several U.S. companies had already begun exploring for the richest mining sites. Howard Hughes' Summa Corporation reportedly possessed the most advanced deep-sea mining technology, possibly aided by CIA funds to build the Glomar Explorer, which attempted secretly to lift a sunken Soviet submarine from the Pacific ocean floor. Kennecott Copper and Deep Sea Ventures, a subsidiary of Tenneco Corporation, also had plans underway to exploit deep-sea hard mineral resources. (See Brian Johnson, "Environmental Controls in the Deep Seabed Under International Jurisdiction," in Robert E. Stein, ed., *Critical Environmental Issues*, p. 33.) The latter two corporations formed international consortia, which included other Japanese, Canadian, British, and Belgian companies. A third international consortium, the "CLB Group," was based upon more than twenty-five major companies from six countries. *Senate Report on Ocean Nodules*, pp. 35-36. Consortia not only shared the capital requirements, but also diminished the risks that a claim staked by a corporation from one nation would be jumped by a competing firm from another country. Claim jumping, of course, was a serious problem in an area owned by no one or everyone. Finally, consortia decreased the number of individual producers,

thus laying the groundwork for possible manipulation of metal prices.

190. Ratiner address of August 9, 1974 in *Senate Report on the Caracas Convention*, pp. 32, 38; Moore, "U.S. Position," p. 400. The U.S. also insisted that expropriation of foreign investment in the 200-mile economic zones be expressly prohibited. Hollick, "Bureaucrats at Sea," pp. 53-54.

191. Stevenson statement, *Senate Status Report on the Law of the Sea Conference*, pp. 853-854; *Senate Report on Ocean Nodules*, p. 94.

192. Ratiner's address of August 9, 1974 in *Senate Report on the Caracas Convention*, pp. 31-32.

193. Ibid., p. 41.

194. Ibid., p. 38.

195. *Senate Report on Ocean Nodules*, pp. 72, 85.

196. Ibid., pp. 85, 97.

197. See the statements of the secretary and assistant secretary of the interior, quoted by Senator Lee Metcalf, *Congressional Record*, February 26, 1975, p. S 2711; *Senate Report on Ocean Nodules*, pp. 82-83.

198. Prominent spokesmen for unilateral action were also active in the House Committee on Merchant Marine and Fisheries, the House Committee on Oceanography, the Senate Commerce Committee, and the Senate Committee on Interior and Insular Affairs.

199. General Assembly Resolution 2574 (XXIV); *Senate Report on Ocean Nodules*, p. 89.

200. U.S. Congress, Senate, Committee on Interior and Insular Affairs, Special Subcommittee on Outer Continental Shelf, *Outer Continental Shelf* (Washington, D.C.: Government Printing Office, 1970), p. 23; *Senate Report on Ocean Nodules*, pp. 63-98.

201. *Congressional Record*, June 23, 1975. Much of Metcalf's language was similar to that of Marne A. Dubs, director of the Ocean Resource Department, Kennecott Copper Corporation. Dubs said the negotiating text was good for the less developed countries, but was "an unmitigated disaster" for the United States. *Geneva Session Hearings*, pp. 37-49.

202. *Senate Status Report on the Law of the Sea Conference*, p. 1162.

203. Text of statement by John M. Murphy, April 15, 1975, reprinted in ibid., pp. 1168-1169. A somewhat more extreme position was taken by Congressman Paul Rogers, who said "the United States should have the right to occupy the ocean floor to the Mid-Atlantic Ridge and assume the responsibility to defend it." Quoted in U.S. Congress, House, Committee on Foreign Affairs, *Exploiting the Resources of the Seabed*, 92nd Cong., 1st Sess. (Washington, D.C.: Government Printing Office, 1971), p. 24.

204. Ratiner, address of August 9, 1974 in *Senate Report on the Caracas Convention*, p. 36.

205. In contrast, advocates of global humanism argue that scarce resources even in national jurisdiction should be seen as part of the common heritage, and a global guidance system should help allocate certain vital resources regardless of their point of origin. In this view, there should not be discrimination by oil producers, for example, against states lacking petroleum resources of their own.

206. Henry Kissinger, "The Law of the Sea: A Test of International Cooperation," address of April 8, 1976 (Washington, D.C.: Bureau of Public Affairs, U.S. Department of State, 1976), p. 5.

207. Ibid., pp. 2, 3, 8.

208. Ibid., pp. 5, 7.

209. Ibid., p. 6.

210. U.S. Congress, Senate, Committee on Interior and Insular Affairs, Subcommittee on Minerals, Materials and Fuels, *Status Report on Law of the Sea Conference*, p. 1662.

211. Ibid., pp. 1639, 1651.

212. U.S. Delegation, "The Third United Nations Conference on the Law of the Sea," New York (March 15-May 7, 1976), p. 7. Text reprinted, ibid., p. 1624.

213. Ibid., p. 1665.

214. Elliot L. Richardson, "Review of the Law of the Sea Conference and Deep Seabed Mining Legislation," p. 751.

215. There was speculation about the possibility that Engo's revisions may have been influenced by conversations with Ratiner, the former U.S. negotiator. Ratiner became an employee of Kennecott the day after resigning his government position. He met socially with Engo and may have cynically encouraged Engo to take a more pro-Third World stance, which would alienate the United States and thereby scuttle the negotiations. This would both enable Kennecott to proceed with mining unilaterally and increase the prospects that the U.S. Congress would pass legislation providing public guarantees for private investment in order to eliminate much of the private corporate risk in deep-sea mining ventures. See "Poker Over Seabed Mining: Tale of the Ubiquitous Lobbyist," *Washington Post*, August 14, 1977.

216. Elliot L. Richardson, "Law of the Sea Conference," p. 390.

217. Hollick, "Bureaucrats at Sea," p. 66.

218. John R. Stevenson, "Lawmaking for the Seas," p. 190.

219. Ratiner address of August 9, 1974 in *Senate Report on the Caracas Convention*, pp. 42-43.

220. See "United States Draft Articles—Protection of the Marine Environment and the Prevention of Marine Pollution," UN Doc. A/AC.138/SC.III/L.40 (1973). The text is reprinted in *Senate Report on the Caracas Conference*, pp. 74-79.

221. Article III (1). See also the statement of Donald L. McKernan, alternate U.S. representative to the Committee on Peaceful Uses of

the Seabed and the Ocean Floor Beyond the Limits of National Jurisdiction, August 17, 1971, reprinted in *Law of the Sea Crisis*, p. 47. See also Moore address of July 20, 1973, UN Doc. A/AC.138/SC.III/SR.41 (1973).

222. See *Third UN Law of the Sea Conference*, pp. 30-31. Flag states, of course, each could set higher standards for their own flag ships, but that was unlikely, as it would put their ships at a competitive disadvantage.

223. U.S. Department of State, "U.N. Law of the Sea Conference 1975," p. 6.

224. Sandbrook and Yurchyshyn, "Marine Pollution from Vessels" in Stein, *Critical Environmental Issues*, p. 26.

225. Stevenson, *Oceanography Hearings*, p. 59.

226. Stevenson, *Senate Status Report on the Law of the Sea Conference*, pp. 5, 38. See also Thomas A. Clingan, deputy assistant secretary of state for Oceans and Fisheries Affairs, ibid., p. 44.

227. Hollick, "Bureaucracies at Sea," p. 67.

228. *Senate Report on the Caracas Conference*, p. 4.

229. Moore, address of July 22, 1974, ibid., p. 23; Article xxiii. The United States did, however, include a provision that military vessels should "act in a manner consistent" with the purposes of the treaty even though they were legally exempt (Article xxiii).

230. Moore, "U.S. Position," p. 400; Robert M. Hallman, "Environmental Regulation of Marine Based Activities in Areas of National Jurisdiction," in Stein, *Critical Environmental Issues*, p. 12.

231. Stevenson, address of July 11, 1974 in *Senate Report on the Caracas Convention*, p. 9.

232. UN Doc. A/AC.138/SC.III/SR.41, p. 3.

233. Article xxiv, text reprinted in *Senate Report on the Caracas Conference*, p. 79. Stevenson, address of July 11, 1974 in *Senate Report on the Caracas Conference*, p. 11.

234. Donald McKernan address of August 17, 1971, *Law of the Sea Crisis*, p. 49.

235. Ibid.

236. Stevenson, address of July 17, 1974 in *Senate Report on the Caracas Conference*, p. 14; UN Doc. A/CONF.62/WP.8/Part I, p. 5. The address is reprinted in *Senate Status Report on the Law of the Sea Conference*, p. 1283.

237. *Third UN Law of the Sea Conference*, p. 31.

238. Johnson, "Environmental Controls" in Stein, *Critical Environmental Issues*, p. 36.

239. "The Third United Nations Conference on the Law of the Sea," Geneva (March 17-May 9, 1975); *Senate Status Report on the Law of the Sea Conference*, p. 1241; "The Third United Nations Conference on the Law of the Sea," Caracas (June 20-August 29, 1974) in U.S. Congress, *Oceanography Miscellaneous*, p. 98.

240. UN Doc. A/CONF.62/C.3/L.15.
241. *Third UN Law of the Sea Conference*, p. 31. See also the statement of Kenya in UN Doc. A/AC.138/SC.III.SR.41, p. 6.
242. *Environmental Quality, Annual Report*, 1972, pp. 80, 93.
243. *Third UN Law of the Sea Conference*, p. 32.
244. *Environmental Quality, Annual Report*, 1972, pp. 80, 93.
245. Ibid., p. 93.
246. Jackson and Dubos, *Only One Earth*, p. 208.
247. Hollick, "What to Expect," p. 68.
248. F. H. Knelman, "What Happened at Stockholm," p. 43.
249. Ibid.
250. *Third UN Law of the Sea Conference*, p. 4. The text of the Truman Proclamation (September 28, 1945) is contained in Shigeru Oda, *The International Law of the Ocean Development* (Leiden: Sijthoff International Publishing Company, 1972), p. 341.
251. Hollick, "What to Expect," p. 71.
252. Hollick, "Bureaucrats at Sea," pp. 52-53; L. F. E. Goldie, "The Management of Ocean Resources: Regimes for Structuring the Maritime Environment," *The Future of the International Legal Order: The Structure of the International Environment*, ed. Cyril E. Black and Richard A. Falk, 4 (Princeton: Princeton University Press, 1972), 210-211; Wenk, *Politics of the Ocean*, p. 280.
253. Goldie, "Management of Ocean Resources" in Black and Falk, *Future of the International Legal Order*, p. 211.
254. Johnson, "Environmental Controls" in Stein, *Critical Environmental Issues*, p. 35.
255. This statement, quoting from Principle 7 of the Declaration of the Stockholm Conference on the Human Environment, is contained in "Statement of the Honorable Russell E. Train," p. 3.
256. *Stockholm Declaration*, Principle 21.
257. Text in Barros and Johnston, *International Law*, p. 251.
258. *Environmental Quality, Annual Report*, 1973, p. 440.
259. John Stevenson, "Department Discusses Progress Towards 1973 Conference on the Law of the Sea," p. 672.
260. Wenk, *Politics of the Ocean*, p. 287.
261. The U.S. delegation even objected to other delegations' use of language depicting an "ocean space" regime, saying that such a sweeping authority was outside the competence of the conference. See Johnson, "Environmental Controls" in Stein, *Critical Environmental Issues*, p. 34; UN Doc. A/CONF.62/C.1/SR.7; R. C. Ogley, "Caracas and the Common Heritage," *International Relations*, 4 (November 1974), 620.
262. Lyndon Johnson, "Remarks at the Commissioning of the Research Ship *Oceanographer*," July 13, 1966, text, Wenk, *Politics of the Ocean*, p. 476.
263. UN Doc. A/6628, Res. 2749 (xxv); *Senate Report on Ocean Nodules*, p. 89.

264. United Nations, General Assembly, *Draft United Nations Convention on the International Seabed Area*, UN Doc. A/AC.138/25 (1970), p. 1.

265. Nixon, "United States Oceans Policy," *Public Papers*, p. 455.

266. Lyndon Johnson, "Report of the President to the Congress on Marine Resources and Engineering Development, Marine Science Affairs—A Year of Transition," U.S. President, National Council on Marine Resources and Engineering Development, *Marine Science Affairs*, 1st Report (Washington, D.C.: Government Printing Office, 1967), pp. v, iii.

267. Nixon, "United States Oceans Policy," *Public Papers*, p. 456.

268. Ratiner, address of August 9, 1974 in *Senate Report on the Caracas Convention*, p. 35.

269. Wenk, *Politics of the Ocean*, p. 262. *Marine Science Affairs*, 1st Report, p. v; Hollick, "Bureaucrats at Sea," pp. 3, 53-54, 70-71.

270. Wenk, *Politics of the Ocean*, pp. 266-267, 274.

271. Nixon, "United States Ocean Policy," *Public Papers*, p. 455.

272. Lynton K. Caldwell, *In Defense of Earth*, p. 237.

273. Goldberg, "Chemical Invasion" in Matthews, Smith, and Goldberg, *Man's Impact*, p. 268.

274. Nixon, "State of the Union Message," in *Environmental Quality, Annual Report*, 1973, p. 440.

275. Nixon, "State of the Union Message," January 30, 1974, *Environmental Quality, Annual Report*, 1974, p. 542.

276. Stevenson, "U.S. Urges Early Conclusion of Law of the Sea Treaty," p. 153.

277. Stevenson, "Lawmaking for the Seas," p. 190.

278. See the Marine Resources and Engineering Development Act of 1966, P. L. 89-454, *U.S. Statutes*, 80 (June 17, 1966); U.S. Commission on Marine Science, Engineering and Resources, *Marine Resources and Legal-Political Arrangements for Their Development* (Washington, D.C.: Government Printing Office, 1969), p. VIII-2.

279. Hollick, "Bureaucrats at Sea," p. 70.

280. Ratiner, address of August 9, 1974 in *Senate Report on the Caracas Convention*, pp. 30, 36-37.

281. Stevenson, "Lawmaking for the Seas," p. 190.

282. U.S. Commission on Marine Science, Engineering, and Resources, *Marine Resources and Legal-Political Arrangements for Their Development*, p. VIII-3.

283. Frank, *Geneva Session Hearings*, p. 58. In order to gain domestic support for a treaty, the United States needed to take a stance less objectionable to U.S. environmental groups. This was accomplished in 1977, as the negotiating text was modified so that it became consistent with U.S. national legislation imposing standards on ships using U.S. ports. However, the other previously noted deficiencies in the treaty remained.

284. Wenk, *Politics of the Ocean*, p. 263; Hollick, "Bureaucrats at Sea," pp. 2, 70-71.

285. For one view of such an agency, see Falk, *Study of Future Worlds*, pp. 268-274.

286. Shinn, *International Politics*, p. 125. Shinn concludes: "The first sign of serious cooperative efforts will be massive consolidation of old organizations or the establishment of new forums with comprehensive capability. Without one or the other, international environmental efforts are reducible to empty rhetoric and meaningless verbiage."

287. See Hollick, "What to Expect," p. 77.

288. On this point, see Hollick, ibid.

289. See John Lawrence Hargrove, *Ocean Pollution*, pp. 127-128.

290. To be sure, the United States has such a large impact on both the political climate and the quantity of pollutants introduced in the seas that strong national legislation would alleviate, although not arrest, the decline of the oceans.

291. Gerald Elliott, "Fishing Control—National Or International," *World Today*, 28 (March 1972), 134-135.

292. O. P. Dwivedi, "The Canadian Government Response to Environmental Concern," p. 15.

293. Controlling radioactive pollution is nearly as difficult as preventing the proliferation of nuclear weapons. William O. Doub and Joseph M. Dukert comment: "If a nation is determined, as India was, to demonstrate the ability to build its own nuclear weapons, probably no international framework can prevent it from doing so; the raw materials and the technology exist, to the point where no amount of international policing consistent with present concepts of national sovereignty . . . can prevent nations from developing and exploding 'devices'" ("Making Nuclear Energy Safe," p. 756).

294. Johnston, "Marine Pollution Control," p. 70; Hardy, "International Control" in Fawcett and Higgins, *International Organization*, p. 110.

295. Shinn, *International Politics*, p. 181.

296. Malarial spraying reportedly accounted for only 15 percent of the general use of DDT in the early 1970s. Quoted in Clyde Sanger, "Environment and Development," p. 118.

297. On this point, see Knelman, "What Happened at Stockholm," pp. 33-34.

298. As Knelman, ibid., has explained: "Economic power thrives on competition. Ecology is based on mutuality and indivisibility. Power is based on zero-sum games. Ecology is based on non-zero-sum games" (pp. 34-35).

299. Richard A. Falk, "Environmental Policy as a World Order Problem," in Albert E. Utton and Daniel H. Henning, eds., *Environmental Policy*, pp. 146, 151.

300. See the statement of Marne Dubs, *Geneva Session Hearings*, p. 45.

466

301. Gordon L. Becker, Counsel, Law Department, Exxon Corporation, *Geneva Session Hearings*, p. 35.

302. These might include, for example, family planning, control of inflation, and improvement of agricultural production.

303. Ambassador Pardo advocated an international regime with three categories of membership for states over 100,000 population: (1) states over 100 million or which meet other criteria, such as length of coastline, catch of fish, and volume of merchant shipping; (2) all other coastal states, and (3) landlocked countries. Decisions would require a majority vote in two of the three categories. All members would have one vote, but could express it only in their own category.

     Hallman, *Towards an Environmentally Sound Law*, offers a brief but relatively comprehensive treatment of the environmental protection that could be satisfied with only a minimum of structural change. Other proposals for an international regime are contained in the following: The Commission to Study the Organization of Peace, *New Dimensions for the United Nations* (New York: UN Plaza, 1968), 17th Report, pp. 44-46; "Malta: Draft Articles on the Preservation of the Marine Environment," pp. 583-590; Borgese, *Pacem in Maribus*; U.S. Congress, Senate, Foreign Relations Committee, *The United Nations at Twenty-One*, Report by Senator Frank Church, 90th Cong., 1st Sess. (Washington, D.C.: Government Printing Office, 1967), p. 25.

304. Jack Davis, Canada's minister of the environment, said that nations will have to agree on international pollution standards for specific industries before the issue of environmental quality versus economic development is resolved. Otherwise, capital will flow to pollution havens. See Sanger, "Environment and Development," p. 104.

305. Jackson and Dubos, *Only One Earth*, p. 201. In the United States alone, dumping of wastes in the oceans multiplied five times during the 1950s and 1960s. According to monitoring surveys of the United States National Oceanographic and Atmospheric Administration, this practice fouled more than one million square miles of the Atlantic and extended into the Caribbean as far as the Yucatan Peninsula. See Hallman, *Towards an Environmentally Sound Law*, p. 6; *MARMAP* Report, NOAA, United States Department of Commerce, January 1974.

306. Jacques Cousteau, "The Perils and Potentials of a Watery Planet," p. 42.

SIX. BUILDING A JUST WORLD ORDER

1. Two sets of tables are relevant here. The first compares professed and implicit values (Tables 2-7, 3-13, 4-2, and 5-3). The second

compares the values implicit in U.S. policy with the values of global humanism (Tables 2-8, 3-14, 4-3, 5-4).

2. There are, of course, additional dimensions that make up a more complete worldview.

3. For a summary of these agreements, see Stockholm International Peace Research Institute, *World Armaments and Disarmament, SIPRI Yearbook, 1977*, pp. 368-380. For an assessment of the impact of these agreements on the arms buildup, see Stockholm International Peace Research Institute, *Armaments and Disarmament in the Nuclear Age*, pp. 217-223; Bernhard G. Bechhoefer, *Postwar Negotiations for Arms Control*; Robert C. Johansen, *Toward a Dependable Peace*.

4. For example, Herbert York, who served as scientific advisor to presidents during three administrations has concluded: "Over the last 30 years we have repeatedly taken unilateral actions that have unnecessarily accelerated the arms race. Our unilateral decisions have set the rate and scale for most of the individual steps in the strategic-arms race." *Race to Oblivion*, p. 230.

5. This concept was developed by Nathan Leites in *A Study of Bolshevism* (Glencoe, Ill.: The Free Press, 1953). Alexander L. George refined it in "The 'Operational Code,'" pp. 190-222. Richard J. Barnet used the concept in *The Roots of War*. Although his study was limited to national security affairs and published before the present studies occurred, the implicit values delineated in the case studies here substantiate many of his findings.

6. These ideas are more fully elaborated in Barnet, *Roots of War*, pp. 95-96, 98.

7. Text, *New York Times*, October 13, 1974.

8. Quoted in Arthur Schlesinger, *A Thousand Days*, p. 481; cited in Barnet, *Roots of War*, p. 106.

9. See Barnet's similar conclusion, *Roots of War*, pp. 93-98; 109-114; 120-129.

10. For elaboration of this point, see ibid., pp. 120-121.

11. For elaboration of this point and general discussion of bureaucratic politics, see ibid., p. 122; Graham Allison, *Essence of Decision*; Graham Allison and Morton Halperin, "Bureaucratic Politics," pp. 40-79.

12. Interview with James Reston, text, *New York Times*, October 13, 1974.

13. One example is the book, *Famine—1975!* (Boston: Little, Brown and Company, 1967). It was written by William and Paul Paddock, two brothers with pertinent experience: one was an agronomist and plant pathologist who headed a tropical research station and also a school of agriculture in Central America; the other was a retired foreign service officer with experience in the developing

countries of Asia and Africa. Part 1 of the book is entitled "Inevitability of Famine in the Hungry Nations."

14. Richard A. Falk has described similar forms of human estrangement as "false consciousness." Such a person "loses the ability to discern his own interests, the conditions of his own fulfillment, or the actuality of his role as a victim or perpetrator of exploitation." See *This Endangered Planet*, pp. 84-85.

15. Many observers would argue that the actions of U.S. officials did not violate reason. To be sure, because their policies were rooted in priorities that differed sharply from those of global humanism did not in itself make their behavior unreasonable. However, to the extent that they were motivated by ideological and material interests which increased selective perception, made them blind to important dimensions of reality, and stimulated unreflective policy responses, to that extent one could say that their behavior "violated reason." The case studies demonstrate that official behavior contained a high degree of such behavior. For both psychological and material reasons, officials resisted modification of their operational code that would bring it into closer harmony with a rapidly changing reality.

16. Barnet, *Roots of War*, p. 126.

17. Of course, the changes may not always be positive. Also, some gaps between rhetoric and behavior may indefinitely disguise normatively deficient policies.

18. Milton Rokeach, *The Nature of Human Values*, pp. 328-330.

19. Although the role of the court system has not been discussed in this study, an example of the judicial branch's national partisanship is the refusal of the federal courts to consider the legality of the war in Vietnam and the legal defense of deserters who claimed to be following the Nuremburg precedent and international treaties prohibiting war crimes.

20. The "balance of power system" does not serve this function. In such a system, one nation may seek to offset another state's potential abuse of power, but usually none of the competing nation-states genuinely promotes the global interest. They pursue different national interests. In contrast to the international system, within most domestic political systems there are many incentives for competing political actors to express different versions of the society's common interest, rather than simply to advance particular vested interests. To be sure, often special interests are disguised as the public interest, but in democratic societies their expression is usually muted and the prospect of their fulfillment less absolute than is the case of superpowers pursuing special interests within the international system.

21. For a discussion of some central guidance possibilities, such as sug-

gested in numbers 3, 6, 9, and 12, see Richard A. Falk, *A Study of Future Worlds*, pp. 224-276.

22. Quoted in Leslie H. Gelb, "The Kissinger Legacy," p. 85.

23. Quoted in Donald McDonald, "American Guilt," p. 30. Commenting upon the influence of the military-industrial complex on national policy, Richard Barnet concluded that "the only force capable of bringing about the conversion of the society is a nationwide movement of Americans who see the militarism of America as our number-one security problem and are prepared to fight for a generation if necessary to free the nation from its grip" (*The Economy of Death*, p. 135).

24. More often than not, on foreign policy issues national governmental rhetoric has been deceptive. This does not mean that all government officials are dishonest, but simply that there is frequently a fundamental contradiction between what they say and what they do. In some instances they *are* dishonest; in others they have faulty perceptions of reality and their own behavior.

25. For a discussion of the possibilities for using nonviolence effectively, see Gene Sharp, *The Politics of Nonviolent Action* and George Lakey, *Strategy for a Living Revolution*.

26. For example, to establish merely a world authority for environmental protection will raise enormous political opposition. Commenting upon the prospects for such an authority, George Kennan concluded: "If the present process of [environmental] deterioration is to be halted, things are going to have to be done which will encounter formidable resistance from individual governments and powerful interests within individual countries." But Kennan did not seem to take his own analysis seriously enough to draw the conclusion that change would need to begin in opposition to present centers of power. In spite of the anticipated governmental and corporate resistance, Kennan offered no plan of action for the creation of a new authority other than to hope that precisely the privileged forces that now resist change will soon implement it. "Only an entity that has great prestige, great authority and active support from centers of influence within the world's most powerful industrial and maritime nations will be able to make headway against such recalcitrance." George F. Kennan, "To Prevent a World Wasteland," p. 409.

27. *New York Times*, February 2, 1975.

28. Although it is impossible to describe precisely how a grass roots popular movement can transform the present institutional structures of the international system, it is useful to outline plausible strategies with feasible steps leading from the present to a preferred system. For discussion of one possible transition strategy aimed at abolishing the war system, see Johansen, *Toward a Dependable Peace*.

470

29. See Falk's "first law of ecological politics," *This Endangered Planet*, p. 353.
30. Rokeach, *Nature of Human Values*, p. 331.
31. As Rokeach commented, the idea that "enduring value changes can be induced by a single experimental session takes on rather awesome . . . political implications." Ibid., p. 324.

    The possibilities for value change, of course, will not automatically serve the values of global humanism, consistent though they are with many psychologists' and religious leaders' understandings of human health, sanity, and spiritual enrichment. Because of an effective socialization process, most people in practice give national loyalty and prevailing subspecific political values priority over the principle of universal compassion which is prescribed by the dominant religious faiths in the United States. In practice, peoples' highest loyalties are to national symbols, even though universal brotherliness and sisterliness are the hallmarks of both Christianity and Judaism.
32. Many critics scoff at the suggestion that foreign policy can, even if it should, reflect extranational humanitarianism. The pervasiveness of self-interest, they say, precludes the transfer of as much as 1 or 2 or 5 percent of GNP to poor states "merely" out of a sense of solidarity with other humans. In the past, the argument goes, national societies have more often than not pursued their own advantages without much regard for, or even at the expense of, other nations. They are likely to continue doing so in the future.

    Such statements are similar to the arguments raised by slave owners in the 1850s who said that some groups, possessing superior skills and racial qualities, had dominated other groups in the past and therefore should continue to do so in the future. The idea of human solidarity between blacks and whites was as unthinkable to such people before the Civil War as is the idea today of human solidarity among all nations of the globe. The past failure to achieve human solidarity transcending either races or nations is not a convincing argument that human solidarity is unachievable. During the last three centuries subnational loyalties in many parts of the world were rapidly replaced with intense feelings of national solidarity. In several noteworthy instances—including the growth of United States nationalism—these new national solidarities transcended previous linguistic, racial, religious, and cultural differences.

471

Bibliography

Aaron, David. "SALT: A New Concept." *Foreign Policy*, No. 17 (Winter 1974-1975), pp. 157-165.

Adede, A. O. "System for Exploitation of the Common Heritage of Mankind at the Caracas Conference." *American Journal of International Law*, 69 (January 1975), 31-49.

Agee, Philip. *Inside the Company: CIA Diary*. London: Penguin, 1975.

Allison, Graham. *Essence of Decision: Explaining the Cuban Missile Crisis*. Boston: Little, Brown and Company, 1971.

Allison, Graham and Halperin, Morton. "Bureaucratic Politics: A Paradigm and some Policy Implications." *World Politics*, 24 (Spring 1972), 40-79.

Artin, Tom. *Earth Talk*. New York: Grossman, 1973.

Baldwin, David A. *Foreign Aid and American Foreign Policy*. New York: Praeger, 1966.

Ball, George. *The Discipline of Power*. Boston: Little, Brown and Company, 1968.

Barnaby, Frank. "The Mounting Prospects of Nuclear War." *Bulletin of the Atomic Scientists*, 33 (June 1977), 11-21.

Barnds, William J. "India and America at Odds." *International Affairs*, 49 (July 1973), 317-384.

Barnet, Richard J. "Dirty Tricks and the Intelligence Underworld." *Society* 12 (March/April 1975), 52-57.

————. *The Economy of Death*. New York: Atheneum, 1970.

————. *Intervention and Revolution*. New York: The World Publishing Company, 1968.

————. *Roots of War*. New York: Atheneum, 1972.

————. *Who Wants Disarmament?* Boston: Beacon Press, 1960.

————, and Mueller, Ronald. *Global Reach: The Power of the Multinational Corporation*. New York: Simon and Schuster, 1974.

Barros, James and Johnston, Douglas M. *The International Law of Pollution*. New York: Free Press, 1974.

Bechhoefer, Bernhard G. *Postwar Negotiations for Arms Control*. Washington, D.C.: The Brookings Institution, 1961.

Bell, Wendell and Mau, James A., eds. *The Sociology of the Future*. New York: Sage, 1971.

Beres, Louis and Targ, Harry. *Reordering the Planet: Constructing Alternative World Futures*. Boston: Allyn and Bacon, 1974.

473

Bernstein, Richard. "Poisoning the Seas." *Saturday Review/World*, 1 (November 20, 1973), 14-16.

Bhagwati, Jagdish N. *Amount and Sharing of Aid*. Washington, D.C.: Overseas Development Council, 1970.

———, ed. *Economics and World Order: From the 1970's to the 1990's*. New York: Macmillan 1972.

Birns, Laurence R. "Allende's Fall, Washington's Push." *New York Times*, September 15, 1974.

———, ed. *The End of Chilean Democracy*. New York: Seabury Press, 1973.

Black, Lloyd. *The Strategy of Foreign Aid*. Princeton: Van Nostrand, 1968.

Blackstock, Paul. *The Strategy of Subversion*. Chicago: Quadrangle, 1964.

Bleicher, Samuel A. "An Overview of International Environmental Regulation." *Ecology Law Quarterly*, 2 (Winter 1972), 1-90.

Bloomfield, Lincoln P. "Nuclear Spread and World Order." *Foreign Affairs*, 53 (July 1975), 743-755.

Borgese, Elisabeth Mann, ed. *Pacem in Maribus*. New York: Dodd, Mead and Company, 1972.

Borgstrom, Georg. *The Hungry Planet*. New York: Macmillan, 1965.

Bowen, V. T. and Sugihara, T. T. "Oceanographic Implications of Radioactive Fallout Distributions in the Atlantic Ocean." *Journal of Marine Research*, 23 (April 1965), 123-146.

Brodkin, E. I. "United States Aid to India and Pakistan." *International Affairs*, 43 (October 1967), 664-677.

Brown, E. D. "International Law and Marine Pollution: Radioactive Waste and Other Hazardous Substances." *Natural Resources Journal*, 11 (April 1971), 221-255.

———. "The Conventional Law of the Environment." *Natural Resources Journal*, 13 (April 1973), 203-234.

Brown, Lester R. *By Bread Alone*. New York: Praeger, 1974.

Brown, Norman W. *The United States and India, Pakistan, Bangladesh*. Cambridge: Harvard University Press, 1972.

Brownlie, Ian. *Basic Documents on Human Rights*. Oxford: Clarendon Press, 1971.

Brynes, Asher. *We Give to Conquer*. New York: Norton, 1966.

Brzezinski, Zbigniew. "The Politics of Underdevelopment." *World Politics*, 9 (October 1956), 55-75.

Caldwell, Lynton K. *In Defense of Earth: International Protection of the Biosphere*. Bloomington: Indiana University Press, 1972.

Carter, Jimmy. "Peace, Arms Control, World Economic Progress, Human Rights: Basic Priorities of United States Foreign Policy." *Department of State Bulletin*, 76 (April 11, 1977), 329-333.

———. "Remarks by President Jimmy Carter Videotaped for Delivery to People of Other Nations." White House Press Release, January 20, 1977, mimeo.

Casey, William J. "A Comprehensive Development Policy for the United States." *Department of State Bulletin*, 69 (December 3, 1973), 688-694.

———. "The Rule of Law in International Economic Affairs." *Department of State Bulletin*, 69 (September 3, 1973), 321-326.

Clark, Grenville and Sohn, Louis B., eds. *Introduction to World Peace Through World Law*. Chicago: World Without War Publications, 1973.

———. *World Peace Through World Law*. Cambridge: Harvard University Press, 1960.

Clark, Ramsey. "The Law and Human Rights in Chile." *Christianity and Crisis*, 34 (July 22, 1974), 161-164.

Clarkson, Kenneth W. "International Law, U.S. Seabeds Policy and Ocean Resource Development." *Journal of Law and Economics*, 17 (April 1974), 117-142.

Clemens, Walter C. "Ecology and International Relations." *International Journal*, 28 (Winter 1972-73), 1-27.

———. "Nicholas II to SALT II: Continuity and Change in East-West Diplomacy." *International Affairs*, 49 (June 1973), 385-401.

Coastal Zone Workshop, Woods Hole, Massachusetts, 1972. *The Water's Edge*. Ed. Bostwich, H. Ketchum. Cambridge, Massachusetts: MIT Press, 1972.

Coffin, Tristan. *The Armed Society*. Baltimore: Penguin Books, 1964.

Commoner, Barry. *The Closing Circle*. New York: Bantam, 1971.

Connor, Walker. "Self-Determination: The New Phase." *World Politics*, 20 (October 1967), 30-53.

Cook, Fred J. *The Warfare State*. New York: Macmillan, 1962.

Cooper, Chester. "The CIA and Decision Making." *Foreign Affairs*, 50 (January 1972), 223-236.

Cousteau, Jacques. "The Perils and Potentials of a Watery Planet." *Saturday Review/World*, 1 (August 24, 1974), 41 ff.

Dillon, Douglas. "The Contribution of Trade to the Cause of Peace." *Department of State Bulletin*, 38 (May 26, 1958), 881-882.

Dornan, James E. "Maybe No Agreement Would be Better." *Armed Forces Journal*, January 1975, pp. 28-32.

Doty, Paul; Garwin, Richard; Kistiakowsky, George; Rathjens, George; Schelling, Thomas. "Nuclear War by 1999?" *Harvard Magazine*, 78 (November 1975), 19-25.

Doub, William O. and Dukert, Joseph M. "Making Nuclear Energy Safe and Secure." *Foreign Affairs*, 53 (July 1975), 756-772.

Dubs, Adolph. "Department Discusses South Asia and U.S. Assistance Programs." *Department of State Bulletin*, 76 (April 19, 1977), 344-346.

Dulles, John Foster. "Peace Without Fear." *Department of State Bulletin*, 24 (May 7, 1951), 726-731.

Dwivedi, O. P. "The Canadian Government Response to Environmental Concern." *International Journal*, 28 (Winter 1972-1973), 134-152.

Eckert, Ross D. "Exploitation of Deep Ocean Minerals: Regulatory Mechanisms and U.S. Policy." *Journal of Law and Economics*, 17 (April 1974), 143-177.

Ehrlich, Paul and Ehrlich, Anne H. *Population, Resources, and Environment*. San Francisco: W. H. Freeman, 1972.

Epstein, William. "Inexorable Rise of Military Expenditures." *Bulletin of the Atomic Scientists*, 31 (January 1975), 17-19.

——. *The Last Chance: Nuclear Proliferation and Arms Control*. New York: Free Press, 1976.

Fagen, Richard R. "The United States and Chile: Roots and Branches." *Foreign Affairs*, 53 (January 1975), 263-313.

Falk, Richard A. "Arms Control, Foreign Policy, and Global Reform." *Daedalus*, 104 (Summer 1975), 35-52.

——. "A New Paradigm for International Legal Studies: Prospects and Proposals." *The Yale Law Journal*, 84 (April 1975), 969-1021.

——. *A Study of Future Worlds*. New York: Free Press, 1975.

——. *This Endangered Planet: Prospects and Proposals for Human Survival*. New York: Vintage, 1971.

——. "Towards a World Order Respectful of the Global Ecological System." *Environmental Affairs*, 1 (June 1971), 25-65.

——, and Black, Cyril E., eds. *The Future of the International Legal Order: Trends and Patterns*. 4 vols. Princeton: Princeton University Press, 1969-75.

——, and Mendlovitz, Saul H. *Regional Politics and World Order*. San Francisco: W. H. Freeman, 1973.

476

Farnsworth, Elizabeth. "Chile: What Was the U.S. Role? More Than Admitted." *Foreign Policy*, No. 16 (Fall 1974), pp. 127-141.

Fawcett, James E. S. and Higgins, Rosalyn, eds. *International Organization: Law in Movement*. London: Oxford University Press, 1974.

Feldman, Herbert. "Aid as Imperialism?" *International Affairs*, 43 (April 1967), 219-235.

Fisher, David W. "Some Social and Economic Aspects of Marine Resource Development." *American Journal of Economics and Sociology*, 32 (April 1973), 113-127.

FAO Technical Conference on Marine Pollution and Its Effect on Living Resources and Fishing, Rome, 1970. *Marine Pollution and Sea Life*. London: Fishing News Books, 1972.

Frank, Richard A. "The Law at Sea." *New York Times Magazine*, May 18, 1975, pp. 14 ff.

Friedheim, R. L. "Quantitative Content Analysis of the U.N. Seabed Debate." *International Organization*, 24 (Summer 1970), 479-502.

Galtung, Johan. *The True Worlds*. New York: The Free Press, forthcoming.

Garcia-Amador, F. V., ed. *The Inter-American System*. Dobbs Ferry, New York: Oceana, 1966.

Garcia Marquez, Gabriel. "Why Allende Had To Die." *New Statesman*, 87 (March 15, 1974), 356-358.

Gaud, William S. "Development—A Balance Sheet." *Department of State Bulletin*, 59 (December 30, 1968), 703-706.

———. "Foreign Aid: What It Is; How It Works, Why We Provide It." *Department of State Bulletin*, 59 (December 9, 1968), 603-606.

Gelb, Leslie H. "The Kissinger Legacy." *New York Times Magazine*, October 31, 1976, pp. 13 ff.

Gelba, Harry M. "Technical Innovation and Arms Control." *World Politics*, 26 (July 1974), 509-541.

George, Alexander L. "The 'Operational Code': A Neglected Approach to the Study of Political Leaders and Decision-Making." *International Studies Quarterly*, 13 (June 1969), 190-222.

Gillette, Robert. "Radiation Spill at Hanford: The Anatomy of an Accident." *Science*, 181 (August 24, 1973), 728-730.

Gilligan, John J. "United States Seeks Improved U.N. Programs

477

to Meet Basic Needs of World's Poor." *Department of State Bulletin*, 77 (August 15, 1977), 204-207.

Goldsmith, Edward et al. *Blueprint for Survival*. Boston: Houghton Mifflin, 1972.

Goldwin, Robert A. *Why Foreign Aid?* Chicago: Rand McNally, 1963.

Goulet, Denis. *The Cruel Choice: A Normative Theory of Development*. New York: Atheneum, 1971.

————, and Hudson, Michael. *The Myth of Aid*. New York: IDOC North America, 1971.

Graham, Frank. *Since Silent Spring*. Boston: Houghton Mifflin, 1970.

Green, Harold P. "Radioactive Waste and The Environment." *Natural Resources Journal*, 11 (April 1971), 281-295.

Green, Philip. *Deadly Logic: The Theory of Nuclear Deterrence*. Columbus, Ohio: Ohio State University Press, 1966.

Greenwood, Ted and Nacht, Michael. "New Nuclear Debate: Sense or Nonsense?" *Foreign Affairs*, 52 (June 1974), 761-780.

Hallman, Robert M. *Towards an Environmentally Sound Law of the Sea*. Washington, D.C.: International Institute for Environment and Development, 1974.

Halperin, Morton H. "Decision-Making for Covert Operations." *Society*, 12 (March/April 1975), 45-51.

Halpern, Manfred. *The Morality and Politics of Intervention*. New York: The Council on Religion and International Affairs, 1963.

Hannah, John A. "Institutional Problems in the Developing Countries." *Department of State Bulletin*, 64 (March 8, 1971), 297-301.

Hansen, Roger D. "The Political Economy of North-South Relations: How Much Change?" *International Organization*, 29 (Fall 1975), 921-947.

Hardin, Garrett. *Exploring New Ethics for Survival*. Baltimore: Penguin, 1972.

Hardy, E. P., Keey, P. W. and Volchok, H. L. "Global Inventory and Distribution of Fallout Plutonium." *Nature*, 241 (February 16, 1973), 444-445.

Hardy, Michael. "International Control of Marine Pollution." *Natural Resources Journal*, 11 (April 1971), 296-348.

Hargrove, John L., ed. "Conference on Legal and Institutional Response to Problems of the Global Environment." *Law, In-*

stitutions, and the Global Environment. Dobbs Ferry: Oceana Publications, 1973.

————, ed. *Who Protects the Ocean?* St. Paul: West Publishing Co., 1975.

Harrison, Selig S., ed. *India and the United States*. New York: Macmillan, 1961.

Heilbroner, Robert L. "Growth and Survival." *Foreign Affairs*, 51 (October 1972), 139-153.

————. *An Inquiry into the Human Prospect*. New York: Norton, 1975.

Herz, John. *International Politics in the Atomic Age*. New York: Columbia University Press, 1959.

————. "The Territorial State Revisited," *Polity*, 1 (September 1968), 11-34.

Hollick, Ann L. "What to Expect From a Sea Treaty." *Foreign Policy*, No. 18 (Spring 1975), pp. 68-78.

————, and Osgood, Robert E. *New Era of Ocean Politics*. Baltimore: Johns Hopkins Press, 1975.

Hollings, Ernest F. "National Ocean Policy Study." *Oceans*, 8 (January/February 1975), 6-7.

Holst, Johan Jorgen. "A Strategic Arms Race: What is Really Going On?" *Foreign Policy*, No. 19 (Summer 1975), pp. 152-162.

Hudson, Michael. *Super Imperialism: The Economic Strategy of American Enterprise*. New York: Holt, Rinehart, and Winston, 1972.

Ingersoll, Robert S. "Economic Interdependence and Common Defense." *Department of State Bulletin*, 71 (October 7, 1974), 473-476.

Inter-American Institute of International Legal Studies. *The Inter-American System: Its Development and Strengthening*. Dobbs Ferry, New York: Oceana Publications, 1966.

International Atomic Energy Agency. *Nuclear Power and the Environment*. Vienna: International Atomic Energy Agency, 1973.

International Colloquium on the European Convention on Human Rights. *Human Rights in National and International Law*. Manchester: Manchester University Press, 1968.

International Institute for Strategic Studies. *The 1974-75 Military Balance*. London: International Institute for Strategic Studies, 1976.

"Interview with William E. Colby." *U.S. News and World Report*, 77 (December 2, 1974), 29-32.

Irwin, John N. "A Strengthened and Revitalized Foreign Aid Program." *Department of State Bulletin*, 64 (May 24, 1971), 657-664.

Jackson, Barbara Ward and Dubos, René. *Only One Earth: The Care and Maintenance of a Small Planet*. New York: Norton, 1972.

Jacobson, Jon. "Caracas 1974: A No-Progress Report on the Law of the Sea." *Oceana*, 7 (November-December, 1974), 66-68.

Johansen, Robert C. "Countercombatant Strategy: A New Balance of Terror?" *Worldview*, 17 (July 1974), 47-53.

———. "A Global Humanist Critique of National Policies for Arms Control." *Journal of International Affairs*, 31 (Fall/Winter 1977), 215-241.

———. *Toward a Dependable Peace: A Proposal for an Appropriate Security System*. New York: Institute for World Order, 1978.

Johnson, Lyndon. "To Build the Peace—The Foreign Aid Program for Fiscal 1969." *Department of State Bulletin*, 58 (March 4, 1968), 322-329.

———. "The Importance of Foreign Aid to U.S. Security and World Peace." *Department of State Bulletin*, 59 (August 21, 1968), 178.

Johnston, Douglas M. "Marine Pollution Control: Law, Science and Politics." *International Journal*, 28 (Winter 1972-73), 69-102.

Kalsi, Swadesh S. "Oil in Neptune's Kingdom: Problems and Responses to Contain Environmental Degradation of the Oceans by Oil Pollution." *Environmental Affairs*, 3, No. 1 (1974), pp. 79-108.

Katzenbach, Nicholas deB. "Foreign Policy, Public Opinion and Secrecy." *Foreign Affairs*, 52 (October 1973), 1-19.

———. "United States Policy Toward the Developing World." *Department of State Bulletin*, 59 (August 26, 1968), 209-213.

Kay, David and Skolinikoff, Eugene B. *World Eco-Crisis*. Madison: University of Wisconsin Press, 1972.

Kennan, George F. "To Prevent a World Wasteland: A Proposal." *Foreign Affairs*, 48 (April 1970), 401-413.

Kennedy, John F. "Message of the President to the Congress." *Department of State Bulletin*, 44 (April 10, 1961), 507-514.

———. "New Opportunities in the Search for Peace." *Department of State Bulletin*, 49 (October 7, 1963), 530-535.

———. "White House Holds Conference on Export Expansion: Address by President Kennedy." *Department of State Bulletin*, 44 (October 14, 1963), 595-599.

Kennedy, Robert, *Thirteen Days*. New York: Norton, 1969.

Kissinger, Henry. "The Foreign Assistance Program and Global Stability." *Department of State Bulletin*, 71 (August 19, 1974), 286-290.

———. "The Foreign Assistance Program: A Vital Tool in the Building of a More Cooperative World." *Department of State Bulletin*, 71 (July 8, 1974), 45-55.

———. "A Just Consensus, a Stable Order, a Durable Peace." *Department of State Bulletin*, 69 (October 15, 1973), 469-473.

———. "Moral Purposes and Policy Choices." *Department of State Bulletin*, 61 (October 29, 1973), 525-531.

———. "Towards a Global Community: The Common Cause of India and America." *Department of State Bulletin*, 71 (November 25, 1975), 740-746.

Klare, Michael T. "The Political Economy of Arms Sales." *Society*, 11 (September-October 1974), 41-49.

Knelman, F. H. "What Happened at Stockholm." *International Journal*, 28 (Winter 1972-1973), 28-49.

Kothari, Rajni. *Footsteps Into the Future: Diagnosis of the Present World and a Design for an Alternative*. New York: Free Press, 1974.

Krasner, Stephen D. "Are Bureaucracies Important? (Or Allison Wonderland)." *Foreign Policy*, No. 7 (Summer 1972), pp. 159-179.

Lagos, Gustavo and Godoy, Horacio H. *Revolution of Being: A Latin American View of the Future*. New York: Free Press, 1977.

Lakey, George. *Strategy for a Living Revolution*. San Francisco: W. H. Freeman, 1973.

Land, Thomas. "Dividing Up the Deep." *The Progressive*, 38 (June 1974), 35-37.

Lapp, Ralph E. *The Weapons Culture*. New York: Norton, 1968.

Laszlo, Ervin. *A Strategy for the Future*. New York: Braziller, 1974.

Laudicina, Paul. *World Poverty and Development: A Survey of American Opinion*. Washington, D.C.: Overseas Development Council, 1973.

Legault, L.J.H. "The Freedom of the Seas: A Licence to Pollute." *University of Toronto Law Journal*, 21 (April 1971), 39-49.

Leggett, Robert L. "Two Legs Do Not a Centipede Make." *Armed Forces Journal*, February 1975, pp. 30-32.

Lerza, Catherine and Jacobson, Michael, eds. *Food for People—Not for Profit*. New York: Ballantine, 1975.

Lewis, John P. *Wanted in India: A Relevant Radicalism*. Center of International Studies, Policy Memorandum No. 36. Princeton, N.J.: Princeton University, 1969.

———. *Quiet Crisis in India: Economic Development and American Policy*. Washington: Brookings, 1962.

McDonald, Donald. "American Guilt," an interview with Richard A. Falk, *Center Magazine*, 7 (January-February 1974), 26-32.

MacEoin, Gary. "The U.S. Government and Chile: An Exercise in Deception." *Christianity and Crisis*, 34 (October 14, 1974), 219-223.

McGarvey, Patrick J. *CIA: the Myth and the Madness*. New York: Saturday Review Press, 1972.

McIntyre, Thomas J. "Security through Détente: Limits and Possibilities," speech before the International Studies Council, University of New Hampshire, May 5, 1975.

McManus, Robert J. "The New Law on Ocean Dumping." *Oceans*, 6 (September-October 1973), 25-32.

———. "New Treaty on Vessel Pollution." *Oceans*, 7 (June 1974), 59-65.

"Malta: Draft Articles on the Preservation of the Marine Environment." A/Ac. 138/SC.III/L.33. *International Legal Materials*, 12 (1973), 583-590.

Marchetti, Victor and Marks, John D. *The CIA and the Cult of Intelligence*. New York: Dell, 1974.

Marx, Wesley. *The Frail Ocean*. New York: Ballantine, 1969.

Matthews, William H.; Smith, Frederick E.; and Goldberg, Edward D. *Man's Impact on Terrestial and Ocean Ecostystems*. Cambridge: MIT Press, 1971.

Mazrui, Ali A. *A World Federation of Cultures: An African Perspective*. New York: Free Press, 1976.

Melman, Seymour. *Pentagon Capitalism: The Political Economy of War*. New York: McGraw-Hill, 1970.

Mendlovitz, Saul H. *On the Creation of a Just World Order: Preferred Worlds for the 1990's*. New York: Free Press, 1975.

Mesarovic, Mihajlo D. and Pestel, Eduard. *Mankind at the Turning Point*. New York: Dutton, 1974.

Millikan, Max F. and Rostow, Walt W. *A Proposal: Key to an Effective Foreign Policy*. New York: Harper and Brothers, 1957.

Mollenhoff, Clark. *The Pentagon: Politics, Profits and Plunder*. New York: Putnam, 1967.

Montagu, Ashley. *The Endangered Environment*. New York: Mason and Lipcomb, 1974.

Moore, John Norton. "U.S. Position on Law of the Sea Reviewed." *Department of State Bulletin*, 70 (April 15, 1974), 397-402.

Moorecraft, Colin. *Must the Seas Die?* Boston: Gambit, 1973.

Moran, Theodore. *Multinational Corporations and the Politics of Dependence: Copper and Chile*. Princeton, N.J.: Princeton University Press, 1974.

Morgenthau, Hans. "A Political Theory of Foreign Aid." *American Political Science Review*, 56 (March 1962), 301-309.

Mostert, Noel. *Supership*. New York: Alfred A. Knopf, 1974.

Moyer, Bill. "Interview for 'Bill Moyer's Journal.' " *Department of State Bulletin*, 72 (February 10, 1975), 165-180.

Myrdal, Alva. *The Game of Disarmament: How the United States and Russia Run the Arms Race*. New York: Pantheon Books, 1976.

———. "The High Price of Nuclear Arms Monopoly." *Foreign Policy,* No. 18 (Spring 1975), pp. 30-43.

———. "International Control of Disarmament." *Scientific American*, 231 (October 1974), 21-33.

Myrdal, Gunnar. *The Challenge of World Poverty*. New York: Pantheon, 1970.

Nacht, Michael L. "The Delicate Balance of Error." *Foreign Policy*, No. 19 (Summer 1975) pp. 163-177.

National Academy of Sciences. Ocean Science Committee of the NAS-NRC Ocean Affairs Board. *Marine Environmental Quality*. Washington, D.C.: National Academy of Sciences, 1971.

National Research Council. Panel on Monitoring Persistent Pesticides in the Marine Environment. *Chlorinated Hydrocarbons in the Marine Environment*. Washington, D.C.: National Academy of Sciences, 1971.

———. Panel on Radioactivity in the Marine Environment. *Radioactivity in the Marine Environment*. Washington, D.C.: National Academy of Sciences, 1971.

———. Study Panel on Assessing Potential Ocean Pollutants. Ocean Affairs Board, Commission on Natural Resources. *Assessing Potential Ocean Pollutants*. Washington, D.C.: National Academy of Sciences, 1975.

Nayar, Baldev Raj. "Political Mainsprings of Economic Planning in the New Nations: The Modernization Imperative Versus Social Mobilization." *Comparative Politics*, 6 (April 1974), 341-366.

―――. "Treat India Seriously." *Foreign Policy*, No. 18 (Spring 1975), pp. 133-154.

Newhouse, John. *Cold Dawn: The Story of SALT*. New York: Holt, Rinehart and Winston, 1973.

Nitze, Paul. "The Strategic Balance Between Hope and Skepticism." *Foreign Policy*, No. 17 (Winter 1974-1975), pp. 136-156.

―――. "The Vladivostok Accord and SALT II." *Review of Politics*, 37 (April 1975), 147-160.

Nixon, Richard. "Foreign Assistance for the Seventies." *Department of State Bulletin*, 63 (October 5, 1970), 369-378.

―――. "Pragmatism and Moral Force in American Foreign Policy." *Department of State Bulletin*, 71 (July 1, 1974), 1-5.

―――. "President Nixon Interviewed for CBS Television." *Department of State Bulletin*, 63 (September 21, 1970), 327-330.

―――. "Reform of the U.S. Foreign Assistance Program." *Department of State Bulletin*, 64 (May 10, 1971), 614-625.

―――. "Special Message to the Congress on Marine Pollution From Oil Spills," May 20, 1970. *Public Papers of the Presidents of the United States*. Washington, D.C.: Government Printing Office, 1971.

―――. "U.S. Foreign Policy for the 1970's: Building for Peace." Report to Congress of February 25, 1971. *Department of State Bulletin*, 64 (March 22, 1971), 341-432.

―――. "United States Policy for the Seabed." *Department of State Bulletin*, 62 (June 15, 1970), 737-738.

Odeen, Philip. "In Defense of the Defense Budget." *Foreign Policy*, No. 16 (Fall 1974), pp. 93-108.

Ohlin, Goran. *Foreign Aid Policies Reconsidered*. Paris: Development Center of the Organization for Economic Cooperation and Development, 1966.

O'Leary, Michael Kent. *The Politics of American Foreign Aid*. New York: Atherton Press, 1967.

Organization for Economic Co-operation and Development. *Development Assistance Efforts and Policies of the Members of the Development Assistance Committee*. Paris: OECD, annual reviews.

―――. *Mercury and the Environment*. Paris: OECD, 1974.

―――. *Resources for the Developing World: Flow of Financial Resources to Less-Developed Countries, 1962-68*. Paris: OECD, 1970.

Packenham, Robert A. "Political Development Doctrines in the

American Foreign Aid Program." *World Politics*, 18 (January, 1966), 194-234.

Pearson, Lester. *The Crisis of Development*. New York: Praeger, 1970.

Petaccio, Victor. "Water Pollution and the Future Law of the Sea." *International and Comparative Law Quarterly*, 21 (January 1972), 15-42.

Petras, James F. and LaPorte, Robert. "Can We Do Business with Radical Nationalists? Chile: No." *Foreign Policy*, No. 7 (Summer 1972), pp. 132-158.

Pirages, Dennis C. and Ehrlich, Paul R. *Ark II*. San Francisco: W. H. Freeman, 1974.

Potter, Van Rensellaer. *Bioethics: Bridge to the Future*. Englewood Cliffs, N.J.: Prentice-Hall, 1971.

Quanbeck, Alton H. and Blechman, Barry M. *Strategic Forces: Issues for the Mid-Seventies*. Washington, D.C.: Brookings Institution, 1973.

Ransom, Harry Howe. "Secret Intelligence Agencies and Congress." *Society*, 12 (March/April 1975), 33-38.

Rathjens, George W. "Flexible Response Options." *Orbis*, 18 (Fall 1974), 677-688.

———. "The Dynamics of the Arms Race." *Scientific American*, (April 1969), pp. 15-25.

Richardson, Elliot. "Law of the Sea Conference: Problems and Progress." *Department of State Bulletin*, 77 (September 19, 1977), 389-391.

———. "Review of the Law of the Sea Conference and Deep Seabed Mining Legislation." *Department of State Bulletin*, 77 (November 21, 1977), 751-756.

Robertson, Arthur Henry. *Human Rights in the World*. Manchester: Manchester University Press, 1972.

Rogers, William. "United States Foreign Policy 1969-70: A Report of the Secretary of State." *Department of State Bulletin*, 64 (April 5, 1971), 465-477.

Rokeach, Milton. *The Nature of Human Values*. New York: Free Press, 1973.

Rosa, Nicholas. "What is Leviation's Future?" *Oceans*, 7 (May 1974), 45-53.

Rostow, Walt W. *The United States in the World Arena*. New York: Simon and Schuster, 1969.

Rotkirch, Holger. "Claims to the Ocean." *Environment*, 16 (June 1974), 34-41.

Russett, Bruce M. "Assured Destruction of What? A Counter-combatant Alternative to Nuclear Madness." *Public Policy*, 22 (Spring 1974), 121-138.

Sanger, Clyde. "Environment and Development." *International Journal*, 28 (Winter 1972-1973), 103-120.

Schachter, Oscar. "Just Prices in World Markets: Proposals *De Sege Ferenda.*" *American Journal of International Law*, 69 (January 1975), 101-109.

————, and Serwer, Daniel. "Marine Pollution Problems and Remedies." *American Journal of International Law*, 65 (January 1971), 84-111.

Schertz, Lyle P. "World Food: Prices and the Poor." *Foreign Affairs*, 52 (April 1974), 511-537.

Schlesinger, Arthur. *A Thousand Days*. Boston: Houghton Mifflin, 1965.

Schlesinger, James R. *Annual Defense Department Report FY 1976*, and *FY 1977*. Washington, D.C.: Government Printing Office, 1975, 1976

Schultze, Charles T. "The Economic Content of National Security Policy." *Foreign Affairs*, 51 (April 1973), 522-540.

Schwelb, Egor. *Human Rights and the International Community*. Chicago: Quadrangle, 1964.

Sewell, John W. *The United States and World Development*. New York: Praeger, 1977.

Sharp, Gene. *The Politics of Nonviolent Action*. Boston: Porter Sargent Publisher, 1973.

Shields, Linda P. and Ott, Marvin C. "Environmental Decay and International Politics: The Uses of Sovereignty." *Environmental Affairs*, 3, No. 4 (1974), 743-767.

Shinn, Robert. *The International Politics of Marine Pollution Control*. New York: Praeger, 1974.

Shultz, George P. "Administration Stresses Importance of U.S. Action on Funding for IDA and ADB Replenishment." *Department of State Bulletin*, 69 (December 17, 1973), 731-736.

Sigmund, Paul E. "Chile: What was the U.S. Role? Less than Charged." *Foreign Policy*, No. 16 (Fall 1974), pp. 142-156.

Singer, Fred, ed. *Global Effects of Environmental Pollution*. New York: Springer-Verlag, 1970.

Sivard, Ruth Leger. *World Military and Social Expenditures, 1974, 1975, 1976, 1977*. Leesburg, Virginia: WMSE Publications, 1974-1977.

Smith, Gerard C. "SALT After Vladivostok," *Journal of International Affairs*," 29 (Spring 1975), 7-18.

Sohn, Louis B. and Buergenthal, Thomas. *International Protection of Human Rights*. New York: Bobbs-Merrill, 1973.

Sommer, John G. *Beyond Charity*. Washington, D.C.: Overseas Development Council, 1977.

Sorensen, Theodore. *Kennedy*. New York: Bantam, 1965.

Stein, Eric. "Legal Restraints in Modern Arms Control Agreements." *American Journal of International Law*, 66 (April 1979), 255-289.

Stein, Robert E., ed. *Critical Environmental Issues on the Law of the Sea*. Washington, D.C.: International Institute for Environment and Development, 1975.

Stevenson, Adlai E. "Working Toward a World Without War." In U.S. Arms Control and Disarmament Agency, *Disarmament: The New U.S. Initiative*. Washington, D.C.: Government Printing Office, 1962, pp. 13-28.

Stevenson, John R. "Conflicting Approaches to the Control and Exploitation of the Ocean." *American Journal of International Law Proceedings*, 65 (Summer 1971), 107-143.

————. "Department Discusses Progress Towards 1973 Conference on the Law of the Sea." *Department of State Bulletin*, 66 (May 8, 1972), 672-679.

————. "Lawmaking for the Seas." *American Bar Association Journal*, 61 (February 1975), 185-190.

————. "U.S. Urges Early Conclusion of Law of the Sea Treaty." *Department of State Bulletin*, 72 (February 3, 1975), 153-154.

————, and Oxman, Bernard H. "The Preparations for the Law of the Sea Conference." *American Journal of International Law*, 68 (January 1974), 1-32.

————. "The Third United Nations Conference on the Law of the Sea: The 1974 Caracas Session." *American Journal of International Law*, 69 (January 1975), 1-30.

Stockholm International Peace Research Institute. *Armaments and Disarmament in the Nuclear Age*. Stockholm: Almqvist and Wiksell International, 1976.

————. *World Armaments and Disarmament, S.I.P.R.I. Yearbook*. Cambridge: MIT Press, various years.

————. *World Armaments: The Nuclear Threat*. Stockholm: SIPRI, 1977.

Stone, Jeremy O. "When and How to Use SALT." *Foreign Affairs*, 48 (January 1970), 262-273.

Strong, Maurice F. "One Year After Stockholm: An Ecological Approach." *Foreign Affairs*, 51 (1973), 690-707.

————, ed. *Who Speaks for Earth?* New York: Norton, 1973.

Study of Critical Environmental Problems. *Man's Impact on the Global Environment*. Cambridge: MIT Press, 1970.

Swing, John Temple. "Law of the Sea at the Brink." *Oceans* (September 1977), pp. 4-5.

Swomley, John M. *The Military Establishment*. Boston: Beacon, 1964.

Symposium on International Relations and the Future of Ocean Space, 1972. *International Relations and the Future of Ocean Space*. Columbia, S.C.: University of South Carolina Press, 1974.

Tansky, Leo. *U.S. and U.S.S.R. Aid to Developing Countries*. New York: Praeger, 1967.

Teclaff, Ludwik A. "International Law and the Protection of Oceans from Pollution." *Fordham Law Review*, 40 (March 1972), 529-564.

Thayer, George. *The War Business: The International Trade in Armaments*. New York: Simon and Schuster, 1969.

Thorp, Willard L. *The Reality of Foreign Aid*. New York: Praeger, 1971.

Tinbergen, Jan. *Reshaping the International Order*. New York: Dutton, 1976.

Train, Russell E. "Statement of the Honorable Russell E. Train Before the Council of the Inter-Governmental Maritime Consultative Organization." Mimeographed. London, June 5, 1973.

United Nations. *Demographic Yearbook of the United Nations*. New York: United Nations, various years.

————. "Draft UN Convention on the Seabed Area." UN Document A/AC. 138/25. *International Legal Materials*, 9 (1970).

————. Department of Economist and Social Affairs, Statistical Office. *Yearbook of National Accounts Statistics*. New York: United Nations, various years.

————. General Assembly. "U.S. Draft Articles on the Protection of the Marine Environment and the Prevention of Marine Pollution." UN Document A/AC. 138/SC.iii/2.40, July 13, 1973.

U. S. Agency for International Development. *The Foreign Assistance Program: Annual Report to Congress*. Washington, D.C.: Government Printing Office, various years

————. *Report to Congress: Foreign Assistance Program Fiscal Years 1962-1971*. Washington, D.C.: Government Printing Office, various years.

————. Program Coordination Staff. *Principles of Foreign Eco-*

nomic Assistance. Washington, D.C.: Government Printing Office, 1963.

————. Statistics and Reports Division. *U.S. Economic Assistance Programs April 3, 1948-June 30, 1963*. Washington, D.C.: Government Printing Office, various years.

————. Statistics and Reports Division. *U.S. Economic Assistance Programs Administered by the Agency for International Development and Predecessor Agencies, April 13, 1948-June 30, 1971*. Washington, D.C.: Government Printing Office, 1972.

————. Statistics and Reports Division. *U.S. Overseas Loans and Grants and Assistance from International Organizations: Obligations and Loan Authorizations, 1945-73, 1945-74, 1945-75, 1945-76*. Washington, D.C.: Government Printing Office, 1974, 1975, 1976, 1977.

U.S. Arms Control and Disarmament Agency. *Arms Control and Disarmament Agreements*. Washington, D.C.: Government Printing Office, 1975.

————. *Disarmament: The New U.S. Initiative*. Washington, D.C.: Government Printing Office, 1962.

————. *The International Transfer of Conventional Arms: Report to the Congress*. Printed for the use of the House Committee on Foreign Affairs, House of Representatives, 93rd Congress, 2nd Session. Washington, D.C.: Government Printing Office, 1974.

————. *World Military Expenditures and Arms Trade, 1963-1973, and 1966-1975*. Washington, D.C.: Government Printing Office, 1975 and 1976.

U.S. Commission on Marine Science, Engineering, and Resources. *Marine Resources and Legal-Political Arrangements for Their Development*. Washington, D.C.: Government Printing Office, 1969.

U.S. Congress. House. Committee on Appropriations, Subcommittee on Foreign Operations and Related Agencies. *Foreign Assistance and Related Agencies Appropriations for 1975*. 93rd Congress, 2nd Session. Washington, D.C.: Government Printing Office, 1974.

U.S. Congress. House. Committee on Armed Services. *Hearings on Military Posture and H.R. 3689 Department of Defense Authorization for Appropriations for Fiscal Year 1976 and 197T*. 94th Congress, 1st Session. Washington, D.C.: Government Printing Office, 1975.

U.S. Congress. House. Committee on Foreign Affairs. *Fiscal Year*

489

1975 Foreign Assistance Request. 93rd Congress, 2nd Session. Washington, D.C.: Government Printing Office, 1974.

———. *Foreign Assistance Act of 1964*. 88th Congress, 2nd Session. Washington, D.C.: Government Printing Office, 1964.

———. *Mutual Development and Cooperation Act of 1973*. 93rd Congress, 1st Session. Washington, D.C.: Government Printing Office, 1973.

———. *Mutual Security Act of 1955*. 84th Congress, 1st Session. Washington, D.C.: Government Printing Office, 1955.

———. *Mutual Security Act of 1958*. 85th Congress, 2nd Session. Washington, D.C.: Government Printing Office, 1958.

———. *Report of Special Study Mission to Pakistan, India, Thailand, and Indochina*. Report No. 412. 83rd Congress, 1st Session. Washington, D.C.: Government Printing Office, 1953.

———. *Status of the U.N. Law of the Sea Conference*. 93rd Congress, 2nd Session. Washington, D.C.: Government Printing Office, 1975.

———. Subcommittee on International Organizations and Movements. *Human Rights in the World Community*. 93rd Congress, 2nd Session. Washington, D.C.: Government Printing Office, 1974.

———. Subcommittee on the Near East and South Asia. *Indian Rupee Settlement Agreement*. 93rd Congress, 2nd Session. Washington, D.C.: Government Printing Office, 1974.

U.S. Congress. House. Committee on Merchant Marine and Fisheries. Subcommittee on Oceanography. *Oceanography Miscellaneous*. 93rd Congress, 2nd Session. Washington, D.C.: Government Printing Office, 1975.

———. Subcommittee on Fisheries and Wildlife Conservation and the Environment. *Ocean Dumping*. 93rd Congress, 1st Session. Washington, D.C.: Government Printing Office, 1973.

U.S. Congress. Senate. Committee on Appropriations. *Department of Defense Appropriations Fiscal Year 1975*. 93rd Congress, 2nd Session. Washington, D.C.: Government Printing Office, 1974.

U.S. Congress. Senate. Committee on Armed Services. *Fiscal Year 1976 and July-September 1976 Transition Period Authorization for Military Procurement, Research and Development, and Active Duty, Selective Reserve, and Civilian Personnel Strengths*. 94th Congress, 1st Session. Washington, D.C.: Government Printing Office, 1975.

U.S. Congress. Senate. Committee on Commerce. *Geneva Session of the Third United Nations Law of the Sea Conference*. 94th Congress, 1st Session. Washington, D.C.: Government Printing Office, 1975.

———. *International Maritime Consultative Organization: 1973 Conference on Marine Pollution*. 93rd Congress, 1st Session. Washington, D.C.: Government Printing Office, 1974.

———. *Offshore Marine Environment Protection Act of 1973*. 93rd Congress, 1st Session. Washington, D.C.: Government Printing Office, 1973.

———. *1972 Survey of Environmental Activities of International Organizations*. 92nd Congress, 2nd Session. Washington, D.C.: Government Printing Office, 1972.

———. *Tankers and the Marine Environment*. 94th Congress, 1st Session. Washington, D.C.: Government Printing Office, 1975.

———. *The Third U.N. Law of the Sea Conference*. 94th Congress, 1st Session. Washington, D.C.: Government Printing Office, 1975.

———. Subcommittee on Oceans and Atmosphere. *Ocean Pollution*. 93rd Congress, 1st Session. Washington, D.C.: Government Printing Office, 1974.

U.S. Congress. Senate. Committee on Foreign Relations. *ACDA Authorization*. 93rd Congress, 2nd Session. Washington, D.C.: Government Printing Office, 1974.

———. *CIA Foreign and Domestic Activities*. 94th Congress, 1st Session. Washington, D.C.: Government Printing Office, 1975.

———. *Foreign Assistance Authorization 1974*. 93rd Congress, 2nd Session. Washington, D.C.: Government Printing Office, 1974.

———. *Mutual Security Act of 1954*. 83rd Congress, 2nd Session. Washington, D.C.: Government Printing Office, 1954.

———. *Mutual Security Act of 1960*. 86th Congress, 2nd Session. Washington, D.C.: Government Printing Office, 1960.

———. *Technical Assistance: Final Report of the Committee on Foreign Relations*. 87th Congress, 1st Session. Washington, D.C.: Government Printing Office, various years.

———. *The Third United Nations Law of the Sea Conference. Report to the Senate*. 94th Congress, 1st Session. Washington, D.C.: Government Printing Office, 1975.

———. *U.S. Participation in ADB and IDA*. 93rd Congress, 1st Session. Washington, D.C.: Government Printing Office, 1974.

491

U.S. Congress. Senate. Committee on Foreign Relations. Subcommittee on Arms Control, International Law and Organization. *Arms Control Implications of Current Defense Budget.* 92nd Congress, 1st Session. Washington, D.C.: Government Printing Office, 1971.

————. Subcommittee on Arms Control, International Law and Organization. *Briefing on Counterforce Attacks.* 93rd Congress, 2nd Session. Washington, D.C.: Government Printing Office, 1975.

————. Subcommittee on Arms Control, International Law and Organization. *U.S.-U.S.S.R. Strategic Policies.* 93rd Congress, 2nd Session. Washington, D.C.: Government Printing Office, 1974.

————. Subcommittee on Multinational Corporations. *The International Telephone and Telegraph Company and Chile, 1970-1971.* 93rd Congress, 1st Session. Washington, D.C.: Government Printing Office, 1973.

————. Subcommittee on Multinational Corporations. *Multinational Corporations and United States Foreign Policy.* 93rd Congress, 1st Session. Washington, D.C.: Government Printing Office, 1973.

————. Subcommittee on U.S. Security Agreements and Commitments Abroad and Subcommittee on Arms Control, International Law and Organization. *Nuclear Weapons and Foreign Policy.* 93rd Congress, 2nd Session. Washington, D.C.: Government Printing Office, 1974.

U.S. Congress. Senate. Committee on Interior and Insular Affairs. *The Law of the Sea Crisis: A Staff Report on the UN Seabed Committee.* 92nd Congress, 1st Session. Washington, D.C.: Government Printing Office, 1972.

U.S. Congress. Senate. Committee on Interior and Insular Affairs. *Ocean Manganese Nodules.* Committee Print prepared by James E. Mielke of the Congressional Research Service. 94th Congress, 1st Session. Washington, D.C.: Government Printing Office, 1975.

————. Subcommittee on Minerals, Materials, and Fuels. *Status Report on the Law of the Sea Conference.* 94th Congress, 1st Session. Washington, D.C.: Government Printing Office, 1975.

U.S. Congress. Senate. Committee on Judiciary. *Refugee and Humanitarian Problems in Chile.* 92nd Congress. 1st Session. Washington, D.C.: Government Printing Office, 1973.

U.S. Congress. Senate. Joint Committee on Atomic Energy. *Development, Growth, and State of the Nuclear Industry.* 93rd Congress, 2nd Session. Washington, D.C.: Government Printing Office, 1974.

U.S. Congress. Senate. Select Committee to Study Governmental Operations with Respect to Intelligence Activities. *Alleged Assassination Plots Involving Foreign Leaders*. 94th Congress, 1st Session. Washington, D.C.: Government Printing Office, 1975.

————. *Covert Action in Chile 1963-73*. 94th Congress, 1st Session. Washington, D.C.: Government Printing Office, 1975.

————. *Foreign and Military Intelligence, Final Report*. 94th Congress, 2nd Session. Washington, D.C.: Government Printing Office, 1976.

U.S. Council on Environmental Quality. *Environmental Quality, Annual Report*. Washington, D.C.: Government Printing Office, various years.

U.S. Council on Environmental Quality. *Ocean Dumping: A National Policy, A Report to the President*. Washington, D.C.: Government Printing Office, 1970.

U.S. Department of Defense. *Annual Report of the Secretary of Defense*. Washington, D.C.: Government Printing Office, various years.

U.S. Department of State. "North-South Dialogue." *Department of State Bulletin*, 77 (March 14, 1977), 235-236.

————. "U.N. Law of the Sea Conference 1975." *Special Report*, Publication 8764, February 1975.

————. Bureau of International and Scientific and Technological Affairs. *United States National Report on the Human Environment*. Washington, D.C.: Government Printing Office, 1971.

————. Bureau of Public Affairs. "Status Report on Law of the Sea Negotiations After Geneva." *Special Report*, May 22, 1975. Washington, D.C.: Government Printing Office, 1975.

"United States Draft of the U.N. Convention on International Seabed Areas." August 3, 1970. *International Legal Materials*, 9 (1970), 1046-1080.

U.S. Secretary of State's Advisory Committee on the 1972 UN Conference on the Human Environment. *Stockholm and Beyond*. Washington, D.C.: Government Printing Office, 1972.

Uribe, Armando. *The Black Book of American Intervention in Chile*. Boston: Beacon Press, 1974.

Utton, Albert E. and Henning, Daniel H., eds. *Environmental Policy: Concepts and International Implications*. New York: Praeger, 1973.

Vance, Cyrus. "Secretary Testifies on Administration's Approach to Foreign Assistance." *Department of State Bulletin*, 76 (March 14, 1977), 236-241.

———. "Secretary Vance Attends Ministerial Meeting of the Conference on International Economic Cooperation." *Department of State Bulletin*, 76 (June 20, 1977), 645-648.

———. "Secretary Vance Emphasizes Importance of Foreign Assistance Programs." *Department of State Bulletin*, 76 (April 11, 1977), 336-340.

———. "Secretary Vance Gives Overview of Foreign Assistance Programs." *Department of State Bulletin*, 76 (March 28, 1977), 284-289.

Van Cleave, William R. and Barnett, Roger W. "Strategic Adaptability." *Orbis*, 18 (Fall 1974), 655-676.

Van Dyke, Vernon. *Human Rights, the United States and the World Community*. New York: Oxford University Press, 1970.

Wagar, Warren. *Building the City of Man: Outlines of a World Civilization*. San Francisco: W. H. Freeman, 1971.

Wagner, Richard H. *Environment and Man*. New York: Norton, 1974.

Wall, David. *The Charity of Nations: The Political Economy of Foreign Aid*. New York: Basic Books, 1973.

Warnke, Paul C. "Apes on a Treadmill." *Foreign Policy*, 18 (Spring 1975), 12-29.

Weissman, Steve R., ed. *The Trojan Horse*. San Francisco: Ramparts Press, 1974.

Wenk, Edward. *The Politics of the Ocean*. Seattle: University of Washington Press, 1972.

Westervelt, Donald R. "The Essence of Armed Futility." *Orbis*, 18 (Fall 1974), 689-705.

Willrich, Mason and Rhinelander, John, eds. *SALT: The Moscow Agreements and Beyond*. New York: Free Press, 1974.

Wilson, Thomas W. *International Environment Action: A Global Survey*. Cambridge, Mass.: Dunellen, 1971.

Wohlstetter, Albert. "How to Confuse Ourselves." *Foreign Policy*, No. 20 (Fall 1975), pp. 170-198.

———. "Is There a Strategic Arms Race?" *Foreign Policy*, No. 15 (Summer 1974), pp. 3-20.

———. "Rivals, But no 'Race.'" *Foreign Policy*, No. 16 (Fall 1974), pp. 48-81.

Workshop on Global Ecological Problems. *Man in the Living Environment*. Madison: University of Wisconsin Press, 1972.

Wurster, C. F. "DDT Reduces Photosynthesis by Marine Phytoplankton." *Science*, 159 (1968), 1474-1475.

494

York, Herbert F. *Race to Oblivion: A Participant's View of the Arms Race*. New York: Simon and Schuster, 1970.

———. "Deterrence Gone M.A.D." *Bulletin of the Atomic Scientists*, 30 (March 1974), 5-8.

Young, Andrew. "Framework for a Dynamic North-South Dialogue." *Department of State Bulletin*, 77 (September 19, 1977), 383-389.

Zener, Robert V. "Environment and the Law of the Sea." *Marine Technology Society Journal*, 11 (May 1977), 27-30.

Index

Books Written Under the Auspices of the
CENTER OF INTERNATIONAL STUDIES
PRINCETON UNIVERSITY
1952-79

Gabriel A. Almond, *The Appeals of Communism* (Princeton University Press 1954)

William W. Kaufmann, ed., *Military Policy and National Security* (Princeton University Press 1956)

Klaus Knorr, *The War Potential of Nations* (Princeton University Press 1956)

Lucian W. Pye, *Guerrilla Communism in Malaya* (Princeton University Press 1956)

Charles De Visscher, *Theory and Reality in Public International Law*, trans. by P. E. Corbett (Princeton University Press 1957; rev. ed. 1968)

Bernard C. Cohen, *The Political Process and Foreign Policy: The Making of the Japanese Peace Settlement* (Princeton University Press 1957)

Myron Weiner, *Party Politics in India: The Development of a Multi-Party System* (Princeton University Press 1957)

Percy E. Corbett, *Law in Diplomacy* (Princeton University Press 1959)

Rolf Sannwald and Jacques Stohler, *Economic Integration: Theoretical Assumptions and Consequences of European Unification*, trans. by Herman Karreman (Princeton University Press 1959)

Klaus Knorr, ed., *NATO and American Security* (Princeton University Press 1959)

Gabriel A. Almond and James S. Coleman, eds., *The Politics of the Developing Areas* (Princeton University Press 1960)

Herman Kahn, *On Thermonuclear War* (Princeton University Press 1960)

Sidney Verba, *Small Groups and Political Behavior: A Study of Leadership* (Princeton University Press 1961)

Robert J. C. Butow, *Tojo and the Coming of the War* (Princeton University Press 1961)

Glenn H. Snyder, *Deterrence and Defense: Toward a Theory of National Security* (Princeton University Press 1961)

Klaus Knorr and Sidney Verba, eds., *The International System: Theoretical Essays* (Princeton University Press 1961)

Peter Paret and John W. Shy, *Guerrillas in the 1960's* (Praeger 1962)

George Modelski, *A Theory of Foreign Policy* (Praeger 1962)

Klaus Knorr and Thornton Read, eds., *Limited Strategic War* (Praeger 1963)

Frederick S. Dunn, *Peace-Making and the Settlement with Japan* (Princeton University Press 1963)

Arthur L. Burns and Nina Heathcote, *Peace-Keeping by United Nations Forces* (Praeger 1963)

Richard A. Falk, *Law, Morality, and War in the Contemporary World* (Praeger 1963)

513

James N. Rosenau, *National Leadership and Foreign Policy: A Case Study in the Mobilization of Public Support* (Princeton University Press 1963)

Gabriel A. Almond and Sidney Verba, *The Civic Culture: Political Attitudes and Democracy in Five Nations* (Princeton University Press 1963)

Bernard C. Cohen, *The Press and Foreign Policy* (Princeton University Press 1963)

Richard L. Sklar, *Nigerian Political Parties: Power in an Emergent African Nation* (Princeton University Press 1963)

Peter Paret, *French Revolutionary Warfare from Indochina to Algeria: The Analysis of a Political and Military Doctrine* (Praeger 1964)

Harry Eckstein, ed., *Internal War: Problems and Approaches* (Free Press 1964)

Cyril E. Black and Thomas P. Thornton, eds., *Communism and Revolution: The Strategic Uses of Political Violence* (Princeton University Press 1964)

Miriam Camps, *Britain and the European Community 1955-1963* (Princeton University Press 1964)

Thomas P. Thornton, ed., *The Third World in Soviet Perspective: Studies by Soviet Writers on the Developing Areas* (Princeton University Press 1964)

James N. Rosenau, ed., *International Aspects of Civil Strife* (Princeton University Press 1964)

Sidney I. Ploss, *Conflict and Decision-Making in Soviet Russia: A Case Study of Agricultural Policy, 1953-1963* (Princeton University Press 1965)

Richard A. Falk and Richard J. Barnet, eds., *Security in Disarmament* (Princeton University Press 1965)

Karl von Vorys, *Political Development in Pakistan* (Princeton University Press 1965)

Harold and Margaret Sprout, *The Ecological Perspective on Human Affairs, With Special Reference to International Politics* (Princeton University Press 1965)

Klaus Knorr, *On the Uses of Military Power in the Nuclear Age* (Princeton University Press 1966)

Harry Eckstein, *Division and Cohesion in Democracy: A Study of Norway* (Princeton University Press 1966)

Cyril E. Black, *The Dynamics of Modernization: A Study in Comparative History* (Harper and Row 1966)

Peter Kunstadter, ed., *Southeast Asian Tribes, Minorities, and Nations* (Princeton University Press 1967)

E. Victor Wolfenstein, *The Revolutionary Personality: Lenin, Trotsky, Gandhi* (Princeton University Press 1967)

Leon Gordenker, *The UN Secretary-General and the Maintenance of Peace* (Columbia University Press 1967)

Oran R. Young, *The Intermediaries: Third Parties in International Crises* (Princeton University Press 1967)

James N. Rosenau, ed., *Domestic Sources of Foreign Policy* (Free Press 1967)

Richard F. Hamilton, *Affluence and the French Worker in the Fourth Republic* (Princeton University Press 1967)

Linda B. Miller, *World Order and Local Disorder: The United Nations and Internal Conflicts* (Princeton University Press 1967)

Henry Bienen, *Tanzania: Party Transformation and Economic Development* (Princeton University Press 1967)

Wolfram F. Hanrieder, *West German Foreign Policy, 1949-1963: International Pressures and Domestic Response* (Stanford University Press 1967)

Richard H. Ullman, *Britain and the Russian Civil War: November 1918-February 1920* (Princeton University Press 1968)

Robert Gilpin, *France in the Age of the Scientific State* (Princeton University Press 1968)

William B. Bader, *The United States and the Spread of Nuclear Weapons* (Pegasus 1968)

Richard A. Falk, *Legal Order in a Violent World* (Princeton University Press 1968)

Cyril E. Black, Richard A. Falk, Klaus Knorr and Oran R. Young, *Neutralization and World Politics* (Princeton University Press 1968)

Oran R. Young, *The Politics of Force: Bargaining During International Crises* (Princeton University Press 1969)

Klaus Knorr and James N. Rosenau, eds., *Contending Approaches to International Politics* (Princeton University Press 1969)

James N. Rosenau, ed., *Linkage Politics: Essays on the Convergence of National and International Systems* (Free Press 1969)

John T. McAlister, Jr., *Viet Nam: The Origins of Revolution* (Knopf 1969)

Jean Edward Smith, *Germany Beyond the Wall: People, Politics and Prosperity* (Little, Brown 1969)

James Barros, *Betrayal from Within: Joseph Avenol, Secretary-General of the League of Nations, 1933-1940* (Yale University Press 1969)

Charles Hermann, *Crises in Foreign Policy: A Simulation Analysis* (Bobbs-Merrill 1969)

Robert C. Tucker, *The Marxian Revolutionary Idea: Essays on Marxist Thought and Its Impact on Radical Movements* (W. W. Norton 1969)

Harvey Waterman, *Political Change in Contemporary France: The Politics of an Industrial Democracy* (Charles E. Merrill 1969)

Cyril E. Black and Richard A. Falk, eds., *The Future of the International Legal Order*. Vol. I: *Trends and Patterns* (Princeton University Press 1969)

Ted Robert Gurr, *Why Men Rebel* (Princeton University Press 1969)

C. Sylvester Whitaker, *The Politics of Tradition: Continuity and Change in Northern Nigeria 1946-1966* (Princeton University Press 1970)

Richard A. Falk, *The Status of Law in International Society* (Princeton University Press 1970)

John T. McAlister, Jr. and Paul Mus, *The Vietnamese and Their Revolution* (Harper & Row 1970)

Klaus Knorr, *Military Power and Potential* (D. C. Heath 1970)

Cyril E. Black and Richard A. Falk, eds., *The Future of the International Legal Order*. Vol. II: *Wealth and Resources* (Princeton University Press 1970)

Leon Gordenker, ed., *The United Nations in International Politics* (Princeton University Press 1971)

Cyril E. Black and Richard A. Falk, eds., *The Future of the International Legal Order*. Vol. III: *Conflict Management* (Princeton University Press 1971)

Francine R. Frankel, *India's Green Revolution: Economic Gains and Political Costs* (Princeton University Press 1971)

Harold and Margaret Sprout, *Toward a Politics of the Planet Earth* (Van Nostrand Reinhold Co. 1971)

Cyril E. Black and Richard A. Falk, eds., *The Future of the International Legal Order*. Vol. IV: *The Structure of the International Environment* (Princeton University Press 1972)

Gerald Garvey, *Energy, Ecology, Economy* (W. W. Norton 1972)

Richard H. Ullman, *The Anglo-Soviet Accord* (Princeton University Press 1973)

Klaus Knorr, *Power and Wealth: The Political Economy of International Power* (Basic Books 1973)

Anton Bebler, *Military Rule in Africa: Dahomey, Ghana, Sierra Leone, and Mali* (Praeger Publishers 1973)

Robert C. Tucker, *Stalin as Revolutionary 1879-1929: A Study in History and Personality* (W. W. Norton 1973)

Edward L. Morse, *Foreign Policy and Interdependence in Gaullist France* (Princeton University Press 1973)

Henry Bienen, *Kenya: The Politics of Participation and Control* (Princeton University Press 1974)

Gregory J. Massell, *The Surrogate Proletariat: Moslem Women and Revolutionary Strategies in Soviet Central Asia, 1919-1929* (Princeton University Press 1974)

James N. Rosenau, *Citizenship Between Elections: An Inquiry Into The Mobilizable American* (Free Press 1974)

Ervin Laszlo, *A Strategy for the Future: The Systems Approach to World Order* (George Braziller 1974)

R. J. Vincent, *Nonintervention and International Order* (Princeton University Press 1974)

Jan H. Kalicki, *The Pattern of Sino-American Crises: Political-Military Interactions in the 1950s* (Cambridge University Press 1975)

Klaus Knorr, *The Power of Nations: The Political Economy of International Relations* (Basic Books, Inc. 1975)

James P. Sewell, *UNESCO and World Politics: Engaging in International Relations* (Princeton University Press 1975)

516

Richard A. Falk, *A Global Approach to National Policy* (Harvard University Press 1975)

Harry Eckstein and Ted Robert Gurr, *Patterns of Authority: A Structural Basis for Political Inquiry* (John Wiley & Sons 1975)

Cyril E. Black, Marius B. Jansen, Herbert S. Levine, Marion J. Levy, Jr., Henry Rosovsky, Gilbert Rozman, Henry D. Smith, II, and S. Frederick Starr, *The Modernization of Japan and Russia* (Free Press 1975)

Leon Gordenker, *International Aid and National Decisions: Development Programs in Malawi, Tanzania, and Zambia* (Princeton University Press 1976)

Carl von Clausewitz, *On War*, edited and translated by Michael Howard and Peter Paret (Princeton University Press 1976)

Gerald Garvey and Lou Ann Garvey, *International Resource Flows* (D. C. Heath 1977)

Walter F. Murphy and Joseph Tanenhaus, *Comparative Constitutional Law: Cases and Commentaries* (St. Martin's Press 1977)

Gerald Garvey, *Nuclear Power and Social Planning: The City of the Second Sun* (D. C. Heath 1977)

Richard E. Bissell, *Apartheid and International Organizations* (Westview Press 1977)

David P. Forsythe, *Humanitarian Politics: The International Committee of the Red Cross* (Johns Hopkins University Press 1977)

Paul E. Sigmund, *The Overthrow of Allende and the Politics of Chile, 1964-1976* (University of Pittsburgh Press 1977)

Henry S. Bienen, *Armies and Parties in Africa* (Holmes and Meier 1978)

Harold and Margaret Sprout, *The Context of Environmental Politics: Unfinished Business for America's Third Century* (University Press of Kentucky 1978)

Samuel S. Kim, *China, The United Nations, and World Order* (Princeton University Press 1979)

S. Basheer Ahmed, *Nuclear Fuel and Energy* (D. C. Heath 1979)

Library of Congress Cataloging in Publication Data
Johansen, Robert C
    The national interest and the human interest.

    Bibliography: p.
    Includes index.
    1. United States—Foreign relations—1945-
2. International organization.   I. Title.
JX1417.J63   327.73   79-83994
ISBN 0-691-07618-9
ISBN 0-691-02196-1 pbk.